Max-Planck-Institut für ausländisches
öffentliches Recht und Völkerrecht

Beiträge zum ausländischen öffentlichen Recht und Völkerrecht

Begründet von Viktor Bruns

Herausgegeben von
Jochen Abr. Frowein · Rüdiger Wolfrum

Band 154

Hanri Mostert

The Constitutional Protection and Regulation of Property and its Influence on the Reform of Private Law and Landownership in South Africa and Germany

A Comparative Analysis

Springer

Berlin Heidelberg New York Barcelona
Hongkong London
Mailand Paris Tokio

ISSN 0172-4770

ISBN 3-540-43006-7 Springer-Verlag Berlin · Heidelberg · New York

Bibliografische Information Der Deutschen Bibliothek

Die Deutsche Bibliothek verzeichnet diese Publikation in der Deutschen Nationalbibliografie; detaillierte bibliografische Daten sind im Internet über <http://dnb.ddb.de> abrufbar.

Printed in Germany

Satz: Reproduktionsfertige Vorlagen vom Autor
Druck- und Bindearbeiten: Konrad Triltsch, Print und digitale Medien GmbH, 97199 Ochsenfurt-Hohestadt
SPIN: 10860339   64/3130 x z – 5 4 3 2 1 0 – Gedruckt auf säurefreiem Papier

Acknowledgements

This book is the product of research done between June 1997 and November 2000 at the University of Stellenbosch in South Africa and the Max Planck Institute for Foreign Public Law and International Law in Heidelberg, Germany. An earlier version of the text was presented in partial fulfillment of the requirements for the Degree of Doctor of Laws at the University of Stellenbosch in November 2000. For purposes of the present publication, and in view of the proliferation of legal developments pertaining to land law, the text has been revised and updated. It also incorporates discussion of a number of South African court decisions, which were handed down during 2001. The text now reflects the legal position as at 31 December 2001, and contains brief references to some scholarly works and court decisions published after this date.

I would like to express my appreciation for the support of many people and institutions that made completion and publication of this research possible. Both my promoters have invested considerable time and efforts in my research. Professor Cornie van der Merwe awakened my interest in property law, encouraged me to undertake the research for this dissertation, and supported me in the decision to conduct most of it in Germany. Professor Juanita Pienaar showed continued interest in the progress of my research, supported my attempts at undertaking research visits abroad, and was always willing to share her knowledge and her literature collection with me. The time they invested in the product of this research as well as in their student is greatly appreciated. Professor André van der Walt, who served as internal examiner, also contributed a great deal to the completion of this research, and deserves a word of gratitude for making several valuable suggestions as to the improvement of the text. I am also grateful to Professor David Carey-Miller for acting as external examiner.

A sincere word of thanks also goes to Professor Jochen Frowein, who agreed to supervise my research in Germany, and who managed to make my time at the Max Planck Institute in Heidelberg an intellectually and personally enriching experience. I am particularly grateful to him and Professor Rüdiger Wolfrum, the directors of the Max Planck Institute, for making the Institute's facilities and library available to me, and for agreeing to support the publication of this text in its present form.

Between 1997 and 2000, several institutions provided financial support for the research on which this text is based, enabling me to cover the study fees and other expenses involved, and to embark upon extensive research visits to Germany. The contributions of the University of Stellenbosch, the Human Sciences Research Council (Centre for Science Development), the *Max Planck Gesellschaft,* the *Deutscher Akademischer Austauschdienst* and the Harry Crossley Foundation are hereby gratefully acknowledged. The opinions expressed in this text should not be attributed to any of these institutions. With regard to the applications for and administering of financial support, I would like to extend a special word of thanks to the staff of the post-graduate bursary office at the University of Stellenbosch, Ms Carin de la Querra and Ms Helena Opperman for their continued assistance. Likewise, the staff of the African desk at the German Academic Exchange Service should also be thanked for their patience in handling all my inquiries. Ms Lazelle Bonthuys and Professor Johan Mouton also assisted me in the drafting of research proposals with the aim of obtaining funds for the overseas research project, and deserve to be thanked here.

A special word of gratitude should be reserved for all the staff of the Max Planck Institute. I would, however, in particular like to thank Mr Ali Zakouri, Ms Michaela Fahlbusch, and Ms Irmgard Bühler, for swiftly managing even the strangest of literature requests. Similarly, I would like to thank Dr Roland Braun, Dr Dietmar Bußmann and the staff of the Information Technologies department for patiently handling all problems connected with computer illiteracy on my part. Mr Klaus Zimmermann and the administrative staff also played an instrumental role in making my stay at the Institute as comfortable as possible. In addition, Ms Angelika Schmidt and Dr Christiane Philipp were instrumental in the preparation of this text for publication, and must be thanked.

Many friends and colleagues have contributed to the content of this dissertation, by reading and commenting on parts of it, by bringing to my attention valuable pieces of literature and/or making suggestions as to interesting courses of inquiry. I appreciate the contributions of all of them. In particular, I would like to thank Professor Lourens du Plessis, Professor Sophie Pirie-Clifton, Dr Loammi Blaauw-Wolf, Dr Christoph Benedict, Dr Dagmar Richter, Mr Vladimir Djeric, Dr Mattias Sahinkuye, Dr Sabine Pittroff, Ms Carin Visser, Dr Erika de Wet and Mr Thilo Grutschnig, who all invested a considerable amount of time and energy in my research and writing endeavours. I am, furthermore, grateful for the continued interest in my progress and the extraordinary support provided by the fellow doctoral students and members of the doctoral research unit at the Max Planck Institute. The members of the Research Unit for Law and Constitutional Interpretation of the Universities of Stellenbosch and the Western Cape should also be thanked for their contributions in evaluating, criticising and commenting upon parts of the research. I would also like to thank Mr Duane Gallie for his assistance in drawing up the bibliography, and Ms Annette King and Ms Elaine van der Merwe for logistic assistance. A special word of thanks is reserved for Mr Peter Mullineux, for editing the text and ironing out some linguistic difficulties, and for Dr Peter McAlister-Smith, who gave me useful pointers on the English grammar and writing style. I am also grateful for the assistance rendered by Ms Melanie Fourie, Ms Agatha Atkins, Ms Chantal Steenkamp, Mr Theuns Möller, Ms Charmaine van der Westhuizen and Mr Gerhard Loots in the preparation of the final draft for this publication.

My husband, Rainer Nowak, went through every painful step and every joyous leap of the research and writing process with me, even at times when he was under immense personal or professional pressure himself. There are not words enough to thank him for his enduring support, even at the most difficult of times.

Likewise, when it came to family matters, my parents, Eugéne and Rettie Mostert, probably would have preferred to have a less absent and a less absent-minded child. However, they never expected anything of me but that I do that to which I have set my mind. They supported me in more ways than one: by nurturing my love of reading, writing and studying, by taking care of the financial aspects of my pregraduate studies, and by continuously voicing their interest in my doings. As a sign of my appreciation, this book is dedicated to them.

Table of Contents

Part Four: The Influence of Social Reform on Land Law in Germany and South Africa

Chapter 9: Meaning of the Constitutional Objective of Land Reform for the South African Property Law

List of Abbreviations*

ANC	African National Congress
Art. / art.	Article(s) / article(s) or *Artikel / artikel*
BGB	*Bürgerliches Gesetzbuch* (German Civil Code)
BGBl	*Bundesgesetzblatt*
BGH	*Bundesgerichtshof* (Federal Court of Justice)
BGHZ	*Entscheidungen des Bundesgerichtshofs in Zivilsachen* (decisions of the Federal Court of Justice in civil matters)
BRD	*Bundesrepublik Deutschland / Bondsrepubliek Duitsland*
BSG	*Bundessozialgericht* (Federal Social Court)
BVerfGE	*Bundesverfassungsgerichtsentscheidungen* (decisions of the Federal Constitutional Court)
BVerwG	*Bundesverwaltungsgericht* (Federal Administrative Court)
CCT	Constitutional Court Trial
CDU	*Christlich Demokratische Union*
Ch. / ch.	Chapter(s) / chapter(s)
DDR	*Deutsche Demokratische Republik / Duitse Demokratiese Republiek*
E.g. / e.g.	For example / for example
Ed	edition or editor
Eds	editors
Et. al. / et. al.	and others
Etc. / etc.	and so on
FC	Final Constitution of the Republic of South Africa, 1996
FDP	*Freie Demokratische Partei*
ff.	and further / following

---

*   Abbreviations of journal titles are used throughout the footnotes. The full titles of journals are provided, together with their abbreviated forms, in the bibliography from page 599 onwards.

FG	*Finale Grondwet*
FRG	Federal Republic of Germany
GDR	German Democratic Republic
GG	*Grundgesetz* (Basic Law of the Federal Republic of Germany)
I.a. / i.a.	Among others / among others
I.e. / i.e.	That is / that is
IC	Interim Constitution, Act 200 of 1993
IG	*Interim Grondwet*
LCC	Land Claims Court
M.n. / m.n.	marginal number *(Randnummer)*
NF	*Neue Fassung* (new version)
NGO	Non-governmental organisation
NP	National Party
Par. / par.	Paragraph(s) / paragraphs
Sec. / sec.	Section(s) / section(s)
SPD	*Sozialdemokratische Partei Deutschlands*
Transl	translated or translation
Vol / vol	Volume(s) / volume(s)
WEG	*Wohnungseigentumsgesetz* (Apartment Ownership Act)

A risk to own anything: a car, a pair of shoes, a packet of
cigarettes. Not enough to go around, not enough cars,
shoes, cigarettes. Too many people, too few things. What
there is must go into circulation, so that everyone can have
a chance to be happy for a day. That is the theory; hold to
the theory and to the comforts of theory.

J.M. Coetzee *Disgrace* (1999) 98

Part One

Research Question, Terminology and Methodology

Chapter 1: Introduction

1. An Introduction to the Basic Problems

Before a new constitutional era dawned on South Africa, the general notions accepted as portraying legal reality best were that private law regulated the acquisition, protection and transfer of private property and that public law regulated the liberty and equality of citizens. The inclusion of the property clauses in the chapters on fundamental rights of the Interim Constitution[1] and Final Constitution[2] challenged this point of departure.[3] More specifically, the reference to public purpose

---

[1]   Sec. 28 (Interim) Constitution Act 200 of 1993.

[2]   Sec. 25 (Final) Constitution, 1996.

[3]   The words *Interim* or *Transitional* in references to the South African Constitution usually denote the Constitution Act 200 of 1993, which was always intended as a temporary measure to be replaced within two years. With the phrase *Final Constitution*, reference is usually made to Act 108 of 1996, which is intended to be of lasting application, even if amended from time to time and therefore not "final" in the absolute sense of the word. See *Budlender* in *Budlender/Latsky/Roux*, New Land Law (1998), ch. 1, 4 note 2. With reference to the erroneous numbering of the Final Constitution as "Act 108 of 1996", see *Van Wyk*, 1997 THRHR, 378-379, where it is explained that the Final Constitution, not being a parliamentary statute, should not have been regarded as part of the body of statutory law accepted by parliament annually and numbered accordingly. The Interim Constitution was numbered as "Act 200 of 1993" because it was technically and formally adopted by the three-cameral parliament, as opposed to a constitutional assembly specifically appointed for this purpose. The Final Constitution has been adopted on 11 October 1996 (after initial rejection of the constitutional text by the Constitutional Court) by the constitutional assembly, which existed independently from parliament. (For

and the public interest as justification for expropriation of property and land reform in the Final Constitution[4] raised questions about the acceptability of the existing scheme of law pertaining to landownership.

In a post-colonial, post-apartheid era, South African common law[5] finds itself at the crossroads as new legal developments endeavour to follow and/or shape the changes in society.[6] From the perspective of private law, the imminent question is what impact the constitutional provisions pertaining to property have on the existing law of property. Prior to the advent of transformation, the land law — in its material form constituting numerous politically inspired statutes[7] — was simply

---

a discussion of the certification of the constitution by the Constitutional Court, see *Malherbe*, 1997 TSAR, 356-370.) The constitutional assembly had one specific assignment: the adoption of the Final Constitution in the manner prescribed by the Interim Constitution. This indicates that reference to the Final Constitution should not support the erroneous numbering thereof. Consequently, further reference to the Final Constitution in this work will ignore the numbering and will simply be indicated with the abbreviation "FC" after the quoted section. For the sake of consistency, reference to the Interim Constitution will be indicated with the abbreviation "IC" after the quoted section.

[4]   Sec. 25 FC. See in particular sec. 25(4) FC.

[5]   The use of the terms *common law* and *civil law* is problematic in the South African context. The term *common law* usually refers to the legal systems in England, Wales and Ireland, which have traditionally been perceived as "flourishing in splendid isolation from those on the European continent." With the term *civil law* reference is made to the legal systems on the European continent, which are, to a larger or lesser extent, influenced by the reception of Roman law in these systems. South Africa has a so-called *mixed legal system*, as a result of its peculiar colonial history, where at first the Dutch province of Holland and later the British Empire enjoyed a particularly influential position with regard to governmental structure and legal regime. A mixed jurisdiction lies at the intersection of civil law and common law. Apart from South Africa, also Scotland, Quebec, Louisiana, Sri Lanka, Botswana, Lesotho, Swaziland, Namibia and Zimbabwe are categorised as mixed jurisdictions. Therefore, the South African *common law* differs in content somewhat from its English counterpart. *Zimmermann/Visser* in *Zimmermann/Visser* (eds), Southern Cross (1996), 2-3; *Beekhuis/Lawson/Knapp et. al.* in *Lawson* (chief ed), International Encyclopaedia of Comparative Law, vol VI (2) (1975), ch. 2, 247-252.

[6]   *Van der Walt*, 1998 THRHR, 401.

[7]   E.g. the Black Land Act 27 of 1913; the Development Trust and Land Act 18 of 1936; and the Group Areas Acts 41 of 1950, 77 of 1957 and 36 of 1966. All these acts were repealed by the Abolition of Racially Based Land Measures Act 108 of 1991.

the most visible embodiment of apartheid and racial discrimination.[8] Many opponents of apartheid wanted to get rid not only of the race laws, but also of the existing land law as such,[9] and vociferously claimed its replacement by a new system of land rights reflecting the ideals of justice and equality under a new constitutional order. No wonder that the South African private law of property had suffered a legitimacy crisis.[10]

Those who did not want to throw out the Roman-Dutch law baby with the dirty apartheid water, argued that the "pure" common law (that is

---

[8]   *Van der Walt* in *Van der Walt* (ed), Land Reform (1991), 22.

[9]   Some authors believed that nationalisation of property would be the adequate solution. See *Marcus*, 1990 SAJHR, 178-194; also *Skweyiya*, 1990 SAJHR, 195-214. However, the debate about transformation of the property law order in South Africa took place more or less simultaneously with the fall of socialism in Eastern Europe. This made it difficult for most scholars to take calls for nationalisation of property in an old-fashioned socialist manner seriously. *Van der Walt* in *Van der Walt* (ed), Land Reform (1991), 29; see in particular *Robertson*, 1990 SAJHR, 215 - 227.

[10]   South African land law as a source for the bitterness and scepticism had several facets: The unfair distribution of land under *grand apartheid* (i.e. the spatial separation of the different races under the policy of *separate development*) resulted, first, in overcrowding, overgrazing and overcultivation of agricultural land. This caused serious environmental damage. It generated controlled urbanisation with the purpose of providing mines and industries with cheap labour. In the second place distribution of land under grand apartheid reduced the activities of all black farmers to subsistence farming (due to acute shortage of land, financing and agricultural markets, as well as the inability to procure agricultural land in so-called white areas because of prohibitory legislation). Furthermore, as the indigenous land law was also used by the apartheid government as an instrument to subordinate blacks, the general disregard for the traditional (civilian) property law also spilled over to this legal sphere. *Gutto*, Property and Land Reform (1995), 17. Finally the statutorily implemented forced removal and resettlement of millions of people in areas according to population group contributed to the growing mistrust in and despise of the existing property law system by the majority of the population. The "colossal social experiment" of separate development (as it was described by the Appellate Division of the South African Supreme Court in *Minister of the Interior v Lockhat* 1961 2 SA 587 (A), 602D) resulted in, first, transport problems for especially people from non-white groups, usually situated outside urban areas and, second, in criminal prosecutions for residential occupation outside the specially demarcated areas. *Van der Walt*, 1995 TSAR, 515-517; *Letsoalo*, Land Reform in South Africa (1987), 3-7, 32-35.

to say the uncodified Roman-Dutch law) was already an embodiment of the required principles of justice and equality.[11] Stripped from the stigma it gathered through legislative alterations, the common law could, according to this argument, serve a post-apartheid society well. The problem with this approach is that a continued reliance on the Roman-Dutch law could impede the development of a "properly *constitutional*" fundamental rights practice and the promotion of land reform.[12] Concepts like reconciliation, reconstruction and development, as well as the notion of constitutionally guaranteed fundamental rights, will cause the South African society to continually scrutinise the legitimacy of the existing common law order.[13]

Even if it is assumed that an equitable solution to the problems created by apartheid land law can only be found in constitutional law, the basic dilemma does not disappear. A compromise still needs to be found between property as an instrument for giving effect to individual freedom and property as an instrument for effecting social equality. If the private law of property would continue to exist unaltered, the unequal distribution of property would remain unchanged and the political and economic inequality present in the South African system would persist. However, private ownership and the security of title coupled with it under private law cannot simply be disregarded for the sake of socio-economic transformation. After all, security of title is an important component of stable socio-economic relations.

2. Objectives of Research

This dissertation is an attempt at reconciling the existing (and until recently predominant) private law concept of ownership and the property rights espoused by the new constitutional order against the background of the land reform programme, in particular the attempts at restitution and redistribution of land in South Africa. The focal point of the expo-

---

[11] *Van der Walt* in *Van der Walt* (ed), Land Reform (1991), 22 (but contrast *Van der Walt*, 1995 SAJHR, 171). *Gutto*, Property and Land Reform (1995), 13, in spite of his criticism of the "colonialist" system of private property promoted by the legal system, shows that "this system of property has been sufficiently indigenised to provide it with 'legitimacy' in the new Africa."

[12] *Van der Walt*, 1998 THRHR, 418.

[13] *Van der Walt*, 1995 SAJHR, 171.

sition will be the influence of the constitutional protection and regulation of property on the private law of ownership. An investigation that affords primary importance to the system of fundamental rights, and which takes governmental policy programmes into account, could provide new insights into the continued relevance or altered significance of the common law concept of landownership in South Africa. It might also be useful in determining the basis of rights created in terms of the new political dispensation, specifically with regard to access to land, and restitution and redistribution of land. Thus, the legal development of the private law of property could be sustained by a paradigm that takes the dictates of the constitution into account.

Such an investigation is also interesting from another perspective. The institution of ownership is meaningful only in relation to the nature of the specific society in which it operates. As such, the scope and content of property rights will always be dependent on the needs of a specific society at a specific point in time. This mostly means that property rights cannot exist in isolation. Moreover, property rights are almost never really absolute in nature. Both in private and constitutional law the scope of these rights is restricted, albeit on different levels. From a private law perspective, property rights are restricted on a "horizontal" level by the rights and interests of third parties. From a constitutional perspective, the scope of a person's property rights is determined by considering limitations in the public interest; that is, on a vertical level *vis-à-vis* the state authority. The interaction of private law and public law limitations of property rights has received little scholarly attention thus far and deserves to be discussed.

2.1. Motivation

At first glance, it seems inevitable that new legal developments initiated by the introduction of an entrenched bill of rights might be incompatible with the property rights enforceable in terms of the South African common law. It is not easy to find viable solutions to undo those injustices that occurred during the apartheid era as a result of forced removals and expropriations for the sake of implementing the policy of racial segregation.

It is, however, important to make an attempt at satisfying the expectations in this regard, and at finding solutions to the socio-political and legal problems that have arisen because of the injustices of the past. An effort of reconciling the notion of fundamental rights (which goes hand in hand with a modern, constitutional state), land reform (which is an imperative of the South African constitutional property clause[14]) and common law (which is the uncodified South African private law rooted in the Roman-Dutch tradition and influenced in some respects by the English common law and the German Pandectists),[15] is important for the establishment of a legitimate new constitutional order. In such a process, at least some of the injustices of the past could be undone.

2.2. Legal Comparison

The extent to which public interest determines how an individual owner is protected in the enjoyment of rights and entitlements pertaining to his or her ownership, is not an issue peculiar to the South African context. Germany was, for instance, confronted with similar problems after the reunification of the Federal Republic of Germany and the German Democratic Republic.[16] The German and South African priorities pertaining to the formulation of a dynamic concept of ownership are, however, linked to the unique historical developments in the respective legal systems. Nevertheless, the process of reformulation and alteration of ownership theory in both systems correspond with each other, in spite of the fact that circumstances that have given rise to these developments in both systems were markedly different.

In South Africa, the transformation of the existing property law must take place as a result of constitutional reform, and has the objective of ensuring security of land tenure, restitution of dispossessed property and equitable access to land.[17] By contrast, the German civil law concept of ownership underwent a gradual adaptation through the decisions of the Federal Constitutional Court *(Bundesverfassungsgericht)*, the Federal Supreme Court *(Bundesgerichtshof)* and the Federal Administrative Court *(Bundesverwaltungsgericht)*. The "social responsibility" embodied in the notion of ownership has been a factor consid-

---

[14] See sec. 25(4)-(9) FC.

[15] *Carey-Miller* in *Barry* (ed), Proceedings of the Conference on Land Tenure (1998), 50, online at http://www.gtz.de/orboden/capetown/cape09.htm [27.05.2000].

[16] See 540 ff. below.

[17] Sec. 25(4)-(9) FC.

ered by the German judiciary practically from the moment the Basic Law came into force.[18] More recently, during the process of reunification, this "social function" of ownership also influenced the drafting of legislation aimed at reconciling the property systems of the Federal Republic of Germany and the German Democratic Republic.[19]

Lessons from German law in the regulation and protection of property, the restitution of property expropriated in the eastern part of Germany during the time of Soviet occupation and German Democratic rule, and in the treatment of such cases by the courts could be a fruitful basis for legal comparison. In this manner, legal-comparative research may contribute to finding solutions to the problems relating to the regulation and protection of property and to land reform, redistribution and restitution under the South African constitutional order. Through legal comparison, a property model that serves the socio-economic and political goals of individual development, societal empowerment and economic growth could be developed. In this exposition, the insights to be gained from the constitutional protection and regulation of property rights by the German legislature and judiciary, and their relevance for the development of a South African property theory which could be employed as an instrument of reform,[20] will take centre stage.

2.3. Delimitation

A focus on the constitutional development of the concept of ownership can, at best, provide only a partial explanation of the intricate system of social, political and historical relations underpinning the legal concept of ownership. For a better understanding of the structure of the legal institution of ownership in both Germany and South Africa, it would be necessary to conduct an in-depth socio-political and historical analysis of the development of this concept in both legal systems. Unfortunately this would go beyond the scope of the current exposition. The primary focus of the thesis is to place into context, from a constitutional perspective, the protection of property rights, expropriation of property and land reform. The discussion of different theories on prop-

---

[18] E.g. BVerfGE 1, 264 *(Schornsteinfeger)*, handed down in 1952.

[19] See 547 ff. below.

[20] See *Munzer*, A Theory of Property (1990), 469.

erty[21] and of the Roman concept of ownership,[22] which lies at the root of the civilian concept of ownership as it is known in both Germany and South Africa, will be confined to the rudimentary.

3. Practical Significance of Research

The aim of this thesis is to determine the extent to which existing rights should yield to the new political policies in property reform legislation and the basis of new rights created by property reform legislation. In this regard it will be of specific interest to examine the extent to which individual property interests could be limited or expanded by the abil-

---

[21] A useful overview over the different theories on property relevant for the South African context can be found in the trilogy of articles by *Van der Walt*, 1995 TSAR, 15-42, 322-345, 493-526.

[22] Among the authoritative sources on the historical development of owner-ship are: *Kaser*, Eigentum (1943); *Diosdi*, Ownership in Ancient and Pre-Classical Roman Law (1970); *Schultz*, Classical Roman Law (1951), 334-380. See also *Daube* in *Cohen & Simon (ed)*, Collected Studies in Roman Law II (1991), 1325-1339. *Van der Walt*, Houerskap (1985) provides an extensive analysis of the historical development of ownership in relation to the concept of holdership from ancient Roman Law, Germanic Law, Medieval Canon Law through the developments in Germany, the Netherlands and France of the six-teenth century and thereafter, and the reception of the Roman Law in Holland and its application in South Africa. *Höft*, Öffentlichrechtliche Eigentumsbe-schränkungen (1952) analyses the public law limitations on ownership in Ro-man Law by using the example of building laws and regulations. This is par-ticularly interesting for the question as to the meaning of common good or public weal in Roman Law pertaining to property. Not only does it provide in-sight into the *mores* governing Roman society pertaining to the individual free-dom and autonomy of the "owners," but also, and more importantly, it indi-cates that the restrictions on ownership for the sake of the common good ex-isting in the various eras were generally quite extensive (72). The restrictions by public building law being least extensive in the classical era of Roman Law, the conclusion is made that the development of limitations to ownership within private law itself made public law restrictions less important (73). On the re-striction of the ownership concept, see also *Birks*, 1985 Acta Juridica 1-37. For the South African context, see *Van der Walt*, 1988 De Jure, 16-35, 306-325; *Visser*, 1985 Acta Juridica, 39-52; *Van der Merwe*, 1998 TSAR, 1-19; *Van der Walt*, 1998 THRHR, 400-422; *Van der Walt*, 1986 THRHR, 305-321; *Van der Walt*, 1993 THRHR, 569-589. For an overview of the development of owner-ship in German law, see *Olzen*, 1984 JuS, 328-335.

ity of a democratically legitimised legislature to interfere with private property interests in the general interest of the public. The extent to which a social responsibility is incorporated into the institution of ownership could also be clarified.

This might, however, create the impression that this research would be simply theoretical and of little importance to the practice of property law in South Africa. On the contrary, a consistent interpretation of the constitutional property clause is practically impossible if the fundamental dogmatic principles on which it is based are unclear or confusing. The purpose of this exposition is to evaluate the current developments in property law in order to determine whether they could serve the socio-economic and political goals of development of individual self-esteem, societal empowerment and economic growth.

Moreover, jurisdictions with longer histories of constitutional property protection than that of South Africa have demonstrated that the harmonisation of individual property rights and the public interest is one of the main issues in judicial evaluation of the state's interference in social or economic matters.[23] The results of the legal-comparative analysis will be specifically targeted at providing guidelines to the South African judiciary (that has to interpret the constitutional and ordinary legislative directives pertaining to property law reform) and the administration (that has to apply these directives).

4. Inquiry Outline

In the following chapters, the existing private law of ownership in both Germany and South Africa will be contrasted with the status of property under the constitutions of these countries. A detailed analysis of the various stages of inquiry into property issues under these constitutions will indicate how the present concepts of ownership in Germany and South Africa have been or will be influenced under a system of constitutional supremacy. Particular attention will be given to the extent to which the existing institution of ownership has been adjusted — in the public interest — by the social function of ownership embodied in the constitutional guarantee of property rights.

---

[23] *Von Brünneck*, Die Eigentumsgarantie des Grundgesetzes (1984), 15.

The restitution processes, both in Germany and in South Africa, will then be discussed as examples of property law reform. As such, the possibility of a new category of adjustments to the private law concept of ownership, apart from the already existing private law limitations, will be considered. However, before embarking on this inquiry, the advantages and disadvantages of the chosen analytical method, and the terminological difficulties that could be encountered in the course of the analysis will be assessed.

Chapter 2: Terminology

1. Possible Terminological Difficulties

Terms such as property, ownership and public interest are not un-known. In fact, they are widely used, not only in the technical language of various legal disciplines, but also in ordinary language. These concepts also differ to various degrees from one society to the other. As Birks remarks:[24]

> "The acquisition and enjoyment of wealth is a social phenomenon, which means at the simplest that it goes on, not in isolation, but in a context in which a plurality of people with competing interests, have to live in physical proximity. The very language of ownership implies the presence of others, albeit others who are to be excluded. It is observable that at different times and places different arrangements are made for locating the selfish drive for wealth and material security in the context of society as a whole."

This statement explains why concepts like property and public interest is so extraordinarily difficult to define. The following paragraphs will indicate the problems that could be experienced with these terms in legal-comparative research.

2. Ownership and Property

Ownership and *property* are the central concepts in an investigation of the constitutional moulding of structures from private law. The meanings of these terms depend on their functions in both private and constitutional law. Without embarking on a detailed analysis of either of these terms, the following introductory statements will attempt to clarify the use of these terms in the rest of this work.

2.1. Ideological Concept

In both Germany and South Africa, ownership is an important legal-sociological institution. On the one hand it recognises the private relationships between individuals in a given community in a unique way.

---

[24] *Birks*, 1985 Acta Juridica, 23.

On the other hand it also recognises the relations between persons and state institutions regarding the control over specific patrimonial objects. In both the German and South African legal systems, the essential function of the institution of ownership is to preserve and propagate the interests of individuals, albeit on different levels. Therefore ownership will continue to shape the structure of society as long as the individual remains the most important basic constructive element of society.[25] Together with agreement, the institution of ownership forms the basis of the modern world economy, and together with labour, property is the constitutive element of modern patrimonial law.[26]

The perception of ownership, nevertheless, differs from one society to the other, depending on the political, legal and economic systems of the various communities. Even within a single community, proprietary relations are transitory in nature: They are not ready-made, fixed or predetermined.[27] Almost like languages, proprietary relations are changeable and are indeed changed as soon as they can no longer meet the needs and interests of the members of the community.[28] Since political theories incorporate ownership in their dogmatic structures, the legal-technical aspects of the ownership concept are furthermore almost invariably ideologically tainted.[29]

The fact that the concept of ownership and property is inextricably linked to the social and political ideologies underlying a specific legal system, renders a universal definition practically impossible. A definition of ownership and property would, therefore, depend on the spe-

---

[25] *Bixio* in *Ferrari (ed)*, Laws and Rights (1991), 969.

[26] *Van der Merwe*, Sakereg (1989), 169-170.

[27] See *Kleyn/Boraine/Du Plessis*, Silberberg & Schoeman's Law of Property (1992), 161; *Pienaar*, 1986 TSAR, 303-306; *Van der Walt*, 1988 De Jure, 17-18; *Domanski*, 1989 THRHR, 433-443; *Van der Walt/Pienaar*, Introduction (1996), 55; *Gutto*, Property and Land Reform (1995), 11.

[28] *Beekhuis/Lawson/Knapp et. al.* in *Lawson* (chief ed), International Encyclopaedia of Comparative Law, vol VI (2) (1975), ch. 2, 273-284 provide a valuable overview of the "grammar" of property law in the different societies. They remark that the differences between property law in various jurisdictions, even within a specific ideological class, can perhaps best be explained in a general way by saying that the various grammars of property law have, like linguistic grammar, been worked out in order to describe and regularise the habitual ways of dealing with problems which predominated in different societies and at different periods.

[29] *Van Maanen*, 1993 Recht & Kritiek, 74.

cific area of investigation, as well as on the prevailing socio-political convictions in the legal systems under scrutiny. In the legal context, attempts at defining the institution of ownership are further complicated by the use of more than one term for the description of more-or-less similar concepts, or the use of a single term for two or more different concepts.

2.2. Legal Concept

Different factors render a definition of property and ownership in law difficult. On the one hand, the inconsistent use of terms denoting proprietary relations in legal English could cause unnecessary hairsplitting. For example, in the First Protocol to the European Convention on Human Rights[30] mention is made of *possessions* in the first paragraph of the English text,[31] whereas the word *property*[32] is used in the second paragraph. The German version of the document treats both these terms as *Eigentum*. These differences have, for instance, resulted in two decisions of the European Court of Justice to the effect that, although different terms are used, one and the same meaning is intended.[33]

On the other hand, the different terms used in English are sometimes used to denote different concepts. In German, like in Afrikaans, one word is generally used with reference to both *ownership* and *property* in the private law sense. *Eigentum* in German and *eiendom* in Afrikaans refer to both *the right of ownership* as well as the *object of such a right*. Then again, the English term *property* is employed differently in public

---

[30] Art. 1, First Protocol to the European Convention on Human Rights: "Every natural or legal person is entitled to the peaceful enjoyment of his *possessions*. No one shall be deprived of his *possessions* except in the public interest and subject to the conditions provided for by law and by the general principles of international law. ... The preceding provisions shall not, however, in any way impair the right of a State to enforce such laws as it deems necessary to control the use of *property* in accordance with the general interest or to secure the payment of taxes or other contributions or penalties." Emphasis added.

[31] The French equivalent is *biens*.

[32] *Propriété* in the French text.

[33] *Frowein/Peukert*, Europäische Menschenrechtskonvention - Kommentar (1996), 766 m.n. 3. *Handyside decision*, EuGRZ 1977, 38, par. 62; *Marckx decision*, EuGRZ 1979, 454, par. 63.

law and in private law. This makes the English terminology of property law rather confusing.

2.2.1. Private Law Terminology

Van der Walt and Pienaar[34] have indicated that the term *property* in its "ordinary sense" refers to a wide variety of assets that make up a person's estate or belongings and which serve as objects of the rights that such a person exercises in respect thereof. In legal English, however, the word *property* is a complex term, the exact meaning of which can only be defined in the context in which it is used. Kleyn and Boraine[35] explain that, even when it is reduced to its most elementary components, *property* has two different meanings. It will always signify two distinct legal concepts: (i) property as the *right of ownership in a thing* and (ii) property as the *thing* to which this right relates.

(i) Property as the *right of ownership* implies a relation of a specific person to a specific object of patrimonial interest. It furthermore implies a relation between a specific person (the holder of the right to ownership) and third parties. The latter can be prohibited from infringing the entitlements of the former to the object.[36] Further, ownership can usually be distinguished in certain respects from other kinds of rights: It is the only *real right* that the person can have with regard to his or her own object.[37] The term *real right* refers to the right of a person *to* a specific kind of object of patrimonial interest, the *res*.[38] *Res* is generally accepted

---

[34] *Van der Walt/Pienaar,* Introduction (1996), 17. They continue by explaining (18) that a person's assets consist partly of tangible, perceptible parts and partly of non-tangible or non-perceptible parts like creditor's rights in terms of a contract, copyright in respect of a book etc.

[35] *Kleyn/Boraine/Du Plessis,* Silberberg & Schoeman's Law of Property (1992), 1. To prevent confusion, the first legal concept to which Kleyn and Boraine refer, that is to say "the right of ownership in a thing," will be described in this work as *ownership* and the second legal concept, or rather "the thing to which this right relates," as *property in its narrow sense,* or by means of the Latin term, *res.* Within the constitutional context, the term *property* will be used, but here in its broader sense, that is to say including all patrimonial interests qualifying for protection under the constitutions.

[36] *Van der Walt,* 1988 De Jure, 17; *Van der Merwe,* Sakereg (1989), 61-63.

[37] I.e. *ius in re sua (in re propria).*

[38] I.e. "thing".

to refer to perceptible and tangible (corporeal) assets only. Various kinds of real rights over *res* exist, but ownership is usually perceived to be the most extensive of these rights. Other real rights are *iura in re aliena*,[39] because they pertain to the *res* of somebody other than the holder of the right. Thus, ownership is described as that real right which provides the subject with potentially the most complete and comprehensive control over an object. In contrast, other real rights are merely limited to a few specific entitlements regarding an object of another.[40] However, this explanation is rather superficial and prone to criticism. This will be indicated in the course of this thesis.

(ii) The term property as *object of a right*[41] was, in the private law context,[42] limited — for scientific purposes — to denote corporeal *res* only.[43] In fact, preference is given to the terms *things* or *res* when denoting the object of the right in private law, as an inconsiderate use of this term creates confusion between references to a person's patrimony or *assets in general* and references to *perceptible and tangible assets only*. The word *property* is even regarded by some as a "foreign" term as far as private property law is concerned.[44] This explains why some authors refrain from referring to this part of the law as "property law," and prefer the term "the law of things."[45] The word *saak* in Afrikaans and the term *Sache* in German both describe the object of the owner's right and correlate with the use of the term *property* in its narrow private law sense (meaning: thing / *res*). Traditionally it was defined very broadly in Roman law,[46] Roman-Dutch law[47] and South African law.[48] However,

---

[39] I.e. rights that persons or legal subjects hold with regard to the *res* of other legal subjects. *Van der Merwe*, Sakereg (1989), 69; *Van der Walt*, 1988 De Jure, 17.

[40] *Van der Walt*, 1988 De Jure, 17; *Van der Merwe*, Sakereg (1989), 171. See 171 ff. below.

[41] When used in the sense of "things" (*res*) as in the second context described by *Kleyn/Boraine/Du Plessis*, Silberberg & Schoeman's Law of Property (1992), 1, i.e. "the object to which the right of ownership relates".

[42] I.e. with reference to *res* / *thing*.

[43] *Van der Merwe*, Sakereg (1989), 63.

[44] *Van der Walt*, Constitutional Property Clause (1997), 53 note 84.

[45] See *Van der Merwe*, Sakereg (1989), 5-7; critical explanation in *Kleyn/Boraine/Du Plessis*, Silberberg & Schoeman's Law of Property (1992), 2.

[46] *Van der Merwe*, Sakereg (1989), 20. Although the Roman texts do not contain a comprehensive definition of *res*, it is indicated in the *Institutiones* of

limiting property to corporeal *res* was apparently the only way in which real rights could be distinguished from other subjective rights.[49] This induces Van der Merwe[50] to declare that, in the law of property, the object of a real right is not as important as the absolute effect of it. This enabled a definition of real rights as those rights that provide the legal subject with direct physical control over a legal object. Nevertheless, several examples from legal practice indicate that incorporeal objects to real rights do indeed exist.[51] Moreover, in the constitutional context this definition becomes problematic.

Gaius 1 8 that things (i.e. *res*) included everything that the private law took cognisance of other than persons and actions. This includes corporeals as well as incorporeals. *Van der Merwe*, Law of Things / LAWSA XXVII (1993), par. 14.

[47]   *Grotius* Inleidinge 2 1 3 (*De Groot*, Inleidinge tot de Hollandsche Rechtsgeleerdheyd (1631)) described property (*Zaken*) as objects which are external to and useful in any way to mankind. *Van der Keessel*, Praelectiones ad Grotius 2 1 3 (Praelectiones Iuris Hodierni ad Hugonis Grotii Introductionem ad Iursiprudentiam Hollandicam, Van Warmelo/Coertze/Gonin/Pont (1961-1967)) adds that objects that are useful and valuable to mankind, except persons and actions, are regarded as things. Voet's definition is even more broadly phrased and includes "*omne id de quo ius dicitur*"-"everything of which the law takes cognisance." *Voet*, Elementa juris (1737), 2 1 1. See *Van der Merwe*, Law of Things / LAWSA XXVII (1993), par. 14 and the accompanying notes for a more detailed discussion.

[48]   These definitions tend to equate the notion of property (*res*) with that of legal object. See *Maasdorp*, Institutes of South African Law (1976), vol 2, 1 "The term property (*res*) is applied in law to everything with respect to which one person may be entitled to a right and another person to a duty." *Van der Merwe*, Law of Things / LAWSA XXVII (1993), par. 14 note 11. *Lee*, Introduction to Roman Dutch Law (1953), 120 uses Voet's definition, but warns that it is "unprofitable to labour to define what is scarcely definable." *Van der Merwe*, Sakereg (1989), 21 note 9.

[49]   *Van der Merwe*, Sakereg (1989), 21, 22. *Kleyn/Boraine/Du Plessis*, Silberberg & Schoeman's Law of Property (1992), 11 argued that, if the definition of *res* would not be limited to corporeal things only, "it would mean that a right can also be the object of a right which is regarded as illogical, inconsistent and jurisprudentially impossible."

[50]   *Van der Merwe*, Sakereg (1989), 23.

[51]   A usufruct, for instance, can be created and registered in connection with registered mineral rights. *Van der Merwe*, Law of Things / LAWSA XXVII (1993), par. 14 note 21. Likewise, a registered long-term lease, a registered per-

2.2.2. Terminology of the Constitution

In the constitutional context the English terminology is possibly not as problematic as the Afrikaans or German terms. Van der Walt[52] indicates that property clauses are usually interpreted liberally and generously in most jurisdictions where constitutional protection of property is found. The term *Eigentum* is, for instance, used in the German constitutional context, although it is quite clear that the constitutional definition of *Eigentum* has very little to do with the narrow definition in the Civil Code.

The terms *eiendom* and *regte in eiendom* are used to refer to proprietary relations in the Afrikaans versions of the Final Constitution and Interim Constitution respectively. The use of *eiendom* in the constitutional context can be confusing, because it can refer either to the object of property rights or to the right of ownership, as it is known in private law. In fact, the Afrikaans word *eiendomsreg* would be technically more appropriate if reference is made to the right of ownership. By contrast, because English prefers use of the terms *thing* and *res* in the private law context, the word *property* is a "foreign" term as far as private property law is concerned. This makes it much easier to accept that *property* in the constitutional context is a wider concept than the private law *ownership* or *things*.[53]

The term *property* in the constitutional context usually designates a broader concept than that of *thing (res)* in private law.[54] It includes not only *ownership* as it is known in private law, but also several other pat-

---

sonal servitude or registered mineral rights can form the object of a real security right *(Pignus / Hypotheca)*. Sec. 65(1), 60, 68(2), 69(4), 71(5) and (6) and sec. 80 of the Deeds Registries Act 47 of 1937; *Van der Merwe*, Sakereg (1989), 22.

[52]   *Van der Walt*, Constitutional Property Clauses - A Comparative Analysis (1999), 21.

[53]   *Van der Walt*, Constitutional Property Clause (1997), 53 note 84. In South Africa, the word *ownership* is usually employed in the private law context and *property*, *rights in property* or *property rights* in the constitutional context, in order to show that the constitutional definition of *property* has a broader scope than the private law definition of *ownership*.

[54]   The South African constitutions and the German Basic Law themselves do not provide definitions of constitutional property, but usually certain requirements have to be complied with before interests not protected by the private law of property can qualify for constitutional protection. See 200 ff. and 224 ff. below.

rimonial and incorporeal rights, regarded as "lesser" rights in private law, and which sometimes do not even qualify as real rights. That does not mean, however, that all rights and interests with even the slightest patrimonial character qualify as property in the constitutional sense. The most difficult questions regarding the constitutional concept of property still concern the protection of intangible property in the form of rights and interests not necessarily recognised or treated as property in the narrow private law sense. Although property rights with regard to the human body, cultural property and religious property have at-tracted some attention in recent years;[55] *intangible* and *commercial* property, as well as the so-called *new property*[56] still remain the most controversial.

(i) Most forms of intangible property and commercial property could qualify for constitutional protection. The best examples are the various forms of intellectual property (that is to say, copyright, patents and trademarks); and even some "rights" based on commercial documents (like shares). The constitutional protection of monetary debts and rights created by legislation (like permits, licences and quotas) is, how-ever, more difficult.

(ii) With the development of the welfare state, access to "state largesse" in the form of benefits, jobs, pensions, housing subsidies, contracts, li-censes, and so on, broadened the scope of individual security connected to property.[57] The increasing economic importance of these "assets" en-visages a notion of property that is — as far as due process issues are concerned[58] — not limited to corporeal *res* only. Although they could

---

[55]   See e.g. *Harris (ed)*, Property Problems from Genes to Pension Funds (1997).

[56]   *Van der Walt*, Constitutional Property Clauses - A Comparative Analysis (1999), 22-23.

[57]   These interests are to a certain extent protected in Germany. See 237 ff. below.

[58]   In the USA, *Reich*, 1964 Yale LJ, 733-787 first propagated the idea of "largesse of government" as a new form of property. See 734-739 for a descrip-tion of this concept and 739-756 for an analysis of the underlying legal struc-ture. This idea found strong support, not only in the USA, where Reich's article has become one of the most frequently cited law review contributions (see *Shapiro*, 1985 California Law Review, 1549), but also in South Africa: e.g. *Van der Walt* in *Van Wyk/Dugard et. al. (eds)*, Rights and Constitutionalism (1996), 457-458, 463, 465-466, 480, 490-493 (criticism); *Davis/Cheadle/Haysom*, Fun-damental Rights in the Constitution - Commentary and Cases (1997), 241;

be covered by the application of existing principles of contract and administrative law, it is difficult to categorise these "rights" in a constitutional sense. If the definition of property under constitutional law would mirror that of private law, these "rights" would not be protected as part of an individual's patrimony, and would not qualify for protection under a constitutional property guarantee. Normally, the constitution does not protect these "rights" or "assets" separately either. If the law was to keep abreast with social development, constitutional protection had to be extended to these types of *new property* by including them within the ambit of the constitutional property concept.[59]

2.2.3. Terminology of Reform

The traditional restriction of the property concept to corporeals might render it impossible to explain the nature of rights created by reform legislation, especially where they are relevant outside the constitutional context. Similarly, the existing model of full ownership as a right elevated above all others, might make it difficult to reconcile the reform policy, portrayed and supported by the constitutions, with the present notion of property in private law.

In the context of the land reform programme in South Africa, reference is sometimes made to the term *land tenure*. This concept includes *land-ownership*, but has a wider scope. The new South Africa has inherited a diversified land tenure system with land control forms varying from race group to race group and region to region depending on the applicable legislation at a specific point in time.[60] Over the past few years, it has become clear that social and economic development in the sphere of land rights depend essentially on *security of tenure*, rather than on ownership. Private law has shown that the latter can be completely stripped of all its inherent entitlements, including the right to use land and the

---

Chaskalson/Lewis in *Chaskalson/Kentridge/Klaaren et. al. (eds)*, Constitutional Law of South Africa (1996), ch. 31, 4. The courts in the USA have, however, accepted the notion of "new property" for purposes of due process, and not for purposes of takings. See the discussion of the US case law (*Goldberg v Kelly* 397 US 254 (1970) and *Flemming v Nestor* 363 US 603 (1960)) in *Van der Walt*, Constitutional Property Clauses - A Comparative Analysis (1999), 441-443.

[59]   *Chaskalson*, 1993 SAJHR, 404.

[60]   *Van der Merwe/Pienaar* in *Jackson/Wilde (eds)*, Reform of Property Law (1997), 364.

power to control that use, without being transformed in the process. However, increasing intervention by the state in several areas related to property demonstrates that unlimited or absolute private ownership does not exist and that all ownership is subject to the state's dual power of regulation and expropriation. The most telling examples are found in the regulation of land use and the creation of new statutory rights to facilitate sectional title ownership, group and cluster housing, as well as property time-sharing. Further examples can be found in the role of the state in the declaration and management of nature reserves and in planning law.

Land tenure implies legally secure access to land and security of its use. Quite often this term is associated with agricultural or rural development. Sometimes it is also used to refer to both urban and rural security of tenure.[61] All rights of tenure, whatever the scope of individual, group or societal rights might be, are subject to the inherent powers of the state. This includes the power to regulate all patrimonial interests (police power / deprivation / legislative interference) and the power to expropriate such interests (eminent domain). The power to regulate includes, for instance, power of taxation, environmental and planning regulation, and compulsory requirements for title to land. In the South African context, the Development Facilitation Act[62] and the Subdivision of Agricultural Land Act[63] contain such state regulatory measures.

2.2.4. Polarisation of the Private Law Property and Constitutional Property

The manner in which property in terms of the constitution is distinguished from private law property is characteristic of the new property order under the constitution. The definition of the South African property concept in terms of the civilian tradition[64] raises the question of whether the constitutional property concept should be restricted in the same way as the private property concept. Although the German legal system is also oriented towards civil law, the Federal Constitutional Court has established a "typically" constitutional interpretation of the

---

[61] See the use of this term in *Gutto*, Property and Land Reform (1995), 26 ff.

[62] 67 of 1995.

[63] 70 of 1970.

[64] I.e. Roman-Germanic law.

term *Eigentum*, which differs from the traditional civil law meaning of this word, with regard to both the objects and the meaning of property rights.[65]

Property therefore means something different from *ownership*. The constitutional *property* concept is much wider than private law *ownership*.[66] The introduction of a wider property concept in terms of the constitution would obviously bring about some changes to the property law order. The consequent polarisation of private law and constitutional law with regard to the concepts of ownership and property raises questions about the inherent characteristics of property and the acceptability of the existing structure of property law.

An important issue is whether aspects or parts of the right of ownership can be judged independently when deciding whether property has been expropriated. Although this issue is older than the new constitutional order in South Africa, it acquires renewed interest because of the widened definition of property under the constitution. Some authors argue that *property* is made up of different characteristic "rights"[67] which could be conceptually severed.[68] In this manner, different ownership entitlements could be withdrawn or removed separately. This *conceptual severance* (also called the *bundle of rights* theory) could influence the fact of expropriation and the amount of compensation. This approach is, in fact, rejected by most scholars in Germany as well as in South Africa. Incorporating elements of such an approach into the theoretical structure of the constitutional concept of property should be avoided.

Certain aspects of both private law property and property in its constitutional sense could be relevant in an investigation of the extent to which existing rights should yield to the new political policies portrayed in, and the theoretical basis of rights created by reform legislation. For purposes of the constitutional interpretation of the property clause it might, for instance, be necessary to distinguish

---

[65] See 224 below.

[66] *Van der Walt*, Constitutional Property Clauses - A Comparative Analysis (1999), 350.

[67] Different "sticks" within a bundle. "Rights" in this sense is used as a general term, not necessarily as a legal term with a specific content.

[68] In *Sandton Town Council v Erf 89 Sandown Extension 2 (Pty) Ltd* 1988 3 SA 122 (A) the Appellate division also seems to adopt an approach based on this theory. See 183 below.

between *rights in property* and *rights in things*.[69] The latter concept is narrower, since it refers to the concept as it is understood in private law. The former includes both real and personal rights in property. This could underscore the extended concept of property in the constitutional context.

3. Public Interest, Common Weal and Public Purposes

The concept of public interest is well known in almost all branches of the law and in almost all jurisdictions, but the formulation of a definition is still problematic. Especially in the case of property law — in both a private and public sense — the meaning of the term *public interest* is perhaps even more difficult to define than the concepts *property* and *ownership* themselves. Attempts at formulating an acceptable definition of *public interest* in the context of property law are complicated by the fact that this term is used in more than one sense. Moreover, other similar terms (like *public use, public weal, public purposes*)[70] are used to denote concepts which either overlap to varying extents with or have a specific relation to the term *public interest.*

In principle, the law allows (or should allow) every individual to realise and propagate his or her full potential, within the limits set by the rights and freedoms of other individuals and the public order. These interests of individuals are protected in private law. When the interests of *individuals as a group ("individuals as all")* are threatened, they are protected by public means. This protection through public means introduces a public element to the protection of the individual's private interests, without depriving the individual of the remedies available for protection of interests in private law.[71] From this, it follows that public *interest* is a general notion used to justify choices of policy. It is a collective term used to refer to all those factors (like economic considerations, state security, as well as administrative and legal interests) which could influence the wellbeing of the community. The state can rely on these factors to justify infringements upon individual rights.

---

69 *Van der Walt*, 1994 THRHR, 193.

70 See *Eisenberg*, 1995 SAJHR, 208-209.

71 *Du Plessis*, 1987 THRHR, 291-293.

To simply say, however, that terms like *public weal, public purposes* or *public interest* are employed in property law to indicate the circumstances under which the state could infringe private rights, would be an inapt generalisation. The following paragraphs explain how these terms can be distinguished and will be employed in the rest of this thesis. An attempt is also made to indicate the kind of problems that might arise in connection with the use of the various terms. Before analysing the use of terms like public interest in the constitutional property clauses in particular, it might be useful to consider how these terms are generally applied in constitutional law.

3.1. Public Interest and Common Weal in the Constitutional Context

In discussing the concept of "sociality" as it is found in existentialist theory, Blaauw[72] draws attention to an important difference between *public interest* and *public weal* (or *common good*). She points out that in public law the state (or a state organ) forms one party to a legal relationship, with either a natural or a juristic person (whether singly or in plurality) constituting the other party. The public at large is only indirectly involved and only in so far as *public interest (salus publica)* is a legal norm applicable in resolving disputes.[73] By contrast, *common good* is a term connected with the philosophy of Rousseau, who determined that the general will *(volonté générale)* of the community is imbued with normative qualities reflecting the content of the *common good*.[74] The *common good* includes the fundamental values of freedom, justice, security, peace and prosperity. This concept is "translated" into "reality" by constitutional mechanisms like fundamental rights, the notion of the *Rechtsstaat* or constitutional state, the notion of the social welfare state and democracy.[75] Still, *common good* is a vague and problem-

---

[72] *Blaauw*, Constitutional Tenability of Group Rights (1988), 179-185.

[73] *Blaauw*, Constitutional Tenability of Group Rights (1988), 180.

[74] The *common good* as a result of the general will of the community is not necessarily the sum of individual wills or interests of specific groups. It can also happen that under specific circumstances the will of a minority in the community reflects the *common good*. *Blaauw*, Constitutional Tenability of Group Rights (1988), 180-182.

[75] *Blaauw*, Constitutional Tenability of Group Rights (1988), 185.

atic term, and renders itself prone to abuse by authoritarian rulers or interest groups.[76]

From Blaauw's analysis it becomes clear that the *public interest* can, in a sense, reflect the *common good*. This would be the case if it is accepted that the *public interest* denotes[77] "a regulative legal principle in terms of which legal interests are integrated on the basis of the recognition of its structural variety and equal value," and that the juridical interests of the public in general should be severed from the interests of the state itself.[78] As such a regulating principle, the *common good* is a valuable element of the constitutional order and, insofar as it is reflected by the *public interest*, important for an analysis of the property concept under the constitution. However, an approach in which *public interest* is equated with *common good*, is unacceptable. This would only serve to camouflage the interests of the state itself.[79]

The consequences of an abuse of the *common good* notion can best be illustrated by the treatment of property in Germany under National Socialism. This experience made Germans sceptical about a concept that is determined in an autocratic way and in reality constitutes nothing but a subterfuge for arbitrary action, which destroys individual freedom.

Scepticism among South African lawyers about the value of a principle like the *common good* for interpretation of the property clause, should also not seem strange in the light of the continuous abuse of executive power under the old regime in South Africa. Some authors have already touched upon the difficulties experienced with terms like *public interest* and *public weal*.[80] The abuse of such terms is perhaps most prevalent in

---

[76] *Blaauw,* Constitutional Tenability of Group Rights (1988), 184.

[77] Translation of the definition in *Pretorius,* Die Begrip Openbare Belang en die Burgervryheidsbeperking (1986), 304 by *Blaauw,* Constitutional Tenability of Group Rights (1988), 183.

[78] *Pretorius,* Die Begrip Openbare Belang en die Burgervryheidsbeperking (1986), 212-213.

[79] *Blaauw,* Constitutional Tenability of Group Rights (1988), 182.

[80] *Eisenberg,* 1995 SAJHR, 221; *Van der Walt,* Constitutional Property Clause (1997), 135-139; *Chaskalson/Lewis* in *Chaskalson/Kentridge/Klaaren et. al. (eds),* Constitutional Law of South Africa (1996), ch. 31, 17-18; *Murphy,* 1995 SAPR/PL, 124-128; *Chaskalson,* 1994 SAJHR, 136-138; *Budlender* in *Budlender/Latsky/Roux,* New Land Law (revised 1998), ch. 1, 48-54; *Reich,* 1964 Yale LJ, 771-783.

the context of expropriation of land. The addition of the term public purposes to the equation increases the confusion.

3.2. Public Interest, Public Purposes and the Property Clauses

Section 25(2)(a) FC provides that property may be expropriated "for a *public purpose* or in the *public interest*,"[81] whereas section 28(3) IC stipulated that "[an expropriation] shall be admissible *for public purposes only.*"[82] The text of the Final Constitution apparently adopted both the concepts of *public purposes* and *public interest* in an effort to eliminate the problem of a limited interpretation[83] stemming from judicial precedent on the matter.[84] This, however, created nothing but further confusion.[85]

In the South African context, the terms *public purposes* and *public interest* are used only with regard to expropriation, and not with regard to deprivations of property. The reason for this is not apparent. Because of the problems with the use of concepts like *public interest, public weal* and *public purposes* in South Africa, comparative legal analysis could in particular on this point have been valuable in suggesting solutions. Instead, problems of translation curtail the value of legal comparison on this point.

In article 14 GG, *public interest* is employed not only with regard to expropriation, but also to refer to the social obligation inherent in property. The official translation of article 14 GG treats both the terms *Wohle der Allgemeinheit* and *Interessen der Allgemeinheit* as meaning *public interest*. Article 14 II GG requires that property should "serve the *public interest*" (*Wohle der Allgemeinheit*).[86] Further, article 14 III GG determines that an expropriation shall only be permissible "in the

---

[81] Emphasis added.

[82] Emphasis added.

[83] *Van der Merwe/Pienaar* in *Jackson/Wilde (eds)*, Reform of Property Law (1997), 358.

[84] See 338 ff. below.

[85] *Van der Walt*, Constitutional Property Clause (1997), 135.

[86] Art. 14 II GG: *(1) Eigentum verpflichtet. (2) Sein Gebrauch soll zugleich dem Wohle der Allgemeinheit dienen.*

public interest" (Wohle der Allgemeinheit)[87] and that the amount of compensation to be paid for expropriation shall "reflect a fair balance between the *public interest (Interessen der Allgemeinheit)* and the interests of those affected."[88]

However, the fact that several authors[89] prefer to translate only *Interessen der Allgemeinheit* with *public interest,* and *Wohle der Allgemeinheit* with *public weal,* again gives rise to the problem of delimiting these concepts. Still, Böhmer J indicated in a minority judgement of the Federal Constitutional Court[90] that the purpose of the term *Wohle der Allgemeinheit* in article 14 II GG is quite distinct from that of the same term in article 14 III GG. In the former it protects the public at large by restricting individual rights, and in the latter it protects the individual by restricting the power of the state to expropriate property.

The definitions of *public interest* and *public weal* developed in the German context could most probably not be applied without further ado to the South African situation. Nevertheless, it would be useful to consider some of the results emanating from the interaction between public interest and property in the German system and which are related to the treatment of the property clause in general. It is submitted that some of these solutions could be adopted in the South African context.

However, one must still determine to what extent *public interest* correlates with the notion of *public purposes* in connection with the South African constitutional property clauses. This is best attempted within the context of the constitutional requirements for expropriation, as the application of the concepts *public interest* and *public purposes* in this field causes many difficulties.

---

[87] Art. 14 III GG: *(1) Eine Enteignung ist nur zum Wohle der Allgemeinheit zulässig.*

[88] Art. 14 III GG: *(3) Die Entschädigung ist unter gerechter Abwägung der Interessen der Allgemeinheit und der Beteiligten zu bestimmen.*

[89] *Kommers,* Constitutional Jurisprudence of Germany (1997), 250; *Finer/Bogdanor/Rudden,* Comparing Constitutions (1995), 134. *Currie,* Constitution of the Federal Republic of Germany (1994), 349.

[90] BVerfGE 56, 249 *(Dürkheimer Gondelbahn),* 273-276.

3.2.1. Public Interest, Public Purposes and Expropriation

In section 25(2)(a) FC both the terms *public purpose* and *public interest* are used with reference to the requirements for expropriation of property. Section 28(3) IC only referred to *public purposes*. This difference in wording shows that the meanings of the terms *public interest* and *public purpose* are neither exact, nor clear. This issue is made more problematic by the fact that the term *public purposes* is used in South African law in a broad as well as in a narrow sense.[91] In discussing *public purposes* as a requirement for expropriation under the South African constitution, it will be indicated[92] that the existing case law on the interpretation of the term *public purposes* is inadequate in the constitutional context, *inter alia* because of the different ways in which the term is applied.

The addition of the term *public interest* in section 25(2)(a) FC lays emphasis on the fact that the courts have limited power to set aside expropriations on the basis of the purpose behind such expropriations. To ensure that the objectives of land reform, redistribution and restitution are also incorporated into an interpretation of the terms *public purposes* and *public interest*, section 25(4) FC incorporates an additional mechanism to ensure that these terms are not "misinterpreted" by the courts. It determines that *public interest* includes the nation's commitment to land reform and to reforms to bring about equitable access to all South Africa's natural resources.

3.2.2. Public Interest, Public Purposes and Land Reform

In other jurisdictions — particularly in those where land reform programmes were introduced — terms like *public interest* and *public purposes* have been debated extensively.[93] One could, therefore, legitimately expect that this topic will be discussed in South Africa in future. However, even the express reference in section 25(4) FC that *public interest* includes the commitment to land reform is not of much help in determining what types of actions would be permissible because of being *in the public interest or for public purposes* and what not.

---

[91] See 333 ff. below.

[92] See 330 ff. below.

[93] In *Eisenberg*, 1995 SAJHR, 216-218 the example of India is discussed, as well as the treatment of this concept in the USA (209-216).

The "deprivations provision" in section 25(1) FC does not refer to the *public interest* or to *public purposes* at all. Consequently, section 25(4)(a) FC cannot be read as referring to deprivations of property. This gives rise to the question of whether it will be possible to attack the validity of a deprivation of property that was imposed for purposes of land reform, or whether section 25(4)(a) FC will cover the situation.[94] The courts can, of course, read a *public purposes* requirement into section 25(1) FC, especially if the view is accepted that expropriations also have to satisfy the provisions of section 36(1) FC, which is wide enough to be regarded as an extended *public purposes* limitation provision. However, the current situation gives rise to the question of whether deprivations of property for *purposes of land reform* would be valid regardless of the question whether they are imposed for *public purposes*. This question will be discussed at a later stage.

4. The Relationship between Property and Public Interest

All branches of the law are, at the least, concerned with property, the individual as a member of a specific community and the state.[95] The omnipresence of property in the law, philosophy and society renders a clear-cut definition of its scope practically impossible. Property takes a central place in the study of constitutional and human rights law, public and private international law, law of delict, criminal law, contract, commercial law, tax law planning and environmental law, mining law, family law, and so on. An exhaustive list cannot be supplied. The relevance of property does not lie only in ascertaining the theoretical and philosophical basis of judicial decisions and statutory provisions. Even more important is the need to understand the dynamics of social processes that underlie the relationship between the law, the state, societal organisation and governance.[96]

For the present inquiry, therefore, it is submitted that a concept of property or ownership can only be transitory in nature. It will be indicated that the regulation and protection of property as a fundamental right under a constitution illustrates that the definition of ownership

---

94 *Van der Walt*, Constitutional Property Clause (1997), 137.

95 *Gutto*, Property and Land Reform (1995), xv.

96 *Gutto*, Property and Land Reform (1995), xv.

varies according to context in which it is used. In this regard, it is possible that the public interest will determine the manner in which ownership is understood in a concrete case. This interaction between public interest and the concept of property or ownership will be elucidated in the course of this exposition, by analysing the way in which property is regulated in Germany and South Africa. For this purpose it will, however, be necessary first to determine the comparability of these two legal systems.

Chapter 3: Legal Comparison and the Course of Inquiry

1. Legal Comparison as Method of Analysis

In an attempt to find a working compromise between protecting the values of liberty and equality in the context of the South African property clause, German law could be a valuable source of comparison for the South African courts. The treatment of the values of individual freedom and social justice through application of constitutional principles and the provisions of article 14 GG have resulted in a clear-cut framework within which the interests of the individual property owner can be weighed against those of the community at large. Thus, German law provides a good example of how the fundamental values of individual freedom and social justice interact in the development of a unique constitutional concept of property. This framework could be important in the South African context. Under the new constitutional order, the legal system will be confronted with the question as to which of these values should enjoy precedence in situations where both are at stake and compete with each other. The analytical method of legal comparison could render valuable service in this regard.

However, the German property model has developed over a period of more than 50 years, and has adapted to the unique political and social circumstances of post-war Germany, whereas the new South African property order is still in its childhood. This might raise the question as to exactly how valuable insights gained from the German legal system could be in the South African context. After all, the best-intended law reform programmes can still be rendered nugatory by social reality, and reform based on the wrong premises could be a waste of time and money. The viability of a comparison of German and South African property law is analysed in the following paragraphs.

2. Comparative Analysis as Constitutional Directive

On the basis of constitutional guidelines for interpretation,[97] the judiciary passes judgements and the legislature is given direction in enacting legislation mandating future legal development. The interpretation of the constitutional property guarantee will determine the extent to

---

[97] Sec. 39 FC.

which existing rights should yield to the new political policies portrayed in legislation aimed at reforming the South African socio-political and legal systems and the theoretical basis of newly created rights in a new political dispensation. The fundamental requirement for constitutional interpretation under the new South African constitution is that[98]

> "[w]hen interpreting the Bill of Rights, a court, tribunal or forum –
> (a) must promote the values that underlie an open and democratic
> society based on human dignity, equality and freedom; (b) must
> consider international law and (c) may consider foreign law."

The Basic Law forms the basis of Germany's democratic and social federal state and is backed up by the decision of the Federal Constitutional Court.[99] It has, moreover, been used as a model[100] in the drafting process of the Interim and Final South African Constitutions. It seems logical that the drafters of the Final Constitution would expect the text to be interpreted by having regard to — among others — those jurisdictions that have provided such important guidelines in formulating the South African constitutional text.

In South Africa, fundamental rights jurisprudence has only recently, after the enactment of the first justiciable bill of rights in the Interim Constitution,[101] gained significance. The enactment of the Final Constitution, which also contains a chapter on fundamental rights,[102] has permanently ingrained this sphere of law in the South African legal system. Given the fact that South African fundamental rights jurisprudence is still young and susceptible to influence, the German jurispru-

---

[98] Sec. 39(1) FC. Sec. 35(1) IC was similar to that of sec. 39(1) FC, in that it provided that a court may "have regard to comparable foreign case law."

[99] *De Waal*, 1995 SAHJR, 1.

[100] See *De Waal*, 1995 SAHJR, 1-29 for a summary of the German influences in the South African Interim Constitution. Also *Van der Walt*, 1993 SAPR/PL, 300-306 for a specific application to the Interim property clause. For similarities with the German Basic Law in the Final Constitution, see i.a. *Grupp*, Südafrikas neue Verfassung (1999); *Van der Walt*, Constitutional Property Clause (1997), 32-35, 47-50, 76-78, 137-139; *Van der Walt*, 1997 SAPR/PL, 284, 301-302, 319-320.

[101] Ch. 3 IC.

[102] Ch. 2 FC.

dence flowing from the Basic Law can undoubtedly play an important role in developing further constitutional theory in South Africa.[103]

The courts have, moreover, already shown their inclination to make use of comparative law for solving legal problems. In the short time span between 1994 and 2000, the Constitutional Court has frequently considered foreign and international law in its decisions.[104] South African constitutional jurisprudence is even developing an international reputation for the exemplary application of legal comparative methodology.[105] This creates the expectation that the insights gained in other jurisdictions concerning most constitutional issues will also in future be applied to reach solutions in the South African context. Until now, however, the courts have had very little opportunity to formulate a theoretical framework within which legislative and administrative actions pertaining to property could take place. Instead, this has been done by academics.[106] Section 39(1) FC paves the way for the reception of foreign law in the constitutional context of South Africa. The German law pertaining to the constitutional protection and regulation of property — where scholarly work and judicial analysis of this topic complement

---

[103] *De Waal*, 1995 SAHJR, 1-3; *Chaskalson*, 1993 SAJHR, 336; *Murphy*, 1994 SAJHR, 388, 392.

[104] It is interesting to note that sec. 39(1)(c) FC does not give the court an injunction to consider foreign law, as is the case with international law in sec. 39(1)(b) FC. In spite of fears that foreign case law might not be a safe guide to the interpretation of the bill of rights, many of the Constitutional Court's decisions contain extensive comparative analyses of constitutional law. See e.g. *S v Makwanyane* (note 363 above), par. 36-37; *Sanderson v Attorney-General, Eastern Cape* 1998 (2) SA 38 (CC), par. 26; and judgement of Ackermann J in *Fose v Minister of Safety and Security* 1997 (3) SA 786 (CC).

[105] See *Grote*, Rechtskreise und ihre Bedeutung für die Rechtsvergleichung (1999), 17.

[106] The following commentary works by South African authors are helpful: *Budlender* in *Budlender/Latsky/Roux*, New Land Law (revised 1998), ch. 1, 1-75; *Van der Walt*, Constitutional Property Clause (1997); *Davis/Cheadle/Haysom*, Fundamental Rights in the Constitution - Commentary and Cases (1997), 237-255; *Devenish*, Commentary on the South African Constitution (1998), 68-72; *Van der Walt*, 1997 SAPR/PL, 275-330; *Van der Walt* in *Van Wyk/Dugard et. al. (eds)*, Rights and Constitutionalism (1996), 455-501; *Chaskalson/Lewis* in *Chaskalson/Kentridge/Klaaren et. al. (eds)*, Constitutional Law of South Africa (1996), ch. 31, 1-21; *Murphy*, 1995 SAPR/PL, 107-130; *Chaskalson*, 1994 SAJHR, 131-139; *Van der Walt*, 1994 THRHR, 181-203.

each other — could be valuable for developing South African law in this regard.

3. Possibilities for Legal Comparison

Several South African scholars have already[107] recognised that German law is particularly suitable for providing insights into the new direction of South African property law. The need for comparative research, with regard to the South African constitutional property guarantee in particular and with human rights law in South Africa in general, is directly related to the need for a theoretic structure for interpretation.

Van der Walt[108] points out that there is ample reason for research: Comparison of the structure and terminology of clauses a bill of rights should be undertaken not only on a smaller scale (by analysing specific provisions), but also on a larger scale (by analysing a number of provisions at a time and comparing them to case law). Since the introduction of the Final Constitution, some commentaries on the Constitution itself,[109] the bill of rights,[110] as well as the property clause in particular[111] have seen the light. Yet, literature on the constitutional

---

[107] *Van der Walt*, 1995 SAPR/PL, 336; *Van Maanen*, 1993 Recht & Kritiek, 74-95; *Van der Walt*, 1993 Recht & Kritiek, 263-297; *Kleyn*, 1996 SAPR/PL, 402-445.

[108] *Van der Walt*, 1998 SAJHR, 586.

[109] *Devenish*, Commentary on the South African Constitution (1998); Chaskalson/Kentridge/Klaaren et. al. (eds), *Constitutional Law* (1996); *Grupp*, Südafrikas neue Verfassung (1999).

[110] *Davis/Cheadle/Haysom*, Fundamental Rights in the Constitution - Commentary and Cases (1997); *De Waal/Currie/Erasmus*, Bill of Rights Handbook (1999).

[111] *Van der Walt*, Constitutional Property Clause (1997); *Budlender* in *Budlender/Latsky/Roux*, New Land Law (revised 1998), and to a lesser extent *Gutto*, Property and Land Reform (1995). See also *Du Plessis/Olivier*, 1997 (1) 5 HRCLJSA, 11-15; *Van der Walt*, 1997 SAPR/PL, 275-330; *Van der Walt*, 1998 SAJHR, 560-586. Most of the existing literature on constitutional property law entail analyses and interpretations of the interim property clause. See *Van der Walt*, 1995 SAPR/PL, 298-345; *Kroeze*, 1994 SAPR/PL, 323-331; *Murphy*, 1995 SAPR/PL, 107-130; *Murphy*, 1994 SAJHR, 385-398; *Van der Walt*, 1993 Recht & Kritiek, 263-297; *Chaskalson*, 1995 SAJHR, 222-240; *Chaskalson/Lewis* in *Chaskalson/Kentridge/Klaaren et. al. (eds)*, Constitutional Law of South Africa

property guarantee in the Final Constitution still needs to address several unanswered questions. As such, the possibilities for comparative research are by no means exhausted.

Questions related to the extent to which existing rights should yield to the new political policy behind reform legislation and the theoretical basis of new rights created by the reform legislation stemming from the constitution have only been touched upon in some of these contributions. Reference to the limitation of property rights in the public interest in these contributions are usually limited to attempts to define the concept "public purpose" or "public benefit," and here opinions differ widely as to exactly what the content of these terms is. On the contrary, the issue of the limitations on ownership in the public interest is to a larger extent — albeit mostly only indirectly — addressed in the ever-growing arsenal of literature on land reform, land restitution and access to land.

4. Similarities in the German and South African Property Orders

One of the most valuable elements of legal-comparative study is that the universality of the laws of different legal systems is recognised, even if the values of the different communities, on which their legal orders are based, differ considerably.[112] In the German and South African property orders there are several comparable elements.

4.1. Bases of the Legal Systems and their Material Law

South Africa has a mixed legal system[113] that contains both characteristic common law[114] and civil law[115] features. Legislation and precedent are the primary sources of law. Beyond these sources, one finds the South African common law, which has, depending on the specific area

---

(1996), ch. 31, 1-21; *Van der Walt*, 1994 THRHR, 181-203; *Chaskalson*, 1994 SAJHR, 131-139; *Chaskalson*, 1993 SAJHR, 388-411.

[112] *Venter/Van der Walt/Van der Walt et al*, Regsnavorsing (1990), 207-208.

[113] *Zimmermann/Visser* in *Zimmermann/Visser (eds)*, Southern Cross (1996), 9-12.

[114] Like the roles of judges and of law reports.

[115] Like the role of legal writers.

of inquiry, been influenced to an equal measure by both English and Roman-Dutch law. Thus, comparison with a great variety of other legal families[116] and specific legal systems[117] is possible.

Especially with regard to the Roman-Dutch roots of the South African legal system, the German legal system — being an important legal system on the European continent and thus also strongly oriented towards civil law[118] — makes it eminently suitable as a comparative model for the South African context. This is particularly so in the field of property law, which has, in contrast to other fields of private law (like the law concerning unjustified enrichment and the law of delict) remained an unassailable stronghold of civilian jurisprudence.[119] On occasion it has even been remarked that South African property law preserves and modernises the *jus commune* of Europe which lies behind the codification of civil law.[120] This also indicates that elements in the South African legal system could serve as comparative agents in the co-ordination, harmonisation and unification of private law within the framework of the European Community.

4.2. Corresponding Legal Problems

Comparative analysis has until now been employed to explain the mechanical as well as the substantive (normative) effect of the two South African constitutions on the concept of ownership. For instance, the Canadian two-stage approach was used as basis for the inquiry into issues related to constitutional property law in South Africa.[121] Comparative analyses of the structure of the constitutional property inquiry have been undertaken by scholars like Kleyn, Van der Walt, and Chaskalson, and many contributions on the meaning of the constitutional

---

[116] I.e. the Anglo-American legal family, the civilian legal systems, and the family of mixed legal systems.

[117] I.e. England, the United States, Germany, France, Scotland, Namibia, etc.

[118] *Murphy,* 1994 SAJHR, 386.

[119] *Zimmermann & Visser* in *Zimmermann/Visser* (eds), Southern Cross (1996) 24-28.

[120] *Beekhuis/Lawson/Knapp et. al.* in *Lawson* (chief ed), International Encyclopaedia of Comparative Law, vol VI (2) (1975), ch. 2, 252.

[121] *Van der Walt,* Constitutional Property Clause (1997), 28 and *Van der Walt,* 1997 SAPR/PL, 277.

guarantees viewed against the insights gained from other jurisdictions have also seen the light.[122] There is no reason why comparative analysis cannot be useful for developing the existing property order and especially the theory of land law in South Africa.

The treatment of social limitations on ownership in other jurisdictions could stimulate innovative ideas about legal reform when the South African experience is placed side to side to that of a legal system where similar problems had to be resolved in the past. The rich collection of German jurisprudence and scholarly work on the institution of ownership could be extremely beneficial in solving practical and dogmatic problems in balancing the interests of individuals with those of the society at large.

4.3. Comparable Legal Methods

Apart from a similarly civil law oriented history, South African legal reasoning also harks back to the abstract and deductive reasoning processes that are characteristic of European civil law systems. This applies not only to constitutional law, but also in other areas of the law.[123] In

---

[122] E.g. *Van der Walt,* Constitutional Property Clause (1997); *Van der Walt,* 1997 SAPR/PL, 275-330; *Van der Walt,* 1998 SAJHR, 560-586; *Van der Walt,* 1995 SAPR/PL, 298-345; *Kroeze,* 1994 SAPR/PL, 323-331; *Murphy,* 1995 SAPR/PL, 107-130; *Murphy,* 1994 SAJHR, 385-398; *Van der Walt,* 1993 Recht & Kritiek, 263-297; *Chaskalson,* 1995 SAJHR, 222-240; *Van der Walt,* 1994 THRHR, 181-203; *Chaskalson,* 1994 SAJHR, 131-139; *Chaskalson,* 1993 SAJHR, 388-411; *Van der Walt,* Constitutional Property Clauses - A Comparative Analysis (1999).

[123] *Van der Walt,* 1995 SAJHR 181 avers that the South African law of property, although conceptually based on the civil-law tradition, has not yet been developed far enough or in sufficient theoretical detail to reveal the full implications of the civil law method. This might be attributed to the fact that, in spite of a general marked reaction against uncritical anglicisation in South Africa, the legal method of the courts is more comparable to the English than to the Continental European pattern. (*Beekhuis/Lawson/Knapp et. al.* in *Lawson* (chief ed), International Encyclopaedia of Comparative Law, vol VI (2) (1975) ch. 2, 252.) *Van der Walt,* however, ascribes this underdevelopment of the civil law method in property law, as compared to other spheres of law like delict and contract, to the fact that the values underlying the civil law method have been worked out in those areas where the protection and enforcement of private law rights were more problematic. This indicates strength of logic and pervasiveness of the civil law method in property law particularly. As such, comparison with a

addition, the traditional division between public and private law in South Africa is also shared by the German system.[124]

In Germany the separate treatment of property in the constitutional context resulted in the parallel existence of both a private law and a public law concept of property. In this scheme, private law property is generally more restricted than the constitutional property concept, and pertains only to corporeal things.[125] Further, constitutional property provisions do not fundamentally influence ownership in private law, except for correcting possible imbalances resulting from an application of private law principles.[126] This approach enables the courts to interpret the meaning of property so as to give more weight either to social justice or to individual freedom, depending on the demands of society at a given moment.[127] In effect, this approach always revolves around a consideration of the boundaries of private and public law, the results of which would be applicable to a similar South African inquiry.

Van der Walt,[128] however, maintains that the situation in South Africa differs considerably from that of Germany in that the division is stricter in the latter jurisdiction. He bases his caution for comparison on three considerations: (i) The existence of a formal civil code in Germany (as opposed to the uncodified common law system of South Africa) exacerbates the strict divide between public and private law and therefore hinders comparative analysis. (ii) The South African Interim Constitution seems more open to an interpretation that overrides the traditional private-public divide (through horizontal application / seepage). (iii) Finally, academics and the courts are both inclined to follow the pur-

---

civil law oriented legal system is recommendable, because of the need to clarify exactly the scope of the private owner's rights, particularly in a new constitutional order. *Van der Walt's* further statement (at 190) that the influence of the Constitution on the development of the civil law tradition should be ascertained, serves as further justification for a study of the German legal system as an example of a civil-law oriented system that has survived constitutional supremacy. See *Murphy,* 1994 SAJHR, 386.

[124] *Chaskalson,* 1993 SAJHR, 336-337.

[125] As traditionally described in the *Bürgerliches Gesetzbuch* par. 90 ff.

[126] E.g. in case of an imminent danger to the common good, or in times of social change, the constitutional provisions will be used to correct the output of private law principles.

[127] *Murphy,* 1994 SAJHR, 388.

[128] *Van der Walt,* 1995 SAPR/PL, 337.

posive approach to interpretation in order to allow the values and re-constructive effects of the constitutions to pervade the whole legal system and to give the constitutional property guarantees broader relevance.

These arguments convincingly caution against an uncalculated comparative approach, but they do not preclude an investigation into German law. The German division between private and public law needs to be considered as one possible solution, or perhaps even merely as an incentive for developing an own approach towards resolving the issues arising from constitutional protection of property in South Africa. This would prevent a one-sided comparative perspective which could result in a transplant of wholesale dogmatic and practical solutions to South African property law from the (by some South African scholars so highly acclaimed)[129] Anglo-American legal family. Even if the South African constitution foresees a more direct application of the constitutional values in the private law sphere, the indirect application of constitutional values to private law in Germany could still provide valuable insights.[130]

---

[129] *Chaskalson,* 1993 SAJHR, 388 remarks that the case law of English speaking jurisdictions will exercise a dominant influence over the development of South African constitutional law because "most South African lawyers share my limitations [i.e. the 'inability to read any international languages other than English']". This argument cannot be supported. The abstract and deductive reasoning processes characteristic of the Romanic legal families of the European continent have frequently been used in South African constitutional law and private law for comparison. See *Murphy,* 1994 SAJHR, 386. Moreover, *De Waal,* 1995 SAHJR, 1-2 note 1 points out that South African legal scholars are "particularly well situated to benefit from the Basic Law and the Federal Constitutional Court's jurisprudence because so many have made use of scholarships to become familiar with the German language and legal system." He mentions the DAAD and BMW scholarships, as well as financial support from the Alexander von Humboldt Foundation and the Max Planck Institutes in Germany. It is however, further acknowledged that traditionally mainly the Afrikaans-oriented universities have maintained relations with the law faculties on the European continent, while English-speaking public-law scholars tended to turn rather to the universities of the United States, Canada and Australia. The consequent gap that has developed between Afrikaans- and English-orientated constitutional literature can only be closed with renewed (and continued) interest by both groups of scholars in the possibilities offered by both the continental and the Anglo-American systems. Other African legal systems are also valuable sources of legal comparison.

[130] See 382 ff. below.

4.4. Constitutional Principles

The principles of German constitutional interpretation correspond largely with those endorsed in the South African Interim and Final Constitutions.[131] The constitutional and social history of the Federal Republic of Germany furthermore supports a notion of property that envisages, on the one hand, wider boundaries of public control and, on the other hand, continued individual security in accordance with the values of liberty and personhood.[132] This has enabled the courts to accord more importance to either social justice or individual freedom, depending on the demands of society at a specific time.[133]

The German treatment of the dichotomy between social justice and individual freedom in cases where property rights are limited for the public benefit must inevitably lead to a better understanding of the South African situation. It is in line with the prevailing property theory in South Africa, which holds that, to be functional, ownership should not only be characterised by the existence of rights and entitlements accruing to the individual owners, but also by inherent duties, limitations and responsibilities toward society.[134] Accordingly, a comparison of South African problems surrounding the property concept with the notion of property as developed under the Weimar Constitution and through article 14 GG seems meaningful.

---

[131] See 123 ff. below.

[132] *De Wet*, Constitutional Enforceability of Economic and Social Rights (1996), 133.

[133] *Murphy*, 1994 SAJHR, 388.

[134] *Cowen*, New Patterns of Landownership (1984); *Pienaar*, Nuwe Sakeregtelike Ontwikkelings op die Gebied van Grondhervorming (1997); *Van der Walt*, 1990 De Iure, 1-45; *Van der Walt*, 1995 SAJHR 169-206; *Van Maanen*, 1993 Recht & Kritiek, 74-95; *Lewis*, 1985 Acta Juridica, 241-266; *Van der Walt*, 1988 De Jure, 16-35, 306-325; *Van der Walt* in *Van Wyk/Dugard et. al. (eds)*, Rights and Constitutionalism (1996); *Kroeze*, Between Conceptualism and Constitutionalism (1997).

5. Differences between the German and South African Systems of Property Law

Despite the several convincing reasons for choosing the German legal system as a comparative source for South African property law, there are also some fundamental differences between the German and South African legal systems. This could prove problematic for such a comparative analysis,[135] as is illustrated in the ruling of *Park-Ross v Director: Office for Serious Economic Offences*.[136] In this decision, it was remarked that legal-comparative analysis should be done with circumspection. The different contexts within which other constitutions were drafted, the different social structures and milieu existing in other countries as compared with those in South Africa, and the different historical backgrounds against which the various constitutions came into being can all be factors dictating against legal comparison. One must be wary of the danger of unnecessarily importing doctrines associated with those constitutions into an inappropriate South African setting.

5.1. Drafting Circumstances

The German constitution, which was adopted after the Second World War, inevitably has a different focus than the South African constitution, which was drafted practically at the end of the twentieth century. Both these documents arose from very unique sets of historical circumstances. As such, both these constitutions tend to place primary focus on values that were important at the time when they came into operation. This will influence the importance attached to the values of individual freedom and social justice in interpreting and applying the constitutional property clause. The initial German constitutional jurisprudence, for instance, granted primary importance to human dignity, whereas both the South African constitutions are strongly oriented towards the value of equality.[137] Particularly in the area of property law,

---

[135] *De Waal*, 1995 SAHJR, 2.

[136] *Park-Ross v Director: Office for Serious Economic Offences* 1995 2 SA 148 (C), 160F-H.

[137] *Du Plessis*, 1996 Stell LR, 7, however, indicates that cognisance has been taken in (the working draft of) the Final Constitution of the consequences in establishing a value of equality unbridled by the demand to realise human dig-

German constitutional case law over the past fifty years indicate that the values underlying the Basic Law have been moulded and shaped extensively by prevailing social circumstances.

The different social structures of South Africa and Germany are, in themselves, grounds for the comparison of constitutional property theory and practice in these jurisdictions. In Germany, for instance, redistribution of land became important after the reunification of the former Federal Republic of Germany and the German Democratic Republic at the beginning of the nineties.[138] By that time, it could draw on a rich collection of constitutional jurisprudence on property that has been developed and refined during the preceding forty years. In South Africa, on the other hand, the redistribution of land has been an issue even before negotiations on the incorporation of a property guarantee in the Interim and Final Constitutions have been initiated. Therefore, land redistribution itself will play an integral part in the development of property law in South Africa.

The social and constitutional history of South Africa will naturally differ from that of Germany. Nevertheless similar issues inevitably arise to some extent, albeit then in differing contexts. A comparison of the German and South African constitutional property issues could help overcome or adjust some of the hurdles still to be crossed, in spite of the different historical contexts at stake. In this regard, the qualification of Tebbutt J to the cautionary approach towards legal comparison propagated in the *Park-Ross* case[139] is significant. Certain fundamental principles and considerations emanating from foreign constitutions which are used as sources of legal comparison in South Africa, can indeed be applied in the South African context as readily as in the interpretation of the foreign constitutions from which those principles originate; notwithstanding the dangers of legal comparison.

---

nity. This is the reason why human dignity is afforded a more central place in the Final Constitution (sec. 1(a) FC) than in the Interim Constitution. Du Plessis explains: "Equality transcends mathematical equations: it needs 'flesh and blood' to breathe a spirit conducive to the promotion of what is peculiarly human. This is best achieved through its symbiotic unison with human dignity." On the relation between equality and dignity, see also *Ackermann*, 2000 ZaöRV, 537-556.

[138] See 535 ff. below.

[139] *Park-Ross v Director: Office for Serious Economic Offences* (note 136 above), 160H-I.

5.2. Wording of South African and German Property Clauses

The South African Interim Constitution contained a positive property guarantee,[140] whereas the property guarantee in the Final Constitution is negatively formulated.[141] In comparison, the property guarantee in article 14 GG has developed into a somewhat more advanced form of protection: The institution of property is guaranteed positively, in contrast to the negative guarantee of individual property rights against state interference.[142] This is sometimes referred to as the institutional and individual guarantees of property in Germany. The guarantee of property as an institution denotes that the very existence of private property in a specific economic and ideological model of state organisation is protected. South African scholars have published several (often contrasting) opinions with regard to whether or not the South African property clauses do protect the institution of property, and if so, to what extent.[143]

But even if direct application of German theory to the South African context would in this regard be limited, it is undeniably true that comparative law, particularly comparative case law, plays an important role in the development of jurisprudence. Moreover, a clear line of reasoning about the nature, interpretation and effects of a constitutional property clause is evident in case law from a large number of jurisdictions.[144] The differences in phrasing or structure also illustrate that approaches to the function and interpretation of property clauses can be more generally applied, even in jurisdictions where the property clauses do not expressly resemble each other.

6. Course of Inquiry

In an attempt to reconcile the existing private law of ownership and the property order propagated by the new constitution against the background of land reform, restitution and redistribution in South Africa,

---

[140] Sec. 28(1) IC: "Every person shall have the right to acquire and hold rights in property and, ... , to dispose of such rights."

[141] Sec. 25(1) FC: "No one may be deprived of property ...".

[142] *Van der Walt*, 1995 SAPR/PL, 302. See also 80 ff. below.

[143] See 85 ff. below and 195 ff. below.

[144] *Van der Walt*, 1998 SAJHR, 584.

the main focus of the inquiry will be the treatment of property in constitutional law. The interaction between the values of individual freedom and social equality in each stage of the constitutional inquiry will be analysed, in order to trace the development of the existing property law under a constitution guaranteeing property and simultaneously limiting it in the interest of the public at large.

Once the treatment of property under the constitution has been analysed, specific attention will be given to adjustments — in the interest of the general public — to the existing property law orders of Germany and South Africa effected by land reform and restitution legislation. These legislative adjustments are the best available examples of the transformation of property law in legal systems characterised by constitutional supremacy. If these legislative adjustments are to be analysed thoroughly, one will have to start with an overview of the principles and values endorsed by the constitutional orders in Germany and South Africa. The drafting histories of, and the principles on which the constitutions of the respective jurisdictions are based will accordingly be discussed in the following chapter. Attention will also be given to certain structural aspects.

Part Two

Background to the Constitutional Protection of Property in Germany and South Africa

Chapter 4: The Drafting Histories of the South African and German Constitutional Property Clauses

1. Relevance of an Historical Inquiry

In order to understand the structure and purpose of the property guarantees in the German Basic Law and the South African Constitutions, it will be necessary to recount the drafting history of the constitutional documents in which the respective provisions appear. It is also necessary to consider the relevance of constitutional property guarantees for the legal systems in which they operate. In this chapter, the historical backgrounds of section 28 IC and section 25 FC respectively, and of article 14 GG, will be discussed. The general relevance of these property guarantees for the respective property orders in which they operate will then be elucidated.

2. Germany: Development of Property Protection Under a Constitution

The German history of constitutionally protected property, covering a period of more than a century, is somewhat more extensive than the South African. Through an overview of the historical highlights of constitutional protection of property, the relevance of the German property clause in the transformation of the ownership concepts will become clear.

2.1. Historical Background of article 14 GG

Article 14 GG forms part of the German bill of rights *(Grundrechtskatalog)*. It provides:[145]

> *(1)* *(1)* *Das Eigentum und das Erbrecht werden gewährleistet.* *(2)* *Inhalt und Schranken werden durch die Gesetze bestimmt. (2)* *(1)* *Eigentum verpflichtet.* *(2)* *Sein Gebrauch soll zugleich dem Wohle der Allgemeinheit dienen. (3)* *(1)* *Eine Enteignung ist nur zum Wohle der Allgemeinheit zulässig.* *(2)* *Sie darf nur durch Gesetz oder auf Grund eines Gesetzes erfolgen, das Art und Ausmaß der Entschädigung regelt.* *(3)* *Die Entschädigung ist unter gerechter Abwägung der Interessen der Allgemeinheit und der Beteiligten zu bestimmen.* *(4)* *Wegen der Höhe der Entschädigung steht im Streitfalle der Rechtsweg vor den ordentlichen Gerichten offen.*

Article 14 GG is characterised by an inherent tension between the liberal view that individual property rights are justified by natural law, and an acknowledgement that property rights are created and restricted by the social context.[146] This tension, which at present forms the backbone of the courts' interpretation[147] of article 14 GG, was also present in the

---

[145] Art. 14 GG consists of three clauses, each containing more than one provision. These provisions are not officially numbered separately, as is the case in South African legislation. However, these provisions have to be clearly identified for purposes of analysis. In this text, reference is made to the various clauses by means of capital Roman numbers (the first clause is therefore indicated with the numeral I; the second with II, and the third with III). Reference to a specific sentence within a clause is then made by means of a consecutive Arabic number, i.e. art. 14 I 1 GG or art. 14 III 2 GG. The official English translation of this text reads: (I) *(1)* Property and the right of inheritance shall be guaranteed. *(2)* Their substance and limits shall be determined by law. (II) *(1)* Property entails obligations. *(2)* Its use should also serve the public interest. (III) *(1)* Expropriation shall only be permissible in the public interest. *(2)* It may only be ordered by or pursuant to a law which determines the nature and extent of compensation. *(3)* Compensation shall reflect a fair balance between the public interest and the interests of those affected. *(4)* In case of dispute regarding the amount of compensation recourse may be had to the ordinary courts. *Press and Information Office of the Federal Government, Foreign Affairs Division* (1994). Numbering of the individual sentences added.

[146] *Van der Walt*, Constitutional Property Clauses - A Comparative Analysis (1999), 122; *Finer/Bogdanor/Rudden*, Comparing Constitutions (1995), 37-38.

[147] In Germany, various courts have jurisdiction in matters pertaining to the property clause. The Federal Supreme Court / Federal Court of Justice in Civil

property clauses preceding article 14 GG. The following paragraphs contain a brief overview of the creation of a constitutional property order in Germany.

2.1.1. First Attempts at Constitutional Protection of Property

The various states in the German Federation received constitutions between 1818 and 1848. However, constitutional development took place predominantly at state level and the monarchic principle[148] lay at its root. The constitutions within the federation of German states guaranteed certain rights, but they were regarded as the rights of the subject, not as human rights. These rights were furthermore confined to the citizens of the particular state in question.[149]

The aims of the middle-class revolution, which began in 1848, were to unite Germany in a new empire and to compel the government to acknowledge fundamental rights. However, the revolution failed and the attempts at unification were unsuccessful. The *Paulskirchenverfassung*[150] that was drawn up during this time never entered into force. Nevertheless, it played a significant role in later developments of a fun-

---

Matters *(Bundesgerichtshof)* has jurisdiction with regard to the compensation that has to be paid for expropriations, whereas the Federal Administrative Court *(Bundesverwaltungsgericht)* has jurisdiction concerning the validity of administrative decisions and actions pertaining to expropriation. The Federal Constitutional Court *(Bundesverfassungsgericht)* has jurisdiction with regard to the question whether legislation, actions of the state or court decisions are in accordance with the Basic Law. This shared jurisdiction in matters pertaining to the property clause opened the system to different interpretations of the property clause and various aspects thereof (for instance the question of when an expropriation or regulation of property could be justifiable), which initially also created confusion in the ranks of property and constitutional lawyers in Germany. See 111 below.

[148] I.e. the sovereignty of the prince, not of the people, was protected.

[149] *Robbers*, Introduction to German Law (1998), 39.

[150] This constitution was named after the venue where the constitutional assembly of the Parliament held their meetings in Frankfurt am Main between 18 May 1848 and 30 May 1849. It is also referred to as the *Frankfurter Reichsverfassung*.

damental rights consciousness in Germany.[151] Paragraph 164 of this constitution contained a property guarantee:[152]

"Das Eigentum ist unverletzlich. Eine Enteignung kann nur aus Rücksichten des gemeinen Besten, nur auf Grund eines Gesetzes und gegen gerechte Entschädigung vorgenommen werden."

This clause was not meant to be a fundamental right in the true sense of the word, but rather a mechanism of control over bureaucratic encroachments on ownership.[153] Nevertheless, it already reflects the dichotomy between a liberal-naturalist justification of private ownership and the social function of property that has in the meantime become a characteristic of all subsequent constitutional property guarantees in Germany.[154]

The German Empire established by Bismarck replaced the German Federation in 1870/71. Its constitution still did not contain express provisions on fundamental rights. However, significant aspects of fundamental rights were incorporated in ordinary statutory law and the different states had constitutions incorporating property guarantees. The lack of an express property guarantee in the Federation's constitution furthermore did not hinder lawyers from elevating the civil concept of ownership — through interpretation based on natural law ideas — to a constitutional level.[155]

2.1.2. Property Protection in the Weimar Republic and Under National-Socialism

It was, however, only forty years later, after Germany's defeat in the First World War,[156] the fall of the monarchy and the introduction of the

---

[151] *Robbers,* Introduction to German Law (1998), 39.

[152] Translation: "Property is inviolable. Expropriation can take place only against a consideration of the public weal, and only in accordance with law and against just compensation."

[153] *Rittstieg,* Eigentum als Verfassungsproblem (1976), 241.

[154] *Kimminich,* Eigentum Enteignung Entschädigung (1976), m.n. 7; *Eschenbach,* Der Verfassungsrechtliche Schutz des Eigentums (1996), 33. See also the Prussian Constitution of 1850, as analysed in *Von Brünneck,* Die Eigentumsgarantie des Grundgesetzes (1984), 21-26.

[155] *Rittstieg,* Eigentum als Verfassungsproblem (1976), 250.

[156] 1914-1918.

Weimar Republic, that the sovereignty of the people and various guaranteed fundamental rights were perceived to be characteristic features of the state.[157] The tradition of constitutional property protection started by the constitution of the *Paulskirche* was continued[158] in article 153 of the Weimar Constitution:[159]

> *"Das Eigentum wird von der Verfassung gewährleistet. Sein Inhalt und seine Schranken ergeben sich aus den Gesetzen. Eine Enteignung kann nur zum Wohle der Allgemeinheit und auf gesetzlicher Grundlage vorgenommen werden. Sie erfolgt gegen angemessene Entschädigung, soweit nicht ein Reichsgesetz etwas anderes bestimmt. ... Eigentum verpflichtet. Sein Gebrauch soll zugleich Dienst sein für das Gemeine Beste."*

Rittstieg[160] points out that this article was initially developed as a tool against direct political interference in the existing order of property law.[161] However, the post-war crisis and the challenges set by the extraordinary inflation rate of the twenties and thirties also brought about extensive jurisprudence on the meaning of *public weal (Wohle der Allgemeinheit)* and the acceptability of infringements on individual property interests for the well-being of the general economy.[162] The jurisprudence of the courts on the property clause in the Weimar Constitution also played a significant role in expanding the concept of property. This can be noticed especially in the area of land utilisation (in particular where the protection of historical monuments is concerned). A fur-

---

[157] *Robbers,* Introduction to German Law (1998), 40.

[158] *Eschenbach,* Verfassungsrechtlicher Schutz des Eigentums (1996), 33.

[159] Translation "Property is guaranteed by the constitution. Its substance and limits are revealed by law. Expropriation can take place only in the public weal and upon a legislative basis. Expropriation is successful against appropriate compensation, unless imperial legislation determines otherwise. ... Property entails obligations. Its use should serve the public interest."

[160] *Rittstieg,* Eigentum als Verfassungsproblem (1976), 256-262.

[161] See *Von Brünneck,* Die Eigentumsgarantie des Grundgesetzes (1984), 32-34.

[162] *Rittstieg,* Eigentum als Verfassungsproblem (1976), 262-265; *Von Brünneck,* Die Eigentumsgarantie des Grundgesetzes (1984), 36 mentions infringements i.a. in the spheres of agriculture, monopolies and restraints of trade, as well as lease and interest rates.

ther example is the treatment of established or exercised commercial activity in terms of constitutional protection of property.[163]

Although the decisions of the German Supreme Court *(Reichsgericht)* mostly lacked a clear theoretical construction and were contradictory and unpredictable in practice,[164] they introduced the practice of judicial examination of legislation according to its material compatibility with the constitution.[165] Furthermore, the academic discourse over the interpretation of article 153 of the Weimar Constitution would also prove to be of importance for similar debates over article 14 GG.[166]

Fundamental rights were not entrenched in the Weimar Constitution, and could therefore be altered or erased by a simple majority.[167] The National-Socialists, who seized power in Germany after 1930, exploited this weakness. The Great Depression and the lack of co-operation between the democratic parties in the Weimar Republic, which caused a system of weak coalitions and fragmentation of party representation, all contributed to the empowerment of the National-Socialists.[168] The era of National Socialism was characterised by a disregard of legal principles and abuse of constitutional structures with binding force in Germany at the time.[169]

---

[163] See *Eschenbach*, Verfassungsrechtlicher Schutz des Eigentums (1996), 34-37 for a discussion of the Federal Court's efforts to expand the constitutional property concept. Also *Rittstieg*, Eigentum als Verfassungsproblem (1976), 266-269; *Von Brünneck*, Die Eigentumsgarantie des Grundgesetzes (1984), 37-38.

[164] *Von Brünneck*, Die Eigentumsgarantie des Grundgesetzes (1984), 39.

[165] *Rittstieg*, Eigentum als Verfassungsproblem (1976), 269.

[166] The various methods of interpretation that were considered are described and evaluated by *Eschenbach*, Verfassungsrechtlicher Schutz des Eigentums (1996), 45-75. It is shown that the difficulties with art. 153 of the Weimar Constitution were not linked with the understanding of art. 153 as such, but rather with the different approaches to constitutional interpretation in general. Thus the discussion revolved around the questions whether the will of the historical legislature, or rather the objective will of the law should enjoy precedence, and what the value of teleological and comparative interpretation methods would be.

[167] *Foster*, German Legal System and Laws (1996), 26.

[168] *Robbers*, Introduction to German Law (1998), 40; *Foster*, German Legal System and Laws (1996), 25, 26.

[169] *Foster*, German Legal System and Laws (1996), 27; *Robbers*, Introduction to German Law (1998), 40.

The property guarantee was annulled in 1933 through a decree of the German president, as a measure of protection against averred communistic acts threatening the security of the state.[170] The courts at first interpreted this legislation as being merely temporary. By contrast, some scholars pointed out that the alterations made to the constitution were not compatible with the idea of fundamental rights and that the annulment of the property guarantee, among other provisions, could not be regarded as being of a passing nature.[171] The consequences of the annulment of the property guarantee soon became clear: The state authorities in the Third *Reich* were enabled to execute several expropriations on racial or political grounds without being exposed to judicial disapproval. The assets of political parties like the KPD and SPD and their supporting organisations, the assets of German emigrants who had lost their citizenship through the *Gesetz über den Widerruf von Einbürgerungen und die Aberkennung der deutschen Staatsangehörigkeit*[172] as well as cinematic material or works of art which were unacceptable *(entartete Kunst)* in the eyes of the National-Socialists were confiscated. The destruction of Jewish property passed unsanctioned after 1933, as the civil-law property order was practically not applicable to Jews after this date. Where judicial investigations were applied for, they simply did not take place. The police also simply turned a blind eye to atrocities connected to the persecution of Jews. As the Jewish persecution intensified, so did the systematic removal of Jewish assets from their owners. Means of production in particular were taken from their true owners and transferred to companies or individuals pursuing the arian ideal.[173]

Still, the administrative and legislative practise of the National-Socialist government afforded property a kind of "quasi-fundamental-right" guarantee. Political institutions assumed the power to determine the contents and limits of property and the obligation to protect it.[174] The expropriation procedure and requirements also remained unchanged during this time — except in political cases like those mentioned

---

[170] *Verordnung des Reichspräsidenten zum Schutz von Volk und Staat,* 28 February 1933, RGBl. I 83.

[171] *Rittstieg,* Eigentum als Verfassungsproblem (1976), 273.

[172] *Aberkennung der deutschen Staatsangehörigkeit,* 14 July 1933, RGBl. I 480.

[173] *Von Brünneck,* 1979 Kritische Justiz, 153; 155-157.

[174] *Von Brünneck,* Die Eigentumsgarantie des Grundgesetzes (1984), 51.

above.[175] However, the National-Socialist aims pursued after 1933 often caused far-reaching interferences with the institution of ownership and other complementary institutions. For instance, the executive and legislative authorities, which continued "guaranteeing" property after annulment of the constitutional provision, could not really solve the problem of whether or not compensation was payable for legislative interference in institutions related to property (namely means of production, industries, etc).[176] This resulted in an inconsistent and confusing system of compensation policies.

2.1.3. Circumstances Influencing the Drafting of article 14 GG

The experience with National-Socialism has to this day been the strongest influence on the law of the Federal Republic of Germany.[177] The Basic Law, that came into force in 1949, is thoroughly pervaded by the determination to prevent anything similar to national-socialism from happening again. Consequently the Basic Law contains extensive provisions on fundamental rights,[178] which were also — in reaction against the loss of freedoms and the repression of individual rights — more strongly oriented towards individual freedom than the fundamental rights of the Weimar constitution. Article 14 GG is, in fact, one of the few fundamental rights provisions which contains references to fundamental duties, and not only to fundamental rights.[179]

The designation "Basic Law" (Grundgesetz) is an expression of the expectation (at the time of its promulgation) that the division of Germany effected by the Allied forces after the Second World War was only a temporary measure and that a permanent constitution for the whole country could soon be created.[180] However, after the commencement of the Cold War, German unification seemed to be out of the question.

---

[175] Fraenkel, Der Doppelstaat (1974), 107-108.

[176] Von Brünneck, Die Eigentumsgarantie des Grundgesetzes (1984), 61-71.

[177] Robbers, Introduction to German Law (1998), 41 explains that the internal self-understanding of Germany is intimately connected to this experience: "[Germany's] political debates, their high points and weaknesses cannot be understood without bearing this background in mind."

[178] Foster, German Legal System and Laws (1996), 28.

[179] Kimminich, Eigentum Enteignung Entschädigung (1976), m.n. 8.

[180] Robbers, Introduction to German Law (1998), 41.

Nevertheless the view that reform could only take place once Germany was reunited impeded the process of reform. The system of property endorsed by the Basic Law thus remained capitalist-oriented, contrary to the ideal of *Neuordnung der Eigentumsverfassung* supported by most political groups in Germany between 1945 and 1949.[181]

This ideal entailed a reformulation of the property guarantee to portray a democratic-socialist order.[182] It would also signify a break with the national-socialist past in which the property order was exploited to serve the aims of the Third *Reich*'s government.[183] However, the Western Allied powers were not in favour of such a reform.[184] America in particular argued strongly that only a unified German legislature could decide whether or not the structure of the German property order should be changed.[185] Simultaneously the Western Allied powers promoted an economy based on private ownership of the means of production.[186]

By 1949, with the drafting of article 14 GG, the political parties already espoused different views on the content of the *Neuordnung der Eigentumsverfassung*. The SPD still favoured socialisation, but the CDU under Adenauer opted rather for a liberal and social market economy *(soziale Marktwirtschaft)*.[187] These different approaches would also eventually influence the wording of the new constitutional property guarantee.[188]

This difference of approach is illustrated by the controversy surrounding the scope of protection to be afforded to property by a constitu-

---

[181] *Von Brünneck*, Die Eigentumsgarantie des Grundgesetzes (1984), 82-83 shows that the SPD, CDU as well as the KPD were in favour of a break with the property order of the past and of socialisation. Only the liberal FDP/LPD/DVP alliance was not in favour of alterations to the existing property order.

[182] *Finer/Bogdanor/Rudden*, Comparing Constitutions (1995), 37-38.

[183] *Rittstieg*, Eigentum als Verfassungsproblem (1976), 275.

[184] *Von Brünneck*, Die Eigentumsgarantie des Grundgesetzes (1984) 85.

[185] In *Rittstieg*, Eigentum als Verfassungsproblem (1976), 278 it is indicated that Britain - where the Labour Party was governing at the time - was more in favour of socialisation than America, but that the American influence in Germany, even in the British occupation zone, was stronger.

[186] E.g. the currency reform (20 June 1948) and the Marshall plan.

[187] *Rittstieg*, Eigentum als Verfassungsproblem (1976), 279.

[188] *Finer/Bogdanor/Rudden*, Comparing Constitutions (1995), 37-38.

tional guarantee. The SPD-representatives disagreed with the FDP and CDU-representatives about the extent to which property interests had to be covered by the constitutional property guarantee in order to aid the development of individual wealth.[189] Further problems were caused by the disagreement about the extent of the social function of property. Another issue that had to be resolved was whether an individual's abuse of his or her property could be constitutionally protected. This was related to the question of whether the use of property should always be in the public interest. In the context of expropriation and compensation, the most contentious issues were the determination of the amount of compensation and the situations under which compensation would be payable.[190]

Eventually the wording of the first two paragraphs was altered to look more like that of article 153 of the Weimar Constitution.[191] After a series of alterations, it was also decided not to make any mention of whether or not owners abusing their property should be protected. The decision as to which property interests would be protected was left to the legislature.[192] These elements clearly illustrate that article 14 GG is characterised by compromises between liberal and socialist ideologies.[193] The drafting process resulted in a constitutional property guarantee, which — although formulated in general terms — still reflects the dichotomy between liberal private ownership and the social obligation inherent in property. The task of finding a working balance between the interests of the individual and the society would in the following years under the Basic Law fall on all levels of government: first and foremost the judiciary, but also to a large extent the legislature and even the administration.

---

[189] *Von Doemming/Füsslein/Matz*, 1951 Jahrbuch des öffentlichen Rechts der Gegenwart (NF), 146.

[190] *Von Doemming/Füsslein/Matz*, 1951 Jahrbuch des öffentlichen Rechts der Gegenwart (NF), 149-154.

[191] Together with the creation of a constitutional court, which would control the Federal legislature, it was expected that the judicial obstruction from the early Weimar period would not be repeated. *Rittstieg*, Eigentum als Verfassungsproblem (1976), 285; *Von Doemming/Füsslein/Matz*, 1951 Jahrbuch des öffentlichen Rechts der Gegenwart (NF), 147.

[192] *Von Doemming/Füsslein/Matz*, 1951 Jahrbuch des öffentlichen Rechts der Gegenwart (NF), 148-149.

[193] *Rittstieg*, Eigentum als Verfassungsproblem (1976), 280.

2.1.4. Constitutional Property Protection in a Reunified Germany

German unification was eventually achieved on 3 October 1990, after the conclusion of the Two-plus-four treaty between Britain, France, the Soviet Union and the United States of America on the one hand and the Federal Republic of Germany and the German Democratic Republic on the other hand. The property law order underpinned by article 14 GG lost its temporary nature and was accepted by the people of the Federal Republic. It was also adopted by the "new" German *Länder* after re-unification.[194] The unification treaty set out the terms upon which unification would take place. It contained several provisions on property. Because of this agreement, a whole new range of problems needed to be addressed. But legal solutions to the newly arisen problems were hampered by the different ideologies underlying the divided German society.[195]

Property law and the transformation of the German Democratic Republic's economy had been particularly problematic in the negotiations preceding the reunification[196] and in the period of transition following upon the reunification.[197] Concepts like property, expropriation, socialisation and compensation were in the theory and practice of the former German Democratic Republic afforded meanings differing quite extensively from those of similar terms used in the Federal Republic of Germany. This gave rise to the question whether the "East-German" and "West-German" property orders could ever be compatible.

It soon became clear that the property order of the German Democratic Republic would not survive the reunification. It was in principle oriented against private property. The flexibility that the property guarantee in article 14 GG acquired through 40 years of jurisprudence was also much better geared for protecting existing property relations in the East of Germany than the property order of the German Democratic Republic itself.[198] This state of affairs nevertheless gave rise to more intricate problems regarding the restitution of property rights lost as a re-

---

[194] *Foster,* German Legal System and Laws (1996), 29; *Robbers,* Introduction to German Law (1998), 41.

[195] *Robbers,* Introduction to German Law (1998), 41.

[196] *Fieberg* in *Rwelamira/Werle (eds),* Confronting Past Injustices (1996), 79.

[197] *Wendt* in *Sachs (ed),* Grundgesetz Kommentar (1996), m.n. 187.

[198] *Kimminich,* Die Eigentumsgarantie im Prozeß der Wiedervereinigung (1990), 69-72.

sult of the division of Germany after the Second World War and the Soviet rule in the East. The issues relating to the existing property order that were discussed, were the following:

(i)   Considerable attention was given to the issue whether property expropriated before 1945, and in the period of Soviet occupation between 1945 and 1949 could be restored.[199]

(ii)   A related issue was the determination of the value of confiscated property and attempts at reaching an agreement on the manner in which the interests of persons entitled to compensation could be better served.[200]

(iii) Further, the differences in social and economic standards in the different parts of Germany gave rise to heated political discussions and challenged the legal and social structures of the reunited Federal Republic.[201]

2.2. Relevance of article 14 GG for the German Property Order

The Basic Law quickly became a "centre of identification for the German people,"[202] and a token of the free, democratic society within which it functions. Within the constitutional system, the protection of property rights is a guiding ethical principle recognised by the Basic Law and of special importance for the system of social relations under the rule of law.[203] Article 14 GG has, mainly through the decisions of the Federal Constitutional Court, obtained a relatively clear basic structure. Nevertheless, the application of the principles incorporated in this section still creates confusion, even for German lawyers, practitioners and students.[204]

---

[199] *Wendt* in *Sachs (ed)*, Grundgesetz Kommentar (1996), m.n. 187-192.

[200] *Badura* in *Benda/Maihofer/Vogel (eds)*, Handbuch des Verfassungsrechts (1994), m.n. 46; *Jeffress*, 1991 Yale LJ, 544-548.

[201] BVerfGE 91, 294 *(Fortgeltung der Mietepreisbindung)*.

[202] *Robbers*, Introduction to German Law (1998), 41.

[203] BVerfGE 14, 263, 277: *"Das Eigentum ist ebenso wie die Freiheit ein elementares Grundrecht; das Bekenntnis zu ihm ist eine Wertentscheidung des Grundgesetzes von besonderer Bedeutung für den sozialen Rechtsstaat."*

[204] See *Von Heinegg/Haltern*, 1993 JuS, 121-122.

In general, it can be said that property is protected in the hands of its owners, and that not only property itself, but also to some extent the value of property, is guaranteed. The function of the property guarantee is to permit the holder of a protected property interest to act freely with the property and to control his or her own economic destiny. From an economic perspective, one can say that the guarantee of ownership in article 14 I GG has a microeconomic and a macroeconomic function. The basic *right of ownership* which is guaranteed in article 14 I GG, results in an economy governed by private-sector autonomy, "actual"[205] competition and decentralised self-regulation.[206] On the other hand, the guarantee of ownership also has the microeconomic function of providing the individual with the freedom to engage in economic activity. Two fundamental characteristics of the German notion of ownership can be deduced from this description of the constitutional property guarantee. First, it indicates that Germany prefers an economic system that recognises individual initiative and responsibility of the entrepreneur in the market economy as essential elements. Second, as a necessary corollary, ownership is guaranteed as an elementary basic right intimately associated with personal freedom. The guarantee of ownership is not merely a guarantee of the value of property, but also a guarantee that the legal entity of ownership will be protected.

3. South Africa: Negotiating a Constitutional Property Clause

The negotiation processes, which preceded the promulgation of both the Interim Constitution and the Final Constitution in South Africa, are well known and well documented.[207] The contentiousness of the right to property as a fundamental right worthy of constitutional protection has enjoyed the attention of many lawyers, politicians and journalists. The following paragraphs briefly summarise the history of the inclusion of a property guarantee in the South African constitutions.

---

[205] In other words not competition determined by regulative policy or theory.

[206] *Ossenbühl* in *Kirchhof/Kommers (eds)*, Germany and its Basic Law (1993), 269.

[207] See *Bennun/Newitt (eds)*, Negotiating Justice (1995); *Chaskalson*, 1995 SAJHR, 222-240; *Friedman/Atkinson (eds)*, Small Miracle (1994); *De Villiers (ed)*, Birth of a Constitution (1994).

3.1. Historical Background to the Property Clauses

The primary object of the bill of rights in the Interim Constitution of South Africa was to find the means and methods of transforming an unjust and deeply divided society.[208] The adoption of this bill of rights was the consequence of political negotiation[209] — in the context of a dialectic interplay between the two opposing, yet complementary human rights traditions of *libertarianism* and *liberationism/ egalitarianism*[210] — at the beginning of the nineties. The protection of human rights as such was proven to be a "site of struggle for political power"[211] in South Africa. Particularly the property clause was contentious right from the outset.[212] In analysing the historical background of the South African constitutional property clauses, these differing ideological influences must be kept in mind.

Libertarianism draws on the ideology of classical liberalism, and is closely related to the idea of restricted government.[213] It tends to rate individual liberty as the core value for purposes of constitutional drafting and interpretation. As such, the value of equality could easily play a subordinate role in libertarian thinking. In South Africa, it was the "white liberals," who expressed their opposition to the authoritarian government and its apartheid regime before 1990 in human rights terms, who initially supported the libertarian tradition. After the fall of

---

[208] *Murphy,* 1994 SAJHR, 391, 394.

[209] *Chaskalson/Lewis* in *Chaskalson/Kentridge/Klaaren et. al. (eds)*, Constitutional Law of South Africa (1996), ch. 31, 1. *Du Plessis/Olivier,* 1997 (1) 5 HRCLJSA, 11; *Chaskalson,* 1995 SAJHR, 229-238; *Du Plessis* in *De Villiers (ed)*, Birth of a Constitution (1994), 89-91.

[210] *Du Plessis,* 1994 SAPR/PL, 2-3 and *Du Plessis* in *De Villiers (ed)*, Birth of a Constitution (1994), 91-92 originally referred to the term "liberationism" to refer to the ideas of "empowerment of the marginalised (majority) by the 'higher hand' of state authority" espoused by certain political groups in South Africa. In a later article, these ideas are referred to as "egalitarianism". See *Du Plessis,* 2000 Scriptura, 34-39.

[211] *Du Plessis,* 1994 SAPR/PL, 1.

[212] *Du Plessis/Olivier,* 1997 (1) 5 HRCLJSA, 11; *Du Plessis* in *De Villiers (ed)*, Birth of a Constitution (1994), 97; *Atkinson* in *Friedman & Atkinson (eds)*, Small Miracle (1994), 134; *Du Plessis,* 1994 SAPR/PL, 17; *Gutto,* Property and Land Reform (1995), 55.

[213] *Du Plessis,* 1994 SAPR/PL, 2-3 and *Du Plessis* in *De Villiers (ed)*, Birth of a Constitution (1994), 91-92.

apartheid, the ranks of the libertarians were expanded and diversified through the joining of "newcomers" on the human rights scene. Ironically, the "old" South African National Party government[214] was probably the most significant newcomer to fervently support the libertarian approach to human rights in ensuing negotiations.

Liberationism/egalitarianism, by contrast, is predominantly underpinned by ideologies ranging from social democracy to democratic socialism.[215] Thus, it takes a more decisive egalitarian stance than its libertarian counterpart, but cannot really be described as being by nature "socialist" or "collectivist" in the true sense of the word. Liberationists are, however, usually more prepared to bear with state intervention for the sake of an equal distribution of means among the members of society. As early as 1943, the ANC adopted a liberationist approach to human rights in South Africa.[216] Strong liberationist elements were also been incorporated into the ANC's proposals[217] presented for negotiations.

Libertarianism and liberationism/egalitarianism can to some extent be complementary. They share a fundamental commitment to a quintessence of time-honoured liberal-democratic values, albeit with a marked difference in emphasis. Among these values are[218]

> *"an unquestioning deference to human life and human dignity, to freedom and security of the person, to freedom of conscience, religion,*

---

[214] Their *Proposals on a Charter of Fundamental Rights* (2 February 1993) is framed in the libertarian tradition. See also the art. 15 of the proposal of the *South African Law Commission,* Working Paper 25, Project 58, Group and Human Rights (1989). This document is printed as Appendix B, vol 21, 1989 *Columbia Human Rights Law Review,* 241-248.

[215] *Du Plessis,* 1994 SAPR/PL, 2-3 and *Du Plessis* in *De Villiers (ed),* Birth of a Constitution (1994), 91-92.

[216] This is apparent from their 1943-document *African Claims in Africa* and the 1955 *Freedom Charter,* online at http://www.anc.org.za/ancdocs/history/keydocs.html [2000.03.12].

[217] *Ready to Govern: ANC Policy Guidelines for a Democratic South Africa* (online at http://www.anc.org.za/ancdocs/history/readyto.html [13.02.2000] and *A Bill of Rights for a New South Africa.* (See Appendix A, vol 21, 1989 *Columbia Human Rights Law Review,* 235-239 which formed the basis of the latter document.)

[218] *Du Plessis,* 1994 SAPR/PL, 2-3; *Du Plessis* in *De Villiers (ed),* Birth of a Constitution (1994), 91-92.

belief and expression (including freedom of the media), to participa-
tory political institutions and to due process of law in its various
forms."

However, in spite of the values shared by the libertarian and liberation-
ist/egalitarianist traditions, it is especially in the field of socio-economic
rights, like those "new" land rights created by section 25(5) to (8) FC,[219]
where the different traditions may be difficult to reconcile. Liberation-
ism/egalitarianism is much more oriented towards the treatment of the
bill of rights as a vehicle for socio-economic upliftment of the marginalised masses than libertarianism. The debate about whether or not
(and the extent to which) socio-economic rights in general should be
entrenched in a bill of rights, thus also had a profound influence on the
discussion about the inclusion of a property clause in a justiciable bill of
rights.[220] The differences between libertarianism and liberation-
ism/egalitarianism therefore become particularly apparent in the debate
about the inclusion of a property clause in the constitution, and the
overview of the compromises that were eventually reached.

3.1.1. The Inclusion of a Property Guarantee in the Constitution

During the negotiations, the different approaches regarding the inclusion of a property guarantee in the Constitution's chapter on fundamental rights were in essence based upon the divisions in the South African society and the fundamental-rights ideologies underpinning these
divisions.[221] This would eventually also determine the wording and
structure of the property clauses, section 28 IC and section 25 FC.

---

[219] *Budlender* in *Budlender/Latsky/Roux,* New Land Law (revised 1998), ch.
1, 69. For a discussion on the enforceability and implementation of the right to
property as a socio-economic right in the South African context, see *De Wet,*
Constitutional Enforceability of Economic and Social Rights (1996), 129-135;
Caiger in *Bennun/Newitt (eds),* Negotiating Justice (1995), 132-137.

[220] *Caiger* in *Bennun/Newitt (eds),* Negotiating Justice (1995), 132; *Budlender,* 1992 SAJHR, 303.

[221] *Chaskalson,* 1995 SAJHR, 222-240 and *Atkinson* in *Friedman/Atkinson
(eds),* Small Miracle (1994), 134-140 provide telling illustrations of the drafting
IC's property clause and the ongoing conflict between the ANC and the NP as
supporters of different human rights traditions and as representatives of conflicting interest-groups in the South African society.

An important and "typically South African" characteristic of the libertarian and liberationist/egalitarian approaches should be mentioned at this stage: Normally, libertarians would — due to their roots in classical liberalism — contend for a minimalist approach towards protection of fundamental rights. They would, for instance assume a "hands-off" attitude with regard to the relation of state authority to individual autonomy. By contrast, liberationists/egalitarianists would — due to social-democratic ideological roots — usually prefer stronger regulatory measures. Further, liberationists normally favour a bill of rights providing mechanisms with which to effect claims premised on second and third generation rights. In South Africa, however, the political positioning of the negotiating parties caused liberationists/egalitarianists to adopt an a-typical minimalist approach, and libertarians to adopt an a-typical "optimalist" stance.[222] This peculiarity had a noteworthy influence on the drafting of section 28 IC in particular, but also on section 25 FC. It is also bound to influence the decisions of the courts in future. Whereas the National Party/Government's negotiators favoured the inclusion of a property guarantee right from the start of negotiations, the ANC's negotiators initially attempted to exclude the right from the interim charter.[223]

The ANC and their supporters believed that a property guarantee would hamper land restitution projects. They were of the opinion that the constitutional protection of property would legitimise the consequences of generations of apartheid and dispossession.[224] Therefore, their proposed bill of rights for the negotiation process did not provide

---

[222] *Du Plessis,* 1994 SAPR/PL, 2-3.

[223] This declares the stronger influence of the NP in determining the initial wording of the property clause. *Chaskalson,* 1995 SAJHR, 222-240; *Atkinson* in *Friedman/Atkinson (eds),* Small Miracle (1994), 134-140.

[224] *Budlender* in *Budlender/Latsky/Roux,* New Land Law (revised 1998), ch. 1, 3; *Caiger* in *Bennun/Newitt (eds),* Negotiating Justice (1995), 113-114; *Atkinson* in *Friedman/Atkinson (eds),* Small Miracle (1994), 135-136; *Van der Walt,* 1992 SAJHR, 450.

for the protection of property as such. The Canadian[225] and Indian[226] situations, where the constitutional drafters for various reasons re-

---

[225] In Canada it was decided to exclude property rights from the Charter of Rights and Freedoms (adopted in 1982), after the topic has been debated extensively. Originally the Canadian Constitution of 1960 contained a non-justiciable Bill of Rights, as part of an ordinary statue, which could be revoked by parliament and which did not provide the court with the power to review statutes. This remains in force and contains specific protection for property rights, by providing guarantees for the right to the enjoyment of property and the right not to be deprived of property except by due process of law. It applies to federal parliament, and seems to be restricted to the property of individual persons. Several provincial bills of rights provide explicit protection of property rights. The guarantee of property was apparently excluded from the 1982 Canadian Charter of Rights and Freedoms by reason of (i) the uncertainty of the range of rights that would be included in the category of property protected by a constitutional property clause; (ii) previous experience with the earlier non-entrenched constitutional provisions regarding property; (iii) the conviction that vital aspects of life, liberty and personal security that are often associated with and protected by the property clause are sufficiently covered by the articles dealing with personal rights; (iv) opposition from provincial governments fearing that the inclusion of a property clause might hamper the solution of specific provincial problems; and (v) the controversy of the question whether property is in fact so fundamental a right that it should rank with other rights that are guaranteed in the charter. Owners, however, are at least protected by a number of common law rules and by procedural provisions which guarantee due process of law. Nevertheless, payment of compensation is not guaranteed, but the relevant statues usually provide for payment of adequate compensation. See *Bauman*, 1992 SAJHR, 345-355; *Van der Walt*, 1993 Recht & Kritiek, 275-277; *Budlender* in *Budlender/Latsky/Roux*, New Land Law (revised 1998), ch. 1, 3. *Gutto*, Property and Land Reform (1995), 31 refers to the Canadian approach to securing property rights and land rights as one of "constitutional abeyance," explaining that this approach of a deliberate omission from constitutional protection is a political strategy not to explicitly incorporate that which is unlikely to receive general consensus, however, with the knowledge that such a *lacuna* would not be fatal to the overall balance of the political and social order in the interests of society. *Van der Walt*, Constitutional Property Clauses - A Comparative Analysis (1999), 86-87 shows that, even without an express property guarantee, the Canadian treatment of property protection is important for comparative purposes, because of the importance attached to the interpretation of the general limitation clause in the Canadian Charter.

[226] The history of constitutional property protection in India is dominated by the constitutional conflict that raged between the legislature and the courts for almost thirty years. Judges asserted property rights to upset schemes of social reform. Land reforms, nationalisation, motor transport, slum clearances and

frained from incorporating a property guarantee in the respective Bills of Rights, were used to justify arguments in favour of the exclusion of property rights from a catalogue of fundamental rights in South Africa.[227]

Instead of showing outright support for property protection, the ANC's proposal set out general principles seemingly imbued with a "communal spirit," affording property a more customary character. According to their proposal, property was to be regarded as something people use and cannot own to the exclusion of others.[228] Their reservations concerning the inclusion of a property guarantee in the new constitution focussed on the unpredictability of consequences flowing from such an inclusion. This could be problematic for the exercise of the government's regulatory functions[229] and legislation aimed at achieving social stability and at addressing the disparities of wealth in the South African society.[230]

On the other hand, the National Party/Government and their supporters from the outset favoured a property guarantee elevating the rights of owners to such a level that the state's power to levy taxes would be subject to the sovereignty of property. Their initially proposed property guarantee would have had the effect that all taxes on property with

---

government take-overs of mismanaged vital industries were struck down in the name of private property. The property clauses contained in the list of fundamental rights (art 19(1)(f) read with 19(5); as well as art. 31), were eventually the most litigated provisions in the Indian Constitution. After a series of constitutional amendments, the inability of the courts and legislature to find common ground on the issue of constitutional property protection resulted in the removal of the property guarantee from the bill of rights in 1978. The Indian experience is relevant for South Africa because of the similar problems of widespread poverty and the aftermath of colonialism that will have to be faced in a democratic order. *Murphy*, 1993 JJS, 38-39; *Chaskalson*, 1993 SAJHR, 389-395; *Van der Walt*, 1993 Recht & Kritiek, 277-278; *Gutto*, Property and Land Reform (1995), 33, *Van der Walt*, Constitutional Property Clauses - A Comparative Analysis (1999), 192 ff.

[227] A discussion on the treatment of the right not to be deprived of property in these jurisdictions, which both are connected to the Commonwealth, can be found in *Allen*, 1993 Int & Comp LQ, 523-552.

[228] *Caiger* in *Bennun/Newitt (eds)*, Negotiating Justice (1995), 130-138.

[229] *Budlender* in *Budlender/Latsky/Roux*, New Land Law (revised 1998), ch. 1, 3; *Atkinson* in *Friedman/Atkinson (eds)*, Small Miracle (1994), 136-139.

[230] *Murphy*, 1993 JJS, 38; *Chaskalson*, 1995 SAJHR, 223.

a confiscatory effect would be invalid. Expropriation against compensation would have been the only interference with property for which the state would have authorisation. They based their view on the proposition that the individual can first and foremost achieve his or her full potential by acquiring property through hard work, thrift and responsibility.[231] They pointed out that the protection of property is fundamental to democracy itself and that such guarantees are present in most modern constitutions.[232] They also indicated that the function of a clause constitutionally entrenching the right to property would be to ban the fears of owners and right holders regarding property confiscation.[233] It was also argued that a property clause would be an effective way of mediating the conflict between free economic activity and the imperatives of social policy.[234]

3.1.2. Compromises Incorporated in Section 28 IC and Section 25 FC

The negotiators eventually agreed that a property clause which both protects existing property rights and recognises property rights which had been taken away by apartheid, should be included in the bill of rights. They could not, however, reach agreement on the way in which, and standards according to which compensation would have to be determined in the event of expropriation. Neither could they agree on a constitutional strategy to provide for the restoration of rights in land to persons who had been dispossessed of such rights as a result of racially discriminatory policies.[235]

---

[231] *Chaskalson*, 1995 SAJHR, 224; *Du Plessis*, 1994 SAPR/PL, 3.

[232] *Budlender* in *Budlender/Latsky/Roux*, New Land Law (revised 1998), ch. 1, 3.

[233] I.e. the withdrawal of property from its owners by the state or public authorities without remuneration. *Du Plessis/Olivier*, 1997 (1) 5 HRCLJSA, 11; *Chaskalson*, 1995 SAJHR, 224.

[234] See the application of the principles in *Munzer*, A Theory of Property (1990), to the South African context in *Lewis*, 1992 SAJHR, 419-430. See also the account of the Democratic Party's lobby at the Multi-Party Negotiating Process in *Atkinson* in *Friedman/Atkinson (eds)*, Small Miracle (1994), 136, 137.

[235] *Du Plessis*, 1994 SAPR/PL, 17; *Caiger* in *Bennun/Newitt (eds)*, Negotiating Justice (1995), 115-116; *Du Plessis/Olivier*, 1997 (1) 5 HRCLJSA, 11; *Chaskalson*, 1995 SAJHR, 229-238; *Atkinson* in *Friedman/Atkinson (eds)*, Small Miracle (1994), 136-140.

It was eventually decided to include a positive property guarantee, section 28 IC, in the chapter on Fundamental Rights of the Interim Constitution. The mandate for land reform and restitution would be framed in sections 121,[236] 122[237] and 123[238] IC,[239] *outside* the chapter on funda-

---

[236] Sec. 121 IC (Claims): "(1) An Act of Parliament shall provide for matters relating to the restitution of land rights, as envisaged in this section and in sections 122 and 123. (2) A person or a community shall be entitled to claim restitution of a right in land from the state if - (a) such person or community was dispossessed of such right at any time after a date to be fixed by the Act referred to in subsection (1); and (b) such dispossession was effected under or for the purpose of furthering the object of a law which would have been inconsistent with the prohibition of racial discrimination contained in section 8(2), had that section been in operation at the time of such dispossession. (3) The date fixed by virtue of subsection (2)(a) shall not be a date earlier than 19 June 1913. (4)(a) The Provisions of this section shall not apply to any rights in land expropriated under the Expropriation Act, 1975 (Act No. 63 of 1975), or any other law incorporating by reference in that Act, or the provisions of that Act with regard to compensation, if just and equitable compensation as contemplated in section 123(4) was paid in respect of such expropriation. (b) In this section "Expropriation Act, 1975" shall include any expropriation law repealed by that Act."

[237] Sec. 122 IC (Commission): "(1) The Act contemplated in section 121(1) shall establish a Commission on Restitution of Land Rights, which shall be competent to-(a) investigate the merits of any claims; (b) mediate and settle disputes arising from such claims; (c) draw up reports on unsettled claims for submission as evidence to a court of law and to present any other relevant evidence to the court; and (d) exercise and perform any such other powers and functions as may be provided for in the said Act. (2) The procedures to be followed for dealing with claims in terms of this section shall be as prescribed by or under the said Act."

[238] Sec. 123 IC (Court orders): "(1) Where a claim contemplated in section 121(2) is lodged with a court of law and the land in question is-(a) in the possession of the state and the state certifies that the restoration of the right in question is feasible, the court may, subject to subsection (4), order the state to restore the relevant right to the claimant; or (b) in the possession of a private owner and the state certifies that the acquisition of such land by the state is feasible, the court may, subject to subsection (4), order the state to purchase or expropriate such land and restore the relevant right to the claimant. (2) The court shall not issue an order under subsection (1)(b) unless it is just and equitable to do so, taking into account all relevant factors, including the history of the dispossession, the hardship caused, the use to which the property is being put, the history of its acquisition by the owner, the interests of the owner and others affected by any expropriation, and the interests of the dispossessed: Provided that any expropriation under subsection (1)(b) shall be subject to the payment

mental rights. Ordinary legislation (more particularly the Restitution of Land Rights Act[240]) would then be passed to give effect to the provisions of these sections.[241] Thus, section 28 IC, while entrenching the right to acquire, hold and dispose of rights in property, also provided for the protection of existing rights in property and for expropriation against payment of compensation. A strong libertarian influence is thus demonstrated. The section provides as follows:

---

of compensation calculated in the manner provided for in section 28(3). (3) If the state certifies that any restoration in terms of subsection (1)(a) or any acquisition in terms of subsection (1)(b) is not feasible, or if the claimant instead of the restoration of the right prefers alternative relief, the court may, subject to subsection (4), order the state, in lieu of the restoration of the said right-(a) to grant the claimant an appropriate right in available alternative state-owned land designated by the state to the satisfaction of the court, provided that the state certifies that it is feasible to designate alternative state-owned land; (b) to pay the claimant compensation; or (c) to grant the claimant any alternative relief. (4)(a)The compensation referred to in subsection (3) shall be determined by the court as being just and equitable, taking into account the circumstances which prevailed at the time of the dispossession and all such other factors as may be prescribed by the Act referred to in section 121(1), including any compensation that was paid upon such dispossession. (b) If the court grants the claimant the relief contemplated in subsection (1) or (3), it shall take into account, and where appropriate, make an order with regard to, any compensation that was paid to the claimant upon the dispossession of the right in question.

[239] Text online at http://www.constitution.org.za/1993cons.htm [28.02.2000].

[240] 22 of 1994.

[241] Note that sec. 121-123 IC and the Restitution of Land Rights Act do not, and were not intended to, deal with land redistribution. *Chaskalson/Lewis* in *Chaskalson/Kentridge/Klaaren et. al. (eds)*, Constitutional Law of South Africa (1996), ch. 31, 2. *Budlender* in *Budlender/Latsky/Roux*, New Land Law (revised 1998), ch. 1, 4 points out that of all the wrongs, injuries and suffering caused by apartheid and racial discrimination, it is only the dispossession of land rights that the legislature is specifically directed to rectify in the Interim Constitution. (The consequences of other human rights abuses are treated in the Postscript to the Constitution, dealing with *National Unity and Reconciliation*. As a result of those provisions and the Promotion of National Unity and Reconciliation Act 34 of 1995, victims of serious human rights abuses do not have an enforceable right to compensation if amnesty is granted in respect of those abuses, even if they constituted illegal conduct.)

28 (Property)

(1) Every person shall have the right to acquire and hold rights in property and, to the extent that the nature of the rights permits, to dispose of such rights.

(2) No deprivation of any rights in property shall be permitted otherwise than in accordance with a law.

(3) Where any rights in property are expropriated pursuant to a law referred to in subsection (2), such expropriation shall be permissible for public purposes only and shall be subject to the payment of agreed compensation or, failing agreement, to the payment of such compensation and within such period as may be determined by a court of law as just and equitable, taking into account all relevant factors, including, in the case of the determination of compensation, the use to which the property is being put, the history of its acquisition, its market value, the value of the investments in it by those affected and the interests of those affected.

The constitutional property clause in the Interim Constitution played an important role in the overall importance of the new constitutional order established after 1994.[242] The compromise embodied in the Interim Constitution was followed by another intense debate in the drafting of the Final Constitution. It was agreed relatively early in the second drafting process that the protection of existing property rights should not render land reform impossible.[243] Divergent opinions were, however, held on what constituted effective land reform, and which measures would render it impossible. The decision to keep the constitutional property guarantee intact remained controversial until the very last moments of the drafting process. It was one of the last issues resolved by the Constitutional Assembly.[244] The property clause in the Final Constitution was eventually phrased more widely so as to include the objectives of access to land, provision of legally secure land tenure, land restitution and land reform in subsections (5) to (8). It provided:

---

[242] *Van der Walt*, Constitutional Property Clauses - A Comparative Analysis (1999), 324.

[243] *Budlender* in *Budlender/Latsky/Roux*, New Land Law (revised 1998), ch. 1, 4.

[244] *Budlender* in *Budlender/Latsky/Roux*, New Land Law (revised 1998), ch. 1, 4-5; *Du Plessis/Olivier*, 1997 (1) 5 HRCLJSA, 11.

25 (Property)

(1) No one may be deprived of property except in terms of law of general application, and no law may permit arbitrary deprivation of property.

(2) Property may be expropriated only in terms of law of general application – (a) for a public purpose or in the public interest; and (b) subject to compensation, the amount of which and the time and manner of payment of which have either been agreed to by those affected or decided or approved by a court.

(3) The amount of the compensation and the time and manner of payment must be just and equitable, reflecting an equitable balance between the public interest and the interests of those affected, having regard to all relevant circumstances, including – (a) the current use of the property; (b) the history of the acquisition and use of the property; (c) the market value of the property; (d) the extent of direct state investment and subsidy in the acquisition and beneficial capital improvement of the property; and (e) the purpose of the expropriation.

(4) For the purposes of this section – (a) the public interest includes the nation's commitment to land reform, and to reforms to bring about equitable access to all South Africa's natural resources; and (b) property is not limited to land.

(5) The state must take reasonable legislative and other measures, within its available resources, to foster conditions which enable citizens to gain access to land on an equitable basis.

(6) A person or community whose tenure of land is legally insecure as a result of past racially discriminatory laws or practices is entitled, to the extent provided by an Act of Parliament, either to tenure which is legally secure or to comparable redress.

(7) A person or community dispossessed of property after 19 June 1913 as a result of past racially discriminatory laws or practices is entitled to the extent provided by an Act of Parliament, either to tenure which is legally secure or to comparable redress.

(8) No provision of this section may impede the state from taking legislative and other measures to achieve land, water and related reform, in order to redress the results of past racial discrimination, provided that any departure from the provisions of this section is in accordance with the provisions of section 36(1).

(9) Parliament must enact the legislation referred to in subsection (6).

3.1.3. Certification of Section 25 FC

The next hurdle to be crossed was the certification of the Final Constitution by the Constitutional Court.[245] The negotiators responsible for drafting the Interim Constitution agreed on thirty-four broad constitutional principles, included in schedule 4 to the Interim Constitution, with which the Final Constitution had to comply. The Constitutional Court had the task of certifying that the text of the Final Constitution complied with all of these principles before the Final Constitution could come into operation.

In the *Certification* case, the court *inter alia* had to decide whether section 25 FC complied with the constitutional principles in schedule 4 IC. With regard to the certification of the property clause, the second constitutional principle played an important role. It determined:

> *Everyone shall enjoy all universally accepted fundamental rights, freedoms and civil liberties, which shall be provided for and protected by entrenched and justiciable provisions in the Constitution, which shall be drafted after having given due consideration to inter alia the fundamental rights contained in Chapter 3 of the [Interim] Constitution.*

Several arguments were presented to the Constitutional Court to indicate that the property clause in the Final Constitution did not comply with the second constitutional principle. The first objection raised against section 25 FC was that the wording adopted by the constitutional assembly did not comply with the requirement of being one of the "universally accepted fundamental rights" and that section 25 FC did not protect the right to "acquire, hold and dispose of property" as was the case with section 28 IC.[246] This argument was dismissed by the court in the light of the many and varied existing versions of property guarantees in other constitutions and human rights documents. The court thus concluded that there is no universally accepted formulation of the right to property and that, although section 25 FC was framed negatively, protection of the right to acquire, hold and dispose of property was implicit in the new text. It was also remarked that a negative formulation of the property guarantee was apparently widely accepted

---

[245] *Certification of the Constitution of the Republic of South Africa* 1996 BCLR 1253 (CC), par. 70-75.

[246] *Certification of the Constitution of the Republic of South Africa* (note 245 above), par. 71.

as appropriate, and that the lack of an express protection for the right to hold and acquire property did not indicate non-compliance with the second constitutional principle.[247]

A further objection against section 25 FC concerned the expropriation provisions. In particular, it was argued that expropriation could also be effected for purposes of land, water or related reform and not only where the use to which the expropriated land would be put would be in the interests of a broad section of the public. It was further argued that compensation should be determined on the basis of market value, and not by having regard to the factors listed in section 25(3) FC. On the first issue, the court found that the aims of expropriation envisaged were not inconsistent with universally accepted approaches to expropriation. With regard to the determination of compensation, the court acknowledged that it was not usual for a constitutional document itself to mention specific criteria upon which compensation could be determined. It found, however, that the approach taken in section 25 FC did not conflict with the universally accepted view that compensation had to be "fair," "adequate," "full," "equitable and appropriate," or "just."[248]

A last objection against section 25 FC was that mineral rights and intellectual property were not expressly afforded protection. The court rejected this argument by indicating that neither of these was regarded as "universally accepted" fundamental rights.[249]

Section 25 FC was not referred to the Constitutional Assembly for amendment. The court thus in principle approved of the compromise reached in the drafting of section 25 FC. In the four years since the enactment of section 25 FC, the government (that is to say the Department of Land Affairs) has published extensive policy declarations on

---

[247] *Certification of the Constitution of the Republic of South Africa* (note 245 above), par. 72.

[248] *Certification of the Constitution of the Republic of South Africa* (note 245 above), par. 73.

[249] *Certification of the Constitution of the Republic of South Africa* (note 245 above), par. 74-75. Mostly, intellectual property or mineral rights are protected by a constitutional guarantee, not because they constitute inherent fundamental rights, but rather because they are regarded as *property* within the wider constitutional meaning of the term.

the property reforms undertaken and intended.[250] Yet, the debate on whether the libertarian or the liberationist tradition[251] of human rights ideology should be preferred continues in the sphere of constitutional interpretation.

3.2. Relevance of the Constitutional Property Clauses for the South African Property Order

The South African provisions on the constitutional protection of property reflect, apart from their hybrid ideological foundations,[252] also a collision between South Africa's unfortunate history of ownership and property rights on the one hand, and the present disparities of wealth in the society on the other. This complicates the court's function of balancing the protection of private property rights against the need for regulation and expropriation of property rights for the sake of the common good. The days are over in which the court could remark that:[253]

> "Whether all this [ie the social transformation envisaged by Parliament in enacting the Group Areas Act] will ultimately prove to be for the common weal of all the inhabitants, is not for the court to decide."

On the one hand, the courts have to abstract a set of values according to which property law — in particular law pertaining to ownership of land — should function under the constitution. On the other hand, they have to monitor compliance with these values. Neither of the constitutional texts provides ample guidance for the fulfilment of these tasks.

The meaning and effect of the interim property clause was, for instance, problematic from the outset. Some scholars regarded section 28(1) IC as

---

[250] Department of Land Affairs *White Paper on South African Land Policy* (1997) online at http://www.polity.org.za/govdocs/white_papers/landwp.html [16.12.1998].

[251] See note 210 above.

[252] See 64 above.

[253] Holmes J in *Minister of the Interior v Lockhat and Others* (note 10 above), 602E-F commenting on the discriminating effect that the Group Areas Act 77 of 1957 would have through substantial partial and unequal treatment of the different race groups, the disrupting effect and substantial inequalities that would arise out of this act clearly having been envisaged by Parliament.

a statement of substantive individual property rights.[254] Others regarded it as a guarantee of the institution of private property, rather than individual property rights.[255] A third group regarded the right to property as a socio-economic right,[256] while some scholars deemed it to be a mere statement of eligibility to hold and deal with rights in property.[257] The divergent interpretations of the function of section 28 IC could possibly be ascribed to the different views on the importance of the human rights ideologies underpinning the compromise reached in the drafting of the property clause.

The dichotomous nature of the values underlying the ownership concept in the new constitutional order persisted in the formulation of section 25 FC. The human rights tradition that enjoys precedence through the interpretation of the constitutional text will therefore also necessarily influence the manner in which existing property rights, and the restitution of land rights, are treated in terms of section 25 FC. This will, in turn, have implications for the understanding of the private law concept of ownership, which is inevitably influenced by the underlying political and social ideologies in the South African society.[258]

The courts in future will have to determine how problems regarding, *inter alia*, the interaction between general and internal limitations of the constitutional property guarantee,[259] the social function of property,[260] the formulation of the constitutional property concept,[261] and the interaction between the property clause and the equality clause of the constitution[262] will be theoretically disposed of. No generally accepted

---

[254] *Murphy*, 1995 SAPR/PL, 107-130.

[255] *Van der Walt*, 1994 THRHR, 181-203.

[256] *Budlender* in *Budlender/Latsky/Roux*, New Land Law (1998), ch. 1, 13-14 for a critical approach; See also in general *Budlender*, 1992 SAJHR, 295-304.

[257] *Budlender* in *Budlender/Latsky/Roux*, New Land Law (1998), ch. 1, 14-15.

[258] See 12 above.

[259] See 270 ff. below.

[260] See 200 ff. below.

[261] *Budlender* in *Budlender/Latsky/Roux*, New Land Law (1998), ch. 1, 13-14; See also *Ackermann*, 2000 ZaöRV, 537-556, and the examples mentioned there.

[262] *Budlender* in *Budlender/Latsky/Roux*, New Land Law (1998), ch. 1, 14-15.

theoretical framework exists at present. Nevertheless, the actual transformation of property law and landownership is not curtailed by the lack
of such a theoretical framework. In the face of severe political pressure, in
anticipation of a new socio-political dispensation and in spite of serious financial difficulties, most of the property practices under apartheid land
law have been altered since 1990.

Compliance with the urgent need for reconstruction and reparation
(which is explicitly demanded in the constitutional property clauses) will
inevitably disturb existing property relations.[263] It is submitted that the judiciary, legislature and administration should try to avoid piecemeal
transformation. A set of principles should rather be abstracted from the
constitutions themselves, according to which land restitution and redistribution can be effected by fully acknowledging the constitutional spirit of
reconciliation, unity and compromise.

In view of the above, it should be clear that the property clause of the
Final Constitution, as well as that of the Interim Constitution are relevant in determining the structure underlying the constitutional property guarantee. This is the result of sections 71, 73 and schedule 4 IC,
which provided that the new Constitution had to comply with certain
principles laid down by the Interim Constitution.[264] Section 28 IC will
continue to be the legal yardstick when determining the constitutional
validity of all property law. Statutes pertaining to property law passed
before the coming into force of the Final Constitution also have to be
measured against section 28 IC.[265] This is illustrated by the decision in
Ferreira v Levin NO, Vryenhoek v Powell[266] where it had to be determined whether a law inconsistent with the Interim Constitution was
automatically invalid through the operation of law, or whether such a
law would have to be declared invalid by a court. The court argued that,
after the coming into force of the Interim Constitution, laws were either objectively valid or invalid[267] — depending on whether or not they

---

[263] *Chaskalson/Lewis* in *Chaskalson/Kentridge/Klaaren et. al. (eds)*, Constitutional Law of South Africa (1996), ch. 31, 21.

[264] A constitutional assembly had to be established in terms of these provisions, and the new constitution had to be passed within two years from the date
of the first sitting of the national assembly in terms of the Interim Constitution.

[265] 4 February 1997.

[266] *Ferreira v Levin NO, Vryenhoek v Powell* 1996 1 SA 984 (CC), par. 27-
28.

[267] And therefore of no force and effect in terms of sec. 4(1) IC.

were consistent with the Constitution — even if a dispute concerning inconsistency would only be decided[268] years afterwards. Therefore, as Budlender indicates,[269] even if they are completely consistent with the Final Constitution, statutes enacted before its promulgation might be inconsistent with the Interim Constitution. In such a case the Court would be obliged to declare them invalid,[270] and may then make any order which is just and equitable,[271] in order to allow the competent authority to correct the defect. Such orders may include limiting the retrospective effect of the declaration of invalidity or suspending the declaration of invalidity for a period and subject to conditions.[272]

4. Constitutionalism and Socio-economic Needs

The purpose of this chapter is to provide an overview of the historic-ideological foundations of the German and South African constitutional property clauses. The historical background can be of valuable interpretative assistance, since it provides information on the nature of a particular property clause and the intention of the drafters thereof.

In both Germany and South Africa, the wording of the constitutional property guarantees was not a matter of chance, but an issue thoroughly debated and negotiated. In both legal systems the products of these negotiations were structured in a manner so as to serve the aims of the drafters of the property guarantees. In both cases, the unique historical circumstances of the respective countries contributed to the process of drafting the constitutional property guarantees. Both in Germany and in South Africa, the foundations of constitutional property protection comprise a compromise between the values of individual freedom and autonomy, on the one hand, and the common good, on the other. The interplay between individual autonomy and the common weal in the compromise between libertarianism and liberationism/egalitarianism forms the basis of section 25 FC and section 28 IC in

---

[268] In terms of sec. 98(5) IC.

[269] *Budlender* in *Budlender/Latsky/Roux*, New Land Law (revised 1998), ch. 1, 6.

[270] In terms of sec. 172(1)(a) FC.

[271] In terms of sec. 172(1)(b) FC.

[272] Sec. 172(1)(b)(i) and (ii) FC.

South Africa. The courts' function of abstracting a set of values from the constitutional property guarantee, according to which property law should function, and of monitoring compliance with these values, is therefore not easy. A similar deduction can be made from the German example.

Apart from the general constitutional principles[273] and the guidelines in the interpretation clause,[274] South African courts have very little material with which to work. In contrast to the German courts, which could, to some extent, rely on the decisions of their predecessors in the Weimar republic, no existing South African case law can provide sufficient guidance in matters pertaining to the constitutional protection of property. Still, major socio-economic issues have to be tackled in South Africa through the chosen method of constitutionalism. Constitutional adjudication in terms of the property clause, the equality clause, or the contentions of property owners that their lives and liberty have been violated by some economic, social or political regulation, require judicial harmonisation of collective and individual interests.[275]

This could be done by relying on legal-comparative analyses of constitutional property protection in other jurisdictions. Here, the German example could be helpful for finding solutions to the South African problems. In the following chapters, it will be indicated to what extent the constitutional values of the German legal system correspond or could be applica-

---

[273] The values on which the constitution is founded are expounded in the Preamble to the constitution. It refers, *inter alia*, to "heal[ing] the divisions of the past," establishing a society "based on democratic values, social justice and fundamental human rights;" and basing government "on the will of the people" and protecting "every citizen ... equally ... by law;" improving "the quality of life of all citizens and free the potential of each person;" and building "a united and democratic South Africa able to take its rightful place as a sovereign state in the family of nations."

[274] Sec. 39 FC (Interpretation of Bill of Rights): (1) When interpreting the Bill of Rights, a court, tribunal or forum-(a) must promote the values that underlie an open and democratic society based on human dignity, equality and freedom; (b) must consider international law; and (c) may consider foreign law. (2) When interpreting any legislation, and when developing the common law or customary law, every court, tribunal or forum must promote the spirit, purport and objects of the Bill of Rights. (3) The Bill of Rights does not deny the existence of any other rights or freedoms that are recognised or conferred by common law, customary law or legislation, to the extent that they are consistent with the Bill.

[275] *Murphy*, 1994 SAJHR, 391, 394.

ble to the South African context. First, however, the property guarantees of Germany and South Africa will be juxtaposed in order to analyse their structural aspects and to identify the apparent similarities and obvious differences between them.

Chapter 5: Structure of the Constitutional Protection and Regulation of Property in Germany and South Africa

1. External Aspects of the Constitutional Property Clauses

The external aspects of a particular property guarantee will inevitably influence the interpretation thereof. These external aspects not only determine the essential features of constitutional property protection in a given jurisdiction, but can also affect the comparative value of specific property guarantees. It will, thus, be necessary to take a closer look at the wording of the constitutional provisions protecting property in Germany and South Africa.

Article 14 GG consists of three clauses, each containing more than one provision:[276]

> *(1) [1] Das Eigentum und das Erbrecht werden gewährleistet. [2] Inhalt und Schranken werden durch die Gesetze bestimmt.*
>
> *(2) [1] Eigentum verpflichtet. [2] Sein Gebrauch soll zugleich dem Wohle der Allgemeinheit dienen.*
>
> *(3) [1] Eine Enteignung ist nur zum Wohle der Allgemeinheit zulässig. [2] Sie darf nur durch Gesetz oder auf Grund eines Gesetzes erfolgen, das Art und Ausmaß der Entschädigung regelt. [3] Die Entschädigung ist unter gerechter Abwägung der Interessen der Allgemeinheit und der Beteiligten zu bestimmen. [4] Wegen der Höhe der Entschädigung steht im Streitfalle der Rechtsweg vor den ordentlichen Gerichten offen.*

The provisions within the respective clauses are not officially numbered separately, as is the South African legislation. For purposes of the present analysis, reference is made to the various clauses by means of capital Roman numbers (the first clause is indicated with the numeral I; the second with II, and the third with III). Reference to a specific sentence within a clause is then made by means of a consecutive Arabic number. So, for instance, article 14 I 1 GG contains the guarantee of property, whereas article 14 I 2 GG acknowledges the ability of the legislature to regulate property. Article 14 II GG mentions the social obligation inherent to property. Article 14 III GG determines the requirements with which expropriation must comply.

---

[276] The official English translation of this text is provided at note 145 above.

Section 28 IC of South Africa also consisted of three clauses. Section 28(1) IC contained the property guarantee, section 28(2) IC stated the circumstances under which property could be regulated (or "deprived"), and section 28(3) IC, almost like article 14 III GG, determined the requirements to be adhered to in the case of expropriation:

Section 28 (Property):

(1) Every person shall have the right to acquire and hold rights in property and, to the extent that the nature of the rights permits, to dispose of such rights.

(2) No deprivation of any rights in property shall be permitted otherwise than in accordance with a law.

(3) Where any rights in property are expropriated pursuant to a law referred to in subsection (2), such expropriation shall be permissible for public purposes only and shall be subject to the payment of agreed compensation or, failing agreement, to the payment of such compensation and within such period as may be determined by a court of law as just and equitable, taking into account all relevant factors, including, in the case of the determination of compensation, the use to which the property is being put, the history of its acquisition, its market value, the value of the investments in it by those affected and the interests of those affected.

Section 25 FC of South Africa constitutes a considerable deviation from the property clause in section 28 IC. Apart from the fact that the property "guarantee" in section 25(1) FC is phrased negatively, and as such perhaps constitutes no real "guarantee" at all, the provisions on the determination of compensation in the case of expropriation are also more detailed. Section 25(4) FC contains a definitions clause and sections 25(5) to (8) FC regulate the state's duty to effect land reform, equitable access of land, security of land tenure and redistribution of property:

Section 25 (Property):

(1) No one may be deprived of property except in terms of law of general application, and no law may permit arbitrary deprivation of property.

(2) Property may be expropriated only in terms of law of general application – (a) for a public purpose or in the public interest; and (b) subject to compensation, the amount of which and the time and manner of payment of which have either been agreed to by those affected or decided or approved by a court.

(3) The amount of the compensation and the time and manner of payment must be just and equitable, reflecting an equitable balance between the public interest and the interests of those affected, having regard to all relevant circumstances, including – (a) the current use of the property; (b) the history of the acquisition and use of the property; (c) the market value of the property; (d) the extent of direct state investment and subsidy in the acquisition and beneficial capital improvement of the property; and (e) the purpose of the expropriation.

(4) For the purposes of this section – (a) the public interest includes the nation's commitment to land reform, and to reforms to bring about equitable access to all South Africa's natural resources; and (b) property is not limited to land.

(5) The state must take reasonable legislative and other measures, within its available resources, to foster conditions which enable citizens to gain access to land on an equitable basis.

(6) A person or community whose tenure of land is legally insecure as a result of past racially discriminatory laws or practices is entitled, to the extent provided by an Act of Parliament, either to tenure which is legally secure or to comparable redress.

(7) A person or community dispossessed of property after 19 June 1913 as a result of past racially discriminatory laws or practices is entitled to the extent provided by an Act of Parliament, either to tenure which is legally secure or to comparable redress.

(8) No provision of this section may impede the state from taking legislative and other measures to achieve land, water and related reform, in order to redress the results of past racial discrimination, provided that any departure from the provisions of this section is in accordance with the provisions of section 36(1).

(9) Parliament must enact the legislation referred to in subsection (6).

At first glance, the obvious question that arises from a comparison of the wording of the German and South African constitutional property clauses is to what extent the formulation of the property guarantee in either a "positive" or "negative" manner influences the interpretation thereof. This question will be addressed in the following paragraphs. Thereafter, the approach followed regarding the object of protection in positively and negatively formulated clauses, and its bearing on the procedure to be followed in an inquiry into the constitutional protection of property as a fundamental right, will be examined.

2. "Positive" and "Negative" Guarantees

The most obvious external characteristic of a property clause lies in the type of property protection it guarantees. The property clause can be formulated either positively or negatively, but neither the positive nor the negative formulation can be described as being the universally recognised version.[277] Most property clauses include at least a negative guarantee of property, which authorises the limitation of property rights subject to certain explicit requirements.[278] Thus, property can be appropriately protected even in the absence of a clause expressly guaranteeing the existence of the right to property.[279] Even so, positive property guarantees are found in the constitutions of several jurisdictions. In the following paragraphs the German and South African constitutional property clauses are discussed as different types of property guarantees.

2.1. The German Property Guarantee

Article 14 I 1 GG is an example of a positive formulation of the property guarantee, since it guarantees the existence of the right to property. However, a positive guarantee does not necessarily establish a right to claim delivery of property from the state.[280] Neither does it guarantee the ability of individuals to acquire property on their own.[281] This may cause confusion, in particular since article 14 I 2 GG already contains an additional ("negative") property guarantee, which provides all the protection that can be claimed in terms of a property clause. It creates the impression that the "positive" guarantee is superfluous, as there is, in effect, no fundamental difference between a positive or negative formulation of the property clause.

---

[277] *Certification of the Constitution of the Republic of South Africa* (note 245 above), par. 72.

[278] *Van der Walt*, Constitutional Property Clauses - A Comparative Analysis (1999), 11.

[279] *Certification of the Constitution of the Republic of South Africa* (note 245 above), par. 72.

[280] *Kleyn*, 1996 SAPR/PL, 414.

[281] *Kimminich* in *Starck (ed)*, Rights, Institutions and Impact of International Law (1987), 82.

The "positive" guarantee of article 14 I 1 GG, nevertheless, plays an important role in German constitutional property theory. Within the context of basic rights *(Grundrechte)*, German constitutional theory distinguishes between fundamental rights and institutional guarantees,[282] thereby giving the basic rights several layers of importance. On the one hand, the basic rights are *subjektive Rechte,* in the sense of fundamental rights accruing to individuals.[283] On the other hand, they are *Elemente objektiver Ordnung,* which means that the basic rights also prescribe the fundamental values of the existing social and legal order.[284] As regards constitutional protection of property in Germany, this two-tiered relevance of basic rights is exemplified particularly well by the existence of both "positive" and "negative" elements within the property guarantee. Indeed, the distinction made in German constitutional theory between fundamental rights and institutional guarantees results in a double property guarantee:[285] On the one hand, individual property[286] rights are guaranteed by means of the negative wording *(Be-*

---

[282] A further distinction is made in German constitutional theory between *Institutsgarantien* and *Institutionellen Garantien. Kimminich,* Eigentum Enteignung Entschädigung (1976), m.n. 92 explains that the former are guarantees of essentially private law institutions, whereas the latter refer to guarantees in the public life, e.g. the institution of civil service with tenure *(Berufsbeamtentum)* or municipal autonomy *(kommunale Selbstverwaltung).* art. 14 I 1 GG is an example of the former, as it sets out to protect private property as a legal institution.

[283] *Hesse,* Grundzüge des Verfassungsrechts (1993), m.n. 279, 283-289.

[284] *Hesse,* Grundzüge des Verfassungsrechts (1993), m.n. 279, 290-299.

[285] The structure of article 14 GG is, however, even more complex than one would think at first glance: Article 14 I 1 GG in effect guarantees two legal institutions, namely private property and inheritance. Simultaneously, two fundamental rights have also been established, namely the right to acquire and own property and the right to establish a will. See *Kimminich* in *Starck (ed),* Rights, Institutions and Impact of International Law (1987), 81. A discussion of the right to establish a will and the guarantee of inheritance falls outside the scope of this work. In the analysis of article 14 GG in later parts of this exposition, focus will be placed only on the right to own property and the guarantee of private property.

[286] The term used in art. 14 GG is correctly translated as *property* and not as *ownership* only. Therefore it includes a variety of proprietary interests. *Kleyn,* 1996 SAPR/PL, 413, 418.

standsgarantie).[287] On the other hand, property as an institution is guaranteed by the positive wording *(Institutsgarantie)*.[288]

The institutional guarantee of article 14 I 1 GG ensures that private property is recognised in an objective sense as a basic component of the social order.[289] It secures the essential elements in the property concept, like its existence, availability and usefulness for individuals. It furthermore and ensures that legislation does not erode or abolish any of these elements.[290] The institutional guarantee thus protects a core of norms that ensures the existence of private property in the broader legal order.[291] In this sense, property is an autonomous legal institution, or, alternatively formulated, an objective constitutional value that the state is obliged to preserve and foster affirmatively.[292] The legislature is directed neither to abolish the institution of ownership, nor to water it down to such an extent that it cannot be characterised as ownership any longer. Such legislation would remove the realm of freedom guaranteed by article 14 GG,[293] lead to the destruction of larger areas of private law and

---

[287] *Badura* in *Benda/Maihofer/Vogel (eds)*, Handbuch des Verfassungsrechts (1994), m.n. 32.

[288] *Kleyn*, 1996 SAPR/PL, 413.

[289] *Badura* in *Benda/Maihofer/Vogel (eds)*, Handbuch des Verfassungsrechts (1994), m.n. 33.

[290] *Van der Walt*, Constitutional Property Clauses - A Comparative Analysis (1999), 129; *Leisner* in *Isensee/Kirchhof*, Handbuch des Staatsrechts VI (1989), m.n. 12; BVerfGE 26, 215, 222; BVerfGE 52, 1, 31.

[291] *Kimminich*, Eigentum Enteignung Entschädigung (1976), 92.

[292] *Kommers*, Constitutional Jurisprudence of Germany (1997), 253 explains that the content of the positive duty of the state in this regard has not yet been fully defined. It may, for instance, require environmental protection legislation preserving the value of property where the productive use would depend on clean water and unspoiled forests. For instance, *Kunig*, 1983 Adel LR, 326-327 remarked that it would be conceivable that the institution of *Anliegergebrauch* – the right of owners or other right holders (e.g. lessees) to use the street adjacent to the land under discussion – could lead to a reactivation of art. 14 GG against measures which endanger the environment; and that art. 14 GG could also be invoked by businesses (for instance the tourist trade) in applying for nature preservation and environmental protection as an important element of property protection.

[293] BVerfGE 58, 300 *(Naßauskiesung)*, 339; BVerfGE 24, 367 *(Deichordnung)*, 389.

would therefore be in conflict with the prohibition of excesses *(Über-maßverbot).*[294]

However, the institutional property guarantee does not mean that the legislature is prevented from interfering with the system of private property. The institutional guarantee does not oblige the state to provide individuals with property,[295] but rather ensures that harmful concentrations of private property can be prevented by legitimate state action. It also places a duty on the legislature to create proper structures in areas where no or only weak proprietary protection exists.[296] Therefore an intrusion of public law into traditionally private law spheres is justified in order to protect and defend aspects of property vital to the well-being of the general public in maintaining the institution of ownership. This does not adversely affect the institutional guarantee.[297]

German constitutional law further also emphasises the subjective character of the right to property. Property is associated with liberty and personhood; it provides space for the exercise of autonomy and development of self-esteem.[298] The Federal Constitutional Court[299] further confirmed that article 14 I 1 GG guarantees private property, not only as legal institution, but also in concrete form in the hands of a specific owner. Logically, individuals cannot be holders of property rights if the institution of property does not exist. The specific purpose of the *Bestandsgarantie* is, however, to entitle individuals to be holders of property rights, and to protect them against undue state interference.[300] The court explained that the right to property is an elementary fundamental right closely related to the guarantee of individual freedom.[301] For the

---

[294] *Kleyn,* 1996 SAPR/PL, 415.

[295] *Leisner* in *Isensee/Kirchhof,* Handbuch des Staatsrechts VI (1989), m.n. 6; *Badura* in *Benda/Maihofer/Vogel (eds),* Handbuch des Verfassungsrechts (1994), m.n. 26; BVerfGE 80, 124, 137.

[296] *Badura* in *Benda/Maihofer/Vogel (eds),* Handbuch des Verfassungsrechts (1994), m.n. 26; *Kleyn,* 1996 SAPR/PL, 415.

[297] BVerfGE 58, 300 *(Naßauskiesung),* 339; See also *Kommers,* Constitutional Jurisprudence of Germany (1997), 259.

[298] *Kommers,* Constitutional Jurisprudence of Germany (1997), 252.

[299] BVerfGE 24, 367 *(Deichordnung),* 389.

[300] *Badura* in *Benda/Maihofer/Vogel (eds),* Handbuch des Verfassungsrechts (1994), 32.

[301] The principle of personal freedom is protected in art. 2 of the German Basic Law and guarantees the development of the individual's personality. Further,

holders of property rights, the article 14 GG guaranteed freedom in the patrimonial sphere. It enables holders of property rights to live independently and to freely take responsibility for their own lives. Therefore private property is said to be an "expression and prerequisite of personal freedom."[302] Accordingly, property not only serves to optimise the product of one's economic efforts, but also forms the basis of a liberal society.[303] In this way, the patrimonial and economic private autonomy of individuals is endorsed. Individuals can control, use and alienate the various objects of their property rights.[304]

In conclusion, the German double property guarantee indicates that, although personal freedom and private property are two separate ethical values, they have reciprocal relations, particularly in modern, industrialised societies.[305] The Federal Civil Court held[306] that the indi-

---

it plays an important role in the interpretation and application of article 14 GG. It reads: *"Jeder hat das Recht auf die freie Entfaltung seiner Persönlichkeit, soweit er nicht die Rechte anderer verletzt und nicht gegen die verfassungsmäßige Ordnung oder das Sittengesetz verstößt."* Translation: "Everybody has the right to self-fulfilment in so far as they do not violate the rights of others or offend against the constitutional order or morality."

[302] *Kimminich* in *Starck (ed)*, Rights, Institutions and Impact of International Law (1987), 81; *Kimminich* in *Abelein/Kimminich (eds)*, Festschrift für Hermann Raschhofer (1977), 105; *Meier-Hayoz* in *Keller (ed)*, Festgabe Karl Oftinger (1969), 171; *Meyer-Abich*, Der Schutzzweck der Eigentumsgarantie (1980), 58 ff.

[303] *Weber* in *Pawlowski/Wieacker (eds)*, Festschrift für Karl Michaelis (1972), 328; *Kimminich* in *Starck (ed)*, Rights, Institutions and Impact of International Law (1987), 81.

[304] *Kleyn*, 1996 SAPR/PL, 414.

[305] Personal freedom is protected and guaranteed in art. 2 GG. It is, however, in relation to art. 14 GG, the general legal rule whenever both apply. Therefore art. 14 GG will take precedence, as it specifically protects freedom in the sphere of al legal titles representing financial assets. (See BVerfGE 19, 206, 225: *"Das Bundesverfassungsgericht hat zwar entschieden, daß die besonderen Grundrechtsnormen für ihren Bereich die Anwendung des Art. 2 Abs.1 GG ausschließen ... Dies gilt aber nur, soweit eine Verletzung des Art. 2 Abs. 1 GG und einer besonderen Grundrechtsnorm unter demselben sachlichen Gesichtspunkt in Betracht kommt, nicht aber, wenn Art. 2 Abs. 1 GG unter einem Gesichtspunkt verletzt ist, der nicht in den Bereich der besonderen Grundrechtsnorm fällt."* See also BVerfGE 6, 32, 37.) If a violation of such titles is combined with an impairment of the free development of one's personality, art. 2 GG may be invoked to prevent further impairments. As activities in a modern, industrialised

vidual, integrated into the community of the State, needs a strictly safe-guarded sphere of property in order to be able to live as a person among equals. This means that the state should enable the individual to be free and responsible for him- or herself, and not merely an object of an overwhelming state power. The court's approach supports the view that the right to private property is a crucial component of the values of freedom and human dignity.

2.2. The South African Property Guarantees

The institutional/individual guarantee theory of German constitutional law has not been adopted or developed in other jurisdictions. Never-theless, the debate has considerably influenced the discussion on con-stitutional property protection in South Africa.[307] The German theory has been referred to several times in the context of the changed struc-ture of the interim and final property clauses, where a noticeably mixed positive/negative guarantee was substituted by one purely negative in formulation.

2.2.1. Section 28 IC

Although section 28(1) IC contains a positive property guarantee, it is unlikely that this section intended to provide individuals with positive claims against the state to provide them with property. The wording of section 28(1) IC rather grants a guarantee to all individuals to become holders of property.

The positive formulation of the property guarantee,[308] together with the fact that the general limitation clause[309] required that the essential con-

---

country often concern financial assets, it often happens that the priority posi-tion art. 14 GG takes, bars recurrence to the protection of freedom by art. 2 GG. Therefore art. 14 GG must also in some circumstances provide protection for personal freedom. This can only be done when property is also guaranteed in the hands of the individual.

[306] BGHZ 6, 276.

[307] *Van der Walt*, Constitutional Property Clauses - A Comparative Analysis (1999), 12.

[308] Sec. 28(1) IC.

tent of all fundamental rights had to be preserved, persuaded most authors[310] to accept that the institution of property was guaranteed in the Interim Constitution. However, diverging opinions existed on the question of in which sections — if any — individual property was guaranteed in the Interim Constitution. According to Van der Walt,[311] and Chaskalson and Lewis[312] the individual property guarantee was to be found in the negative guarantees of section 28(2) and (3) IC. Then again, Murphy[313] accepted that the positive guarantee in section 28(1) FC empowered all individuals with the right to acquire, hold and dispose of rights in property. This viewpoint has been criticised by Chaskalson and Lewis,[314] because it supported an interpretation through which all existing rights in property and therefore also privileges extended during the apartheid era would be protected. Kleyn's[315] reply to this line of argument was, however, that existing rights would even be protected under the negative guarantees of sections 28(2) and (3) IC. Privilege based on apartheid would, therefore, not be entrenched only by reliance on section 28(1) IC as individual guarantee. He furthermore indicated that section 28(1) IC would not necessarily entrench privilege based on apartheid at all, as such a guarantee could not immunise private property against the operation of section 28(2) and (3) IC or against sections 121 to 123 IC.

---

[309] Sec. 33(1)(b): "(1) The rights entrenched in this Chapter may be limited by law of general application, provided that such limitation-... (b) shall not negate the essential content of the right in question, ..." The effect of this is that *rights in property* may not be abolished as institutions of the legal system to which individuals can have access.

[310] *Kleyn*, 1996 SAPR/PL, 418; *Van der Walt*, 1995 SAPR/PL, 302, 308; *Murphy*, 1995 SAPR/PL, 112; *Chaskalson/Lewis* in *Chaskalson/Kentridge/ Klaaren et. al. (eds)*, Constitutional Law of South Africa (1996), ch. 31, 8.

[311] *Van der Walt*, 1995 SAPR/PL, 302-303; 308.

[312] *Chaskalson/Lewis* in *Chaskalson/Kentridge/Klaaren et. al. (eds)*, Constitutional Law of South Africa (1996), ch. 31, 7-8.

[313] See *Murphy*, 1992 SAJHR, 362-388; *Murphy*, 1995 SAPR/PL, 107-130.

[314] *Chaskalson/Lewis* in *Chaskalson/Kentridge/Klaaren et. al. (eds)*, Constitutional Law of South Africa (1996), ch. 31, 8.

[315] *Kleyn*, 1996 SAPR/PL, 417.

2.2.2. Section 25 FC

In terms of section 25 FC, individuals are still not provided with positive claims for the provision of property against the state. The wording of section 25 FC also still raises the issue of whether or not individual property and the institution of property are protected. Nevertheless, the structure of the South African property clause has in many respects undergone a metamorphosis since 1994.

Contrary to section 28(1) IC, section 25(1) FC is formulated negatively. Moreover, section 25(1) FC can be deemed a so-called *specific* negative guarantee. In this section, the provision for limitation of rights is negatively phrased within a sentence prohibiting deprivations. This specific negative guarantee, which includes references to the conditions for limitations on property, has to be seen as a clause directly restricting the scope of the right that is protected. By contrast, a *general* negative guarantee could still have been regarded as an indirect guarantee of property.[316] This could result in some complications during a process of interpretation.[317] The choice of a negative formulation could give rise to the argument that section 25 FC in reality protects something "less than property,"[318] namely the right not to be deprived of property and the right not to be expropriated except as provided for in the property clause itself.

Nevertheless, the Constitutional Court indicated a preference for an interpretation of section 25 FC that upholds the idea of an individual property guarantee, even if this terminology is not used explicitly. According to the *First Certification Case*,[319] a negative formulation such as

---

[316] After explaining (297) that the difference between *specific* and *general* negative guarantees lies in the fact that in the former case, both the guarantee as well as the limitations provision are phrased negatively within one sentence, whereas the latter would be characterised by two separate phrases, *Van der Walt*, 1997 SAPR/PL, 301-302 points out that this difference is probably merely a question of linguistic preference by the drafters of the constitution, instead of a conscious attempt to protection something less than property.

[317] The right not to be subjected to slavery, servitude or forced labour (sec. 13 FC); the right to citizenship (sec. 20 FC) and the right to participate in cultural, religious and linguistic communities (sec. 31 FC) are phrased negatively and do not involve the same complications as sec. 25 FC.

[318] See the explanation of this argument in *Van der Walt*, 1997 SAPR/PL, 295-313.

[319] *Certification of the Constitution of the Republic of South Africa* (note 245 above), par. 72.

employed in section 25 FC appears to be widely accepted as an appropriate formulation of the right to property. The assumption that the full content of property — and not something "less than property" — is protected by section 25 FC, is therefore well founded. Moreover, the court remarked that the right to hold property is implicit in section 25 FC. The court therefore could not support the argument that section 25 FC failed to meet the requirements of constitutional principle II in schedule 4 IC simply because of its negative formulation and because it lacks express recognition of the right to acquire and dispose of property. This also indicates that the court supports the protection of an individual right to acquire, hold and dispose of property.

The negative formulation of the property guarantee in section 25(1) FC also makes it more difficult to assume that the *institution of property* is guaranteed, as was the case under section 28(1) IC. Van der Walt[320] is of the opinion that the positive element of the property clause in section 28(1) IC was omitted from the final property clause specifically to avoid the debate about an institutional guarantee. However, Kleyn's[321] submission that such a guarantee still exists and the reasons he advances for this, are convincing.[322] He argues that the commitment to land reform, access to resources, restitution of land and the security of tenure all point to the creation of a mixed economy in which newly-empowered "deprived" section of the South African society can benefit from an institutional guarantee. He points out that these issues reflect the duty upon the state to safeguard the institution of property. Accordingly, it would be senseless to protect property in a bill of rights if the institution of property as a fundamental right in the objective sense is not protected.

The idea that the constitutional property clause protects the institution of property as such can to a certain extent also be inferred from the decision in the *First Certification Case.*[323] The Constitutional Court accepted that there is no fundamental difference between a positive or negative formulation of the property clause, and concluded that even a negative property clause would be an appropriate way of providing (implicit) protection for the right to hold property. This indifference of

---

[320] *Van der Walt*, 1997 SAPR/PL, 303.

[321] *Kleyn*, 1996 SAPR/PL, 418.

[322] See, however, *Van der Walt*, 1997 SAPR/PL, 303 note 45.

[323] *Certification of the Constitution of the Republic of South Africa* (note 245 above), par. 70-75.

the court towards the type of formulation used could point to an implicit adoption of the institutional guarantee of property. The court could, however, also have found that the institution of property is protected on the basis of the general limitation clause of the Final Constitution. Section 36 FC provides justification for the protection of property as an institution, even though the *essential content* provision in the limitation clause of the Interim Constitution[324] has been omitted in the final text. The proportionality requirement is implicit[325] in section 36 FC. It is specifically foreseen that the constitutionality of a particular infringement on property depends on the existence of certain formal elements. A law of general application can restrict the fundamental right only to the extent prescribed in the Constitution.[326] Furthermore, the constitutionality of a particular infringement also depends on whether the restriction complies with the three requirements (namely suitability, necessity and moderation[327])[328] of the proportionality test itself. The restriction should, in other words, be reasonable and justifiable in an open and democratic society and the same purpose should not have been achievable by less restrictive means. Upon this analysis, it can be submitted that an abolition of private property would infringe human dignity, equality and freedom beyond reasonableness and justifiability. It would at the same time be excessive. It would, therefore, be in conflict with the constitutional requirement of proportionality.

2.3. *Legal-comparative Evaluation*

In South Africa, a clear distinction is not always made between individual and institutional guarantees when the question as to the scope of protection in terms of the property clause is discussed. Therefore, the situation in South Africa might differ from that of Germany with regard to the protection of individual property or property as an institution. This theoretical distinction is more apparent in scholarly work

---

[324] Sec. 33(1)(b) IC.

[325] See 135 above; *Blaauw-Wolf,* 1999 SAPR/PL, 209 ff.; 31-32; contra *De Waal,* 1995 SAHJR, 7.

[326] Sec. 36(1) FC.

[327] I.e. not disproportionate.

[328] See 128 above.

than in the reasoning of the Constitutional Court. However, it could have an important influence on the manner in which an inquiry into the provisions of a particular constitutional property clause is conducted. In the course of this exposition, this influence will be pointed out.

The idea that — in spite of the negatively phrased constitutional property clause — at least some private property in a free (or mixed) market economy is guaranteed, might be valuable in the South African context. Van der Walt[329] has, in this regard, pointed out that the circumstances, in which individuals are empowered to acquire, hold and dispose of rights in property, form the basis of the market system. It is submitted that the mixed market economic policy of the present government could benefit from an approach by which private property is protected to that extent in which it can serve the individual's initiatives to attain self-fulfilment, and the initiatives of the state to bring about social upliftment and development. This matter will be discussed in more detail in the next chapter.[330] At this point it is necessary to provide a brief overview of the basic structure of an inquiry into the constitutional property clause, and the manner in which the approach to such an inquiry is influenced by the view taken on the matters concerning the object of property protection and the nature of such protection.

3. Basic Structure of an Inquiry into the Constitutional Property Clause

In order to undertake an analysis of the constitutional protection and regulation of property in Germany and South Africa, it is necessary to understand the general structures of human rights litigation and the role of the different courts in these systems. These issues will be dealt with in the following paragraphs.

3.1. Structure of Human Rights Litigation in General

In general, litigation pertaining to human rights occurs in a number of distinct stages in which procedural and substantive issues, as well as the remedies available are considered. Initially a court must decide whether

---

[329] *Van der Walt,* 1995 SAPR/PL, 303.

[330] See 160 ff. below.

a particular kind of legal relationship is subject to a fundamental rights review. This means that certain procedural issues such as the *locus standi* of the applicant, the justiciability of the issue, the jurisdiction of the court and the application of the bill of rights to the subject-matter of the litigation must be investigated.[331] The subsequent stages concern the substance of the case. If the chapter on fundamental rights applies to a given legal relationship, the court must decide whether the applicant's constitutional right has been infringed. If the court finds that the applicant has a right falling within the ambit of constitutional protection, and that this right has been infringed, it must decide whether the limitation placed upon the right is justifiable.[332] Finally, if the court finds that a violation of a right is not a justifiable limitation, it will have to consider the proper remedy to deal with the unconstitutional infringement of a fundamental right.[333]

The three-tiered investigation is in principle applicable in Germany, as well as in South Africa. Nevertheless some differences exist, in particular with regard to the procedures followed by the courts in these legal systems. The procedural differences are due mainly to the fact that the inquisitorial court system and the adversarial court system are preferred in Germany and in South Africa respectively, and the consequent influence on the power of the court to investigate or consider certain issues.[334] Where these issues have an influence on the comparison undertaken in this exposition, they will be discussed in more detail.

---

[331] These issues are discussed in *De Waal/Currie/Erasmus*, Bill of Rights Handbook (1999), 20-21, 26-121; *Chaskalson/Kentridge/Klaaren* in *Chaskalson/Kentridge et. al. (eds)* Constitutional Law of South Africa (1996), ch. 1.

[332] *De Waal/Currie/Erasmus*, Bill of Rights Handbook (1999), 21-22 describe the substantive questions generally relating to constitutional litigation as follows: "The court must assess the merits of this allegation. This assessment primarily involves the interpretation of the provisions of the Constitution in general and the Bill of Rights in particular." It must first be determined whether a particular interest of the applicant is protected under the bill of rights. Then it must be determined whether the law or the conduct challenged impairs that interest. If the court has thus determined that a law or the conduct of the respondent impairs a fundamental right, it must be considered whether the infringement is nevertheless a justifiable limitation of the right under discussion.

[333] *De Waal/Currie/Erasmus*, Bill of Rights Handbook (1999), 21 depicts this as the third stage of human rights litigation.

[334] See *Kötz*, 1987 TSAR, 35-43.

One important point of distinction between human rights litigation in South Africa from that of Germany is the presence of a general limitation clause[335] in the South African bill of rights and the lack of something similar in the German Basic Law. This issue is apparently also influenced by the formulation of the constitutional propety clause in either negative, positive or mixed (positive and negative) terms.[336] In the discussion about the limitation of rights at a later stage,[337] it will be indicated that certain principles of rights limitation in Germany are applicable to all the basic rights. The function of these provisions differs from that of the South African section 36 FC. Nevertheless, the German approach to the object of protection and the nature of limitation of the right hold interesting possibilities for the South African context, as will be pointed out in the course of this exposition.[338]

It is not within the scope of the present exposition to provide a detailed discussion of the procedural stage of constitutional litigation. Hence, in commenting on the application of the property guarantees, focus will be placed mainly on the substantive issues at hand, and to a lesser extent on the remedies available. At the outset, however, a few explanatory comments on the application of the principles of human rights litigation in general to the specific inquiry into constitutional protection of property are necessary. The following paragraphs contain a brief discussion of the possible claims that could arise from a constitutional property guarantee, and the manner in which the courts could deal with these issues.

3.2. Substantive Issues Relating to the Property Clause

At this point, a few remarks about the substantive issues in the inquiry based on the constitutional property guarantee will have to suffice. In the following paragraphs, the views on the object of protection in terms of the constitutional property clause and the claims arising from such protection will be briefly discussed. The influence of these views on the

---

[335] Sec. 36 FC.

[336] See *Van der Walt,* 1997 SAPR/PL, 275-330 for an overview of the different approaches emanating from the understanding attached to the nature of the object of protection and limitation of the right of constitutional property.

[337] See 258 below.

[338] See 393 ff. below.

inquiries into the constitutional validity of property regulation will then be indicated.

3.2.1. Claims Arising from the Constitutional Property Clause

A constitutional property clause could give rise to a variety of possible claims. The categorisation of possible claims depends largely on the approach taken regarding the object of protection and the influence of the limitation provisions on the constitutional property clause.[339] For the moment, these differences in opinion will be set aside in an attempt to cover this issue from more than one angle. Thus, the most important categories of possible claims for present purposes are (i) claims to have property, (ii) claims of eligibility to hold property, (iii) claims to immunity against uncompensated expropriation of private property, and (iv) claims of insulation against state interference with private property. The extent to which these claims exist in the South African and German context will be discussed in the following paragraphs.

3.2.1.1. The Claim to Have Property

The claim to have property would be premised on the argument that all people have a moral right to have at least enough property to enable them to survive or to lead a dignified existence. If they do not have this minimum, it should be provided to them (usually by the state). It will be indicated in the course of this exposition that such a claim is not acknowledged by section 25 FC, nor by article 14 GG.[340]

---

[339] E.g. *De Waal/Currie/Erasmus,* Bill of Rights Handbook (2000), 381 discuss some of the possible claims that could emanate from the constitutional protection of property. Their view is based on the idea that the term "property" refers to "the set of legal rules governing the relationship between individuals and physical property" (at 383). This idea they explain (at 384) as that "property ... encompasses at least some of the component rights making up what is termed the 'bundle of rights' that constitute ownership" which they refer to (at 383) as "the closest to the traditional conception of property in South African law." The problems with such an approach are pointed out at 183 ff. below.

[340] See 80, 85 and 87 above.

3.2.1.2. Eligibility to Hold Property

If a claim to the eligibility to hold property were acknowledged, it would create a constitutional right not to be excluded from a class of property holders. In other words, the claim to eligibility points to the right to acquire and hold property rights. However, the claim of eligibility to hold property does not entitle a person to become a holder of property simply on the basis of the constitutional provisions. It merely would protect the position of existing holders of property. In German terminology, this would point to the opinion that the constitutional right to property is not a *Teilhaberecht*, but rather a *Freiheitsrecht*.[341]

Because of its formulation partly as a "positive" guarantee,[342] article 14 I 1 GG (like section 28(1) IC) could be regarded as an embodiment of the claim of eligibility to hold property.[343] It is often argued that section 25(1) FC does not provide any basis for a claim of eligibility to hold property, because it is phrased negatively.[344] The choice of a negative formulation could give rise to the argument that section 25 FC in reality protects something "less than property,"[345] namely the right not to be deprived of property and the right not to be expropriated except as provided for in the property clause itself. Exponents of this argument draw strongly on the fact that most[346] of the other provisions in chapter 2 of the Final Constitution are phrased positively, while section 25(1) FC is phrased negatively. Additionally, the negative formulation of section 25(1) FC as opposed section 28(1) IC indicates a conscious decision against incorporation of claims for eligibility to hold property under the constitutional property clause. Furthermore, section 25(1) FC comprises a single provision, which combines the prohibition against unconstitutional deprivations with the requirements for consti-

---

[341] See 242 below.

[342] For a discussion of the positive and negative formulations of property clauses, see 80 above.

[343] See *De Waal/Currie/Erasmus*, Bill of Rights Handbook (2000), 381.

[344] *De Waal/Currie/Erasmus*, Bill of Rights Handbook (2000), 394 note 40.

[345] See the explanation of this argument in *Van der Walt*, 1997 SAPR/PL, 295-313.

[346] Apart from sec. 25(1) FC, the following sections in ch. 2 FC are also framed negatively: sec. 13 FC (slavery, servitude and forced labour), sec. 20 FC (citizenship), and sec. 31 FC (linguistic communities).

tutional deprivations of property.[347] These factors all seemingly point to an intention of the drafters of the constitution that the eligibility to hold property was not envisaged as a possible claim falling under section 25(1) FC, and that the intention was, in fact, to guarantee a right that was something less than property.[348] The most important effect of such an argument is that it can be employed to support the idea that section 36(1) FC only in exceptional circumstances applies to an inquiry into the constitutional validity of a regulation of property.[349]

However, a few considerations may be advanced against such an approach.[350] The constitutional court has accepted in the *First Certification Case*,[351] that the positive or negative phraseology of the property clause will make no fundamental difference to the appropriateness in terms of universal recognition of the clause. The court even went further and accepted that the right to hold property (or rather, the claim for eligibility to hold property) is implicit in the negatively formulated section 25(1) FC. This argument is in line with the tendency to interpret specific provisions of the Constitution in the light of the constitutional text in its entirety.[352] Moreover, from a comparative point of view, there is no indication in any other jurisdiction making use of negatively formulated property clauses that something "less than property" is envisaged for protection. It seems to be accepted (or at least not strange or unusual) that a property clause, unlike most other fundamental right guarantees, launches into the limitation provision and qualifications without any introduction of founding statement of the right that is to be protected. Even the fact that section 25(1) FC is a so-called *specific*

---

[347] Section 25(1) FC has, in other words, deliberately not been phrased: "Nobody may be deprived of property except as provided for by the Constitution. Deprivations of property are only allowed in terms of law of general application. No law may provide for arbitrary deprivations of property." Instead, the combined negative phraseology of sec. 25(1) FC includes the limitation provisions that apply in the given case.

[348] I am grateful to Prof Frank Michelman for pointing this out to me. *Van der Walt*, 1997 SAPR/PL, 294-298 has also articulated these arguments very clearly.

[349] See *Van der Walt*, 1997 SAPR/PL, 298, 291-293. See also 270 below.

[350] See *Van der Walt*, 1997 SAPR/PL, 299-312.

[351] *Certification of the Constitution of the Republic of South Africa* (note 245 above), par. 72.

[352] See 119 below.

negative guarantee[353] does not flout the overwhelming indications from comparative law that the formulation of the property clause does not really influence the content of its guarantee. In fact, from a comparative view there seems to be no dramatic difference between a ("general") negatively phrased guarantee with limitations spread over two or more sentences, and a ("specific") negatively phrased clause that condenses guarantee and limitations into one sentence. As has been indicated above,[354] the avoidance of a positive formulation or statement in a property clause supposedly displays the desire not to get caught in the complexities of theories about institutional guarantees, as is the case with article 14 GG, which contains some positive elements. However, this cannot be justification for the view that a negatively formulated property clause does not envisage the eligibility to hold property. It merely indicates that the debate about the existence of an institutional guarantee of property is more suitable in a jurisdiction with codified private law than in the uncodified South African system. Besides, from the other negatively formulated provisions in the South African bill of rights no indication of an intention to protect something less than the right mentioned in each[355] can be deduced.

3.2.1.3. Insulation of Private Property from State Interference

For exponents of the idea that section 25(1) FC does not provide for claims of eligibility to hold property, it may seem strange that an argument in favour of claims of eligibility to hold property is immediately followed with a statement that the property clause can also cater for claims of to insulate of private property from state interference. Superficially, this would exactly be the substitute argument offered by supporters of the "less than property" argument.[356] However, the submission above is that simply that, should the question arise for adjudication, the courts need not shy away from upholding a claim of eligibility

---

[353] See 87 above. In a "general" negative guarantee, the conditions for limitation are stated in a separate phrase or sentence, whereas a "specific" negative guarantee combines the guarantee of the right with the conditions for limitation in a single sentence. See *Van der Walt*, 1997 SAPR/PL, 297-298, 301.

[354] See 87 above.

[355] I.e. in particular the right to citizenship (sec. 20 FC) and the rights of participation in cultural, religious and linguistic communities (sec. 31 FC).

[356] See 94 above.

to hold property merely on the basis of the negative formulation of the property clause. Even in its present negative form, section 25(1) FC protects and guarantees property in the constitutional context.

As is indicated by the example of article 14 I GG read with article 14 II GG, this does not mean that property rights are entrenched in absolute fashion. In fact, they are subject to many immanent restrictions embodied in legislation, private law (codified or uncodified) and the constitutional provisions themselves. For the purposes of constitutional interpretation and application of the property clause, it should submittedly be accepted that a constitutional property clause can simultaneously protect and guarantee property, and limit its protection not only generally, but also in specific ways from case to case.[357] Thus, claims of eligibility to hold property could, to some extent be regarded as going hand in hand with claims of insulation against state interference with private property. In some instances, these claims could even fulfill the same function.

For purposes of clarity, however, it should be mentioned that support of claims of insulation against state interference could be a separate purpose of a constitutional property clause. Section 25(1) FC should be a clear example of this point. It may be more difficult to abstract the same kind of example from article 14 GG. However, in the course of this exposition it will be indicated[358] to what extent article 14 GG, like section 25(1) FC does, in fact, provide insulation against state interference. In order to understand this function of the constitutional protection of property, it is necessary to review a final purpose of the constitutional property clause, namely to support claims of immunity against uncompensated expropriation.

3.2.1.4. Immunity against Uncompensated Expropriation

Claims of immunity against uncompensated expropriation of private property would, in the South African context, typically be based on section 25(2) FC and section 25(3) FC. In the German context, these claims would typically be based on article 14 III GG. Immunity against uncompensated expropriation means that the state cannot lawfully

---

[357] See the description of the constitutional right to property as "derivative" by *Michelman*, 1981 Wash & Lee LR, 1099.

[358] See 278 ff. below.

withdraw property from the control of a private person unless that person is remunerated for the withdrawal. Claims of this nature would, therefore, involve an inquiry into the constitutional validity of a specific action by the state, or an inquiry into the payment of compensation, or both. Although the question of compensation can, in other words, form part of the inquiry into the justifiability of a specific regulation, it can also by itself form the basis of an inquiry into constitutional validity of a specific regulation. For the purposes of the current exposition, the question of compensation will be discussed as one of the requirements for constitutional validity of an expropriation.[359] With regard to this category of claims, it will henceforth be necessary to distinguish between different kinds of regulatory actions with private property. It can then be determined whether and to what extent regulation of property needs to be compensated.

Regulation of property is the general term referring to all permissible state interferences with patrimonial interests. The reference to *deprivation* of property in the South African context usually refers to regulation of property taking place without remuneration of the deprived holder. In Germany, this kind of regulation is referred to as the *Inhalts-und Schrankenbestimmung* (determination of the content and limits of property), as it is found in article 14 I 2 GG. By contrast, *expropriation* (the German equivalent being *Enteignung*) of property usually takes place against payment of compensation to the deprived holder. It is a very severe form of regulation, through which the property in its entirety (and not only specific patrimonial interests pertaining to it) is withdrawn.

The issue of compensation is thus important in many respects. It is often difficult to determine whether an extensive regulation of ownership entitlements amounts to partial expropriation (in which case fair compensation should be paid) or qualifies merely as a regulation of property (in which case compensation is not obligatory). In these cases, the basic question is whether ownership is diminished through the act of infringement to a *nudum ius* or whether the infringement pertains to a separate element of ownership that can be treated independently without damaging the essence of the ownership concept. The focus should, furthermore, be on whether the patrimonial interests of an individual or

---

[359] See 300, 304, 342 ff. below.

those of a specific group are infringed. This issue will be discussed at a later stage.[360]

3.2.2. Stages of Inquiries Based on the Constitutional Property Clause

The categorisation of the claims that could be brought in terms of a constitutional property clause could have a profound influence on the content of the different stages of an inquiry based on the constitutional clause protecting property. In the following paragraphs, reference will be made to inquiries aimed at determining the constitutional validity of a specific interference with private property, and to inquiries aimed at determining the payment of compensation. Thereafter, the influence of the different views as to the object of protection and the purpose of limitation will be briefly indicated.

3.2.2.1. Inquiries into the Constitutional Validity of an Interference with Property

Three basic questions determine the outcome of the constitutional validity of an interference with private property:[361] (i) the question whether the affected property right is at all protected by the constitutional property guarantee; (ii) the question whether the action curtails the freedom of the particular holder of the right; and (iii) the question whether the infringing action is constitutionally justifiable. The determination of the constitutional concept of property, as well as the investigation into the question of whether an infringement has taken place, outlines the scope of the guarantee, whereas the question to justifiability serves as a qualification on the results of the first two questions. These issues will be dealt with in detail in chapters 7 and 8 with regard to both the jurisdictions in the present comparison. The following discussion merely points out some basic differences between the approaches followed by the German and South African courts.

In Germany, each of these three questions forms a separate stage of the inquiry as to the constitutional validity of a specific interference with

---

[360] See 304 ff. below.

[361] See *De Waal/Currie/Erasmus*, Bill of Rights Handbook (1999), 20-25.

property.[362] By contrast, the South African Constitutional Court has in its first few decisions[363] shown an inclination towards the Canadian "two-stages" approach to an inquiry concerning the constitutional (in)validity of statutes. Assuming that the Canadian "two-stages" approach will also be followed in a constitutional dispute about property, Van der Walt[364] has formulated the structure of an inquiry into section 25 FC also in two stages (although the Canadian Charter of Rights and Freedoms does not explicitly protect the right to property along with the other categories of protected legal rights).[365] The applicants first bear the onus of proving that an infringement of a property right, which is protected by section 25 FC, has taken place. As such the applicants would have to affirm (i) that the interest under discussion must qualify for protection under section 25 FC, and (ii) that an infringement of this interest has taken place. Once these issues have been established, the state (or the party relying on the validity of the relevant act), has the onus of proving that the infringement is justified, either in terms of section 25 FC or in terms of section 36 FC or both.

This (admittedly small) difference in the preference of how the constitutionality inquiry should be conducted, could perhaps be ascribed to the fact that the German courts are in general more inclined to adopt an inquisitorial approach than their South African counterparts.[366] In Germany, owing to the preference of an inquisitorial approach, the judge can consider issues and arguments not raised by either of the parties to the case. In the South African system, the party bearing the onus of proof has to lead the evidence and introduce the arguments necessary to lift that onus. The importance attached to this procedural fact under the South African adversarial system, resulted in South African schol-

---

[362] See *Pieroth/Schlink*, Grundrechte (1998), 237-239 for a schematic representation of this three-staged inquiry.

[363] I.e. *S v Makwanyane* 1995 3 SA 391 (CC), par. 100-102; *Ferreira v Levin; Vryenhoek v Powel NO* 1996 1 BCLR 1 (CC), 26H.

[364] *Van der Walt*, Constitutional Property Clause (1997), 28 and *Van der Walt*, 1997 SAPR/PL, 277.

[365] See *Bauman*, 1992 SAJHR, 344-361 for a description of the circumstances giving rise to the exclusion of a property guarantee from the Canadian Charter of Rights and Freedoms. See also note 225 above.

[366] *Kötz*, 1987 TSAR, 35, 37-38.

ars[367] combining the question as to which rights enjoy protection in terms of a constitutional property guarantee, and the question as to whether infringement has taken place, into a single stage of the investigation. The investigation into constitutional validity of an interference with property in South Africa will then most probably consist of only two stages.

Regardless of the number of stages in the formal structure of a constitutional property inquiry, the elements[368] investigated during the inquiries of both the German and South African legal systems remain similar. The application of these different elements to the constitutional protection of property will be briefly described in the following paragraphs.

3.2.2.1.1. "Threshold Question"

The first element in a determination of the constitutional validity of a specific interference with private property is connected to the question whether the interest upon which the applicant bases the claim qualifies for protection under the constitutional property guarantee. In other words, the court must determine whether the applicant's interest is "property" in terms of the constitution. Some proprietary interests qualify more easily for protection than others. Nevertheless, this "threshold" question,[369] which attempts to clarify the *existence* of a

---

[367] *Kentridge/Spitz* in *Chaskalson/Kentridge* et. al. *(eds)*, Constitutional Law of South Africa (1996), ch. 11, 32; *Van der Walt*, Constitutional Property Clause (1997), 28. In *Chaskalson/Kentridge/Klaaren* in *Chaskalson/Kentridge et. al. (eds)*, Constitutional Law of South Africa (1996), ch. 1, 2-4 the question of the applicability of specific human right guarantees on the facts in a given case is placed in the second stage of the investigation (i.e. under "Interpretation") and the question of "application" is reserved only for issues dealing with the horizontal / vertical operation of the Bill of Rights. See *De Waal/Currie/ Erasmus*, Bill of Rights Handbook (1999), 21-22 where it is implied that the infringement question must be treated separately from the question concerning the protective ambit of a specific fundamental right.

[368] These are: (i) The inquiry as to whether a specific interest qualify for protection (that is, the "threshold question"); (ii) the question of whether a specific action constituted an infringement upon a specific protected interest; and (iii) the inquiry as to whether a specific infringement of a protected interest can be constitutionally justified.

[369] *Van der Walt*, Constitutional Property Clause (1997), 57 uses this term.

property right qualifying for protection under a constitutional property guarantee in a constitutional dispute, arises regardless of the degree of difficulty attached to identifying the property interests at stake.

The acknowledgement of the purpose of a constitutional property clause to support claims for the eligibility to hold property would influence this stage. As has been indicated above,[370] convincing reasons exist for upholding the eligibility to hold property through interpretation of the constitutional property clause, even in cases where the property clause itself is phrased in negative terms. A further consideration would be the extent to which support for an "institutional" guarantee of property can be deduced from the treatment of the threshold question in a specific jurisdiction.[371] It has been indicated already[372] that a negative formulation of the property clause does not exclude the possibility of an institutional guarantee arising from the property clause. The convincing arguments of some authors[373] in favour of upholding a guarantee similar to that of article 14 GG in the South African context have also been discussed, and will not be repeated here. At this point it can simply be mentioned that these kinds of issues will contribute to determining the outcome of the "threshold" test. In the comparative evaluation of the following chapters, the influence of these issues on the "threshold" question in the different jurisdictions will again be referred to.

Once it has been ascertained that the interest for which the applicant seeks constitutional protection indeed pass the "threshold" test, one can proceed with the inquiry to determine whether the constitutionally protected interest has been curtailed.

3.2.2.1.2. Infringement Question

The protective ambit of the property guarantee is then determined by the effect the curtailment of the freedom has on the holder of the property right in terms of the constitutional property guarantee.[374] The main

---

[370] See 94 above.

[371] See 80 above for a discussion of the terms "institutional guarantee" and "individual guarantee" of property.

[372] See 87 above.

[373] I.e. *Kleyn*, 1996 SAPR/PL, 418.

[374] *Lerche* in *Isensee/Kirchhof (eds)*, Handbuch des Staatsrechts V (1992), m.n. 45.

aim of this enquiry is to determine whether the freedom of the holder of the property right has been affected by the action of one of the state powers. The constitutional justifiability of the action is only tested once it is certain that the holder's freedom has indeed been affected.

In the South African "two-stage" approach,[375] this element still forms part of the first stage. In other words, the property right holder has the onus of proving that he has a protected property right, and that this right has been infringed by state action. Apparently it is more problematic to prove the right or interest at stake (that is, to answer the "threshold question") than to identify the existence of an infringement.[376] However, this does not mean that the question of infringement can simply be ignored in the South African context. This element forms an important link between the content of the protection afforded to right holders by the constitution and the restriction of the scope of protection. It therefore deserves careful consideration. In the case of *Re Munhumeso*[377] a valuable guideline was formulated to determine whether or not a protected right has been affected:

> "*The test in determining whether an enactment infringes a fundamental freedom is to examine its* effect *and not its object or subject-matter. If the* effect *of the impugned law is to abridge a fundamental freedom, its object or subject-matter will be irrelevant.*"

An application of the *Munhumeso* test in the context of the constitutional property guarantee would mean that the inquiry would be satisfied if it can be demonstrated that either the purpose or the effect of the state action (whether of legislative or administrative kind) was to encroach upon the property rights protected in terms of the guarantee. An encroachment must, in other words, exist before the question of justifiability arises.

In Germany, where the court has to consider all important points regardless of whether they were raised by the parties or not, this element constitutes the second phase of the constitutionality enquiry. The purpose of the state action affecting the right holder's freedom is mostly the result of an attempt by the state to balance conflicting interests. The

---

[375] *Van der Walt,* Constitutional Property Clause (1997), 28; *Van der Walt,* 1997 SAPR/PL, 277 based on *S v Makwanyane* (note 363 above), par. 100-102; *Ferreira v Levin and Others; Vryenhoek and Others v Powel NO and Others* (note 363 above), 26H. See 100 above.

[376] *Van der Walt,* Constitutional Property Clause (1997), 28.

[377] *Re Munhumeso* 1995 1 SA 551 (ZS), 561D-E. Emphasis added.

interests can be those of two individuals, or those of an individual on the one hand and society on the other, or they can even be conflicting interests of the same individual.[378] This requires the legislature to keep the dual function of the property guarantee in mind: On the one hand, property must be useful to or aimed at serving the private individual. On the other hand, it must also be useful to the public in general. Harmonising the functions of private use and public usefulness is difficult. The success of such a venture depends on the legislature's ability to combine these functions in such proportions that a balance between the interests at stake can be worked out.[379] It should be added, though, that the application of either a normative concept of infringement or a concept that investigates more material requirements of infringement has given rise to divergent views concerning the content of this stage of the constitutionality enquiry in German law, which will be referred to again later in the present discussion.[380] Be that as it may, the most important question for determination at this stage of the inquiry is still whether or not a certain sovereign measure affects a legal position protected by article 14 I 1 GG. Only once such an infringement is identified, does the inquiry turn to the question whether the action by the state is justified or not.

The question of curtailment depends on the state action involved and the legal position that is affected.[381] Usually, the freedom of the property-right holder would be affected by a positive action by one of the state organs. A right holder's position could, however, also be affected by the non-compliance with a legal duty by an organ of state. A legislative infringement occurs if ownership entitlements are abstractly or generally (that is to say not with regard to a specific right holder) limited by the legislation. Legislation can, by itself, already concretely re-

---

378 *Lerche* in *Isensee/Kirchhof (eds)*, Handbuch des Staatsrechts V (1992), m.n. 47.

379 *Schuppert* in *Karpen (ed)*, Constitution of Germany (1988), 115.

380 *Von Heinegg/Haltern*, 1993 JuS, 123. See the different approaches followed by different branches of the judiciary as discussed at 311 ff. below.

381 If it is, for instance, a legislative measure affecting the legal position in the sphere of intellectual property, the legislative measure will affect the freedom of the right holder if the copyright holder of a specific work is in general or with regard to specific parts of the relevant legal position curtailed to draw on the fruits of his or her labour and performance. *Von Heinegg/Haltern*, 1993 JuS, 124.

move individuals' property rights completely or partially.[382] Alternatively, one of the state's executive organs can be authorised by law to enforce a removal of property rights.[383]

The question whether the conduct complained of was the result of a legislative act, an administrative action or a decision of a court of final instance is, however, not only important because it could influence the outcome of the investigation as to constitutional justifiability of such conduct, but also because it could help to determine the consequences of a possible infringement. At this stage it could already in principle be determined whether any of the two basic permissible forms of infringement, expropriation[384] or regulation[385] of property are at stake. In both South Africa and Germany these two forms of infringement are mentioned in the constitutional text.

3.2.2.1.3. Justifiability

Once the effect of a specific state action on the fundamental right to property has been identified, one can continue with the last stage of the constitutionality enquiry: determining whether the specific state action constituted a justified limitation of property rights or not.

In South Africa, the party relying on the validity of a specific infringement would, in this phase, bear the onus of proving that all the requirements justifying the infringement on property rights were met. The infringement has, in other words, to qualify either as a deprivation of property or as an expropriation. Also in German law, the basic

---

[382] These curtailments are referred to as *"Eingriffe durch Gesetz"* - see *Lerche* in *Isensee/Kirchhof (eds)*, Handbuch des Staatsrechts V (1992), m.n. 48.

[383] Such a curtailment is called *"Eingriff auf Grund Gesetzes"* - see *Lerche* in *Isensee/Kirchhof (eds)*, Handbuch des Staatsrechts V (1992), m.n. 48.

[384] Sec. 28(3) IC; sec. 25(2) FC. It is also sometimes referred to as *compulsive acquisition* of property. The German term is *Enteignung*. See *art.* 14 III GG.

[385] In South Africa, this is usually referred to as deprivation of property, due to the choice of terminology in the constitutions. Sec. 28(2) IC determines that "No deprivation of any rights in property shall be permitted otherwise than in accordance with a law." Sec. 25(1) FC determines that "No one may be deprived of property except in terms of law of general application, and no law may permit arbitrary deprivation of property." Similarly, this concept is referred to as *Inhalts- und Schrankenbestimmung* in Germany, because of this phrase being used in art. 14 I 2 GG.

premise is that a legislative infringement can only be constitutionally justifiable if it represents either a legislative regulation of property in terms of article 14 I 2 GG *(Inhalts- und Schrankenbestimmung),*[386] or an expropriation *(Enteignung)* of property in terms of article 14 III GG.

However, whereas the main issue during the previous stage of the investigation would have been whether or not a specific action constitutes an infringement, the focus in the final stage is on the question of the manner and extent to which the constitutionally protected right to property can be limited by such an infringement. In order to establish whether these requirements are met, it is necessary to take the relation between the constitutional provisions for regulation of property and the provisions for limitations of rights in general into account. In principle, the justifiability of a specific limitation of a fundamental right must be examined with reference both to formal and material requirements for limitation. The requirements for limitation in Germany and South Africa are similar in that if a limitation on the right to property must take place *pursuant to a law,* the law should *apply generally* and should not permit arbitrary limitation of the right to property.

In end effect, and if all other possibilities have been exhausted, it is the issue of proportionality *(Verhältnismäßigkeit)* that determines whether a specific infringement was *justifiable* or not. As will be indicated in the next chapters, the South African proportionality test differs slightly from its German counterpart with regard to content and application. In the course of this exposition, it will be argued that, although the proportionality test is applied correctly in the South African context as a very final stage of the inquiry regarding the constitutional protection and regulation of property, the considerations underlying this test should pervade the entire inquiry. For the moment, this approach can

---

[386] Even in English literature on German constitutional law, the term "deprivation" as it was used in terms of sec. 28 IC of South Africa, is not employed. Usually, authors refer to this phenomenon as the "legislative competence to determine the contents and limits of the property guarantee" or the "legislative interference with property". See i.a. *Kimminich* in *Starck (ed),* Rights, Institutions and Impact of International Law (1987); *Schuppert* in *Karpen (ed),* Constitution of Germany (1988); *Frowein,* Protection of Property in Relation to Taxation (1996); *Kommers,* Constitutional Jurisprudence of Germany (1997). The use of these phrases stems from the wording of art. 14 I 2 GG, which grants the legislature capacity to indeed pass statutes determining what the range and intensity of the constitutional property guarantee should be.

best be illustrated with reference to the manner in which the second element of the inquiry of constitutional validity of an interference with property is treated in Germany. The most important question for determination at this stage is still whether or not a certain sovereign measure affects a legal position protected by article 14 I 1 GG. Only once such an infringement is identified does the inquiry turn to the question whether the action by the state is justified or not. However, it has been pointed out[387] that the purpose of the state action affecting the right holder's freedom is mostly the result of an attempt by the state to balance conflicting interests.[388] In this process, the legislature has to take into account the dual function of the property guarantee of serving the needs of the private individual and of being useful to the public in general. Harmonising the functions of the private use and public usefulness of property can only be successful if the legislature is able to combine these functions in such proportions that a balance between the interests at stake can be worked out.[389] In such a process, similar considerations to those that appear in the proportionality test can be used, but mostly in different combinations and for different reasons.

3.2.2.2. Inquiries Regarding the Payment of Compensation

The question concerning the payment of compensation can follow on an inquiry into the constitutional validity of a specific interference, if it is found that such interference amounts to an expropriation of property for which no compensation has been paid. However, mostly the question of compensation is an independent issue which has very little to do with the constitutional validity of the expropriation itself. A thorough discussion of the issues of valuation connected to the determination of a compensation amount is unfortunately outside the scope of this exposition. In the course of this exposition, the compensation issue will therefore only be treated in its function as one of the validity requirements for valid interference of a specific kind in South Africa and Germany. It is especially in this area of the law where the borderlines be-

---

[387] See 102 above.

[388] I.e. the interests of two individuals, or those of an individual on the one hand and the society on the other, or the conflicting interests of the same individual. See *Lerche* in *Isensee/Kirchhof (eds)*, Handbuch des Staatsrechts V (1992), m.n. 47.

[389] *Schuppert* in *Karpen (ed)*, Constitution of Germany (1988), 115.

tween private law and constitutional law might be confusing or unclear, due to the grey area of interferences with property that are difficult to classify as either expropriations *(Enteignungen)* or deprivations *(Inhalts- und Schrankenbestimmungen)*.

3.2.3. Summary: Object of Protection and Nature of Limitation

In the course of the preceding discussion, reference was made on several occasions to the influence that the approach towards the object of constitutional protection of property and the nature limitation could have on the substantive issues to be incorporated in an inquiry based on the constitutional property clause. This section contains a summary of the most important points touched upon.

The understanding of the function attached to a specific formulation of the constitutional property clause will influence the approach to the object of protection. In this regard, the formulation of section 25(1) FC as "absolutely" negative, in contrast to article 14 I GG (which is a positively formulated clause with negative elements), causes some scholars to hold the opinion that something "less than property" is protected by section 25(1) FC. The fallacies of this view have been pointed out above.[390] However, the influence of this view on later stages of the inquiry into the constitutional validity of an interference with property deserves further attention.

De Waal, Currie and Erasmus[391] point out, that the application of section 36 FC can have no meaningful application to section 25 FC. The gist of their argument is that the criteria justifying the limitation of rights have been included in the demarcation of the rights in section 25 FC themselves, with the effect of making the basis for justifying the infringement of section 25 FC the very reason why section 25 FC was infringed in the first place. This obviously must be illogical. However, the incongruity does not stem from the two-stage approach to the limitation of section 25 FC, but rather from the starting point of their investigation. If the *object* of the right protected by section 25 FC is limited to something less than property, section 36 FC would become obsolete, because of the built-in limitations in section 25 FC. A number

---

[390] See 87, 94, 96 above. *Van der Walt*, 1997 SAPR/PL, 275-330 contains extensive analyses of all the variations of this approach, as well as counterarguments.

[391] *De Waal/Currie/Erasmus*, Bill of Rights Handbook (2000), 393-394.

of considerations militate against such an approach. These are discussed at a later stage.[392] It must, nevertheless, be pointed out here that section 7(3) FC excludes the possibility that the limitation provisions of section 36 FC could simply not be applicable on section 25 FC. In fact, section 7(3) FC supports a reading of the bill of rights in which section 25 FC and section 36 FC are applied cumulatively. This would mean that the starting point of the investigation should be altered, so as not to make the application of section 36 FC illogical.

Such an alteration could be effected by viewing the object of the right protected in section 25 FC as the eligibility to hold an interest with economic value, which deserves constitutional protection by reason of its purpose of assisting an individual to live a self-fulfilled life and to make responsible choices regarding his or her patrimonial interests. There are many examples in German law relating to article 14 GG where such an approach was sucessfully followed. These examples will be discussed and applied to the South African context in due course.[393]

3.3. The Structure of the Judicial System and its Relevance for a Constitutional Property Inquiry

In both South Africa and Germany various courts have jurisdiction in matters related to the constitutional protection and regulation of property. The following paragraphs provide a brief overview.

3.3.1. The South African Judicial Hierarcy and the Property Clause

Since 1910,[394] the judicial authority in South Africa was divided between the Supreme Court, which consisted of an Appellate Division and several provincial and local divisions, and a number of lower courts, of which the magistrates' courts were the principal contingent. Certain courts were also created by statute for a specific purpose. Of these statutory courts, the Land Claims Court[395] is important for purposes of this thesis. In the Interim Constitution,[396] the Constitutional

---

[392] See 270 below.

[393] See 224 ff. below.

[394] With establishment of the Union of South Africa.

[395] Established in terms of the Restitution of Land Rights Act. See 429 below.

[396] Sec. 98 and 99 IC.

Court was created, which would function as the court of final instance in constitutional matters. The Constitutional Court had the same status and ranking as the Appellate division. Neither court was empowered to hear appeals from the other. The Appellate Division was the court of final instance in all matters where constitutional issues were not raised, and had no jurisdiction to confer constitutional remedies such as declaring legislation invalid on the basis of unconstitutionality.[397] This system was changed slightly with promulgation of the Final Constitution.

The Final Constitution determined that all courts operating immediately prior to its commencement would remain intact thereafter.[398] The structure of the courts would also remain as it was in terms of the Interim Constitution, except for the changes introduced by the Final Constitution.[399] Accordingly, section 166 FC determines the new hierarchy of the South African judicial system. The magistrates' courts and the statutory courts (including the Land Claims Court) remained unchanged. However, under the Final Constitution, the former provincial and local divisions of the Supreme Court (and various superior courts of the former TBVC[400] states) were converted into the High Courts, which have constitutional jurisdiction, limited to matters arising in specific geographical areas. In terms of section 166 FC, read with item 16 of Schedule 6 FC, the Appellate Division was converted into the Supreme Court of Appeal, and acquired constitutional jurisdiction. The Constitutional Court remains intact, and has, together with the Supreme Court of Appeal, jurisdiction over the whole of the Republic of South Africa. Both the Constitutional Court and the Court of Appeal are appellate courts. The former decides constitutional appeals, and the latter all other appeals, including those in which both constitutional and non-constitutional matters have to be considered. The Constitutional

---

[397] Sec. 101 read with sec. 102 IC.

[398] Item 16, schedule 6, FC.

[399] Sec. 165-180 FC.

[400] The territories of Transkei, Bophuthatswana, Venda and Ciskei were regarded as "independent states" by the apartheid government. Consequently, their judiciaries functioned "independently" from that of South Africa, although the Appellate Division of the former Supreme Court was also the final instance for cases referred by the courts of these territories.

Court has, additionally, non-appellate jurisdiction and may sometimes function as a court of first instance.[401]

In general, jurisdiction is to be exercised concurrently between the Constitutional Court, the Supreme Court of Appeal and the High Courts in respect of all forms of legislation. Although a dispute over the constitutionality of an Act of Parliament, provincial legislation or delegated legislation can thus be heard by any of these courts, it would normally be heard in the first instance by the High Court. Concurrent jurisdiction is, however, limited by section 167(5) FC which determines that any order made by the Supreme Court of Appeal or the High Court invalidating an act of Parliament, a provincial Act, or conduct of the President, has to be confirmed by the Constitutional Court.

Concurrent jurisdiction means that all courts within the South African hierarchy theoretically have the ability to pronounce on issues pertaining to the constitutional protection and regulation of property. In issues related to the expropriation of property and land reform and restitution measures, the Land Claims Court would, however, usually be the court of first instance, because it specialises in these matters. In matters concerning the regulation of property, the High Court would probably be the court of first instance, whereas the Supreme Court of Appeal and the Constitutional Court would probably function as appellate courts.

3.3.2. Shared Jurisdiction in Property Issues within the German Judicial Hierarchy

The judicial system[402] in Germany encompasses a compromise between maintaining the independence of the different *Länder* in judicial matters and the desire for legal unity. After reunification, the courts which existed in the former German Democratic Republic had to be incorporated in the structure of the Federal Republic.[403] The German court

---

[401] I.e. matters in which the court has exclusive jurisdiction in terms of 167(4) FC.

[402] The main piece of legislation regulating the judicial structure and organisation is the *Gerichtsverfassungsgesetz*.

[403] *Gesetz zur Anpassung der Rechtspflege im Beitrittsgebiet*, 30 June 1992, BGBl I Sec. 1147.

structure is complex, since it is based on the principles of specialisation and decentralisation.[404]

Specialisation points to the division of the courts into different fields of jurisdiction. Thus, article 95 GG provides for courts with ordinary jurisdiction, administrative courts, labour courts, social courts and revenue courts. The constitutional courts of the different *Länder* and the Federal Constitutional Court provide control over the courts of the other jurisdictions. Specialisation has the advantage that specific issues can be decided by a court which was specifically created to solve matters of a particular kind. Because of the specialist knowledge of the judges, the individual can be assured that his or her case will be heard by an expert in the specific field of law. However, it might be difficult to determine which court will have jurisdiction in a specific case.

Decentralisation arises from the division between the federal and "provincial" *(Länder)* courts.[405] Each *Land* has an own court structure in accordance with the general provisions of the Basic Law and is responsible for administration of justice within its territory, but the overall structure of the courts is regulated on a federal level. The federal courts (that is, the Federal Court of Justice *(Bundesgerichtshof)*, the Federal Administrative Court *(Bundesverwaltungsgericht)*, the Federal Labour Court *(Bundesarbeitsgericht)*, the Federal Social Court *(Bundessozialgericht)* and the Federal Tax Court *(Bundesfinanzhof)*) are at the top of the judicial hierarchy. They act as final courts of appeal, and have to ensure that the law in Germany is interpreted and developed uniformly.

From the German judicial structure it appears that, normally, only one set of courts would have jurisdiction over a given area of the law. In the field of property law, however, jurisdiction is divided between administrative courts (where the Federal Administrative Court or *Bundesverwaltungsgericht* is the court of final instance) and ordinary courts (where the Federal Court or *Bundesgerichtshof* is court of final instance). The administrative courts have authority to deal with the (administrative) matters concerning the actual expropriation. When, however, the amount of compensation is contested, the ordinary courts have jurisdiction. Because these issues are interlinked, both tribunals have been forced to define the "common good" and a "compensable expro-

---

[404] *Foster,* German Legal System and Laws (1996), 39-41.

[405] Art. 92 read with art. 95 GG.

priation."[406] As a result of this, the Federal Court of Justice and the Federal Administrative Court share the jurisdiction on the standards according to which public and private interests in the field of property regulation are balanced. Due to this shared jurisdiction, several possible analytical approaches have been developed as aids in determining the intention of the legislature where infringements on property rights are concerned.[407] Moreover, the Federal Constitutional Court has the function of protecting, interpreting and applying the Basic Law,[408] and does not function as another higher instance of the other branches of the judiciary. It has developed its own interpretation of the property clause, which does not always coincide with either that of the Federal Court of Justice or the Federal Administrative Court.

4. Structure and Interpretation

In this chapter, some of the structural aspects of constitutional property protection in Germany and South Africa have been discussed in order to ascertain their influence on the interpretation of the constitutional property clauses. Focus was placed on the formulation of the provisions of the property clause in positive or negative terms. The influence of different approaches to interpreting the property clauses according to their external appearances on the inquiry into substantive issues of constitutional property protection have also been highlighted. In particular, reference was made to the object of the constitutional right to property and the manner of limiting such a right. These issues will also enjoy further attention in chapters 7 and 8. The issue of application of certain elements resembling those involved in the very last phase of inquiries related to the constitutional protection and regulation of property — the proportionality test — has also been mentioned. In the course of the next three chapters, this issue will surface again.

External appearance of a constitutional property clause is, however, only one of many factors that might influence interpretation thereof. It

---

[406] *Kommers,* Constitutional Jurisprudence of Germany (1997), 253 and note 34 to ch. 6, 568. See also *Dolzer,* Property and Environment (1976); and *Badura* in *Benda/Maihofer/Vogel (eds),* Handbuch des Verfassungsrechts (1994), 653-696.

[407] *Kommers,* Constitutional Jurisprudence of Germany (1997), 253.

[408] *Foster,* German Legal System and Laws (1996), 48.

is mostly closely connected with other factors influencing interpretation. As has been indicated, the historical background can also give an indication as to the nature of a particular property clause and the intention of the drafters thereof. Furthermore, the interpretation of the property guarantees in both Germany and in South Africa is linked to certain basic principles of constitutional interpretation. The property guarantees should, for example, not be read in isolation, but with regard to the constitution as a whole. This means that interpretation of the property clauses can only be embarked upon when certain principles of state, like the constitutional state *(Rechtsstaat)* and social welfare state *(Sozialstaat)*, are taken into account. Once the importance of these factors has been established, an attempt can be made to structure the constitutional property inquiry. The next chapter contains an overview of the constitutional principles and their significance for the interpretation of the constitutional property clauses in Germany and South Africa.

Chapter 6:
Basic Principles of a Constitutional Order and Interpretation of a Constitutional Property Clause

1. Relevance of Constitutional Values for the Property Order

The legitimacy of the traditional protection of property in South African common law needs to be examined in view of the new legal order that has arisen after the advent of a new constitutional order. Such an examination should be guided by the values underlying the new constitutional dispensation. The Interim and Final Constitutions are the embodiment of the new legal order in South Africa. The main virtue of this constitutional order is its potential to correct the injustices integrated in existing law. The principles that form the basis of the constitutional order in South Africa, like republicanism and democracy,[409] federalism,[410] constitutional state[411] and social welfare state,[412] are to some extent comparable with the values underlying the German Basic Law.

In both systems these principles or values are vital for interpreting the basic rights *(Grundrechte)* or fundamental rights in general and the constitutional property clauses in particular. This chapter is aimed at analysing the significance of some of these general constitutional principles for the interpretation of property guarantees like section 28 IC, section 25 FC and article 14 GG. The focus is on the approach that regards the whole constitutional text as a unity. In particular, two of the fundamental constitutional principles on which an interpretation of a bill of rights is based, and which are relevant for the interpretation of the property guarantees in particular, are discussed. They are the constitutional state *(Rechtsstaat)* principle and the social welfare state *(Sozialstaat)* principle.

---

[409] See note 416 and note 435 below.

[410] See note 417 and note 436 below.

[411] See 123 below.

[412] See 137 below.

2. The Unity of the Constitution

The *unity of the constitution* refers to the practice of interpreting all constitutional provisions by applying certain general principles that are derived from the constitution as a whole. This approach is apparently important from both the German and the South African points of view. In Germany, the importance of this type of interpretation became apparent through the jurisprudence of the Federal Constitutional Court, whereas in South Africa this idea was directly included in both the Interim and Final Constitutions. The following paragraphs illustrate the meaning of an interpretation based on the unity of the constitutional text.

2.1. *"Innere Einheit" of the German Constitution*

The Federal Constitutional Court has developed certain rules of constitutional interpretation — in view of the special political values contained in the Basic Law — which are applicable over and above the normal rules of legislative interpretation. Very early[413] in the jurisprudence of the Federal Constitutional Court, it was determined that the constitutional text contains certain general and fundamental constitutional principles which appear from a reading of the constitution as a whole, and which are superior to the specific provisions of the constitution. The Federal Constitutional Court stated in 1951:[414]

> *"Eine einzelne Verfassungsbestimmung kann nicht isoliert betrachtet und allein aus sich heraus ausgelegt werden. Sie steht in einem Sinnzusammenhang mit den übrigen Vorschriften der Verfassung, die eine innere Einheit darstellt. Aus dem Gesamtinhalt der Verfassung ergeben sich gewisse verfassungsrechtliche Grundsätze und Grundentscheidungen, denen die einzelnen Verfassungsbestimmungen untergeordnet sind."*

---

[413] The decision in BVerfGE 1, 14 was handed down on 23 October 1951, two years after the enactment of the Basic Law.

[414] In BVerfGE 1, 14, 32. Translation: "A single constitutional provision cannot be viewed in isolation and cannot be interpreted only with reference to itself. Such a provision is to be understood in coherence with the other constitutional provisions, which establish an inner unity. From the contents of the complete constitution certain constitutional principles, to which the single constitutional provisions are subject, arise."

This means that single constitutional provisions are to be interpreted in accordance with general fundamental constitutional principles,[415] like republicanism and democracy,[416] federalism,[417] *Rechtsstaat*,[418] *Sozial-*

---

[415] *Kunig*, 1990 Jura, (Special edition) 52-60; *Avenarius*, Rechtsordnung der Bundesrepublik Deutschland (1997), 16-25; *Freckmann/Wegerich*, German Legal System (1999), 56-62; *Ebke/Finkin (eds)*, Introduction to German Law (1996), 45-56; *Robbers*, Introduction to German Law (1998), 57-67; *Foster*, German Legal System and Laws (1996), 146-153 all provide detailed discussions of the principles of the German state.

[416] Art. 20 I GG and 79 III GG show that the German state is founded upon this principle, apparently, according to *Foster*, German Legal System and Laws (1996), 147, to ensure that the German people would not put too much faith, and eventually power, in one person. The Basic Law does not attempt to outline a complete model or example of what democracy should be or consist of in state government, but rather require the presence of certain characteristics usually associated with democracy. Art. 20 II GG requires representative government. Further characteristics of democracy and basic rights of democratic participation, like free speech, press, free opinion, independent media (art. 5 GG) freedom of assembly (art. 8 GG) freedom of association (art. 9 GG), political parties (art. 21 GG) elections (art. 38 GG) and parliamentary organs (art. 39 GG) are guaranteed. Detailed analyses in *Kunig*, 1990 Jura, (Special edition) 52-54, 60; *Ebke/Finkin (eds)*, Introduction to German Law (1996), 46-47; *Freckmann/Wegerich*, German Legal System (1999), 57-58; *Avenarius*, Rechtsordnung der Bundesrepublik Deutschland (1997), 17-21.

[417] The federalist structure of the German state has its origins in the Holy Roman Empire of the ninth century and is important for constitutional theory as well as for political practise. Both the separate *Länder* as well as the *Bund* have sovereign status. The political weight of the Federal Government is, however, greater. Legislation is, in principle, the task of the separate *Länder* (according to art. 70 GG), although the several particularly important issues (like international relations, defence, citizenship, currency) are subject to the legislative authority of the *Bund* (art. 71-75 GG). In other fields (like civil law, criminal law, procedure, law relating to foreigners, etc) the *Länder* and the *Bund* have concurrent legislative authority (art. 72 GG). However, if the *Bund* exercises its power to legislate on a particular subject, as it has happened in most fields, the competence of the *Länder* to legislate on the same subject is terminated. The *Bund* can also pass framework legislation *(Rahmengesetzgebung)*, which leaves open the possibility for the *Länder* to legislate on the subject in order to fill in the details of such framework legislation. The *Bund* can also in certain areas prescribe principles to ensure consistency *(Grundsatzgesetzgebung)*. The *Länder* are in principle responsible for administration, even in matters which have been regulated by the Federal legislature (art. 83 GG ff.). The *Bund* is assigned the administrative duties pertaining to the armed forces, for-

staat,[419] environmental protection[420] and subsidiarity.[421] Although these rules in themselves constitute no basis for substantiating individual claims,[422] they are binding on all courts and state organs that are expected to interpret the Basic Law. They are considered regardless of the fundamental right at stake in a specific case. Thus, effect is given to the principle of the unity of the constitution. The constitution not only binds the state authority to uphold procedural safeguards, but also obliges the legislature to act in accordance with the requirements of substantive justice when exercising its legislative function.

In interpreting the constitution as a unity, it could happen that fundamental rights conflict with one another. In such circumstances, the Federal Constitutional Court determines how each right reciprocally limits the other. Both (or all) rights are given the greatest possible relative protection. By thus harmonising the protection of conflicting rights, a result is obtained which affects all the rights at stake to the least possible extent. The court will also respect the basic rights, norms or freedoms, and the fact that all the organs of state are integrated, as far as possible. It will not follow an interpretation that will isolate a particular

---

eign service etc (art. 32 GG). In all other matters the *Bund* can merely provide guidelines for the administration. For more information on German federalism, see *Kunig*, 1990 Jura, (Special edition) 58-60; *Avenarius*, Rechtsordnung der Bundesrepublik Deutschland (1997), 23-25; *Ebke/Finkin (eds)*, Introduction to German Law (1996), 49-54; *Freckmann/Wegerich*, German Legal System (1999), 61-62.

[418] See 123 below.

[419] See 137 below.

[420] *Environmental protection* is, according to *Foster*, German Legal System and Laws (1996), 152, a recent addition to the fundamental principles. Art. 20a GG was introduced into the Basic Law on 27 October 1994 and requires the three branches of the state to protect the natural surroundings. In South Africa, environmental rights are incorporated into the Bill of Rights and protected under section 24 FC and section 29 IC.

[421] *Subsidiarity* refers to the openness of the Basic Law to the European integration, as introduced (also recently) by art. 23 GG. In promoting the unification of Europe, Germany may confer sovereign rights upon European Institutions, but without giving up its own existence as a state: sovereign rights of material significance must remain. *Foster*, German Legal System and Laws (1996), 153.

[422] *De Waal*, 1995 SAHJR, 8.

organ of the state.[423] In this way the basic "principles of state" (or rather constitutional values) enshrined in the Basic Law are constantly taken into account as interpretative devices.

The basic principles are — through the inner unity *(innere Einheit)* of the Basic Law — the *Leitmotifs* that guide the legislature in performing its main function, and against which all state action should be measured. Article 14 GG, like all other provisions in the Basic Law, cannot be interpreted in isolation, but should be seen against the Basic Law as a whole.

2.2. *"Conformity with the Constitution" in South Africa*

Section 39 FC contains an interpretation clause pertaining to the bill of rights. Section 239 FC contains definitions of certain terms and is applicable to the Final Constitution in its entirety. However, neither of these provisions can completely regulate constitutional interpretation, and to some extent they even require interpretation themselves.[424]

The Constitutional Court continually lays down guidelines for the interpretation of the Constitution in general and the bill of rights in particular. These guidelines are based on a variety of interpreting techniques. The court invokes the mechanisms of grammatical,[425] systematic (contextual),[426] teleological (purposive),[427] historical[428] and compara-

---

[423] *Foster*, German Legal System and Laws (1996), 145.

[424] *De Waal/Currie/Erasmus*, Bill of Rights Handbook (1999), 123.

[425] This technique of interpretation regards the language of the text as the mediator of meaning. The language therefore conveys and creates the meaning of a specific provision or text. Other contextual factors are then decisive of the meaning of a text. *Du Plessis*, 1999 Saskatchewan Law Review, 310.

[426] This technique of interpretation attempts to find the meaning of a specific provision by drawing on the system of the text as a whole, and, according to some scholars, even by considering other legal precepts and institutions, the legal system, the political and constitutional order, the international legal order and so on. *Du Plessis*, 1999 Saskatchewan Law Review, 310; *De Waal/Currie/Erasmus*, Bill of Rights Handbook (1999), 133-135.

[427] This technique is much acclaimed among South African constitutional lawyers. It entails that the core values underpinning the listed fundamental rights in an open and democratic society based on human dignity, equality and freedom are "teased out" and that preference is given to an interpretation of a specific provision that best promote those values. *De Waal/Currie/Erasmus*,

tive[429] interpretation. However, the court does not always seem to recognise that the different techniques have to be considered in relation to one another. Moreover, these techniques have not been ranked according to a specific priority. From the application of the different techniques, it nevertheless becomes apparent that the court favours the idea that the constitutional text as a whole is employed in order to determine the meaning of a specific provision. At least some of the court's guidelines to interpretation of the Constitution are based upon this premise. The technique of *purposive interpretation* serves as an example: The Constitution, particularly the chapter on fundamental rights, is viewed as being of a different legal *genus* than ordinary legislation.[430] It constitutes a set of constitutional principles in terms of which the whole text has to be interpreted.

Already under the South African Interim Constitution it was clear that the values stated in the Preamble and the Postscript[431] would influence constitutional interpretation.[432] This practice is continued under the Fi-

---

Bill of Rights Handbook (1999), 125. *Du Plessis*, 1999 Saskatchewan Law Review, 311 indicates that teleological interpretation is not quite the same as purposive interpretation. It rather involves the discovery of a purpose that has to be realised.

[428] This technique of interpretation entails, on the one hand, a consideration of the circumstances surrounding the drafting of a specific provision, and on the other hand, could also refer to the political history of a specific text. *De Waal/Currie/Erasmus*, Bill of Rights Handbook (1999), 130-133. As such, this technique is prone to abuse and should be employed with circumspection.

[429] This technique involves comparison of the treatment of similar provisions or texts in different jurisdictions in order to reach solutions. It is widely employed in South African constitutional jurisprudence. Sec. 39(1) FC authorises, but does not require, comparative interpretation. *Du Plessis*, 1999 Saskatchewan Law Review, 312.

[430] *Davis/Chaskalson/De Waal* in *Van Wyk/Dugard et. al. (eds)*, Rights and Constitutionalism (1996), 126.

[431] The portion of the Interim Constitution headed *National Unity and Reconciliation*, sometimes referred to as the "Post-amble" or "Afterword."

[432] Cases where the Postscript and Preamble have been employed for constitutional interpretation include: *S v Makwanyane* (note 363 above), par. 262-264 (Mahomed J), and 363 (Sachs J); *S v Mhlungu* 1995 3 SA 867 (CC), par. 112 (Sachs J); *Khala v Minister of Safety and Security* 1994 4 SA 218 (W), 221F-G; *Qozeleni v Minister of Law and Order* 1994 3 SA 625 (E), 632A-G; *Holomisa v Argus Newspapers Ltd* 1996 2 SA 588 (W), 597G-598B; *Du Plessis and Others v De Klerk and Another* 1996 3 SA 850 (CC), par. 75, 123, 125-126.

nal Constitution, as is apparent from the wording of the Preamble and the fact that the values and principles are repeated in sections 1 and 2 FC.[433] This indicates that the property clauses — like all other provisions — cannot be treated in isolation from the rest of the Constitution.

Moreover, section 39(2) FC (which corresponds more or less with section 35(3) IC) provides that the "spirit, purport and objects" of the bill of rights must be taken into account by courts, tribunals or forums when interpreting legislation.[434] This also applies to cases where the common or customary law needs to be developed. The spirit, purport and objects of the bill of rights are best identifiable against a consideration of the bill of rights as a whole, and not only upon those provisions that might be applicable in a specific case.

The result of interpreting certain provisions upon a reading of the Constitution as a whole is that certain principles inherent in the constitutional order (namely republicanism and democracy,[435] federalism,[436]

---

[433] The "Afterword" has fallen away.

[434] "Law" in terms of sec. 35(3) FC.

[435] Sec. 1 IC and sec. 1 FC in principle subscribe to the republican form of government. (However, certain forms of traditional monarchy are acknowledged within the borders of South Africa. See sec. 211(1) FC that recognises institution, status and role of traditional leadership according to customary law, however, still subject to the Constitution, and sec. 212 FC that envisages the provision by national legislation of traditional leadership as an institution at local level on matters affecting local communities. This section further foresees that national or provincial legislation may provide for the establishment of houses of traditional leaders, and that national legislation may establish a council of traditional leaders.) Sec. 1 FC also provides the values on which a democratic South African state will be founded: (a) Human dignity, the achievement of equality and the advancement of human rights and freedoms; (b) Non-racialism and non-sexism; (c) Supremacy of the constitution and the rule of law; and (d) Universal adult suffrage, a national common voters roll, regular elections and a multi-party system of democratic government, to ensure accountability, responsiveness and openness.

[436] In South Africa the questions of federalism and regionalism were hotly debated during the multi-party negotiations. See *Humphries/Rapoo/Friedman* in *Friedman/Atkinson (eds)*, Small Miracle (1994), 150-177; *Friedman/Humphries (eds)*, Federalism and its Foes (1993). With regard to the Interim Constitution, *Watts* in *De Villiers (ed)*, Birth of a Constitution (1994), 78-86 has indicated that many of the characteristics underlying a federal system (i.e. two orders of government, legislative and executive competence of the provinces, representation of regional views through the senate, a supreme written constitu-

constitutional state[437] and social/welfare state[438]) will have specific relevance for interpretation of the constitution in general and of fundamental rights provisions in particular. These principles make up the constitutional framework of the state and government. They will shape the political and legal machinery of South Africa in the same way as similar principles have done in Germany. They will influence the direction of all state functions and will legitimise the use of state power and the exercise of governmental duties. They could also be employed to prevent the abuse of state power.

3. Principles Inherent in a Constitutional Order

The constitutional state principle and the social welfare state principle are of particular importance when individual freedom and social justice have to be harmonised in the sphere of property rights. In the following paragraphs, these constitutional values (or "principles of state"), which

---

tion, existence of a constitutional court) are present in the new South African constitutional order. However, the form of the distribution of the legislative and executive powers and of financial resources between the national and provincial governments reminds more of a regionalised unitary system. The Constitution of the Republic of South Africa Amendment Act 2 of 1994 strengthened the federal character of the Interim Constitution. In the Final Constitution, sec. 41 FC makes provision for *co-operative government*, which apparently resulted from the influence of the German notions of *Bundestreue* (as explained in BVerfGE 12, 205, 254), *Kooperativer Föderalismus* and *Paktierender Föderalismus*. The National Council of Provinces created by sec. 42(1)(b) FC has also been inspired by the German example (i.e. *Bundesrat*). However, *Venter*, 1997 ZaöRV, 61-73 shows also that, in spite of the "thoroughly regulated constitutional foundation" which has been laid for the development of a composite state in South Africa, it is at this time still unclear whether the principles in sec. 41 FC (which contain the notion of co-operative government and which can be categorised into (i) principles emphasising national unity; (ii) principles defending areas of competence; and (iii) principles promoting good government and service to the public) will aid the development of a centrifugal or centripetal state. He nevertheless remarks that, against the background of constitutionalism, the possibility of "regional states" is not far-fetched. This view can be supported. See contra, however, *Booysen*, 1997 Loy LA Int'l & Comp LJ, 800, 808.

[437] See 123 below.

[438] See 137 below.

are to some extent present in both the German and South African systems, will be compared briefly.

3.1. Constitutional State ("Rechtsstaat") and Rule of Law

Blaauw[439] has shown that the concept of *Rechtsstaat* in effect incorporates the *constitutional state* principle and that it must be distinguished from the *Rule of Law* principle. The *Rule of Law* originated in England as a symbol of resistance against attempts by the Stuart kings to institutionalise an absolutist regime at the cost of sovereignty of Parliament.[440] By contrast, the notion of a *constitutional state* — evolving from the principle of *Rechtsstaat*, which in turn originated in Germany as a solution to unchecked power[441] — denotes a rigid, written constitution (as opposed to parliamentary sovereignty) as highest directing normative principle.[442]

However, Blaauw[443] also pointed out that, although the historical influences on the development of the concepts of *Rule of Law* and *Rechtsstaat* differ quite extensively from each other, modern versions of these concepts overlap to a certain extent. Her discussion of the distinctions between the concepts of *Rechtsstaat* and *Rule of Law* shows that both these concepts contain the ideals of equality before the law,

---

[439] *Blaau,* [sic] 1990 SALJ, 89-90. This article (88-92) contains a short, but helpful exposition of the differences between the concepts *Rule of Law* and *Rechtsstaat* against their unique historical backgrounds.

[440] Parliament was regarded as the representative of the people.

[441] *Mohnhaupt,* 1993/94 Acta Facultatis Politico-Iuridicae Universitatis Scientiarum Budapestinensis de Rolando Eötvös Nominatae, 45 shows that the *Rechtsstaat* was developed as a counterpoint against, on the one hand, the police state (i.e. in the sense of the welfare state) and, on the other hand, against a system of despotic rule and absolutism. The meaning of the *Rechtsstaat* principle has changed drastically over the last two centuries. In the 19th century it originated from Kant's concept of the state (that freedom had to be governed by law), thus denoting the importance of legality in a legal system. After the World War II, the principle became associated with the state's commitment to the realisation of justice. In Germany this is sometimes described as the progression from the formal *Rechtsstaat* to the material *Rechtsstaat*. BVerfGE 9, 137, 146. See *De Waal,* 1995 SAHJR, 4-5.

[442] *Sobota,* Das Prinzip Rechtsstaat (1997), 27 ff.; 39 ff.

[443] *Blaau,* [sic] 1990 SALJ, 96.

substantive liberties and rights, and the notion of law as a general principle.[444]

Although the term *Rule of Law* is used in the Final Constitution of South Africa, it is placed in section 1(c) FC directly after the value of constitutional supremacy.[445] It is submitted that this phrase should, therefore, be regarded as denoting a concept similar to that of the *constitutional state*, which builds upon the principles of the German *Rechtsstaat*.[446] *Rule of Law* as it appears in the South African Constitution should therefore not be understood in its traditional sense as upholding parliamentary sovereignty, but rather as a mechanism for upholding constitutional supremacy.

Since at least some of the elements of the German *Rechtsstaat* concept are present in the South African concept of the constitutional state, this concept can prove valuable for the interpretation of the constitutional property guarantee. These elements warrant a brief discussion.

3.1.1. The "Rechtsstaat" Concept in German law

Sobota[447] indicates that attempts to define the *Rechtsstaat* in Germany usually result in either fragmentary, vague descriptions of this term, or

---

[444] *Blaau*, [sic] 1990 SALJ, 92.

[445] Sec. 1 FC: "The Republic of South Africa is one, sovereign, democratic state founded on the following values: (a) Human dignity, the achievement of equality and the advancement of human rights and freedoms. (b) Non-racialism and non-sexism. (c) *Supremacy of the constitution and the rule of law.* (d) Universal adult suffrage, a national common voters roll, regular elections and a multi-party system of democratic government, to ensure accountability, responsiveness and openness." Italics added.

[446] *Robbers*, Introduction to German Law (1998), 60 translates the *Rechts-staatsprinzip* with as "the principle of constitutional government under the rule of law," which indicates an indifference towards the finer historical distinctions between these concepts. Nevertheless the importance of this principle is illustrated clearly by the author when he writes: "Together with the comprehensive protection of Fundamental Rights, this principle expresses the ideal self-image of the Federal Republic of Germany to an even greater extent than the principle of democracy."

[447] *Sobota*, Das Prinzip Rechtsstaat (1997), 21-24.

in an unintended expansion of the concept.[448] Therefore most authors refrain from defining the concept, but embark on an enumeration of the components of the formal concept[449] of the German *Rechtsstaat*. The following paragraphs provide an overview of these components.

3.1.1.1. Elements Comprising the "Rechtsstaat" Concept

Among the most important components that are mentioned by Sobota, the following can be isolated as especially relevant to the proceedings in terms of article 14 GG and for the related *constitutional state* concept in South Africa:

(i) Separation of powers *(Gewaltenteilung)* is required. This means that the three arms of state authority[450] should not have overlapping functions.[451] In other words, the legislature is the only body that has the power to limit fundamental rights and that the independent judiciary should protect fundamental rights,[452] including the right to property.

(ii) The principle of legality *(Gesetzlichkeit; Vorrang des Gesetzes; Vorbehalt des Gesetzes)* must be adhered to. This means that the representatives of the people should have adopted the legislation; that statutes find general application and that the legislature itself is bound by such

---

[448] Problems such as those mentioned by *Sobota,* Das Prinzip Rechtsstaat (1997), 21-24, as well as the fact that most Western democratic governments tend to refer to their regimes as complying with the *Rechtsstaat* concept, caused *Mohnhaupt,* 1993/94 Acta Facultatis Politico-Iuridicae Universitatis Scientiarum Budapestiensis de Rolando Eötvös Nominatae, 45 to refer to its characteristic of *"Janusköpfigkeit."*

[449] *Blaauw-Wolf/Wolf,* 1996 SALJ, 268 indicates that a coherent concept of the *Rechtsstaat* has not been developed yet. In this regard a theoretical distinction is drawn between the formal *Rechtsstaat* concept, on the one hand, and the material *Rechtsstaat* concept, on the other hand. The formal concept consists of certain elements for which no uniformly accepted definition exists. The material concept is based on the idea of justice in law and in administrative decisions.

[450] I.e. the legislature, executive and judiciary.

[451] *Sobota,* Das Prinzip Rechtsstaat (1997), 70-77; *Foster,* German Legal System and Laws (1996), 149; *Blaau,* [sic] 1990 SALJ, 81. art. 1 III, 20 III, 97 III GG points to this principle in German Law.

[452] Art. 80 I GG.

legislation until it has been repealed or amended.[453] An important formal safeguard flowing from the *Rechtsstaat* principle is entrenched by the Basic Law:[454] the democratically elected legislature must authorise all limitations of fundamental rights. This is relevant in terms of article 14 I 2 GG, as the legislature is given the power to determine the scope and content of the property concept.

(iii) The principle of legal certainty *(Rechtssicherheitsgrundsatz / Bestimmtheitsgrundsatz)* must be observed. This means that legal measures and legal rules must be clear and consistently applied and that state action must be sufficiently defined in order to remain predictable.[455] Adherence to this principle is important in the context of the constitutional property clause in evaluating the effect of certain legislative measures on private property. Because of the difference in intensity of legislative measures creating regulatory interference with property and those resulting in expropriation, article 14 GG provides for certain precautionary measures in the formulation of legislation to this effect.[456]

(iv) According to the principle of trust *(Vertrauensschutz)*, legitimate expectations are protected. If the state has created a specific situation and a person has acted on the reasonable assumption that this situation will remain unchanged, then he or she can rely on such an assumption.[457]

(v) The principle of proportionality *(Verhältnismäßigkeitsgrundsatz)* is also an important aspect of the *Rechtsstaat* concept[458] applicable to the

---

[453] *Sobota,* Das Prinzip Rechtsstaat (1997), 77-85, 104-131; *Robbers,* Introduction to German Law (1998), 60; *Foster,* German Legal System and Laws (1996), 149; *Blaau,* [sic] 1990 SALJ, 81; *Blaauw-Wolf/Wolf,* 1996 SALJ, 268.

[454] Art. 19 II GG.

[455] *Sobota,* Das Prinzip Rechtsstaat (1997), 132-139; 154-188; *Kleyn,* 1996 SAPR/PL, 407; *Robbers,* Introduction to German Law (1998), 61; *Blaau,* [sic] 1990 SALJ, 81; *Blaauw-Wolf/Wolf,* 1996 SALJ, 268.

[456] See 300 ff. below.

[457] This principle, together with that of legal certainty, give rise to the general prohibition of retrospective legislation. *Robbers,* Introduction to German Law (1998), 61; *Kleyn,* 1996 SAPR/PL, 407; *Foster,* German Legal System and Laws (1996), 150; *Blaau,* [sic] 1990 SALJ, 81; *Blaauw-Wolf/Wolf,* 1996 SALJ, 269.

[458] BVerfGE 23, 127, 133; BVerfGE 6, 389, 439; BVerfGE 16, 194, 201 ff.; BVerfGE 17, 108, 117 ff.; BVerfGE 17, 306, 313; BVerfGE 19, 342, 348; BVerfGE 20, 45, 49. The Court, however, deviated from this viewpoint in a few decisions and tried to substantiate the foundation of the principle of proportionality

interpretation of article 14 GG (and all other basic rights) of the German Basic Law.[459] Proportionality is a method for determining whether the reasons advanced by the state to justify limitation of a specific fundamental freedom outweigh the values which underlie the constitutional commitment to the protection of that freedom. It is only employed once it is clear that the state's actions conflict with the scope of protection offered by the right,[460] and thus constitutes the very last stage in an enquiry into the constitutionality of a particular infringement on fundamental freedoms.[461] It entails that laws, actions and measures of state organs should not exceed those strict limits within

---

with specific reference to certain articles or a part of the Basic Law. Against this background, the Court held that the principle of proportionality is implicitly evident in fundamental rights as such, or in provisions allowing for the limitation of such rights. (BVerfGE 19, 342, 348 ff.; BVerfGE 27, 344, 352.) This gave rise to the argument that principle of proportionality arose from the essential-content guarantee. In more recent decisions, however, the court has apparently returned to its initial view that the principle of proportionality is based upon the *Rechtsstaat* concept. See BVerfGE 38, 348, 368 and BVerfGE 59, 275, 278.

[459] See *Blaauw-Wolf*, 1999 SAPR/PL, 193 ff. where the Federal Constitutional Court's uncertainty as to whether this principle is founded in the *Rechtsstaat* concept or whether it is implicitly evident in the fundamental rights themselves, is discussed. It is surely more acceptable, from a methodological perspective, to regard the principle of proportionality for the purposes of constitutional interpretation as part of the *Rechtsstaat* concept rather than part of the essential content of each fundamental right, as the function of the latter is not particularly clear when contemplating the reasons for the application of the proportionality principle.

[460] Although the link between the "constitutional state" concept and "proportionality" has become somewhat blurred during the drafting of the Final Constitution, the proportionality test is also the final stage in an inquiry concerning the constitutional validity of an interference with human rights in South Africa. See 132 ff. below. *De Waal*, 1995 SAHJR, 7 points out that, because the doctrine of proportionality is rooted in the material freedoms, it can be used to measure the constitutionality of the state's limitations of fundamental rights and freedoms. It is, however, more difficult to apply it in the context of the state's constitutional commitment to substantive equality or the furtherance of socio-economic rights.

[461] Very often the inquiry does not even need to go as far as applying the proportionality test. Constitutional disputes can also be resolved simply by demarcating or defining the right properly, rather than by reliance on proportionality.

which a specific legal purpose is pursued.[462] Proportionality is usually tested by having regard to the objective suitability *(Geeignetheit)* of the law, action or measure;[463] the question of its necessity *(Erforder-lichkeit)*;[464] and the question of its reasonableness or its "proportionality" in the narrow sense *(Angemessenheit[465])*.[466] By applying the proportionality principle at the point in the constitutionality inquiry where the justifiability of a specific restriction has to be determined, the Court endeavours to come to an optimal decision, based on the hypothetical relationship between an intended infringement and the intended goals to be attained by it. The intended infringement is compared with an alternative measure that could attain the same result.[467] This mechanism is important for determining whether curtailment of rights under the property clause is justifiable and will be discussed in more detail in the course of the thesis.

---

[462] *Foster,* German Legal System and Laws (1996), 150.

[463] This means that the restriction which is being tested against the constitutional provisions should be appropriate or suitable to achieve the objective intended. The intended aim of the legislation under discussion must be measured against the possible means to achieve it, to determine whether a rational relation exist between them. *Degenhart,* Staatsrecht I (1998), m.n. 278.

[464] A cost-benefit analysis: the measure taken must not, in other words, be harsher than is necessary to achieve the specified goal. *Degenhart,* Staatsrecht I (1998), m.n. 279.

[465] In relation to the importance and meaning of the fundamental right, no less far-reaching restriction would have achieved the same result. This element is also sometimes referred to as proportionality in the narrow sense *(Verhält-nismäßigkeit im engeren Sinne)*. *Degenhart,* Staatsrecht I (1998), m.n. 281. The proportional evening out of the interests of the involved parties (i.e. the proportionality in the wider sense) should not be confused with the classical investigation into the *Angemessenheit* (i.e. proportionality in the narrow sense) of a specific infringement with a concrete purpose. The proportionality in the (wider) sense of the appropriateness of the relation between the concepts of private property and social interest is rather a purpose of the wide leeway of the legislature in enacting infringing legislation than is the case with the classical determination of the proportionality of a specific infringement. *Thormann,* Abstufungen in der Sozialbindung des Eigentums (1996), 210.

[466] *Robbers,* Introduction to German Law (1998), 61; *Blaau,* [sic] 1990 SALJ, 82.

[467] *Blaauw-Wolf,* 1999 SAPR/PL, 195.

3.1.1.2. "Rechtsstaat" and Property Under the German Basic Law

The relation between article 14 GG and the *Rechtsstaat* concept in general becomes clearly influential (i) in cases where the judiciary is confronted with the problem of judicial development of the law, or (ii) when the balancing process requires a consideration of three or more protected positions (instead of the usual two fundamental rights at stake), or (iii) in cases where the courts have to determine for themselves the measure and intensity of the control they can exercise.[468] The right protected by article 14 GG places a duty on the judiciary to provide effective factual protection. This duty would also include a procedure that effectively guarantees the interests of the owner or holder of the relevant property right. In this manner, effect is also given to the notion of the *Rechtsstaat*. The following paragraphs contain some examples.

The Federal Constitutional Court has on occasion held[469] that it is constitutional in terms of article 14 GG (and that it does not amount to inadmissible judicial development of the law) to use the municipal *Mietspiegel* in legal practice to determine a rent increase. The *Mietspiegel* is a document compiled by or at least acknowledged by a municipality or landlord and tenant associations within the municipal borders. In this document, the different "normal" rent levels for residential premises within the municipal area are published. The location, size, nature, and manner in which the accommodation is equipped are factors taken into account when determining the rent level. According to the Regulation of Rent Increase Act *(Gesetz zur Regelung der Miethöhe)*, the lessor can only increase the rental up to the amount prescribed in the *Mietspiegel*.

The court has, for instance, also indicated that the constitutional principles involved in the notion of the *Rechtsstaat* apply when land is sold at an auction.[470] The court also had to heed the notion of the *Rechtsstaat* in considering whether a date for the sale in execution of the debtor's property could be postponed due to the debtor's illness.[471] In this particular case, the court committed itself to the process of balancing the interests of both the creditor and the debtor, with particular reference

---

[468] *Buchwald*, Prinzipien des Rechtsstaats (1996), 384.

[469] BVerfG (1.K) 03.04.1990 (1 BvR 269/90, 1 BvR 270/90).

[470] BVerfGE 51, 150, 156.

[471] BVerfG KTS 1988, 564-565 (3.K).

to the protection of the debtor's interests by paragraph 67 of the Sale in Execution Act.[472]

In another decision, the first senate of the Federal Constitutional Court had to pronounce on the banking practice of inducing official authorities in the German Democratic Republic to agree on certain non-commercial payment transactions by freezing bank accounts of German Democratic Republic citizens held in the Federal Republic of Germany. It was decided that, upon a consideration of the *Rechtsstaat* principle and article 14 I GG, this practice was constitutional.[473]

The application of the *Rechtsstaat* concept in the context of constitutionally protected property rights is also apparent in the treatment of the question whether social security claims qualified for protection in terms of article 14 GG. The first senate of the Federal Constitutional Court[474] decided that a patrimonial interest could qualify for protection under the property clause if the interest is so strong that a deprivation without compensation *(ersatzlose Entziehung)* of the interest would be in contradiction with the *Rechtsstaat* notion underlying the Basic Law. In the case of social security claims,[475] the interests to be protected would comply with this requirement if they:[476] (i) befall the holder of such interests as exclusive rights for private use;[477] (ii) are based on considerable individual efforts of the holder;[478] and (iii) serve the purpose of securing the livelihood of the holder.[479]

---

[472] *Zwangsversteigerungsgesetz (Gesetz über die Zwangsversteigerung und Zwangsverwaltung vom 24.03.1897, zuletzt geändert am 18.2.1998.)*

[473] BVerfGE 62, 169-189.

[474] BVerfGE 16, 94, 112; BVerfGE 18, 392, 397.

[475] BVerfGE 76, 220, 247 has indicated that least claims for maintenance or transitional maintenance *(Unterhaltsgeld oder Übergangsgeld)* in terms of par. 44 II 1(2) and par. 59 II 2(2) of the Labour Development Act *(Arbeitsförderungsgesetz)* qualify for protection. The question whether unemployment insurance and other claims in terms of the same legislation also qualify for protection, was left open by the court. In BVerfGE 72, 9, 18 this question has been affirmed with certain qualifications pertaining to the minimum period required for payments into the unemployment insurance fund.

[476] BVerfGE 72, 9, 18-19.

[477] *"[V]ermögenswerte Rechtsposition, die nach Art eines Ausschließlichkeitsrechts dem Rechtsträger als privatnützig zugeordnet ist, ... "*.

[478] *"[A]uf nicht unerheblichen Eigenleistungen des Versicherten beruht, ...".*

[479] *"[D]er Sicherung seiner Existenz dient."*

3.1.2. "Constitutional State" in South Africa

For almost two decades before the new constitutional order was introduced in 1994, South African lawyers recognised the European *Rechtsstaat* concept. However, the idea could not really become part of public law doctrine in a system where the sovereignty of Parliament was fundamental and where an easily amendable statute was employed as a constitution.[480] Venter shows that the absorption of this concept into the new constitutional order in South Africa is all the more surprising when it is borne in mind that:[481]

> "[t]he main role-players in the multi-party constitutional negotiations that produced the 1993 Constitution were representatives of a liberation movement on the one hand, and on the other hand, of an order that was established and was functioning under a constitutional dispensation founded in English legal thinking."

Nevertheless, the preamble to the Interim Constitution recognised the need to create[482]

> " 'n nuwe bestel ... waarin alle Suid-Afrikaners geregtig sal wees op 'n gemeenskaplike Suid-Afrikaanse burgerskap in 'n soewereine en demokratiese regstaat ... "

The fact that this recognition of the constitutional state *(regstaat)* appeared in the Preamble, but was not incorporated in one of the "real" constitutional provisions, induced some authors[483] to argue that no constitutional state was created in the Interim Constitution. Instead, they

---

[480] *Venter*, 1997 ZaöRV, 73.

[481] *Venter*, 1997 ZaöRV, 74.

[482] Translation: "a new order in which all South Africans will be entitled to a common South African citizenship in a sovereign and democratic constitutional state...". The Afrikaans text is cited here to show the use of the term *regstaat* (as opposed to *constitutional state* in the English version). Sec. 15, Constitution of South Africa Amendment Act 2 of 1994 determines (in the context of the Interim Constitution) that the Afrikaans text is a source of reference in matters of constitutional interpretation. Here it might help clear up the uncertainty caused with the use of the term *Rule of Law*. The German *Rechtsstaat* cannot be directly translated into English and *Rule of Law* cannot really be regarded as its equivalent (see 123 above). The most acceptable expression is therefore *constitutional state*, although this should not be confused with the German concept of *Verfassungsstaat*, which forms part of the *Rechtsstaat* idea in that a rigid constitution is required.

[483] *De Waal*, 1995 SAJHR, 4.

argued, an unenforceable directive for the creation of the constitutional state has been given to the Constitutional Assembly. In spite of the provision in section 232(4) IC,[484] it could perhaps still be contended that the statement in the Preamble alone, however significant it might have been, could not be sufficient to firmly establish the notion of the constitutional state *(regstaat)* in the new constitutional order.

If any doubt still existed with regard to whether or not the Interim Constitution embraced a notion similar to that of the *Rechtsstaat*, the inclusion of section 1(c) FC has dispelled the uncertainty, accepting that this section does not intend to refer to the *Rule of Law* in its "traditional" sense,[485] but supports the notion of constitutional supremacy.[486] Moreover, in both the Interim and Final Constitutions the principles and elements characteristic of the *Rechtsstaat* (both in the formal and in the substantive sense) were prescribed in the substantive provisions.[487] However, it does not follow from the incorporation of certain elements typical of a constitutional state in the Final Constitution of South Africa that a constitutional state does exist in practice. The following paragraphs will show how fragile the constitutional state notion in South Africa really is.

3.1.2.1. Latent Support of a "Constitutional State" in the Constitution

The following principles are apparently adhered to in both the Interim Constitution and the Final Constitution, as well as in Schedule 4 IC that dictated the content of the Final Constitution:

(i) The separation of state powers principle is supported by section 96(2) IC, which established an independent and impartial judiciary. Principle VII of schedule II IC also made the separation of powers an indispensable requirement, binding the Constitutional Assembly. The impartiality and independence of the judiciary is now endorsed by sec-

---

[484] Which determined that, for purposes of interpretation, the provisions contained in schedules to the Interim Constitution and the "Postscript" of the Interim Constitution should not have a lesser status than other "normal" provisions, and could therefore also well be applicable to the Preamble of the Interim Constitution.

[485] I.e. assuming sovereignty of Parliament.

[486] See 124 above.

[487] *Kleyn,* 1996 SAPR/PL, 407; *Venter,* 1997 ZaöRV, 75.

tion 165 FC. Moreover, several of the provisions in schedule II IC supported the inclusion of a democratic system of government and representation on all levels of government in the Final Constitution.[488] Provision also had to be made for the horizontal separation of powers[489] and the definition of the powers and functions of government at national and provincial level.[490] Sections 44(4), 83 and 165(2) FC, among others, adhere to these requirements by providing for the separation of powers and reinforcing the requirement that government authority is to be exercised in accordance with and subject to the Constitution.[491]

(ii) The legality principle appears from section 4(1) IC read with section 7(1) IC and sections 1(c), 2 and 8(1) FC,[492] where the Constitution is declared to be the supreme law.[493] Also, the limitation of a fundamental right is only allowed in accordance with "a law of general application."[494] The reason for this is that the constitutional state ensures that the legislature is the only body with the necessary legitimacy to limit the use of the fundamental freedoms[495] and that legislation has to define administrative powers clearly. A further indication of the intention to create a constitutional state appears from the characteristic of rigidity that is ascribed to the Constitution. This is particularly noticeable in the provision for a two-third majority for constitutional amendments in

---

[488] Principles I (democratic system of government), XVII (democratic representation on all levels of government), VIII (multi-party democracy), schedule II, IC.

[489] Principle VI, schedule II, IC.

[490] Principle XVIII, schedule II, IC.

[491] *Venter*, 1997 ZaöRV, 79.

[492] *Kleyn*, 1996 SAPR/PL, 407 note 25.

[493] Further support of this element is found in sec. 237 FC, that determines that all constitutional obligations must be performed diligently and without delay. *Grupp*, Südafrikas neue Verfassung (1999), 31-32.

[494] Sec. 33(1) IC and sec. 36(1) FC.

[495] In this regard, the question arises in South African context whether the fundamental rights may also be limited by or pursuant to the common law. Because of codification in the German legal system, no need exists for a distinction between statutory law and common law. Section 33(2) IC seems to indicate that fundamental rights may also be limited by the common law in South Africa. In other Common-law jurisdictions, such as Canada, the phrase *prescribed by law* is used instead of *law of general application* in order to make clear that common law limitation can take place. See *De Waal*, 1995 SAHJR, 5 note 10.

section 62(1) IC and principle XV of schedule II IC (requiring special majorities and special procedures for constitutional amendments). Section 74 FC serves as a further indication of rigidity, requiring 75% of the National Assembly members and at least six of the provinces to support constitutional amendments.[496]

(iii) The principle of legal certainty is endorsed in the special procedural constitutional guarantees that are found in the Interim and Final Constitutions.[497] Moreover, the provision for the appointment of a Public Protector in sections 112(1) IC and 181(1)(a) FC not only strengthens the constitutional democracy, but also supports the development of a system in which maladministration, corruption, administrative injustice and inefficiency on the part of public functionaries can be exposed. How effective this will be in practice, is yet to be determined.

(iv) The principle of trust is also embraced by section 25(3)(f) IC and section 35(3)(m) FC.

(v) From the wording of the limitation clauses[498] and decisions of the Constitutional Court on this matter, it is also apparent that a principle resembling that of the German *Verhältnismäßigkeitsprinzip* is endorsed. According to Chaskalson P in the watershed decision of *S v Makwanyane*,[499] it is implicit in section 33(1) IC that the limitation of constitutional rights for a purpose that is reasonable and necessary in a democratic society "involves the weighing up of competing values, and ultimately an assessment based on proportionality." The court used the treatment of this issue in the constitutional courts of Canada, Germany and the European Court of Human Rights to show that proportionality is an essential requirement of any legitimate limitation of an entrenched right and to justify its application in the South African context.[500] The decisions of *Makwanyane* and *Zuma*,[501] however, influ-

---

[496] *Grupp*, Südafrikas neue Verfassung (1999), 98-99.

[497] E.g. in the Interim Constitution: sec. 22 IC (recourse to impartial judges), 25(3)(d) IC (right to be heard), 25(3)(f) IC (*nulla poena sine lege*), 25(3)(g) IC (prohibition on double jeopardy), 25(3)(b) IC (right to a speedy trial). See *De Waal*, 1995 SAHJR, 6. Also in the Final Constitution: sec. 33(3)(a) FC (recourse to impartial judges), 35(3)(i) FC (right to be heard), 35(3)(l) FC (*nulla poena sine lege*), 35(3)(m) FC (prohibition on double jeopardy), 35(3)(d) FC (right to a speedy trial).

[498] Sec. 33 IC; sec. 36 FC. *Kleyn*, 1996 SAPR/PL, 407 note 25.

[499] *S v Makwanyane* (note 363 above).

[500] *S v Makwanyane* (note 363 above), par. 104 note 130.

enced the formulation of the limitation clause in the Final Constitution[502] and therewith also the adoption of a South African version of the proportionality principle.[503] Since then, many others have followed the same reasoning and used the same terminology when pronouncing on the limitation of rights.[504] In the case of *De Lange v Smuts*[505] the approach to limitation of rights propounded by Chaskalson, P in the *Makwanyane* case (and pertaining to the limitation clause in the Interim Constitution) was endorsed with regard to the limitation clause in the Final Constitution. Further, Blaauw-Wolf[506] shows convincingly that the proportionality principle is also implicit in the procedure for limiting rights under the Final Constitution, by classifying the requirements of *a law of general application* restricting the right only *to a certain extent*[507] as the formal elements which must be clarified before proportionality can be determined. The requirements that the restriction should be *reasonable* and *justifiable* in an open and democratic society then resembles elements of the proportionality principle (that is to say *Geeignetheit, Erforderlichkeit*).[508] The third element (*Angemessenheit*) of the proportionality principle is evident in section 36(1)(e) FC that requires a consideration of whether less restrictive measures could have been invoked to achieve the objective. On the basis of this analysis, it can be submitted that, even though the roots of the South African pro-

---

[501] *S v Makwanyane* (note 363 above); *S v Zuma* 1995 2 SA 642 (CC).

[502] *Blaauw-Wolf*, 1999 SAPR/PL, 208. Section 36(1) FC determines: "The rights in the Bill of Rights may be limited only in terms of law of general application to the extent that the limitation is reasonable and justifiable in an open and democratic society based on human dignity, equality and freedom, taking into account all relevant factors, including – (a) the nature of the right; (b) the importance of the purpose of the limitation; (c) the nature and extent of the limitation; (d) the relation between the limitation and its purpose; and (e) less restrictive means to achieve the purpose."

[503] See 264 ff. below.

[504] An overview of these decisions is found in *Blaauw-Wolf*, 1999 SAPR/PL, 208 and note 106.

[505] *De Lange v Smuts* 1998 3 SA 785 (CC), par. 86-88.

[506] *Blaauw-Wolf*, 1999 SAPR/PL, 209 ff.; see contra *De Waal*, 1995 SAHJR, 7.

[507] "[T]o the extent that the limitation is reasonable and justifiable in an open and democratic society based on human dignity, equality and freedom" sec. 36(1) FC.

[508] See 128 above.

portionality test are mostly sought in its Canadian counterpart,[509] the German Basic Law remains the best comparative agent as far as the content and nature of the proportionality test in South Africa is concerned.

3.1.2.2. The "Constitutional State" Principle and Property in South Africa

The South African constitutional order seems to subcribe to most of the characteristics of the formal and material *Rechtsstaat*. South Africa can thus be regarded as a *constitutional state*. Wiechers,[510] however, refers to the present situation of South Africa as a "*Rechtsstaat*-at-rest." He explains that the principle of the constitutional state is set in motion as a result of unbalanced political forces, unfulfilled socio-economic needs, unkept promises on the part of the government, frustration and outrage on the part of the citizens, conflict, strife, corruption, dirty tricks and law-breaking.[511] He quite validly questions the strength and resilience of the South African model of the constitutional state to maintain its essential theoretical features in practice, and then remarks:[512]

> "*The answer to this question depends on the political forces in our country, and more particularly ... on the capacity and will of politicians and political leaders to deal with conflict within the ambit and scope of* Rechtsstaatlichkeit.*"*

Exactly how the proportionality principle and the other elements constituting the South African constitutional state will be used in future in interpreting the property clause, is to a large extent still open to speculation. One can only expect that this issue will be particularly contentious in cases where the restriction of property as well as other fundamental rights must be dealt with in the same context. The reason for this is that the internal limitations of the property clause mirror the general limitations provision to some extent. The same holds for cases in which the constitutionality of restrictions will to a certain extent require political decisions. The inherent tension between liberty and

---

[509] See *Van der Walt*, Constitutional Property Clauses - A Comparative Analysis (1999), 339-340 and note 94.

[510] *Wiechers*, 1998 THRHR, 624-634.

[511] *Wiechers*, 1998 THRHR, 627.

[512] *Wiechers*, 1998 THRHR, 630.

equality in the South African constitutional state lies at the heart of these decisions. Wiechers[513] cautions:

"Suid-Afrika moet die toon aangee om die sogenoemde Afrika-renaissance aan te moedig en te inspireer. So 'n Afrika-renaissance is egter tot 'n misgeboorte verdoem as Afrika-lande nie die gelykheids-grondslag van die moderne regstaat met die ewe wesenlike vryheids-grondslag kan paar nie."

Some academics endeavoured to explain how the limitation clause and the property clause are supposed to interact against this underlying tension between liberty and equality.[514] These views are important for the interpretation of the property clause and will be discussed when the more concrete provisions of the property clause itself are analysed in the following chapters. The connection between the constitutional state, the social state and the property clause first has to be established.

3.2. "Sozialstaat" and Social Welfare State

The term *social welfare state* is used in this thesis to indicate either the German notion of *Sozialstaat*, or to refer to a South African concept comparable to that of the *Sozialstaat*. Technically speaking *social welfare state* as a concept in English-speaking countries may denote a concept which differs in some regards from the German *Sozialstaat* concept. However, such particularities of the concept will be ignored. The thesis will focus mainly on the relation between the concept of the *social welfare state / Sozialstaat* and the enforcement of socio-economic rights.

---

[513] *Wiechers*, 1998 THRHR, 634. Translation: "South Africa must set the pace to foster and inspire the so-called African Renaissance. However, such an African Renaissance is doomed to miscarriage if African states are incapable of finding a compromise between the essential bases of equality and freedom of the modern constitutional state."

[514] *Van der Walt*, 1997 SAPR/PL, 275-330; *Rautenbach*, General Provisions of the South African Bill of Rights (1995), 84-89, 105-109; *Woolman* in *Chaskalson/Kentridge et. al. (eds)*, Constitutional Law of South Africa (1996), ch. 12, 1-34; *Van der Walt*, 1995 SAPR/PL, 303 ff.; *Du Plessis/Corder*, Understanding South Africa's Transitional Bill of Rights (1994), 122-133.

Apart from the linguistic difficulties inherent in this term, a definition thereof is also problematic. The famous statement of Zacher[515] that it is the business of politics to define the *social welfare state* concept, summarises the difficulties experienced with this term. Indeed, this principle is mainly substantiated through legislation and is consequently more dependant on the political process and also more difficult to grasp than any other principle.[516] In spite of its vagueness, however, the notion of the social welfare state can be an important tool for interpretation and limitation of fundamental rights. It is also of importance for the goals and values chosen by the legislature and administration when enacting legislation and executing state policies respectively.[517]

The social welfare state principle embodies the state's designs for the political future, reflects experiences of a political past and enables the state to form a workable structure in order to cope with present realities.[518] This does not mean that the political goals or programmes have to be enumerated in the Constitution itself, but rather that they must be left open to the political process. A constitution may, for instance, explicitly or implicitly legitimise the pursuit of a certain policy by granting state authorities certain competencies and regulating them. A state could, however, also pursue the creation of a social state policy even though no express reference has been made of it in the constitution. In such a case the state's action would indicate the existence of certain elements of social policy;[519] namely social security, a just social order and, where possible, an increase in the general standard of living.

Social security could be described as the prevention of individual and general need in society. It is aimed at preserving a community during times of crisis by supplying a comprehensive system of social insurance, by alleviating liabilities caused by general disasters and by regulating certain essential services and the prices on essential goods, or by pro-

---

[515] *"Den Sozialstaat zu definieren, ist ein politisches Geschäft."* *Zacher* in *Stödter/Thieme (eds)*, Festschrift für Hans Peter Ipsen (1977), 266.

[516] *De Waal*, 1995 SAJHR, 8 note 21.

[517] *De Wet*, Constitutional Enforceability of Economic and Social Rights (1996), 17; *Kunig* in *Karpen (ed)*, The Constitution of the Federal Republic of Germany (1988), 197-198.

[518] *Kunig* in *Karpen (ed)*, The Constitution of the Federal Republic of Germany (1988), 194.

[519] See 141 and 150 below for a detailed discussion.

tecting specific industries.[520] *Social justice* is directed particularly at the protection of socially vulnerable groups in order to prevent exploitation and unfair dominance. It ensures more equitable bargaining positions for parties in socio-economic relations, by eliminating or reducing the weaker party's dependence on and exposure to the stronger party. This can be done either by a radical levelling of all inequalities, or by systematically reconciling diverse social interests, such as those of employer / employee, husband / wife, or owner / tenant. The ultimate aim is a balance in community interests.[521] The third element, the *raising of living standards* by the state, depends on the means available: in times of economic crisis the means of the state would probably be limited and the demand for higher living standards would have to make way for combating of more pressing needs.[522] In fulfilling the objectives inherent in these elements, the state attempts to guarantee a dignified existence for all, to minimise the difference between rich and poor, and to control or eliminate relationships of dependence in society.[523]

The principle of the social welfare state acts as a counterbalance to the constitutional state or *Rechtsstaat* principle[524] and can rectify injustices brought about by the neglect of socio-economic processes in system based on classical liberalism.[525] In the following paragraphs adherence to the notion of the social welfare state in Germany and South Africa will be analysed.

3.2.1. The "Sozialstaatsprinzip" in Germany

The Basic Law does not mention the "*Sozialstaatsprinzip*" as such: this term was created through constitutional theory and political discus-

---

[520] *De Wet,* 1995 SAJHR, 30-49, 36-39.

[521] *De Wet,* 1995 SAJHR, 39-40.

[522] *De Wet,* 1995 SAJHR, 42.

[523] *Kunig* in *Karpen (ed),* The Constitution of the Federal Republic of Germany (1988), 189; *De Waal,* 1995 SAHJR, 8 note 21.

[524] *Stern,* 1981 TSAR, 241-250.

[525] According to *Kunig* in *Karpen (ed),* The Constitution of the Federal Republic of Germany (1988), 190-191, the general idea of social justice as a goal to be pursued by the state originate in the tendency to compensate for socially unacceptable consequences originating from the development of liberal individual rights.

sion.[526] Yet, the Basic Law defines the Federal Republic of Germany as a social federation (*sozialer Bundesstaat*)[527] and as a social constitutional state under the rule of law (*sozialer Rechtsstaat*).[528]

The initial controversy surrounding the existence of the *Sozialstaatsprinzip* as a constitutional value (or "principle of state") subsided after the Federal Constitutional Court expressly recognised the existence of this principle.[529] Further, the social welfare character of the German state was firmly established during the 1950s and the beginning of the 1960s, with the political and economic stabilisation of Germany. During this time, the German legislature also enacted comprehensive social welfare legislation, independent from deciding whether or not it had a constitutional duty to do so.[530] Today, the social welfare state principle enjoys equal status with the other principles of state, even though the social welfare state principle is not manifested by a single constitutional norm, but rather through a variety of statutes and administrative policy.[531]

The principle of the social welfare state has been employed repeatedly to establish the positive aspect of fundamental rights, namely that they are entitlements to benefits.[532] But this principle also imposes an obligation on the state to work towards the common good. This means that it provides an appropriate doctrinal basis for the limitation of individual interests.[533] In this way:[534]

---

[526] *Kunig* in *Karpen (ed)*, The Constitution of the Federal Republic of Germany (1988), 188.

[527] Art. 20 I GG.

[528] Art. 28 I GG.

[529] See BVerfGE 1, 97, 105; BVerfGE 3, 377, 381; BVerfGE 6, 32, 41.

[530] For a discussion of the early academic debate regarding the existence of the social state principle in Germany and its historical relevance, see *Kunig* in *Karpen (ed)*, The Constitution of the Federal Republic of Germany (1988), 192-194.

[531] *Kunig* in *Karpen (ed)*, The Constitution of the Federal Republic of Germany (1988), 193.

[532] Because the boundaries of rights stemming from the *Sozialstaatsprinzip* are unclear and problematic, it is discussed and reflected in connection with several of the basic rights-arts 1, 3, 6, 7, 9, 12, 14, and 15 GG. *Foster*, German Legal System and Laws (1996), 151.

[533] *Robbers*, Introduction to German Law (1998), 62.

"social security as an institution created by the state, the 'social rights' of the Weimar constitution, global steering in the context of a free market economy grown to a 'social market economy', state welfare providing social welfare benefits as well as other social facilities and welfare institutions all are the result and expression of a contradiction, which is elementary to an order guaranteeing broad individual freedoms to a person and leaving it to his or her individual mental physical and economic capabilities, how far these freedoms contribute to personal success."

Over the past 50 years the social welfare state concept has in a variety of cases shaped governmental policy in Germany.

3.2.1.1. Elements of the "Sozialstaat"

Although the Federal Constitutional Court has not yet given an explanation of the content of the *Sozialstaat* principle as such, it is possible to construct the basic substance of this principle by analysing the decisions on "socially unjust conduct" in a number of cases.[535] In this way it can be identified how the three elements of social welfare policy in Germany, namely social security, social justice and the raising of general living standards, were realised.

In the context of *social security*, the first important component of the social state is social insurance. In 1952 the German Federal Constitutional Court obliged the state to guarantee a human existence to all persons who were in need as a result of the war.[536] This guarantee was later extended to grant *all* persons in need a dignified existence.[537] It is now accepted in Germany that every individual has a subjective right to a minimum subsistence level in the social welfare state.[538] However, the

---

[534] *Kunig* in *Karpen (ed)*, The Constitution of the Federal Republic of Germany (1988), 191.

[535] This has been done by *De Wet* in her doctoral dissertation of 1995, also published as *De Wet*, Constitutional Enforceability of Economic and Social Rights (1996). In the following discussion the structure of this work is used as point of departure.

[536] BVerfGE 1, 97.

[537] BVerfGE 40, 121, 133.

[538] This viewpoint is usually supported by reading art. 2 II with the social state provisions. See *De Wet*, Constitutional Enforceability of Economic and Social Rights (1996), 21.

court went even further and declared that state protection stretches beyond those in need: comprehensive accident insurance whereby the safety risks inevitably associated with specific occupations are covered, should be shared by the individual and the state.[539] Similarly, unemployment insurance,[540] medical insurance[541] and the granting of old-age pensions to previously self-supporting persons who are unable to continue supporting themselves because of changed social circumstances,[542] constitute basic functions of the social state.

To realise social security, the state in the second place has to regulate certain essential services, the prices of essential goods, and specific industries vital to the community. Directly after the second World War prices of certain goods were fixed by legislation, thereby influencing the cost of living.[543] The Federal Constitutional Court ruled that such regulation did not violate the notion of freedom of contract, because the restrictions were proportional to the crisis at hand and because the legislation clearly determined the aim, contents and extent of these restrictions.[544] Price regulation was also allowed long after the war, whenever it was in the general interest of the public. Thus the Federal Constitutional Court decided in 1964 that the regulation of the milk price and the imposition of specific taxes on processed dairy products to alleviate the losses resulting from the regulation of the milk price did not

---

[539] BVerfGE 45, 376, 387.

[540] This was acknowledged in BVerfGE 51, 115, 125, although the court added that this kind of insurance was aimed at compensating a person for losses suffered because of the fact of his or her unemployment and was not intended to place the person in a position in which he or she could maintain a previously attained standard of living through earning extra income.

[541] BVerfGE 16, 286, 304; BVerfGE 68, 193, 209. The German state must ensure that people have access to proper medical services without exposing them to excessive costs. For this purpose compulsory medical insurance has been introduced. People under a certain income level are obliged to be members of a state-subsidised insurance company.

[542] BVerfGE 11, 105, 114 and 117. See also BVerfGE 62, 320, 332 where it was determined that widow's pension could also be seen as a further manifestation of the social state principle.

[543] BVerfGE 8, 277, 277 and 278.

[544] BVerfGE 8, 277, 328. The legislation was transitional and was aimed at establishing normal price rations. Besides, it was clear that price fixing would rather be the exception than the rule. This specific legislation was also repealed once the markets retained their normal state.

affect freedom of competition to such an extent as to make the regulation of the dairy market unconstitutional, because it was necessitated by the public interest.[545] Cost regulation is also justified in connection with medical care[546] and housing.[547]

In realising social security, the state in the third place also has to alleviate economic liabilities caused by general disasters which affect some people more severely than others.[548] Thus the Federal Constitutional Court decided that the state was obliged to compensate individuals as far as possible for patrimonial losses suffered during the second World War. This did not presume full compensation: the notion of the social welfare state also implied that individuals themselves had to bear a reasonable share of the burden.[549]

In order to establish a system of *social justice*, the Federal Constitutional Court identified certain socially vulnerable groups where a reconciliation of social interests would lead to unequal treatment in favour of these social groups. It was, for instance, ruled that employees should be protected against exploitation of their labour abilities.[550] In order to grant needy persons particular protection in the community, tax exempting legislation concerning the investments of people with limited income (as opposed to the same investments by people falling in higher income groups) was also considered reconcilable with the principle of equality.[551]

Women benefited from the social justice element too: Legislation enabling women to claim pensions from the age of 60, as opposed to the usual age of 65, was justified by the Federal Constitutional Court on the basis that this amounted to compensating persons for past discrimination.[552] However, the court also made it clear that social justice did

---

[545] BVerfGE 18, 315.

[546] BVerfGE 53, 366, 410.

[547] BVerfGE 72, 175, 198.

[548] *De Wet*, 1995 SAJHR, 39.

[549] BVerfGE 27, 253, 283; BVerfGE 7, 129, 152; BVerfGE 13, 248, 259.

[550] Measures had to be taken to protect employees from inhuman working conditions, like a health-affecting working environment, hazardous working conditions, unwarrantably long working hours, insufficient leave and inadequate remuneration. BVerfGE 35, 85 206.

[551] BVerfGE 50, 57, 107-108.

[552] BVerfGE 74, 12, 179; BVerfGE 22, 180, 204; BVerfGE 5, 85, 198.

not mean that only the interests of a specific group should be considered. Legislation promulgated in the sole interest of a particular group must be necessitated by the public good and could not result in an indiscriminate neglect of the interests of other groups in society.[553]

The Federal Constitutional Court confirmed that the state was obliged to guarantee equal education opportunities for all pupils.[554] In addition, the Bavarian Constitutional Court held that the social welfare state principle compels the state to attain a high employment rate.[555] In this way the third element of the social welfare state — the raising of living standards where possible — has also been addressed, albeit only indirectly.

3.2.1.2. "Sozialstaat" and Constitutional Protection of Property

Article 14 II GG represents the point where the *Sozialstaatsprinzip* and the constitutional protection of property in Germany meet. In terms of this provision, property imposes duties and should serve the public interest. Society thus has an interest in the individual's exercise of his or her right to property. This is an expression of fundamental ethical values recognised by the Basic Law: the creation of social justice.

The creation of social justice in the area of property law is described in constitutional terms as the "social function" or the "social obligation" *(Sozialbindung)* of property. Article 14 II GG thus refers to an attribute of property that exists irrespective of specific legislation. In practice, there is no difference between legislation based on article 14 I 2 GG and legislation based on article 14 II GG. In theory, however, a difference does exist. This can be explained as follows: In both the case of article 14 I 2 GG and article 14 II GG a certain degree of legislative interference with property rights is anticipated, and has to be tolerated if justifiable in terms of the constitution. However, the "social obligation" of property as expressed in article 14 II GG goes much further than article 14 I 2 GG, as it symbolises some of the fundamental ethical values recognised by the Basic Law. Legislation promulgated in terms of article 14 I 2 GG might activate the social obligation described in article 14 II GG, but does not create it. The "social function" of property

---

[553] BVerfGE 74, 12, 179; BVerfGE 4, 7, 16.

[554] BVerfGE 72, 278, 290.

[555] BayVfGH 13, 141 (b).

will exist irrespective of specific legislation, and is given effect by the courts.[556] On the contrary, legislative determination of the content and limits of the property concept (in terms of article 14 I 2 GG) is to a much larger extent expected to fulfil a defining and delimiting function. The theoretical connection between the legislative competence of article 14 I 2 GG and article 14 II GG is described by the Federal Constitutional Court as the realisation of the social model by the legislature in the determination of the contents and limitations of property in terms of article 14 I 2 GG. The normative elements of the social model result, on the one hand, from the constitutional recognition of private property in article 14 I 1 GG and, on the other hand, from the binding guideline of article 14 II GG.[557]

Thus, the social function of property has two important consequences:

(i) It provides the legislature with guidelines concerning the extent to which it may restrict the powers of disposal of the individual owner for reasons of public purpose. The more distinct the social function of property is in a certain area, the greater leeway the legislature has to regulate use of property.

(ii) The social function of property also enables one to distinguish between different types of property, because the social relevance of various objects of ownership differ widely. There are kinds of property with a very distinct social character (for instance land or industrial property), while others have less social relevance.[558] Thus the degree of constitutional protection afforded to a specific type of property can also be determined. Upon the question whether an act establishing parity between management and labour in a board of directors violated the constitutional property guarantee, the Federal Constitutional Court[559] for instance remarked that the social function of property demanded more restrictions on property than the individual or personal function

---

[556] *Kimminich* in *Starck (ed)*, Rights, Institutions and Impact of International Law (1987), 86.

[557] BVerfGE 37, 132, 140: *"Der Gesetzgeber steht bei der Erfüllung des ihm in Art. 14 Abs. 1 Satz 2 GG erteilten Auftrages, Inhalt und Schranken des Eigentums zu bestimmen, vor der Aufgabe, das Sozialmodell zu verwirklichen, dessen normative Elemente sich einerseits aus der grundgesetzlichen Anerkennung des Privateigentums durch Art. 14 Abs. 1 Satz 1 GG und andererseits aus der verbindlichen Richtschnur des Art. 14 Abs. 2 GG ergeben."*

[558] *Schuppert* in *Karpen (ed)*, The Constitution of Germany (1988), 110.

[559] BVerfGE 50, 290 (*Mitbestimmung*).

would allow. In this specific case it was, however, decided that the substance and allocation of property would be preserved under article 14 I GG in any event, regardless of the extent of a restriction on property in terms of the social obligation.

The right to property was, of course, also subject to the social interest in terms of article 153 of the Weimar Constitution: a provision which was strongly emphasised during the national-socialist regime. But, whereas the right to property could during this time be exercised only as far as it served the aims of the National-socialist state,[560] the right to property in post-war Germany means that individual freedom must enjoy precedence. The premise was that owners needed the liberty to determine the purpose of their property rights for themselves.[561] During the seventies, with the switching of political power from the Christian Democrats to the Social Democrats in Germany, a stronger awareness of the social obligation of ownership became apparent in political circles and in the legislation drafted during this period.[562] Henceforth, property may not be used to damage the public interest, just as it may be regulated in the public interest. Yet, the regulation of property may not infringe the essence of ownership, even if it would be in the interest of society.[563] It is in this context that the interaction of protection of property in private law and protection of property under the Basic Law is best illustrated.

The rent control in Germany serves as an example of the manner in which the leeway of the legislature to enact legislation restricting the right to property is influenced by the socio-economic interests involved. The Federal Constitutional Court ruled that a tenant could be protected against termination of a contract of lease that is not based on

---

[560] *Leisner* in *Isensee/Kirchhof*, Handbuch des Staatsrechts VI (1989), m.n. 31, 32. See also 51 above.

[561] *Leisner* in *Isensee/Kirchhof*, Handbuch des Staatsrechts VI (1989), m.n. 33.

[562] *Von Brünneck*, Die Eigentumsgarantie des Grundgesetzes (1984), 125.

[563] BVerfGE 14, 263. The condemnation of private property might, for instance, fundamentally change the structure of important social and personal relationships. The collectivisation of agriculture is possibly one example of such a fundamental change. In this situation, it is suggested that article 19 II GG could possibly be invoked to deny government the power to recast these relationships. This would leave the wealth of the affected individuals intact. *Kommers*, Constitutional Jurisprudence of Germany (1997), 253.

a well-founded interest of the landlord not specified in the contract.[564] Legislation endorsing this notion was held constitutional in terms of article 14 I 2 GG. Here the court expressly focussed on the role of the social obligation of property in determining whether specific interests should be protected under the constitutional property guarantee or not. The court remarked:[565]

> *"Ebensowenig wie die Eigentumsgarantie eine die soziale Funktion eines Eigentumsobjekts mißachtende Nutzung schützt, kann Art. 14 Abs. 2 GG eine übermäßige, durch die soziale Funktion nicht gebotene Begrenzung privatrechtlicher Befugnisse rechtfertigen... ."*

Legislation regulating the right to property has to protect the owner's freedom and implement a socially just order of property. Thus it must reflect a balance between the interests of all parties involved.[566] On this basis, several lower court decisions were invalidated in 1974 by the Federal Constitutional Court for the harsh manner in which a federal rent control statute *(Wohnraumskündigungsschutzgesetz)* had been applied to owners of rental units. The court decided that the disputed rent increase control legislation[567] constituted a lawful restriction of the property rights of the landlord/owner of a residential unit, as the property guarantee stipulated explicitly that the property rights should be exercised in the general interest.[568]

The *Contergan* decision[569] is another striking example of an important social concern overriding a claim based on a traditional property right. In this case, a federal benefit plan to assist children seriously deformed by a contraceptive drug marketed in Germany was contested. This entailed the nationalisation of a trust fund for the victims of *Contergan*,

---

[564] BVerfGE 68, 361, 367.

[565] BVerfGE 68, 361, 368. (First stated in BVerfGE 37, 132 140-141.) Translation: As little as the property guarantee can protect use of the object of ownership that ignores the social function, can art. 14 II GG justify an excessive restriction on the private law entitlements of ownership not required by its social function.

[566] BVerfGE 37, 132, 140-141.

[567] I.e. legislation determining that owners of residential units could only raise the rent of such residences in compliance with the average rent in a particular area and thereby could not ask more rent for a residence than the normal rental for similar residences in the specific area.

[568] BVerfGE 37, 132, 141.

[569] BVerfGE 42, 263.

and consequently it nullified settlement agreements concluded in terms of private law that were to the exclusive benefit of the parties to the settlement agreement and not to all victims of *Contergan*. The court upheld the legislation nationalising the *Contergan* trust fund and converting it into a public law foundation as constitutional in terms of the property clause, in spite of objections from individual right holders in terms of the settlement agreement.

In conclusion, it can be remarked that the German Federal Constitutional Court successfully moulded the egalitarian effect of the social state principle into a legal structure that could prevent unrestricted state action and thus also totalitarianism. The limitation of freedom in the general interest is emphasised by employing the requirements of proportionality and legal certainty. In order to realise a fundamental social goal, the aim as well as the means of the limitation must be clear, relevant and necessary. In this way the court balances freedom and equality and seeks to guarantee a certain basic sphere of free activity.[570]

3.2.2. The Social Welfare State Principle in South Africa?

It is still not clear to what extent the social welfare state principle will be endorsed in South Africa. This term is not specifically mentioned in either the Interim or the Final Constitution. Nevertheless, several provisions in both Constitutions support some objectives similar to those explained above in the German context. This could be interpreted as indications that the notion of the social welfare state may be applicable in the South African context.

For instance, effect could be given to the objectives of the social state by enacting ordinary legislation. In South Africa, governmental policy and recent legislation seem to support the aims of social security, social justice and the eventual raising of living standards. The treatment of property is in this context a key element to socio-economic reconstruction in South Africa. Another possible mechanism of promoting the establishment of a social welfare state is to entrench so-called socio-economic rights in a constitution. Several socio-economic rights find protection in the bills of rights of both the Interim and Final Constitutions. Some of these rights, like the right to restitution of land and redistribution of property, are also contained within section 25 FC.

---

[570] *De Wet*, 1995 SAJHR, 46.

One of the most important effects of socio-economic rights is that they act as a counterbalance to other rights. Thus, socio-economic rights provide constitutional authority or protection for legislation or administrative action aimed at introducing social reform. Enforcement of socio-economic rights is also a mechanism of empowerment for the individual. These rights can be used to test and invalidate legislation or administrative action at the instance of individuals affected. They could also be used as an interpretative device, to slant the interpretation of statutes so as to put the poor or disadvantaged in a more favourable position.[571] However, a challenge to the constitutionality of legislation attempting to bring about social reform could be countered by reliance on the social and economic rights in the Constitution.

In the following paragraphs, the possibility of successfully establishing a social welfare state in South Africa will be discussed. Focus will be placed on the viability of social reform policies and giving effect to socio-economic rights in the South African context.

3.2.2.1. Constitutional Entrenchment of the Social Welfare State

De Wet[572] recognised that some provisions in the Interim Constitution indicated acceptance of the social welfare state. The provisions of the limitation clause[573] in the Interim Constitution were — for the sake of upholding the democratic values of the constitution as a whole — applicable to, *inter alia*, the equality clause (section 8(3) IC)[574] and the

---

[571] *Budlender* in *Budlender/Latsky/Roux*, New Land Law (revised 1998), ch. 1, 69.

[572] *De Wet*, 1995 SAJHR, 47-48.

[573] Sec. 33(1) IC.

[574] This subsection determines that the right to equality (sec. 8(1) IC) and the freedom from discrimination (sec. 8(2) IC) "(a) shall not preclude measures designed to achieve the adequate protection and advancement of persons or groups or categories of persons disadvantaged by unfair discrimination, in order to enable their full and equal enjoyment of all rights and freedoms" and that "(b) [e]very person or community dispossessed of rights in land before the commencement of this Constitution under any law which would have been inconsistent with subsection (2) had that subsection been in operation at the time of the dispossession, shall be entitled to claim restitution of such rights subject to and in accordance with section 121, 122 and 123."

right to freely engage in economic activity (section 26(2) IC).[575] Read with Constitutional Principle V[576] of Schedule II IC, this was an indication of the presence of the social welfare state concept in the South African context.

Although no direct mention is made of the social welfare state principle in the Final Constitution,[577] the evidence of the incorporation of this concept in the Final Constitution is more substantial than in the Interim Constitution.[578] For instance, the preamble of the Final Constitution recognises the establishment of a society based on "social justice" and the "improvement of the quality of life of all citizens" as constitutional aims.

A further indication of the existence of the social welfare state principle in the South African context is the inclusion of socio-economic rights in the bill of rights. Already in terms of the Interim Constitution some rights could clearly be classified as social and economic rights.[579] These included environmental rights,[580] children's rights[581] and educational rights.[582] However, the issue of entrenching socio-economic rights was dealt with rather incompletely and provisionally in the Interim Constitution.[583] In the debates and negotiations preceding the drafting of the two South African Constitutions, many politicians and scholars wres-

---

[575] This subsection determines that the right to freely engage in economic activity guaranteed in sec. 26(1) IC "shall not preclude measures designed to promote the protection or the improvement of the quality of life, economic growth, human development, social justice, basic conditions of employment, fair labour practices or equal opportunity for all, provided such measures are justifiable in an open and democratic society based on freedom and equality."

[576] This principle determines: "The legal system shall ensure the equality of all before the law and an equitable legal process. Equality before the law includes laws, programmes or activities that have as their object the amelioration of the conditions of the disadvantaged, including those disadvantaged on the grounds of race, colour or gender."

[577] *Kleyn*, 1996 SAPR/PL, 408.

[578] *Du Plessis*, 1996 Stell LR, 7.

[579] *Budlender* in *Budlender/Latsky/Roux*, New Land Law (revised 1998), ch. 1, 68.

[580] Sec. 29 IC.

[581] Sec. 30 IC.

[582] Sec. 21 IC.

[583] *Du Plessis*, 1996 Stell LR, 13; See also 60 above.

tled with the question of whether and to what extent socio-economic rights should be entrenched.[584] In view of the implications that the entrenchment and enforceability of socio-economic rights could have for the establishment of a social welfare state, these questions need to be elucidated here.

Due to the vast demands that would be made on public resources to give effect to these rights, direct enforcement of socio-economic rights is problematic. Enforcing socio-economic rights directly, without limiting the claims of prospective beneficiaries, could undermine the confidence in the bill of rights. It could also subvert the legitimacy of the bill of rights.[585] That is why various alternatives were suggested during the negotiations preceding the promulgation of the Interim Constitution:

(i) The National Party and the Law Commission were, for instance, in favour of social and economic rights in a constitution *only* if they would be negatively enforced.[586] Positive claims against the state would, according to this view, not be entrenched in the Constitution as fundamental rights.

(ii) Proponents in favour of the entrenchment of social and economic rights argued that such rights could be made legally enforceable once the legislature has qualified or circumscribed their scope.[587] In addition, they argued that the fact that social and economic rights cannot be enforced should not be decisive in resolving whether or not such rights should be entrenched in a bill of rights.[588] The value of such rights for the community and the possibility to enforce such rights at a particular stage would, so the argument went, be more important.[589] It has also been argued that the mere formulation of these rights in a bill of rights

---

[584] *De Wet,* Constitutional Enforceability of Economic and Social Rights (1996), 92-104 gives an overview of this debate. See also i.a. *Haysom,* 1992 SAJHR, 451-463; *Mureinik,* 1992 SAJHR, 464-474; *Davis,* 1992 SAJHR 475-490.

[585] *Mureinik,* 1992 SAJHR, 465-467; Corder, Kahanovitz, Murphy et. al. *A Charter for Social Justice* (1992) 21; *Du Plessis,* 1996 Stell LR, 13.

[586] *De Wet,* Constitutional Enforceability of Economic and Social Rights (1996), 103.

[587] *Haysom,* 1992 SAJHR, 461 call such right "framework rights" and remarks: " 'Framework' rights include those that entitle citizens to forms of relief but the content of which can be left to statutory expansion."

[588] *De Vos* in *Bennun/Newitt (eds),* Negotiating Justice (1995), 106.

[589] *Haysom,* 1992 SAJHR, 461.

is advantageous, because it would oblige the state to progressively realise socio-economic fundamental rights.[590] At the very least, it would
give the individual the possibility of claiming revision of legislation in
order to test the reasonableness of the legislature's conduct.[591]

(iii) Other possible ways for such rights to be included in a bill of rights
would be either to incorporate them under a single notion defining the
role of the state as "social provider,"[592] or to clothe them as "directives
of state policy" that envision the achievement of specific socio-
economic goals.[593]

These suggested alternatives to directly enforceable socio-economic
rights all attempt to solve the problems brought about by a lack of resources. It is sad but true that the success of giving direct effect to socio-economic rights is inextricably linked to adequate financial backing.
In a developing country like South Africa the lack of resources could
compromise the introduction of a social welfare state to such an extent
that it should be considered whether it is worth the trouble to entrench
socio-economic rights at all. Still, the drafters of the Final Constitution
decided to include an even more comprehensive list of such rights. Section 27 FC guarantees the right to health care, food, water and social security, and also provides for appropriate social assistance in specific circumstances. Furthermore, access to housing,[594] the right to education,[595]
and environmental rights[596] are guaranteed.[597] Moreover, the relevant

---

[590] *Sachs*, Advancing Human Rights (1992), 35.

[591] *Mureinik*, 1992 SAJHR, 471.

[592] E.g. the German *Sozialstaatsprinzip*, as described at 139 above. *Du Plessis*,
1996 Stell LR, 13.

[593] E.g. the Indian example: See *Corder/Kahanovitz/Murphy*, Social Justice
(1992), 20. *Du Plessis*, 1996 Stell LR, 13; *De Villiers*, 1992 SAJHR, 29-49, 188-
199; *De Vos* in *Bennun/Newitt (eds)*, Negotiating Justice (1995), 83-85.

[594] Sec. 26 FC.

[595] Sec. 29 FC.

[596] Sec. 24 FC.

[597] In discussing the certification of the Final Constitution, *Sachs*, 1996 NYU
J Int'l L & P, 702-703 referred to the objection raised that the inclusion of social
and economic rights (i) would bring the court into the position of usurping the
legislative function and (ii) would submerge first generation fundamental rights
under such claims. After dealing with these objections, it was remarked that:
"Our job was simply to ensure that all universally accepted rights were included, and that they were viewed as a platform – a minimum, and not a ceil-

organs of state are accountable to the Human Rights Commission in that they are required to furnish the commission with information on the measures undertaken towards the realisation of fundamental rights related to housing, health care, food, water, social security, education and the environment.[598]

The increased emphasis on social and democratic rights in the Final Constitution may warrant the description of South Africa as a *social democracy*,[599] thereby acknowledging the state's role in the regulation of the market, the provision of social welfare services and the protection of institutions and mechanisms of political democracy. The new South African state can therefore also be seen as "providing an enterprising and caring administration of the social market."[600] This not only includes the achievement of equality, but also requires diligent reorganisation of resources.[601]

However, these socio-economic rights protected in the South African bill of rights are subject to quite comprehensive limitations, in terms of the general limitation clause and the clauses providing for these rights themselves. In terms of internal limitations, which are quite typical to the socio-economic rights in the Final Constitution, the (progressive) realisation of many of these rights is made subject to the availability of resources.[602]

The right to medical treatment, which was the subject of two recent court cases, serves as an example of how the courts understand this kind of internal limitation. In both *Van Biljon v Minister of Correctional Services*[603] and *Soobramoney v Minister of Health, KwaZulu-Natal*[604] orders were sought for the provision of expensive medical treatment at the expense of the state. In both cases the applicants relied on provisions of the bill of rights. In the *Soobramoney* case the applicant relied on section 27 FC. In the *Van Biljon* case, section 35(2)(e) FC was the

---

ing." See *Certification of the Constitution of the Republic of South Africa* (note 245 above), par. 76-78.

[598] Sec. 184(3) FC.

[599] *Du Plessis*, 1996 Stell LR, 7.

[600] *Corder/Kahanovitz/Murphy*, Social Justice (1992), 28.

[601] *Du Plessis*, 1996 Stell LR, 7.

[602] See sec. 26(2) FC; sec. 27(2) FC.

[603] *Van Biljon v Minister of Correctional Services* 1997 4 SA 441 (C).

[604] *Soobramoney v Minister of Health, KwaZulu-Natal* 1998 1 SA 765 (CC).

basis of the claim, as the applicant was a prisoner. In both cases the state raised the lack of funds as a defence. Furthermore, in both cases the medical treatment sought by the applicants would not cure their ailments, but would extend their life expectancies and enhance their quality of life. In spite of the similarities upon the facts, the court came to opposing decisions. The main reason for this can be found in the fact that the right to medical care for prisoners is differently phrased than in the case of section 27 FC. Section 35(2)(e) FC does not contain qualifying phrases like "within its available resources" and "progressive realisation of these rights." It might, therefore, have been easier for the state to get away with the lack-of-resources argument in the case of *Soobramoney* than in the case of *Van Biljon*. In the context of section 27 FC it was also for the court easier to pronounce upon a limitation of the rights protected, as this section contains an internal limitation. In the case of section 35(2)(e) FC the court would have to be convinced, in terms of the general limitations clause (s 36 FC), that it was authorised by law of general application to limit the applicant's rights to adequate medical treatment.[605]

3.2.2.2. Social Welfare State and the Protection of Property Rights

The interaction between the principle of the social welfare state and the fundamental right to property in the South African context depends on the perception of the rights to restitution and redistribution of land and the right to reform of land tenure. These "new land rights" created by section 25(5) to (8) FC and the legislation resulting from section 25(9) FC could act as internal counterbalances to the constitutional protection of existing property rights. This is the premise upon which the analysis in the following paragraphs is based. It is intended to indicate the elements of the social state prevalent in the constitutional property clause, and to consider the question of how successful the establishment of a social welfare state through application of the constitutional property clause could be.

Section 25(5) FC not only provides strong protection to the state in actions aimed at promoting equitable access to land, but could also be used in litigation to compel the state to enact legislation of this kind if it

---

[605] See *Ka Mdumbe*, 1998 SAPR/PL, 460-470; *Moellendorf*, 1998 SAJHR, 327-333.

failed to do so in the first place.[606] However, it is more likely that section 25(5) FC would be used as a shield against challenges to administrative actions or fiscal measures aimed at promoting equitable access to land, than as a sword in the hands of those who need access to land.[607] In the first instance, therefore, section 25(5) FC will be used as justification for the social reform programmes designed by legislature.

Section 25(6) FC provides a contingent right to security of land tenure or comparable redress for tenure made insecure because of past racially discriminatory laws or practices. The fact that the right is contingent in the sense that it must first be given effect by an act of Parliament, does not mean that it is an empty right: If Parliament fails to fulfil this duty, it may be held in breach of its constitutional obligations. If such legislation is enacted, however, it enjoys constitutional protection against challenge. It must also be interpreted in accordance with the constitutional obligation in section 25(6) FC.[608] Social and economic development in the area of land tenure requires that the narrower issue of land and property rights *per se* must be transcended and that issues like social justice in the context of agrarian law and agricultural land distribution need to be addressed.[609] The possibilities for analysing and discussing the legal and institutional aspects relevant for social and economic development in the area of property law can only then be fully exploited.

The interpretation of the phrase *past discriminatory laws and practices* will be especially problematic in this context. On the one hand, it will influence the formulation of reform legislation. On the other hand, it will also determine how legislation of the apartheid era has to be treated in a new constitutional dispensation.

---

[606] This brings about problems connected with the separation of state powers. The court, for example, does not have the competence to draft the legislation. Other problems include the remedy for non-compliance. The solution in this instance would be for the court to issue nothing but a declaratory order that the state is in breach of its constitutional obligations. *Budlender* in *Budlender/Latsky/Roux*, New Land Law (revised 1998), ch. 1, 69-70.

[607] *Budlender* in *Budlender/Latsky/Roux*, New Land Law (revised 1998), ch. 1, 70.

[608] *Budlender* in *Budlender/Latsky/Roux*, New Land Law (revised 1998), ch. 1, 70.

[609] *Gutto*, Property and Land Reform (1995), 25.

Explicit racial discrimination was — by content and/or purpose — inherent in some of the laws, policies and practices of the apartheid era,
whereas racial discrimination was not explicitly intended by others, but
resulted from them. It is nowadays permissible in terms of the "affirmative action" provision of section 9(2) FC to formulate new legislation — like laws promoting tenure security — on an explicitly racial basis. However, some authors[610] believe that legislation broadly promoting tenure security will go beyond addressing the results of past discriminatory laws and practices, and will therefore not be phrased so as
to favour specific races within the South African borders explicitly. A
possible consequence of such an approach would be that the legislation
would no longer be protected by section 25(6) FC. However, such an
interpretation should be avoided, except if compliance with the constitutional obligation in section 25(6) FC is not the major purpose of the
legislation.[611]

The procedures for securing land tenure introduced in the course of the
upgrading of land tenure rights can also be jeopardised by the treatment
of past discriminatory laws and practices. The recent case of *DVB Behuising (Pty) Ltd v North West Provincial Government and others*,[612]
albeit only indirectly, raises the issue of how the courts should treat
legislation perceived to be a continuance of the racially based property
order, without endangering rights created on the basis of such legislation.

The legal question in this case revolved around the legislative competencies of the provincial and national legislatures. The facts involved the
enactment of section 6 of the North West Local Government Laws
Amendment Act[613] by the legislature of the North West Province. This
section purported to repeal in its entirety a proclamation[614] issued in
terms of the Black[615] Administration Act.[616] The Black Administration

---

[610] *Budlender* in *Budlender/Latsky/Roux*, New Land Law (revised 1998),
ch. 1, 70-71.

[611] *Budlender* in *Budlender/Latsky/Roux*, New Land Law (revised 1998), ch.
1, 71.

[612] *DVB Behuising (Pty) Ltd v North West Provincial Government and others* 2000 4 BCLR 347 (CC).

[613] 7 of 1998.

[614] R293 of 1962.

[615] The term "Native" was used in the earliest racial segregatory legislation to
refer to matters pertaining to Black South Africans. This had been replaced later

Act was one of two infamous statutes[617] that effectively made it impossible for the majority of (black) South Africans, to own land in some 87% of the country. Even upon a cursory reading, this proclamation conveys the demeaning and racist nature of the system of which it was a part.[618]

The constitutional validity of section 6 of the North West Local Government Laws Amendment Act was challenged on the basis that the purported repeal of certain provisions of the proclamation was beyond the legislative competence of the North West Province. It was claimed that a repeal of certain sections in this proclamation would make it impossible for persons to whom the applicant had sold houses in a township established under the proclamation, to have their deeds of grant registered, or to mortgage their properties in order to finance their purchases.[619]

In issues of property law reform and social justice, the outcome of the decision is not as important as the fact that some remarks were made, in a minority judgement by Goldstone, O'Regan and Sachs JJ, about the constitutional obligation that s 25 FC places on the national legislature to provide redress by legislative means for past discrimination in relation to land. Section 25(6) FC is read by the minority to imply that insecure forms of land tenure arising from discriminatory legislation of the past regime could not be abolished or reformed by any legislature other than Parliament.[620] It is then conceded that the jurisprudence of the transitional era necessarily involves a measure of contradiction, as

---

with the term "Black". The latter term will be used in this analysis if reference needs to be made to any of the acts initially promulgated to deal with the issues of so-called Natives.

[616] 38 of 1927.

[617] The other statute was the Black Land Act, 27 of 1913.

[618] See decision of Ngcobo, J, *DVB Behuising* case (note 612 above), par. 2.

[619] In the court of first instance (Bophuthatswana High Court), the application was upheld, upon the reasoning that the purported legislative repeal dealt with a question of land tenure, which fell exclusively within the competence of the national legislature. The majority of the Constitutional Court (*DVB Behuising* case (note 612 above), par. 65, 72) refused to confirm this order of invalidity, except insofar as it related to provisions concerning registration of title, which were regarded by the court as the only matter pertaining to which the provincial legislature did not have the power to repeal the proclamation.

[620] *DVB Behuising* case (note 612 above), par. 103.

"fundamental fairness" at times requires that aspects of the old discriminatory order have to survive immediate removal from the statute
books, pending their replacement by appropriate mechanisms under a
new, more equitable order.[621]

In essence, the minority of the court puts forward an argument in favour of upholding certain forms of "lesser" property rights which were
created under the laws of the apartheid regime and which can still be
created under the same laws at present. Certain mechanisms (like the
Upgrading of Land Tenure Rights Act[622]) have already been introduced
to "upgrade" tenuous and insecure land rights, by gradually converting
them into full ownership or secure property rights, thus establishing a
more expeditious way of acquiring land. If the law on the basis of
which these rights were initially created is abolished, so the argument
goes, "underprivileged communities"[623] would no longer have access to
the speedy and accessible form of registration coupled with the deed of
grant tenure.[624]

According to the view of the minority, therefore, the "meritorious desire" manifested in the majority judgement "for a clean sweep of the
past in the name of modernisation and de-racialisation,"[625] has the unintended and ironic consequence of depriving underprivileged communities from gaining access to a cheap form of land tenure that in terms
of present national legislation could be upgraded to full ownership. The
minority thus argued that a repeal of the (admittedly demeaning and
racist) proclamation would not promote the constitutional objective of

---

[621] *DVB Behuising* case (note 612 above), par. 110. In the judgement of
Ngcobo J, (par. 66-71) this issue is dealt with by referring to the provisions of
the Less Formal Township Establishment Act, 113 of 1991 and the Development Facilitation Act, 67 of 1995. It is argued that these statutes do provide the
necessary mechanism for promoting development of land in urban and rural areas for residential purposes, granting land tenure rights and shortening and
simplifying procedures for the designation, provision and development of land
and establishment of townships. In turn, the minority argued (at par. 106) that
the purpose of the Upgrading of Land Tenure Rights Act, 112 of 1991, is to
transform existing insecure title to freehold, and to permit continued granting
of those forms of land tenure as well as their upgrading.

[622] 112 of 1991.

[623] *DVB Behuising* case (note 612 above) par. 110.

[624] *DVB Behuising* case (note 612 above) par. 111.

[625] *DVB Behuising* case (note 612 above) par. 110.

fostering access to land. According to their argument, quite the reverse would be the case.

This argument was used to indicate that legislation pertaining to land tenure should fall within the exclusive competence of the national legislature. It might be debatable whether this line of reasoning is appropriate or not. The point here is that the minority judgement of *DVB Behuising (Pty) Ltd v North West Provincial Government and others* indicates that it is questionable whether pure liberationist ideology can by itself ensure socio-economic upliftment of the marginalised masses of South Africans. At the very least, this case shows the need to carefully consider the nature and function of the specific property rights which are to be protected.

Section 25(7) FC is in a sense the successor of sections 121 to 123 IC, although the restitution of property (or equitable redress) to people or communities dispossessed of property after 19 June 1913 is now a right directly incorporated in the bill of rights itself. This right is, furthermore, broader than those under the Interim Constitution are. It applies to all forms of property and not only to deprivation of "rights in land" as under section 121 IC. Furthermore, whereas the entitlement under the Interim Constitution arises from dispossession under or for the purpose of furthering the object of a discriminatory law, section 25(7) FC broadens that to dispossession under either a racially discriminatory law or such a practice.[626]

The extent and content of the right to restitution are determined by the Restitution of Land Rights Act,[627] which creates a very broad right to restitution. It applies to the dispossession of:[628]

> *"any right in land whether registered or unregistered and may include the interest of a labour tenant, a share cropper, a customary law interest, the interests of a beneficiary under a trust arrangement and beneficial occupation for a continuous period of not less than ten years."*

The fact that the statutory right to restitution is clearly broader than that accorded the Constitution should not lead to statutory invalidity. The Constitution only states the minimum rights that the state must

---

[626] *Budlender* in *Budlender/Latsky/Roux*, New Land Law (revised 1998), ch. 1, 71-72.

[627] 22 of 1994.

[628] Sec. 1 (Definitions): "Right in land".

establish. As long as an expansion of these rights do not compromise any other constitutional right, there should be no reason why such an expansion should not be permissible.[629]

Other evidence of the acceptance of a social welfare state is perhaps noticeable in section 25(8) FC, which serves as an internal limitation on the property clause. The relation between this provision and the general limitation clause in section 36(1) FC continues to puzzle interpreters of the property clause.[630] One possible explanation of the relevance of this subsection is that it acts as a directive to the courts that land, water and related reforms are especially valuable as a result of the aim to redress the results of past racial discrimination.[631] This interpretation is consistent with the broad purposive approach supported by the Constitutional Court in interpretation and application of the bill of rights.[632] If it were supported, it would be a further indication of the presence of social welfare state in the South African context.

4. Social Welfare State, Constitutional State and Property Guarantee

The relation between the principles of the constitutional state and the social welfare state may be described as an ongoing interaction, aimed at creating a balance between liberty and equality. This interaction is characterised by a relationship of challenged interdependence rather than exclusivity.[633] A strict theoretical division between the principles of the

---

[629] Budlender in Budlender/Latsky/Roux, New Land Law (revised 1998), ch. 1, 72.

[630] See Rautenbach, General Provisions of the South African Bill of Rights (1995), 105-110; Van der Walt, 1997 SAPR/PL, 275-330; Budlender in Budlender/Latsky/Roux, New Land Law (revised 1998), ch. 1, 72-73; Van der Walt, Constitutional Property Clause (1997), 72-100; De Waal/Currie/Erasmus, Bill of Rights Handbook (1999), 160-162 and 413-415.

[631] Budlender in Budlender/Latsky/Roux, New Land Law (revised 1998), ch. 1, 73.

[632] De Waal/Currie/Erasmus, Bill of Rights Handbook (1999), 125-127.

[633] Zacher in Stödter/Thieme (eds), Festschrift für Hans Peter Ipsen (1977), 260-261: "Ein politisch und prozeßhaft verstandener Sozialstaat steht zu Rechtsstaat und Demokratie im Verhältnis der wechselseitigen Verwiesenheit und Herausforderung, nicht aber im Verhältnis des Überwindens oder der Ausschließlichkeit."

constitutional state and the social welfare state would not advance the practical application of these principles in practice. It would also undermine the inherent objectives of the Constitution by playing off two different concepts of state against each other, instead of reconciling them.[634]

In general, the constitutional state principle acts as an objective normative principle rather than as a basis for substantiating specific claims. The constitutional state principle in conjunction with fundamental freedoms serve as a counterbalance to limit the increasing re-interpretation of rights as demands. The social welfare state principle, on the other hand, incorporates a social welfare philosophy into constitutional law and sets limits to liberal aspirations of an autonomous society. Moreover, the social welfare state principle does not in itself provide individuals with a basis for substantiating claims either.[635] No law may conflict with either of these principles and all law should be interpreted in the light thereof. Thus the state can serve not only the freedom of the individual, but also his or her welfare.

The constitutional and social welfare state, therefore, reflect different sides of the same coin. De Wet[636] explains that they both have the same centre of gravity, namely the protection of liberty, security, equality and human dignity:

> "[I]n a law state emphasis falls on liberty, security, equality and assistance in need — in that sequence. The same elements exist in a social state, but in the opposite sequence viz assistance in need, equality, security and liberty."

The fundamental individual freedom inherent in a system based on the constitutional state principle would usually prevent the social welfare state from getting out of control. This is crucial, because of the tendency towards collectivism inherent in the social welfare state principle. An unchecked policy of state intervention could easily develop into a totalitarian regime. Thus, the principles of the constitutional state and

---

[634] *De Wet*, Constitutional Enforceability of Economic and Social Rights (1996), 34.

[635] *De Waal*, 1995 SAJHR, 8 note 21.

[636] *De Wet*, Constitutional Enforceability of Economic and Social Rights (1996), 34.

the social welfare state are in a fragile equilibrium with each other. Wiechers[637] explains:

"[S]osiaalstaatlikheid, in die sin van maatskaplike en ekonomiese opheffing, [hoef] in geen opsig teen regstaatlikheid ... in te druis nie. As so 'n opheffing egter grondwetlike waarborge en prosedures verkrag en die belange van minderhede op 'n ongrondwetlike wyse aantas, bestaan daar inderdaad 'n gevaar dat regstaatlikheid bedreig kan word."

Especially in a young democracy like South Africa, the greatest potential challenge to the survival of the constitutional state lies in the undercurrent of social values which could be abused through overemphasis. Venter[638] mentions the potential of communalism overshadowing individualism, *Sozialstaatlichkeit* gaining the upper hand over *Rechtsstaatlichkeit* and the remedial promotion of the disadvantaged undermining the ideals of equality.

The role of the state is primarily to foster the ideals of governance through legality, the promotion and protection of fundamental rights and the constitutional state principle. The state must also heed this ideal in formulating and implementing policies on social and economic development. This can be done either through legal regulation, or through providing the necessary infrastructure, or both. In this regard, the German and South African systems are comparable, although by no means similar. Ownership of land can, for instance, be a stabilising element in society. However, this stabilising role can also be undertaken by the state through the provision of *inter alia* social security, licences and permits. The extent to which the state assumes responsibility for providing in the socio-economic needs of individuals influence the importance attached to private ownership in a given society.

In a democratic-social-constitutional-state system, proprietary relations must always be characterised by an interaction between equality and liberty. A constitutional property guarantee[639] can be a particularly good example of the necessary interaction between the principles of the

---

[637] *Wiechers*, 1998 THRHR, 632. Translation: "The social welfare state, in the sense of socio-economic upliftment, need not clash with the constitutional state. However, if such upliftment were to disregard the constitutional guarantees and processes, and were to affect the interests of minorities, the constitutional state could be under imminent threat".

[638] *Venter*, 1997 ZaöRV, 82.

[639] Like sec. 28 IC; sec. 25 FC and art. 14 GG.

constitutional and social welfare state.[640] In terms of their social function, property rights are important in providing individuals with a sense of possessing an immediate personal stake in the public realm, a sense of belonging to a community with whom they identify.[641] In a liberal society supported by the constitutional state principle, the individual can acquire property according to his or her own free choice, thereby enlarging his or her sphere of freedom. However, without regulation, this process could lead to misuse of property and abuse of discretionary powers by owners. Freedom under the constitutional state should therefore not be without limits. These limits are provided by the social welfare state principle. Thus, property as a constitutional right means that the individual should be provided with the necessary sphere of liberty in the patrimonial sphere with which he or she is responsible for creating his or her own way of living.[642]

In the context of the constitutional property guarantee, like in the field of private law property, it is necessary to demarcate the borders of individual power and to determine the consequences of an infringement of these borders by other individuals. Sometimes, existing proprietary relations can cause inequality in the chances of participation in social life to such an extent that "justice" would require state intervention. In a legal system in which the constitutional state principle is supposed to interact with the social welfare state principle, a purely legalistic interpretation of property and ownership is not possible. The demands of equity shape the approach to property to such an extent that the material needs, historical changes and the social function of property rights qualify the definition and application of a constitutional property guarantee.[643]

---

[640] *Kunig* in *Karpen (ed)*, The Constitution of the Federal Republic of Germany (1988), 191; *De Wet*, Constitutional Enforceability of Economic and Social Rights (1996), 34.

[641] *Salter* in *Harris (ed)*, Property Problems from Genes to Pension Funds (1997), 271. See also BVerfGE 24, 367.

[642] See BVerfGE 30, 292; also BGHZ 6, 276.

[643] This approach reminds of that in *Hegel*, Grundlinien der Philosophie des Rechts (1896) / transl *Dyde*, Philosophy of Right (1996). Although first published at the end of the nineteenth century, some of the elements present in Hegel's account of property law have retained contemporary relevance. Hegel's core contention is that liberty cannot be separated from order and that an interconnection between all parts of the body politic is vital to the common good and public interest. This philosophy has often been abused to justify the opin-

This approach is best illustrated in the decisions of the Federal Constitutional Court in Germany, where the fundamental purpose of the constitutional property guarantee is used as the starting point of almost all important decisions on this aspect. It thus provides the basis for interpretation and application of article 14 GG in its entirety. The property guarantee is accordingly described as:[644]

> "(a) a fundamental (human) right, (b) which is meant to secure, for the holder of property, (c) an area of personal liberty (d) in the patrimonial sphere, (e) to enable her to take responsibility for the free development and organisation of her own life (f) within the larger social and legal context."

As for the South African property clause, the courts still have to determine to what extent the principles of the constitutional and social welfare state will be realised through section 25 FC. Given the requirements for deprivation and expropriation of property and the new (socio-economic) rights created by sections 25(5), (6), (7) and (8), the South African constitutional property clause certainly has the potential to support the introduction of a constitutional and social welfare state in the South African context.

Social and economic development implies the increase of wealth and the effective and equitable distribution of wealth within a society so as to enhance material, cultural, intellectual and spiritual well-being.[645] For proprietary relations in South Africa, this means that legal change will have to influence and promote the individual's ability to participate in important societal changes. Several issues could be raised in this regard:[646]

(i) The relations of power existing in the South African society need to be restructured in order to establish equality. A programme supporting

---

ion that national leaders should possess absolute freedom in realising what they perceive to be the world-historical mission of their nation. Hegel's analysis nevertheless re-opens the question of which areas of social life should fall within the domain of private property rights, thus providing a starting point in answering the question concerning the ambit of private property and the extent to which it can be limited for the sake of public interest. *Salter* in *Harris (ed)*, Property Problems from Genes to Pension Funds (1997), 257.

[644] *Van der Walt*, Constitutional Property Clauses - A Comparative Analysis (1999), 124.

[645] *Gutto*, Property and Land Reform (1995), 26.

[646] Adapted from *Gutto*, Property and Land Reform (1995), 26-27.

the redistribution of property would be important in this regard. Furthermore, rights of tenure and proprietary relations that were in the past not recognised, or not protected by law, need to be strengthened. The unequal division of wealth between rural and urban inhabitants of South Africa also needs to be narrowed. This is a challenging task, as addressing regional inequalities has to be coupled with a strengthening of national cohesion, while simultaneously respecting diversity of culture and lifestyle. A matter of particular urgency, however, is gender inequality. This issue needs to be addressed, for instance, through programmes empowering women to become owners of land (especially in rural areas).

(ii) Productivity needs to be promoted. In this regard it will be important to recognise individual autonomy in the use land and business property. The state would, for instance, have to carefully consider the wisdom of introducing regulation hampering free enterprise. Instead, the state could be involved on another level, by increasing its participation in the organisation and provision of material, technological and institutional support, whilst curbing excessive state power and bureaucracy. In other words, the state should allow reasonable scope for entrepreneurial initiatives in fulfilling its duty of promoting social and economic development.

(iii) It is, furthermore, vital that ecological balance is promoted and that the environment is protected within a system of diversified land tenure and land use relations. This will ensure an increase in the value of land in years to come.

However, the success of ventures like these will be determined by the ability of the courts and legislature to resolve the inherent conflict between freedom and equality and to strike a working balance between the protection of property and its regulation.

5. Individual Freedom, Social Justice and Proportionality

The purpose of this chapter was to provide a brief overview of the interaction of the constitutional property clauses in Germany and South Africa and the constitutional values that form the basis of the respective legal orders. The interplay between the constitutional state, the fundamental right to property and the social welfare state ought to form an integral part of the discourse on property and its place in society. This, once again, raises the question as to the place and function of the proportionality test in the system of constitutional property litigation.

The tension between individual freedom and social justice is apparently inherent to the concept of constitutional property. It has already been indicated[647] that it is practically impossible to consider any aspect of the constitutional property concept without simultaneously considering this tension between different interests and conducting a process of balancing them. This approach does not have to mean that the proportionality test, which is supposed to constitute the very last phase in an inquiry about the constitutional validity of an interference with property, needs to be uprooted and re-applied earlier in the investigation. It also does not attempt to overthrow the two-stage inquiry into constitutional validity of interference with fundamental rights.[648] It rather advocates the proper application of the principles of the constitutional and social state as elements of interpretation throughout the inquiry, so as to establish a less formalistic, more result-oriented approach towards the protection and regulation of property.[649] This simply means that one or the other form of interest-balancing is part of each stage of the entire process, and that the nature and function of the balancing process will differ according to the stage of the inquiry in which it is employed. The following chapters will indicate that, in some instances, this kind of balancing of interests in earlier stages of the inquiry as to the constitutional validity of an interference with property will be similar — but by no means equal — to the elements of proportionality.

The crucial question arising from this survey is what significance the courts and the legislature will attach to the underlying values of individual freedom and autonomy, on the one hand, and social justice and equality, on the other hand. This in turn opens an enquiry into the interaction between the private law concept of ownership and the constitutional concept of public interest. In the following chapters, an attempt will be made to address these issues by analysing the operation of the German and South African constitutional property clauses and the areas where the private law and constitutional regulation and protection of property overlap. The

---

[647] See 105 above.

[648] For a discussion of this two-stage approach, see *De Waal/Currie/Erasmus*, Bill of Rights Handbook (2000), 23-30.

[649] Such an approach could have been particularly useful in deciding the questions posed by the case of *Harksen v Lane* 1998 1 SA 300 (CC). See discussion at 350 ff. below.

different elements of the constitutionality enquiry in South Africa and Germany respectively will be examined, with reference to the different procedures followed by the courts in these jurisdictions. The manner in which compensation for expropriation of property is determined under the constitutional order, will also be discussed.

Part Three

The Constitutional Inquiry into Property Protection and its Relevance for the Existing Property Order

Chapter 7: The Relevance of the Concept of Property for Protection Under Constitutional and Private Law

1. The "Threshold Question"

In both South Africa and Germany, the constitutional concept of property differs in some respects from the private law concept. Some proprietary interests also qualify more obviously for constitutional protection than others. This has, of course, implications for the kind of protection afforded to right holders under private law and under the constitutional provisions. In this chapter, this distinction will be discussed with a view to analysing the function of property in the constitutional and private law contexts of Germany and South Africa.

2. Ownership and Property in South Africa

Compared to the extensive attempts at giving content to the concept of property under the German Basic Law, many unanswered questions pertaining to the constitutional concept of property in South Africa still exist. Land reform and redistribution policies in particular still need to be scrutinised. The first socio-political steps towards transforming the South African concept of land have been taken through land-use policies and programmes and innovative legislative reforms.[650] Legal theory

---

[650] E.g. Abolition of Racially Based Land Measures Act 108 of 1991; the Restitution of Land Rights Act 22 of 1994; the Land Reform Pilot Programme of 1995; the Land Affairs General Amendment Act 11 of 1995; the Upgrading

should attempt to place the current socio-political function of property within an acceptable legal theoretical framework and simultaneously set the conceptual scope for future legal and social development.

The meaning of property under the constitutional order has not yet been fully explored in South Africa. Some guidelines do exist, but for the moment the private law remains one of the most important sources of reference in determining the type of protection that could be afforded to property right holders under the constitutional provisions. The private law of property and land rights that preceded the Interim Constitution is vital to a better understanding of legal and social structures inherited from the old order. It will also continue to influence the objectives to be pursued within a constitutional framework.[651] The following paragraphs contain an analysis of the existing private law concept of property in South Africa with the purpose of indicating the possible development of a constitutional concept of property reaching beyond the traditional boundaries of private law.

2.1. Ownership and Property Under Private Law

The South African private law concept of ownership is based mainly on the principles of Roman-Dutch law and influenced to some extent by Pandectism.[652] Unlike the German private law of property, the South African law is not codified. This means that the sources of property law in South Africa stretch beyond that of a written code and supplementary statutes. It includes, for instance, the law of precedent. Nevertheless, the South African and German principles are still comparable, if not identical.

In order to explain the private law system of rights, and the place of ownership within that system, it is necessary to consider the relevance of the theory of subjective rights for the property order. Thereafter, one can determine the characteristics of ownership, the need for reform and the initiatives undertaken in the private law context.

---

of Land Tenure Rights Amendment Act 34 of 1996; the Interim Protection of Informal Land Rights Act 31 of 1996; the Extension of Security of Tenure Act 62 of 1997 etc.

[651] *Gutto,* Property and Land Reform (1995), 57.

[652] *Van der Walt,* 1995 SAJHR 175-179.

2.1.1. General Structure of Ownership and Property Under Private Law

The "law"[653] is, first and foremost, a system of norms of conduct.[654] These norms are formulated by competent bodies in order to regulate the relations between members of a specific society in a just and peaceful manner. The *person* is the basic constitutive element of society. The objective law bestows rights and duties upon a person to be exercised in relation to other persons within a given society.[655] Apart from being a system of rules, the law also constitutes a dual network of legal relationships (i) between the members of a society *(persons / legal subjects)* and objects which they regard as bearing economic value *(legal objects)*, and (ii) among the members of a society mutually *(legal subjects inter se)*. In other words, the *law* also consists of a system of subjective *rights*. Legal norms (the "objective law") determine the content and limits of every *right*.[656]

In the South African private law, the *institution of ownership* is described within the context of this subjective rights theory as a product of (i) the relation between a person (legal subject) and a thing[657] (legal object), on the one hand, and (ii) relations between persons (legal subjects) *inter se*, on the other hand.[658] The legal object is juridically destined to comply with the juridical needs of the legal subject.[659] This is done to the exclusion of third persons. In other words, the individual legal subject (per-

---

[653] I.e. "Objektiewe reg" / Positive law.

[654] *Barnard/Cronjé/Olivier*, The South African Law of Persons and Family Law (1990), 3; *Davel/Jordaan*, Personereg Studentehandboek (1995), 1.

[655] *Van der Vyver* in *Strauss (ed)*, Huldigingsbundel vir WA Joubert (1988), 231.

[656] *Barnard/Cronjé/Olivier*, The South African Law of Persons and Family Law (1990), 4; *Davel/Jordaan*, Personereg Studentehandboek (1995), 1.

[657] In the legal technical sense, the word *thing (res)* signifies a corporeal or tangible object external to persons, which is further an independent entity, subject to juridical control by a legal subject, for whom it is useful and valuable. *Van der Walt/Pienaar*, Introduction (1996), 19; *Van der Merwe*, Sakereg (1989), 23; *Kleyn/Boraine/Du Plessis*, Silberberg & Schoeman's Law of Property (1992), 9.

[658] *Van der Walt*, 1988 De Jure, 17, where *Van Zyl* and *Van der Vyver*'s theory of subjective rights is discussed in relation to ownership.

[659] *Van der Vyver* in *Strauss (ed)*, Huldigingsbundel vir WA Joubert (1988), 231.

son) can by law prohibit other members of the society (other legal subjects / third persons) from infringing his or her entitlements to the legal
object.[660] The holder of the right can, in other words, enforce the right
against anyone and everyone. The legal object in this relation is a thing
(res), and that is why the relation is then classified as a *real right (ius in
re)*. If this real right amounts to a relation between the legal subject and
an object belonging to him or her, the relation is called *ownership (ius in
rem suam)*. If the real right amounts to a relation between a legal subject
and the property of another, a *limited real right (ius in re aliena)* is at
stake.

The relation between these different aspects of ownership within the
theory of subjective rights is exemplified by the decision of *Elektrisiteitsvoorsieningskommissie v Fourie en Andere*.[661] In this decision,
an attempt was made to explain the nature and structure of subjective
rights, because the case raised the question of whether the "right" of a
landowner to the lateral and surface support of the land is a subjective
right, and then more particularly a real right (which can be expropriated), or whether it is something completely different.

The case involved land owned by the first respondent (Fourie). The
other respondents (Matla/the collective enterprise)[662] held prospecting
and mining rights pertaining to coal deposits in the land. In terms of an
agreement between them and the applicant (ESKOM), who was the
public authority responsible for the provision of electricity in South
Africa, all coal mined on the land would be supplied to the applicant,
for the operation of a power station. In order to produce sufficient coal
for that purpose, unconventional high-recovery mining methods would
have had to be applied. This would have disturbed the surface of
Fourie's land. The prospecting and mining agreements between Fourie
and Matla/the collective enterprise provided that the mining operation
should leave the surface of the land intact. ESKOM offered to purchase
the right of lateral and surface support from Fourie. The latter, however, refused to sell these rights separately and offered, instead, to sell
his land as such to ESKOM. As the parties could not agree on a price,
ESKOM subsequently purported to expropriate the owner's right of

---

[660] *Van der Walt*, 1988 De Jure, 17; *Van der Merwe*, Sakereg (1989), 61-63.

[661] *Elektrisiteitsvoorsieningskommissie v Fourie en Andere* 1988 2 SA 627 (T).

[662] The second, third and fourth respondents were mining companies, referred to as "die gesamentlike onderneming" in the decision. The fifth respondent (Matla Coal Ltd) was a coal mining company.

lateral and surface support pursuant to section 43 of the Electricity Act.[663] Thereupon the parties approached the court.

The matters to be determined were (i) whether the "right" of lateral and surface support was susceptible to expropriation in terms of the Electricity Act and (ii) whether ESKOM (which was not the registered holder of mineral and mining rights) was eligible to acquire such a "right." The court decided that a landowner's "right" to lateral and surface support is *not* a separate or independent "right."[664] Kriegler J explained that in this case the issue entailed the relations between two legal subjects and a legal object in the following structure:

It involved the relations between A (Fourie, the owner), and B (Matla/the collective enterprise, the mining right holder), and the thing, C (the land as an entity).[665] Both A (the owner) and B (the mineral right holder) have certain specific entitlements to the land as a consequence of their relation to it. The relation between the owner and the land (AC-relation) contain those entitlements pertaining to ownership. Fourie's entitlements with regard to the land result *ex lege* from his ownership of it. They are "natural," "common" or "incident to the ownership of the soil," but do not necessarily constitute "rights in" the land.[666] The relation between the mining right holder and the land (BC-relation) is far more limited in content and stems from an agreement with the owner (A), enabling the holder of the right (B) to enforce certain entitlements. Certain mutual claims and obligations also exist be-

---

[663] 40 of 1958. In terms of sec. 43 of this act, a "compulsory purchase" may be sought by "an authorised undertaker or any person entitled to cause electricity to be generated or to supply electricity in a particular area" for the acquisition of "such land or any such right in, over or in respect of land as such undertaker or person may require for the exercise of the power." The formalities preceding such a compulsory purchase included a public hearing to be conducted by the Electricity Control Board in order to "determine whether the land or right in question is so required ...". The public hearing was held, pursuant to which the Board reserved its finding and requested ESKOM to seek a declaration of rights in respect of the legal feasibility of expropriating the "right" to surface and lateral support in the specific case.

[664] *Elektrisiteitsvoorsieningskommissie v Fourie en Andere* (note 661 above), 641C-642A.

[665] *Elektrisiteitsvoorsieningskommissie v Fourie en Andere* (note 661 above), 641G-H.

[666] *Elektrisiteitsvoorsieningskommissie v Fourie en Andere* (note 661 above), 641H-I.

tween the owner and the holder of the mineral right (AB-relation). The owner's *entitlements* with regard to the land result *ex lege* from his ownership of it and are, therefore, natural, common or incident to the ownership of the soil. However, they do not necessarily constitute *rights* in the land.[667] It was, henceforth, held that the right to surface and lateral support is, in fact, not really a "right" *stricto sensu* (AC-relation), but rather an incident of the relation between the landowner and the holder of the mineral right (AB-relation).[668]

Kriegler J's explanation shows that the *owner* of a *res* has, through the subject-object relationship between the owner and the thing *(res)*, certain rights and entitlements. In this sense, the term *right* would refer to the claim of a legal subject as against other persons to a legal object; whereas the term *entitlement* would refer to the contents of such a right, denoting what a person, by virtue of having a right to a legal object, may lawfully do with the object of his or her right.[669] The *rights* and *entitlements* of the owner are manifested in different ways in the different relations that exist between the owner and other legal subjects, be that persons with some kind of interest in the thing (like holders of mineral rights), or persons with no interest in the thing whatsoever (like ESKOM, in the *Fourie* case). Lateral and surface support is, for instance, a manifestation of the relation between the landowner as legal subject and the land as legal object, relevant for the relation between the landowner (as legal subject) and the mining right holder (as another legal subject). The landowner's claim to maintenance of the surface is, therefore, inextricably linked to the relation between him or her and the mining right holder (AB-relation). There is a tripartite relation between the mining right holder (legal subject with *ius in re aliena*) and the land (legal object / *res*) and the owner (legal subject with *ius in rem suam / dominium*) in that the owner must permit the mining right holder to exploit the land's mineral resources. However, the relation between the landowner and the holder of mineral rights again requires that the latter should respect the right of ownership — and all the incidents thereof —

---

[667] *Elektrisiteitsvoorsieningskommissie v Fourie en Andere* (note 661 above), 641H-I.

[668] *Elektrisiteitsvoorsieningskommissie v Fourie en Andere* (note 661 above), 641J-642A.

[669] *Van der Vyver*, 1988 SALJ, 6.

of the former. Consequently, this entitlement[670] can only vest in either the owner or the mining right holder. A third party — one with no interest in the use and enjoyment of the land surface — cannot sensibly acquire or hold the use and enjoyment of the *land surface by itself* in any way, because this would strip the entitlement of lateral and surface support of its economic basis.[671]

Ownership thus comprises more than a mere *physical relation* between owner and object, but rather — and more particularly — a network of *juridical relations* between a specific legal subject and other legal subjects in general, to a legal object.[672] Moreover, instead of merely signifying the relation between two (or more) legal subjects *inter se (personal right)*, the *real right* signifies the relation between a *specific person* and a *specific thing*, as well as the relation between a *specific person* and *other legal subjects in general.* Ownership thus symbolises a claim of a specific type: the claim of a legal subject to a particular kind of legal object.[673]

Within these general confines, ownership comprises various aspects. It has a specific "formal make-up" which distinguishes it from other juridical relations. Van der Vyver,[674] in reliance on Dooyeweerd, explains:

> *"Ownership is founded on certain substrata; that is, conditions that must essentially be satisfied before the concept of ownership would be*

---

[670] *Entitlement* is used in the sense that *Van der Vyver* in *Strauss (ed)*, Huldigingsbundel vir WA Joubert (1988), 209 attributes to it: "*entitlement*, which constitutes the contents of a *right* [in the sense of the claim of a legal subject as against other persons to a legal object] and denotes what a person, by virtue of having a right to a particular legal object, may lawfully do with the object of his right."

[671] It would result in the situation where the mining right holder would be exempted from the obligation towards the landowner to respect his or her entitlements of ownership, and that the land would become "*onverkoopbaar, onverbindbaar [en] onverbruikbaar*" (*Elektrisiteitsvoorsieningskommissie v Fourie en Andere* (note 661 above), 640G-H) to the owner. Further, the "holder" of a separate "right" to surface and lateral support (other than the owner or mining right holder) would not be able to enforce it either, since the duties and rights flowing from surface and lateral support (because of it being an incidence of ownership) would not befall him or her.

[672] *Van der Merwe*, Sakereg (1989), 1.

[673] *Van der Vyver*, 1988 SALJ, 9.

[674] *Van der Vyver*, 1988 SALJ, 10. Emphasis added.

possible. For instance, being the claim of a legal subject to a legal object, ownership presupposes the historical *power base included in the notion of disposition ('beskikking') over an object; being a claim enforceable against other persons, ownership is conditioned by the existence* of inter-individual social relations; *the protection afforded to the owner's claim by the law implies relative scarcity, in the* economic *sense, of the objects of ownership; the multiplicity of persons in the owner-third-parties relationship presupposes the modal aspect of* number; *the protection of ownership is confined to a particular territory and thus implies the modal aspect of* space; *the object of ownership is taken from* physical *reality; ownership belongs to living persons and is thus conditional upon the* biotical *[sic] aspect of reality; and so on."*

The essence of ownership is inextricably linked to this formal make-up or basic substrata. These components make up the *structure* of ownership. The *content* of ownership entitlements, related to its history or social basis might be subject to change, but the *structure* as such will remain constant. On the other hand, the *material content* of ownership is comprised in a number of juridical entitlements, which might vary from time to time and case to case. In the following paragraphs, the various ways in which ownership in private law is conceptualised with regard to its *material content* will be discussed.

2.1.2. The Material Content of Ownership in Private Law

A description of the true nature, identity and scope of the institution of ownership that elaborates upon the definition of ownership in the context of the subjective rights theory is problematic. In South Africa, most modern scholarly definitions of ownership follow that of Van der Merwe, being[675]

"[Eiendom is] ... die mees omvattende reg oor 'n saak omdat dit in vergelyking met beperkte saaklike regte, wyer bevoegdhede ten

---

[675] *Van der Merwe*, Sakereg (1989), 173. A similar definition is found in *Van der Merwe*, Law of Things / LAWSA XXVII (1993), par. 104: "Ownership is potentially the most extensive private right that a person can have with regard to a corporeal thing." See *Van der Walt* in *Van der Walt (ed)*, Land Reform and the Future of Landownership in South Africa (1991), 1; *Kroeze*, Between Conceptualism and Constitutionalism (1997), 5; *Kleyn/Boraine/Du Plessis*, Silberberg & Schoeman's Law of Property (1992), 161.

aansien van die saak verleen, hoewel dit steeds aan beperkings on-
derhewig is."

This definition was formulated with reference to: (i) the scope of the owner's capability to enforce the unique ownership entitlements;[676] and (ii) the characteristic qualities of ownership.[677] Thus, it indicates at least two very important aspects of the ownership concept: the owner's capacity to freely act with the *res* at will, but within the limits set by the law,[678] and the unique entitlements accruing to the owner because of his or her specific legal position. As such, Van der Merwe's definition can serve as a starting point for distinguishing the characteristics of ownership[679] from the characteristics of other rights and to ascertain the elements exclusive[680] to ownership. This will be referred to as a "nature-identity description"[681] of ownership. The above definition is also useful where a description of ownership is guided by the ambit of the owner's rights and entitlements.[682] This will be referred to as the "scope description" of ownership. Unfortunately, the combination of two different modes of defining ownership could also confuse the distinctions between a scope-based and a character-based definition of ownership. The following paragraphs provide an overview of the different ways in which the material content of ownership can be defined, and the problems related to it.

---

[676] As opposed to a description of the entitlements themselves (see note 677 below). *Van der Walt*, 1988 De Jure, 22-23.

[677] See *Lewis*, 1985 Acta Juridica, 242-258; and *Honoré* in *Guest (ed)*, Oxford Essays in Jurisprudence (1961), 112-128.

[678] Sometimes referred to as the "*Uitoefeningsaspek*" of ownership. *Van der Walt*, 1988 De Jure, 22-23.

[679] *Van der Walt*, 1988 De Jure, 20-21 mentions the characteristics of abstractness (residuary or indeterminate nature), completeness (totality), elasticity, exclusivity (individuality) and independence (the *moederreg* characteristic).

[680] *Van der Walt*, 1988 De Jure, 21-22 mentions here the owner's capacities to dispose of and alienate the *res*, the right to manage the *res*, the capacity to use and enjoy the *res*, and the capacity to vindicate. In such a definition, it is usual to indicate that ownership entails more than just the mere sum of the owner's entitlements.

[681] The terms used to describe the different approaches to defining the ownership concept are borrowed from *Van der Walt*, 1988 De Jure, 23 ff.

[682] *Van der Walt*, 1988 De Jure, 23; *Gien v Gien* 1979 2 SA 1113 (T).

2.1.2.1. The Scope of Ownership

Attempts at conceptualising the content of ownership focusing on a description of its scope, do not define or classify the entitlements of ownership themselves, but rather concentrate on the ways in which ownership entitlements are exercised. The decision of *Gien v Gien*[683] illustrates a scope-based definition of ownership:

> *"Die uitgangspunt is dat 'n persoon ... met en op sy eiendom kan maak wat hy wil. Hierdie op die oog af ongebonde vryheid is egter 'n halwe waarheid. Die absolute beskikkingsbevoegdheid van 'n eienaar bestaan binne die perke wat die reg daarop plaas."*

The owner can thus do with the thing *(res)* what he or she wants, within the limits set by the law. This means that the material content of the ownership concept is by no means absolute or unlimited in practice. Public and private law limitations are clearly defined in most cases, but they are seen as "unnatural" or "exceptional" burdens on ownership.[684] An owner who exercises his or her rights and entitlements with regard to a thing *(res)* acts in accordance with the law, except when the law renders his or her actions unlawful.

In *Gien v Gien*, unlawful action with the *res* was determined by the *malicious motive*, and the objective unreasonableness, of the owner in the use of an apparatus producing explosive noises at regular intervals on his farm to scare away baboons from a vegetable garden. From the facts of the case it was apparent that the erection of the apparatus was the consequence of a long rivalry between brothers on neighbouring farms. Another indication of objective unreasonableness in the exercise of ownership entitlements was, *inter alia*, the *relatively small benefit* for the owner from the use of the apparatus against the *considerably larger disadvantage* and discomfort for his neighbour.[685]

---

[683] *Gien v Gien* (note 682 above), 1120C-E. Translation: The point of departure is that a person can do with and upon his property as he [sic] likes. This apparently unlimited freedom is, however, only partially true. The absolute capacity of an owner in dealing with his property exists within the limits of the law.

[684] *Van der Walt*, 1988 De Jure, 23.

[685] *Gien v Gien* (note 682 above), 1121 F-G.

2.1.2.2. The Nature and Identity of Ownership

In a description of the nature and identity of ownership, two aspects are important: (i) the characteristics usually pertaining to ownership; and (ii) the entitlements connected to the right of ownership. In the following paragraphs, a brief overview is provided of the problems resulting from such a description.

2.1.2.2.1. Characteristics of Ownership

In the "traditional" private law property order, ownership is sometimes described as being characterised by certain qualities: originality, elasticity, duration and independence. These qualities then, according to the description, give the institution a position superior to all other rights, whether real or personal. Other characteristics, which are also mentioned in this context, include totality, absoluteness and exclusivity. An overview of the different characteristics influencing the nature and identity of ownership indicates that this institution indeed takes a hierarchical position superior to that of other limited real rights.[686] However, it also indicates that scholars by no means agree on the basic material elements constituting ownership.

(i) The term *originality* refers to the fact that ownership is described as the right from which all other real rights can be derived. Therefore, ownership is sometimes described as a so-called *"moederreg"* or "mother right."[687] An owner has the ability to dispose of many of the incidents of the use and enjoyment of his or her *res* by granting limited real rights to others, without losing the ownership itself in the process. As such, ownership is an abstract right: it always will be more than the mere sum total of the entitlements pertaining to it.[688] Another element of this characteristic is that, because any collection of ownership entitlements per se would not necessarily constitute ownership itself, own-

---

[686] *Van der Walt*, 1988 De Jure, 19 refers to this aspect of the definition as the *"Identiteitsaspek."* This entails the definition of ownership according to the characteristics that distinguishes it from other (limited) real rights.

[687] *Van der Merwe*, Sakereg (1989), 175; *Kleyn/Boraine/Du Plessis*, Silberberg & Schoeman's Law of Property (1992), 162.

[688] *Van der Walt*, 1988 De Jure, 20; contra *Honoré* in *Guest (ed)*, Oxford Essays in Jurisprudence (1961), 107, 112, 113; *Lewis*, 1985 Acta Juridica, 241-243.

ership is a complete right. This is sometimes referred to as the characteristic of *totality*.[689]

(ii) The *elasticity* of ownership is also referred to by some authors as its *residuary character*.[690] In terms of this characteristic, all other real rights pertaining to specific *res* are viewed as unnatural burdens on ownership. When these other real rights (that always infringe the rights and entitlements of the owner of the specific *res*) expire, the owner's entitlements revert to their original content. Thus, no matter how many entitlements the owner disposes of, a reversionary right to those entitlements is always retained. Once those entitlements are extinguished, the ownership automatically becomes unencumbered again. This makes the concept of ownership inherently elastic.[691] Lewis[692] considers this characteristic as the distinguishing element of ownership.

(iii) In principle, ownership is also *not of limited duration* like many other rights. Other (limited) real rights expire after a certain time: Usufruct, for instance, expires with the death of the holder of the right; real security rights (like pledge and mortgage) expire with repayment of the debts on which these rights depend.[693]

(iv) Van der Walt[694] describes the characteristic of *exclusivity* as one of the most important elements of ownership. This characteristic entails that the owner can exclude others from the occupation, use and enjoyment of his or her property.[695] In this way, the owner exercises a "unique power of individual moral autonomy." In any contest about control, ownership is always superior to any other right.

---

[689] *Cowen*, New Patterns of Landownership (1984), 8 refers to this characteristic under the latin title of *plena in re potestas*. See also the description of the various entitlements to ownership in *Lewis*, 1985 Acta Juridica, 243-258 and the definition of ownership in *Gien v Gien* (note 682 above), 1120C et seq.; *Van der Walt*, 1988 De Jure, 20.

[690] *Kleyn/Boraine/Du Plessis*, Silberberg & Schoeman's Law of Property (1992), 163.

[691] *Van der Merwe*, Sakereg (1989), 175. See also the discussion of the viewpoints of various authors in *Lewis*, 1985 Acta Juridica, 257-258 concerning the primary importance attached to this characteristic.

[692] *Lewis*, 1985 Acta Juridica, 257.

[693] *Van der Merwe*, Sakereg (1989), 175.

[694] *Van der Walt*, 1995 SAJHR, 179. See also *Chetty v Naidoo* 1974 3 SA 13 (A), 20-23.

[695] *Van der Walt*, 1988 De Jure, 21.

(v) The *independence* quality entails that ownership (because it is considered as the right from which all other real rights originate) needs no further legal construction for its existence. Unlike limited real rights, for instance, ownership is not dependent on or derived from any other right. Van der Merwe[696] describes this as the distinguishing element of ownership.

2.1.2.2.2. Entitlements Pertaining to Ownership

Sometimes ownership is also described by focussing on the entitlements that pertain to it: that is, the *entitlements that cannot be transferred to holders of real rights* and thus cause ownership to be more than the mere sum of the entitlements that *can* be transferred to other right holders.[697] Such a description implies that these non-transferable entitlements are characteristic of ownership and distinguish it from other real rights. The following entitlements are mentioned in this regard:[698]

(i) The owner can *dispose* of the *res*. This means he or she can alienate, abuse or destroy it. It also entails that the owner can decide who may use or control the *res*, and therefore includes the owner's capacity to grant rights in the *res* to third parties.

(ii) The maxim *nemo plus iuris ad alium transferre potest quam ipse habet*, has the consequence that only the owner has the capacity to alienate his or her ownership as such. Holders of limited real rights might be able to alienate their real rights or the entitlements pertaining to it, but ownership remains with the owner. Ownership is, in other words, "superior to" limited real rights. The holder of a limited real right cannot alienate more than that which he or she has.

(iii) The owner can *vindicate* the *res*. This means that he or she can claim the res from any person, merely by proving that he or she is owner thereof, and that it is under the control of the person against whom he or she institutes the claim. The onus is then on the defendant to prove the lawfulness of his or her control.

---

[696] *Van der Merwe*, Sakereg (1989), 176.

[697] *Lewis*, 1985 Acta Juridica, 243; *Honoré* in *Guest (ed)*, Oxford Essays in Jurisprudence (1961), 107.

[698] *Van der Walt*, 1988 De Jure, 21-22. The owner's capacity to use and enjoy the *res* technically does not belong to this categorisation, as it can be transferred by the owner to another legal subject.

2.1.2.3. Problems Arising from Attempts to Define the Content of
Ownership

Several problems are encountered in defining the material content of
ownership. The reason for this is that the choice of description of the
ownership concept that focuses either on the nature and identity or the
scope of ownership is closely related to the theoretical approach that
forms the basis of private law rights.

Van der Vyver[699] points out that the distinction between real and personal rights can be based on *the manner in which real and personal
rights are enforced.* That would entail an application of the *personality
doctrine.* In such a case, emphasis is more readily placed upon the *obligations of persons other than the holder of the right* to respect (in the
case of real rights) or to execute (in the case of personal rights) the right.
In terms of the personality doctrine, real rights distinguish themselves
from personal rights by the fact that they operate *vis-à-vis* all persons
generally and not only against particular individuals (or groups of persons).[700] As the personality doctrine supports the absoluteness of real
rights in the context of enforceability, it shows preference for a *scope*
description of ownership.

The distinction between real and personal rights can also be based on
*the objects of the rights as portraying the essential difference between
real and personal rights.*[701] This would entail an application of the *classical theory* of rights. In such a case, emphasis is placed on the *object of
the right rather than on its absoluteness or relativity.*[702] A definition of

---

[699] *Van der Vyver* in *Strauss (ed),* Huldigingsbundel vir WA Joubert (1988),
222.

[700] See *Van der Vyver* in *Strauss (ed),* Huldigingsbundel vir WA Joubert
(1988), 220; *Van der Merwe,* Sakereg (1989), 61 where the view of *Von Savigny,*
System des heutigen römischen Rechts (1840), vol I at 373, is quoted as example
of the personality doctrine. See also *Van der Walt/Pienaar,* Introduction
(1996), 39.

[701] *Van der Vyver* in *Strauss (ed),* Huldigingsbundel vir WA Joubert (1988),
222.

[702] Usually, the view of *Landsberg,* Das Recht des bürgerlichen Gesetzbuches vom 18. VIII. 1896 (1906), vol I at 68 is quoted to portray the classical
rights theory's point of departure: Real rights afford legal control over things,
creditor's rights afford legal control over persons. See *Van der Merwe,* Sakereg
(1989), 62 note 27. However, in the work of *Van der Linden,* Regtsgeleerd,
Practicaal en Koopmans Handboek (1806), 1 6 1, that was in principle also
based on the classical theory, mention is made in a secondary sense of the ab-

ownership in terms of its nature and identity is usually based on the classical theory of rights.

The divergent theories underlying the nature of private law rights, however, create various problems in defining the concept of ownership. For one, a focus on the different entitlements of ownership may lend support to the idea that ownership consists merely of the sum of its entitlements at a given point in time. Another related problem is the question of which characteristics of ownership are decisive for its material content. The apparent absoluteness of ownership, arising from a description of its scope, could also be problematic. These problems could have implications for the formulation of a constitutional concept of property and deserves closer scrutiny.

2.1.2.3.1. Ownership is more than a Sum of its Entitlements

An attempt to describe ownership by means of the different entitlements that it comprises, might lead to the view that ownership equals the sum of its entitlements, or that ownership constitutes a "bundle" of smaller component rights. According to this *bundle of rights theory*, property should be regarded as a variable set of legally enforceable claims upon resources, instead of a simple claim pertaining to a thing *(res)*.[703] A property right may consist of a number of constituent rights, for example the right to hold, the right to use, the right to occupy, the right to alienate, the right to bequeath, and so on. Each of these would then be a separate property right, a separate "stick in the bundle" or, possibly, according to some authors, a separate *right in property*.[704] Property rights are, thus, conceived as economic relationships between legal subjects with regard to the exploitation of natural resources.

The Appellate Division implicitly adopted this trend in the case of *Sandton Town Council v Erf 89 Sandown Extension 2 (Pty) Ltd*,[705] by remarking that

---

solute and relative operation of real rights and personal rights respectively. See *Van der Vyver* in *Strauss (ed)*, Huldigingsbundel vir WA Joubert (1988), 221.

[703] *Davis/Cheadle/Haysom*, Fundamental Rights in the Constitution - Commentary and Cases (1997), 241.

[704] *Budlender* in *Budlender/Latsky/Roux*, New Land Law (1998), ch. 1, 16.

[705] *Sandton Town Council v Erf 89 Sandown Extension 2 (Pty) Ltd* (note 68 above).

> *"[o]wnership of land connotes the existence of an aggregate of distinct and valuable rights inhering in the owner. These include not only the right to exclusive possession and the right of disposal, but also the right to the use and enjoyment of the land for all lawful purposes."*

The facts concerned a claim for compensation[706] against the town council after it had laid stormwater pipes over an erf belonging to the respondent. The court had to decide whether the town council had to reward the respondent for damages other than for losses due to direct physical damage to the land. In this case consequential losses, like diminution of the land's value, sustained as a result of the municipality installing a drainage system on the property affected, were at stake. It was held that the presence of the pipes had rendered the exploitation of the business rights attaching to the relevant piece of land less profitable to the respondent. Therefore the value of the land was reduced. Consequently, the respondent company (present owner) had been partially divested (without its consent) of one of its "rights to" ownership.[707] It was further held that the action taken by the appellant was clearly akin to expropriation.

The possibility of alienating or expropriating specific "portions" of ownership, separately from the ownership in a specific thing *(res)* itself, seems to be an issue that keeps recurring in case law and academic writing.[708] The treatment of this issue under the new constitutional order in South Africa will be dealt with in the following chapters. However, a few remarks need to be made concerning the view that property consists only of different component entitlements.

The *Fourie* case[709] pointed out the difference between, on the one hand, the structural relationship of a legal subject and a legal object as against third persons, and, on the other hand, the entitlement of the owner (and of other persons in the case of certain limited real rights) to use and

---

[706] In terms of sec. 134(b) of the Local Government Ordinance 17 of 1939 (T), which entitled an owner of property, over or on which a drainage system was installed by the municipal council, to claim compensation "for any damage done."

[707] *Sandton Town Council v Erf 89 Sandown Extension 2 (Pty) Ltd* (note 68 above), 129F-H.

[708] *Lewis*, 1985 Acta Juridica, 243; *Honoré* in *Guest (ed)*, Oxford Essays in Jurisprudence (1961), 107.

[709] *Elektrisiteitsvoorsieningskommissie v Fourie en Andere* (note 661 above).

enjoy the thing *(res)* concerned. Only the structural relationship can be called *ownership*.[710] The owner can transfer a portion of the ownership (or several entitlements pertaining to ownership) to a third party, making it legally permissible for that party to exercise the entitlement(s) concerned. That entitlement "belongs" then to a person other than the owner, by virtue of a right other than ownership *(ius in re aliena)*. However, the entitlement does not change its nature. It simply fits into another, different kind of structural relationship, which does not qualify as *ownership*. Van der Merwe[711] explains this phenomenon with reference to the granting of servitudes by the owner to third parties:

> *"Bepaalde inherente bevoeghede [sic] van eiendomsreg kan wel aan 'n ander oorgedra word deur die vestiging van 'n saaklike reg. Maar selfs wanneer 'n eienaar byvoorbeeld 'n serwituut aan iemand anders verleen, staan hy nie sommige van sy regte aan iemand anders af nie. Hy stem slegs toe dat sy eiendomsbevoegdhede op 'n bepaalde manier opgeskort word. Wanneer 'n serwituut tot niet gaan, val die beperking weg en groei die eiendom weer tot sy volle omvang uit. Daar is geen sprake van teruggawe van verleende regte nie."*

The entitlements comprising ownership are, therefore, viewed as a unity, and the fact that some of those entitlements might at a given point in time be lawfully enforced by someone other than the owner, does not amount to the conclusion that ownership equals the sum of its entitlements and nothing more. Such a viewpoint loses sight of the unique structural relation (between the owner, third parties and the *res)* which forms the basis of the concept of ownership.

2.1.2.3.2. The Seminal Characteristic of Ownership

In analysing the description of the different characteristics of ownership, scholars differ as to which single characteristic is the most impor-

---

[710] *Van der Vyver*, 1988 SALJ, 8.

[711] *Van der Merwe*, Sakereg (1989), 174. Translation: "Certain inherent entitlements of ownership may indeed be transferred to another by the vesting of a real right. However, even when an owner confers a servitude, for instance, to someone else, he does not concede his rights to someone else. He merely agrees that his ownership entitlements are restricted in a certain manner. When the servitude terminates, the restriction falls away and ownership grows back to its full scope. Returning of conceded rights is not at stake here."

tant. Van der Merwe[712] chooses the independence quality of ownership as the distinguishing characteristic; Van der Walt[713] focuses on exclusivity; and Lewis[714] on elasticity. However, no single characteristic can by itself distinguish ownership from other legal institutions. It is the combination of all the characteristics that secure the superior position of ownership in private law.

The material content of ownership depends on all these characteristics, because they are all indispensable components for the ownership concept. Neither the originality nor the elasticity of ownership is *per se* sufficient to define ownership. Likewise, the independence characteristic is distinctive only in relation to the characteristics of originality, elasticity and duration. In addition, the feature of ownership making it endure for an indeterminable time also arises from — and can only be effective within — the sphere of the other inter-related distinctive qualities of ownership. The different characteristics are, therefore, inextricably linked.

2.1.2.3.3. The Absoluteness of Ownership

It has been indicated that the definition of the material content of ownership in private law depends to a large extent on whether the classical theory or the personality doctrine forms the basic premise. In the case of application of the personality doctrine, the question regarding the absoluteness in the context of enforceability has never been clearly distinguished from the question of absoluteness in the context of the owners' entitlements. Any discussion about the content of ownership that does not recognise this delicate distinction, could fall prey to the mistaken assumption[715] that ownership is by nature unlimited.[716]

Absoluteness, being one of the basic general principles underlying the law of things,[717] indicates the security provided to all holders of real rights. This principle places the holder of a real right, therefore also the

---

[712] *Van der Merwe*, Sakereg (1989), 176.

[713] *Van der Walt*, 1995 SAJHR, 179.

[714] *Lewis*, 1985 Acta Juridica, 257.

[715] *Van der Merwe*, Sakereg (1989), 173 expressly warns against such an assumption.

[716] See e.g. *Kroeze*, Between Conceptualism and Constitutionalism (1997), 5.

[717] See *Van der Merwe*, Sakereg (1989), 10-16.

owner, in an unassailable juridical relation regarding the enforcement of the right. However, when it is averred that ownership by nature can endure even the most severe limitations without being mutilated by them, reference is made only to the characteristic "elasticity" of ownership.[718] Together with the other characteristics of originality, duration, independence, exclusivity and totality – the "elasticity" of ownership enables the owner to exercise quite extensive powers over the object of the right and over fellow legal subjects. But even if the owner has quite extensive powers over the object, the exercise of the ownership entitlements does not make ownership *by nature* absolute.

Viewed from a scope-perspective,[719] ownership becomes a mechanism through which the individual can preserve and propagate the idea of freedom, which is one of the basic entitlements of a legal subject. However, legal subjectivity also incorporates the notion of responsibility of the legal subject, which has, of course, implications for the understanding of the concept of ownership. The distinction between the enforceability of an owner's right and the content of the right of ownership should not be disregarded. Though it may be true that an owner can enforce his or her right of ownership against the entire world, it does not provide the owner with an unlimited capacity to act with the *res* at will. The owner's capacity to exercise ownership entitlements is still limited by law and by the rights of others.

2.1.3. Limitations on the Content of Ownership

In the present century, growing socialist tendencies, increased control of property in the spheres of public law in general and administrative law in particular, and expansion of rights of parties other than the owner,[720] have contributed considerably to the demise of the once sacred, inviolable right of ownership. Ownership has been regarded as sacred and inviolable since the French Revolution, because of the individualism proclaimed through the natural law ideology of the late eighteenth and early nineteenth centuries and the then prevalent *laissez-faire* principle of economic control.[721] Nevertheless, it should be obvious that no

---

718 *Van der Merwe*, Sakereg (1989), 175. See 180 above.

719 See *Van der Walt*, 1988 De Jure, 23 ff. See also 178 ff. above.

720 E.g. Lessees, possessors etc.

721 *Van der Merwe*, Sakereg (1989), 176.

community can tolerate ownership literally unrestricted in its content. For the sake of socio-political morality, ownership needs to be restricted to some extent.[722]

The significance of the categories of limitations on ownership existing under common and statutory law lies therein that the interests of the community in general, or specific groups within the community, dictate how private property should under certain circumstances be regulated or limited by the state or through legislation. In this manner, the question of protection of private property under the Constitution becomes relevant. Therefore, the different categories of limitations on ownership must be kept in mind when determining the extent to which the protection of ownership in terms of the constitutional property clauses overlap with the protection of property under private law.

There are numerous examples of limitations on ownership entitlements in private law. The scope of this work does not allow a complete descriptive catalogue of the existing limitations and the different categories of limitations will be discussed only briefly. These categories are (i) limitation of ownership by contractual rights and limited real rights; (ii) limitation of ownership by the rules of neighbour law; and (iii) statutory limitation of ownership.

(i) An owner's entitlements can be limited by *contractual rights* that third parties have against such an owner.[723] Limitations like these are usually created by agreement between the owners and the holders of such personal rights. These contractual rights are enforceable against the owner personally, and can entail any infringement on the property rights of the owner that is not *contra bonos mores*, impossible or illegal in terms of the law of contract. Rights like these, being enforceable against a specific owner in his or her personal capacity, do not influence the essence of the ownership institution as such, although the infringement on a specific owner's entitlements could be quite extensive. The *limited real rights* that other parties may have regarding the res can also limit an owner's entitlements. Such limitations are enforceable against the owner *qua* owner,[724] and because such limitations constitute *subtractions from the dominium* they are enforceable against all subsequent owners of the *res*. For this reason the owner's entitlements are curtailed to a larger extent than in the former case, although the infringement on

---

[722] *Birks*, 1985 Acta Juridica, 1.

[723] *Van der Walt/Pienaar*, Introduction (1996), 117.

[724] *Ex parte Geldenhuys* 1926 OPD 155, 164.

ownership by a limited real right might in content be similar to a personal right. In the case of *iura in re aliena* the limitation attaches to the object of the right to ownership and not to the person of the owner. Therefore, the ownership in a specific *res* is in principle limited until the *res* is destroyed or until the limited real right comes to an end. In the case of limited real rights pertaining to immovable property, registration of these rights against the relevant title deed will have the effect that subsequent owners will also be bound.

(ii) Neighbour law can also limit an owner's entitlements. The owner's exercise of entitlements in respect of land is limited in the interest of the community of neighbouring landowners or users of adjacent or nearby land. The principle *sic utere tuo ut alienum non laedas* which determines that land must be used in such a way that other persons are not prejudiced or burdened, forms the basis of this branch of law.[725] Neighbour law is based, on the one hand, on the principle of nuisance[726] and therefore includes the criterion of *reasonable use*, limiting an owner's entitlements with regard to the property to those acts that should be tolerated by the neighbours, as set out in the case of *Gien v Gien*.[727] On the other hand, there are also some specific (or "traditional") remedies of neighbour liability (like lateral support, encroachments, overhanging branches and interference with the natural flow of water).[728] According to these "traditional" remedies of neighbour liability, the owner could under certain circumstances be liable to compensate the neighbour on the basis of damages already incurred. These remedies usually approximate the aquilian action, but with a narrower scope. The bases of liability accordingly vary depending on the nature of the specific remedy and the requirements applicable.[729] However, the "traditional" remedies of

---

[725] *Van der Merwe*, Sakereg (1989), 185. See also *Holland v Scott* 1882 EDC 307.

[726] This principle is derived from the tort principles of English law. *Van der Merwe*, Sakereg (1989), 197; *Kleyn/Boraine/Du Plessis*, Silberberg & Schoeman's Law of Property (1992), 168.

[727] *Gien v Gien* (note 682 above).

[728] These were mostly handed down from Roman law, but were in some cases also influenced by English law. Some are of English origin. See *Van der Merwe*, Sakereg (1989), 197-213; *Kleyn/Boraine/Du Plessis*, Silberberg & Schoeman's Law of Property (1992), 168-193; *Van der Walt/Pienaar*, Introduction (1996), 120-131.

neighbour liability are mostly aimed at preventing pending (or further) harm by invoking a prohibitory interdict or declaratory order.

(iii) Finally, a number of *ordinary statutory provisions* limit the owner's entitlements regarding the use of property, usually in the interest of the community. Here a distinction can be made between limitations on movable and immovable property. In the case of *movable property*, the use of certain objects like motor vehicles as well as radio transmitters, radios and television sets are regulated by the National Road Traffic Act[730] and the Telecommunications Act[731] respectively. The Animals Protection Act[732] prohibits owners of animals to abuse, neglect, over-burden, overwork or frighten their animals and makes such behaviour criminally punishable. The possession, acquisition or distribution of certain objects, like (i) oil and precious metals by private individuals in terms of the Minerals Act;[733] (ii) certain photographic material in the Films and Publications Act;[734] (iii) certain substances in terms of the Abuse of Dependence-producing Substances and Rehabilitation Centres Act;[735] and (iv) objectionable publications or objects in terms of the Publications Act; [736] is also prohibited. The Arms and Ammunition Act[737] also limits the entitlements of owners of weapons or ammunition

---

[729] In the case of a claim for the loss of lateral support, the owner is vicariously liable for damages already suffered by the neighbour. In the case of encroachments, the award of damages is but one alternative at the disposal of the court, which is expected to balance the interests of both parties involved and to make a discretionary order. In the case of the *actio aquae pluviae arcendae* (which is a remedy for a prohibitive interdict), the payment of damages only becomes relevant if damage has been incurred after *litis contestatio*. Damages can be claimed with the *interdictum quod vi aut clam*, but, again, on the basis of vicarious liability. A person is also entitled to damages caused by dilapidated buildings, but only if a notice of protest was issued in terms of the *cautio damni infecti*, which is then also the basis of this claim for damages. *Van der Merwe, Sakereg* (1989), 197-212.

[730] 93 of 1996.

[731] 103 of 1996.

[732] 71 of 1962.

[733] 50 of 1991.

[734] 65 of 1996.

[735] 140 of 1992.

[736] 65 of 1996.

[737] 75 of 1969. See also Arms and Ammunition Amendment Act 15 of 1999.

in various ways. Several limiting mechanisms exist also in the case of *immovable property*. The Expropriation Act[738] and the Physical Planning Act[739] are two examples of specific legislation that has far-reaching consequences for the limitation (or even dispossession) of the property rights of landowners. Besides these, the Environment Conservation Act,[740] the Advertising on Roads and Ribbon Development Act,[741] the Agricultural Pests Act[742] and the Conservation of Agricultural Resources Act[743] limits the entitlements of owners of rural land. Various provincial town planning ordinances[744], as well as legislation dealing with township establishment,[745] the nature and standard of buildings,[746] and other issues[747] affect the entitlements of owners of urban land.

2.1.4. Import of Private Law for Property and Ownership in Constitutional Law

In the light of the debate concerning horizontal application of fundamental rights on private law relations, one should examine the definition of property in both private and constitutional law. The difference between property in private law and in the constitutional context is closely related to the fact that property has a different function in each

---

[738] 63 of 1975.

[739] 125 of 1991.

[740] 73 of 1989.

[741] 21 of 1940.

[742] 36 of 1983.

[743] 43 of 1983.

[744] E.g. the Town Planning and Township Ordinance 15 of 1986 (Transvaal); Land Use Planning Ordinance 15 of 1985 (Cape); Townships Ordinance 9 of 1969 (OFS); and the Town Planning Ordinance 27 of 1949 (Natal).

[745] E.g. the Less Formal Township Establishment Act 113 of 1991; Provision of Land and Assistance Act 126 of 1993 and the Development Facilitation Act 67 of 1995.

[746] E.g. National Building Regulations and Building Standards Act 103 of 1977.

[747] The Atmospheric Pollution Prevention Act 45 of 1965; Black Communities Development Act 3 of 1966 and 4 of 1984; Health Act 63 of 1977 and the Slums Act 76 of 1979 (which has been repealed by sec. 20 of the Housing Act 107 of 1997).

of these areas of the law. In private law, the interests of owners are protected against interference by third parties. The purpose of property as a fundamental right is to protect the holders of property rights against interference with their rights by the state, and to determine the circumstances under which such interference would be justified in the interests of the public in general. If this divide is ignored, the whole of private law might be invaded by the notion of property.[748] Nevertheless, it is noticeable that the definition of ownership in private law broadened over a number of years. The circumstances giving rise to this broadening of the private law definition need to be examined in order to determine the meaning of private law property for the constitutional context.

The past two decades have witnessed a considerable expansion of the concept of ownership under private law. The Sectional Titles Act[749] and the "new patterns of landownership" are illustrations of this tendency.

(i) Since the introduction of the first South African Sectional Titles Act on 10 June 1971 (and even more so after the coming into force of this act on 31 March 1973), the legislature has set the pace for fundamental changes to property law, more particularly the law pertaining to landownership.[750] The enactment of sectional title legislation led to the first reconsideration of the common law concept of ownership, as it existed at that time. Initially, the question of whether sectional ownership could qualify as "true" ownership had to be resolved. In considering this issue, Van der Merwe[751] declared that the concept of *dominium* as it was understood in the eighteenth and early nineteenth century cannot pass muster any more. In the eighteenth and early nineteenth century, ownership was regarded as a sacred, inviolable right. All limitations on the ownership concept, albeit in neighbour law or public law, were regarded as irreconcilable with the true nature of this institution. However, it was recognised that the institution of ownership has been irreversibly altered by several factors such as the industrial revolution, the rise of the workers' classes and the two world wars. Indicating that sectional ownership should be seen as true ownership against the background of a more dynamic definition of ownership that takes the particular nature of the object of the right,

---

[748] *Kleyn*, 1996 SAPR/PL, 423.

[749] Act 66 of 1971. This has in the mean time been replaced by the Sectional Titles Act 95 of 1986. The latter has also been amended several times.

[750] *Cowen*, New Patterns of Landownership (1984), 12.

[751] See 187 above.

as well as the extent of the limitations upon the right for the sake of the public weal into account, Van der Merwe declared:[752]

> *"Die talryke privaatregtelike en publiekregtelike beperkings wat in die jongste tyd in belang van die gemeenskap aan eiendom en veral aan grondeiendom opgelê word, moet dus nie as onverenigbaar met die eiendomsbegrip beskou word nie, maar as omstandighede wat die omvang en inhoud van eiendom in 'n konkrete geval bepaal."*

Van der Merwe's analysis of the sectional title legislation thus anticipated the acceptance by the legislature of an ownership concept that includes a distinct social function, as opposed to one supporting a theory of individualism. Although several acts and regulations contain provisions limiting the ownership concept, the Sectional Titles Act was the first concise reflection of direct approval by the South African legislature of the "new" ownership concept, namely ownership as a right exercised against acknowledgement of the correlative duties towards a community. In the narrow sense, duties to the community would in this context indicate a sectional owner's responsibility towards the other sectional owners (in the sectional title community). However, the interests of the community at large are also considered through sectional title legislation, particularly its interest in affordable housing and the expansion of the category of home owners in the community.

(ii) Since the coming into force of the Sectional Titles Act, several alterations to the common law concept of ownership as it existed in South Africa[753] were made to accommodate specific contemporary needs or to solve specific problems connected with the public weal.[754]

---

[752] *Van der Merwe*, 1974 THRHR, 122.

[753] E.g. Share Block Control Act 59 of 1980 introducing share block schemes, Property Time-Sharing Control Act 75 of 1983 introducing property time-sharing. More examples of such an extension of the common law concept of landownership in the shape of air space development, nature conservation and planning laws followed.

[754] *Van der Walt* in *Van der Walt* (ed), Land Reform (1991), 27. See also *Van der Walt*, 1999 Koers, 259-294, where it is argued that the statutory deviations from the "traditional" system of property law in terms of private law, like the "new patterns of landownership", served the purposes of high-finance development and the provision of upper-class housing, holiday accommodation and commercial premises and that non of these developments were really aimed at serving the needs of the underprivileged, homeless, poor or dispossessed under the apartheid regime. They also did not really constitute an alteration of the underlying principles of private property law, as all alterations could still be clas-

This development has become known as the "new patterns of landownership," on the basis of a paper delivered by Cowen at the University of the Witwatersrand in 1984.[755] Cowen's presentation gave the development of a dynamic concept of ownership in South Africa a new force. It attempted to adjust the "well-trodden and somewhat outdated territory of established and traditional theory"[756] of ownership, defined and described in terms of the terminological, theoretical and dogmatic legacy of Grotius, Van Leeuwen and Van der Linden. In Cowen's opinion the concept of ownership was partly extended by these "new patterns of landownership,"[757] while it was simultaneously subjected to a growing tendency to restrict landownership in the interests of society.[758]

Several scholars[759] have, since these early observations in the context of sectional title legislation and the "new patterns of landownership," commented on the concept of ownership. Numerous new ideas have been explored. Yet, most writers seem to agree that ownership should be a functional institution, thereby indicating that the definition, nature, content, characteristics and protection of ownership are all influenced and shaped by the social implications of this institution, as well as by prevalent ideologies and beliefs. They have explored the possibility of a diversification of property rights within the field of private law,[760] and indicated repeatedly that ownership is not only characterised by the existence of rights and entitlements accruing to the individual owners, but also by inherent duties, limitations and responsibilities toward

---

sified within the existing hierarcical system of land rights. It is also argued that most of the early land reform efforts, especially those introduced by the former National Party government in 1991, did not succeed in breaking down the structural and dogmatic privilege of the common-law ownership paradigm.

[755] See in general *Cowen*, New Patterns of Landownership (1984); *Van der Walt* in *Van der Walt (ed)*, Land Reform and the Future of Landownership in South Africa (1991), 3, 26.

[756] *Van der Walt* in *Van der Walt (ed)*, Land Reform and the Future of Landownership in South Africa (1991), 1.

[757] *Cowen*, New Patterns of Landownership (1984), 15-50.

[758] *Cowen*, New Patterns of Landownership (1984), 51-80.

[759] E.g. *Pienaar*, 1986 TSAR, 295-308; *Corder/Davis* in *Corder (ed)*, Law & Social Practice (1988), 1-30; *Van der Walt*, 1995 TSAR, 322-345; *Van der Walt*, 1995 SAPR/PL, 1-30; *Van der Walt*, 1995 SAJHR, 169-206; *Lewis*, 1992 SAJHR, 389-430.

[760] *Van der Walt*, 1995 TSAR, 322-345; *Van der Walt*, 1995 SAPR/PL, 1-30; *Van der Walt*, 1995 SAJHR, 169-206.

society. However, the question as to the exact meaning of the "social function" of ownership is only indirectly referred to.

The constitutional protection and regulation of property could solve some of the problems in this regard. Private and constitutional law will most definitely influence each other, and the incorporation of elements from customary property law can be expected. Moreover, in view of the fact that direct horizontal application of the fundamental-rights provisions of the Final Constitution on all law, the constitutional property provisions would for reasons of policy be applicable directly to certain private law relations.[761] A glance at the development of the German concept of property clearly indicates that the definition of property is not the exclusive domain of private law.[762] In the following paragraphs, the development of a constitutional concept of property in South African law will be discussed, with a view to comparison with the German law.

2.2. The Constitutional Concept of Property

The expansion of the property concept in South African private law provides a useful stepping stone for incorporation of the constitutional definition of property into the property concept. Moreover, the constitutional protection and regulation of property would avoid entrenching property rights acquired during the apartheid era where their protection can no longer be justified as a matter of public policy or morality.[763] Ideally, a constitutional concept of property should, in the South African context, limit the scope of property to advance economic development. This ideal is not easily attainable. The realisation of this task is complicated by the fact that the property clauses of the Interim and Final Constitutions provide few guidelines, if any, for defining the constitutional concept of property.

The South African constitutional property concept is even more complex than its German counterpart, owing to the incorporation of the land reform and restitution objectives in the constitutions from the out-

---

[761] *Kroeze*, 1994 SAPR/PL, 324 quoting *Rautenbach/Malherbe*, Staatsreg (1993), 114.

[762] BVerfGE 58, 300 *(Naßauskiesung)*, 339.

[763] *Chaskalson/Lewis* in *Chaskalson/Kentridge/Klaaren et. al. (eds)*, Constitutional Law of South Africa (1996), ch. 31, 4-5.

set. Furthermore, neither the Interim Constitution nor the Final Constitution provides a definition of "property." In fact, different terms are employed in the Interim Constitution and Final Constitution to refer to proprietary relations protected by them.

2.2.1. Meaning of the Term "Rights in Property"

Section 28 IC used the term *rights in property*[764] and section 25 FC uses the term *property*,[765] neither of which are properly defined in either of the constitutions. The judiciary and legislature have to give content and meaning to these terms, depending on the supposed function of the constitutional property guarantee in the South African society. The uncertainty concerning the function of property in the Constitution is apparent when these terms are interpreted.

The term *rights in property*, which was used in section 28 IC, was puzzling from the start,[766] since this term was not known or acknowledged in either private or public law.[767] This caused Chaskalson and Lewis,[768] among others, to warn against the dogmatic inconsistencies that could flow from such uncertainty:

> *"Although it has up till now been clear in South Africa that incorporeals can be the objects of rights and are regarded as property, is this changed by the phrasing of s 28, which allows for the right to acquire and hold rights in property? Can one have a right to a right in a right? The answer should clearly be yes: but the awkward wording may leave room for the argument that only corporeals are protected."*

The origin of the phrase *rights in property* was also not clear. Presumably the phrase was inserted in the constitutional text to ensure that *property* was not equated with *ownership*, thus widening the scope of constitutional protection to rights beyond those protected in terms of

---

[764] *Regte in eiendom* in the Afrikaans text.

[765] *Eiendom* in the Afrikaans text.

[766] *Chaskalson*, 1994 SAJHR, 131-139; *Van der Walt*, 1994 THRHR, 181-203; *Murphy*, 1995 SAPR/PL, 107-130.

[767] *Chaskalson/Lewis* in *Chaskalson/Kentridge/Klaaren et al. (eds)*, Constitutional Law of South Africa (1996), ch. 31, 5.

[768] *Chaskalson/Lewis* in *Chaskalson/Kentridge/Klaaren et al. (eds)*, Constitutional Law of South Africa (1996), ch. 31, 6.

the private law of property.[769] However, this intention was not apparent from the interim property clause itself. Hence, it was argued that this term could have either a progressive or a reactionary meaning:[770] It could, on the one hand, be interpreted so as to treat all rights as being on an equal footing with the traditionally elevated right of ownership. On the other hand, it could also be interpreted so as to support the notion of conceptual severance,[771] which could provide a reactionary court with the right ammunition to boycott any attempt at social reform.

At first glance, the phrase seems to refer only to real rights, as opposed to personal rights.[772] Then only the "traditional" real rights such as ownership, mortgage, pledge (in respect of movable things), servitudes, water rights, mineral rights and liens would be protected under section 28 IC. This interpretation would also exclude rights that were not traditionally recognised as real — like labour-tenants' "rights" of occupation, or "rights" of squatters to undisturbed possession of their shacks. However, the protection of real rights only would conflict with the general international idea that a constitutional property guarantee usually incorporates protection for a wider range of rights based on a broader definition of property than that employed in pure private law issues. Moreover, a wide interpretation of *rights in property* would avoid the dilemma facing a court that has to choose between widening the concept of ownership (as known in private law) or discarding it altogether.[773]

Nevertheless, the view soon prevailed that the drafters of the Interim Constitution intended a more extensive interpretation of the property clause so as to include not only real rights but also personal rights for constitutional protection.[774] In its extreme, this could mean that prop-

---

[769] According to *Du Plessis/Corder*, Understanding South Africa's Transitional Bill of Rights (1994), 56, this phrase was used to appease the concerns of traditional leaders that the Western notion of individual ownership does not cater for communal ownership.

[770] *Davis/Cheadle/Haysom*, Fundamental Rights in the Constitution – Commentary and Cases (1997), 239-242.

[771] See 183 ff. above.

[772] *Chaskalson/Lewis* in *Chaskalson/Kentridge/Klaaren et al. (eds)*, Constitutional Law of South Africa (1996), ch. 31, 5.

[773] *Kroeze*, 1994 SAPR/PL, 326.

[774] *Van der Walt*, 1994 THRHR, 193. See also *Administrator, Natal v Sibiya* 1992 4 SA 532 (A), 539A-B where Hoexter JA already (obiter) anticipated that

erty rights would encompass the whole of private law.[775] This even the negotiating parties could not have foreseen. However, Van der Walt[776] pointed out that the function of the court was not to determine whether *rights in property* should be interpreted extensively. It was rather to determine how far the courts could and should go in extending the guarantee of rights in property to non-real rights in incorporeals. In other words, the problem in reality was the scope of the court's interpretative competence. Whether the Constitution used the term *property* or *rights in property* would not make a substantial difference to the solution of this problem.

In view of the dispute about the meaning of the term *rights in property*, section 25 FC has been phrased to refer only to *property*. By this time, however, most South African lawyers realised that the exact terminology was probably less important than the overall structure and function of the property clause in the bill of rights as a whole.[777] Therefore, the change in terminology might have evaded some of the dogmatic problems, but did not simplify the "threshold" question in the South African context. The courts are still faced with the problem of how far they should extend the guarantee of rights in property to non-real rights in incorporeals.

By now, it seems clear that, regardless of whether the term *property* instead of *rights in property* is used,[778] the constitutional protection of property will extend beyond the limits of private law rights. Perhaps the social welfare rights (like the rights to housing, food, water and security) already included in the Final Constitution point to the preference of a wider approach. However, the wording of sections 26 FC[779]

---

property could under certain circumstances (here in the context of applying the *audi alteram partem* rule in decisions by public officials) be wider than the traditional concept of *ownership*.

[775] *Kleyn*, 1996 SAPR/PL, 423.

[776] *Van der Walt*, 1994 THRHR, 193.

[777] *Van der Walt*, Constitutional Property Clauses - A Comparative Analysis (1999), 351.

[778] *Certification of the Constitution of the Republic of South Africa* (note 245 above), par. 70-75.

[779] Sec. 26 FC, Housing: "(1) Everyone has the right to have access to adequate housing. (2) The state must take reasonable legislative and other measures, within its available resources, to achieve the progressive realisation of this right. (3) No one may be evicted from their home, or have their home demol-

and section 27 FC,[780] which both require the state to take reasonable measures "within its available resources, to achieve the progressive realisation of these rights," emphasise, at least for the time being, the relative status of such social welfare rights.[781] Although there should be reservations concerning the classification of the rights protected in section 25 FC as socio-economic rights, the true socio-economic rights in the Constitution could anticipate an interpretation of the constitutional property concept which would acknowledge the limits of constitutional property protection.

Property law, especially land law, which was contorted most during the apartheid era, is in dire need of reconstruction to mirror the spirit, goal and objectives of the new constitutions. The socio-economic function of the property clause is therefore clearly to protect existing property relations while, at the same time, consciously endeavouring to correct historical imbalances.[782] Obviously, private law will serve as a point of departure and orientation, but protection of proprietary relations against the state should be based on the Constitution itself, taking into account the fundamental purpose of the constitutional bill of rights in general and the property clause in particular. In other words, the protection of the property clause must always function in the broader framework of establishing and maintaining a just and equitable balance between the protection of existing property rights and the protection of the public interest in regulating the use of property.[783] This balance, to-

---

ished, without an order of court made after considering all the relevant circumstances. No legislation may permit arbitrary evictions."

[780] Sec. 27 FC, Health care, food, water and social security: "(1) Everyone has the right to have access to - (a) health care services, including reproductive health care; (b) sufficient food and water; and (c) social security, including, if they are unable to support themselves and their dependants, appropriate social assistance. (2) The state must take reasonable legislative and other measures, within its available resources, to achieve the progressive realisation of each of these rights. (3) No one may be refused emergency medical treatment."

[781] See *Pienaar/Muller*, 1999 Stell LR, 373, where it is pointed out that South Africa has one of the worst records in the world in terms of income equality and social indicators like health, education, safe water and fertility. The inclusion of socio-economic rights in the bill of rights might represent a strong commitment to overcome this legacy, but could well remain an empty promise if the state is unable to turn around the economic tide.

[782] *Kroeze*, 1994 SAPR/PL, 325.

[783] *Van der Walt*, Constitutional Property Clause (1997), 71.

gether with the values of an open and democratic society based on human dignity and the promotion of equality and freedom, should determine the extent to which rights are protected.

2.2.2. Interests Included in the Protective Ambit of Section 25 FC

Although section 25(4) FC[784] functions as a definition clause within the property guarantee, it does not address all problems of interpretation. The new property clause further does not contain a *numerus clausus* of proprietary interests that deserve protection, and it is still up to the courts and the legislature to define the limits of constitutional property.

Constitutions usually do not create new property rights.[785] The rights already exist in law. The function of the constitution is to restrict itself to describing the circumstances under which those rights may be limited or removed. In South Africa, like in most other jurisdictions, the minimum requirement for an interest to qualify as constitutional property seems to be that it must have vested in the claimant. In other words, the right must have accrued according to the relevant principles of common or statutory law. It is, therefore, something more than a mere expectation. Further, the interest must, of course, have some kind of patrimonial value.[786]

The likelihood of certain proprietary interests being protected or not, enables one to create different categories of interests. In what follows, the protection of various possible categories of rights will be discussed.[787] To determine whether a specific interest qualifies for protection, the most important point to remember is that a balance must be struck between private property interests and the public weal. Therefore, the inclusion of a specific proprietary interest within the protective ambit of the constitutional property clause will depend — at least

---

[784] Sec. 25(4) FC: "For the purposes of this section - (a) the public interest includes the nation's commitment to land reform, and to reforms to bring about equitable access to all South Africa's natural resources; and (b) property is not limited to land."

[785] *Budlender* in *Budlender/Latsky/Roux*, New Land Law (1998), ch. 1, 10.

[786] *Van der Walt*, Constitutional Property Clauses - A Comparative Analysis (1999), 353.

[787] The categorisation of *Van der Walt*, Constitutional Property Clause (1997), 63-66 is used as point of departure for the following discussion.

to some extent — on the influence that protecting such an interest will have on the common good.

2.2.2.1. Traditional "Private Law" Property Rights

The first category would contain those instances where rights would so obviously exist, and those interests that can so clearly be regarded as constitutional "property," that the "threshold" question would barely need to be asked.[788] This category would then at least include the traditional private law rights to movable or immovable corporeal things and real rights.[789] Most probably, rights of use (as opposed to ownership) with regard to immovable property would also be included in this category, even though they are usually derived from contract or legislation. Although these rights are not covered by the term "property" in the traditional (private law) sense of the word, they are usually protected in other jurisdictions once they have vested and their protection is socially justifiable.[790]

2.2.2.2. Other "Private Law" and Commercial Rights

The second category contains those interests which would probably only be protected once it is proved that the "right" at stake exists and that it is worthy of being included in the protective ambit of the property clause. Proof of such a right would usually be sufficient qualification for protection.

Intellectual property rights (like copyright, patents, trademarks, confidential commercial information, and so on) could for instance form an important part of this category. Furthermore established and well-known commercial rights based on contract (like debts, claims, goodwill and shares in a company) could also be included. Among these, land-use rights based on contract, court orders or legislation are especially important in the context of the Final Constitution. Such rights can even be protected vis-à-vis a private landowner if it is in the interest of the public at large.

---

[788] *Van der Walt,* Constitutional Property Clause (1997), 63.

[789] *Van der Walt,* 1994 THRHR, 193.

[790] *Van der Walt,* Constitutional Property Clause (1997), 63.

2.2.2.3. Benefits Granted by the State

The third category could contain debts and claims against the state not based on contract.[791] In this context, one should distinguish between incorporeal participation rights (like rights to receive pensions and social security) and rights connected to corporeal property, such as land. The protection of both kinds of rights as "property" in terms of a constitutional guarantee could be problematic, but the latter category in particular could be a rather difficult nut to crack. Therefore, these subcategories of rights will be discussed separately.

2.2.2.3.1. Incorporeal Participation Rights

Incorporeal participation rights include a variety of claims emanating from what is usually understood to be the field of public law. Licences, permits and quotas are included in this category, as well as some rights pertaining to the social security and welfare of citizens. Licences, permits and quotas issued by the state would probably be regarded as property and protected if they have vested in the claimant and if they are regarded as valuable assets. However, protection of social security rights through a mechanism like the constitutional property clause needs further reflection.

Some scholars utilise the broad definition of property provided by section 25(4) FC to extend constitutional protection to pensions, social and unemployment security, medical benefits and similar grants.[792] However, protection in this area is mostly problematic, and the qualifying criteria differ slightly in various comparable jurisdictions. The courts will, however, first have to consider these interests carefully before any clear guidelines in this regard can be assumed. Here the application of the social welfare state principle could play a significant role in the South African context.

Up to now the South African courts have treated the definition of constitutional property with great caution. This is illustrated by the decision in *Transkei Public Servants Association v Government of the Re-*

---

[791] *Reich,* 1964 Yale LJ, 734-739 calls these interests the "new property" based on "state largesse." See note 57 above.

[792] *Devenish,* Commentary on the South African Constitution (1998), 71; *Davis/Cheadle/Haysom,* Fundamental Rights in the Constitution - Commentary and Cases (1997), 255; *Underkuffler,* 1990 Yale LJ, 127, 130 et seq.

public of South Africa.[793] In this case the High Court *inter alia* had to deal with the question of whether or not housing subsidy benefits that were formerly granted to Transkeian civil servants[794] were fundamental property rights protected by section 28 IC. The validity of various provisions of the Public Service Staff Code[795] relating to housing subsidies was at stake. Although the court refrained from determining whether a state housing subsidy was covered by the meaning of "property" in section 28 IC,[796] it made some valuable *obiter* observations about the scope of the constitutional property concept.

The court acknowledged that the meaning of "property" in section 28 IC might well be sufficiently wide to encompass a housing subsidy

---

[793] *Transkei Public Servants Association v Government of the Republic of South Africa* 1995 9 BCLR 1235 (Tk).

[794] These housing subsidies were found to be considerably higher than similar subsidies for Public Service employees in South Africa, Bophuthatswana, Ciskei and Venda. Therefore the Staff Code determined that the higher housing subsidies would still be afforded to the Transkeian civil servants for a period of six months, and that they would thereafter receive the uniform amount laid down in the Code.

[795] This code was issued in fulfilment of sec. 42 of the Public Service Act of 1994 (promulgated by Proclamation 103 of 1994) which required the Public Service Commission (established by sec. 209 IC) to devise a Public Service Staff Code, the provisions of which would be binding upon all government departments and the public servants employed by these departments. This was supposed to establish uniformity in the terms and conditions of employment of all public servants in the whole of South Africa's national territory, therefore also in the formerly "independent" states of Venda, Bophuthatswana, Ciskei and Transkei, which each had its own statute governing the conditions of employment in the Public Service.

[796] *Transkei Public Servants Association* (note 793 above), 1247A. The application failed on other grounds. It was determined (1247 B-G) that the Interim Constitution did not intend protecting property rights in the broad sense flowing from the employment relationship between civil servants and the State during the transitional period. The bases of the decision was sec. 236(4) IC, which provided for the enactment of laws to establish uniformity of terms and conditions of employment of civil servants and sec. 236(5) IC, which expressly precluded the reduction of the pensionable salary or pensionable salary scale of civil servants below that which prevailed immediately before the commencement of the Constitution. The latter provision was the only protection of this kind afforded to civil servants. No other protection was intended by the Interim Constitution. Besides, the court reasoned that certain reductions in benefits were inevitable in order to achieve uniformity.

benefit.[797] The language of the Constitution had to be given a generous and purposive interpretation,[798] especially since academics have on the basis of comparative legal analysis expressed the view that the constitutional property concept was not restricted to corporeal things, but rather extended to a variety of social and economic interests and benefits.[799] However, the court also remarked that, even if it could be decided that housing subsidies could be included within the protective scope of section 28 IC, the reduction of the Transkeian housing subsidy by the Staff Code[800] would be a reasonable and justifiable limitation of the right. It would, furthermore, not negate the essential content of that right, the purpose being to effect uniformity of housing subsidy grants in the South African civil service.

2.2.2.3.2. Rights Granted by the State and Based on Traditional Corporeal Property

Another problem is posed by the intricate system of land rights, which has developed in South Africa over the past century. The land tenure system based on the ideology of apartheid resulted in the vast majority of the population being able to hold land only in accordance with customary law (or purported codifications of it), or in terms of other statutory regimes, like the permits-based system of land rights. Statutory permits were usually issued in terms of subordinate legislation defining the rights and obligations of the permit holder and those who occupy the land through him or her.[801] Such a permit conferred a statutory right to occupy land, which resembled a personal right rather than a real right. The circumstances under which these permit-based rights could be withdrawn from the holders were extensively defined in legislation. Moreover, under almost all of these systems, holders of land did not have the capacity to dispose of it.[802] Constitutional analysts are con-

---

[797] *Transkei Public Servants Association* (note 793 above), 1246J-1247A.

[798] *Transkei Public Servants Association* (note 793 above), 1245H.

[799] *Transkei Public Servants Association* (note 793 above), 1246B-J.

[800] Chapter D XX.

[801] E.g. proclamation R293 and the case of *DVB Behuising* (note 612 above) ensuing from a continued reliance upon the permit-based right established through proclamation R293. See 440 ff. below. *Budlender/Latsky*, 1990 SAJHR, 155.

[802] *Budlender* in *Budlender/Latsky/Roux*, New Land Law (1998), ch. 1, 20.

sequently faced with the question of whether these land rights should be protected, and, if so, to what extent. For instance, in terms of customary law, an individual's interests in land consist of (i) the "right to avail" — an entitlement of a member of a tribe to claim an allotment of land — and (ii) the individual's right to benefit from land already allotted.[803] The latter could be included within the protection of the constitution, as it is based on the right to exclude others. The "right to avail" could be construed as analogous to a benefit granted by the state,[804] and protected as such.

The concept "rights in land" is certainly not limited to *ownership of land*. It is submitted that the new constitutional property concept can be extended to bring the right to hold land in terms of a statutory permit or customary law under its protection.[805] These rights should qualify for constitutional protection, because they constitute special benefits granted by the state that fall within the protective ambit of the constitutional property clause.

2.2.3. The Nature of Property Under the Constitution

From a traditional liberalist viewpoint, property is regarded not only as the most important private law right, but also as the most important fundamental right.[806] The constitutional concept of property might therefore overlap in some respects with the private law concept of ownership. These two concepts should, nevertheless, be kept apart as far as possible, as the purpose of the constitutional protection of property differs considerably from that of the protection of property in private law. The latter aims at insulating the rights under discussion from an invasion or interference not based on the owner's permission. The former aims at striking a just and equitable balance between the interest of private property holders and the public interest in the control and regulation of the use of property.[807]

---

[803] *Bennett*, Human Rights & African Customary Law (1995), 133, 144-145.

[804] *Budlender* in *Budlender/Latsky/Roux*, New Land Law (1998), ch. 1, 20.

[805] See e.g. the minority decision in the *DVB Behuising* case (note 612 above). See 411 ff. below.

[806] *Kroeze*, 1994 SAPR/PL, 326 and sources quoted there.

[807] *Van der Walt*, Constitutional Property Clause (1997), 67.

It is, therefore, submitted that the material content of property in the Constitution differs from the property concept in private law. These concepts may, however, overlap to some extent. In principle, the *structural relation* (owner – third parties – *res*) underlying property and ownership in private law remains unaltered in the constitutional context. However, the *kind of protection* afforded to holders of property rights change as soon as the state (as representative of the public interest) is involved in the property relations. The material concept of property is, therefore, much broader in terms of the constitutional provisions than under private law. The main reason for this is that the social function of property is an important consideration in determining which kinds of rights should be protected under the constitutional guarantee of property, thus allowing a more diversified description of property.

According to one of the first commentaries on the new South African Constitution,[808] the drafting of section 28 IC was inspired by the modern concept of property as a *bundle of rights*. This has induced some authors[809] to equate the *bundle of rights theory*[810] (or *conceptual severance*, as it is sometime referred to in constitutional law circles) with the movement towards a diversified and socially functional concept of ownership. The bundle of rights theory was juxtaposed against the "now rather outdated conception of property as thing-ownership." These authors cited the use of the term *rights in property* in the Interim Constitution as support for their argument. Although the term *rights in property* does not occur in the Final Constitution, supporters of *conceptual severance* claim that this theory is still applicable.[811]

However, if one accepts that the constitutional concept of property is in principle much broader than the private law concept of property, the *bundle of rights theory* has very little to contribute to the development of the constitutional concept of property. Moreover, such an approach is not in line with the objectives of the Constitution regarding the property clause. If property is to be interpreted in the constitutional context according to the *bundle of rights theory*, a regulatory action by

---

[808] *Cachalia/Cheadle/Davis et al*, Fundamental Rights (1994), 91-92.

[809] *Visser/Roux* in *Rwelamira/Werle (eds)*, Confronting Past Injustices (1996), 95.

[810] See 183 above.

[811] *Van der Walt*, Constitutional Property Clauses - A Comparative Analysis (1999), 24.

the state affecting one of the "rights" in the "bundle" may have unanticipated consequences. It can happen that the state removes one of the entitlements constituting ownership, without intending it to be an expropriation, for which compensation needs to be paid.

An illustration would be the case where the state introduces rent control and thus removes the right of the owner to determine the rent or the right to terminate a tenancy. In terms of the private law concept of ownership, actions like these are not regarded as expropriation and consequently no compensation needs to be paid. However, if the *bundle of rights theory* is applied to the situation, it could mean that the withdrawal of one of the "sticks" (in this case the powers of termination or setting the rent) constitute an expropriation of that particular "right in" property. This would give rise to the duty to compensate.[812] Thus, any form of regulation of the exercise of rights in property — for example town planning regulations, zoning laws, environmental regulation and public health regulations — could be susceptible to the argument that it is an expropriation of one of the rights in property, which would be unlawful unless compensation is provided.[813] This would not be conducive to the common good, because it affords right holders more liberty than the state (and also the public in general) could uphold.

2.3. Evaluation

From the analysis of the provisions of the property clauses in the South African constitutional order, it seems that the private law concept of property will be a mere stepping stone to a broader, more extensive constitutional concept of property. The public interest as well as the social function attributed to property in the constitutional context will require a broader interpretation of this term. This will have certain implications for the land reform and redistribution initiatives of the South African government, which will be briefly mentioned in the following paragraphs.

---

[812] *Van der Walt*, Constitutional Property Clauses - A Comparative Analysis (1999), 24.

[813] *Budlender* in *Budlender/Latsky/Roux*, New Land Law (1998), ch. 1, 17-18.

2.3.1. The "Social Importance" of Property for Purposes of Definition

Section 28(1) IC referred explicitly to the right to "acquire and hold rights in property and, to the extent that the nature of the right permits, to dispose of such rights." This indicated that the extent of the entitlements is determined by their nature and social function. This is in line with the development of a so-called "socialised" or functional property concept, which has developed in private law since the 1970's. It is of particular importance for the two-stage approach to human rights issues that was adopted by the Constitutional Court.[814]

The remarks made in the case of *Transkei Public Servants Association v Government of the Republic of South Africa and Others* about the protective ambit of the constitutional property guarantee indicate the inevitable general tendency to consider the purpose and social function of constitutionally protecting intangible assets as *property*. The categorisation of interests possibly worthy of protection also indicate that the more difficult it is to justify constitutional protection of an interest on the basis of its "traditional" protection in private law, the more reliance will be placed on the social importance of that interest as justification for its constitutional protection.

Different considerations apply in the determination of the constitutional concept of property and the private law definition of property. In terms of private law, interests qualifying as "property" (or rather as things or *res*) are unconditionally and absolutely insulated against interference and invasion not consented to by the owner.[815] For the constitutional concept of "ownership" or "property," the inquiry has to go further than merely recognising the obvious protection usually afforded to owners in a private-rights context. The land-use rights envisaged for historically disadvantaged communities and individuals by section 25 FC are in this regard of particular interest and will therefore be discussed in the context of the effect of the constitutional concept of public interest on private law rights concerning land.

---

[814] *Van der Walt*, Constitutional Property Clauses - A Comparative Analysis (1999), 351.

[815] *Van der Walt*, Constitutional Property Clause (1997), 66.

2.3.2. Property and the Public Interest

Section 25 FC protects and guarantees property in a way characteristic of the new constitutional order in general and the bill of rights in particular. Property is included and protected in the bill of rights, in spite of the negative formulation of the guarantee. Property is, therefore, a genuine constitutional right. The broad scope of the property concept under the Constitution may raise the question of whether apartheid-based property rights are also constitutionally entrenched.[816]

It is submitted that the augmented scope of property protection in terms of the Constitution does not necessarily mean that all rights are unconditionally entrenched. Due to its broader material content, the constitutional property concept differs from the private law concept of property. It is merely by chance that the two concepts sometimes overlap. The constitutional property clause does not really insulate or entrench "private law ownership" as such. It rather protects existing rights in the form of derivative rights: by way of a guarantee that attaches only to a certain entitlement which in fact arises, under existing laws that make provision for it, and that protect the specific (contingent but actual) entitlement against certain kinds of governmental impairment.[817] This view corresponds essentially with the German notion of property rights that are subject to immanent restrictions as embodied in legislation.

The spirit and values of the South African bill of rights indicate that the aim of section 25 FC is to establish a just and equitable balance between the protection of private property and the promotion of the public interest. Section 25 FC, in other words, guarantees property without necessarily falling foul of the liberalist view that the main function of the bill of rights is to insulate private property from state interference and transformation programmes.[818]

The tension between individual autonomy and the collective good is an element inherent to the concept of constitutional property. It is impossible to consider any aspect of the constitutional property concept without simultaneously considering this tension between and balancing of different interests. This approach does not have to mean that the

---

[816] *Chaskalson/Lewis* in *Chaskalson/Kentridge/Klaaren et. al. (eds)*, Constitutional Law of South Africa (1996), ch. 31, 4-5.

[817] See *Michelman*, 1981 Wash & Lee LR, 1099.

[818] *Van der Walt*, 1997 SAPR/PL, 304.

proportionality test, which is supposed to constitute the very last phase in an inquiry about the constitutional validity of an interference with property, needs to be uprooted and re-applied earlier in the investigation. It also does not attempt to overthrow the two-stage inquiry into constitutional validity of interference with fundamental rights. It rather advocates the proper application of the principles of the constitutional and social state as elements of interpretation throughout the inquiry,[819] so as to establish a less formalistic, more result-oriented approach towards the protection and regulation of property.[820] This simply means that one or the other form of interest-balancing is part of the entire process, and that the nature and function of the balancing process will differ according to the stage of the inquiry in which it is employed. In some instances, this kind of balancing of interests will be similar — but by no means equal — to the elements of proportionality.

The challenge awaiting the courts is that of finding an equitable balance between individual interests and the public interest. The inclusion of a property clause in the bill of rights does not *per se* mean that private property is privileged in relation to the public interest or some public benefit. Instead, it indicates that the court deems it necessary to proceed to the substantive issues raised in the second stage of the constitutional dispute rather than rule them out of order in the first stage on the basis of a conceptualist approach to the meaning of the term *property*.[821]

3. "Eigentum" Under German Law

In Germany, the same term *(Eigentum)*[822] is used in private and constitutional law to indicate the proprietary relations that receive protection. It will be shown in the following paragraphs that the use of this term in

---

[819] See ch. 6, 115 ff. above.

[820] Such an approach could have been particularly useful in deciding the questions posed by the case of *Harksen v Lane* 1998 1 SA 300 (CC). See discussion at 350 ff. below.

[821] *Van der Walt,* Constitutional Property Clause (1997), 42.

[822] See *Kleyn,* 1996 SAPR/PL, 413 where it is indicated that the correct translation of *Eigentum* in art. 14 GG is "property" rather than merely "ownership." This is furthermore clear from the official translation and from the fact that a far wider range of proprietary interests than ownership in the private law sense is protected under this article.

constitutional law differs considerably from its use in private law, even though the constitutional concept of *Eigentum* and the private law concept of *Eigentum* have some elements in common.

3.1. *"Eigentum" in the German Civil Code*

The German Civil Code *(Bürgerliches Gesetzbuch)*, which came into force on 1 January 1900, is based on classical liberal ideology.[823] It fosters private autonomy and ownership. The German Law on property is primarily contained in the third book *(Dritter Abschnitt)* of the Civil Code.[824] Here, the allocation of property *(Sachen)* to legal subjects who may have either ownership[825] or possession[826] of this property is regulated. Other property rights, like rights of use and security rights, are also regulated.

The third book of the Civil Code is divided into five parts *(Titel)*. These different parts deal with (i) the content of ownership; (ii) regulations for the acquisition and loss of ownership in immovable property; (iii) regulations for the acquisition and loss of ownership in movable property; (iv) the protection of property; and (v) co-ownership. Outside the Civil Code a number of statutes deal with special aspects of real rights, like the *Wohnungseigentumsgesetz*,[827] the *Erbbauverordnung*[828] and the *Pachtkreditgesetz*. The provisions of the Civil Code on property law pertain to material (substantive) law only. It does not deal with procedural questions. These are mainly dealt with in the *Grundbuchordnung*. Most of the material law on property in the Civil Code is based on Roman law.[829]

---

[823] See *Olzen*, 1984 JuS, 328-335.

[824] Par. 854-1296. Par. 90-103 BGB provide definitions of the basic legal terms, such as "thing" *(Sachen)*, "component" *(Bestandteile, Zubehör, Inventar)*, and "fruit" *(Früchte)*.

[825] *Eigentum*, that is, legal control over an object.

[826] *Besitz*, that is, factual control over an object.

[827] *Gesetz über das Wohnungseigentum und das Dauerwohnrecht.*

[828] *Gesetz über Maßnahmen zur Verbesserung der Agrarstruktur und zur Sicherung land- und forstwirtschaflicher Betriebe.*

[829] *Foster*, German Legal System and Laws (1996), 278. The land registration system in Germany has its own origin: After political unification of Germany in 1871, a cadastral survey was undertaken, on the basis of which the whole of

In view of its constitutionally destined social function, ownership —
especially landownership and ownership of means of production — is
subject to several economically inspired limitations, or limitations pertaining to building regulations, town planning and environmental protection.[830] The following paragraphs contain a description of the place
of ownership within the structure of German property law, the characteristics of ownership and its significance for property protection under
the German Basic Law.

3.1.1. General Structure of Rights *in rem* Under the Civil Code

According to paragraph 903 BGB read with paragraph 90 BGB, the
rights *in rem* pertain to both corporeal movables and immovables.[831]
Because of the different rules applicable to immovable and movable
property, these two subject areas are usually treated separately in commentaries on the Civil Code. The distinction between movable and
immovable property is relevant with respect to the modes of acquisition
and the types of real rights available, as well as with regard to the kind
of publicity required in order to protect third parties or the public in
general.[832] Although the distinction does not have any noticeable theoretical effect as to the quality of property rights, it does have practical
implications due to the impact of public law — especially planning and
environmental laws — on land.

Under the civil law, the owner has a "right" of control *(Herrschaftsrecht)* over the object at stake, which means that he or she can uphold

---

the German territory was divided into numbered plots. This survey, together
with its associated taxation registers, is the foundation of the land registration
system. In case of a numbered plot belonging to a private persons, the name of
the owner is entered into the land register *(Grundbuch)*. Such an entry can indicate a change of legal position, and is constitutive of ownership. Erasures or
strikings through of any kind are prohibited. If an entry has to be cancelled, it
needs to be underlined in red, and a cancellation note needs to be made.
Southern, 1993 ICLQ, 691.

[830] *Avenarius*, Rechtsordnung der Bundesrepublik Deutschland (1997), 168.

[831] *Schuppert* in *Karpen (ed)*, Constitution of Germany (1988), 108.

[832] Publicity is integrated into the act of transferring or establishing a real
right. With movables, for instance, publicity entails the actual handing over of
the *res*. With immovables, the publicity requirement is met with entry of the
change in the legal position in the land register *(Grundbuch)*.

the rights and entitlements pertaining to the *res* against anyone and everyone. In this sense, ownership (like all other rights *in rem*) is theoretically absolute. This should be contrasted with the effect of contractual
or obligatory rights, which bind only parties to the agreements that give
rise to such rights.[833] The absolute legal effect of real rights on third
parties poses a risk to the public in general. In order to enable third
parties to assess the scope of possible risks arising from another person's "absolute" rights, the instances recognised by law as having absolute legal effect need to be defined clearly. This is done in the Civil
Code by, on the one hand, allowing only a limited category of real
rights to exist,[834] and, on the other hand, prescribing limitations on the
so-called *full* rights.[835]

Herrschaftsrechte are, therefore, restricted by law and standardised to a
large extent. The freedom to develop new categories of rights, characteristic for the law of obligations, does not exist in the property law under the Civil Code. Variations that do not fall within the categories of
rights in terms provided by the Civil Code are considered void. In order to have absolute effect, particular forms of rights must be observed.
This results in a *numerus clausus* of real rights contained in the Civil
Code,[836] which is also known as the principles of *Typenzwang* and *Typenfixierung*. The principle of *Typenzwang* means that *only* those forms
of the right that have been established by law can be created and exercised.[837] *Typenfixierung* determines that the content or the substance of
a particular real right cannot be varied. The effect of this is that property rights can only be established in the way provided for by the Civil
Code and supplementary legislation, making property law rather
rigid.[838]

Nevertheless, the Federal Court of Justice protects certain relative (personal) rights by affording them "real effect." This happens when a specific relative right is consistent with a specific legal position. For instance, the lessee of an apartment enjoys legal protection against the in-

---

[833] *Ebke/Finkin (eds)*, Introduction (1996), 229.

[834] *Baur/Stürner*, Sachenrecht (1999), 27; contra *Wieling*, Sachenrecht (1994),
6, 8.

[835] *Seiler* in Staudingers Kommentar - 3. Buch Sachenrecht (1996), m.n. 7.

[836] *Westermann*, BGB-Sachenrecht (1994), m.n. 4; *Ebke/Finkin (eds)*, Introduction (1996), 230.

[837] *Wieling*, Sachenrecht (1994), 8.

[838] *Foster*, German Legal System and Laws (1996), 280.

fringement of his or her rights pertaining to occupation of that apartment, which is quite similar to the protection afforded an owner of such an apartment. The lessee holds a "quasi-real right," which can be enforced even against the owner of the apartment. Such "quasi-real rights" do not qualify as real rights in the true sense of the word, as they only have some of the characteristics of real rights.[839]

Another example is found in the treatment of so-called *Sondernutzungsrechte*. These are rights of exclusive use over the common property, which forms part of an apartment ownership scheme to an apartment building. According to paragraphs 10 I and 15 I WEG,[840] these rights are contractual in nature, but paragraph 10 II WEG provides that these rights can be registered in the *Grundbuch* upon request by the interested parties. Accordingly, the Federal Court of Justice determined[841] that, when a *Sondernutzungsrecht* has been registered, the right is not "purely contractual" in nature any more, but through registration has acquired real effect *(dingliche Wirkung)*. The theoretical tenability of distinguishing between "real" real rights and personal rights "with real effect" is questionable and has been debated extensively by the German authors.[842]

3.1.2. The Concept of "Eigentum" Under the Civil Code

Ownership is described in paragraph 903 BGB as the right to dispose of a *res* at will and, to the extent that the law and the rights of third parties permit, exclude others from interference with the *res*:[843]

> *903 [Befugnisse des Eigentümers] Der Eigentümer einer Sache kann, soweit nicht das Gesetz oder Rechte Dritter entgegenstehen, mit der Sache nach Belieben verfahren und andere von jeder Einwirkung ausschließen.*

---

[839] *Baur/Stürner*, Sachenrecht (1999), 28.

[840] *Wohnungseigentumsgesetz* (Apartment Ownership Act).

[841] BGHZ 73, 146 148.

[842] *Schnauder*, Festschrift für Johannes Bärmann und Hermann Weitnauer (1990), 567 ff.

[843] Translation: "[Entitlements of the owner] The owner of a thing *(res)* can, as far as the law or the rights of third parties do not prohibit, act with that thing *(res)* at will and can exclude others from interfering with it."

According to most of the commentators,[844] this provision technically contains no definition of ownership. The circumscription of the owner's entitlements and their limitation by law and by the rights of third parties is not regarded as a technical definition of ownership.[845] It is also apparently accepted in most of the recent commentaries that a technical definition of *Eigentum* would be merely of theoretical significance, and therefore the issue is mostly avoided.[846] Instead, focus is placed on the object of ownership, the entitlements of the owner and the limitations on ownership, in an attempt to sever the *concept* of ownership from its *content*.[847] The following paragraphs provide a brief overview of the object of ownership and the entitlements of the owner under German law, as well as the limitations on the right of ownership.

3.1.2.1. Object of Ownership and Entitlements of the Owner

Paragraph 90 BGB determines that only *corporeal* objects can qualify as things (res) within the meaning of the law. This includes movable as well as immovable objects, but is still a much narrower definition of property than that which is found in the constitutional context.[848] Moreover, in terms of the Civil Code, ownership can vest only with regard to these corporeal objects. By contrast, other real rights — like *Nießbrauch* (usufruct) or *Pfandrecht* (pledge) — can also have a right as object.[849]

---

[844] See *Seiler* in Staudingers Kommentar - 3. Buch Sachenrecht (1996), m.n. 6; *Seiler/Roth/Kohler* in Staudingers Kommentar - 3. Buch Sachenrecht (1996), § 903 m.n. 2; *Baur/Stürner*, Sachenrecht (1999), 268 provides a discussion of its characteristics without providing a definition.

[845] Contra *Wieling*, Sachenrecht (1994), 81.

[846] *Baur/Stürner*, Sachenrecht (1999), 268; *Seiler/Roth/Kohler* in Staudingers Kommentar - 3. Buch Sachenrecht (1996), § 903 m.n. 7; *Eckert*, Sachenrecht (1999) m.n. 114. See *Olzen*, 1984 JuS, 328-336 for an historical overview of the development of the concept of ownership in civil law and the polemical discussion (around 1973) about the continued relevance of the concept of ownership in view of the increasing number of public law limitations on ownership. See also *Sontis*, 1973 Festschrift Larenz, 981 ff.

[847] *Olzen*, 1984 JuS, 328-329.

[848] See 224 below.

[849] *Seiler/Roth/Kohler* in Staudingers Kommentar - 3. Buch Sachenrecht (1996), § 903 m.n. 3.

The identity of the ownership concept is read into paragraph 903 BGB by the commentators, who regard ownership as the most comprehensive right of control permitted by law with regard to the *res*.[850] As such, *Eigentum* has a position superior to that of other real rights. It is the all-embracing right *in rem*. According to paragraph 903 BGB, the owner can act with his or her *res* at own discretion and can exclude others from infringing upon the *res*. This provision thus ascribes a positive and a negative nucleus of meaning to the entitlements of the owner: Property rights can be used actively, allowing the owner to use the property in specific ways, but it can also be used in defence, to preclude third parties from interfering with it. This constitutes a description of ownership on the basis of the entitlements, combined with the decisive characteristic of exclusivity.[851]

(i) The owner's ability to act with the *res* upon own discretion constitutes the positive "power" *(Rechtsmacht)* of ownership. It includes, *inter alia*, use and abuse, alteration, consumption, and destruction of the *res*. The owner can also transfer, encumber, bequeath or abandon the *res*.[852]

(ii) The negative component of the owner's "power" *(Rechtsmacht)* comprises the characteristic of exclusivity that is attributed to ownership. The owner can exclude all arbitrary infringements on the *res* by third parties, for instance, change of possession, use and abuse, alterations, consumption, damage or destruction of the *res* by the third party, or infringement of the owner's legal position pertaining to the *res*. Several legal remedies are at the disposal of the owner in case of infringement by third parties: On the one hand, the owner can act in self-defence and self-help (for instance, acting under *Notwehr*,[853] *Notstand*[854] or *Selbsthilfe*.[855]) On the other hand, several legislative mecha-

---

[850] *Baur/Stürner*, Sachenrecht (1999), 269; *Seiler* in Staudingers Kommentar - 3. Buch Sachenrecht (1996), m.n. 6; *Eckert*, Sachenrecht (1999), m.n. 114; *Westermann*, BGB-Sachenrecht (1994), m.n. 103.

[851] *Westermann*, BGB-Sachenrecht (1994), m.n. 42; *Seiler/Roth/Kohler* in Staudingers Kommentar - 3. Buch Sachenrecht (1996), § 903 m.n. 2.

[852] *Seiler/Roth/Kohler* in Staudingers Kommentar - 3. Buch Sachenrecht (1996), § 903 m.n. 10. See also BGH NJW 1994, 188.

[853] Par. 277 BGB.

[854] Par. 228, 904 BGB.

[855] Par. 229 BGB.

nisms (like claims for vindication of the *res*,[856] claims for abatement of hindrance,[857] and claims for correction of entries in the land register,[858]) ensure extensive protection of the owners' rights and entitlements.[859]

However, it is also agreed that even a comprehensive right of control over certain objects cannot be without limits. Therefore, the Civil Code immediately after stating the entitlements of the owner determines the limitations on those entitlements.[860] Further, in the case of neighbouring pieces of land or pieces of land situated close to each other, it can also happen that the positive "powers" of one landowner can collide with the negative "powers" of his or her neighbours or the other owners of adjacent land. Here the law has placed some restrictions on the entitlements of owners.

3.1.2.2. Limitations on the Right of Ownership

In paragraph 903 BGB it is provided that the owner of a thing may, *so far as the law and the rights of other do not oppose*, manage the thing as he or she likes and may exclude others from interfering with it. This phrase means that certain laws and rights of third parties give content to the right of ownership and set the limits of an owner's entitlements,[861] so that he or she can only exercise the inherent positive and/or negative "powers" to a certain degree. Paragraph 903 BGB foresees two kinds of limitations on the right of ownership: limitations by normative law and limitations by the interests of third parties. Normative law includes constitutional law, statutory law as well as subordinate legislation.[862]

Most limitations by normative law stem from public law, and are contained in legislation of either the Federation or the different *Länder*, or

---

[856] Par. 985, 823 BGB.

[857] Par. 1004 BGB.

[858] Par. 894 BGB.

[859] *Seiler/Roth/Kohler* in Staudingers Kommentar - 3. Buch Sachenrecht (1996), § 903 m.n. 11-12.

[860] Par. 903-924 BGB *(Erster Titel)*.

[861] *Seiler/Roth/Kohler* in Staudingers Kommentar - 3. Buch Sachenrecht (1996), § 903 m.n. 13.

[862] *Seiler/Roth/Kohler* in Staudingers Kommentar - 3. Buch Sachenrecht (1996), § 903 m.n. 14.

both. In the field of building and construction law[863] *(Bauordnungs-recht, Bauplanungsrecht, Bundesbaurecht)* several building and security regulations[864] can result in a limitation of the owner's right. Further, in agricultural law *(Agrarrecht)*[865] strict provision[866] on the alienation and subdivision of land limits the subdivision of agricultural land into units that are not economically viable. According to forestry laws *(Forst-recht)*,[867] owners of forestland have to abide by timber felling quotas, and have to reafforest in keeping with prescribed rules. Similarly, many environmental law provisions[868] limit the rights of owners. For instance, owners of dangerous industrial and nuclear plants need special permission for establishment, in accordance with the Federal Act on Protection against Intromission[869] and the Atom Act.[870] Certain buildings are protected as ancient or historical monuments by provincial legislation.[871] Provisions in these statutes can have a restrictive effect on the entitlements of the owners, as can the statutes in traffic law.[872]

In the field of private law, the neighbour law provisions of the Civil Code and corresponding legislation contain certain limitations on the right to ownership. The Civil Code itself contains only rudimentary provisions pertaining to the limitation of an owner's rights with regard to immovable property by that of his or her neighbours. Paragraph 905 BGB contains the principle *cuius est solum, eius est usque ad caelum et ad inferos.* However, it also states that the owner cannot prohibit infringements in the area above or below his or her land if he or she has no interest in the exclusion of such infringements. More specific regulations on the mutual rights and duties of neighbours are contained

---

[863] See *Baugesetzbuch.*

[864] E.g. par. 14, 15, 19-23, 24 and 85, *Baugesetzbuch.*

[865] *Grundstücksverkehrsgesetz.*

[866] Par. 2, 9, *Grundstücksverkehrsgesetz; Flurbereinigungsgesetz.*

[867] *Bundeswaldgesetz.*

[868] E.g. *Bundesnaturschutzgesetz; Wasserhaushaltsgesetz.*

[869] *Bundesimmissionsschutzgesetz.*

[870] *Atomgesetz.*

[871] E.g. *Hamburger Denkmalschutzgesetz.*

[872] E.g. *Luftverkehrgesetz; Bundeswasserstraßengesetz; Telegraphenwegege-setz.*

in the legislation of the different German *Länder*.[873] Paragraphs 905 to 924 BGB deal with various aspects of neighbour law: emission, encroachment of buildings and plants and various duties to eliminate dangers. In principle the effect of these provisions is that the limitation of the owner's entitlements constitutes an assertion of the ownership entitlements of his or her neighbour.

Another general limitation is found in paragraph 904 BGB, which deals with the infringement on property rights by a third party in cases of urgent necessity *(Notstand)*. Simultaneously, this paragraph, read with paragraph 228 BGB, provides justification for infringing the property of another.[874]

However, the most important general limitation on ownership under the Civil Code appears in paragraph 903 BGB itself. The absolute rights of third parties that affect ownership in a specific case determine the content of the right to ownership. The rights of third parties pertaining to a specific object of ownership are external limitations on the right to property.[875] Such rights would include the limited real rights with regard to the thing *(res)*, like *Erbbaurecht* (heritable building right), *Dienstbarkeiten* (servitudes) and *Pfandrechte* (pledge). As these rights enable the holders thereof to exercise some entitlements in terms of the thing *(res)*, they limit the power of disposal of the owner.[876] However, personal rights are not regarded as limitations on ownership as such, as these rights are not absolutely enforceable and only bind the owner in his capacity as party to the agreement which gives rise to rights like these.[877]

---

[873] See *Seiler* in Staudingers Kommentar - 3. Buch Sachenrecht (1996), m.n. 8 and the reference provided there.

[874] See *Müller*, Sachenrecht (1997), m.n. 302-317.

[875] *Pieroth/Schlink*, Grundrechte-Staatsrecht II (1991), m.n. 997.

[876] *Müller*, Sachenrecht (1997), m.n. 291; *Seiler/Roth/Kohler* in Staudingers Kommentar - 3. Buch Sachenrecht (1996), § 903 m.n. 25; *Wieling*, Sachenrecht (1994), 82.

[877] *Seiler/Roth/Kohler* in Staudingers Kommentar - 3. Buch Sachenrecht (1996), § 903 m.n. 25.

3.1.3. The Civil Code's Ownership Concept from the Perspective of the Basic Law

It is generally accepted that, under the German Civil Code, ownership has a standardised base *(einheitliche Basis)* as formulated (but not defined) by paragraph 903 BGB. As for the question of enforceability, ownership is seen as an absolute right *(Vollrecht / Herrschaftsrecht)*, but that does not mean that ownership is also absolute with regard to content. Many restrictions on ownership, whether it is as a result of public law, private law or the rights of third parties, have to be tolerated by the owners.[878]

One of the most basic aspects of the German society is that individuals are given the freedom to set and fulfil their own goals, thus freely developing their personalities. This is not possible without a substratum of objects over which the individual can exercise control.[879] Ownership is seen as personal freedom to exercise control over things or objects.[880] However, acknowledgement of the right of ownership (that is, the freedom to control own objects) vis-à-vis other legal subjects does not explain how the interest of the owner should be balanced against the interests of public at large. That is a question of legal policy, the content of which is in Germany determined by the Basic Law. The legislature is allowed to determine the content and limits of ownership, but is not allowed to negate the essence of the right. However, since a social function is ascribed to ownership, certain entitlements flowing from ownership are sometimes restricted without being compensated.

In principle, therefore, the Basic Law determines the relation between owners and the state. On the one hand, it determines the extent to which the state can infringe the owners' entitlements. On the other hand, it also determines to what extent owners can protect themselves against infringement by the state. Especially with regard to the latter part of the equation the Civil Code's conception of ownership plays an important role. Article 14 GG provides no definition of *Eigentum*. This raises the question as to the importance of the meaning attached to ownership in the Civil Code for the constitutional context.

---

[878] *Seiler* in Staudingers Kommentar - 3. Buch Sachenrecht (1996), m.n. 6.

[879] *Wieling*, Sachenrecht (1994), 79; BVerfGE 50, 290, 339; BVerfGE 68, 193, 222.

[880] BVerfGE 24, 389; BVerfGE 31, 239; BGHZ 6, 276.

Although it has formerly been acknowledged in Germany that the nature of ownership had to be determined mainly by private law,[881] the more recent common opinion is that the notion of property ascribed by private law cannot be equally authoritative for constitutional purposes.[882] The property concept prevalent in constitutional law is dualistic. On the one hand article 14 GG limits the protection of property to that which guarantees a minimum of patrimonial rights enabling an adequate flexibility of activity. In other words, it constitutes an institutional guarantee of property. On the other hand article 14 GG also contains an individual guarantee of property, through which the property concept is enlarged. This harks back to article 153 of the Weimar Constitution, which contained a property clause almost identical to that of article 14 GG. Under article 153 of the Weimar Constitution, an enlarged concept of property rights was applied for purposes of interpretation. The extent of the constitutional guarantee in the Constitution of the Weimar Republic included not only material things *(res)*, but also financial assets (including all categories of titles to movable and immovable things), creditor's rights and "rights" of membership in associations.[883]

---

[881] *Leisner* in *Isensee/Kirchhof*, Handbuch des Staatsrechts VI (1989), m.n. 73-74. The Federal Constitutional Court of Germany declared in 1952 (BVerfGE 1, 264, 278-279) that the notion of property, as used in the Basic Law constitutes the legal institution of property, as it has been formed by civil law and by the views prevailing in society *("das Rechtsinstitut Eigentum, so wie es das bürgerliche Recht und die gesellschaftlichen Anschauungen geformt haben")*. German civil law defines property rights as the sum of legally permitted dominance over an object: The relevant section (par. 903 I BGB) reads: *"Der Eigentümer einer Sache kann, soweit nicht das Gesetz oder Rechte Dritter entgegenstehen, mit der Sache nach Belieben verfahren und andere von jeder Einwirkung ausschließen."* (Translation: The owner of a thing may, in as far as the law and the rights of others do not oppose, manage the thing according to his pleasure, and may exclude others from any interference with it). However, the scope of application of the Civil Law Code is limited to material objects only (par. 90 BGB). These definitions nevertheless do not lead to the conclusion that the Basic Law protects only ownership rights directed at material objects, i.e. movable and immovable things. *Kimminich* in *Starck (ed)*, Rights, Institutions and Impact of International Law (1987), 76.

[882] *Schuppert* in *Karpen (ed)*, Constitution of Germany (1988), 108.

[883] *Kimminich* in *Starck (ed)*, Rights, Institutions and Impact of International Law (1987), 76; RGZ 109, 319 and confirmed by RGZ 111, 320; RGZ 129, 146.

After the Basic Law came into force, the Federal Court of Justice continued to apply this more extensive concept of property for purposes of interpreting the Basic Law.[884] The Federal Court of Justice reasoned that property should be interpreted in the light of its historical development under the Civil Code. This reasoning was supported by the early decisions of the Federal Constitutional Court.[885] In this line of reasoning, the *Deichordnung* decision[886] is the most telling example of the Federal Constitutional Court's earlier emphasis on the overriding importance of private law in defining the content and limits of property. The logic of these cases was eroded when the Federal Constitutional Court decided to develop a constitutional concept of property that is derived from the Constitution itself.

3.2. The Shift from a Private Law Based Concept of Property to a "Purely" Constitutional Meaning of Property

In 1981, with the handing down of the famous *Naßauskiesung* decision,[887] the court departed from its own previous view (to consider property in the light of its historical development under the Civil Code) and expounded the boundaries of public control. The Federal Supreme Court questioned the validity of the Water Resources Act,[888] a federal statute interfering with the right of an owner to dispose of the groundwater under his or her property. Designed to preserve public water supplies against contamination or other uses damaging to the public welfare, the Federal Water Resources Act required any person whose activities affected the quantity or quality of groundwater to procure a permit granted for limited periods and specified purposes sanctioned by law. The plaintiff owned and operated a gravel pit near Münster. For decades he had freely used the groundwater beneath his property for the purpose of extracting gravel. This unlimited use of groundwater was restricted in 1968 with the creation of a new water conservation district by the city of Rheine. The quarry was located within the district and near the city's water wells. Because these wells were threatened by the

---

884 BGHZ 6, 270.

885 BVerfGE 1, 264, 278; BVerfGE 11, 64, 70; BVerfGE 28, 119, 142.

886 BVerfGE 24, 367.

887 BVerfGE 58, 225 (*Naßauskiesung*), 300.

888 *Wasserhaushaltsgesetz* (in its amended version of 16.10.1976).

quarry operation, the city denied the operator a permit to use the water beneath his property. After exhausting his administrative remedies, the plaintiff sued the province of North Rhine-Westphalia for damages, claiming that the denial of the permit for wet gravel extraction violated his right to property as well as his right to pursue his profession. He was successful in the court of first instance. The court there relied on the traditional kind of property protection afforded to owners under paragraph 903 BGB, and argued that the right to property encompasses every possible and economically reasonable utilisation of that property. On appeal, the Federal Court of Justice referred the case to the Federal Constitutional Court for adjudication. The decision of the Constitutional Court at the time came as somewhat of a surprise to property lawyers.

The Federal Supreme Court, on the basis of paragraph 905 BGB,[889] held that the right to dispose of the groundwater found on the premises is part of the property rights inherent to ownership and that the Water Resources Act[890] therefore violated a right which was intrinsic to property.[891] The Constitutional Court rejected this decision.[892] It concluded that the objections raised against the legal regulation of groundwater was based on the mistaken assumption that groundwater would be legally inseparable from the right to property.[893] In the constitutional context, this argument did not assist the plaintiff. According to the

---

[889] This section is the embodiment of the Roman Law principle *Cuius est solum, eius est usque ad caelum et ad inferos*, and reads: *"Das Recht des Eigentümers eines Grundstücks erstreckt sich auf den Raum über der Oberfläche und auf den Erdkörper unter der Oberfläche..."* Translation: "The right of the owner to a piece of land extends to the space above the surface and to the terrestrial body under the surface...".

[890] *Wasserhaushaltsgesetz.*

[891] In the eyes of the Federal Supreme Court, the Water Resources Act amounted to an expropriation of property because it constituted an *Eingriff in die Privatrechtssphäre*, that is to say an "infringement in the private sphere".

[892] BVerfGE 58, 300 *(Naßauskiesung)*, 332-333. This rejection was based on the argument that, in spite of sec. 905 BGB, the right to control the flow of groundwater has been reserved for the provincial legislatures in that the power to regulate Water Law lay within their exclusive competence.

[893] BVerfGE 58, 300 *(Naßauskiesung)*, 335.

court, it was incorrect to assume that the Water Resources Act would lead to erosion of the substance of the right to property.[894]

It was held that the constitutional meaning of ownership could neither be deduced from ordinary statutes, which ranked lower than the Constitution, nor could the scope of the property guarantee be determined on the basis of private law regulations.[895] The significance of this decision for the German concept of property becomes clear through an analysis of the concept of property in terms of the Basic Law.

3.3. "Eigentum" in the German Basic Law

The Basic Law does not contain a definition of the concept of ownership in the constitutional context.[896] Article 14 I 1 GG is phrased in general terms: The guarantee could in principle encompass all conceivable forms of property[897] and it is left to the legislature to determine which proprietary interests would qualify for protection.[898] Judicial interpretation is not mentioned in article 14 I GG as a possible means of

---

[894] The court explained (348) that property ownership does not result in the loss of usufruct simply because the owner's right to use groundwater would be subject to governmental approval. The property owner's right had always been primarily the right to use the surface of the property, whereas the right to take material buried in the ground had always been subject to far-reaching restrictions. Even the right to dispose of surface property was in many ways subject tot constitutional restriction. The possibility of making meaningful economic use of property as a rule does not depend on whether or not groundwater can be brought to the surface or used by the owner.

[895] BVerfGE 58, 300 (Naßauskiesung), 335. "Der Begriff des von der Verfassung gewährleisteten Eigentums muß aus der Verfassung selbst gewonnen werden. Aus Normen des einfachen Rechts, die im Range unter der Verfassung stehen, kann weder der Begriff des Eigentums im verfassungsrechtlichen Sinn abgeleitet noch kann aus der privatrechtlichen Rechtsstellung der Umfang der Gewährleistung des konkreten Eigentums bestimmt werden."

[896] Papier in Maunz/Dürig, GG Kommentar (1994), m.n. 63; BVerfGE 36, 281, 290; BVerfGE 42, 263, 292-293; BVerfGE 51, 193, 218; BVerfGE 58, 300 (Naßauskiesung), 335.

[897] Private property and productive property (Produktiveigentum); immovables and movables; as well as small commercial enterprises and large corporations are protected in terms of art. 14 GG. See Thormann, Abstufungen in der Sozialbindung des Eigentums (1996), 63-75.

[898] Art. 14 I 2 GG.

determining the scope and content of property, although the competence of the ordinary courts to interpret statutory law and the competence of the Constitutional Court to interpret the Basic Law has never been doubted.[899]

The general perception is that article 14 GG protects only existing property relations,[900] but the lack of a constitutional definition of *"Eigentum"* opens the system of constitutional protection to the dynamics of development in the German society.[901] This means that the legislature and the Federal Constitutional Court must allow changes in common perceptions to be channelled into law, while maintaining the Basic Law as a guideline to measure such changes.[902] Thus, the constitutional property guarantee anticipates a differentiation between the various kinds of property, according to the kind of the protection it deserves.[903]

---

[899] See, however, *Kimminich* in *Starck (ed)*, Rights, Institutions and Impact of International Law (1987), 82.

[900] The right to engage in the acquisition or the transfer of property rights has to be derived by way of interpretation, usually by making use of art. 2 GG (the right to personal freedom) or of the property guarantee itself, by evaluating the nature of different proprietary interests. art. 2 I GG is, with relation to the property guarantee, the *lex generalis* and art. 14 I GG the *lex specialis*. It is therefore preferable to deduce the right from the institutional guarantee of private property itself. *Kimminich* in *Starck (ed)*, Rights, Institutions and Impact of International Law (1987), 82.

[901] BVerfGE 20, 351 *(Tollwut)*, 355.

[902] BVerfGE 24, 367 *(Deichordnung)*, 389; BVerfGE 25, 112 *(Niedersächsisches Deichgesetz)*, 117: *"Inhalt und Funktion des Eigentums sind dabei der Anpassung an die gesellschaftlichen und wirtschaftlichen Verhältnisse fähig und bedürftig; es ist Sache des Gesetzgebers, Inhalt und Schranken des Eigentums unter Beachtung der grundlegenden verfassungsrechtlichen Wertentscheidung zu bestimmen."* Translation: "The contents and functions of property are capable and in need of adaptation to social and economic conditions. It is the task of the legislature to undertake such adaptation while taking into account the fundamental constitutional guideline concerning ethical values."

[903] This layering or categorising of the differentiated limits of the property guarantee according to the object of the right at stake is sometimes in German legal literature referred to as the *Abstufung der eigentumsrechtlichen Grenzen*. See *Thormann*, Abstufungen in der Sozialbindung des Eigentums (1996), 214-218.

3.3.1. Property Interests Included in the Protective Ambit of Article 14 GG

The German constitutional property guarantee as such does not contain any information on the scope of the protection that it provides. The court thus has to decide which patrimonial interests are included or excluded from the constitutional guarantee. Here the crucial question is whether the inclusion of specific patrimonial interests in the protective sphere of article 14 GG would serve the fundamental constitutional purpose of securing a sphere of personal liberty for the individual. Protection of a specific interest should, in other words, enable the individual to act on his or her own initiative and to take responsibility for his or her actions, while participating in the development and functioning of the broader social and legal community.[904]

The decisions of the Federal Constitutional Court on the constitutional protection of property have enabled legal writers to draw up a system of protected rights.[905] Private law and public law entitlements would qualify to a similar extent for the protection of article 14 GG, insofar as such property interests could be described either as (i) *Leistungseigentum* (that is to say, property acquired by an owner on the ground of his

---

[904] *Badura* in *Benda/Maihofer/Vogel (eds)*, Handbuch des Verfassungsrechts (1994), m.n. 2; *Van der Walt*, Constitutional Property Clauses - A Comparative Analysis (1999), 151; *Papier* in *Maunz/Dürig*, GG Kommentar (1994), m.n. 1.

[905] The following categorisation is borrowed from *Leisner* in *Isensee/Kirchhof*, Handbuch des Staatsrechts VI (1989), m.n. 85-95. It must be added, however, that not all writers share Leisner's view of the *characteristics* belonging to constitutional property. The main point of distinction is that Leisner views the inclusion of public law patrimonial rights or interests into the protective ambit of art. 14 GG not as an extension to the constitutional concept of property, but rather as a natural consequence of the scope of the property guarantee as laid down in art. 14 GG. On the contrary, some writers view the inclusion of public law patrimonial interests into the protective ambit of art. 14 GG as a development or extension of the scope of art. 14 GG. (*Van der Walt*, Constitutional Property Clauses - A Comparative Analysis (1999), 152.) Regardless of the theoretical implications and the different approaches towards the characteristics of constitutional property, it seems as if many authors implicitly follow the *categorisation* of constitutionally protected patrimonial interests into *Leistungseigentum, Sicherungseigentum* and *Vertrauenseigentum*. See *Wendt* in *Sachs (ed)*, Grundgesetz Kommentar (1996), m.n. 28.

or her own efforts,[906] whether in money or labour),[907] as (ii) *Sicherungs-eigentum* (in other words, those objects required to maintain a subsistence level),[908] or as (iii) *Vertrauenseigentum* (that is to say, legal positions that objectively require protection because of the legitimate reliance placed upon such protection).[909]

3.3.1.1. Expanded Category of Private-law Rights and Patrimonial Interests

The premise adopted in German constitutional law is that the property guarantee includes, but is not restricted to, rights in corporeal things. In fact, the property guarantee embraces almost all private law rights, as well as interests with economic value.[910] Thus, all patrimonial rights enabling the holder thereof to determine how they can serve his or her interests best are protected.[911] Rights relating to corporeal as well as incorporeal objects are therefore incorporated in the protective ambit of article 14 GG.

The application of article 14 GG to private law interests and rights are restricted by certain general principles:[912]

(i) Only *specific individual* rights or assets are protected,[913] not patrimony, wealth or estate in general.[914] This point is important, because it

---

[906] Such a performance can consist of either a monetary contribution or of labour, but should in all circumstances be rendered by the owner himself or herself.

[907] E.g. BVerfGE 14, 288, 293.

[908] E.g. BVerfGE 32, 111, 142.

[909] E.g. BVerfGE 14, 263, 278 read with BVerfGE 58, 81, 121.

[910] *Pieroth/Schlink*, Grundrechte-Staatsrecht II (1991), m.n. 999.

[911] *Van der Walt*, Constitutional Property Clauses - A Comparative Analysis (1999), 152.

[912] *Badura* in *Benda/Maihofer/Vogel (eds)*, Handbuch des Verfassungsrechts (1994), m.n. 37.

[913] See BGHZ 62, 96; BGHZ 72, 211, 218 ff.; BGH 1975 *NJW* 1017; BGH 1976 *NJW* 1313; BGH 1980 NJW 387.

[914] BVerfGE 74, 129, 148. See also *Pieroth/Schlink*, Grundrechte-Staatsrecht II (1991), m.n. 1003; *Papier* in *Maunz/Dürig*, GG Kommentar (1994), m.n. 8; *Kimminich*, Eigentum Enteignung Entschädigung (1976), m.n. 57; BVerfGE 4, 7 (*Investitionshilfe*), 17.

determines, for instance, whether the duty to pay taxes is subject to the provisions of article 14 GG. The assumption that taxes pertain to general wealth and not to specific objects of property, renders an application of article 14 GG to the limitation of property by tax law and practice difficult.[915] The Federal Constitutional Court tried to escape this dilemma by first arguing[916] that taxation generally does not affect the constitutional guarantee of property. An infringement of the property guarantee could therefore only be considered if the tax burden is excessive or if his or her wealth is fundamentally affected. This decision resulted in the perception that article 14 GG is no effective bulwark against the avaricious exercise of the state's power of taxation.[917] The Federal Constitutional Court has, in the mean time, modified its view to the extent that tax laws may in principle be reviewed on the basis of the constitutional property guarantee. However, a violation of article 14 GG would only apply in extreme cases. Article 14 GG would, for instance, apply when — notwithstanding the effect it might have in individual cases[918] — the taxation *in general* would have a strangulating effect or would amount to confiscation. The tax burden is said to have a strangulating effect *(Erdrosselungssteuer)* when it makes it impossible for an individual to continue a lawful professional activity.[919] The tax burden has a confiscatory effect *(Konfiskatorische Steuern)* when it completely deprives a person of a specific property right.[920] The Federal Constitutional Court does not offer a clear explanation of the term *confiscation* in this context. From the literature on the subject it seems

---

[915] It is, moreover, problematic to determine the proportionality of taxation, as taxes are usually collected to provide money for the general budget and not for financing definite policy objectives. *Schuppert* in *Karpen (ed)*, Constitution of Germany (1988), 112.

[916] BVerfGE 4, 7 *(Investitionshilfe)*.

[917] *Schuppert* in *Karpen (ed)*, Constitution of Germany (1988), 112.

[918] BVerfG 1976 NJW 101 *(Vermögenssteuer)*.

[919] BVerfGE 16, 147, 161; BVerfGE 82, 159, 190. *Frowein*, Protection of Property in Relation to Taxation (1996), 16-17.

[920] BVerfGE 23, 288, 315 states: *"Ein Verstoß gegen Artikel 14 GG kann allenfalls dann in Betracht kommen, wenn die Geldleistungspflichten den Pflichtigen übermäßig belasten und seine Vermögensverhältnisse grundlegend beeinträchtigen würden, also eine Konfiskation darstellen würden."* Translation: "A violation of article 14 GG could only be considered where the obligations to pay money would be an unreasonable burden on the debtor fundamentally affecting his economic conditions, amounting in fact to a confiscation."

that taxes on assets are considered confiscatory if they force the owner to surrender these assets over a certain period. The tax will be considered confiscatory if it is impossible to finance it out of the revenue normally received from the assets.[921]

(ii) Further, expectancies or contingent "rights"[922] are as a rule not guaranteed: only vested rights which have been acquired[923] already are protected.[924] The property clause would thus only provide protection for existing rights. It also does not provide for the acquisition of rights.[925] Consequently, the wide concept of property recognised for purposes of article 14 GG does not simply include all rights or interests which have some patrimonial value.[926]

(iii) The use of property is protected by article 14 GG: the holder of the right can retain, alter, use or consume his or her property. Negative use is also guaranteed: the freedom *not* to use the property.[927] Protection of the use of property will, however, only be under discussion if some

---

[921] *Frowein*, Protection of Property in Relation to Taxation (1996), 15-16; *Mußgnug*, 1991 JZ, 996.

[922] *"[N]icht bloße Umsatz- und Gewinnchancen, Hoffnungen, Erwartungen und Aussichten."* BVerfGE 68, 193, 222 and BVerfGE 74, 129, 148.

[923] The so-called *Bestandsschutz*.

[924] *Wendt* in *Sachs (ed)*, Grundgesetz Kommentar (1996), m.n. 44 points out that in some cases, a vested property interest can include, for example, the right to acquire future profits. This is distinguishable from the case (e.g. BGHZ 23, 235; BGHZ 55, 261) where a person relies merely on an existing favourable legal situation in basing its claim for protection of a future interest. BVerfGE 78, 205, 211 ff.

[925] *Erwerbschutz. Kleyn,* 1996 SAPR/PL, 414 note 71.

[926] However, the rights and interests falling within the protective ambit of article 14 GG are guaranteed in several ways. Not only is the continued existence of these rights-and therewith the freedom of the owner to retain his or her property-protected, but the owner's freedom to use, consume, and dispose of the property at will also falls within the ambit of article 14 I 1 GG. The enforcement of these rights in the constitutional context nevertheless takes on another dimension than in private law: The social obligation related to property requires a balancing of individual and social interests in the definition of constitutional property.

[927] *Pieroth/Schlink*, Grundrechte-Staatsrecht II (1991), m.n. 1007.

other fundamental right does not protect the action of the holder of the right.[928]

(iv) Further, the right holder's right to defend his or her interests in administrative or court proceedings, also against third parties, is included in article 14 GG.[929]

It is beyond the scope of this work to discuss each private law right that falls within the protective ambit of the property clause in Germany separately. However, the following rights could be mentioned by way of example. In general things *(das Sacheigentum)*, real rights *(dingliche Rechte)*,[930] real security rights,[931] possession *(der Besitz)*,[932] the right to heritable lease of land *(das Erbbaurecht)*,[933] most personal (contractual) rights *(Forderungsrechte)*,[934] rights of membership with patrimonial value *(vermögenswerte Mitgliedschafts- und Gesellschaftsrechte)* like shares *(Aktien)*,[935] and copyright, patents and registered trademarks *(Urheberrechte, eingetragene Warenzeichen)*[936] among others,[937] fall within the protective ambit of the property guarantee. The protection of incorporeal property and certain rights to develop land will be discussed in more detail in the following paragraphs as specific examples

---

[928] E.g. reading of a bought magazine is protected in terms of art. 5 I 1 GG, not in terms of art. 14 GG. Similarly, use of an automobile vehicle is protected in terms of art. 2 I GG. However, use of a piece of land for purposes of securing a loan (mortgage), would be protected in terms of art. 14 GG.

[929] Verfahrensgarantie. *Pieroth/Schlink*, Grundrechte-Staatsrecht II (1991), m.n. 1010.

[930] *Wendt* in *Sachs (ed)*, Grundgesetz Kommentar (1996), m.n. 24.

[931] *Hypotheken, Grundschulden, Pfandrechte*: BVerfGE 1991 DVBl 376 ff.

[932] *Papier* in *Maunz/Dürig*, GG Kommentar (1994), m.n. 200.

[933] BVerfGE 79, 174, 191.

[934] BVerfGE 68, 193, 222; BVerfGE 42, 263 *(Contergan)*; BVerfGE 83, 201 *(Vorkaufsrecht)*; BVerfGE 45, 142, 179.

[935] BVerfGE 14, 262, 276.

[936] Copyright: BVerfGE 79, 29, 40. Patents: BVerfGE 36, 281, 290. Trademarks: BVerfGE 51, 193, 216 ff. See also BVerfGE 79, 174, 191; BGHZ 77, 179, 182; BVerfGE 25, 371, 407; BVerfGE 31, 229; BVerfGE 36, 281.

[937] See *Badura* in *Benda/Maihofer/Vogel (eds)*, Handbuch des Verfassungsrechts (1994), m.n. 35-39; *Bryde* in *Von Münch/Kunig*, GG Kommentar (1992), m.n. 11-24; *Wendt* in *Sachs (ed)*, Grundgesetz Kommentar (1996), m.n. 24.

of the extension of the category of protected private law rights by the courts and authors.

3.3.1.1.1. Incorporeal Assets

Incorporeal assets include certain patrimonial rights, which are protected in private law, but not necessarily as *property*. The inclusion of these interests within the protective ambit of article 14 I 1 GG therefore constitutes a remarkable deviation from the private law concept of ownership. Examples are tenants' rights, which are in private law governed by contract, the right to goodwill in established and operating business concerns,[938] and intellectual property.

The Federal Constitutional Court held that the right of a tenant to live in a rented apartment constitutes "property" within the meaning of article 14 I GG.[939] The tenant would thus be protected against termination of a contract of lease by the landlord if termination is not based on a well-founded interest of the landlord[940] and if such an interest is not specified in the contract.[941] The Federal Constitutional Court justified its decision to place a tenant's right of occupation within the protective ambit of article 14 I 1 GG as follows:[942]

> *"Die Wohnung ist für jedermann Mittelpunkt seiner privaten Existenz. Der Einzelne ist auf ihren Gebrauch zur Befriedigung elementarer Lebensbedürfnisse sowie zur Freiheitssicherung und Entfaltung seiner Persönlichkeit angewiesen. Der Großteil der Bevölkerung kann zur Deckung seines Wohnbedarfs jedoch nicht auf Eigentum zurückgreifen, sondern ist gezwungen, Wohnraum zu mie-*

---

[938] *"Eingerichteter und ausgeübter Gewerbebetrieb."*

[939] BVerfGE 89, 1 *(Besitzrecht des Mieters)*; Judgement of 18 October 1993 I BvR 1335/91 1994 Neue Justiz 25.

[940] BVerfGE 89, 1, 10.

[941] Judgement of 18 October 1993 I BvR 1335/91 1994 Neue Justiz 26.

[942] BVerfGE 89, 1, 6. Translation: "A dwelling place is the centre of every person's private existence. The person is dependant on a place of dwelling for complying with elementary needs of living, as well as for securing his freedom and for self-fulfilment. However, the largest part of the population cannot afford to fulfil this need through ownership. Instead, they are forced to rent living space. The possessory right of a lessee, under these circumstances, has the same function of ownership of things."

ten. Das Besitzrecht des Mieters erfüllt unter diesen Umständen Funktionen, wie sie typischerweise dem Sacheigentum zukommen."

On the other hand, the Federal Constitutional Court in 1974 overruled several decisions of the courts of lower instance on account of the unduly harsh application of a federal rent control statute to owners of apartments occupied by tenants.[943] The court stressed that the social function of property is important when it needs to be determined whether specific interests should be protected under the constitutional property guarantee or not. However, the court also remarked that[944]

"*Ebensowenig wie die Eigentumsgarantie eine die soziale Funktion eines Eigentumsobjektes mißachtende Nutzung schützt, kann Art. 14 Abs. 2 GG eine übermäßige, durch die soziale Funktion nicht gebotene Begrenzung privatrechtlicher Befugnisse rechtfertigen.*"

The right to goodwill in a commercial enterprise ("established and exercised commercial activity"[945]) is an example of a private law right which is regarded by many authors,[946] as well as the Federal Supreme Court[947] and the Federal Administrative Court,[948] as "property" in terms of article 14 GG. However, it has not been acknowledged as a right qualifying for constitutional protection by the Federal Constitutional Court.[949] The notion of "commercial enterprise" (established and exercised commercial activity) is usually defined in very broad terms to recognise the fact that business property is more than the mere sum of

---

[943] BVerfGE 37, 132 *(Wohnraumkündigungsschutzgesetz).*

[944] BVerfGE 37, 132, 140-141. Translation: "As little as the property guarantee can protect a function of the object of ownership that disregards the social obligation of property, can art. 14 II GG justify a disproportionate limitation of private law entitlements that are not necessitated by the social obligation."

[945] "*Eingerichteter und ausgeübter Gewerbebetrieb.*" BVerfGE 4, 7 *(Investitionshilfe),* 17.

[946] *Wendt* in *Sachs* (ed), Grundgesetz Kommentar (1996), m.n. 26; *Kimminich,* Eigentum Enteignung Entschädigung (1976), m.n. 75; *Van der Walt,* Constitutional Property Clauses - A Comparative Analysis (1999), 153-154.

[947] BGHZ 23, 157, 162 ff.; BGHZ 92, 34, 37.

[948] BVerwGE 62, 224 226.

[949] In BVerfGE 77, 84, 118, the Federal Constitutional Court excluded goodwill of this kind (that is to say, *bestehende Geschäftsverbindungen, einen erworbenen Kundenstamm oder die Marktstellung eines Unternehmens*) from the protective ambit of article 14 I GG.

its individual property holdings.[950] Commercial activity often entails the capability to make profits, thus giving rise to a whole range of so-called *business property* rights. Business property might, for instance, be affected if the state decides to withhold certain vital licences or permits. However, the Federal Constitutional Court[951] held (without explicitly deciding this point)[952] that, seen from a property law perspective, the enterprise *de facto* comprises all those objects and rights forming part of its patrimony. However, the court did not want to acknowledge that the business enterprise as an entity enjoyed legal protection in terms of the property clause,[953] because its patrimonial interests and rights in themselves already fell within the ambit of the constitutional guarantee.[954] As such, rights relating to business concerns would not comply with the requirement that only specific (vested and existing) patrimonial rights will be protected by article 14 GG. Consequently, an investigation into the protective scope of article 14 GG is not mandated in cases where a legislative alteration or rescission influences economic and financial policy measures. These measures might hold factual advantages for commercial enterprises, but they do not necessarily hold legal advantages.[955]

The Federal Constitution Court has, in a number of decisions,[956] furnished the legal basis upon which the patrimonial aspects of "intellec-

---

[950] *Van der Walt*, Constitutional Property Clauses - A Comparative Analysis (1999), 154.

[951] BVerfGE 51, 193, 221 ff.

[952] *Kimminich*, Eigentum Enteignung Entschädigung (1976), m.n. 77; *Van der Walt*, Constitutional Property Clauses - A Comparative Analysis (1999), 154.

[953] BVerfGE 51, 193 221 ff.: *"Es ist die Frage, ob der Gewerbebetrieb als solcher die konstituierenden Merkmale des verfassungsrechtlichen Eigentumsbegriffs aufweist. Eigentumsrechtlich gesehen ist das Unternehmen die tatsächliche – nicht aber die rechtliche – Zusammenfassung der zu einem Vermögen gehörenden Sachen und Rechte, die an sich schon vor verfassungswidrigen Eingriffen geschützt sind."*

[954] BVerfGE 51, 193 *(Schloßberg)*, 221.

[955] BGHZ 45, 83 *(Knäckebrot)*.

[956] Copyright see BVerfGE 31, 229, 239; BVerfGE 49, 382; BVerfGE 79, 29, 40 ff.; BVerfGE 81, 12, 16; Patents see BVerfGE 36, 281, 290; Trademarks see BVerfGE 51, 193, 216 ff.; BVerfGE 78, 58, 71.

tual property"[957] enjoy constitutional protection. According to the court, the protection of intellectual property under article 14 GG did not follow from the statutory protection of copyright as such, as this includes protection of non-patrimonial aspects.[958] Instead, intellectual property enjoys constitutional protection in terms of article 14 GG, because of the functions of the property clause. For instance, the function of the property clause as an individual guarantee will result in protection of the holder of copyright in a specific work, in the case where legislation orders the free distribution of that work.[959] The patrimonial aspects of intellectual property are means by which an individual determines his or her economic destiny, and exercises his or her independence and freedom.[960] Therefore, intellectual property deserves constitutional protection.

3.3.1.1.2. Development of Rights with Regard to Land

Property protection within the category of rights to land has always been particularly complicated, mainly on account of the fact that rights and benefits granted by public authorities are not traditionally included in the ambit of ownership entitlements. These entitlements hover on the boundary between private and public law. The property guarantee clearly covers land-use rights lawfully acquired and exercised. However, certain land-use rights which are unlawful or which have not been exercised, can also be protected in terms of the constitutional property guarantee. This would require, at least, that the "holder" of these rights has the permission for exercising them, and that such permission has been acquired legally. The withdrawal of such a land-use right would then affect the holder thereof so severely its constitutional protection is warranted.[961] It is not always easy to determine whether a land-use right like this complies with all the requirements for protection. The protec-

---

[957] *Geistiges Eigentum* which includes patents and copyright of printed material.

[958] See BVerfGE 31, 229, 241; BVerfGE 79, 1, 25.

[959] See *Von Heinegg/Haltern*, 1993 JuS, 123; BVerfGE 31, 229, 239.

[960] *Badura* in *Benda/Maihofer/Vogel (eds)*, Handbuch des Verfassungsrechts (1994), m.n. 2.

[961] *Van der Walt*, Constitutional Property Clauses - A Comparative Analysis (1999), 154; *Leisner* in *Isensee/Kirchhof*, Handbuch des Staatsrechts VI (1989), 105.

tion of *Baufreiheit* and *Anliegergebrauch* respectively serve as examples.

(i) The question whether the right to erect buildings on land[962] fell within the protective ambit of article 14 I 1 GG, has given rise to varying opinions. Some authors are of the opinion that this *Baufreiheit* is an element inherent in the concept of private ownership of land, and that it should be protected on this basis.[963] Another opinion is that the right to erect buildings on land depends on a grant by a public authority[964] and that the numerous building law limitations result in this right being practically without content.[965] If this view is followed, building law regulations would not be monitored in terms of the constitutional property guarantee, and landownership would be stripped of part of its functions, namely free and exclusive use. Alternatively, if the guarantee of article 14 GG is aimed at preserving the function of property expounding private individual use, a particular kind of use could not simply be excluded from protection of the property guarantee. Moreover, it is dogmatically unsound to construct the freedom to erect buildings on land as "*Nutzungszuweisung.*"[966] Instead of investigating the constitutionality of limitations on the right to erect buildings on land, the issue is investigated from the premise that *Baufreiheit* is *ab initio* excluded from protection. Consequently, all more strictly limited fundamental rights would be reduced to mere state-granted (or state-approved) activities. This would, in turn, make the socialisation of land provided for in article 15 GG[967] impossible. As such, it would be in breach with the social welfare state principle underlying the Basic Law.

---

[962] See BVerfGE 35, 263, 276.

[963] *Papier* in *Maunz/Dürig*, GG Kommentar (1994), m.n. 58; *Badura* in *Benda/Maihofer/Vogel (eds)*, Handbuch des Verfassungsrechts (1994), m.n. 79.

[964] "*Baubefugnis als öffentlich-rechtliche Nutzungszuweisung.*"

[965] "*Schrumpfung der Freiheit auf Null.*" See *Papier* in *Maunz/Dürig*, GG Kommentar (1994), m.n. 60; *Leisner* in *Isensee/Kirchhof*, Handbuch des Staatsrechts VI (1989), m.n. 104.

[966] *Leisner* in *Isensee/Kirchhof*, Handbuch des Staatsrechts VI (1989), m.n. 104.

[967] "*Grund und Boden, Naturschätze und Produktionsmittel können zum Zwecke der Vergesellschaftung durch ein Gesetz, das Art und Ausmaß der Entschädigung regelt, in Gemeineigentum oder in andere Formen der Gemeinwirtschaft überführt werden. Für die Entschädigung gilt Artikel 14 Abs. 3 Satz 3 und 4 entsprechend.*" Translation: "Land, natural resources and means of pro-

(ii) The right to use roads and public spaces adjacent to private land *(Anliegerrecht und Anliegergebrauch)*,[968] is regarded as part of the landed property flowing from the nature and location of the land.[969] Access to public roads, and free access of air and light from the adjoining street are thus guaranteed for the local residents.[970] The concept of *Anliegergebrauch* includes, for instance,[971] the use of the windows and outer wall of the building facing the street for purposes of advertising by resident shop owners (that is to say, for placing overhanging advertisement boards or posters in view of passing pedestrians and traffic); use of the adjoining street and pavement for loading purposes within reasonable limits;[972] and use of the adjoining pavement and street for purposes of parking bicycles or motor cars.[973] In this sense, *Anliegergebrauch* can be viewed a form of public use limited to the residents of a specific area.[974] However, *Anliegergebrauch* does not allow a business concern (like a restaurant) to place tables or a vending machine on the adjoining pavement or to place free-standing poster boards there to advertise on behalf of a third party. These activities are consequently not protected by article 14 I 1 GG.[975] The owner, possessor or holder of land adjoining a public road or street therefore is entitled to use it, subject to reasonable use by the public. Temporary limitations on the right to use of and access to public roads adjoining landed property (due to, for instance, road repairs or building renovations) usually have to be

---

duction may be transferred to public ownership or other forms of public enterprise by a law which determines the nature and extent of compensation. In respect of compensation the third and fourth sentences of paragraph (3) of Article 14 shall apply mutatis mutandis."

[968] As well as the limitations on the use of property brought about by the public use of such roads.

[969] *Badura* in *Benda/Maihofer/Vogel (eds)*, Handbuch des Verfassungsrechts (1994), m.n. 87; *Van der Walt*, Constitutional Property Clauses - A Comparative Analysis (1999), 154.

[970] *Papier* in *Maunz/Dürig*, GG Kommentar (1994), m.n. 115.

[971] *Papier*, Recht der öffentlichen Sachen (1998), 19-20.

[972] The reasonableness of this action will depend on the local customs, frequency, and measure to which traffic is hindered thereby.

[973] Provided that the possibility of parking exists.

[974] *Papier*, Recht der öffentlichen Sachen (1998), 19; *Papier* in *Maunz/Dürig*, GG Kommentar (1994), m.n. 120.

[975] See BGHZ 30, 241; BGHZ 48, 65.

tolerated by the local residents. They are, however, protected against limitations of a more permanent nature in terms of the constitutional property guarantee.[976] In terms of the guideline formulated by the Federal Administrative Court,[977] protection in terms of article 14 GG is afforded if it can be reasonably expected that the limitation of the local resident's rights of use will continue permanently. However, if it could at the outset be reasonably foreseen that use of a specific area would cause nuisance due to the nature or natural, probable development of a specific residential or industrial area, the use would be unreasonable and unworthy of constitutional protection. If the nature and use of the public road or street is materially changed, the benefit thereof for the public in general prevails over the interests of the owners of adjacent land.[978] It is only in exceptional circumstances that a local resident could claim that the *status quo* be continued.[979]

3.3.1.2. Public Law Rights and Benefits as "Property" in Terms of Article 14 GG

It is problematic to determine the concept of property in cases where public law *rights* with economic value are at stake or where ordinary legal rules attribute specific *benefits* only to a specific person who has obtained some form of official authorisation for holding those benefits. However, a similar threshold test as applied with regard to private law rights with economic value is applied where *public law rights or benefits* with economic value are at stake. It has to be determined whether protection of the particular right in question would serve the purpose of the property guarantee. The right or benefit for which protection is sought must, in other words, secure an individual's personal development in society. Similar to the question in the context of private law rights with economic value, protection is afforded only if the individual has, at least, acquired a vested right (or benefit). The inquiry into the scope of the protection afforded by article 14 I 1 GG is, however, usu-

---

[976] *Papier* in *Maunz/Dürig*, GG Kommentar (1994), m.n. 116.

[977] BVerwGE 38, 209 219.

[978] *Badura* in *Benda/Maihofer/Vogel (eds)*, Handbuch des Verfassungsrechts (1994), m.n. 87; *Papier* in *Maunz/Dürig*, GG Kommentar (1994), m.n. 117.

[979] *Badura* in *Benda/Maihofer/Vogel (eds)*, Handbuch des Verfassungsrechts (1994), m.n. 87.

ally more intensive than is the case with private law rights with economic value.

Private and public law entitlements qualify to a similar extent for the protection of article 14 GG. The latter need not qualify as entitlements in terms of the private law definition of ownership, but they at least have to fall within the patrimony of private individuals,[980] being either characteristically *Leistungseigentum, Sicherungseigentum,* or *Vertrauenseigentum.*[981] Because the threshold question is usually investigated more intensively where public law rights or benefits are involved, the characteristics of *eigene Leistung, Existenzsicherung* and *Vertrauen* play a more important role in determining whether constitutional protection will be afforded than in the case of private law rights. However, this does not mean that these characteristics are of no consequence in the private law context. These characteristics of constitutionally protected property merely surface more readily in an inquiry where public law rights or benefits are at stake.

Claims for pension or unemployment benefits,[982] which exemplify social welfare titles emanating from public law, are for instance in appropriate circumstances included within the protective scope of article 14 GG.[983] The courts have determined that these public law claims must meet certain requirements to qualify for protection. Constitutionally protected social welfare benefits must be (i) exclusively assigned to the insured for his or her private use; (ii) based on considerable personal efforts *(eigene Leistung)* of the insured;[984] and (iii) aimed at securing the continued well-being *(Existenzsicherung)* of the insured.[985]

---

[980] E.g. claims for tax refunds: BVerfGE 70, 278, 285; child allowance: BSG 1987 NJW 463; subsidies: BVerfGE 72, 175, 193 ff.

[981] *Leisner* in *Isensee/Kirchhof,* Handbuch des Staatsrechts VI (1989), m.n. 85-95; *Wendt* in *Sachs (ed),* Grundgesetz Kommentar (1996), m.n. 28. See *note* 905 above.

[982] BVerfGE 58, 81, 112; BVerfGE 72, 9.

[983] E.g. Social security (national insurance): BVerfGE 58, 81, 109 and BVerfGE 66, 234, 247; Unemployment benefits: BVerfGE 72, 9 19 and BVerfGE 74, 203 213.

[984] BVerfGE 1, 264, 277 ff.; BVerfGE 50, 290, 340; BVerfGE 58, 81, 112.

[985] Decision of 7 July 1985, 1985 DVBl 1015; BVerfGE 69, 272, 300 ff.; BVerfGE 72, 9, 18 ff.

The concept of *eigene Leistung* (personal efforts) could create some interpretative difficulty.[986] However, fears that this concept could be interpreted either too strictly or too widely were proved to be unfounded.[987] The importance of this criterion as mechanism for determining which state-granted benefits qualify as "property," and as a general justification for the protection of certain interests as constitutional property[988] has been established.

In the context of medical aid insurance, the concept of *Existenzsicherung* has been expressly acknowledged by the Federal Constitutional Court[989] as an element of the constitutional property concept:[990]

> *"Konstituierendes Merkmal einer Sozialversicherungsrechtlichen Position ist es schließlich, daß sie der Existenzsicherung des Berechtigten zu dienen bestimmt ist."*

Claims based on medical aid insurance would for instance qualify as property if they promote the well-being of the majority of the population and if these grants have been provided as an essential service over a long period. According to the courts, the insured can, in other words, count on it as an additional source of securing his or her personal well-being.[991]

Apart from indicating how the criterion of *Existenzsicherung* is applied in the process of determining the threshold question, this example also indicates the caution of the courts in setting these criteria as general rules for the determination of constitutional protection of property. Almost all forms of property are aimed at advancing the material well being of the individual in one way or the other. Nevertheless, it is ar-

---

[986] See the criticism of *Meyer-Abich,* Der Schutzzweck der Eigentumsgarantie (1980), 50-57; *Wendt,* Eigentum (1985), 113-120, 86-90.

[987] *Leisner* in *Isensee/Kirchhof,* Handbuch des Staatsrechts VI (1989), m.n. 86-88.

[988] *Leisner* in *Isensee/Kirchhof,* Handbuch des Staatsrechts VI (1989), m.n. 89.

[989] Judgement of 16.7.1985-1 BvL 5/80 reported in 1985 BB 1537-1540.

[990] Judgement of 16.7.1985-1 BvL 5/80 reported in 1985 BB 1538. Translation: "A characteristic feature of a right emanating from social insurance is, after all, that it is aimed at securing the continued well being of the holder of the right."

[991] See also BVerfGE 40, 65, 84; BVerfGE 53, 257, 294.

gued that the requirement of *Existenzsicherung* should only be applicable to a limited category of patrimonial interests, namely interests based on social welfare policies, or perhaps more generally to public law interests with economic value.[992] However, such an argument could too easily result in a confusing system of differing criteria for constitutional protection, depending on the nature of the contended right or interest. This would make the threshold question too complicated and could flout many claims for constitutional protection simply because the nature of the right or interest is contentious.

It is submitted that the criterion of *Existenzsicherung* in the context of constitutional protection of property should be viewed against the interplay between the *Rechtsstaat* and the *Sozialstaat* principles within the German constitutional order.[993] It is, in other words, not a full-fledged requirement for constitutional protection, but rather an indication of possible constitutional protection that has to be seen in the light of the combined individual and social function of property within the German constitutional order. The quoted dictum of the Federal Constitutional Court, therefore, acknowledges that when certain interests have the effect of advancing the continued well-being of those who benefit therefrom, these interests could also qualify as constitutional property.[994]

This reasoning provides the necessary link between protection of "new" (public law) property relations and "traditional" (private law) property relations. All interests that advance the well-being of an individual will qualify for constitutional property protection; provided that they are appropriated (that is, that they have vested in or have been assigned to a specific person for his or her exclusive use). This holds true, not only for property interests arising from social welfare policies, but also for property relations in private law and elsewhere. Land, patents and trademarks — even money — can have the effect of advancing per-

---

[992] *Leisner*, Eigentum (1996), 57-59 point out, for instance, a too broad definition of *Existenzsicherungseigentum* could considerably infringe individual freedom, and could complicate the already difficult "threshold question" even further by introducing a layered protection of property interests.

[993] See 115 ff. above.

[994] *Leisner* in *Isensee/Kirchhof*, Handbuch des Staatsrechts VI (1989), m.n. 92.

sonal well-being.[995] Those elements indicating whether a particular patrimonial interest in the sphere of public law, especially in the context of social welfare, qualifies for constitutional protection are thus also present in the context of private law rights. However, private law rights mostly qualify so obviously for constitutional protection in terms of the property clause, that these indications of *eigene Leistung, Existenzsicherung* and *Vertrauen* hardly ever need to be considered in the course of determining the threshold question.

3.4. Evaluation: Property in the German Constitutional Order

From an analysis of the concept of property under the German Civil Code and under the Basic Law, it becomes clear that the German concept of property in constitutional law has been developed into something quite different from the private law concept of property. This can be ascribed to the changes in the German social order since the promulgation of the Basic Law, as well as to the interpretation of article 14 GG in the light of the basic constitutional principles like the *Rechtsstaat* and the *Sozialstaat*. Article 14 GG thus guarantees a subjective constitutional right, not a subjective private right.[996]

In this sense, property protection under the constitution has to be distinguished from property protection in the sphere of private law. Nevertheless, private law property rights are controlled by the German Civil Code and related statutes, which have to comply with the requirements of article 14 GG. If these private law rules determine or protect the proprietary relations between individuals in such a manner that the basic constitutional right to property of either party is affected, the court can be approached with a complaint based on the probable unconstitutionality of that particular rule of private law directly.[997]

---

[995] *Leisner* in *Isensee/Kirchhof,* Handbuch des Staatsrechts VI (1989), m.n. 93.

[996] *Leisner* in *Isensee/Kirchhof,* Handbuch des Staatsrechts VI (1989), m.n. 4.

[997] *Van der Walt,* Constitutional Property Clauses - A Comparative Analysis (1999), 126 accordingly shows that it is therefore unnecessary to revert to the theory of *Drittwirkung* or to a horizontal constitutional complaint against another private party - the complaint is directed at the statute itself.

3.4.1. Property and Development of the Social Order

The lack of a definition of property rights in the Basic Law opens the system of constitutional protection to the dynamics of developments in the society.[998] This places great responsibility on the shoulders of the legislature and the Federal Constitutional Court. The Basic Law must be maintained as the mechanism by which changed public perceptions can be channelled into law.[999] In German law, the process of defining constitutional property was characterised by different phases. Initially, efforts were made to formulate a suitable principle for the definition of property. In subsequent phases, the definition was applied in ways that took the values and political ideology pervasive in society at a particular point in time into account.

Article 14 GG does not guarantee protection of a set of individual property rights, but rather property in general.[1000] The ownership guarantee itself makes no distinction between different kinds of property or different types of ownership. Although the ownership protection afforded by article 14 GG is not graded or differentiated,[1001] variable degrees of restriction on ownership protection arise from the social welfare function of ownership.[1002]

The property guarantee in the German legal system covers those actions that facilitate freedom for the citizen in the economic sphere. In this way, provision is also made for the functional change of the right to property. Formerly the basis of the individual's well-being was the ownership of land or the family enterprise. The individual's well-being is now gradually being linked rather to the proceeds of his or her own labour, which is reflected in his or her right to participate in the benefits

---

[998] BVerfGE 20, 351 *(Tollwut)*, 355.

[999] See BVerfGE 24, 367 *(Deichordnung)*, 389.

[1000] *Leisner* in *Isensee/Kirchhof*, Handbuch des Staatsrechts VI (1989), m.n. 46. "*In erstaunlicher Kontinuität ist in der Judikatur aller obersten Gerichte stets von 'dem' Eigentum die Rede. 'Bodeneigentum' etwa oder urheberrechtliches Eigentum sind demgegenüber deutlich untergeordnete Spezialbegriffe.*"

[1001] *Leisner* in *Isensee/Kirchhof*, Handbuch des Staatsrechts VI (1989), m.n. 46; *Ossenbühl* in *Kirchhof/Kommers (eds)*, Germany and its Basic Law (1993), 270.

[1002] *Ossenbühl* in *Kirchhof/Kommers (eds)*, Germany and its Basic Law (1993), 270. See 296 ff. below.

of the social welfare system.[1003] This change in the function of the property guarantee is at best illustrated by the decisions of the Federal Constitutional Court on social welfare benefits. The court determined that social insurance pensions fall within the protection of the property guarantee, on the basis that the function of social security is to safeguard the personal well-being of individuals.[1004] The court also took into account the fact that pension benefits are not granted by the government as a measure of social assistance. These benefits are to a large extent based on the individual's personal efforts and should therefore fall within the ambit of the constitutional property guarantee.[1005]

Papier[1006] ascribes the intensified inquiry to the transformation of constitutional property protection by the claims set by public law rights from a so-called *Abwehr- (Freiheits)recht* into a so-called *Teilhaberrecht*. He explains the difference between them as follows:[1007]

> *"Grundrechtliche Teilhaberrechte können aber nie die dem Freiheitsrecht eigene Stringenz, Verbindlichkeit und anspruchskonstituierende Unmittelbarkeit aufweisen. Sie geben dem Gesetzgeber eher Direktiven und partielle Zielvorgabe im komplexen legislatorischen Abwägungsvorgang."*

The term *Abwehrrechte* indicates the function of fundamental rights pertaining to the protection afforded to individuals against unjustified curtailment of their constitutional status by the state. The term *Freiheitsrechte* denotes that the function of fundamental rights is to afford constitutional protection to individuals to arrange their lives freely and to take responsibility for their own actions, thereby contributing to the affairs of society at large. Reference to *Teilhaberechte* focuses on the

---

[1003] *Hesse*, Grundzüge des Verfassungsrechts (1993), m.n. 443: *"Mit Recht ist deshalb davon gesprochen worden, daß unter den Bedingungen der modernen Industriegesellschaft soziale Sicherheit weniger eine Frage privatrechtlicher Verwendung des produktiven Eigentums sei als eine solche der öffentlichen Austeilung von Bezugsrechten und daß die publizistischen Eigentumssurrogate entscheidend geworden seien."*

[1004] BVerfGE 53, 257, 289.

[1005] BVerfGE 53, 257, 289.

[1006] *Papier* in *Maunz/Dürig*, GG Kommentar (1994), m.n. 129.

[1007] Translation: "Constitutional participation rights can, however, never display the same stringency (rigorousness), commitment and immediacy of claiming capacity as freedom rights. Much rather do they provide legislature with directives and partial goals in the complex process of legislative balancing."

function of fundamental rights to ensure that the individual has access to state resources and the services[1008] that the state is in the financial position to provide when fulfilling its responsibility to the public by balancing its divergent public functions.[1009] In this regard, the social welfare state principle assumes great importance in determining the scope of the constitutional definition of property.

3.4.2. Property and the Basic Constitutional Principles

Article 14 I 2 GG confers on the legislator the authority to determine the "content and limits" of property, but read with article 19 II GG, the Constitutional Court is required to define the essence of property in order to protect the freedom associated with it.[1010] The court has tended to approach this problem of definition by considering the property guarantee within the framework of the Constitution as a whole. In reality, however, it has relied more heavily on the historical development of the concept of property in the Civil Code than on any systematic or teleological approach to constitutional interpretation.[1011] One problem in this regard was the continuing tendency of the Federal Supreme Court to define the right to property more broadly than the Federal Constitutional Court, occasionally bringing the two tribunals into confrontation.[1012]

From the court's treatment of the "threshold" question it is clear that some of the requirements applied in determining the constitutional concept of property are not limited to questions relating to the property guarantee exclusively.[1013] As happens with all fundamental rights, the elements of the *Rechtsstaat* principle[1014] are employed time and

---

[1008] *Hesse*, Grundzüge des Verfassungsrechts (1993), m.n. 287-289.

[1009] *Papier* in *Maunz/Dürig*, GG Kommentar (1994), m.n. 129.

[1010] BVerfGE 42, 263 *(Contergan)* 292.

[1011] *Kommers*, Constitutional Jurisprudence of Germany (1997), 254.

[1012] See BVerfGE 3, 58 where the Constitutional Court declined the Supreme Court's invitation to regard civil service tenure and its associated job benefits as "property" within the meaning of the Basic Law.

[1013] *Leisner* in *Isensee/Kirchhof*, Handbuch des Staatsrechts VI (1989), m.n. 75.

[1014] In particular the principles of legal certainty *(Rechtssicherheit / allgemeine Bestimmtheit)*, proportionality *(Verhältnismäßigkeit)* and necessity *(Erforder-*

again to determine how far the state conduct is limited by virtue of the objects of the fundamental property right. But the constitutional property concept should be defined more specifically than by merely applying the values underlying the *Rechtsstaat*. This is indicated by the importance attached to the institution of property as such.[1015]

The characteristic element of trust *(Vertrauensschutz)* inherent in the *Rechtsstaat* principle assumes a deeper meaning within the constitutional property guarantee. Especially within the sphere of patrimonial public law interests, it is clear that trust in the state's maintenance of the *status quo* is an important constitutive element of the constitutional property concept. Where it can reasonably be expected that a legal position would be protected as property in the constitutional context, the legislature should have legitimate reasons for the curtailment of rights that could stem from such a legal position.[1016] The principle that social security benefits granted by the state are not by nature objects creating trust,[1017] therefore becomes an important factor for limitation of the property concept.[1018] This point will also be mentioned again in the next chapter.

3.4.3. Property as a Fundamental Right

In determining the constitutional concept of property in German law, the focus is on the question of whether the object of the right is an asset of economic value, rather than on the question of exclusive domi-

---

lichkeit), and the duty to conduct a balancing of interests *(Abwägungsverpflichtung)* See 125 ff. above.

[1015] BVerfGE 45, 142, 173 determines that the core of ownership should not be affected. BVerfGE 58, 300 *(Naßauskiesung),* 338 determines that the constitutional recognition of private ownership should be heeded when determining the limits of the property guarantee. BVerfGE 62, 169, 183 focuses on the correspondence between the purpose of the infringement and the social function of the object of ownership when determining that any infringement on ownership should not excessively burden or unreasonably influence the patrimonial sphere of the owner.

[1016] BVerfGE 58, 81, 121.

[1017] *"Soziale Staatsgeschenke sind eben ihrem Wesen nach schon kein Gegenstand von Vertrauen."*

[1018] *Leisner* in *Isensee/Kirchhof,* Handbuch des Staatsrechts VI (1989), m.n. 95.

nance.[1019] In constitutional law, the concept of property is, therefore, wider than in private law. Nevertheless, a concept of property that is as wide as to include all rights representing economically valuable assets, also needs to be limited. Some of the most important limitations entail that contractual claims are protected by the constitutional property guarantee only if they are not connected with an activity contrary to public policy.[1020] Furthermore, claims emanating from the public law sphere are considered to be property rights only if they have been acquired by the holder as a result of his or her own efforts[1021] or if they serve to advance his or her well-being.

The Federal Constitutional Court has over years abstracted certain elements of a constitutional property concept in particular. Thus, the relation between the object and the subject of ownership — the *Zuordnungselement* — has been acknowledged by the court on several occasions:[1022] Owners' rights of disposal and alienation of their property at will are liberties which should, in principle, be protected by the property guarantee. Reference has furthermore been made to the object's value or usefulness — the *Substanz* of ownership — as an element of the constitutional concept.[1023] In this regard, the Federal Constitutional Court provided clear insight into the reasons for constitutional protection of property when it decided that the municipality of Sasbach could not rely upon an averred infringement of article 14 I 1 GG in attempts to prevent the erection of a nuclear power station by the *Kernkraftwerk Süd GmbH* and the *Ministerium für Wirtschaft, Mittelstand und Verkehr* of Baden-Württemberg on the district borders. The municipality is a public law juristic person and therefore does not fall within the category of juristic persons whose fundamental rights would traditionally be guaranteed.[1024] It could in any event not claim the protection of article 14 GG. However, the court in any event decided that insofar

---

[1019] This question pertains to the protection of property in private law and under the Civil Code.

[1020] I.e. Prostitution. *Kimminich* in *Starck (ed)*, Rights, Institutions and Impact of International Law (1987), 77.

[1021] BVerfGE 18, 392.

[1022] BVerfGE 31, 275, 285; BVerfGE 42, 263 *(Contergan)*, 294, BVerfGE 31, 229, 240-241.

[1023] *Leisner* in *Isensee/Kirchhof*, Handbuch des Staatsrechts VI (1989), m.n. 81, 82, 84.

[1024] I.e. private law, natural juristic persons. BVerfGE 61, 82, 100-101.

as municipal property — in this case agricultural land — is used for public purposes, it does not fall within the protective ambit of the property guarantee. The court also added that, even if the municipal property is not employed for public purposes, it would in any event not enjoy the protection of article 14 I 1 GG. The reason for this was that the municipal property would still not fulfil the function of property that the constitutional guarantee intends to protect. Property should serve the owner's private interests and should be the basis of the owner's private initiative if it is to qualify for constitutional protection.[1025]

3.4.4. Property as a "Purely Constitutional" Concept

The *Naßauskiesung* decision indicated that the constitutional concept of property should be deduced from the constitutional context itself and not from the concept of ownership as defined in the civil law and through ordinary legislation. Nevertheless, this is hard to accomplish. The "truly constitutional" requirements applicable in defining the concept of property — the principles of legal certainty *(Rechtsicherheit / allgemeine Bestimmtheit)* and necessity *(Erforderlichkeit)*, the proportionality principle *(Verhältnismäßigkeit)*, and the duty to conduct a balancing of interests *(Abwägungsverpflichtung)* — are not limited to questions relating to the property guarantee.[1026] Moreover, the role that the civil law concept of ownership in Germany has played in the development of a constitutional concept of property cannot be denied. It is, however, not the civil law rules themselves, but rather the underlying principles of classical property law, that are noticeable in the constitutional concept of ownership.[1027] For instance, in cases where the characteristic exclusivity quality of ownership — prevalent both in the constitutional context and in the civil code — is under discussion, the civil law remains the most important analogous source for constitutional interpretation. Similarly, in cases where private relations have to be determined, the private use requirement of the constitutional property

---

[1025] BVerfGE 61, 82, 108 ff.

[1026] *Leisner* in *Isensee/Kirchhof*, Handbuch des Staatsrechts VI (1989), m.n. 75.

[1027] *Leisner* in *Isensee/Kirchhof*, Handbuch des Staatsrechts VI (1989), m.n. 73-74.

clause can also only be understood against the background of the civil law concept of ownership.

Further, in spite of the Federal Constitutional Court's aim of developing an "independent" constitutional property concept, ordinary legislation plays an important role in the determination of the constitutional concept of property. Through article 14 I 2 GG, the legislature is given the capacity to determine the contents and limits of property. This gives rise to two conceptual possibilities. Leisner[1028] explains that the legislature could proceed from the premise that the constitutional contents of property are already stipulated, in which case it should determine the limitations upon the concept. Alternatively, the legislature could define the concept itself, and then determine the limitations upon it.[1029]

The question of which of these conceptual possibilities are to be preferred, depends in principle on the political orientation of the state and of the constitutional court and the extent to which the property concept can be reformed in terms of the political convictions of the government.[1030] Some authors accept that property is a creation of the legal order and that the content of ownership cannot be predetermined.[1031] This would mean that the Basic Law simply protects that concept of property which has been defined by ordinary legislation. This view could, however, be misunderstood.[1032] The ordinary legislature, in defining the concept of property, still has to legislate in accordance with the prescriptions of the constitution.

Ordinary legislation, in defining the constitutional property concept, therefore does not influence the "independence" of the constitutional property clause, but plays an important interactive role between the

---

[1028] *Leisner* in *Isensee/Kirchhof,* Handbuch des Staatsrechts VI (1989), m.n. 54.

[1029] *"Entweder der einfache Gesetzgeber 'findet den verfassungsrechtlichen Eigentumsinhalt vor' und zieht diesem Schutzbereich Schranken, oder er definiert ihn, er bringt ihn hervor und beschränkt ihn (sodann)."*

[1030] *Badura* in *Benda/Maihofer/Vogel (eds),* Handbuch des Verfassungsrechts (1994), m.n. 3; *Leisner* in *Isensee/Kirchhof,* Handbuch des Staatsrechts VI (1989), m.n. 55.

[1031] *Leisner* in *Isensee/Kirchhof,* Handbuch des Staatsrechts VI (1989), m.n. 57.

[1032] See the explanation of *Leisner* in *Isensee/Kirchhof,* Handbuch des Staatsrechts VI (1989), m.n. 57-58.

constitution and the public policy.[1033] The Basic Law assigned the function to the legislature in article 14 I 2 GG to define the property concept in order to protect the interests of the individual and of the public in general.[1034] The legislature consequently has a twofold responsibility: On the one hand, it has to make the rules of private law governing the protection and transfer of property. On the other hand, it should safeguard public interests by giving them consideration in drafting legislation.

The *Naßauskiesung* ruling was the first decision in which equal weight was attached to public law and private law in setting boundaries to the use of property. This is what makes this decision important. The court supported the view that private law and public law contribute to the determination of the constitutional legal position of the property owner. The body of property law represented in the Civil Code does not exclusively define the constitutional concept of property. All regulations of property existing at a particular point in time determine which specific rights the property owner enjoys.[1035] If these regulations divest the property owner of a certain control over his or her property, then this control is not included in his or her constitutional right to property.[1036] In the context of constitutional property, the limitations imposed by public and private law regulations are therefore not regarded as external and additional, but rather as necessary ingredients of the definition of constitutional property.[1037] An owner in terms of private law would thus in terms of constitutional law not necessarily always be able to exercise those entitlements with regard to the property that would promise the greatest possible economic advantage.

Furthermore, the Federal Constitutional Court made it clear that, in determining the question of whether a specific proprietary interest qualifies for constitutional protection, the purpose and function of the

---

[1033] See *Von Brünneck*, Die Eigentumsgarantie des Grundgesetzes (1984), 163 ff. for a discussion of the role of ordinary legislature in expanding or limiting the entitlements of ownership in terms of the constitution since the coming into force of the Basic Law. It is shown that the developments effected by legislation mirror those of the politics and economic policy at specific points in time.

[1034] BVerfGE 58, 300 *(Naßauskiesung)*, 335.

[1035] *Pieroth/Schlink*, Grundrechte-Staatsrecht II (1991), m.n. 997.

[1036] BVerfGE 58, 300 *(Naßauskiesung)* 335-336.

[1037] *Pieroth/Schlink*, Grundrechte - Staatsrecht II (1991), m.n. 997.

property guarantee has to be considered against its place in the German constitutional order as a whole.[1038] This affirms the influence of civil law and ordinary legislation on the formation of a constitutional property concept, while simultaneously explaining that constitutional law relations act as another important co-determinative force.[1039] These factors all contribute to the establishment of a constitutional concept of property in the genuine sense of the word.

4. The Continued Role of Private Law Ownership in the Constitutional Context?

Together with concepts like person, family and agreement, the institution of private property is part of the core of modern South African private law.[1040] This is also the case in German law. In the German private law of property, corporeal *res* are susceptible of becoming objects of ownership. Incorporeals are, mostly, regulated through other legal mechanisms. As a result of its strong civil law tradition, the South African private law of property, too, is characterised by the conceptual domination of corporeals as the main proprietary objects. This explains the use of the term *law of things* when denoting that part of the patrimonial law in which the relations between legal subjects and legal objects are regulated.[1041] Moreover, the structural domination of ownership as the most comprehensive and most valuable of all property rights was seen as the basis of property in private law.

In both South Africa and Germany, however, the introduction and interpretation of a constitutional clause protecting property changed the direction of property law quite dramatically.[1042] An important aspect of this change of direction is the nature and content of the property concept. Criteria as to the scope and content of that which is supposed to

---

[1038] *Papier* in *Maunz/Dürig*, GG Kommentar (1994), m.n. 63; BVerfGE 36, 281 290; BVerfGE 42, 263 292-293; BVerfGE 51, 193 218; BVerfGE 58, 300 (*Naßauskiesung*), 335.

[1039] *Leisner*, 1983 DVBl, 64.

[1040] *Van der Merwe*, Sakereg (1989), 169.

[1041] *Van der Merwe*, Law of Things / LAWSA XXVII (1993), par. 5.

[1042] *Van der Walt*, Constitutional Property Clauses - A Comparative Analysis (1999), 350.

be protected under the constitutional property guarantees can be a structural characteristic valuable for interpretation of the relevant property clauses. However, in neither the German, nor in either of the South African Constitutions[1043] an explicit definition of the constitutional property concept is given, thus leaving the concept of property under the Constitution open to the influences of socio-political pressure in both these systems.

The adoption of a constitutional property clause in the South African context once again raised the question whether a concept of ownership cast in the mould of the Roman-Dutch authors and the Pandectists sufficiently meets the needs of society.[1044] The needs of the present-day South African society are now to a large extent portrayed by the objectives of the Constitution. In this sense, the introduction of the constitutional property clause in South Africa resembles another step in the process of transformation and rejuvenation of the property concept initiated by scholars like Van der Merwe, Cowen and Van der Walt. More than twenty years have passed since the need for change was first recognised.[1045] In the mean time, South African lawyers have increasingly accentuated the political and social role of property against the backdrop of a new political dispensation.[1046] Property is increasingly being regarded as a bond, rather than a barrier, between the individual and society.[1047] The need for a concept of ownership which can explain the many and varied existing real relationships, and which can conform to the different functions of property, is increasingly expressed,[1048] causing lawyers to doubt the primacy of owner-

---

[1043] Interim Constitution Act 200 of 1993; Final Constitution, 1996.

[1044] See e.g. the discussions of *Erasmus,* Interaction between Property Rights and Land Reform in the New Constitutional Order in South Africa (1998), 452-453, *Kroeze,* Between Conceptualism and Constitutionalism: Private-law and Constitutional Perspectives on Property (1998), 267-269.

[1045] See discussion of *Van der Merwe*'s work in the field of sectional title, and *Cowen*'s analysis of the understanding of ownership as *plena in re potestas* at 191 ff. above.

[1046] *Cowen,* New Patterns of Landownership (1984), 10, 78; *Milton* in *Zimmermann/Visser (ed),* Southern Cross (1996), 699.

[1047] *Rycroft* in *Corder (ed),* Law & Social Practice (1988), 274; *Cowen,* New Patterns of Landownership (1984), 10, 78.

[1048] *Van der Walt,* 1995 SAJHR 205-206; *Milton* in *Zimmermann/Visser (ed),* Southern Cross (1996), 699; *Cowen,* New Patterns of Landownership (1984), 9, 76.

ship in relation to other real rights.[1049] Many South African authors have joined in the propagation of the idea that most of the social limitations on ownership are indeed not only exceptions to the rule.[1050] The introduction of a new property order with the promulgation of the Interim Constitution in 1994 underscored the need to rethink the content and function of ownership, also in private law. Moreover, in a legal order where constitutional supremacy is the highest value, and the aim of the Constitution is to "[h]eal the divisions of the past and establish a society based on democratic values, social justice and fundamental human rights"[1051] the legitimacy of the concept of ownership as an essentially private law institution, which was violated by statute upon statute in order to serve the purpose of racial segregation, is constantly questioned.[1052]

An analysis of the concept of property and its relevance for protection of holders proprietary rights in private law and in constitutional law indicates that the concept of property under the Constitution differs considerably from that concept in private law. Therefore, right after the coming into effect of the "interim" property clause, focus was placed almost exclusively on the property interests that could or could not be included under the term *rights in property* in section 28 IC.[1053] Traditional private law conceptualism induced lawyers to concentrate on the question of how the new property concept should be interpreted,[1054] and this resulted in a list of rights that would, according to common opinion, most probably fall within the protective ambit of the property clause. Most of these speculations have not been confirmed by the South African courts yet. Nevertheless, it is submitted that the most important new categories of property that could probably enjoy protection are: (i) personal rights related to proprietary interests; (ii) customary land law rights; (iii) informal land rights; (iv) rights

---

[1049] *Cowen*, New Patterns of Landownership (1984), 19, 73; *Van der Walt*, 1988 De Jure 325; *Milton* in *Zimmermann/Visser (ed)*, Southern Cross (1996), 698-699.

[1050] *Milton* in *Zimmermann/Visser (ed)*, Southern Cross (1996), 698.

[1051] Preamble to the Final Constitution.

[1052] *Van der Walt* in *Van der Walt* (ed), Land Reform (1991), 21-22.

[1053] *Van der Walt*, 1995 SAPR/PL, 298-345; *Kleyn*, 1996 SAPR/PL, 419-423; *Van der Walt*, 1994 THRHR, 181-203; *Van der Walt*, 1995 SAJHR, 169-206; *Chaskalson*, 1994 SAJHR, 132-134; *Kroeze*, 1994 SAPR/PL, 325-327; *Lewis*, 1992 SAJHR, 393-411.

[1054] *Van der Walt*, 1995 SAPR/PL, 298-299.

aimed at land reform; (v) immaterial property; (vi) commercial property (rights related to business enterprises); and (vii) interests in terms of social welfare policies (also known in other jurisdictions as "new property" rights or "public law" rights).

In Germany, the concept of ownership has also been broadened considerably: to such an extent that an overview of the interests protected under article 14 I 1 GG can, by itself, fill volumes.[1055] In spite of the need to formulate a "purely constitutional" concept of property as propagated by and after the *Naßauskiesung* decision, the "traditional" civilian concept of property still forms the basic premise of any inquiry.[1056] However, through the decisions of the German Federal Constitutional Court, the concept was expanded, so as to include not only corporeal objects, but also (almost) all rights which can form part of a person's estate. Property in terms of the Basic Law's *"erweiterte" Eigentumsbegriff* includes not only ownership in things *(res)*, but also other (limited) real rights in things *(res)*, immaterial and intellectual property rights, creditor's rights, rights to pension, shares and other shareholder's rights, and even certain claims pertaining to a person's profession or occupation. Consequently, it appears that also in Germany the discussion about the content and limits of the civilian concept of ownership is not over.[1057] To some extent, the problem of acknowledging a more diversified concept of ownership in the private law context, or of affording more rights the kind of protection that absolutely enforceable rights should have, is more problematic because of the closed category of rights acknowledged by the Civil Code. The discrepancy that has arisen in the practice of the Federal Court of Justice and the provisions of the Civil Code, for instance, with regard to the retention of title constructed as pledge without possession, cannot be overlooked.

This once again raises the question of whether the concept of property in private law, and therefore also the property order in general, needs to be adapted. A good case can be made for the abolishment of the civilian concept of ownership as it is found in South Africa on the basis that the "ordinary" Roman-Dutch law principles of property as they are found at present in the South African common law, are subordinate to the constitutional principles. Further, it can also be argued that the "standard"

[1055] See *Papier* in *Maunz/Dürig*, GG Kommentar (1994), m.n. 56-203; *Kimminich*, Eigentum Enteignung Entschädigung (1976), 55-84.

[1056] *Kimminich* in *Von Mangoldt/Klein*, Bonner Kommentar (1992), m.n. 31.

[1057] *Olzen*, 1984 JuS, 335.

private law view of property law is too eurocentricised for the majority of South Africans who have no interest in the Roman-Dutch heritage of South African property law.[1058]

It is submitted, however, that these arguments need not result in the view that the Roman-Dutch/Pandectist principles of property are of no consequence in matters pertaining to the constitutional protection of property. From a practical point of view, it would simply be impossible to eradicate the existing structure of property law without further ado. The law of property and the system of land rights, which preceded the new constitutional order in South Africa, are vital to an understanding of legal and social structures inherited from the old order. They will continue to influence the transformation pursued within constitutional framework and the prevailing social reality.[1059] Moreover, certain provisions in the Interim and Final Constitutions provide for legal continuity.[1060] In a reform of the structure of property law in South Africa, the Roman-Dutch/Pandectist approach could therefore still influence the interpretative approach to property.[1061]

The influence that the Roman-Dutch/Pandectist tradition could still have on the development of law under the new constitutional order in South Africa need not be negative. It can provide an acceptable interpretative structure for the provisions of private law. Moreover, the principles of a critical analytical approach are already present in the Roman-Dutch legal thinking.[1062] The Roman-Dutch/Pandectist tradition can still reflect the sense of justice endorsed by the Constitution. There can be no doubt that this is indispensable for proprietary relations in the new legal order.

Nevertheless, the function of the Roman-Dutch law within the legal system in general and the property law order in particular should be adapted. It should not be used as the instrument for rationalising the existing scheme of policy and principle, but rather as the source from which logical and just changes to the existing scheme should be effected. The interpretative significance of Roman-Dutch law in the

---

[1058] See e.g. a similar argument in the case of *S v Makwanyane* (note 363 above) where certain typically "African" values were used as considerations in the abolishment of the death penalty in South Africa.

[1059] *Gutto,* Property and Land Reform (1995), 57.

[1060] Sec. 4, 229 IC; Sec. 2, Items 2 and 3 of Schedule 6 FC.

[1061] *Van der Merwe,* 1998 TSAR, 11.

[1062] *Van der Merwe,* 1998 TSAR, 14.

South African context therefore does not lie in its aptitude for teleological pragmatism, which is described as the method of creating a "productive misunderstanding of historical material to force it into the service of present day needs" in order to design "alternative trajectories of institutional and policy change."[1063]

It is submitted that such an approach will not, in future, establish the necessary credibility for the Roman-Dutch law as an authoritative source of law in a constitutional order. Roman-Dutch law is not to be the tool with which to provide law reformers with a "constructed reality."[1064] The abuse of, in particular, the Roman-Dutch law of property under the previous regime excludes such a possibility. Of all the constitutional resources[1065] with which Roman-Dutch law is, in our time, on equal footing, it can least afford the doubts that such an approach might raise. The universal and timeless elements to be deduced from this source of law could still supply law reformers with principles by which to adapt the law to comply with modern day needs of society. However, transposing existing legal principles to serve institutional and policy issues in the interests of the modern South African society does not require "interpretative misunderstandings." Instead, what is needed is an equilibrium between the values portrayed by the specific constitutional resource and the values embodied by the Constitution itself, that is to say the values of human dignity, equality and freedom that "underlie an open and democratic society."[1066]

The guiding principles for evaluation of the civil legal tradition and the new constitutional order are, therefore, found in the Constitution itself. The Constitution provides a historic bridge between the past of a deeply divided society characterised by strife, conflict, suffering and injustice, and a future founded on the recognition of human rights, democracy and peaceful co-existence and development opportunities for

---

[1063] *Van der Merwe*, 1998 TSAR, 15.

[1064] In the words of *Van der Merwe*, 1998 TSAR, 5 who explains this term by saying that "The passage of time has imbued the 'old authorities' with larger-than-life dimensions and, even as codification in the Netherlands (in 1809) reduced them to cultural artefacts, their fame and their value increased in their adopted country i.e. South Africa."

[1065] I.e. customary law, legislation, as well as foreign law and international law as prescribed by sec. 39 FC (Interpretation clause).

[1066] Sec. 39(1)(a) FC.

all South Africans, irrespective of colour, race, class or sex.[1067] This could mean that some of the existing civil law principles might fall into disuse or be replaced by more adequate mechanisms from other resources, like customary law or foreign law. But those principles that do survive the scrutiny of the Constitution would have, by themselves, more to contribute to the development of the property order.

The function of the constitutional property clause should, however, not be confused with traditional protection of property in private law. In private law, the purpose of the protection of property is to insulate the right in question absolutely from an invasion or interference not based on the owner's permission. In constitutional law, the purpose of the property clause is to ensure that a just and equitable balance is struck between the interests of private property holders and the public interest in the control and regulation of the use of property.[1068]

Property as a constitutional right differs fundamentally from property as a right in private law. The differences between the property in its constitutional and private law senses are not restricted to the concept of property or to the range of property interests that can be included under the property clause in the Constitution. They also extend to the kind of protection that each right can get and, most importantly, the reasons why and the consideration in terms of which the protection is afforded in an individual case.[1069] Property as a right in terms of the Constitution does not mean that each entitlement recognised or protected by private law is insulated from state interference. Existing entitlements can be changed, restricted, and subjected to new or stricter controls, limitations and levies without compensation. These alterations should only be justified by the public interest. The legislature will inevitably be faced with the social need to regulate the use of property. However, it is not restricted to either leaving existing rights intact or expropriating them against compensation. The state's power to regulate proprietary relations can be employed to introduce the necessary social control over individual property rights.[1070] Further, property interests that are not recognised or protected by private law can be acknowledged and protected by the constitutional property clause, if that pro-

---

[1067] Post-amble, IC.

[1068] *Van der Walt*, Constitutional Property Clause (1997), 67.

[1069] *Van der Walt*, Constitutional Property Clause (1997), 70-71.

[1070] *Van der Walt*, Constitutional Property Clause (1997), 70.

tection is justified by the constitutional function of the property clause and the public interest.

Chapter 8: Constitutional Limitations on Property Rights: Regulation, Expropriation and the Property Order

1. General Remarks

Once it is established that the constitutional concept of property over-reaches the concept of ownership in private law, it is necessary to determine to what extent the constitutional guarantee of property will tolerate limitation by the legislature or administration. An answer to this question will determine the extent to which existing rights would recede to accommodate new policies. A further interesting aspect concerns the extent to which the interests of right holders in terms of the constitutional property guarantee can be protected from interferences by actions of private persons. This raises the issue of horizontal application of the property clause. This chapter contains a discussion of the different methods by which constitutional rights in general and the fundamental right to property in particular can be restricted in Germany and South Africa.

2. Limitation of Rights in General

The Interim Constitution's limitation clause, although exclusively South African, contained certain aspects relating to the limitation of the constitutional property right found in Germany (and Canada).[1071] Section 33(1) IC reminds of the German manner of limitation by providing that rights entrenched in the chapter on fundamental rights could be limited by *law of general application*, provided that such a limitation would be permissible only to the extent that it was *reasonable* and *justifiable* under specific pre-conditions. Further, a limitation was not supposed to negate the *essential content* of the right in question. Limitation of certain rights[1072] was further subject to the requirement of *necessity*.

[1071] *Blaauw-Wolf*, 1999 SAPR/PL, 201.

[1072] I.e. rights entrenched in sec. 10, 11, 12, 14(1), 21, 25 or 30(1)(d) or (e) or (2) IC. Similarly, limitations of rights entrenched in sec. 15, 16, 17, 18, 23 or 24 IC, also were subject to the requirement of necessity, in so far as these rights related to free and fair political activity.

However, the South African Constitutional Court chose not to follow the German approach to limitation of rights blindly. The court observed that, although the way in which the rules for limitation of fundamental rights are applied in Germany (and Canada) may well be of assistance in the South African context, there was no reason why the South African analysis should be fitted into either of these modes.[1073] The observations of the Constitutional Court in *S v Zuma* and *S v Makwanyane* concerning the interpretation of the general limitation clause in the Interim Constitution, [1074] apparently influenced the drafting of section 36 FC to a large extent. Thereby, reliance on the general limitation provision of the Canadian Charter of Rights and Freedoms of 1982[1075] and the decision of *R v Oakes*[1076] was important. The Canadian treatment of fundamental rights limitation was in turn influenced considerably (through the decisions of the European Court of Human Rights) by German theory on proportionality and the limitation of rights.[1077] Since the Canadian Charter contains no property clause, and the German Basic Law no general limitations provision, the South African limitation of property rights is in some ways quite unique from the perspective of legal reception. In fact, for a better understanding of the application of section 36 FC, the South African law relating to constitutional property rights limitation needs to be juxtaposed with property rights limitation in both Germany and Canada. However, the scope of the present inquiry only allows a comparison between the South African and German positions.[1078] The following discussion will therefore endeavour to explain the differences and similarities in the German and South African methods of limitation.

[1073] See Kentridge J in *S v Zuma* (note 501 above), par. 35; Chaskalson P in *S v Makwanyane* (note 363 above), par. 110.

[1074] See *Blaauw-Wolf,* 1999 SAPR/PL, 201-208; *Woolman,* 1997 SAJHR, 107.

[1075] *Van der Walt,* Constitutional Property Clauses - A Comparative Analysis (1999), 357.

[1076] *R v Oakes* 1986 19 CRR 308.

[1077] *Van der Walt,* 1997 SAPR/PL, 319; *Rautenbach,* General Provisions of the South African Bill of Rights (1995), 96.

[1078] Valuable discussions of the Canadian theory of property rights limitations can be found in *Van der Walt,* Constitutional Property Clauses - A Comparative Analysis (1999), 93-95 and 353-358; *Van der Walt,* Constitutional Property Clause (1997), 84-86; *Allen,* 1993 ICLQ, 536 ff.; *Bauman,* 1992 SAJHR, 344 ff.

2.1. Requirements for Limitation of Rights Under the Basic Law

One of the most important functions of the Basic Law is to limit the powers of the legislature in order to create effective guarantees of fundamental rights.[1079] However, no general limitation clause appears in the first nineteen articles of the Basic Law, which constitute the German catalogue of basic rights. The degree in which the different fundamental rights are restricted is usually determined by the guarantees of the different rights provided in articles 1 to 19 GG themselves.[1080] The separate guarantees of basic rights in the German Basic Law are usually restricted through one or more of the following methods:[1081]

2.1.1. Restriction Directly through Legislation

In some cases guarantees are explicitly *restricted by or pursuant to a law*.[1082] This means that the legislation may restrict the fundamental right directly,[1083] or that a fundamental right may be limited in terms of administrative discretion explicitly sanctioned by a statute.[1084] In the latter case the legislature still has to determine the conditions to be complied with for the restriction to be constitutional. In both instances, the restriction will be either *simple* or *qualified* in nature. A simple restriction does not list any further particular conditions to be complied with,[1085] whereas a qualified restriction requires specific conditions to be complied with.[1086] Certain rights may not be restricted at all by or

---

[1079] See *Limpens*, Funktion & Grenzen der Inhaltsbestimmung des Eigentums (1973), 69 concerning the limitations inherent to all the constitutional norms in general and the limitations with regard to the preservation of the concept of private property in particular.

[1080] *Blaauw-Wolf/Wolf*, 1996 SALJ, 271.

[1081] *Blaauw-Wolf*, 1999 SAPR/PL, 187-191. *Pieroth/Schlink*, Grundrechte - Staatsrecht II (1991), m.n. 292 ff.

[1082] E.g. art. 8 II GG.

[1083] Only the legislature may formulate such a restriction; the executive and the judiciary are precluded from such action.   ·

[1084] E.g. art. 10 II GG.

[1085] E.g. art. 2 II GG; art. 8 II GG.

[1086] E.g. art. 13 III GG: "Intrusions and restrictions ... shall otherwise only be permissible to avert danger to the public or to the life of an individual or, pur-

pursuant to a law.[1087] In case of a simple limitation, the freedom of the legislature to restrict a fundamental right has the widest scope. In case of a qualified restriction, the scope is not as wide, and in the last instance where no restriction is allowed, the legislature has practically no freedom to restrict the fundamental right.[1088]

However, for the constitutionality of legislation restricting fundamental rights, several general conditions must be fulfilled. The Federal Constitutional Court describes this process as an interaction between the fundamental rights, which protect individual freedom, and the limitation provisions, which enable adequate consideration of the public interest.[1089] These general guidelines for limiting the legislature's capacity to restrict fundamental rights can be found in article 19 I GG,[1090] which constitute the so-called *Schranken-Schranken* in the German constitutional dogmatic structure. This term refers to the fact that the legislature, in exercising its capacity of limiting specific basic rights, can only act within the borders of limitation set by the Basic Law.

In terms of article 19 I GG, the following conditions for legislative restriction of rights must be fulfilled: (i) A right can be restricted only *by or pursuant to a law*. (ii) A right so restricted must be based upon a law that has *general application*.[1091] (iii) A law enabling restriction of a right has to *specify* the fundamental right concerned and *explicitly mention* the part of the guarantee against which the restriction operates.[1092] Further, article 19 II GG requires that the essence (or "essential con-

---

suant to a law, an acute threat to public safety and order, in particular to relieve a housing shortage, to prevent an epidemic or to protect young persons at risk."

[1087] E.g. art. 4 III GG: "Nobody may be forced against their conscience into military service involving armed combat. Details shall be the subject of a federal law." art. 5 III GG: "Art and science, research and teaching, shall be free. Freedom of teaching shall not absolve anybody from loyalty to the Constitution." art. 8 I GG: "All Germans have the right to assemble peacefully and unarmed without prior notification or permission."

[1088] *Pieroth/Schlink,* Grundrechte-Staatsrecht II (1991), m.n. 299.

[1089] BVerfGE 7, 198, 208 ff.

[1090] Art. 19 I GG: *"Soweit nach diesem Grundgesetz ein Grundrecht durch Gesetz oder auf Grund eines Gesetzes eingeschränkt werden kann, muß das Gesetz allgemein und nicht nur für den Einzelfall gelten. Außerdem muß das Gesetz das Grundrecht unter Angabe des Artikels nennen."*

[1091] Art. 19 I 1 GG: *Verbot des einschränkenden Einzelfallgesetzes.*

[1092] Art. 19 I 2 GG: *Zitiergebot.*

Part Three: Constitutional Inquiry into Property Protection

tent") of a fundamental right may not be affected.[1093] This essential content requirement applies to all rights without exception.[1094] The proportionality principle[1095] stems from the basic constitutional principle of the *Rechtsstaat*, and will thus also be invoked by the court to determine whether and to what extent a restriction is to be allowed,[1096] regardless of the specific basic right at stake.

2.1.2. Restriction by Basic Rights Mutually

In some cases, different fundamental rights might come into conflict with each other. In these cases, the collision of rights[1097] has to be resolved by means of legislation or by giving the constitutional provisions a specific meaning. Where a fundamental right (which may be restricted) has to be balanced against a legitimate public interest provided for in the Basic Law, the Federal Constitutional Court[1098] tries to give partial effect to each right and attempts not to sacrifice either the specific right or the public interest completely. Thus, both the fundamental right and the public interest are "optimised" in a relative way. Hesse[1099] refers to this practice as the *Herstellung praktischer Konkordanz*. The achievement of so-called *practical concordance* is also important in the context of conflicting rights in relations among private individuals.[1100] In such a case the courts should apply the principle of equality assiduously, as practical concordance of the rights aims at creating a situation

---

[1093] Art. 19 II GG *(Wesensgehaltsgarantie): "In keinem Falle darf ein Grundrecht in seinem Wesensgehalt angetastet werden."*

[1094] This provision was the result of the treatment of limitations of fundamental rights under the Weimar constitution. The specialised order of limitation in the Weimar Constitution lead the Weimar judges to interpret the constitution in such a manner that the legislature was said not to be bound by the fundamental right. Consequently the legislature could negate the right completely and undermine the protection offered by such fundamental rights.

[1095] *Verhältnismäßigkeit (Übermaßverbot)*.

[1096] *Blaauw-Wolf*, 1999 SAPR/PL, 191.

[1097] See the explanation of the terms "collision of rights" and "competition of rights" in *Blaauw-Wolf/Wolf*, 1996 SALJ, 273-274.

[1098] BVerfGE 41, 29, 51; BVerfGE 41, 65, 78.

[1099] *Hesse*, Grundzüge des Verfassungsrechts (1993), m.n. 317-320.

[1100] See 383 ff. below.

in which both (or all) the rights at stake can be exercised as far as possible to their full potential.[1101]

2.1.3. Internal Modifying Components

Sometimes the guarantees of specific basic rights themselves contain some internal modifying components, which help determine the scope of a specific right and thus also the extent to which it can be limited.[1102] Hesse[1103] refers to these limits as the *Grundrechtsimmanenten Grenzen* that are to be determined by interpretation of the different basic rights. The limits to an individual's basic rights are thus determined with reference to the rights of other individuals in society, or the *boni mores* as interpreted in the light of the Constitution.[1104]

2.2. General Limitation of Rights in South Africa

The investigation into the limitation of rights in South Africa differs somewhat from the limitation inquiry in Germany. The main distinction is the presence of a general limitation clause[1105] in the South African bill of rights, and the absence of a similar provision in the German Basic Law. In Germany, as has been indicated,[1106] the limitation of rights is effected by legislation (within which the *Schranken-Schranken* doctrine operates and to which the essential content principle has to be applied), other basic rights, and/or internal modifying components. In South Africa, limitation of fundamental rights is effected by the provisions of section 36 FC read with section 7(3) FC, as well as certain internal

---

[1101] *Rautenbach*, General Provisions of the South African Bill of Rights (1995), 74.

[1102] An example of such immanent limits to a right would be the qualification in article 8 I which states that the right to *peaceful and unarmed* assembly is guaranteed. Logically, no constitutional protection is afforded to violent and armed assembly. Similarly, article 8 II subjects only *open-air* meetings to restriction, and not meetings in closed-off rooms.

[1103] *Hesse*, Grundzüge des Verfassungsrechts (1993), m.n. 310.

[1104] See *Blaauw-Wolf/Wolf*, 1996 SALJ, 275.

[1105] Sec. 36 FC.

[1106] See 260 ff. above.

modifiers[1107] and specific limitation provisions[1108] within the different
fundamental right provisions.[1109] The following paragraphs are aimed at
giving an overview of this process and applying it specifically to the
constitutional property clause.

2.2.1. The General Limitation Clause of the Final Constitution

The function of the general limitation clause is mainly to stipulate the
constitutional authority for limiting fundamental rights, and to provide
the controlling requirements for such a limitation.[1110] The Interim and
Final Constitutions both contain general limitation clauses.[1111] For present purposes, only section 36 FC will be discussed. This provision
reads:

> "The rights in the Bill of Rights may be limited only in terms of law
> of general application to the extent that the limitation is reasonable
> and justifiable in an open and democratic society based on human
> dignity, equality and freedom, taking into account all relevant fac-
> tors, including – (a) the nature of the right; (b) the importance of the
> purpose of the limitation; (c) the nature and extent of the limitation;
> (d) the relation between the limitation and its purpose, and (e) less
> restrictive means to achieve the purpose."

Section 7(3) FC lays down the general rule that all the rights in the bill
of rights are limited in principle:

> "The rights in the Bill of Rights are subject to the limitations con-
> tained in or referred to in section 36, or elsewhere in the Bill."

This provision clearly determines that the rights in the bill of rights are
not absolute and that constitutional protection of the fundamental

---

[1107] These are also sometimes referred to as "demarcations." See *De Waal*,
1995 SAJHR, 25.

[1108] These are also sometimes referred to as "special limitations." See *Van der
Walt*, 1997 SAPR/PL, 279.

[1109] The terminology might be somewhat confusing in certain sources. E.g. in
Panel of Constitutional Experts, Memorandum (Re: panel memo on "special
limitations"/"qualifiers" and general limitation) of 20-02-1996. Reference is
made to both special limitations and internal qualifiers without that a distinction is drawn between these two concepts.

[1110] *Van der Walt*, 1997 SAPR/PL, 284.

[1111] Sec. 33 IC, sec. 36 FC.

rights is subject to certain constitutionally determined limitations. In the constitutional context, therefore, the absolute enforceability of a right like *dominium* — as it is encountered in private law — is not acknowledged. In fact, the existence of a general limitation provision indicates that the protection of fundamental rights — also those rights endorsed by section 25 FC — are in principle restricted. In other words, in spite of the guarantee contained in each fundamental right provision, authorised restrictions on those rights can exist. These authorised restrictions are not imposed by the constitution itself, as the function of the constitutional limitation clause is to stipulate the constitutional authority and provide the controlling requirements for a limitation, and not to limit the rights of own accord.[1112]

Moreover, the existence of a single, separate limitation clause in the Final Constitution does not mean that its principles should mechanically and without distinction apply to the limitation of all rights and freedoms protected in the chapter on fundamental rights. The fact that specific limitations have been included within certain guarantees to simplify the inquiry shows that the words of the general limitation clause could have a variety of meanings within the different contexts of separate rights and freedoms. After the meaning and function of specific limitations and internal modifying components have been pointed out in the following paragraphs, it will be indicated that the justifiability of all interferences[1113] with property should be determined by cumulatively considering the limitation provisions of section 36 FC and the more specific limitations and internal modifying components of section 25 FC.

2.2.2. Specific Limitations and Internal Modifying Components

Although both specific limitations and internal modifying components appear in certain provisions of the chapter on fundamental rights, a specific limitation differs from an internal modifying component in that the former does much more than simply demarcating the right. Whereas an internal modifying component is inserted with the purpose of providing greater clarity in respect of some of the vague and indeterminate words used in describing the protected conduct and inter-

---

[1112] This consideration is important in categorising the kind of claims endorsed by the constitutional property clause. See 93 above.

[1113] I.e. deprivations and expropriations.

ests,[1114] a specific limitation provides the legislature with special grounds to limit that right.[1115]

Specific limitations were incorporated in the right to equality,[1116] the guarantees of freedom of religion, belief and opinion,[1117] and freedom of economic activity[1118] and also the right to property.[1119] In the Final

---

[1114] The following provisions in the Final Constitution serve as examples of internal modifying components: Sec. 14 FC (Privacy): "Everyone has the right to privacy, *which includes the right not to have – (a) their person or home searched; (b) their property searched; (c) their possessions seized; or (d) the privacy of their communications infringed.* S 32 FC (Access to information): "(1) Everyone has the right of access to – (a) *any* information *held by the state*; and (b) any information that is *held by another person and that is required for the exercise or protection of any rights.*" Emphasis added.

[1115] *Rautenbach*, General Provisions of the South African Bill of Rights (1995), 105-106; *De Waal*, 1995 SAHJR, 25; *Van der Walt*, 1997 SAPR/PL, 281. The language is usually couched in negative terms and directed at the state. The provisions cannot therefore be considered as mere demarcations.

[1116] Sec. 8(2) IC: "No person shall be unfairly discriminated against, directly or indirectly, and, without derogating from the generality of this provision, on one or more of the following grounds in particular: race, gender, sex, ethnic or social origin, colour, sexual orientation, age, disability, religion, conscience, belief, culture or language."

[1117] Sec. 14 IC: "(1) Every person shall have the right to freedom of conscience, religion, thought, belief and opinion, which shall include academic freedom in institutions of higher learning. (2) Without derogating from the generality of subsection (1), religious observances may be conducted at state or state-aided institutions under rules established by an appropriate authority for that purpose, provided that such religious observances are conducted on an equitable basis and attendance at them is free and voluntary. *(3) Nothing in this Chapter shall preclude legislation recognising – (a) a system of personal and family law adhered to by persons professing a particular religion; and (b) the validity of marriages concluded under a system of religious law subject to specified procedures.*" (Emphasis added).

[1118] Sec. 26 IC: "(1) Every person shall have the right freely to engage in economic activity and to pursue a livelihood anywhere in the national territory. *(2) Subsection (1) shall not preclude measures designed to promote the protection or the improvement of the quality of life, economic growth, human development, social justice, basic conditions of employment, fair labour practices or equal opportunity for all, provided such measures are justifiable in an open and democratic society based on freedom and equality.*" (Emphasis added).

[1119] Sec. 28 IC: "(1) Every person shall have the right to acquire and hold rights in property and, to the extent that the nature of the rights permits, to dis-

Constitution, this practice has been continued by the express mention made of it in section 7(3) FC. Therefore, some of the specific limitation clauses have been retained and some others have been included in the final text. The guarantees of equality,[1120] freedom of religion, belief and opinion,[1121] and expression[1122] are a few examples of the kind of clauses containing special limitations.

---

pose of such rights. (2) No deprivation of any rights in property shall be permitted otherwise than *in accordance with a law*. (3) Where any rights in property are expropriated pursuant to a law referred to in subsection (2), such expropriation shall be *permissible for public purposes only and shall be subject to the payment of agreed compensation* or, failing agreement, to the payment of such compensation and within such period as may be *determined by a court of law as just and equitable*, taking into account all relevant factors, including, in the case of the determination of compensation, the use to which the property is being put, the history of its acquisition, its market value, the value of the investments in it by those affected and the interests of those affected." (Emphasis added).

[1120] Sec. 9 FC: "(3) The state may not unfairly discriminate directly or indirectly against anyone on one or more grounds, including race, gender, sex, pregnancy, marital status, ethnic or social origin, colour, sexual orientation, age, disability, religion, conscience, belief, culture, language and birth. (4) No person may unfairly discriminate directly or indirectly against anyone on one or more grounds in terms of subsection (3). National legislation must be enacted to prevent or prohibit unfair discrimination."

[1121] Sec. 15 FC: "(1) Everyone has the right to freedom of conscience, religion, thought, belief and opinion. (2) Religious observances may be conducted at state or state-aided institutions, provided that – (a) those observances follow rules made by the appropriate public authorities; (b) they are conducted on an equitable basis; and (c) attendance at them is free and voluntary. *(3) (a) This section does not prevent legislation recognising – (i) marriages concluded under any tradition, or a system of religious, personal or family law; or (ii) systems of personal and family law under any tradition, or adhered to by persons professing a particular religion. (b) Recognition in terms of paragraph (a) must be consistent with this section and the other provisions of the Constitution.*" (Emphasis added).

[1122] Sec. 16 FC: "(1) Everyone has the right to freedom of expression, which includes – (a) freedom of the press and other media; (b) freedom to receive or impart information or ideas; (c) freedom of artistic creativity; and (d) academic freedom and freedom of scientific research. *(2) The right in subsection (1) does not extend to – (a) propaganda for war; (b) incitement of imminent violence; or (c) advocacy of hatred that is based on race, ethnicity, gender or religion, and that constitutes incitement to cause harm.*" (Emphasis added).

The state bears the onus of showing that it exploited a specific limitation,[1123] whereas the complainant bears the onus of showing that his or her activity fell within the scope of a demarcated right.[1124] Internal modifying components or demarcations would then typically be important in the first phase of the constitutionality inquiry, where the scope of the guarantee is examined.[1125] The function of specific limitation provisions is, on the contrary, more important when the justifiability of an infringement has to be determined. Therefore, the language used in such specific limitation clauses often reminds of the general limitation clause,[1126] whereas an internal modifying component usually, linguistically, takes the form of an adjectival or adverbial phrase. The property clause provides a good example.

The generally accepted purpose of a specific limitation provision is to express one or more of the elements usually contained in limitation clauses in more specific terms with regard to a particular fundamental right.[1127] In this way, the specific limitation provision indicates how the general limitation provision should be applied to a particular fundamental right. Thus, although each right is not limited separately within the South African Constitution, the presence of specific limitations could have the consequence that the limitation of single fundamental rights differs slightly from each other.[1128] In the context of constitu-

---

[1123] Logically, the individual cannot be burdened with the onus of showing that the state "did not exploit the specific limitation clause".

[1124] *De Waal,* 1995 SAJHR, 26.

[1125] *Woolman,* 1997 SAJHR, 108 indicates the difficulties that arise if internal modifying components are to be treated as part of the inquiry concerning justifiability: "[T]he limitation stage [i.e. the inquiry into the justifiability of an infringement upon a fundamental right] directs our attention primarily, if not exclusively, to the reasonableness and justifiability of a limitation in an open and democratic society based upon human dignity, freedom and equality. Consideration of the nature and scope of the right is something that should already have taken place. To engage the question of a right's nature a second time would seem to invite analytical confusion."

[1126] *De Waal,* 1995 SAJHR, 25-26.

[1127] *Rautenbach,* General Provisions of the South African Bill of Rights (1995), 106.

[1128] Contra *Blaauw-Wolf,* 1999 SAPR/PL, 210. However, *Rautenbach,* General Provisions of the South African Bill of Rights (1995), 107 correctly points out that the presence of a specific limitation clause could, as a result of careless drafting or of complicated compromises struck during the negotiations,

tional property protection, internal modifying components in section 25 FC will help to define the content of the right protected by section 25 FC. By contrast, specific limitations will control limitations of the protected right.[1129]

In the field of constitutional property in particular, many varying analyses[1130] could provide insight into the nature of the provisions affecting property protection in section 25 FC. In sections 25(1), (2) and (3) FC alone, there are several provisions affecting the protection of property in one way or the other:[1131]

(1) No one may be deprived of property *except in terms of law of general application*, and no law may permit *arbitrary deprivation* of property.

(2) Property may be expropriated only *in terms of law of general application* – (a) for a *public purpose or in the public interest*; and (b) subject to *compensation*, the amount of which and the time and manner of payment of which have either been agreed to by those affected or decided or approved by a court.

(3) The amount of the compensation and the time and manner of payment must be *just and equitable*, reflecting an *equitable balance between the public interest and the interests of those affected*, having regard to all relevant circumstances, including – (a) the current use of the property; (b) the history of the acquisition and use of the property; (c) the market value of the property; (d) the extent of direct state investment and subsidy in the acquisition and beneficial capital improvement of the property; and (e) the purpose of the expropriation.

It is important to determine whether these provisions amount to internal modifying components or to specific limitations, as this will provide clarity about their function and application in the constitutionality inquiry. In this regard the relationship and differences between internal

---

in some instances simply repeat elements of the general limitation clause without adding or qualifying anything. In such a case the specific limitation would, naturally, have no influence on the application of the general limitations clause to a specific fundamental right.

[1129] *Van der Walt*, 1997 SAPR/PL, 281-282.

[1130] See the discussion of *Van der Walt*, 1997 SAPR/PL, 275-330.

[1131] Emphasis added.

modifying components, specific limitations and the general limitation clause must be examined.

2.2.3. Section 25 FC and the General Limitations-Clause, Specific Limitations and Internal Modifying Components

Many divergent views exist on the effect of the general limitation provisions on section 25 FC in view of the specific limitations and/or internal modifying components present in this provision. The approaches diverge not only concerning the classification of the different "limiting elements" in section 25 FC, but also concerning the manner in which section 25 FC should interact with section 36 FC. The following paragraphs provide an overview.

2.2.3.1. Classification of the Provisions in Section 25 FC

Exponents of the view that section 25 FC does not guarantee property itself, but only the right not to be deprived of property exept if in accordance with the provisions of section 25 FC hold the opinion section 25 FC contains no specific limitations. All "limiting elements" should accordingly be regarded as internal limiting components.[1132] This approach cannot be tenable. It has been indicated[1133] that the function of a specific limitation clause is, first and foremost, to determine the effect of section 36(1) FC on a specific case. The provisions in section 25(1) and (2) FC therefore would rather amount to specific limitations, and not to internal modifying components. The provisions of section 25(1) and (2) FC determine the requirements for a limitation of property, rather than define the right that is to be protected. By contrast, the provision in section 25(5) FC, that the state must take *reasonable* legislative and other measures, *within its available resources*, to foster conditions that will enable citizens to gain access to land on an equitable basis, can perhaps be seen as an internal modifying component.[1134] Further, the

---

[1132] *Van der Walt*, 1997 SAPR/PL, 293; *De Waal/Currie/Erasmus*, Bill of Rights Handbook (2000), 393.

[1133] See 265 above.

[1134] See mention made by the *Panel of Constitutional Experts'* Memorandum (Re: panel memo on "special limitations"/"qualifiers" and general limitation) of 20-02-1996, where this provision is described as being a "special limitation or internal qualifier." From the definition provided in this document for the

provisions of section 25(3)(a), (b), (c), and (d) FC necessitate an inquiry into the permissible actions or entitlements of the property holder, and can therefore be regarded as internal modifying components describing the outer scope of the protected right.[1135]

Accordingly, it could be said that section 36 FC provides the structural and value-based framework within which the specific terms of section 25 FC should be interpreted. Section 25 FC confirms the general provisions of section 36 FC. This would explain the repetition of certain requirements, and place section 25 FC in line with the provisions of section 7(3) FC. Section 25 FC thus renders certain provisions of section 36 FC more specifically applicable to the property clause, and states additional requirements only applicable to situations where section 25 FC has to be invoked.[1136]

2.2.3.2. Interplay between Section 25 FC and Section 36 FC

Different theories exist regarding the interplay between section 25 FC and section 36 FC. Because the approach to this issue will determine the applicability of the proportionality principle to the South African property clause, an overview of the different theories is necessary.

(i) Some scholars argue that section 36 FC should not be applicable to section 25 FC at all.[1137] This is indeed the inevitable conclusion that will be reached if a process is followed by which the provisions of section 25 FC themselves are first exhausted before turning to an examination of

---

term(s), it becomes apparent that focus is placed only on the so-called internal modifying components.

[1135] *Van der Walt*, 1997 SAPR/PL, 312 explains: "while the market value of the property is taken into account when determining compensation, certain current uses of the property, certain practices relating to the history of the acquisition and use of the property and certain state investments and subsidies which enhanced the value of the property are excluded from the protection against expropriation and will not be included in just and equitable compensation. These provisions exclude certain aspects or possible entitlements from the protection of section 25(2) FC and 25(3) FC generally and *ab initio*, and can therefore be described as internal modifiers."

[1136] *Van der Walt*, 1997 SAPR/PL, 327.

[1137] *De Waal/Currie/Erasmus*, Bill of Rights Handbook (2000), 393 ff.

the influence of section 36 FC on a specific matter. De Waal, Currie and Erasmus[1138] explain:

> "*It seems then that s 36 can have no meaningful application to s 25. The rights in s 25 have been qualified to such an extent that it is unlikely that any violation of those rights can be justified. Put another way, if an applicant is able to discharge the difficult burden of showing that the rights in s 25(1)-(3) have been violated, the state will be unable to justify the violation in terms of s 36.*"

Several considerations dictate against such an approach. For one, section 7(3) FC determines that the rights in the bill of rights are limited by section 36 FC. No express exclusion of section 25 FC from the effect of section 7(3) FC is provided. The mere existence of specific limitations within section 25 FC does not justify a deviation in this regard.[1139] In fact, the specific limitations within section 25 FC points to the existence of a functional relationship between section 25 FC and section 36 FC. A general limitation clause might contain elements describing (i) the organ of state empowered to impose a restriction, (ii) the procedures to be followed to impose a limitation, (iii) the purpose for which the limitation may be imposed, and the relationship between the purpose and the limitation, and (iv) the conditions and circumstances under which a limitation may be imposed.[1140] A specific limitation provision can either exclude, amend, explain, repeat or provide detail about these elements of the general limitation clause. Depending on the particular function of the specific limitation provision, the provisions of the general limitation can be superseded by it or not. In the case of section 25 FC, no indications exist that the specific limitation provisions are aimed at excluding some or all of the elements of the general limitation provision. Instead, an analysis[1141] of the provisions of section 25 FC and section 36 FC rather indicates that the specific limitation provisions in section 25 FC are aimed at repeating[1142] or explaining or pro-

---

[1138] *De Waal/Currie/Erasmus,* Bill of Rights Handbook (2000), 394.

[1139] *Rautenbach,* General Provisions of the South African Bill of Rights (1995), 106-107.

[1140] *Rautenbach,* General Provisions of the South African Bill of Rights (1995), 84-85.

[1141] See the analysis of *Van der Walt,* 1997 SAPR/PL, 288 ff.

[1142] I.e. the provision in sec. 25(1) FC that "no one may be deprived of property except in terms of law of general application" repeats the similar phrase in sec. 36(1) FC. The only difference is that limitations in terms of sec. 25(1) FC

viding more detail[1143] with regard to the elements contained in section 36 FC.[1144] This, together with the inclination to interpret the separate provisions of the bill of rights in the light of the Constitution as a whole,[1145] confirms that section 36 FC is not only applicable to section 25 FC, but that it is applicable cumulatively, and not disjunctively. In contrast to the argument of De Waal, Currie and Erasmus as set out above,[1146] the application of section 36 FC to the property clause does not introduce a third stage into the constitutionality inquiry in which the onus of proving justifiability reverts to the party challenging the constitutional validity of a specific interference with property.

(ii) It can also be argued that section 36 FC will only apply to section 25 FC in exceptional cases. This argument is also based on the view that the provisions of section 25 FC should be exhausted before the analysis turn to section 36 FC. If the state cannot justify the limitation on the basis of the specific limitation provisions in section 25 FC, a third phase is introduced, in which the state (or the party relying on the validity of the limitation) gets another chance to justify the limitation in terms of

---

are called "deprivations", but these terms basically mean the same. This provision therefore does not add to or alter any of the elements of the general limitation provision. Similarly, sec. 25(2) FC provides that property "may be expropriated in terms of a law of general application". In this case, an addition is made in the sense that the interference must assume the form of an "expropriation", which is a rather severe form of limitation. It thus also provides detail about the limitation, as is explained in note 1143 below.

[1143] I.e. the provision in sec. 25(1) FC that no law "may permit arbitrary deprivaiton of property", which would have been covered by sec. 36(1) FC anyway, even if not expressly mentioned in sec. 25 FC. The express inclusion of this phrase merely serves the purpose of making the application of the elements of sec. 36 FC more particular in the context of sec. 25(1) FC. In the case of sec. 25(2) FC, which requires that limitations should be in the form of "expropriations", the requirements for justification are provided. These provisions affect the purpose of the limitation as well as the procedures to be followed. As such, they specify the way in which tow of the elements of the general limitation clause have to be seen in the case of property.

[1144] The provision in sec. 25(8) FC that none of the provisions in sec. 25 FC may impede land reform, as long as any deviation from the provisions of sec. 25 FC is still in line with sec. 36 FC further confirms the applicability of the general limitation clause on sec. 25 FC.

[1145] See 119 above.

[1146] See note 1137 and 1138 above.

the more general provisions of section 36 FC.[1147] However, the inconsequence of such an approach has been pointed out by De Waal, Currie and Erasmus, and quoted above.[1148] Moreover, such an approach would also require that section 25 FC is read in isolation from section 36 FC, which goes against the reading of single provisions in conformity with the constitutional text in its entirety.[1149] It would require that the courts override non-compliance with the specific limitation provisions of section 25 FC if compliance with the more general provisions of section 36 FC can be indicated. The practical possibility of such an approach is questionable.[1150]

(iii) A third argument against cumulative application of section 25 FC and section 36 FC emanates from the view that section 25 FC does not entrench property rights as such, but merely guarantees the right not to be deprived of property.[1151] Exponents of this line of thought argue that the "limiting elements" in section 25 FC all constitute internal modifying components, which restrict the right that is protected in section 25 FC. According to this view, there can only be a question of a limitation of the right in section 25 FC when deprivation or expropriation other than as provided for in section 25 FC has already been established. Then, only, section 36 FC enters the scene. The merits of this "less than property" argument have been discussed elsewhere[1152] and will not be repeated here. For present purposes, a discussion of the implication of this argument for limitation of property right must suffice. Van der Walt[1153] explains:

> "[T]he 'less than property' thesis does not ... necessarily exclude the general application of section 36 to the property clause. It is possible, however, to argue that the 'less than property' thesis effectively restricts the general application of section 36 to the property clause to

---

[1147] Woolman in Chaskalson/Kentridge et. al. (eds), Constitutional Law of South Africa (1996), ch. 12, 14.

[1148] See note 1137 and 1138 above.

[1149] See 119 above.

[1150] See Van der Walt, 1997 SAPR/PL, 292.

[1151] This view is based on the "less than property" argument in the context of the object of protection of section 25 FC, which is discussed at 87, 94, 96 and 108 above.

[1152] See 87, 94, 96 and 108 above.

[1153] Van der Walt, 1997 SAPR/PL, 312-313.

certain special cases, in the sense that in terms of this thesis section 36 will not find application to the property clause as long as a restrictive law or state action that affects property rights complies with the more or less formal provisions of section 25 ... "

According to this approach, limitations of property will only be subjected to scrutiny in terms of section 36 FC if it appears that they do not comply with the limitation requirements in section 25 FC. Such an approach leaves practically no scope for the consideration and balancing of the interests of the individual and society, because the parameters of such an interest-balancing venture have to be determined by the provisions of section 25 FC in colaboration with section 36 FC. What is more, the exclusion of section 36 FC from the inquiry into the constitutional validity of an interference with property would effectively oust the proportionality test from the process, as this test is incorporated or "codified" in section 36 FC.[1154]

(iv) In the view of Van der Walt[1155] the point of departure in a determination of the effect of section 36 FC on section 25 FC is article 36 FC itself. This approach is based on the structure and functions of limitation provisions and on the proportionality test as it appears in section 36 FC. It indicates that the assumption that the specific limitation provisions should be applied before the general limitation provision, is wrong. Section 36 FC should be the standard upon which section 25 FC elaborates. This would mean that the provisions of section 36 FC would, for instance, be employed to determine whether an interference with property is arbitrary or not. As such, section 36 FC *read with* section 25 FC would determine the constitutional limits of property. This view seems to be most acceptable, although it could raise concerns about the time and manner in which the proportionality test should be applied in an inquiry as to the constitutional validity of an interference with property. This issue will be dealt with in the discussion on the principle of proportionality with reference to the property clause.[1156]

[1154] See 352 ff. below.

[1155] *Van der Walt,* 1997 SAPR/PL, 327-329.

[1156] See 352 ff. below.

2.2.3.3. Evaluation

The aforegoing discussion should have indicated that constitutional property protection and limitation in South Africa involve all three possible kinds of limitations: internal modifying components or demarcations within section 25 FC; specific limitation provisions within section 25 FC; and the provisions of the general limitation clause of the Final Constitution. This raises the vexing question of why some of the more "formal" requirements[1157] for limiting the right to property are repeated in section 36 FC and section 25 FC. This repetition could even support the argument that section 36 FC does not apply to section 25 FC, simply because of the specific limitation already present in the latter. However, the principle of conformity[1158] requires that no provision — and this includes the property clause — can be treated in isolation from the rest of the constitution. Given the importance of section 36 FC, which is a strong embodiment of the values underlying the constitution as a whole, the argument that the provisions of section 25 FC exclude those of section 36 FC should be rejected. Besides, nothing in section 25 FC indicates that the general provisions of section 36 FC do not apply to the property clause. The specific limitations that can be identified in section 25 FC do not conflict with any of the requirements in section 36 FC. They simply repeat, explain, clarify and extend the elements of the general limitation clause.[1159] Therefore the inclusion of a specific limitation within section 25 FC also does not point to the intention to confer a right, only to deny the right straight afterwards.[1160] It simply makes it easier for the legislature to limit the right within the enumerated circumstances.

Indeed, section 36 FC applies to the property clause, and it applies in all circumstances. Theories favouring the idea that section 36 FC only applies in some cases, as a kind of "very last resort" or because it is indirectly excluded through the negative formulation of the right in section 25 FC,[1161] should also be rejected. The argument that section 36 FC will

---

[1157] I.e. limitation only in terms of a law of general application.

[1158] See 119 above.

[1159] *Rautenbach*, General Provisions of the South African Bill of Rights (1995), 106-107; *Van der Walt*, 1997 SAPR/PL, 289.

[1160] See *De Waal*, 1995 SAHJR, 25-26.

[1161] This argument is based mainly on the theory that section 25(1) FC guarantees something "less than property." See *Van der Walt*, 1997 SAPR/PL, 295-299; also 87 above.

only apply once all other possibilities have been exhausted, and that it therefore is a very last resort that is not always available to either or both of the parties involved, is (like the first argument) in conflict with the principle of conformity. Arguments based on the negative formulation contained in section 25 FC fail on an extended version of basically the same counter-argument. The conformity principle (or rather, the tendency of the court to follow a purposive interpretation of the constitutional provisions) renders a narrow distinction between negative and positive formulations of rights in one and the same bill illogical. Moreover, comparison with other jurisdictions indicates that a positive or negative formulation — or, for that matter even a general or specific negative formulation[1162] — of the guarantee to property, does not cause a significant difference in the protection afforded to property in the various legal systems.[1163] In fact, the Constitutional Court found that a negative formulation such as that of section 25 FC appears to be widely accepted as an appropriate formulation of the right to property.[1164]

The exact function of the proportionality principle in the South African context is closely related to the issue of how section 25 FC and section 36 FC interact with each other. Therefore, reference will again be made to the different theories about the interplay between these provisions when the issue of proportionality is discussed[1165] in the course of the analysis of the limitation of property rights. From a study of section 25 FC in its relation to section 36 FC, the more formal requirements of such a limitation should be quite clear, as they appear in both these clauses. To be constitutional, a deprivation or an expropriation of property (that is to say a limitation on the right to property) has to be effected *in terms of a law*,[1166] which must be *of general application*.[1167] Moreover, such a law *may not permit arbitrary limitation*[1168] of the right

---

[1162] See note 316 above.

[1163] *Van der Walt*, 1997 SAPR/PL, 299-301.

[1164] *Certification of the Constitution of the Republic of South Africa* (note 245 above), par. 72.

[1165] See 352 ff. below.

[1166] Sec. 25(1) and (2) FC; Sec. 36(1) FC.

[1167] Sec. 25(1) and (2) FC; Sec. 36(1) FC.

[1168] Sec. 25(1) FC. Expropriation is regarded as a special subcategory of deprivation. This means that expropriatory actions would also be subject to the requirement of non-arbitrariness.

to property.[1169] Furthermore, an expropriation in particular must be *for a public purpose or in the public interest*,[1170] and is subject to the payment of *compensation*,[1171] the amount of which should be either agreed to by the affected parties, or determined by a court, in which case it has to be just and equitable.[1172] In any event, all limitations of the right to property need to be *reasonable and justifiable* in an open and democratic society based on human dignity, equality and freedom. Moreover, the general limitation clause compels the court to take certain factors into account in order to determine whether a limitation would comply with this requirement.[1173] These requirements will enjoy further scrutiny in the course of this chapter.

3. Limitation through "Vertical Application": Regulation and Expropriation of Property

In both South Africa and Germany, provision is made for two basic types of infringement upon private property rights that could qualify as justifiable if certain requirements are met. In South Africa, the infringement has to qualify either as a deprivation of property in terms of section 25(1) FC, or as an expropriation in terms of section 25(2) FC. Similarly, the basic premise under German law is that a legislative infringement[1174] can only be constitutionally justifiable if it represents ei-

---

[1169] Sec. 25(1) FC.

[1170] Sec. 25(2)(a) FC.

[1171] Sec. 25(2)(b) FC. *Van der Walt*, Constitutional Property Clause (1997), 115. Similar requirements were set in the Interim Constitution: Section 28(3) IC laid down two explicit requirements for expropriations: they would be permissible *for public purposes only*, and they would be subject to the payment of *compensation*. Further, expropriations had also to comply with the more general requirement for deprivations as stated in section 28(2) IC as well as with the limitation provisions of section 33 IC.

[1172] Contrary to the situation in most other legal systems, the South African property clause also provides some indications of how the justness and equability of the compensation amount should be determined. See sec. 25(3) FC.

[1173] Sec. 36(1)(a)-(e) FC.

[1174] An infringing administrative act is justified if it is based on an enabling statute and still within the authorised limits set by this statute. The same principle applies to court decisions (of the final instance) creating an infringement.

ther a legislative regulation of property in terms of article 14 I 2 GG *(Inhalts- und Schrankenbestimmung)*,[1175] or an expropriation *(Enteignung)* of property in terms of article 14 III GG.

Although the requirements that render deprivation (regulation) and expropriation of property permissible might differ, the methods by means of which these infringements on property rights are instituted in Germany and South Africa bear a considerable degree of resemblance. Therefore, it is always important to determine which type of infringement was intended. This is sometimes easier said than done.

3.1. Difference between Regulation of Property and Expropriation

Particularly in cases where the infringements on property rights were initiated through legislation, or where the constitutionality of an act enabling administrative or judicial infringement must be tested, the outcome of the decision might be influenced by the type of infringement intended. Both in Germany and in South Africa, determining whether the infringement was intended to be either a regulation of property or an expropriation will not only be decisive for the question as to the admissibility requirements applicable to a specific infringement, but also for the question of whether compensation has to be paid. As a rule, compensation is paid in the case of expropriation, but not in the case of

---

However, in the latter case an additional question must be considered, i.e. whether the relevant court has misjudged the meaning and scope of article 14 GG. Consequently, in the case of infringement through administrative actions or final-instance court decisions stemming from specific legislation, the constitutionality of the legislation itself should also be tested. *Von Heinegg/Haltern*, 1993 JuS, 124.

[1175] In English literature on German constitutional law, the term "deprivation" as it was used in terms of sec. 28 IC, is not employed. Usually, authors refer to this phenomenon as the "legislative competence to determine the contents and limits of the property guarantee" or the "legislative interference with property". See i.a. *Kimminich* in *Starck (ed)*, Rights, Institutions and Impact of International Law (1987); *Schuppert* in *Karpen (ed)*, Constitution of Germany (1988); *Frowein*, Protection of Property in Relation to Taxation (1996); *Kommers*, Constitutional Jurisprudence of Germany (1997). The use of these phrases stems from the wording of art. 14 I 2 GG, which grants the legislature capacity to indeed pass statutes determining what the range, and intensity of the constitutional property guarantee should be.

deprivation.[1176] In addition, the circumstances permitting deprivation of property are generally perceived to be broader in scope than in the case of expropriation.[1177] It is therefore necessary to distinguish between regulation (in the narrow sense of deprivation) of property and expropriation already when determining whether a curtailment of the protected interests has taken place. This will enable the investigation to proceed to the last stage of the constitutionality inquiry and beyond.

At its simplest, the distinction between regulation and expropriation in both Germany and South Africa lies in the extent of the infringement: If the owner's freedom is curtailed, but not completely eliminated, a regulation of property has occurred. If the ownership itself is entirely withdrawn (either through discontinuation or through transfer to another legal subject), an expropriation has occurred. In general, expropriation is also distinguished from regulation of property by two related aspects: Expropriation is specific whereas regulation of or legislative interference with property is abstract in nature. This also has the consequence that expropriation has a direct effect on specific individuals, whereas legislative interference applies more generally.[1178] As a legislative interference could, however, be so extensive that it could have the same effect as an expropriation, a further distinction between these two concepts are often needed. This issue has already been discussed by both German and South African courts.[1179]

Regulation (in the narrow sense of deprivation) and expropriation of property are, both in Germany and in South Africa, only permissible or justifiable if the requirements provided for in the respective constitutions are met. The following paragraphs compare the requirements for regulation (in the sense of deprivation) and those for expropriation of property in German law and in South African law. This will be followed by a description of how limitations on property can be effected by the administration or the legislature in German and South African

---

[1176] In Germany, however some cases of legislative regulation of property demand payment of a financial settlement. This does not amount to compensation for expropriation in its true sense and does not cause a change in the nature of the infringement.

[1177] *Budlender* in *Budlender/Latsky/Roux*, New Land Law (revised 1998), ch. 1, 38.

[1178] *Schuppert* in *Karpen (ed)*, Constitution of Germany (1988), 113; BVerfGE 52, 1 *(Kleingärten); Pieroth/Schlink*, Grundrechte (1998), m.n. 923.

[1179] See also 378 ff. and 311 ff. below.

law. The problems of distinguishing between the different types of limitation in both legal systems will then be discussed.

3.2. The Justifiability of Limitations on Property Under German Law

Article 14 I 2 GG authorises the legislature to "determine the contents and limits" of the property guarantee, and thereby grants the legislature the ability to regulate property. However, the legal position protected by article 14 I 1 GG, should essentially remain intact. According to article 14 III GG, an infringement on property can also occur by expropriation *(Enteignung).*[1180] This is a more intensive infringement on property rights, as it does not merely limit the property rights but removes them altogether from the holder's sphere of influence. It must be kept in mind that legislative regulation of the contents and limits of property, and expropriation, are both mechanisms through which *intended* infringements on property rights can be justified.

Sometimes, actions of state also affect the right holder's freedom and property rights without it having been intended as a curtailment.[1181] If a measure directly[1182] and sufficiently[1183] intrudes upon the ownership of the affected individual to such an extent that he or she is expected to make a special sacrifice, an expropriatory infringement *(enteignender Eingriff)* is said to have taken place. This is probably the most a-typical, unintended and unexpected side effect of a legitimate administrative ac-

---

[1180] Art. 14 III 1 GG and 14 III 2 GG: *"Eine Enteignung ist nur zum Wohle der Allgemeinheit zulässig. Sie darf nur durch Gesetz oder auf Grund eines Gesetzes erfolgen, das Art und Ausmaß der Entschädigung regelt."*

[1181] *"Man kann finale Grundrechtseinwirkungen, die als solche vom Hoheitsträger als 'Griff' in den grundrechtlichen Bereich gewollt sind, von sonstigen Grundrechtseinwirkungen gleichen Effekts unterscheiden, die dann also 'eingriffsgleich' wirken."* Lerche in *Isensee/Kirchhof* (eds), Handbuch des Staatsrechts V (1992), m.n. 50.

[1182] An infringement is direct if it follows from a state-created objective, if it puts into effect a situation created by the state, or if it would result in a responsibility for the state. BGHZ 92, 34, 41 ff.

[1183] I.e., if an individual right holder *(Sonderopfer)* suffers because the general borderlines on the limitation of individual rights have been crossed and the curtailment would be of a unreasonable and unbearable intensity *(hinreichende Intensität).*

tion, and gives rise to a claim for compensation.[1184] On the contrary, had the administration acted illegally or had it omitted to act where a legal duty existed, and had an infringement arisen as result of this action or omission, a quasi-expropriatory infringement (*enteignungsgleicher Eingriff*) occurred.[1185] For instance, reparation work to roads and streets can bring about severe infringements on the rights of businesses in areas where the reparation work is being done. If the infringements result from the fact that the maintenance authority has not announced, prepared and executed the intended maintenance properly and in the least harmful way, the infringement would be illegal and therefore quasi-expropriatory. If the relevant authority, however, did everything within its power to reduce the effects of such an infringement, and the consequences are still harsh, the infringement would nevertheless be legal and therefore expropriatory.[1186]

Within the structure of article 14 GG, such unintended restrictions upon the holder of a right can be problematic: Article 14 III 2 GG requires that the legislature should be aware of the full effect of a curtailment of the freedom protected in the property guarantee. It is not clear whether the concepts of *enteignender Eingriff* and *enteignungsgleicher Eingriff* will survive the latest trends in the decisions of the Federal Constitutional Court pertaining to expropriation under article 14 GG. Authors are further not in agreement about the legitimacy and applicability of these concepts.[1187] In fact, *enteignende Eingriffe* and *enteignungsgleiche Eingriffe* should be dealt with on the basis of the *Staats-*

[1184] *Schoch*, 1990 Jura, 141.

[1185] *Schoch*, 1990 Jura, 140-141.

[1186] *Pieroth/Schlink*, Grundrechte - Staatsrecht II (1991), m.n. 1019a. For further examples, see BGHZ 37, 44 (forest fire resulting from artillery shooting exercises); BGHZ 97, 369 (traffic noise infringing on the rights of landowners); etc.

[1187] See *Bryde* in *Von Münch/Kunig*, Kommentar (1992), m.n. 56 ff., 100-108; contra *Papier* in *Maunz/Dürig*, GG Kommentar (1994), m.n. 377, 406 ff., 687 ff. The German Federal Court of Justice is, in terms of article 14 III 4 GG, the court of final instance in questions regarding the amount of compensation to be paid. This court is of the opinion that concepts of *enteignender Eingriff* and *enteignungsgleicher Eingriff* should remain intact. BGHZ 90, 17 at 20; BGHZ 91, 20 at 26 ff. See also BGH NVwZ 1986, 76 at 78; *Maurer*, Allgemeines Verwaltungsrecht (1997), m.n. 87 ff. For an exposition of the different solutions to this discussion, see *Von Heinegg/Haltern*, 1993 JuS, 215-217.

haftungsrecht (state liability law).[1188] This issue will, therefore, for purposes of the present chapter, be ignored. Instead, it will be indicated how the general principles of limitation of fundamental rights in the German legal system translate into certain requirements for regulation (in the sense of deprivation) and expropriation of property when read with the specific requirements of limitation provided by article 14 GG.

3.2.1. By or Pursuant to a Law

The authorisation for the German legislature to regulate property can be found in article 14 I 2 GG, which determines that the scope and content of property has to be determined by law. Regulation of property thus occurs *"durch die Gesetze"*.[1189] This refers mostly to formal law in the sense of statute; but requirements for the nature and content of legislation might differ depending on whether a legislative regulation or a full-fledged expropriation of property was intended. In the case of expropriation in particular, such a severe limitation of the right to property can only be successful if it is contained in formal legislation. It is argued that legislature alone has the capacity to determine which actions would be for the public good[1190] and to determine for which purposes, situations and exigencies expropriation would be acceptable.[1191]

3.2.1.1. "Legalenteignung" and "Administrativenteignung"

The legislature itself can infringe upon property rights, or it can authorise an infringement by the executive. In order to comply with the requirements of article 14 III 2 GG, an expropriation can take place through the expropriatory legislation *itself*, in which an individuals' property rights are (completely or partially) specifically removed by a

---

[1188] See *Von Heinegg/Haltern*, 1993 JuS, 123 where it is argued that the question concerning expropriatory and quasi-expropriatory infringements should not be relevant in the constitutionality inquiry, because it *only* serves the purpose of determining *exceptional* compensation claims.

[1189] *Pieroth/Schlink*, Grundrechte (1998), m.n. 928.

[1190] BVerfGE 56, 249, 261.

[1191] BVerfGE 74, 264, 285.

legislative enactment.[1192] This is usually referred to as *Legalenteignung*. Alternatively, one of the state's executive organs can be empowered by legislation to enforce a removal of existing individual property rights of a determined or determinable person or group of persons *on the basis of* expropriatory legislation.[1193] This is usually referred to as *Administrativenteignung*.

A legislative expropriation *(Legalenteignung)* is characterised by the fact that the enactment of the legislation itself, immediately, without any further administrative performance, withdraws existing individual rights of a determined or determinable person or group of persons.[1194] Because of its harsh effect, and because *Legalenteignung* also excludes the possibility of revision by the administrative courts,[1195] this kind of expropriation is only permissible under certain very limited circumstances. The *Deichordnungsbeschluß*[1196] can be used as example. This case arose from the damages caused by the flood in the city-state of Hamburg in 1962. The disaster resulted in the passing of the Dikes and Embankments Act,[1197] which provided for the conversion of immovable property classified in the land register as *Deichgrund* (dikeland) into public property. Thus, the land of owners adjacent to the dikes was expropriated directly by the relevant legislation. All private rights over the property were terminated and provision was made for compensation of the former owners. The former owners alleged that their fundamental rights in terms of article 14 GG had been violated. The Federal Constitutional Court, however, decided that consideration of the common weal sometimes require an interference with the rights of owners. According to the court, the fundamental constitutional values would prohibit a revision of the legal order that would remove constitutional protection of certain activities relating to property or substantially curtail or suspend the sphere of individual liberty protected by

---

[1192] These curtailments are referred to as *"Eingriffe durch Gesetz"* - see *Lerche* in *Isensee/Kirchhof (eds)*, Handbuch des Staatsrechts V (1992), m.n. 48.

[1193] E.g. BVerfGE 56, 249 *(Dürkheimer Gondelbahn)*, 261; BVerfGE 74, 264 *(Boxberg)*, 285 ff. Such a curtailment is called *"Eingriff auf Grund Gesetzes"*- see *Lerche* in *Isensee/Kirchhof (eds)*, Handbuch des Staatsrechts V (1992), m.n. 48.

[1194] E.g. BVerfGE 45, 297, 326.

[1195] Because no administrative act is at stake.

[1196] BVerfGE 24, 367.

[1197] *Hamburg Deichordnungsgesetz 1964.*

the fundamental right to property.[1198] However, despite the broad principles, which protected property and were mentioned by the court,[1199] it held[1200] that the state could in this instance legitimately place the dikeland properties under public control.

In the case of an administrative act of expropriation *(Administrativenteignung)* the legislation under discussion empowers an administrative organ to execute the expropriation,[1201] which must still result in a withdrawal of existing individual rights of a determined or determinable person or group of persons. Administrative expropriation can be effected upon the basis of ordinary legislation, or subordinate legislation.[1202] This approach does not warrant an equitable outcome in each individual case. Therefore the act would probably not amount to expropriation, but rather to legislative interference with property, if ownership entitlements enabling the owner to use the property responsibly remain.[1203]

3.2.1.2. Limitation and Exercise of the Legislature's Ability to Limit Property Rights

The legislature's capacity to determine the content and limits of property rights could give rise to various dogmatic problems. One might

---

[1198] BVerfGE 24, 367, 389.

[1199] The court declared (389) that the right to hold property is an elementary constitutional right which must be seen in close context with the protection of personal liberty. This decision established that property is secured in the hands of its owners, and that property itself, but also to some extent the value of property, is guaranteed. The court explained that the function of the property guarantee was to secure a sphere of economic liberty for the holder of a protected property interest, thereby enabling him or her to lead a self-governing life. Then the court indicated that property could not be effectively secured if the legislature were empowered to replace private property with something no longer qualifying as *ownership* in the true sense of the word.

[1200] BVerfGE 24, 367, 392.

[1201] E.g. par. 11 I, *Energiewirtschaftsgesetz*; par. 19 read with par. 17, *Bundesfernstraßengesetz*; par. 85 ff., *Baugesetzbuch*. See also provincial legislation, e.g. par. 1 *Landesenteignungsgesetz von Rheinland-Pfalz*; *Landesenteignungsgesetz von Baden-Württemberg*.

[1202] *Jung*, Das deutsche und das koreanische Enteignungsinstitut (1990), 29.

[1203] BVerfGE 58, 300, 301; *Pieroth/Schlink*, Grundrechte (1998), m.n. 922.

ask, for instance, whether the competence to determine the *contents* of property could be distinguished from the competence to determine *limits* of property rights. Further, the dialectic relation between article 14 I 2 GG and article 14 I GG could give rise to the argument that no effective constitutional protection of property rights can possibly exist, as the state can later take back by law that which has been conferred by the constitution at the outset.

As far as the competence of the courts is concerned, it has been argued that article 14 I 2 GG contains only a uniform authorisation: defining the contents would accordingly fix the limits; and setting the limits would also determine the contents.[1204] Others have contended that the Basic Law clearly distinguishes between these two activities,[1205] even though the two competencies became so confused through the jurisprudence of the Federal Constitutional Court that it is almost impossible to isolate them from each other.[1206] Nevertheless, legislation legalising encroachments upon property rights[1207] are considered to determine limitations,[1208] while legislation necessary to create property rights and aiming exclusively at rendering possible the protection of property[1209] is considered to be an instance of the determination of contents. Although the legislature can with respect to the latter largely exercise discretion in defining property, it should be sensitive to social change and the needs of the common good. Above all, the legislature must be guided by a constitutional perspective in these matters, to create conditions in which this right can flourish. If technological, economic, or social change begins to endanger or threaten guaranteed rights, proper corrective measures may be required as a matter of constitutional law.[1210]

[1204] *Kimminich* in *Starck (ed)*, Rights, Institutions and Impact of International Law (1987), 83.

[1205] *Limpens*, Funktion & Grenzen der Inhaltsbestimmung des Eigentums (1973), 66 ff., 109 ff.; *Wendt*, Eigentum und Gesetzgebung (1985), 147 ff.

[1206] *Limpens*, Funktion & Grenzen der Inhaltsbestimmung des Eigentums (1973), 71.

[1207] I.e. legislation which allows curtailments of the legal position of the holder of specific property rights.

[1208] *Kimminich* in *Starck (ed)*, Rights, Institutions and Impact of International Law (1987), 83; *Wendt*, Eigentum und Gesetzgebung (1985), 148-149.

[1209] I.e. legislation which stipulates who is to be protected, and to what extent.

[1210] *Kommers*, Constitutional Jurisprudence of Germany (1997), 297.

As to the apparently inherent discrepancy between article 14 I 1 GG and article 14 I 2 GG, it is acknowledged that legislative intervention will almost always affect existing rights.[1211] However, the theory of *Schranken-Schranken* ensures that a right is only limited to the extent prescribed by the Basic Law. It is thus well accepted that, in the context of the German property guarantee, the constitutional guarantee contained in article 14 I 1 GG and the social welfare function inherent in property in terms of article 14 II GG provide limits to the legislative powers to regulate property.[1212] The legislature's powers are not as extensive as they appear to be at first glance. Although article 14 I 2 GG does not explicitly mention the limits on the competence of the legislators as such, jurisprudence and jurisdiction unanimously assert these inherent limits. In this regard, the Federal Constitutional Court[1213] has indicated that, in regulating the content and limits of property under article 14 I GG, the legislator is required to accord due weight to the framers' fundamental value decision in favour of private property.[1214] As with other fundamental rights, balancing is the order of the day, as any legislative regulation is subject to certain overarching values that influence the meaning of the entire Basic Law. These are the principles of human dignity, personality, and equality, which are enshrined, respectively, in the first three articles of the Basic Law. It is the legislature's responsibility to harmonise these values in practice, even if it means that more weight is attached to some property rights than to others. Finally, the principles of rule of law (*Rechtsstaatlichkeit*), social justice (*Sozialstaatlichkeit*) and proportionality (*Verhältnismäßigkeit*)[1215] must be fed

---

[1211] *Thormann*, Abstufungen in der Sozialbindung des Eigentums (1996), 143-147.

[1212] BVerfGE 58, 300, 338; *Kimminich* in *Starck (ed)*, Rights, Institutions and Impact of International Law (1987), 82-83.

[1213] BVerfGE 14, 263 *(Feldmühle)*, 277-278: *"Der Regelungsbefugnis des Gesetzgebers scheinen nach dem Wortlaut des Art. 14 Abs. 1 Satz 2 GG keine Schranken gesetzt zu sein. Es ist jedoch selbstverständlich, daß jede gesetzliche Inhalts- und Schrankenbestimmung sowohl die grundlegende Wertentscheidung des Grundgesetzes zugunsten des Privateigentums im herkömmlichen Sinne zu beachten hat als auch mit allen übrigen Verfassungsnormen in Einklang stehen muß, also insbesondere dem Gleichheitssatz, dem Grundrecht auf freie Entfaltung der Persönlichkeit und den Prinzipien der Rechts- und Sozialstaatlichkeit."*

[1214] *Kommers*, Constitutional Jurisprudence of Germany (1997), 254.

[1215] Although no direct reference is made in the quotation from the *Feldmühle* case (see note 1213 above) these words were repeated in subsequent deci-

into the equation.[1216] The legislature is supposed to find the guidelines according to which the contents and limits of property rights are determined by observing the current ideas and perceptions in society.[1217] The function of the Constitutional Court in reviewing an alleged intrusion into the right of property is to determine whether lawmakers have adequately considered and properly weighed these competing values.[1218]

The orientation of the legislature towards a determination of the contents and limits of property against the changing demands of the society is noteworthy. Upon scrutinising the legislation enacted since the promulgation of the Basic Law in 1949, Von Brünneck[1219] has identified three phases in the German legislature's exercise of its competence to determine the content and limits of property.[1220] In the first phase (from 1949 until the 1960s) the legislature — in fostering a liberal and social economy *(soziale Marktwirtschaft)* — concentrated on securing property rights by promoting private property with a wide range of entitlements for the holder.[1221] In the second phase more focus was placed on the social elements in the same economic system. Private property was still promoted, but only within the framework of state regulations de-

---

sions with the addition that the legislator must not determine contents and limitations in a grossly inappropriate manner encroaching upon the interests of the persons concerned without necessity or excessively. "*[Der Gesetzgeber] darf Inhalt und Schranken des Eigentums nicht in einer Weise bestimmen, die grob sachwidrig ist und in die Interessen der Beteiligten ohne Grund oder übermäßig eingreift.*" BVerfGE 18, 121, 132; also BVerfGE 21, 150, 155.

[1216] *Kommers*, Constitutional Jurisprudence of Germany (1997), 254.

[1217] BVerfGE 20, 351 *(Tollwutentscheidung)*, 355-366.

[1218] *Kommers*, Constitutional Jurisprudence of Germany (1997), 255. In this regard, the treatment by the Federal Constitutional Court of the various competing interests at stake is illustrated in BVerfGE 14, 263 *(Feldmühlebeschluß)*; BVerfGE 37, 132 *(Wohnraumkündigungsschutzgesetz)*; BVerfGE 42, 263 *(Conterganentscheidung)*; BVerfGE 52, 1 *(Kleingärten)*; BVerfGE 89, 1 *(Besitzrecht des Mieters)*.

[1219] *Von Brünneck*, Die Eigentumsgarantie des Grundgesetzes (1984), 163 ff.

[1220] In *Von Brünneck*, Die Eigentumsgarantie des Grundgesetzes (1984), 163 ff. no distinction is made between the different competencies of the legislature in determining, on the one hand, the scope, and on the other hand, the limitations of property. See contra *Limpens*, Funktion & Grenzen der Inhaltsbestimmung des Eigentums (1973), and *Wendt*, Eigentum und Gesetzgebung (1985).

[1221] *Von Brünneck*, Die Eigentumsgarantie des Grundgesetzes (1984), 163.

signed to keep the competitive market working efficiently and to secure social protection. Therefore more restrictions on private property were acknowledged.[1222] The second phase ended in the time of the change-over of political power from the social-liberal coalition to the CDU/CSU-FDP coalition at the beginning of the eighties. This introduced the third identifiable phase in property legislation. Some individual property rights were broadened to correlate with the policy of less state control and more individual rights and duties,[1223] but (contrary to the treatment of property rights in the first phase) the broadening of individual property rights and correlative duties depended much more on the type of property at stake.[1224] The development of the legislature's regulatory competence can therefore not be described as a simple broadening, nor a systematic limitation of property rights. Legislation regulating property varies according to the type of property involved and the relevant moment in history.

3.2.2. Specific Requirement for Regulation of Property: Proportionality

The constitutionality of particular regulations of property is premised on adherence to the principle of proportionality. By and large, proportionality is tested by considering the objective suitability *(Geeignetheit)* of the law, action or measure; the question of its necessity *(Erforderlichkeit)*; and the question of its reasonableness or its "proportionality" in the narrow sense *(Angemessenheit)*. Objective suitability means that the restriction, which is being tested against the constitutional provisions, should be appropriate or suitable to achieve the objective intended. The intended aim of the legislation under discussion must be measured against the possible means to achieve it, to determine whether a rational relation exist between them. Necessity implies that the measure taken must not, in other words, be harsher than is necessary to achieve the specified goal. Reasonableness (or "proportionality" in the narrow sense) means that, in relation to the importance and meaning of

---

[1222] *Kimminich* in *Starck (ed)*, Rights, Institutions and Impact of International Law (1987), 83; *Von Brünneck*, Die Eigentumsgarantie des Grundgesetzes (1984), 163.

[1223] *Von Brünneck*, Die Eigentumsgarantie des Grundgesetzes (1984), 163.

[1224] *Von Brünneck*, Die Eigentumsgarantie des Grundgesetzes (1984), 164.

the fundamental right, no less far-reaching restriction would have achieved the same result.[1225]

The principle of proportionality is the basis for binding legislature in determining the relationship of fundamental rights and their restriction. It is, in other words, the method used to determine whether the reasons advanced by the state to limit a freedom outweigh the values that underlie the constitutional commitment to the protection of the freedom.[1226] The principle of proportionality also binds the executive in the exercise of its discretionary powers.[1227] As such, proportionality gives rise to the prohibition of excesses *(Übermaßverbot)*, which means that it monitors and culls legislation, tempering harsh statutory provisions and substantiating exceptions to the general rule without compromising the general applicability of the legislation.[1228] Thus, the Federal Constitutional Court has determined[1229] that public authorities can limit the citizens' general claim for freedom against the state only insofar as it is necessary for the protection of the public interest.

3.2.2.1. Proportionality and the Property Clause

With reference to the property clause, the Federal Constitutional Court has deduced the applicability of the proportionality principle from article 14 I 2 GG read with article 14 I 1 GG, particularly because they appear within one paragraph of the guarantee, and follow each other.[1230] Further, the social welfare function of property as it appears from article 14 II GG read with article 14 I GG gives the proportionality test a unique structure in the context of the property guarantee.[1231] The proportionality principle requires that legislation infringing upon property rights acknowledges the holders' freedom and limit it reasonably,

---

[1225] *Degenhart,* Staatsrecht I (1998), m.n. 278, 279, 281; *Robbers,* Introduction to German Law (1998), 61; *Blaau,* [sic] 1990 SALJ, 82.

[1226] However, constitutional disputes are often resolved by demarcating or defining the right properly, rather than by reliance on the doctrine of proportionality. *De Waal,* 1995 SAHJR, 6 note 17.

[1227] *Blaauw-Wolf/Wolf,* 1996 SALJ, 269.

[1228] *Blaauw-Wolf,* 1999 SAPR/PL, 194.

[1229] In BVerfGE 19, 342, 348-349.

[1230] BVerfGE 52, 1, 29.

[1231] BVerfGE 34, 210, 138 ff., 211 ff.

namely only as far as it is necessary and suitable. At the same time, the infringing legislation should allow only proportional (suitable, necessary and proportionate/moderate) neglect of the social welfare obligation.[1232]

In effect, this means that the German *Übermaßverbot*[1233] on the one hand, and the *Gebot sachgerechter Abwägung* on the other should be complied with. The Federal Court has explained these requirements.[1234] It entails that, when enacting legislation in terms of article 14 I 2 GG, the legislature has to consider both elements contained in the constitution: (i) the relationship between constitutionally protected legal positions, and (ii) the demand of a social welfare system of property ownership. It has to balance the different interests meriting protection. Neither one-sided preference nor discrimination is in line with the constitutional idea that private property has to serve the society in which it operates. Corresponding therewith is the commitment of the legislature to the constitutional principle of proportionality. The public good is not only the motive, but also the limit up to which restrictions can be imposed on the owner. To be constitutional, these restrictions must be necessary within the ambit of the regulated sphere and structurally applicable to the property under discussion. Restrictions of the power of disposition of the owner may not go beyond that what is necessary for the achievement of the purpose that the regulation serves.

[1232] *Pieroth/Schlink*, Grundrechte (1998), m.n. 929.

[1233] *"Der allgemeinen rechtsstaatlichen Eingriffsschranke des Übermaßverbots ... entsprochen hat."* Von Heinegg/Haltern, 1993 JuS, 125. See 290 above.

[1234] BVerfGE 52, 1 *(Kleingarten)*, 29: *"Der Gesetzgeber muß bei Regelungen im Sinne des Art. 14 Abs. 1 Satz 2 GG beiden Elementen des im Grundgesetz angelegten Verhältnisses von verfassungsrechtlich garantierter Rechtsstellung und dem Gebot einer sozialgerechten Eigentumsordnung in gleicher Weise Rechnung tragen; er muß die schutzwürdigen Interessen der Beteiligten in einen gerechten Ausgleich und ein ausgewogenes Verhältnis bringen. Eine einseitige Bevorzugung oder Benachteiligung steht mit den verfassungsrechtlichen Vorstellungen eines sozialgebundenen Privateigentums nicht in Einklang. Dem entspricht die Bindung des Gesetzgebers an den verfassungsrechtlichen Grundsatz der Verhältnismäßigkeit. Das Wohl der Allgemeinheit ist nicht nur Grund, sondern auch Grenze für die dem Eigentümer aufzuerlegenden Beschränkungen. Um vor der Verfassung Bestand zu haben, müssen sie vom geregelten Sachbereich her geboten und auch in ihrer Ausgestaltung sachgerecht sein. Einschränkungen der Eigentümerbefugnisse dürfen nicht weiter gehen, als der Schutzzweck reicht, dem die Regelung dient."*

The dual task of the legislature created by article 14 I 2 GG must be seen against the dual function of the property guarantee.[1235] On the one hand, property must serve the needs of the private individual and, on the other hand, it must also be useful to the public in general. The legislature has the difficult task of harmonising these requirements of private use and public usefulness. Its success depends on its ability to obtain a proper proportional combination of these functions, which would create equilibrium in the interests under discussion.

3.2.2.2. Proportionality and Balancing of Interests Under the Property Clause

In determining whether a fair balance has been struck between the individual interest at stake and the public interest in general, the fundamental purpose of the property guarantee will be taken into account by the courts. In several decisions the court indicated what a proper balance between the interests of the community and the individual interests would be, and then reached the conclusion that the particular statutes were invalid because they violated the the principle of balancing competing interests. However, many recent decisions of the Federal Constitutional Court are not consistent with each other.[1236]

The Federal Constitutional Court, for instance, held that copyright legislation providing for the possibility to print protected materials for educational purposes is as such compatible with article 14 GG, but found that the exclusion of any royalties for this publication was a violation of article 14 II GG. The Court explained in detail that the exclusion of royalties was not demanded by the public interest.[1237] In a further decision,[1238] the Court held that it is in accordance with article 14 GG to legalise performance of protected musical works in church services without the permission of the author. However, the exclusion of

---

[1235] See 104 above.

[1236] *Pieroth/Schlink*, Grundrechte - Staatsrecht II (1991), m.n. 986a remarks that the latest decisions of the Federal Constitutional Court indicates that the ownership concept is in transit. Cases mentioned include: BVerfGE 37, 132 *(Wohnraumkündigung)*; BVerfGE 45, 297 *(Hamburger U-Bahn-Bau)*; BVerfGE 50, 290 *(Mitbestimmung)*; BVerfGE 52, 1 *(Kleingarten)*; BVerfGE 58, 137 *(Pflichtexemplar)*; BVerfGE 58, 300 *(Naßauskiesung)*.

[1237] BVerfGE 31, 229.

[1238] BVerfGE 49, 382.

any royalty for such a performance was also found to be in violation of article 14 GG. In another matter, the court found that a change of legislation that prohibited the continued use of lawfully acquired trademarks for wines is in violation of article 14 GG. It therefore invalidated the legislation concerned.[1239] The court also held that specific rules requiring publishers to provide copies for official libraries is in principle compatible with article 14 GG. However, this is not so where a limited edition of a specific public ation at extremely high costs is involved.[1240]

The (classical) *Verhältnismäßigkeit* test can, *inter alia*, involve an investigation into the social welfare function embodied in article 14 II GG. Therefore the *Gestaltungsspielraum* (that is, the legislative scope or leeway) of the legislature is an important factor. Proportionality (in the wide sense) is a general rule of constitutional interpretation. It should not be confused with the balancing of conflicting rights[1241] *(Güterabwägung)* which is applied by some administrative and civil courts, but not endorsed by the Federal Constitutional Court.[1242]

In terms of the theory of *Güterabwägung*, the "abstract ranking" of rights and values depend on their source. Constitutional rights rank higher than rights accorded by other statutes, just like federal law is more important than the law of the *Länder*.[1243] For present purposes, the hierarchical ranking of fundamental rights, which are proposed by this theory, needs to be mentioned.[1244] According to this hierarchy, individual freedom would, for instance, rank higher than property rights and other rights which protect objects, because individual freedom is inextricably connected to the person. Furthermore, the importance of a right depends, *inter alia*, on its relevance to the community, which in

---

[1239] BVerfGE 51, 193.

[1240] BVerfGE 58, 137.

[1241] E.g. *De Waal*, 1995 SAHJR, 6 note 17 indicates that proportionality can also be employed in cases where the court is called upon to balance conflicting rights, because balancing is a form of limitation of rights. This is an over-simplification of the process which really takes place when invoking the proportionality principle.

[1242] BVerfGE 7, 198 *(Lüth)*, 208 ff.

[1243] Art. 31 GG.

[1244] *Blaauw-Wolf*, 1999 SAPR/PL, 198-199 provides an excellent overview of this theory of *Güterabwägung*. The present discussion is based on her exposition of the matter, but the sources quoted by her are omitted in order to avoid duplication.

turn links with the importance of individual freedom. This theory basically foresees that the more fundamental a right is for the maintenance of values in a democratic state, the higher its position in this pyramid of fundamental rights will be. Freedom of expression or occupational freedom, would, for instance, rank higher than property rights. In addition to this "abstract ranking" there is a "concrete ranking" of rights which can be applied in a particular instance to determine which right enjoys preference over another, or which right has to give way to another. This depends on the "values" or "interests" at stake, the intensity of the infringement and the degree to which a right deserves protection. A right with a low ranking, from an abstract perspective, could be awarded a higher ranking in a specific case, depending on a number of other factors involved.[1245] The actual number of values or interests can thus also play a role in the specific situation. In principle, more interests take precedence over a single interest; the public interest is more important than an individual interest and multiple freedoms come before a single freedom. The extent to which one right enjoys preference over another is not specifically delimited by the theory of abstract or concrete ranking. A number of other criteria still has to be considered, namely interpretation in conformity with the constitution, the principle of equality, the *Rechtsstaat* concept and the principle of proportionality. These criteria are also applied when two rights have the same ranking.[1246]

Blaauw-Wolf[1247] shows that the principle of proportionality and this balancing-of-conflicting rights theory *(Güterabwägung)* overlap and might even sometimes lead to the same results. The latter is, nevertheless, based upon a system of weighed or ranked fundamental rights where the general importance of a certain right or freedom depends on its relevance for the community.[1248] Proportionality in the (wider) sense

---

[1245] For example, the owner of a factory with relatively high pollution emissions must be willing to accept a 'depreciation' of his property rights. In the concrete case his property is less deserving of protection than the property rights of others, even in another context.

[1246] See *Blaauw-Wolf*, 1999 SAPR/PL, 198-199 and the sources quoted there.

[1247] *Blaauw-Wolf*, 1999 SAPR/PL, 198 – 201.

[1248] This theory determines that the more fundamental a right is for the maintenance of values in a democratic state, the higher its position is in the hierarchy of fundamental rights ("abstract ranking"). Moreover, the factors applicable in a concrete case determines the value attached to fundamental rights for that specific case only ("concrete ranking"). *Blaauw-Wolf*, 1999 SAPR/PL, 198.

of propriety in the relation between the concepts of private property and social interest is much rather a function embodied in a broad legislative competence *(Gestaltungsspielraum)* to determine the content and scope (framework) of the property guarantee.[1249]

In the constitutional context, the disadvantage of the theory of *Güterabwägung* is that it encourages subjective assessment of constitutional norms and often even replaces a true interpretation of the constitutional norms. This amounts to a denial of the *Rechtsstaat* concept, which is the origin of the proportionality principle.[1250] It also confuses the distinction between the proportional leveling of the interests of the parties involved (in other words, proportionality in the wider sense) and the classical investigation into the *Angemessenheit* (that is, proportionality in the narrow sense) of a specific infringement with a specific purpose.[1251] Therefore, *Güterabwägung* or the balancing of conflicting interests should only be resorted to if the elements of suitability and necessity have been investigated in a specific case and could provide no clear answer as to the constitutionality of the restriction. Moreover, even if the case requires a "real" balancing of interests in the sense that the proportionality in the narrow sense should be investigated, a predestined hierarchical ranking of the different rights, freedoms and values, should not be endorsed:[1252]

> *"Vielmehr stellt das Prinzip der Einheit der Verfassung die Aufgabe einer Optimierung: Beiden Gütern müssen Grenzen gezogen werden, damit beide zu optimaler Wirksamkeit gelangen können. ... 'Verhältnismäßigkeit' bezeichnet in diesem Zusammenhang eine Relation Zweier variabler Größen, und zwar diejenige, die jener Optimierungsaufgabe am besten gerecht wird, nicht eine Relation zwischen einem konstanten 'Zweck' und einem oder mehreren variablen 'Mitteln'."*

[1249] *Thormann*, Abstufungen in der Sozialbindung des Eigentums (1996), 210.

[1250] *Blaauw-Wolf*, 1999 SAPR/PL, 199.

[1251] *Thormann*, Abstufungen in der Sozialbindung des Eigentums (1996), 210.

[1252] *Hesse*, Grundzüge des Verfassungsrechts (1993), m.n. 72. Translation: "The principle of the unity of the constitution rather requires an optimisation: Both interests should be limited, as both should be optimally effective. ... 'Proportionality' in this sense signifies a relation between two interests which could vary in importance, a relation which would serve the required optimisation best, not a relation between a constant 'purpose' and one or more varying 'means'."

This would mean that proportionality in the (wider) sense of the appropriate relation between the concepts of private property and public interest is something different from the classical determination of the proportionality of a specific infringement.[1253] It represents the purpose of granting the legislature wide capacities in enacting legislation that creates interference with private property.

3.2.2.3. Property, Legislative Structuring and Levels of Scrutiny

Because of the different elements of proportionality, the provision on legislative determination of the contents and limits of property in article 14 I 2 GG is in a sense also intertwined with the social welfare function, although these two provisions pursue different aims in the context of article 14 GG as a whole. The case law on the matter shows that, even where the Federal Constitutional Court found that the purpose of the legislation was to serve the general interest, the concomitant hardship caused to the individual may lead to a violation of article 14 GG.[1254]

The constitutional property guarantee is to a large extent dependent on legislative structuring (*Gestaltung*). In fact, the constitutional property guarantee is made specific and is given effect through the enactment of ordinary legislation. In the context of the property guarantee, legislature is assigned the task of putting the social model of property, the normative elements of which are stipulated in article 14 I 1 GG and article 14 II GG, into practice.[1255] Proportionality in the narrow sense involves in particular the taking into account of, *inter alia*, the social

---

[1253] *Thormann*, Abstufungen in der Sozialbindung des Eigentums (1996), 210, 143: "*Dort ist die richtige Stelle, um zu fragen, ob der Gesetzgeber ausgewogen genug zwischen Eigentum und Sozialgebot abgewogen hat, mit anderen Worten, ob er sowohl die Freiheit nicht mehr als verhältnismäßig verkürzt als auch die Sozialbindung nicht mehr als verhältnismäßig vernachlässigt hat.*" See, however, also BVerfGE 52, 1, 29 ff.; BVerfGE 72, 66, 78 ff.; BVerfGE 87, 114, 138 ff. and note 1256 below.

[1254] BVerfGE 58, 137; BVerfGE 31, 229; BVerfGE 49, 382. *Frowein*, Protection of Property in Relation to Taxation (1996), 8.

[1255] BVerfGE 52, 1, 29. See also BVerfGE 37, 132, 140, where the dialectic relation between constitutionally guaranteed freedoms and a socially just property order is mentioned.

welfare function of property in terms of article 14 II GG.[1256] It is here that the wide scope of the legislature in enacting legislation affecting the rights of holders of patrimonial rights can be questioned. The interests worthy of protection of the parties involved must be justly balanced and brought into equilibrium. The specific type of patrimonial interest, with its particular characteristics, should also be taken into account.

The kind of restriction imposed upon the property guarantee is closely connected to the perception of the function of ownership under given circumstances. If the function of ownership is primarily perceived to be the securing of the private freedom of the individual, legislative restrictions operate within a narrow set of limits. If, however, the function of ownership is perceived to be that of social benefit, the legislature's powers to determine the content and limits of property (protection) are more extensive.[1257]

The specific object of a property right for the holder thereof is relevant in considering the justifiability of regulations upon the property, because of the approach of the Federal Constitutional Court. Property is made subject to varying levels of scrutiny,[1258] depending on the nature of the object of a specific property right and its importance for the individual as well as society at large. The court tests constitutional justifiability against a higher standard when the function of ownership as the means through which the individual can secure his or her material wellbeing, independence and freedom is at stake.[1259] By contrast, the court tends to grant the legislature more scope in the enactment of constitu-

---

[1256] See note 1253 above. *Thormann*, Abstufungen in der Sozialbindung des Eigentums (1996), 143. See, however, also BVerfGE 52, 1, 29 ff.; BVerfGE 72, 66, 78; BVerfGE 87, 114, 138 ff. *"Das Wohl der Allgemeinheit ist nicht nur Grund, sondern auch Grenze für die dem Eigentümer aufzuerlegenden Beschränkungen. Um vor der Verfassung Bestand zu haben, müssen sie vom geregelten Sachbereich her geboten und auch in ihrer Ausgestaltung sachgerecht sein. Einschränkungen der Eigentümerbefugnisse dürfen nicht weiter gehen, als der Schutzzweck reicht, dem die Regelung dient."*

[1257] BVerfGE 53, 257, 292.

[1258] *Thormann*, Abstufungen in der Sozialbindung des Eigentums (1996), 211-225; *Van der Walt*, 1997 SAPR/PL, 318.

[1259] BVerfGE 50, 290, 340. The legislature's legislative ability is therefore more limited in cases concerning property interests acquired through the holder's own labour or performance, as well as in cases concerning the alienation of property (because the capacity to dispose of property is elementary to the owner's freedom). *Pieroth/Schlink*, Grundrechte (1998), m.n. 933.

tionally justifiable regulating legislation when the social function[1260] of ownership — the social responsibility of the state and the power to control the dangers and disadvantages of private autonomous use of property — is involved.[1261] Ownership of means of production, which provides power over third parties, would typically fall into this category.[1262] Landownership is also treated with caution, because of the argument that land, which is an indispensable but limited resource, cannot be made completely subject to the free will and power of the individual owner. In a just legal and social order, the public weal is much closer connected to land than to many other kinds of patrimonial interests.[1263]

The social relevance of a specific kind of property is dependent on time and place, and has no influence on the concept of property in general. "Socially relevant" property should not be regarded as being either less or more valuable than property without any particular social relevance.[1264] It merely influences the courts' and legislature's obligation to consider certain issues when attempting to regulate specific kinds of property: In the *Kleingärten* case,[1265] for example, the court struck down a federal statute that sought to limit the right of landowners to terminate garden plot leases. Garden plots rented from landowners on the fringes of large cities were a major feature of German social organisation and once played an important role in feeding the population. It

---

[1260] An earlier draft by the Parliamentary Council that harbours the intent of this broad language reads: "Ownership entails a social obligation. Its use shall find its limits in the living necessities of all citizens and in the public order essential to society." This suggests that the legislator has been given a wide berth for the regulation of private property in the public interest. *Kommers*, Constitutional Jurisprudence of Germany (1997), 253.

[1261] Albeit without giving detailed reasons: BVerfGE 80, 137, 150; BVerfGE 8, 71, 80; BVerfGE 21, 73, 83; BVerfGE 50, 290, 340 and 347. This trend is also echoed in literature on the topic of art. 14 GG. See *Bryde* in *Von Münch/Kunig*, GG Kommentar (1992), m.n. 63; *Leisner* in *Isensee/Kirchhof*, Handbuch des Staatsrechts VI (1989), m.n. 60, 61.

[1262] See BVerfGE 79, 29, 41. *Pieroth/Schlink*, Grundrechte (1998), m.n. 933. *Papier* in *Maunz/Dürig*, GG Kommentar (1994), m.n. 298 ff.

[1263] BVerfGE 21, 73, 82 ff.; BVerfGE 52, 1, 32 ff. See similar reasoning in BGHZ 23, 30, 35; BGHZ 80, 111, 116; BGHZ 90, 4, 15.

[1264] *Leisner* in *Isensee/Kirchhof*, Handbuch des Staatsrechts VI (1989), m.n. 115; *Thormann*, Abstufungen in der Sozialbindung des Eigentums (1996), 211.

[1265] BVerfGE 52, 1.

was argued by the state that limiting the landowners' right to terminate garden plot leases was consistent with the social welfare function of property and an emerging national policy against urban sprawl. In the light of changed economic conditions and developments in commercial agriculture, however, the court deemed the burden on the property owner disproportionately heavy in relation to the value of the protected interest. From this example, it should be clear that the legislature must carefully have considered either the specific nature of the property interest at stake, or the meaning of the property interest for the right holder, or even both.

In this manner — through the interplay of the liberty and social functions of property and the legislature's scope to regulate property — a system of differentiated (or "scaled") protection of various property interests has developed from the constitutional directives. In this regard, Thormann[1266] points out that the more the public interest is taken into account in the regulation of property, the less the interests of individual owners will, as a rule, be heeded. *Vice versa*, the situation is similar. Accordingly, each differentiation made between the requirements for justifiable regulation of various kinds of property rights would simultaneously have the effect of layering (or "scaling") the protection of property and of differentiating between the social relevance of various kinds of property rights.

The ability of the legislature of translating the constitutional requirements into specific terms and categorising property accordingly should not be curtailed to the extent that it cannot fulfil the functions placed upon it by the Basic Law and meet the expectations created by a democratic order. It must still be possible for the legislature to be creative in order to be functional. This so-called *Gestaltungsspielraum*[1267] of the legislature is of the utmost importance in the context of the limitation of property rights in the public interest, and should therefore always be taken into account by the courts when considering whether or not a specific regulation of property is constitutionally justifiable. The assessments of the legislature cannot simply be thrown overboard and be replaced at whim and fancy when constitutional interpretation is at stake.[1268]

[1266] *Thormann*, Abstufungen in der Sozialbindung des Eigentums (1996), 38.

[1267] I.e. the legislative scope or leeway.

[1268] *Thormann*, Abstufungen in der Sozialbindung des Eigentums (1996), 209.

3.2.3. Specific Requirements for Expropriation of Property

Apart from the requirement which applies to both legislative regulation (in the narrow sense of deprivation) and expropriation of property that the infringement should be undertaken by or pursuant to a law (which, in the case of expropriation means formally enacted legislation), additional requirements determine the justifiability of an expropriation. These are that (i) the legislation must provide for compensation, and the type and extent of compensation must be stipulated;[1269] (ii) the expropriation must be for the public weal;[1270] and (iii) the determination of the amount of compensation must follow from a fair balancing of interests of the society as a whole on the one hand and of the affected individuals on the other.[1271] If these requirements are not met, the basic right to property is violated. The owner's duty to tolerate an intrusion of his or her basic right to property is determined by the Basic Law itself. These limits are fixed and permanent. The legislature is not empowered to change them.[1272] These requirements need closer scrutiny.

3.2.3.1. Provision for Compensation ("Junktimklausel")

Once it is certain that a specific expropriation is justified and valid in terms of the requirements set out in article 14 GG, the constitutional guarantee of property in German law embodies a "guarantee of value" (Wertgarantie). This entitles the individual to receive compensation

---

[1269] Art. 14 III 2 GG.

[1270] Art. 14 III 1 GG.

[1271] Art. 14 III 3 GG. This so-called *"Abwägungsgebot"* does not allow the allocation of mere nominal compensation. However, it also does not require that compensation should always equal the full market value of the property. Instead, the type and extent of compensation must be determined through a consideration of all the interests at stake. See BVerfGE 24, 367 *(Deichordnung)*, 421; BGHZ 39, 198, 199. *Pieroth/Schlink*, Grundrechte (1998), m.n. 944. *Richter/Schuppert*, Casebook (1996), 378 ff. The act can determine the manner in which the different interests should be rated and balanced, but should at least contain a set framework within which the compensation amount could be determined and which provides for the consideration of the specific circumstances of each case. See BVerfGE 24, 367, 419. *Richter/Schuppert*, Casebook (1996), 379.

[1272] BVerfGE 24, 367, 396; *Kommers*, Constitutional Jurisprudence of Germany (1997), 251.

upon the expropriation of his or her right to property by the state.[1273] The requirement that provision must be made for compensation and that the type and extent of such compensation must be stipulated, is found in article 14 III 2 GG. This is the so-called *Junktimklausel* (linking-clause provision), which applies to all legislation enacted after the promulgation of the Basic Law in 1949.[1274] It obliges the state to compensate owners whose special rights and privileges are forcibly sacrificed for the common good. Compensation can be in money or in kind,[1275] but the authorising statute must determine the nature and measure (or amount) of compensation.[1276] Although it need not provide a general formula for the calculation of compensation, this is the general trend in practice. The statute may also specify a *definite* measure if such is indicated and justified by the nature of the property in question. If no provision is made for compensation, and/or if the statute does not determine the type and extent of the compensation, the expropriation would be unconstitutional and therefore void.[1277]

The *Junktimklausel* has a two-pronged warning function. For the individual owner it must ensure that expropriation takes place only once the compensation question has been cleared by the democratically elected legislature. Furthermore, it must protect the public (or more specifically the national budget) from being burdened with expenses not foreseen by the legislature.[1278] Therefore, the *Junktimklausel* cannot be impliedly incorporated into a statute, but it has to be expressly stipulated.[1279]

[1273] BVerfGE 24, 367 *(Deichordnung)*, 405; BVerfGE 74, 264 *(Boxberg)*, 283; *Van der Walt*, Constitutional Property Clauses - A Comparative Analysis (1999), 129.

[1274] The *Junktimklausel* does not apply to pre-constitutionally enacted legislation. BVerfGE 56, 249 *(Dürkheimer Gondelbahn)*, 261.

[1275] *Van der Walt*, Constitutional Property Clauses - A Comparative Analysis (1999), 150.

[1276] BVerfGE 24, 367 *(Deichordung)*.

[1277] BVerfGE 24, 367, 418; *Ipsen* in *Von Hippel/Ipsen/Voigt et al*, Verhandlungen der Tagung der Deutschen Staatsrechtslehrer (1952), 96 ff.; *Bryde* in *Von Münch/Kunig*, GG Kommentar (1992), m.n. 87 ff. *Wendt* in *Sachs (ed)*, Grundgesetz Kommentar (1996), m.n. 167.

[1278] BVerfGE 47, 268, 287.

[1279] *Bryde* in *Von Münch/Kunig*, GG Kommentar (1992), m.n. 89; *Pieroth/Schlink*, Grundrechte (1998), m.n. 939.

3.2.3.2. Expropriation in the Public Interest

Article 14 III 1 GG expressly stipulates that expropriation is only possible in the public interest. Accordingly, the legislature must lay down the specific purpose for which expropriation may be employed and this purpose must be in the public interest.[1280] The legislature must, with regard to this question, determine what is meant by "public weal." This involves a consideration of the proportionality principle (*Verhältnismäßigkeit*) and is intimately connected with the constitutionality test.[1281] Therefore, a *Legalenteignung* will be tested against the question whether or not legislature has defined the public weal correctly. An *Administrativenteignung* will again be tested against the question whether or not the public interest has been served correctly by the executive.[1282]

Competent courts must in the final instance decide whether a specific measure is in the public interest.[1283] In this regard, once again, proportionality *(Verhältnismäßigkeit)* is of supreme importance.[1284] Applied to the context of expropriation, the proportionality principle contains the following basic components:

(i) Expropriation must be *suitable*: a specific public purpose is therefore required to justify the expropriation.[1285] Not all public purposes warrant the expropriation of ownership; only those that, according to the proportionality principle, justify the withdrawal of all ownership entitlements.[1286] Some authors require an urgent state purpose.[1287] Expropriation is, for instance, neither justifiable on mere fiscal grounds, nor on the basis of promoting individual interests.[1288] On the other hand, the question about the extent to which expropriation is permissible in favour of private enterprises has been left open by the Federal Consti-

---

[1280] *Frowein*, Protection of Property in Relation to Taxation (1996), 11.

[1281] See BVerfGE 24, 367 *(Deichordnung)*, 404.

[1282] *Pieroth/Schlink*, Grundrechte (1998), m.n. 942.

[1283] *Frowein*, Protection of Property in Relation to Taxation (1996), 11.

[1284] BVerfGE 24, 367 *(Deichordnung)*, 404.

[1285] See Böhmer's minority judgement in BVerfGE 56, 249, 279.

[1286] *Richter/Schuppert*, Casebook (1996), 373.

[1287] See Böhmer's minority judgement in BVerfGE 56, 249, 279.

[1288] BVerfGE 38, 175, 180.

tutional Court.[1289] In terms of the *Deichordnung* case,[1290] the public-purpose requirement was satisfied because of the pressing need to build an effective system of dikes and embankments to avert a disaster similar to the Hamburg flood of 1962. The court accentuated that article 14 III GG permits expropriation if the common good requires it, and that the common good therefore limits the state's power to expropriate property in terms of article 14 GG.

(ii) Expropriation must be *requisite*, which means that no other more lenient or less serious method would have been appropriate. An *Administrativenteignung* is, for instance, more lenient than its stricter counterpart, *Legalenteignung*. Therefore the latter is permissible only under specific circumstances, since far less legal protection is afforded to the affected owner(s) and since the constitutional order prefers legislation to be generally applicable.[1291]

(iii) The expropriation should also be *appropriate*: a fair balance between the public purpose and the withdrawal of ownership must therefore exist. Both the Federal Court of Justice and the Federal Administrative Court have worked out the standards governing the attempt to balance public and private interests in the field of expropriation.[1292] In the *Feldmühle* case[1293] the Federal Constitutional Court also had the opportunity to pronounce on this issue. It sustained the validity of a company reorganisation statute, which permitted shareholders who owned more than three fourths of the capital stock to convert their joint-stock company into a new company in spite of the opposition of the stockholder minority group. The court reasoned that the legislature was acting in the general interest by fostering the creation of

---

[1289] See BVerfGE 66, 248 *(Hochspannungsleitung)*, 257; BVerfGE 74, 264 *(Boxberg)*, 286. See also *Von Heinegg/Haltern*, 1993 JuS, 126; *Bryde* in *Von Münch/Kunig*, GG Kommentar (1992), m.n. 81-84.

[1290] BVerfGE 24, 367, 396.

[1291] *Bryde* in *Von Münch/Kunig*, GG Kommentar (1992), m.n. 73-75.

[1292] Normally only one set of courts in Germany has jurisdiction over a given subject area of law. In the field of property, however, jurisdiction is divided between administrative and ordinary courts: the former have authority to decide whether property has been expropriated, the latter to decide the amount of compensation. Because these issues are intertwined, both tribunals have been forced to define the "public good" and "expropriation." *Kommers*, Constitutional Jurisprudence of Germany (1997), 253 and note 34 to ch. 6, 568.

[1293] BVerfGE 14, 263.

larger business enterprises and that the three-fourths conversion rule was not manifestly disproportionate to the severity of the encroachment on the property interest of minority shareholders.[1294]

3.2.3.3. Determination of Compensation

According to article 14 III 3 GG, compensation for expropriation should reflect a fair balance between the public interest and the interests of those affected. In practice this entails that expropriatory legislation can determine the manner in which the different interests should be rated and balanced, and should at least contain a set framework within which the compensation amount could be determined according to the specific circumstances of each case.[1295] A court adjudicating a dispute about compensation will have to pay careful attention to this provision.

In the following paragraphs, some of the problems that could arise in the course of this balancing of competing interests to determine equitable compensation will be briefly mentioned. For instance, the unconstitutionality of legislation permitting an administrative expropriation could influence the affected property holders' ability to claim compensation. Likewise, legislation can in principle not leave the determination of the amount of compensation to the discretion of the state. Another issue is the importance of market value as an indication in the determination of the amount of compensation.

3.2.3.3.1. Balancing of Interests and Market Value

Under normal circumstances the balancing of interests will also mean that *full compensation* has to be paid for the value of the expropriated property.[1296] It is difficult to justify the allocation of mere nominal compensation on the basis of article 14 III 3 GG. Full compensation entails that the *market value* of a specific object has to be established, and that this will usually constitute the amount of compensation to be paid. However, the *Abwägungsgebot* of article 14 III 3 GG does not require that compensation should *always* equal the full market value of

---

[1294] BVerfGE 14, 263, 277.

[1295] BVerfGE 24, 367, 419. *Richter/Schuppert,* Casebook (1996), 379.

[1296] *Frowein,* Protection of Property in Relation to Taxation (1996), 12-13.

the property.[1297] It is more important to determine the type and extent of compensation by considering all the interests at stake to achieve a fair balance.[1298]

Of course, the market value of the property and the financial loss of the owner will have to be considered in order to establish a fair balance of the interests at stake. But these considerations are not the sole determinants. They also have to be weighed against other interests (like the public interest) and all relevant surrounding circumstances. The Federal Constitutional Court has occasionally held that there may be special reasons why full compensation need not be paid for lawful expropriation. In the *Deichordnung*[1299] case, for instance, the court held that, despite the broad principles protecting the right to private property[1300] the state could legitimately place the land adjoining the dikes in Hamburg

---

[1297] *Papier* in *Maunz/Dürig*, GG Kommentar (1994), m.n. 642-643; *Bryde* in *Von Münch/Kunig*, GG Kommentar (1992), 882 ff.; *Badura* in *Benda/Maihofer/Vogel (eds)*, Handbuch des Verfassungsrechts (1994), 367 ff.; *Wendt* in *Sachs (ed)*, Grundgesetz Kommentar (1996), m.n. 170; BVerfGE 24, 367 *(Deichordnung)*, 421.

[1298] BVerfGE 24, 367 *(Deichordnung)*, 421; BGHZ 39, 198, 199. *Pieroth/Schlink*, Grundrechte (1998), m.n. 944. *Richter/Schuppert*, Casebook (1996), 378 ff.

[1299] BVerfGE 24, 367 *(Deichordnung)*.

[1300] It was acknowledged that art. 14 I GG guarantees property both as a legal institution and as a concrete right held by the owner and that the right to hold property is an elementary constitutional right which must be seen in close context with the protection of personal liberty. The function of the property guarantee was further acknowledged as securing for the holder of a property a sphere of liberty in the economic field, and thus also as enabling the holder of a property right to lead a self-governing life. It followed that the protection of property as a legal institution therefore serves to secure the basic right to property. The constitutional right of the individual is, in other words, conditioned upon the legal institution of property. Property could thus not be effectively secured if lawmakers were empowered to replace private property with something no longer deserving the label "ownership". Therefore, the legislature's task is to regulate property in the light of fundamental constitutional values. It was, however, further mentioned that the institutional guarantee prohibits any revision of the private legal order which would remove the fundamental catalogue of constitutionally protected activities relating to the area of property and which would substantially curtail or suspend the protected sphere of liberty protected by the fundamental right to property.

under public control. The court went even further and argued[1301] that the *Abwägungsgebot* of article 14 III enables (and also obliges) the legislature to take cognisance of the peculiarities of the specific situation. The court thus arrived at the conclusion that *just compensation* refers to an equitable amount of compensation as at the time of the expropriation, which does not necessarily amount to market value. This confirms that compensation need not be based on market value.

3.2.3.3.2. Consequences of Unconstitutional Legislation on Administrative Expropriation

Article 14 III 3 GG provides that the interests involved must be balanced in order to determine a fair amount of compensation.[1302] This applies to legislative expropriation as well as to expropriation through administrative acts *(Verwaltungshandlungen)*. In the case where the administrative authority cannot support its action by underlying legislation permitting infringement of property interests protected by article 14 GG, two possibilities arise: (i) The situation could be that the administrative organ acts without legislative authority at all. (ii) Alternatively, the administrative organ could be acting upon legislative authority, but one that does not permit an infringement of article 14 GG's scope.[1303] The individual whose rights are infringed by unconstitutional legislation cannot choose between legal action (that is, attacking the law or act on the basis of illegality) and compensation. It is not possible to accept the infringement on condition that compensation is paid.[1304] The affected holders of rights should therefore object to the action itself.

3.2.3.3.3. The State's Discretion to Determine the Amount of Compensation

Acts permitting *Legal-* or *Administrativenteignung* will be unconstitutional if they contain *"salvatorische Entschädigungsklauseln,"* that is, clauses that permit compensation for expropriation at the discretion of

---

[1301] BVerfGE 24, 367 *(Deichordnung)*, 421.

[1302] *Pieroth/Schlink*, Grundrechte (1998), m.n. 944.

[1303] *Von Heinegg/Haltern*, 1993 JuS, 214.

[1304] BVerfGE 58, 200 *(Naßauskiesung)*.

the expropriating authority.[1305] This covers the possibility that a statute could have an eventual — until then unforeseen and unintended — expropriatory effect. Though invalid in cases of expropriation, *"salvatorische Entschädigungsklauseln"* are permissible and valid in the case of regulation (deprivation) of property.[1306] In the latter case, however, compensation is not a requirement for validity of the infringement on property rights in terms of the constitution.

Regulation of property *(Inhalts- und Schrankenbestimmung)* in principle does not require the payment of compensation. It might, however, happen in exceptional circumstances that, a monetary reimbursement must be offered to the affected owner(s) because the legislation constitutes an excessive inroad on specific property rights and thus is in conflict with the *Übermaßverbot*. According to the Federal Constitutional Court, the state will have exceeded its capacity to regulate property without compensating the holders of the property rights if the regulation intrudes upon the proceeds of the personal efforts of the affected person in establishing his or her property rights, or if the provision for equality in the Basic Law is violated.[1307]

If the burden of a regulation seriously affects an *individual* owner (for example by depriving him or her completely of the use of the property), and if the regulation only benefits the public at large, the state is obliged to compensate the owner. No compensation is due if a uniformly imposed regulation confers benefits on all owners against limited sacrifices by all for the sake of the common good. If an individual affected by a general regulation is part of the public, and if he or she benefits from the regulation, he or she is also expected to bear the costs thereof, in which case the loss is not compensable.[1308] For instance, a landowner forced to sacrifice a property interest for the sake of the higher social

---

[1305] *Bryde* in *Von Münch/Kunig*, GG Kommentar (1992), m.n. 90; *Ipsen* in *Von Hippel/Ipsen/Voigt et al*, Verhandlungen der Tagung der Deutschen Staatsrechtslehrer (1952), 96.

[1306] *Leisner* in *Isensee/Kirchhof*, Handbuch des Staatsrechts VI (1989), m.n. 173-179; BVerwG DVBl 1990 585; BGH NJW 1990 898; *Bryde* in *Von Münch/Kunig*, Kommentar (1992), m.n. 65; *Maurer*, Allgemeines Verwaltungsrecht (1997), m.n. 83; *Papier* in *Maunz/Dürig*, GG Kommentar (1994), m.n. 307 ff.

[1307] BVerfGE 58, 137 *(Pflichtexemplar)*; *Pieroth/Schlink*, Grundrechte (1998), m.n. 934-935.

[1308] *Kommers*, Constitutional Jurisprudence of Germany (1997), 253.

good of his or her neighbour is entitled to compensation.[1309] This approach is based on the principle that burdens should be borne equally, and the affected owner can claim an appropriate amount of compensation from his or her neighbour. This so-called *Ausgleichsanspruch* (claim for equalisation payment) should, however, not be confused with a "real" claim for compensation pursuant to expropriation in terms of article 14 III GG.

Special arrangements are also made where a legislative infringement upon property falls within the legislative competence to regulate property, but nevertheless deprives the affected owner of a subjective right or some other right that has been acquired *on the basis of existing law*. In such cases, the legislation must contain either a transitional provision or must provide for some kind of compensation in the form of so-called *Schadensersatz* to be constitutional. Nevertheless, such legislation still does not amount to expropriation.[1310]

A regulatory measure with private property will not necessarily be transformed into an expropriation if provision is made for compensation.[1311] Monetary reimbursement is simply connected to the question of proportionality *(Verhältnismäßigkeit)* and should also be considered at that stage of the investigation. Furthermore, a claim to monetary reimbursement can only be brought if it was provided for in ordinary legislation. If no provision for reimbursement is made, the affected holders of rights will not be able to claim reimbursement. Any claim they might have must be directed against the infringing statute itself. If the legislative interference with property rights is found to be unlawful, the former owner has to be reimbursed for profits lost on account of the infringement *(lucrum cessans)*.[1312]

3.2.4. Institution of Property Retained (Essential Content)

In the final instance the regulation (that is, deprivation or expro-

---

[1309] *Kommers*, Constitutional Jurisprudence of Germany (1997), note 35 to ch. 6, 568.

[1310] *Maurer*, Allgemeines Verwaltungsrecht (1997), par. 26 m.n. 65.

[1311] BVerfGE 52, 1, 27 ff.; BVerfGE 58, 137, 145; BVerfGE 58, 300, 320; BVerfGE 70, 191, 199; BVerfGE 79, 174, 192; *Bryde* in *Von Münch/Kunig*, Kommentar (1992), m.n. 52.

[1312] *Frowein*, Protection of Property in Relation to Taxation (1996), 12-13.

priation) of property is only justifiable if the institutional guarantee of article 14 I 1 GG is maintained. When read with the essential content provision of article 19 II GG, the institutional guarantee secures the existence of certain basic norms.[1313] Together these norms amount to an institution which could appropriately be referred to as "property." However, the relation between the institutional guarantee of property and article 19 II GG is not as self-evident as it might seem at first glance.

The true function and place of the essential content provision within the structure of basic rights in Germany is probably one of the most complicated theoretical issues in the German legal system, and it is beyond the scope of this work to elaborate extensively upon it.[1314] For purposes of interpreting the property clause, however, one can safely assume that article 19 II GG is an extension of the institutional guarantee already present in article 14 GG. This would move the focus to the question concerning the intensity of limitations permitted by the essential-content / institutional guarantee. The roles attributed to the principle of proportionality and the process by which the interests concerned are balanced are central to this debate.

The Federal Constitutional Court has held that article 14 I 1 GG entails a fundamental value decision of the Basic Law in favour of private

---

[1313] *"Grundbestand von Normen"*.

[1314] For summaries of the different issues, see *Blaauw-Wolf*, 1999 SAPR/PL, 181-187. In BVerfGE 7, 198 *(Lüth)*, 204 ff., the Court held that fundamental rights are first and foremost rights of the subject which accrue to the individual as *Abwehrrechte* (i.e. as freedom from state interference). This would then be the purpose of the protection of the essential content of fundamental rights in terms of art. 19 II GG. However, the Court also emphasised that the Basic Law was not intended to be a neutral constitutional system. It rests upon the constitutional norms of a democratic *Rechtsstaat* and these objective basic norms *(objektive Grundsatznormen)* also act as an institutional guarantee of fundamental rights. Thus, instead of looking at fundamental rights as rights of the subject accruing to the individual who can exercise them against the organs of state, the court viewed them as the boundaries of state competencies to limit rights in a negative sense *(negative Kompetenzbestimmungen)*. The positive scope of the individual rights guaranteed by the bill of rights therefore objectively restricts the scope of action left to the state irrespective of the fact whether a specific individual asserts his/her rights. Accordingly, the objective function of the bill of rights enhances the meaning and content of the individual rights as rights of the subject.

ownership.[1315] It bars legislature from withdrawing elements that form an elementary part of constitutionally protected participation in the patrimonial sphere from the legal order,[1316] even if the social welfare function of property is taken into account. Thus, it constitutes one of the so-called *Schranken-Schranke*. No determination of the limits of property can ignore the fact that, in essence, the institution of property should be retained. In effect, legislation has to acknowledge the institution of property[1317] by leaving the basic content of the property concept intact.[1318] However, this still leaves the question as to the manner of adherence to the institutional guarantee unanswered. Would application of the proportionality principle suffice in securing the the essence of the protected right, or would not even a consideration of the public interest justify that the right is hollowed out leaving only an empty shell? Up to now the Federal Constitutional Court have not really had the opportunity to give a clear answer to this question.[1319]

However, the approach of the Federal Constitutional Court concerning the application of article 19 II GG could be transplanted to the institutional guarantee of the property clause, since it is accepted that the institutional guarantee of article 14 GG amounts to a specialised essential-content requirement. This would mean that the guarantee of the institution of property has the function of protecting individual right holders against an unjustified curtailment of their constitutional status by the state powers.[1320] Nevertheless, the institutional character of the right to property does not elevate the fundamental right to the level of an independent objective legal norm.[1321] The true function of the institutional property guarantee still is to curtail the powers of state authority to encroach upon the individual's right to property. The institutional property guarantee is, in other words, a *Schranken-Schranke*. The result is that the inviolable core of the property right may not be encroached even if an overriding public interest exists. The principle of proportionality therefore comes into play only once it is clear that the essential

---

[1315] *"[G]rundlegende Wertentscheidung des Grundgesetzes zugunsten des Privateigentums."* BVerfGE 21, 150, 155.

[1316] BVerfGE 24, 367, 389.

[1317] BVerfGE 58, 300, 338.

[1318] BVerfGE 24, 367 *(Deichordnungsbeschluß)*, 389.

[1319] *Pieroth/Schlink*, Grundrechte - Staatsrecht II (1991), m.n. 1047.

[1320] I.e. an *Abwehrrecht*.

[1321] See BVerfGE 50, 290, 337.

core of the right to property is secure.

3.3. The German Judiciary's Methods of Establishing Type of Infringement

It has been indicated that both the German administrative courts and the "ordinary" German courts (Federal Court of Justice or *Bundesgerichtshof*) are involved in matters pertaining to expropriation. The administrative court deals with (administrative) matters concerning actual expropriation. When, however, the amount of compensation is contested, the "ordinary" courts have jurisdiction. The Federal Constitutional Court in principle has the function of protecting, interpreting and applying the Basic Law.[1322]

Due to the shared jurisdiction of the administrative and "ordinary" courts in Germany in matters pertaining to expropriation, several possible analytical approaches have been developed as aids in determining the intention of the legislature where infringements of property rights are concerned. This means that the decisions pertaining to regulation and expropriation of property are not always consistent. The different courts also apply different theories in determining issues related to regulation and expropriation of property.[1323]

(i) The Doctrine of Individual Sacrifice *(Sonderopfertheorie)* of the German Federal Court of Justice determines that an infringement constitutes an expropriation if, through it, the principle of equality is breached. The specific owner (or group of owners) is thus forced to make a special sacrifice.[1324] Since its introduction into the German property law system, this doctrine has been criticised mainly because its effect depends on the application of a very formal criterion.

(ii) The Doctrine of Intensity or Tolerable Sacrifice *(Schweretheorie)* of the Federal Administrative Court, by contrast, entails that the intensity of the administrative measure directed against the property, together with the weight of the burden placed upon the individual owner, determines whether the limits of the social welfare function of property

---

[1322] *Foster,* German Legal System and Laws (1996), 48.

[1323] See, e.g. BVerwGE 3, 335, 337-338; BVerwGE 4, 57, 60; BVerwGE 32, 135, 137; BGHZ 23, 30, 32; BGHZ 30, 338, 341-342.

[1324] BGHZ 6, 270, 280 (*NJW* 1952, 972).

have been overstepped.[1325] An affirmation of this question would mean that there is no justification for regulation of property without compensation. This doctrine is widely recognised in theory and practice, since it orients the protection and regulation of property on specific values of a civil society.[1326] Moreover, it enables an application of more general constitutional rules by which legality of the state's actions against individuals can be tested.[1327] Therefore, this doctrine is more widely supported than the theory of individual sacrifice.

(iii) The Federal Constitutional Court has declined to emphasise either of these principles above the other, but considers them in tandem.[1328] Further, the court also applies the so-called Doctrine of Situational Commitment. In terms of this approach, the concepts of regulation (in the sense of deprivation) and expropriation are more formally circumscribed.[1329] The general rule in Germany is that the expropriation of private property is admissible only when adequate compensation is paid.[1330] In addition, property can be regulated, but only to a tolerable degree.[1331] The Federal Constitutional Court decided that particular legislative acts amount to a regulation if they affect certain rights and duties that fall within the ambit of the protective scope of article 14 GG. In essence, the legal position protected by article 14 I 1 GG, should remain intact. However, the owner's entitlements

---

[1325] *Kimminich* in *Starck (ed)*, Rights, Institutions and Impact of International Law (1987), 87-88; *Maurer*, Allgemeines Verwaltungsrecht (1997), § 26 m.n. 28; BVerwGE 5, 143, 145 ff.

[1326] BVerwGE 5, 143, 145.

[1327] *Dolzer*, Property and Environment (1976), 25.

[1328] *Kommers*, Constitutional Jurisprudence of Germany (1997), 254; BVerfGE 25, 112, 121.

[1329] In this sense, it seems as if the Federal Constitutional Court is more inclined towards the approach of the Federal Court of Justice (which has jurisdiction in cases where "fair compensation" has to be determined). This demarcation has been controversial ever since, although there seems to be agreement on the point that the competence of the legislature to determine the contents and limits of the property guarantee must be defined formally (as opposed to materially). *Pieroth/Schlink*, Grundrechte (1998), m.n. 921. *"Sie legen generell und abstrakt die Rechte und Pflichten des Eigentümers fest."* BVerfGE 58, 300, 330; BVerfGE 72, 66, 76.

[1330] *Kommers*, Constitutional Jurisprudence of Germany (1997), 254; BVerfGE 4, 219.

[1331] BVerfGE 21, 150.

to use and enjoyment of his or her property are subject to the obligations imposed by article 14 II GG.[1332] Accordingly, emphasis is placed on the fact that some objects of property rights are by nature burdened with higher social obligations than others, and are therefore affected at an earlier stage than in the case of property rights which by nature have a lesser social function. The protected area of property rights can, therefore, not be determined by abstract reasoning, but presupposes that the owner's legal position is changeable, depending upon the location and circumstances surrounding the property.[1333] This doctrine by which the protected area of property rights is dependent on external factors is most frequently applied in the spheres of zoning and planning law; pollution control; conservation of nature and the protection of historic sites.[1334]

Both the doctrine of individual sacrifice and the doctrine of intensity have in the past been subject to intense criticism. They do not explain why certain owners are obliged to suffer curtailment of their property rights without compensation, while others are entitled to compensation, or do not have to suffer the same kind of curtailment. The Federal Constitutional Court's treatment of this issue shows that the social welfare function of property determines whether regulation (in the sense of deprivation) or expropriation has taken place. The higher the value of a specific object of property rights is for society at large, the more likely it is that regulation, for which no compensation will be offered in return for the individual freedom or private autonomy sacrificed in the process, is at stake. However, the social welfare function of property is not expressly emphasised by either the Basic Law or the courts, and the broad language in which article 14 II GG is formulated reduced its immediate and practical effect. On a more theoretical level, the social welfare function inherent in the concept of property is intrinsically connected with that of expropriation. By defining expropriation, the scope of the social function of property is delimited, which in turn demarcates the area of public activity in which no compensation is payable. For instance, the Federal Constitutional Court has in its *Naßaus-*

[1332] *Kimminich* in *Starck (ed)*, Rights, Institutions and Impact of International Law (1987), 87.

[1333] *Dolzer*, Property and Environment (1976), 23.

[1334] *Kimminich* in *Starck (ed)*, Rights, Institutions and Impact of International Law (1987), 88.

kiesung decision[1335] held that, in distinguishing between the regulation of property and expropriation, the starting point is the question whether ownership is diminished through the act of infringement to a *nudum ius*. Furthermore, it needs to be determined whether the infringement pertains to an element of ownership that can be separated from the concept and treated independently without damaging the ownership concept itself in the process.[1336] From this, the court deduced that the Water Resources Act does not constitute expropriation by law. The Act merely defines the content of property in relation to groundwater, as a matter of objective law. Since the change in the law effected by this act did not result in a deprivation of a specific legal interest protected by the institutional guarantee of article 14 I GG, it does not constitute an expropriation of property.[1337]

However, the real importance of article 14 II GG stems from the fact that it forms the constitutional basis for legislative restrictions on the exercise of property rights *without compensation* to the owner.[1338] The legislature has, in other words, been given broad leeway for the regulation of private property in the public interest.[1339] For example, the court sustained a federal restriction on the cultivation of new vineyards not only because the regulation helped to maintain the quality of German wine, but also because it contributed to the economic position of the German wine industry as a whole, particularly wine-growers. The burden imposed by the regulation was therefore not excessive.[1340]

[1335] BVerfGE 58, 200 (*Naßauskiesung*).

[1336] *"Ohne diese Verselbständigungsfähigkeit fehlt das Objekt, das jeder Vorgang der Güterentziehung wie auch der Güterbeschaffung voraussetzt."* *Pieroth/Schlink*, Grundrechte (1998), m.n. 923.

[1337] BVerfGE 58, 200 (*Naßauskiesung*), 338.

[1338] An earlier draft by the German Parliamentary Council, which harbours the intent of this broad language, provided: "Ownership entails a social obligation. Its use shall find its limits in the living necessities of all citizens and in the public order essential to society."

[1339] *Kommers*, Constitutional Jurisprudence of Germany (1997), 253.

[1340] *Kommers*, Constitutional Jurisprudence of Germany (1997), 254.

3.4. Justifiability of Limitations on Property Rights Under South African Law

In South Africa, by reason of the wording of the constitutions, and the principle of the unity of the constitution for interpretative purposes, several possible variations on the infringement concept exist. "Deprivation" of property is justifiable under certain circumstances. Moreover, both the Interim Constitution and the Final Constitution also permit expropriation as a justified infringement of the right to property, provided that certain requirements are met. In view of the arguments in favour of a cumulative application of section 25 FC and section 36 FC, these requirements need to be determined with reference not only to the provisions of the property clause itself, but also to the provisions of the general limitations clause. Moreover, these requirements need to be deduced from a simultaneous reading of these two provisions, and not by reading section 36 FC subsequent to section 25 FC.[1341]

In the South African context, a *deprivation* is usually described as a broader genus of interference with (or regulation of) property, with *expropriation* as one of its species.[1342] The term *deprivation* implies a loss of enjoyment or of benefits. It is a generic term, which circumscribes a whole range of possible *regulatory interferences*[1343] with the rights of citizens to their property.[1344] If a deprivation of property takes place through the exercise of administrative power (as is mostly the case),[1345] the deprivations clause[1346] has to be read with the administrative justice clause[1347] in the constitution for purposes of interpretation and analysis of the regulation. An administrative deprivation of property rights will

---

[1341] See the discussion at 108, 271 ff. above.

[1342] *Murphy*, 1995 SAPR/PL, 115-116. See, however, the arguments against this view that deprivation and expropriation forms a conceptual continuity at 327 ff. below.

[1343] This term is also sometimes used to refer to "deprivations" in terms of section 28(2) IC, sec. 25(1) FC. Similar terms like "acts of police power" have also been used on occasion. See *Murphy*, 1995 SAPR/PL, 116; *Murphy*, 1993 JJS, 45; *Budlender* in *Budlender/Latsky/Roux*, New Land Law (revised 1998), ch. 1, 23.

[1344] *Murphy*, 1995 SAPR/PL, 116.

[1345] *Chaskalson/Lewis* in *Chaskalson/Kentridge/Klaaren et. al. (eds)*, Constitutional Law of South Africa (1996), ch. 31, 9.

[1346] I.e. sec. 28(2) IC; sec. 25(1) FC.

[1347] I.e. sec. 24 IC; sec. 33 FC.

have to be procedurally fair. Moreover, the reasons furnished by the administrative authority, whose action affected the rights of a specific person, have to substantively justify the infringement. Deprivations of property can, however, also be effected directly through legislation.[1348] Legislative deprivation of rights in property is also subject to the due-process principle. Deprivation can thus only take place in accordance with validly enacted legislation.[1349] *Expropriation* can be described as a deprivation by the state with the specific characteristic that a right is completely withdrawn from the owner. The right can then be appropriated without the consent of the owner by means of transfer or extinction of the use exclusively assigned to the former owner. This is done for the benefit of the public.[1350]

It can be expected that social reform legislation would encroach on existing property rights. Restrictions of property rights could, for instance, include rent control legislation, orders of the Land Claims Court creating lesser rights in land without expropriating the land from its present owners,[1351] industrial court incursions into the managerial prerogative, zoning regulations and restrictions imposed under legislation protecting the environment and authorisation for demolition of buildings presenting health hazards.[1352] In order to determine which of these restrictions constitute mere deprivations, for which no compensation is payable, and which of these restrictions are so severe that they amount to compensable expropriation, it will be necessary to take a

---

[1348] *Chaskalson/Lewis* in *Chaskalson/Kentridge/Klaaren et. al. (eds)*, Constitutional Law of South Africa (1996), ch. 31, 9 refer to these as "non-administrative" deprivations.

[1349] However, this principle does not necessarily mean that due process must be substantive, but merely the certain procedural safeguards should be heeded. See *Chaskalson/Lewis* in *Chaskalson/Kentridge/Klaaren et. al. (eds)*, Constitutional Law of South Africa (1996), ch. 31, 9.

[1350] Some authors, noteably *Murphy*, 1995 SAPR/PL, 116 define expropriation with reference to elements like the acquisition of title and permanency. See, however, the discussion at 350 below.

[1351] Up to now, no such order has been made. However, the Land Claims Court does have the capacity to make any order it deems fit upon adjudicating a specific claim. This theoretically renders it possible for the court to create new rights, or adapt existing rights to such an extent that their content is not comparable to that of the original rights.

[1352] *Murphy*, 1993 JJS, 45.

closer look at the requirements applicable to the different kinds of interference with property rights.

3.4.1. Law of General Application (Not Permitting Arbitrary Deprivation)

In the Interim Constitution, the requirement that the law establishing an infringement (on property, *inter alia*) should be of general application, was expressed in the limitations clause,[1353] but not repeated in the property clause.[1354] Now the requirement that only a law of general application may limit property rights appears not only in the general limitation clause of the Final Constitution,[1355] but also in the property clause itself: in section 25(1) FC, where deprivations of property are regulated, as well as in section 25(2) FC,[1356] where expropriation is regulated. Section 25(1) FC in addition provides that no law may permit arbitrary deprivation of property. This provision is not repeated in section 25(2) FC, dealing with expropriation. The questions that arise from this formulation are: (i) the meaning of the phrase "in accordance with law" or "in terms of law"; (ii) the meaning of "arbitrary" in the context of section 25(1) FC; and (iii) whether deprivation and expropriation of property should be regarded as two separate mechanisms, or whether expropriation can still be described as a genus of deprivation.

3.4.1.1. Meaning of "in Accordance with Law" / "in Terms of Law"

The phrase *in accordance with law* as it appeared in section 28(2) IC, was subject to three fundamentally different interpretations:

[1353] Sec. 33(1) IC.

[1354] There it was only required that "[n]o deprivation of any rights in property shall be permitted otherwise than *in accordance with a law*." Sec. 28(2) IC, emphasis added.

[1355] Sec. 36(1) FC.

[1356] The general reference in section 28(3) IC to property rights that have been "expropriated *pursuant to a law* referred to in subsection (2)" was amended in section 25(2) FC to the more explicit requirement that property may be "expropriated *only in terms of law of general application*."

(i) It could, on the one hand, denote the proper statutory authority of the legislature to pass the specific legislation.[1357] However, this interpretation does nothing but to endorse the trite common law principle that deprivations of property require lawful authority. This interpretation therefore deprives section 28(2) FC of any real meaning.[1358]

(ii) This phrase could, on the other hand, indicate that something equivalent to the American "substantive due process" is required.[1359] Under these circumstances, the phrase would require that, in order to test justifiability, the courts would have to consider both the compliance with formal procedural requirements, as well as the merits of the deprivation. However, the South African Constitutional Court has already in Ferreira v Levin[1360] referred to the pitfalls of this approach, and is not likely to follow it in future.

(iii) A third explanation is that this phrase could refer to the notion of fairness inherent in the constitutional state principle.[1361] This would require that the court rejects a purely formalistic approach, and accepts a measure of legal protection against arbitrary interference by public

---

[1357] See *Park-Ross v Director: Office for Serious Economic Offences* (note 136 above), 168G-H.

[1358] *Budlender* in *Budlender/Latsky/Roux*, New Land Law (revised 1998), ch. 1, 24.

[1359] This approach was adopted by the US Supreme Court during the period of "Lochnerism" and its application to the South African constitutions was propagated by certain South African scholars. See *Budlender* in *Budlender/ Latsky/Roux*, New Land Law (revised 1998), ch. 1, 25; *Murphy*, 1995 SAPR/PL, 117; *Chaskalson/Lewis* in *Chaskalson/Kentridge/Klaaren et. al. (eds)*, Constitutional Law of South Africa (1996), ch. 31, 10; *Chaskalson*, 1993 SAJHR, 411.

[1360] *Ferreira v Levin NO, Vryenhoek v Powell NO* (note 266 above), par. 182. This approach especially causes problems in the area of division of powers. It expects the court to judge legislation on its merits, or wisdom. For this the court lacks political authority and legitimacy problems will arise. *Chaskalson/ Lewis* in *Chaskalson/Kentridge/Klaaren et. al. (eds)*, Constitutional Law of South Africa (1996), ch. 31, 11. Moreover, this approach caused a constitutional crisis involving a dispute between the legislative and judicial branches of government concerning their respective roles. *Chaskalson*, 1993 SAJHR, 395-404; *Budlender* in *Budlender/Latsky/Roux*, New Land Law (revised 1998), ch. 1, 25-26.

[1361] *Budlender* in *Budlender/Latsky/Roux*, New Land Law (revised 1998), ch. 1, 26.

authorities, as the European Court of Human Rights did. If this is the case, application in the South African context would be subject to two conditions:[1362] the law should be adequately accessible, and it should be formulated with sufficient clarity to enable the citizen to foresee the consequences of his or her conduct and to regulate it accordingly.[1363] Budlender[1364] views this approach as the most acceptable, and predicts that it will also be followed by the South African courts.

In view of the fact that (at least) the deprivations clause in the Final Constitution additionally requires a law of general application *not to permit arbitrary deprivation* of property, it can be argued that Budlender's approach is also in line with the specific limitation provision in section 25 FC. These two requirements give content and set limits to the state's power to deprive individuals of their property rights.[1365]

In *Park-Ross v Director: Office for Serious Economic Offences*[1366] it has been accepted that legislative interference *per se* can constitute a deprivation of property. This case concerned the Mossgas project for exploration and production of oil and gas off the Mossel Bay coastline. The crucial question to be considered was whether sections 5, 6 and 7 of the Investigation of Serious Economic Offences Act[1367], which provided for the seizure and removal of documentation pertaining to alleged economic offences, were constitutional. The applicants *inter alia* averred that section 6 of this act (which provided for the search and seizure of documentation) conflicted with section 28 IC and was therefore unconstitutional. In his decision, Tebbutt J emphasised that in terms of section 28 IC a deprivation may occur *in accordance with a law*, and found that section 6 of the Investigation of Serious Economic Offences Act

---

[1362] The requirement applied in ECHR case law that the interference must be based in domestic law (see *Silver v United Kingdom* (1983) 5 EHRR 347, par. 86 to 88) makes sense on an international level, but does not bring the interpretation process further in South Africa.

[1363] *Sunday Times v United Kingdom* (1980) 2 EHRR 245, par. 49.

[1364] *Budlender* in *Budlender/Latsky/Roux*, New Land Law (revised 1998), ch. 1, 31.

[1365] *De Waal/Currie/Erasmus*, Bill of Rights Handbook (1999), 408.

[1366] *Park-Ross v Director: Office for Serious Economic Offences* (note 136 above).

[1367] 117 of 1991.

was such a law. Consequently, seizure constituted a (permissible) legislative infringement of property rights.[1368]

3.4.1.2. Meaning of "Arbitrary Limitation"

In addition to requiring (in terms of both section 36 FC and section 25 FC)[1369] valid interference with property to be pursuant to a law of general application, the property clause provides a more specific requirement for limitation and requires a deprivation of property not to be *arbitrary*.[1370] In *S v Makwanyane*,[1371] Ackermann J provides an explanation of this term viewed against the historical background and social structure of South Africa:[1372]

> "We have moved from a past characterised by much which was arbitrary and unequal in the operation of the law to a present and a future in a constitutional State where State action must be such that it is capable of being analysed and justified rationally. The idea of the constitutional State presupposes a system whose operation can be rationally tested against or in terms of the law."

Ackermann J explains that arbitrariness, by its very nature, is dissonant with these core concepts of our new constitutional order. He remarks:[1373]

> "Neither arbitrary action nor laws or rules which are inherently arbitrary or must lead to arbitrary application can, in any real sense, be tested against the precepts or principles of the Constitution. Arbitrariness must also inevitably, by its very nature, lead to the unequal treatment of persons."

Arbitrary action or decision-making is thus incapable of providing a rational explanation as to why similarly placed persons are treated in a

---

[1368] *Park-Ross v Director: Office for Serious Economic Offences* (note 136 above), 168G-I.

[1369] See 271 ff. above for a discussion on the cumulative application of these provisions.

[1370] Sec. 25(1) FC.

[1371] *S v Makwanyane* (note 363 above).

[1372] *S v Makwanyane* (note 363 above), par. 156.

[1373] *S v Makwanyane* (note 363 above), par. 156.

substantially different way. The absense of a rational justifying mechanism will inevitably lead to unequal treatment.

In general, therefore, it can be said that the requirement of non-arbitrariness harks back to the principle of the constitutional state,[1374] and that arbitrariness is inconsistent with values that underlie an open and democratic society based on freedom and equality.[1375] Accordingly, arbitrary restrictions of the fundamental right to property would not pass constitutional scrutiny.

The *arbitrary deprivation* provision in section 25(1) FC is aimed at the legislative provision permitting the deprivation, not necessarily at the deprivation itself. Because an alleged arbitrary deprivation will have to be attacked on the basis of the provision allowing deprivation, one must determine exactly what is meant by the term *arbitrary* in this context. In several recent decisions the South African courts were faced with the interpretation of the term "arbitrary", although it was not always in connection with interference with property.[1376] In the following discussion, the impact of these decisions on the constitutional regulation of property will be discussed by making use of the requirements in the Canadian interpretation of this term, as suggested by Budlender.[1377]

3.4.1.2.1. Lack of Criteria Governing the Exercise of the Deprivation

A first requirement is that arbitrariness will be indicated by the lack of (express or implied) criteria governing the exercise of the deprivation. Stated simply, as was done in the case of *Woolworths (Pty) Ltd v*

[1374] This was clearly stated in *New National Party of South Africa v Government of the Republic of South Africa and Others* 1999 3 SA 191 (CC), par. 24: "Arbitrariness is inconsistent with the rule of law which is a core value of the Constitution."

[1375] *S v Lawrence; S v Negal; S v Solberg* 1997 4 SA 1176 (CC), par. 33.

[1376] See the discussion of *Joubert v Van Rensburg* 2001 1 SA 753 (W) at 522 ff. below. In the recent Constitutional Court judgement of *First National Bank v South African Revenue Service* 2002 7 BCLR 702 CC, the interpretation of the term "arbitrary" in the context of property deprivation enjoyed attention (cf. par. 64-73 and 105-117 of the decision). Ackermann J treats the non-abitrariness question as a form of ("thin") rationality review.

[1377] *Budlender* in *Budlender/Latsky/Roux*, New Land Law (revised 1998), ch. 1, 34-35.

Whitehead,[1378] this would mean that the word *arbitrary*[1379] denotes "the absence of reason, or, at the very least, the absence of a justifiable reason."[1380] Also, if legislation would, for instance, lack specific provisions permitting deprivation, it could be arbitrary.

The case of *Dawood v Minister of Home Affairs,*[1381] in which it had to be decided whether section 25(9)(b) of the Aliens Control Act[1382] was in conflict with the Final Constitution,[1383] illustrates this point. The applicants were spouses, one of whom was South African and the other a foreigner who sought an immigration permit to settle in South Africa. Section 25(9)(b) of the Aliens Control Act provided that an immigration permit could be granted to the spouse of a South African citizen who was in South Africa at the time *only* if that spouse was in possession of a valid temporary residence permit. Accordingly, if the foreign spouse did not have such a permit, he or she would either have to separate until the application for the permit was processed, or the South African spouse would have to leave the country. After having found that the right to family life (which is not expressly included in the South African bill of rights) forms an integral part of the right to human dignity,[1384] O'Regan J held that, even though the purpose of section 25(9)(b) of the Aliens Control Act might be to grant a privilege to foreign spouses, its effect is uncertain in any specific case because of the discretionary powers contained in s 26(3) and (6) of the same act. The latter provisions render the grant of an immigration permit subject to the grant of a valid temporary permit. However, the statutory provisions contemplate the possible refusal of a temporary permit, but contain no indication of the considerations that would be relevant to such

---

[1378] *Woolworths (Pty) Ltd v Whitehead (Women's Legal Centre Trust Intervening)* 2000 3 SA 529 (LAC), par. 128.

[1379] In this case it was employed in terms of item 2(1)(a) of Schedule 7 to the Labour Relations Act 66 of 1995.

[1380] Ironically, in this case, it was found that the pregnancy of the respondent, coupled with the wish of the appellant to establish continuity within the ranks of its employees, was a justifiable reason for refusing to offer her a contract of permanent employment and instead offering her a temporary position terminating exactly when her confinement would start.

[1381] *Dawood v Minister of Home Affairs* 2000 3 SA 936 (CC).

[1382] 96 of 1991.

[1383] Inter alia, the right to human dignity (sec. 10 FC).

[1384] *Dawood v Minister of Home Affairs* (note 1381 above), par. 36-37.

refusal. Accordingly, it was held that the failure to identify the criteria relevant to the exercise of the discretionary powers contained in section 26(3) and (6) of the Alien Control Act introduces an "element of arbitrariness" to their exercise that is inconsistent with the constitutional protection of the right to marry and establish a family.[1385]

From the example of the *Dawood* case, it can be inferred that the provision against arbitrariness in the context of section 25(1) FC would mean that the interference of property must be based on a law that provides the standards for the exercise of discretion as to the deprivation of property. This could be issued in the form of a number of criteria, which should be met in order to give effect to the deprivation.

3.4.1.2.2. Rational Connection between Interference and Purpose

A second requirement is that the deprivation should be justifiable. In the cases of *S v Lawrence; S v Negal; S v Solberg*[1386] and *Prinsloo v Van der Linde*[1387] this requirement was explained as meaning that a rational connection must exist between means and ends,[1388] in the respective contexts of limitation on the right to engage in economic activity[1389] and the right to equality.[1390] Non-compliance with this requirement, according to the court, would be arbitrary and "incompatible with ... a society [based on freedom and equality]".[1391]

This requirement for non-arbitrariness was repeated in *New National Party of South Africa v Government of the Republic of South Africa and Others*[1392] where the effective exercise of the right to vote was at

---

[1385] *Dawood v Minister of Home Affairs* (note 1381 above), par. 58.

[1386] *S v Lawrence; S v Negal; S v Solberg* (note 1375 above).

[1387] *Prinsloo v Van der Linde* 1997 3 SA 1012 (CC).

[1388] *S v Lawrence; S v Negal; S v Solberg* (note 1375 above), par. 40.

[1389] Sec. 26 IC.

[1390] Sec. 8 IC.

[1391] *S v Lawrence; S v Negal; S v Solberg* (note 1375 above), par. 40.

[1392] *New National Party of South Africa v Government of the Republic of South Africa and Others* (note 1374 above), par. 24. In this case it was decided, within the context of the national elections of 1999, that the requirement of the bar-coded identity document as the principal method of identification was, on the face of it, rationally connected to the legitimate governmental purpose of enabling the effective exercise of the vote. The bar-code on the document facilitated quick, easy and reliable verification of the fact that the name of the per-

stake. The two-stage process through which (non-)arbitrariness was determined in this case is interesting for present purposes: first, it was determined whether a "facial analysis of the provisions in issue, in relation to the Constitution, has been shown to lack rationality"; whereafter the circumstances existing as at the date of the adoption of the statute at stake were taken into account to determine whether it was capricious or arbitrary.[1393] The inquiry into the arbitrariness of legislative action is, thus, in essence an objective one.[1394]

In the case of *Harksen v Lane*[1395] this requirement for (non-)arbitrariness was applied in the context of the attachment of the assets of a solvent spouse in terms of section 21 of the Insolvency Act. The appellant argued that the vesting of the property of the solvent spouse in the hands of the master (and thereafter in the hands of the trustee) constituted a drastic and arbitrary invasion upon the proprietary rights of citizens. Nevertheless, the court held that, although such divesting of the assets of the solvent spouse might be inconvenient, potentially prejudicious and embarrassing, and even drastic, such measures are not arbitrary or without rationality. The court argued that the legislature acted rationally in enacting remedial provisions for the insufficient provision — in the eyes of the legislature — made in common and statutory law for ensuring that all the property of the insolvent spouse found its way into the insolvent estate. However, the question with regard to the interim property clause that had to be considered by the court in the *Harksen* case, was whether the interference with property

---

son had been entered on the population register. In addition, it was argued that it was much easier for officers charged with the verification of the necessary particulars at the point of registration and voting to perform this task if they were to do so consistently by reference to a single type of identity document. Recognition of a multiplicity of documents for this purpose could be potentially confusing, give rise to error and slow down the process. Accordingly, there could be nothing irrational, arbitrary or capricious about the bar-coded identity document serving as the main identification instrument, showing at a glance the citizenship and the age of the holder.

[1393] *New National Party of South Africa v Government of the Republic of South Africa and Others New National Party of South Africa v Government of the Republic of South Africa and Others* (note 1374 above), par. 25-30.

[1394] See also *Pharmaceutical Manufacturers Association of SA and Another: In Re Ex Parte President of the Republic of South Africa and Others* 2000 2 SA 674 (CC), par. 86.

[1395] *Harksen v Lane* (note 820 above), par. 58.

encompassed in section 21 of the Insolvency Act constituted an expro-priation of property, for which compensation would be payable. In fo-cussing on the questions of expropriation and compensation in par-ticular, the court largely skipped the more important questions related to the requirement of non-arbitrariness and its relation to the propor-tionality requirement of section 36(1) FC. This will be elucidated at a later stage of the present exposition.[1396]

3.4.1.2.3. Procedural Safeguards

A deprivation would, in the third place, be arbitrary if it is not preceded by a proper hearing or other procedural safeguards. It must, therefore, also be procedurally justified. It is submitted that procedural fairness in the context of a non-arbitrary deprivation of property would have to be determined on a case by case basis. The circumstances of a specific case would thus determine whether stricter or more lenient rules of proce-dure need to be applied in order eliminate arbitrariness from the proc-ess of interference.

In this regard, it can be argued that application of a principle or legal requirement on a case by case basis would naturally bring about a dif-ferentiation of approach from one case to the other, which could render the process of decision-making unjust. In the case of *Pretoria City Council v Walker*[1397] this objection was treated with the statement that[1398]

> "[A]ny form of systematic deviation from the principle of equal and impartial application of the law ... might well have to be expressed in a law of general application which would be justiciable according to the criteria of reasonableness and justifiability as set out in s 33 [of the Interim Constitution]."

This case arose from the differentiated manners[1399] in which tariffs for the actual consumption of water and electricity in different areas within

---

[1396] See 375 below.

[1397] *Pretoria City Council v Walker* 1998 2 SA 363 (CC).

[1398] *Pretoria City Council v Walker* (note 1397 above), par. 140.

[1399] The council had charged the residents of the former municipal area of Pretoria on the basis of a tariff for the actual consumption of water and elec-tricity supplied which was measured by means of meters installed on each property in such area, whereas it had charged residents in the former Mamelodi and Atteridgeville municipal areas (where no meters had been installed) a flat

the territory of the Pretoria City Council were determined. The respondent objected to the enforcement of a debt owed by him to the city council, on the grounds that the flat rate for water and electricity charges in the former municipal areas of Mamelodi and Atteridgeville was lower than the metered rate charged to the respondent and other persons in the former municipal area of Pretoria and that this meant that the latter were subsidising the former; that the differentiation in the tariffs continued even after meters had been installed on some properties in Mamelodi and Atteridgeville; that only residents of old Pretoria had been singled out for legal action to recover arrears whilst a policy of non-enforcement was followed in respect of Mamelodi and Atteridgeville; and that the imposition of differential rates was, inter alia, inconsistent with section 8(2) IC.

The court found that respondent had to settle the debt owed to the council.[1400] For present purposes, the reasoning[1401] of the court in making this finding is not as important as the court's recognition of the fact that the selective institution of legal proceedings by the city council amounted to a breach of the constitutional right not to be unfairly discriminated against.[1402] One could assume that, in the context of section 25(1) FC, the procedural safeguards in the context of ensuring non-arbitrariness would include, for instance, avoiding the selective applica-

---

rate based on the amount of water and electricity supplied to such areas divided by the number of residences therein.

[1400] As to the question whether the conduct of the city council amounted to unfair discrimination, it was held that the operation of the flat rate and its continued application on properties where meters had been installed in Mamelodi and Atteridgeville, as well as the cross-subsidisation which might have resulted from any delays in implementing a metered tariff, did not impact adversely on the respondent in any material way: there was no invasion of the respondent's dignity nor was he affected in a manner comparably serious to an invasion of his dignity. *Pretoria City Council v Walker* (note 1397 above), par. 68.

[1401] The court held that the debt that was owed by the respondent remained. Upon the question whether its payment should be enforced, it was remarked that the finding that the conduct of the city council's officials amounted to unfair discrimination was an intimation that the city council had acted incorrectly and that it should put its house in order; it was not a vindication of the respondent's refusal to pay for services rendered. *Pretoria City Council v Walker* (note 1397 above), par. 94.

[1402] *Pretoria City Council v Walker* (note 1397 above), par. 81.

tion of certain legislative measures that could constitute an interference with property.

Reference should also be made to case of *Transvaal Agricultural Union v Minister of Land Affairs*,[1403] where the validity of the Restitution of Land Rights Act was contested on the basis of, inter alia, section 28 IC and the just administrative action provision of section 24 IC. It was alleged by the applicants that the provisions in the Restitution of Land Rights Act relating to the manner in which the claims for resitution were to be treated by the Commission for the Restitution of Land Rights impaired the rights of the owner of the land, as it did not provide the owner with an opportunity of being heard by the regional land claims commissioner before any decision is taken in regard to the publication of the notice of restitution. Eventually, the decision resolved only the procedural issue of direct acces to the constitutional court, and there was no need to pronounce on the justifiability of the interference with property. However, the court remarked *obiter* that the restitution of land rights was a complex process in which the rights of registered owners and other persons with an interest in the land had to be balanced against the constitutional injunctions to ensure that restitution be made where this was just and equitable. It further indicated that Parliament was given a discretion by the Interim Constitution to decide how this process was to be carried out. Provisions in such legislation that were designed to protect claimants and maintain the status quo pending determination of a claim therefore served a legitimate purpose. The court further remarked that, even if it were assumed in favour of the applicant that the contested provisions in the Restitution of Land Rights Act infringed rights protected under, inter alia, section 28 IC, there was prima facie justification in terms of section 33 IC for such infringement.[1404]

3.4.1.3. Conceptual Continuity of Deprivation and Expropriation?

In the Final Constitution the property clause was reformulated with regard to the requirement of the infringing law's general applicability. The aim of this reformulation was probably to rule out any uncertainty

---

[1403] *Transvaal Agricultural Union v Minister of Land Affairs* 1997 2 SA 621 (CC).

[1404] *Transvaal Agricultural Union v Minister of Land Affairs* (note 1403 above), par. 36-37.

about whether or not a broader meaning should be attached to the word *law*.[1405] However, the reformulation did not exclude all problems. Because of the repetition of the general applicability requirement in sections 25(1) and (2) FC, and the ommission of the reference to arbitrariness in section 25(2) FC, the new section dealing with expropriation[1406] is not as clearly linked to the deprivation provision[1407] as the old section 28(3) IC was linked to section 28(2) IC. Consequently, it is not as easy to argue that expropriations are just one special subcategory of deprivations. Instead, it is possible to argue that the drafters of the constitution intended sections 25(1) and (2) FC to be separate provisions which have very little in common.

Such an interpretation would have implications for the assumption that the requirements for deprivation of property should implicitly also apply to expropriation. In fact, it would destroy the conceptual continuity on which a theory of regulatory expropriation could be construed.[1408] It is, furthermore, possible that the requirement of general applicability involves the preclusion of laws designed to single out certain or easily ascertainable individuals.[1409] Thus, this requirement might in future pose the problem of distinguishing between laws which would be unconstitutional because they affect a particular class of persons and laws that are aimed at particular individuals, describing them by means of a class, but are nevertheless constitutional.[1410] A cumulative reading of section 36 FC and section 25 FC might clarify some of the problems in this regard. Even if the deprivation requirements of section 25(1) FC do not apply to situations in which expropriation of property is at stake, section 36 FC still provides that expropriatory interferences with property must be subject to a law of general application.

[1405] See the discussion of this issue in *Budlender* in *Budlender/Latsky/Roux*, New Land Law (revised 1998), ch. 1, 35.

[1406] Sec. 25(2) FC.

[1407] Sec. 25(1) FC.

[1408] *Van der Walt*, Constitutional Property Clauses - A Comparative Analysis (1999), 341.

[1409] *Woolman* in *Chaskalson/Kentridge et. al. (eds)*, Constitutional Law of South Africa (1996), ch. 12, 17 note 4 gives an account of the drafting history of this phrase in connection with section 33(1) IC which indicates that the drafters had the so-called "bill of attainder" in mind when drawing up this provision.

[1410] *Budlender* in *Budlender/Latsky/Roux*, New Land Law (revised 1998), ch. 1, 34.

However, it would be anomalous to distinguish between interferences with property against which the (additional) requirement of non-arbitrariness would be applicable and those against which it would not be applicable. Henceforth, it is submitted that, even if the wording of section 25(1) and (2) FC compared with section 28 IC could be prone to a different interpretation, expropriation should nevertheless be linked to, and regarded as a species of deprivation. Accordingly, the requirements of section 25(1) FC should also apply — in addition to those of section 25(2) FC — to cases of expropriation. In determining whether an infringement on the right to property is justified on the basis of section 36 FC read with section 25 FC, the first question to be answered will be whether the infringement took place in terms of a law of general application.

3.4.2. Additional Requirements for Expropriation

Apart from the requirement that expropriation can only be effected pursuant to a law of general application, both the Interim and Final Constitution in South Africa prescribe certain requirements applicable to expropriations only. However, the *public purposes* requirement was formulated more broadly in the Final Constitution, and the *compensation* requirement was moved to a separate subsection.[1411] Although the texts differ, these requirements are present in both constitutions.

The meaning of the concept expropriation will determine the approach to confiscation and regulation of property. Expropriation could, for example, be regarded as a narrow concept requiring the state to actually acquire or obtain some benefit.[1412] The effect of this view of section 25(3) FC on confiscation and forfeiture of property is devastating: If the term expropriation is interpreted so narrowly that it includes only formal expropriation, then confiscation and forfeiture of property would have to be regarded as deprivations of property. Consequently, it would be possible for the legislature to "regulate" property to such an extent that the property rights of individuals can be completely withdrawn without the duty of compensation arising. Thus, the question of regulatory expropriation would be raised with regards to some kinds of

---

[1411] Sec. 25(3) FC.

[1412] See the stance taken in *Harksen v Lane* (note 820 above), par. 32.

confiscation or forfeiture, especially in the case where the loss affects an innocent owner in an exceptionally harsh and unfair manner.[1413]

It is, however, also possible to follow a less restrictive interpretation of the term expropriation. Then the fact that the state actually acquires some benefit or gain from a confiscation or forfeiture would be an indication of the fact that a specific infringement amounts to an expropriation, without appropriation by the expropriator being necessary. Subject to the validity requirements of section 25(3) FC and the proportionality principle, it might also indicate that compensation is payable (for instance, when the owner whose property is confiscated or forfeited was not involved in and innocent of the crime resulting in the confiscation or forfeiture).[1414]

In a discussion of the *constitutional* requirements for expropriation, it must be kept in mind that the Expropriation Act[1415] is still valid, and therefore also the court rulings pertaining to this Act before the Interim and Final Constitutions were promulgated. Nevertheless, the existing law is only valid in so far as it does not conflict with the explicit provisions of sections 25(2) FC or 25(3) FC.[1416]

3.4.2.1. Public Purpose / Public Interest

Section 25(2) FC provides that property may be expropriated only in terms of law of general application, more specifically *for a public purpose or in the public interest*. Section 28(3) IC contained a similar provision, but only made reference to the term *public purpose*. The requirement of *public purposes* was stated in general terms.[1417] This raised the question of whether land reform measures would be incorporated into the idea of expropriation for public purposes. The amended property

---

[1413] *Van der Walt*, Constitutional Property Clauses - A Comparative Analysis (1999), 342.

[1414] *Van der Walt*, Constitutional Property Clauses - A Comparative Analysis (1999), 342.

[1415] 63 of 1975.

[1416] *Van der Walt*, Constitutional Property Clauses - A Comparative Analysis (1999), 342-343.

[1417] Sec. 25(3) FC: "Where any rights in property are expropriated pursuant to a law referred to in subsection (2), such expropriation *shall be permissible for public purposes only* ..." Emphasis added.

clause in the Final Constitution explicitly addresses this problem.[1418] In neither of the constitutions an extensive definition of the terms *public purpose* or *public interest* is given, but section 25(4) FC determines that, for the purposes of the property clause, the *public interest* "includes the nation's commitment to land reform." The meaning of terms like public interest and public purposes in the context of the constitutional property guarantee is an issue debated in many legal systems. It also deserves closer scrutiny in the South African context.

Both the terms *public interest* and *public purposes* have, over the past century, been subject to varying interpretations in South African property law.[1419] It seems, however, as if this terminology has not been exceptionally contentious, nor subjected to rigorous legal analysis.[1420] Still, the case law on this matter is not adequate for application in the constitutional context. On the one hand, expropriation for racially discriminatory and social restructuring purposes in South Africa has in the past simply been upheld — or not questioned — as constituting a *public purpose* or being in the *public interest* or for the *public weal*. On the other hand, the cases in which the courts did attempt to interpret the terms public purposes and public interest can at best provide only rather vague guidelines for interpretation of these terms in the new constitutional order. Here, the vexing problem is trying to distinguish between applications of the term *public purposes* interpreted *broadly* or *narrowly*.

3.4.2.1.1. Public Interest and Racial Discrimination Under Apartheid

The Expropriation Act[1421] was used to expropriate white property for the purposes of homeland consolidation and for the removal of certain "blackspots," such as Cerman in Natal.[1422] Legislation aimed at giving effect to the segregation policy under apartheid also frequently made

---

[1418] *Van der Walt*, Constitutional Property Clauses - A Comparative Analysis (1999), 340.

[1419] See *Rondebosch Municipal Council v Trustees of the Western Province Agricultural Society* 1911 AD 271; *Fourie v Minister van Lande en 'n Ander* 1970 4 SA 165 (O); *White Rocks Farm (Pty) Ltd and Others v Minister of Community Development* 1984 3 SA 774 (WLD).

[1420] *Eisenberg*, 1995 SAJHR, 208.

[1421] 63 of 1975.

[1422] *Eisenberg*, 1995 SAJHR, 219 note 74.

specific reference to *"public purpose."*[1423] The courts also frequently upheld legislation permitting expropriation for purposes of social restructuring which were racially discriminatory for being in the *public
interest* or for the *public weal.*[1424] Alternatively, racially discriminatory
actions by the state were not questioned by the courts on the basis of
public purpose or public interest.

However, in submissions to the Truth and Reconciliation Commission
some members[1425] of the judiciary admitted:[1426]

> *"Apartheid was defined by law and enforced by law. It is necessary,
> therefore, to acknowledge the role of the legal system in upholding
> and maintaining apartheid and injustices associated with it. ...
> Apartheid caused poverty, degradation and suffering on a massive
> scale. It denied to the overwhelming majority of the population ac-
> cess to ownership and occupation of land, ... and to fundamental
> rights and freedoms which are essential for the development of self-
> esteem. ... What is striking is the way in which these provisions were
> treated as 'normal law'. It was very rare to find a judicial officer re-
> marking on the racist and unacceptable character of apartheid law.
> ... Even where legislation could not, as a matter of law, be ignored,
> judges should have acknowledged situations where law and justice
> diverged. The divergence between law and jusitice was only rarely
> acknowledged by judges."*

The case of *Minister of the Interior v Lockhat and Others*[1427] is a telling
example of this attitude. In this case, an expropriation by the state for
purposes of effecting the policy of racial segregation followed by the
government around 1961 had to be evaluated. The court, however,
avoided becoming involved in a discussion about the virtues of the
social transformation envisaged by Parliament in enacting the *Group*

[1423] I.e. s 13(3) Development and Trust Land Act 18 of 1936.

[1424] See also 71 above.

[1425] I.e. Ismail Mohamed (Chief Justice); Arthur Chaskalson (President of the
Constitutional Court); Michael Corbett (former Chief Justice); Hennie van
Heerden (Deputy Chief Justice); and Pius Langa (Deputy President of the Con-
stitutional Court).

[1426] *The Sunday Independent* (19.10.1997) 11 (edited version of the submission made to the Truth and Reconciliation Commission by Mohamed, Chaskalson, Corbett, Van Heerden and Langa).

[1427] *Minister of the Interior v Lockhat and Others* (note 10 above).

Areas Act,[1428] and remarked that it did not have the power to determine whether the legislation was for the ultimate *common weal* of all South Africans.[1429] Under the new constitutional order, the courts should attempt counteracting similar arbitrary legislative or executive action, should it arise. The interpretation of these terms by the courts under apartheid legislation will not provide many helpful examples.

3.4.2.1.2. Different Applications of the Terms Public Purposes and Public Interest

The cases in which the courts did attempt to interpret the terms *public purposes* and *public interest* can, at best, provide only rather vague guidelines for interpretation of these terms in the new constitutional order. This is due to: (i) reservations concerning the question of whether these terms should be interpreted broadly or narrowly; (ii) uncertainty about whether precedent on the meaning of these terms outside the context of expropriation legislation would have an influence on its interpretation within the context of expropriation; and (iii) uncertainty about the questions whether these terms in the context of expropriation requires actual use of the land by the expropriator and whether expropriation of one individual for the benefit of another would qualify as being in the public interest or for public purposes.

The term *public purposes* has been used in South African law in a broad sense as well as in a narrow sense. The reason for this, according to Innes J in the case of *Rondebosch Municipal Council v Trustees of the Western Province Agricultural Society*[1430] lies in the application of the modifiying adjective *public:*[1431]

> "[t]he word public *is one of wide significance, and it may have several meanings, between some of which, in spite of their common origin, there are very real differences."*

This decision indicates that the adjective *public* in terms like *public purposes, public use,* and *public interest* is broadly applied to matters that

---

[1428] 77 of 1957.

[1429] *Minister of the Interior v Lockhat and Others* (note 10 above), 602E-F.

[1430] *Rondebosch Municipal Council v Trustees of the Western Province Agricultural Society* (note 1419 above).

[1431] *Rondebosch Municipal Council v Trustees of the Western Province Agricultural Society* (note 1419 above), 283.

pertain to or affect *the people of a country or a local community*. It is, however, as frequently employed in a more restricted sense to denote matters that pertain *not to the people directly but to the State or the Government* representing the people.

However, the interpretation of the term *public purposes* as a requirement for expropriation has by itself caused problems because of the tendency in earlier jurisprudence to interpret this term in contrast with *public use* on the one hand, and *public interest* on the other.[1432] An analysis of the South African case law on the matter shows that *public purposes* originally denoted a benefit in the sense of any specific advantage, as opposed to actual physical use required by *public use*.[1433] In more modern conceptions of the former term no distinction is made between these two terms, especially when *public use* is employed in its broader sense as denoting an advantage for the public, but not necessarily actual physical use of the property. It can therefore be accepted that both *public use* and *public purpose* anticipated a direct public advantage as requirement for expropriation, through either actual use of, or access to the property. By contrast, *public interest* (in the context of limitations on property rights in particular) required only that the public derive some indirect benefit from the expropriation of the property.[1434]

In the *Rondebosch*-case, for instance, *public purpose* had to be interpreted in the context of section 115 of the Municipal Act.[1435] The court unanimously decided that the term *public purposes*, when pertaining to the question whether land qualifies as "rateable property," must be interpreted in the narrower sense as denoting matters pertaining to the

---

[1432] *Eisenberg*, 1995 SAJHR, 208.

[1433] Previously been defined narrowly in the United States of America and India (see *Karesh v City Council* 247 SE 2d 342; *City of Ownensboro v McCormack* 581 SW 2d 3 (Ky 1979); *State of Bihar v Kameshwar Singh AIR* (1952) SC 252; *Poletown Neighbourhood City Council v City of Detroit* 304 NW 2d 455), public use indicated benefit through the actual physical use by the public of the property. Recently this term has rather been employed in a broader sense as requiring some public advantage without actual physical use of the property. *Eisenberg*, 1995 SAJHR, 208 note 9.

[1434] *Eisenberg*, 1995 SAJHR, 209.

[1435] 45 of 1882.

state or government.[1436] Here, clearly, the term *public purposes* was intended to have the meaning of *governmental purposes*. However, later decisions pertaining to expropriation of particular plots of land follow a broader interpretation of *public purposes*.[1437] The decision in *Slabbert v Minister van Lande*,[1438] that the intention of the legislature in enacting section 2 of the Expropriation of Lands and Arbitration Clauses Proclamation[1439] was that the words *public purposes* had to be understood in their unrestricted sense, apparently implies that these words assume a broader meaning in all expropriation cases.[1440]

In *Slabbert v Minister van Lande*[1441] the court had to determine whether an expropriation of private land adjoining the official residence of the Prime Minister (as the head of state was then called) was *for public purposes* in terms of the Expropriation of Lands and Arbitration Clauses Proclamation.[1442] The apparent purpose of the expropriation was to enlarge the premises in order to provide more security and privacy for the Prime Minister. The court reasoned that the proclamation was phrased in such wide terms that both the restricted meaning (in the sense of governmental purposes) *and* the wide meaning (in the sense of interests of the community in general) of the phrase *public purposes* was intended. *Public purposes* should, in the opinion of the court, thus only be contrasted with the phrase *private and/or personal purposes*.[1443] Thereby it is implied that an expropriation is for *public purposes* as long as it is not for *private and/or personal purposes*.

[1436] De Villiers CJ, 280; Innes J, 286. Laurence J, 292 also founded that "it is not sufficient, to make purposes public, that they should be altruistic, neither must the object in view be merely sectional, however large or important the section concerned" and confirmed the strict interpretation of the term.

[1437] *Fourie v Minister van Lande* (note 1419 above), 175D; *White Rocks Farm (Pty) Ltd v Minister of Community Development* (note 1419 above), 794B-D.

[1438] *Slabbert v Minister van Lande* 1963 3 SA 620 (T), 621; see *Fourie v Minister van Lande* (note 1419 above), 173H-174E.

[1439] 5 of 1902 (Transvaal) as amended by the Expropriation Amendment Act 31 of 1958.

[1440] E.g. *Fourie v Minister van Lande* (note 1419 above), 174C-D.

[1441] *Slabbert v Minister van Lande* (note 1438 above).

[1442] 5 of 1902 (Transvaal) as amended by the Expropriation Amendment Act 31 of 1958.

[1443] *Slabbert v Minister van Lande* (note 1438 above), 621H.

This line of reasoning provides little help in clarifying the difference in meaning between *public purposes* in the narrow sense of *governmental purposes* and *public purposes* in the wide sense of *public interest*. In fact, it is stated in *Slabbert v Minister van Lande* that expropriating private lands adjoining the official residence of the Prime Minister has the purpose of improving state administration (or rather serves governmental purposes[1444] by improving the security and privacy of the Prime Minister) *and therefore* is also of general *public interest*.[1445] By arguing along the lines of *public interest in general*, the court fails to give an acceptable explanation of the reasons for expanding the *public purpose* concept to include *public interest*, and fails to clarify the possible distinction between *public purpose* in the broader sense and *public interest*.

In the context of expropriation, *public purposes* is usually understood to denote issues whereby the whole population or the local public are affected, and not only matters pertaining to the state or the government.[1446] The wider interpretation of *public purposes* in expropriation questions is explained in the case of *Fourie v Minister van Lande*.[1447] The court argued that the term public purposes is interpreted differently in matters pertaining to expropriation, on the one hand, and matters pertaining to legislation "not concerned with expropriation," on the other. It was pointed out that, with the promulgation of the Expropriation Act, the term public purposes already had a meaning attributed to it by a long line of earlier court decisions. The court is obliged to take cognisance of this established meaning on the supposition that the legislature will use a term in the same sense when incorporating it without further qualification into later enactments.[1448]

This illustrates the court's intention to interpret the term *public purposes* in the context of expropriation by having regard not only to previous expropriation cases, but also to other decisions that interpreted the term. In the *Fourie* case, an extensive analysis of both sets of the existing case law was undertaken. The court also described the procedure to determine the meaning of the words *public purpose* in a specific context. A historical survey of the use of the phrase should be undertaken,

---

[1444] Referring to *public purposes* in the narrow sense.

[1445] *Slabbert v Minister van Lande* (note 1438 above), 622A-B, 622D-E.

[1446] *White Rocks Farm (Pty) Ltd v Minister of Community Development* (note 1419 above), 793I.

[1447] *Fourie v Minister van Lande* (note 1419 above), 170D.

[1448] *Fourie v Minister van Lande* (note 1419 above), 170F-G.

and once the established meaning has been ascertained, it is presumed that through subsequent use of such a term in an act which is *in pari materia* with previous legislation, the legislature intended to use the term in its already established sense.[1449] This procedure and its results were endorsed in the later decision of *White Rocks Farm v Minister of Community Development*.[1450]

Some decisions[1451] hold the opinion that the term *public purposes* does not imply that the expropriator actually uses the land. Other decisions do not regard the expropriation of one individual's private property for the benefit of another private individual as sufficiently complying with the requirement of *public purpose*. In the case of *Administrator, Transvaal v J van Streepen (Kempton Park) (Pty) Ltd*,[1452] for instance, the Appellate Division of the Supreme Court (as it was then called) gave an extremely wide meaning to the phrase "any purpose in connection with the construction or maintenance of a road" in section 7(1) of the Transvaal Roads Ordinance.[1453] The decision resulted directly in an interpretation of the specific provision that included any purpose reasonably expedient to the main purpose for the specific expropriation in terms of the ordinance (namely the building of roads). The indirect effect of the decision was that an expropriation of one individual's property for what was essentially the benefit of another, could still be *for public purposes or in the public interest*.[1454]

[1449] *Fourie v Minister van Lande* (note 1419 above), 170G-H, 174H-175A.

[1450] *White Rocks Farm (Pty) Ltd v Minister of Community Development* (note 1419 above), 793I. See, however, the differing approach of Watermeyer, J in *Durban City Council v SA Board Mills Ltd* 1961 3 SA 392 (C), 397C-E: In absence of indications to the contrary, it was held that expropriation of a piece of land for the purpose of widening a road in accordance with a town planning scheme was in the public purpose. It was said that the municipality performing the expropriation was the authority charged with the duty of planning the town, and in doing so were performing a public function. If an expropriation was necessary to enable the municipality to perform a public function, it had to be in the public interest.

[1451] E.g. *African Farms and Townships Ltd v Cape Town Municipality* 1961 3 SA 392 (C), 396H.

[1452] *Administrator, Transvaal v J van Streepen (Kempton Park) (Pty) Ltd* 1990 4 SA 644 (A).

[1453] 22 of 1957.

[1454] *Van der Walt*, Constitutional Property Clauses - A Comparative Analysis (1999), 343.

The *Van Streepen* case could be used in support of an argument that an interpretation making expropriation of one private individual for the benefit of another, forms the basis of the purported intention behind section 25(2)(a) FC read with section 25(4)(a) FC. However, it is still questionable to what extent the guidelines existing in South African case law in general can really make a substantial contribution in formulating the concepts of *public purpose* or *public interest* with regard to the constitutional property guarantee. Many of the earlier decisions would probably also be counterproductive in the context of testing the constitutionality of reform legislation.

3.4.2.1.3. The Inadequacy of Existing Judicial Precedent for Constitutional Interpretation

The existing judicial precedent on the terms *public purposes* and *public interest* poses a few pitfalls for their interpretation of these terms under the constitutional property clause. It raises the question of how governmental manipulation of the law for purposes of social restructuring should be handled by the courts, in which regard the choice of terminology and interpretation thereof poses problems.

The application of the term *public purposes* to expropriation under apartheid legislation does not provide any helpful guidelines for application in the constitutional context. Instead, they sound a clear warning that the judiciary cannot simply accept that manipulation of the law by the government for purposes of social restructuring is necessarily always in the *public interest or for public purposes*. No matter how honourable the intentions of the legislature might be in a specific case where property rights are limited in the public interest or for public purposes, a constitutional standard should still be applied. The crucial question is what this constitutional standard of *public interest / public purposes* should be.

Further, the choice of terminology and the interpretation thereof can be controversial in view of the land-redistribution objectives of the government. A restrictive definition of *public interest* or *public purpose* will preclude the possibility of expropriation for the sake of transfer to private parties and thereby render the land redistribution programme ineffective. A too liberal definition of *public purpose* or *public interest* might, by contrast, leave the legislature with unlimited capacity to control private property at its own discretion, leaving it to the courts to determine normative limits to this legislative capacity.

Most foreign jurisdictions attribute a broad meaning to the term *public purposes*.[1455] The Expropriation Act[1456] also defines *public purposes* broadly so as to include any purpose connected with the administration of any law by an organ of state. However, the meanings attached to the terms *public interest, public purposes,* and so on, could still depend on the context in which they are used. It is thus possible that the meanings of these terms may vary from one situation to the other.

In *Park-Ross v Director: Office for Serious Economic Offences*[1457] the purpose of the search-and-seizure infringement on the right to property and the right to privacy in terms of section 28 IC and section 13 IC respectively was considered. Tebutt J remarked:[1458]

> "... it must ... be accepted that, for the preservation of law and order and the proper investigation and combating of crime, as well as for the protection of society and of rights of the members of that society, searches may have to occur at times ... even if the right to privacy is affected thereby."

The court concludes that it must be accepted that property can be seized and removed pursuant to such (permissible) searches. Thus the court indicates that a consideration of the public good is present in the enquiry as to whether or not an infringement of property rights has occurred.

For purposes of limiting property rights in South Africa under the Final Constitution, the inclusion of the term *public interest* in section 25(2) FC suggests that the provision in the Final Constitution is of wider import. It can thus include expropriations that might have been *ultra vires* in terms of the narrower *public purpose* concept of the Interim Constitution.[1459] Section 25(4)(a) FC also underscores this approach.

Nevertheless, it could be argued that the addition of the term *public interest* in section 25(2)(a) FC emphasises that the courts' powers to set aside expropriations on the grouds of their purpose are limited. Chas-

---

[1455] *Eisenberg*, 1995 SAJHR, 216 ff.

[1456] 63 of 1975. Sec. 1 of the act contains a definitions clause.

[1457] *Park-Ross v Director: Office for Serious Economic Offences* (note 136 above).

[1458] *Park-Ross v Director: Office for Serious Economic Offences* (note 136 above), 168F-G.

[1459] *Van der Walt*, Constitutional Property Clauses - A Comparative Analysis (1999), 341.

kalson and Lewis[1460] regard the inclusion of this term as a warning to the judiciary to respect the choices made by the legislature or the executive as to where the public interest lies. Such an approach to the interpretation of the terms *public interest* and *public purposes* in the property clause does not realise that the legislative and executive powers inherent in these concepts can easily be abused. The sanctioning powers of the judiciary should be increased beyond merely respecting the decisions of the legislature and executive. After all, to ensure that the objectives of land reform, redistribution and restitution are also incorporated into an interpretation of the terms public purposes and public interest, section 25(4) FC incorporates an additional mechanism to ensure that these terms are not "misinterpreted" by the courts. It states expressly that *public interest* includes the nation's commitment to land reform and to reforms to bring about equitable access to all South Africa's natural resources.

So, even if it were uncertain whether expropriation for purposes of redistribution of land would have been permissible in terms of section 28(3) IC, it is now clear that such an expropriation is permissible in terms of section 25(2) FC. Expropriation for the purpose of land redistribution, which involves the withdrawal of property from one private person in order to transfer it to another private person, will now probably be *in the public interest*. The public interest in this case is the general interest of the society in the implementation and promotion of an equitable, effective and successful programme of transformation and land reform.[1461]

In this sense, it is advisable that *public purposes* and *public interest* be attributed a broad meaning in the constitutional context of expropriation. A narrow interpretation of the *public interest / public purposes* requirement in the constitutional property clause would be contrary to the trends in constitutional law of other jurisdictions. Further, a narrow approach would render several politically uncontroversial and commercially efficacious legislative provisions[1462] potentially unconstitutional.[1463]

[1460] *Chaskalson/Lewis* in *Chaskalson, Kentridge, Klaaren et al. (eds)*, Constitutional Law of South Africa (1996), ch. 31, 21.

[1461] *Van der Walt*, Constitutional Property Clauses - A Comparative Analysis (1999), 341-342.

[1462] E.g. sec. 440K, Companies Act 61 of 1973, which provides for the compulsory acquisition of minority shareholdings by a successful take-over bidder

3.4.2.1.4. The Land Claims Court's Definition of "Public Interest"

Recently, in *Ex Parte North Central and South Central Metropolitan Substructure Councils of the Durban Metropolitan Area*,[1464] the Land Claims Court developed the concept of *public interest* in the context of the court's capacity to order[1465] that certain land must be excluded from restitution.[1466] The court will only make an order with the effect that certain land is excluded from restoration if it is satisfied that it is in the public interest and that the public or any substantial part thereof will suffer substantial prejudice unless such an order is made.[1467] The case arose from the purported development of Cato Manor, an area from which a large group of persons have forcibly been removed during the apartheid regime. They applied for the order of exclusion from restitution, and were opposed by claimants claiming restoration. During the proceedings, the parties started negotiations and finally reached an agreement, which they then wanted to incorporate into the court order under section 34(5)(d) of the Restitution of Land Rights Act. The settlement entailed an agreement to proceed with the development as planned, but subject to the proviso that where restoration was feasible any respondent who wished to pursue a claim, would be entitled to do so. Respondents who wished to return to the area without insisting on restoration or for whom restoration was not a viable option were also able to benefit from the development.

Consequently, in order to determine whether the requirements of section 34(6) of the Restitution of Land Rights Act had been met, the court had to scrutinise the concept of *public interest*.[1468] The court found that both development of the land and restoration of it would be

---

who owns 90 per cent of the shares in the company; sec. 24, Minerals Act 50 of 1991, providing for the compulsory acquisition of landowner's rights in the interests of mining activities on the land.

[1463] *Chaskalson/Lewis* in *Chaskalson, Kentridge, Klaaren et al. (eds)*, Constitutional Law of South Africa (1996), ch. 31, 21.

[1464] *Ex Parte North Central and South Central Metropolitan Substructure Councils of the Durban Metropolitan Area* 1998 1 SA 78 (LCC).

[1465] Sec. 34 of the Restitution of Land Rights Act.

[1466] See the discussion of *Pienaar*, Land Reform (2000), 44 ff.

[1467] Sec. 34(6) of the Restitution of Land Rights Act.

[1468] *Ex Parte North Central and South Central Metropolitan Substructure Councils of the Durban Metropolitan Area* (note 1464 above), 83B-C, E-F.

in public interest in the instant case. It indicated that, due to the devastation caused and hardship suffered as a result of the dispossession and removal, restoration would be a logical step to address the historical injustice, and that it therefore would be in public interest. However, the court further argued that a blanket restoration would result in the loss of the intended development. This could ultimately also be in public interest, as becomes clear from, *inter alia,* the provision of affordable housing for a disadvantaged community, opportunities for employment, the upgrading of informal settlements, foreign investments and economic upliftment for the whole area that would emanate from the development.[1469] The court thus found that any agreement that accommodated both development and restoration, with the consent of all the parties concerned, would eminently be in the public interest.[1470]

3.4.2.2. Compensation

Section 25(2)(b) FC only provides in general for compensation, determining that expropriation is subject to compensation and that the amount, as well as the time and also the manner of payment either have to be agreed upon by those affected, or have to be decided or approved by a court. A more detailed provision is contained in section 25(3) FC. The amount of compensation and the manner and time of payment have to be just and equitable, reflecting an equitable balance between the public interest and the interests of those affected, upon taking into account "all relevant circumstances."

[1469] *Ex Parte North Central and South Central Metropolitan Substructure Councils of the Durban Metropolitan Area* (note 1464 above), 86H-87D.

[1470] A section 34(5) order was consequently granted. In *Singh and Others v North Central & South Central Local Councils* 1999 1 All SA 350 (LCC) another application was brought before the court by participants and other claimants in respect of land in Cato Manor who were not party to the agreement that was incorporated into the sec. 34 court order. The applicants claimed that the respondents were in breach of numerous obligations under the said agreement and claimed, in most instances, orders of specific performance. The application was dismissed on the facts.

3.4.2.2.1. Compensation Agreed upon by the Affected Parties or Determined by Court

As in section 25(2)(b) FC, section 28(3) IC provided that expropriation was subject to the payment of *agreed* compensation. If no agreement could be reached, the court — taking account of all relevant factors — had to determine the amount and time limit for payment of compensation. Section 25(2)(b) FC contains an extension of the preceding section 28(3) IC in the sense that provision is also made for approval by a court of the *manner of payment* of allocated or agreed compensation. This is an improvement of the Interim Constitution's provisions, because it enables a consideration of alternative forms of payment, for example payment by means of state bonds.[1471]

3.4.2.2.2. Taking into Account of All Relevant Circumstances

Section 28(3) IC provided that a court, when having to determine an amount of compensation, had to take into account

> "*all relevant factors, including ... the use to which the property is being put, the history of its acquisition, its market value, the value of the investments in it by those affected and the interests of those affected.*"

Reference to "all relevant factors" indicates merely that the enumerated factors do not form part of a *numerus clausus* of factors.[1472] Simultaneously, it indicates the general relevance and relative importance of the other listed factors.[1473] Section 25(3) FC also comprises a list of "relevant circumstances" to be taken into account in the determination of compensation, but they differ from those listed in section 28(3) IC. In particular, the new list of factors includes the importance of considering the history of the property during the apartheid era, especially if the expropriation was in one way or other connected to the new regime's land reform initiatives:[1474]

[1471] *Van der Walt*, Constitutional Property Clauses - A Comparative Analysis (1999), 346.

[1472] *Budlender* in *Budlender/Latsky/Roux*, New Land Law (1998), ch. 1, 64.

[1473] *Van der Walt*, Constitutional Property Clauses - A Comparative Analysis (1999), 345.

[1474] *Van der Walt*, Constitutional Property Clauses - A Comparative Analysis (1999), 344.

Section 25 (Property) ...

(3) The amount of the compensation and the time and manner of payment must be just and equitable, reflecting an equitable balance between the public interest and the interests of those affected, having regard to all relevant circumstances, including – (a) the current use of the property; (b) the history of the acquisition and use of the property; (c) the market value of the property; (d) the extent of direct state investment and subsidy in the acquisition and beneficial capital improvement of the property; and (e) the purpose of the expropriation.

The factors which have remained are "current use of the property" and the "market value."

(i) The use to which the property is being put can, according to Budlender,[1475] play an important role when the property at stake is a scarce resource not being used in a socially productive manner. For instance, in the case of speculative hoarding of land in a location where access to land for housing is critical, the need for land and the owner's speculative exploitation of the land should not be allowed to increase the amount of compensation payable.

(ii) Section 12 of the Expropriation Act,[1476] which is still valid and constitutes the main statutory provision controlling the calculation and payment of compensation for expropriation, is based mainly on the notion of market value as measure for compensation. In this regard, the Expropriation Act conflicts with the purpose and intention of section 25(3) FC. The market value of the property is, obviously, a relevant factor, but in view of the whole constitution and the property clause, it cannot be the only or most important factor in determining the just and equitable amount of compensation.[1477] Existing legislation has to be interpreted in accordance with the new constitutions. This will probably result in an adaptation of the focus on section 12 of the Expropriation Act to mirror the intention displayed by the constitutional property clause. In *Khumalo v Potgieter*,[1478] the Land Claims Court adopted a two-tiered approach by first establishing the market value of the prop-

---

[1475] *Budlender* in *Budlender/Latsky/Roux*, New Land Law (1998), ch. 1, 58.

[1476] 63 of 1975.

[1477] *Kerksay Investments (Pty) Ltd v Randburg Town Council* 1997 1 SA 511 (T), 522E-G.

[1478] *Khumalo and others v Potgieter and others* 1999 1 All SA 10 (N).

erty at stake,[1479] and only thereafter considering the influence of the constitutional indications for valuation of property to be expropriated on the determined amount.[1480] The court expressly excluded the possible influence that the presence of the labour tenants on the land to be valuated could have on the eventual determination of the market value of the land, on the basis of the "Pointe Gourde" principle.[1481] In considering the "current use of the property" in terms of section 25(3) FC as a factor influencing the amount of compensation, the court found that the presence of labour tenants, who are almost absolutely insulated against eviction, can result in the present owner not being capable of deriving any benefit from the land. It consequently warrants a limited upward adjustment of the compensation amount.[1482]

The investments made by the parties affected,[1483] and the interests of the affected parties[1484] are not mentioned in the list of considerations in

---

[1479] *Khumalo and others v Potgieter and others* (note 1478 above), par. 72-92.

[1480] *Khumalo and others v Potgieter and others* (note 1478 above), par. 93 ff.

[1481] According to this principle, the increase or decrease in value of the land, which is attributable to the scheme underlying the acquisition, should not be taken into account in the assessment of the market value of land acquired in an expropriation. This principle emanated from the Privy Council decision of *Pointe Gourde Quarrying and Transport Co Ltd v Sub-intendent of Crown Lands* [1947] AC 565.

[1482] *Khumalo and others v Potgieter and others* (note 1478 above), par. 94.

[1483] The value of the investments in the property can affect the amount of compensation either positively or negatively, depending on the circumstances. The market value will normally already reflect any positive influence that investments might have had, and investments that do not raise the market value should probably not be compensated. There are, however, the extraordinary circumstances where compensation should perhaps be higher than market value because of investments. *Budlender* in *Budlender/Latsky/Roux*, New Land Law (1998), ch. 1, 63 mentions two examples: (i) cases where market value is depressed by negative influences not of the owner's making, like land invasions; and (ii) cases where someone else than the owner (the lessee, an unlawful occupant) has made investments that should be considered for compensation.

[1484] It is difficult to interpret the factor referring to the "interests of those affected," although it most probably establishes a balancing factor similar to that found in German law. The compensation should therefore not be so high that it makes expropriation and therewith the benefits (land or housing) to be received in terms of land reform programmes impossible. Further, it should not be so low that it causes substantial detriment for the current owners and holders of

section 25(3) FC, whereas they seemed to be important enough to be worthy of explicit mention under section 28 IC. However, some factors have been broadened:

(i) Section 25(3)(b) FC does not refer only to the "history of acquisition", as was the case in section 28(3) IC, but also to "use" of the property. The history of the acquisition of the property is a fairly obvious consideration in cases where compensation has to be determined for land which is to be expropriated now, and which was obtained by forced removals and made available to white farmers at low prices, with heavy state subsidies and/or favourable loans. It should logically affect the amount of compensation in cases where the land is later expropriated again for restitution or redistribution purposes. Housing subsidies provided by the state in urban areas could, arguably, also fall within the ambit of this provision. In the Khumalo case, an analysis of the "history of the acquisition" of the land indicated that the owner who was to be expropriated bought the land in question at a time when the value thereof was already depressed and expropriation was likely. This influenced the purchase price, and consequently, at expropriation, justified a downward adjustment of the compensation amount.[1485]

(ii) Further, explicit reference is made (in section 25(3)(d) FC) to the extent of direct state investment and subsidy in the acquisition and beneficial capital improvement of property. The extent of direct state investment and subsidy in the acquisition and beneficial capital improvement of the property probably excludes indirect subsidies such as tax incentives and drought or marketing subsidies. This factor has arguably also replaced the general factor of investments in property as it appeared in section 28(3) IC. This has the effect that investments in property can be taken into account when it affects the amount of compensation negatively. Investments increasing the compensation amount now have to be regarded under the general heading of "all relevant factors." Land that was expropriated from blacks during the apartheid era was often made available to whites with the assistance of very beneficial state loans and subsidies. This often made it possible to acquire or improve land, from which the current owner could benefit if the effect of state investment was not taken into account. Moreover, this requirement is in line with the general principles of expropriation and compen-

---

rights in or to that land. *Budlender* in *Budlender/Latsky/Roux,* New Land Law (1998), ch. 1, 64.

[1485] *Khumalo and others v Potgieter and others* (note 1478 above), par. 95.

sation, as it is normally considered improper to allow compensation to be influenced by state actions and developments or plans related to the expropriation.[1486]

(iii) The "purpose of the expropriation" is now explicitly mentioned in section 25(3)(e) FC as a factor to be considered. Consideration of the purpose of an expropriation probably allows the courts to ensure that the social importance of the expropriation is taken into account. When an expropriation is in the public interest but not essential, a stricter measure may be applied, but when an expropriation is for an essential public purpose (such as land reform or housing), the courts should ensure that the amount of compensation does not prevent the state from addressing the critical situation that requires the expropriation.[1487] If the purpose of expropriation is the restitution of the property to a formerly dispossessed claimant, the scales could be tipped against the private owner. An investigation of the *history of acquisition* of the property might, for instance, include a consideration of the fact that the property was obtained during apartheid era for less than its true (market) value. If consistent with the principles inherent in the land restitution programme, compensation should in such a case be determined on a basis where "just and equitable" is seen in the context of effecting social justice rather than rewarding the individual owner for the loss of his or her property and security of title. This implies that, in the case of expropriation for purposes of land reform, compensation at a level lower than market value would be highly likely. It is, however, questionable whether expropriation for purposes of land reform *without any* compensation would be possible. Section 25(8) FC creates at least the impression that it would be possible to deviate from the provisions of section 25 FC for purposes of land reform, as long as the deviation is still in accordance with section 36(1) FC.[1488] It would, obviously, not be possible to effect an expropriation that would not be in accordance with the requirements in section 36(1) FC. An expropriation would therefore always have to be in accordance with a law of general application, and can never be arbitrary, even if the expropriation is aimed at land

---

[1486] *Van der Walt*, Constitutional Property Clauses - A Comparative Analysis (1999), 346 note 124.

[1487] *Van der Walt*, Constitutional Property Clauses - A Comparative Analysis (1999), 347.

[1488] *Van der Walt*, Constitutional Property Clauses - A Comparative Analysis (1999), 347.

reform. The expropriation also has to be for public purposes or in the public interest. Section 25(3)(e) FC, however, suggests that the purpose of the expropriation (in this case land reform) may influence the amount of compensation payable, especially if weighed against the public interest.[1489] Although this might support arguments for a diminished amount of compensation, it does not, in itself, justify the complete denial of an expropriated owner's right to compensation.[1490]

In the *Certification* case[1491] it has been mentioned that it is not usual for a constitutional document itself to mention specific criteria upon which compensation for expropriation could be determined. It found, however, that the approach taken in section 25 FC were not in conflict with the universally accepted view that compensation had to be "fair," "adequate," "full," "equitable and appropriate," or "just."[1492] The fact that the drafters of both the Interim and Final Constitutions resorted to this approach towards the determination of compensation indicates that market value is not the only (or even most important) criterion to be considered in the determination of the amount of compensation.[1493] The explicit listing of market value as one of the possible factors to be taken into account is, furthermore, clearly a sign that market value by itself is not the only or even the most important factor. There is no simple equation which would enable an easy evaluation of all the relevant factors. The facts and circumstances of each case accordingly has a great influence on the outcome of the process.

The overall standard is that compensation should be just and equitable, taking into account *all relevant factors*. What "just and equitable" means in a specific context, and which factors would be relevant, should be determined with reference to the overall structure and purpose of the Constitution, including the property clause and the limitation clause.

[1489] *Van der Walt*, Constitutional Property Clauses - A Comparative Analysis (1999), 347.

[1490] See *Khumalo and others v Potgieter and others* (note 1478 above), and the discussion of this decision at 345 above.

[1491] *Certification of the Constitution of the Republic of South Africa* (note 245 above), par. 70-75.

[1492] *Certification of the Constitution of the Republic of South Africa* (note 245 above), par. 73.

[1493] See *Claassens*, 1993 SAJHR, 422; *Budlender* in *Budlender/Latsky/Roux*, New Land Law (revised 1998), ch. 1, 56 ff. where the factors enumerated in sec. 28(3) IC are discussed.

Moreover, the specific factors enumerated in section 28(3) IC and section 25(3) FC, are not the only relevant factors to be considered: they simply constitute examples of what kind of considerations might be important under certain circumstances.

3.4.2.2.3. Expropriation without Compensation?

Van der Walt[1494] has indicated that expropriation without compensation would only be possible if the requirements of section 25(3) FC are complied with. This would render section 25(8) FC a dead letter. Expropriation without compensation would, therefore, be possible only in the case where the court (ruling upon a consideration of all the relevant factors, including the circumstances of the acquisition, use and expropriation of the property) would find that payment of compensation would be unnecessary, and that it is justifiable and equitable to withhold compensation completely.[1495] However, even under such circumstances, the court could probably award nominal compensation, in order to pay lip service to the compensation requirement.

The issue of compensation in cases of constructive expropriation,[1496] deserves some attention. The argument that state interference with private property which is not structured formally as an expropriation (for instance when the action is not undertaken in terms of expropriation legislation or procedures, and no provision is made for compensation), but nevertheless has the same effects and impact as an expropriation, could be used to extract compensation for regulatory deprivations of property of this kind. In this regard, the idea that compensation should indeed be paid in cases that qualify as constructive expropriation, seems less in dispute as the question whether specific scenarios would qualify as constructive expropriation. However, even under these circumstances the guidelines in section 25(3) FC should provide the courts with the necessary information on the basis of which compensation amounts should be determined.

[1494] *Van der Walt*, Constitutional Property Clauses - A Comparative Analysis (1999), 347.

[1495] No such decision has been made yet.

[1496] See 378 ff. below.

3.4.2.3. Additional Requirements from Judicial Precedent?

Certain points raised in the decision of *Harksen v Lane NO*,[1497] where the court had to consider the constitutionality of section 21 of the Insolvency Act,[1498] could have far-reaching consequences for the concept of expropriation as described in the South African constitutions. Therefore, this decision needs further discussion.

3.4.2.3.1. Appropriation by the Expropriator

In the *Harksen* case the court reasoned on the basis of previous and foreign case law,[1499] that an expropriation amounts to more than a mere dispossession of property, and that *appropriation by the expropriator* is a requirement.[1500] Although the authority[1501] upon which the ruling was based was not on all fours with the *Harksen* case, it was nevertheless decided that, in the case of section 21 of the Insolvency Act, the temporary vesting of ownership in the Master or trustee did not sufficiently fulfil the requirement of appropriation by the expropriator.[1502] The court argued that the purpose of section 21 of the Insolvency Act was to ensure that all property that belonged to the insolvent spouse is contained in his or her estate at the point of liquidation. The property rights of both the insolvent spouse and the solvent spouse are thus temporarily "suspended" by the operation of law. The law also creates a procedure for the release of the property belonging to the solvent spouse.[1503] The court, in reaching this decision, held it to be unnecessary

---

[1497] *Harksen v Lane* (note 820 above).

[1498] 24 of 1936. It was decided that section 21 of the Insolvency Act did not constitute an expropriation of property and therefore was not subject to section 28(3) of the Constitution (par. 37). The case was eventually decided on the basis of the equality clause (section 8 IC). It was held that section 21 of the Insolvency Act was not in conflict with the equality guarantee or the prohibition against discrimination. *Harksen v Lane* (note 820 above) par. 68. See also 371 ff. above.

[1499] *Beckenstrater v Sand River Irrigation Board* 1964 4 SA 510 (T) 515A-C; *Hewlett v Minister of Finance* 1982 1 SA 490 (ZSC); *Davies v Minister of Lands, Agriculture and Water Development* 1997 1 SA 228 (ZSC).

[1500] *Harksen v Lane* (note 820 above), par. 32.

[1501] See *note* 1499 above.

[1502] *Harksen v Lane* (note 820 above), par. 35.

[1503] *Harksen v Lane* (note 820 above), par. 36.

to decide whether the expropriation was for a public purpose as required by section 28(3) IC, and whether the vesting of the property involved a public authority. Thereby it assumed that the appropriation by a public authority is a constitutional requirement for expropriation.

Whereas the result of the ruling might be correct, the courts' pronouncements on the requirement of *actual dispossession or acquisition of the property by the expropriator* as an element of expropriation should be rejected. Such a requirement restricts the action of expropriation to tangible property only. The constitution does not support such an approach. Further, restricting the action to actual expropriations in the formal sense by requiring appropriation by the expropriator, is an unnecessarily rigid requirement.[1504] The state need not have acquired a benefit from the specific action, and even if this had been the case, the state nevertheless need not necessarily have acquired exactly the same benefit or right that has been lost by the expropriated party. In this regard, Van der Walt and Botha's[1505] comparative analysis on this issue indicates that as far as constitutional property guarantees are concerned, the scope of the term *expropriation* or *compulsory acquisition* cannot be reduced or restricted to either physical dispossession or actual acquisition by the state.

3.4.2.3.2. Permanent Nature of Expropriation

On the basis of the temporary nature of section 21 of the Insolvency Act, the court argued[1506] that, even if this section does result in a transfer of the ownership of the solvent spouse's property to the master or trustee of the insolvent estate, the purpose of the section is not to acquire the property. Instead, it is aimed at ensuring that the insolvent estate is not deprived of property actually belonging to it. Therefore, it was held, section 21 of the Insolvency Act cannot be described as permitting expropriation. This is another justified point of concern. The mention made by the court of the fact that the limitation in section 21 of the Insolvency Act is only of a temporary nature, could result in an interpretation of the expropriation provisions in the constitution that

---

[1504] *Van der Walt*, Constitutional Property Clauses - A Comparative Analysis (1999), 338.

[1505] *Van der Walt/Botha*, 1998 SAPR/PL, 20-21.

[1506] *Harksen v Lane* (note 820 above), par. 35-37.

imports a requirement of permancy of expropriation. Such a requirement is not explicitly mentioned in either of the constitutions.[1507]

3.4.3. Proportionality in Terms of the General Limitations Clause

The inquiry into the proportionality of a specific restrictive action by
the state has first been described by Chaskalson, P[1508] in the case of *S v
Makwanyane*,[1509] with regard to the constitutional validity of the death
penalty in terms of the Interim Constitution:[1510]

> "*[An assessment based on proportionality] is implicit in the provisions
> of section 33(1) [IC]. The fact that different rights have different im-
> plications for democracy, and in the case of our Constitution, for "an
> open and democratic society based on freedom and equality", means
> that there is no absolute standard which can be laid down for deter-
> mining reasonableness and necessity. [Proportionality] ... calls for the
> balancing of different interests. In the balancing process, the relevant
> considerations will include the nature of the right that is limited, and
> its importance to an open and democratic society based on freedom
> and equality; the purpose for which the right is limited and the im-
> portance of that purpose to such a society; the extent of the limitation,
> its efficacy, and particularly where the limitation has to be necessary,
> whether the desired ends could reasonably be achieved through other
> means less damaging to the right in question. In the process regard
> must be had to the provisions of section 33(1) [IC], and the underly-
> ing values of the Constitution, bearing in mind that, as a Canadian*

[1507] *Van der Walt*, Constitutional Property Clauses - A Comparative Analysis
(1999), 338.

[1508] With reference to the limitation of rights in Canada and Germany and
under the European Convention of Rights of 1950. However, the South African
Constitutional Court also asserted its independence at an early stage by observing that the way in which the criteria relating to the principle of proportionality, or more specifically the theory of interpretation and limitation of fundamental rights are applied in Germany and Canada "may well be of assistance"
to a South African court, but there was no reason to attempt to fit its analysis
into the Canadian mode (or the German, for that matter). See Kentridge J in *S v
Zuma* (note 501 above), par. 35; Chaskalson P in *S v Makwanyane* (note 363
above), par. 110.

[1509] *S v Makwanyane* (note 363 above).

[1510] *S v Makwanyane* (note 363 above), par. 104. Footnotes omitted.

Judge has said, "the role of the Court is not to second-guess the wisdom of policy choices made by legislators."

With this approach, the court on the one hand refrained from seriously considering the impact of the essential-content guarantee.[1511] On the other hand, the theory of a balancing of interests, which apparently encompasses the principle of proportionality, but also some other elements, was introduced.[1512] The factors mentioned in the *Makwanyane* case were later included in the limitation clause of the Final Constitution,[1513] thereby codifying the South African proportionality test within section 36(1) FC.[1514] Hence, a review of the structure of the general limitations clause is important for an understanding of the proportionality principle in South Africa.[1515] In the following sections, this issue will enjoy closer scrutiny. A distinction will also be made between proportionality and the balancing of interests, whereafter the function of proportionality and the balancing of interests in the South African constitutional context will be discussed.

3.4.3.1. Proportionality and the Limitation Clause

Together with section 7(3) FC, section 36 FC lays down the general requirements for limitations with regard to all the rights in the bill of rights. Briefly, these requirements entail that[1516] (i) the rights in the bill of rights are not absolute, even in principle, but can be limited in terms

---

[1511] See 362 ff. below for a more detailed discussion.

[1512] See *Blaauw-Wolf,* 1999 SAPR/PL, 203 for a more detailed discussion.

[1513] *Blaauw-Wolf,* 1999 SAPR/PL, 202 indicates that in both the *Makwanyane* decision (note 363 above) and the *Zuma* decision (note 501 above), the Constitutional Court made a number of key pronouncements which directly influenced the manner in which the limitation clause of the Final Constitution was formulated.

[1514] This test, as set out in the *Makwanyane* case (note 363 above), is strongly rooted in Canadian jurisprudence. However, there are strong indications that the German theory of *Verhältnismäßigkeit* influenced the development of the Canadian proportionality test through the jurisprudence of the European Court of Justice. In the *Makwanyane* case, reference is also made to the German and European Convention law in the discussion of proportionality.

[1515] See 264 above. See also *Woolman,* 1997 SAJHR, 102-134 for an analysis of the limitation clause.

[1516] *Van der Walt,* 1997 SAPR/PL, 314-315.

of the limitation provisions in section 36 FC, or elsewhere in the bill of rights;[1517] (ii) no law may limit a right entrenched in the bill of rights except as provided for in section 36(1) FC or elsewhere in the text of the Final Constitution;[1518] (iii) the rights in the bill of rights may be limited only in terms of law of general application;[1519] and (iv) the rights in the bill of rights may only be limited to the extent that the limitation is reasonable and justifiable in an open and democratic society based on human dignity, equality and freedom, taking into account all relevant factors, including those mentioned in section 36(1)(a) to (e) FC.[1520] It has been indicated[1521] that, contrary to the opinion held by some scholars,[1522] the general limitations clause applies in all cases of inquiry into the limitation of the rights to property. Consequently, it must be determined — in case of both deprivation as well as expropriation — whether the infringement was reasonable and justifiable in an open and democratic society based on human dignity, equality and freedom, taking into account all relevant factors including the nature of the right, the importance of the purpose of the limitation, the nature and extent of the limitation, the relation between the limitation and its purpose, and less restrictive means to achieve the purpose.[1523] This, in brief, is the South African version of the proportionality principle.[1524] There is, however, more to this principle than might meet the eye.

As opposed to the method of the German Federal Constitutional Court for limiting rights by applying the principle of proportionality, section 36(1) FC simultaneously circumscribes the legislature's capacity to limit fundamental rights and provides some guidelines for interpretation of this provision. The first part of the limitation clause, for instance, provides the constitutional reference for limitation by the legislature: [1525]

"The rights in the Bill of Rights may be limited only in terms of law *of general application* to the extent that the limitation is *reasonable*

[1517] See sec. 7(3) FC.

[1518] See sec. 36(2) FC.

[1519] See sec. 36(1) FC.

[1520] See sec. 36(1) FC.

[1521] 270 ff. above.

[1522] See in this regard also 93 ff., 271 ff. above.

[1523] Sec. 36(1) FC.

[1524] Contra *De Waal*, 1995 SAHJR, 7-8.

[1525] Sec. 36(1) FC. Emphasis added.

and justifiable *in an open and democratic society based on human dignity, equality and freedom.*"

The second part of section 36(1) FC provides that all relevant factors must be taken into account when limiting a fundamental right. These factors include the nature of the right, the importance of the purpose of the limitation, the nature and extent of the limitation, the relation between the limitation and its purpose, and less restrictive means to achieve the purpose. In this way, focus is placed on the interpretation of constitutional norms in a given case. Thus, two different aspects of the principle of proportionality are combined within section 36(1) FC, through the involvement of both the legislature and the courts.[1526]

The presence of a general limitation clause in a constitutional text need not mean that the proportionality principle has to be applied mechanically to the limitation of all rights and freedoms. The fact that the proportionality principle is also an instance of the constitutional state,[1527] together with the existence of a structure of specific limitation provisions[1528] within the constitution, requires that the proportionality inquiry can be adapted to the particularities of the clause under discussion. As a matter of course, proportionality in the case of socio-economic rights will differ from proportionality applied to material freedoms.

3.4.3.2. Proportionality and the Balancing of Interests

In spite of differences in formulation and application, the function of the proportionality principle in South Africa remains similar to that of Germany, namely to examine the question whether the purpose of a specific limitation is proportionate in view of its consequences. In this regard, the following remark[1529] of Chaskalson, P in the *Makwanyane* case needs closer scrutiny:

> "*Principles can be established, but the application of those principles to particular circumstances can only be done on a case by case basis. This is inherent in the requirement of proportionality, which calls for the balancing of different interests.*"

[1526] *Blaauw-Wolf*, 1999 SAPR/PL, 210-211.

[1527] See 123 ff. above.

[1528] See 265 ff. above.

[1529] *S v Makwanyane* (note 363 above), par. 104.

This statement seems to equate proportionality with the balancing of interests in the South African context. However, the construction of a *balancing of interests* could be misleading and have different meanings, depending on the circumstances:[1530]

(i) The weighing up of competing values could be regarded as a balancing of interests, in the sense that one interest or right takes precedence over another and that the preference determines that the other interest or right is subordinate and should give way to the one taking priority.[1531] Woolman[1532] refers to this type of balancing as "the 'head-to-head' comparison of competing rights, values or interests," which can assume the form of a balancing of one right, interest or value against another. There are indications of such an approach in the *Makwanyane* case.[1533] However several points of criticism can be brought against this approach.[1534] For one, if different constitutional norms are weighted and ranked, and some regarded as more important than others, the inner cohesion of the principles upon which the Constitution rests is endangered. The equality of fundamental rights and the basic premises of democracy are played off against each other, thereby seriously compromising the notion of the constitutional state. Furthermore, an interpretation which allows for one interest or right to take precedence over another, resulting in the subordination of one right to another, does not comply with the requirement that all the rights in the bill of rights must be respected and promoted in the process. Such a balancing of interests could at most have its foundation in secondary considerations and is not directly based upon an analysis "in conformity with the Constitution."[1535]

[1530] *Blaauw-Wolf,* 1999 SAPR/PL, 178.

[1531] *Blaauw-Wolf,* 1999 SAPR/PL, 213. She equates this approach with the *Güterabwägung* of German jurisprudence and indicates (at 199) that, although it is followed by some administrative and civil courts in Germany, this approach is controversial and has not been endorsed by the Federal Constitutional Court (BVerfGE 7, 198, 208 ff.). Only a few academics support this theory in a constitutional context. Many eminent academics have rejected this theory out of hand. See 292 above.

[1532] *Woolman,* 1997 SAJHR, 102-103.

[1533] See the discussion of *Blaauw-Wolf,* 1999 SAPR/PL, 206-208.

[1534] *Blaauw-Wolf,* 1999 SAPR/PL, 214-215.

[1535] See 119 ff. above.

(ii) The court could alternatively opt for an approach that would attain a harmonious concretisation or practical concordance of the relevant provisions. In the terminology of Woolman,[1536] this would be the procedure of "striking a balance" between competing rights or interests. This kind of "optimisation" of the relevant provisions would mean that each of the relevant provisions co-influences the solution of the disputing rights *without* ranking them.[1537] The German theory of *praktische Konkordanz* can here provide valuable examples.[1538]

(iii) Another possible approach can be found in the method of interpretation "in conformity with the Constitution."[1539] Upon a comparison of the German counterpart rule of an interpretation giving effect to the *"innere Einheit"* of the constitutional text,[1540] this approach would mean that a statutory provision must be interpreted in such a manner that it complies with the normative principles endorsed by the Constitution: If it is possible to interpret a statutory provision in more than one way, the interpretation which is in conformity with the Constitution should be preferred. This principle of constitutional interpretation links the interpretation of legal norms (*Normauslegung*) with a judicial inquiry into the constitutionality of the legal provisions (*Normenkontrolle*). If the point of departure is that the Constitution is supreme and that all the branches of state authority are bound to respect, promote, and fulfil the rights in the Bill of Rights, the constitutional text is, as a matter of course, the most important source for the concretisation of fundamental rights. This is probably also the meaning that Van der Walt[1541] attaches to interest-balancing when explaining that "[i]n the Constitution there are reasons for the protection of rights and for the limitation of rights, and the proportionality question involves a balancing or consideration of the relative weight of these reasons in the specific context."

The term *proportionality*, on the other hand, is usually described in less uncertain terms. In terms of German[1542] and Canadian[1543] jurisprudence,

---

[1536] *Woolman*, 1997 SAJHR, 102-103.

[1537] *Blaauw-Wolf*, 1999 SAPR/PL, 214.

[1538] See 262 above.

[1539] *Blaauw-Wolf*, 1999 SAPR/PL, 214. See also 119 above.

[1540] BVerfGE 8, 210, 221; BVerfGE 34, 165, 199 ff.

[1541] *Van der Walt*, 1997 SAPR/PL, 321-322.

[1542] See 125 ff., 289 ff. above.

it consists of three elements:[1544] (i) The limitation must be necessary *(erforderlich)* to promote the public purpose served by it. (ii) The limitation must be suitable *(geeignet)* to promote or serve that purpose. (iii) Finally, the limitation must be moderate *(zumutbar)* — or rather, it must not be disproportionate — in its effects. There are strong indications that the test as formulated in the Makwanyane case,[1545] and "codified" in section 36(1) FC are based on German and Canadian jurisprudence, even though Chaskalson, P expressed his reservations concerning the use of foreign jurisprudence in this regard.[1546]

The fact that Chaskalson, P uses the process of interest-balancing to describe the proportionality test, as in the *dictum* quoted above, must indicate that the former concept is used rather in a figurative sense than in any of the legal-technical meanings that can be attached to it. Blaauw-Wolf explains:[1547]

> "It would appear, though, that the emphasis of the Court ... is no longer on the 'weighing of values' in the sense of the doctrine of Güterabwägung. Instead, the terminology of 'balancing of interests' is invoked in the context of the principle of proportionality. In this 'balancing process' the age-old likeness of Justitia and her scales which balances [sic] in favour of justice is used."

This view is endorsed by the dictum of Ackermann, J in the case of *De Lange v Smuts*,[1548] where an exposition of the application of section 36(1) FC is provided:

[1543] In the decision of *R v Oakes* (note 1076 above) it was held that, in order to be valid in terms of the general limitation clause (sec. 1 of the Canadian Charter of Rights and Freedoms, 1982), a limitation had to satisfy two separate requirements: (i) The limitation has to be aimed at an objective that is important enough to justify the limitation of the right. (ii) It has to be justified in terms of a proportionality test, which consists of three elements, i.e. that the limitation has to be rationally connected to the objective and designed to achieve that objective; that the means chosen to achieve the objective should impair the right as little as possible; and that there must be proportionality between the effect of the measures and the objective they are aimed at achieving.

[1544] See the summary of *Van der Walt*, 1997 SAPR/PL, 319.

[1545] See 353 above.

[1546] See 353 ff. above.

[1547] *Blaauw-Wolf*, 1999 SAPR/PL, 209.

[1548] *De Lange v Smuts* (note 505 above), par. 86-88.

"The balancing of different interests must still take place. On the one hand there is the right infringed, its nature; its importance in an open and democratic society based on human dignity, equality and freedom; and the nature and extent of the limitation. On the other hand there is the importance of the purpose of the limitation. In the balancing process and in the evaluation of proportionality one is enjoined to consider the relation between the limitation and its purpose as well as the existence of less restrictive means to achieve this purpose."

Inevitably, the conclusion must be that the term interest-balancing surfaces in several shapes and sizes in the process of determining the constitutional validity of specific interferences with fundamental rights. One can go even further and say that proportionality is a very specific kind of interest-balancing, which does not exclude other kinds of interest-balancing at other stages of the inquiry into the constitutional validity of a specific interference with a fundamental right such as property. This will be further elucidated in the following paragraphs.

3.4.3.3. Application of the Proportionality Test in the South African Context

It has been indicated above[1549] that the South African proportionality test as formulated in the *Makwanyane* case and codified in section 36(1) FC was to some extent based on the German and Canadian approaches towards the determination of the proportionality of interferences with fundamental rights. However, Blaauw-Wolf[1550] drew attention to the fact that the provisions of section 36(1) FC goes further — in some regards — than the "common" proportionality inquiries of Canada and Germany. According to this analysis, the conditions for a valid limitation of rights as set out by section 36(1) FC are: (i) that the restriction must be in terms of law of general application;[1551] (ii) that such a limita-

---

[1549] See 353 ff., 355 ff. above.

[1550] *Blaauw-Wolf*, 1999 SAPR/PL, 178 ff.

[1551] "Generally applicable law" can only be statutes made by the legislature and not administrative regulations or decrees. The reason for this provision is that the democratically elected legislature must authorise the limitation, being the organ of state endowed with legislative powers. However, the legislature must still remain within the ambit of what has been authorised by the Constitution: it may only restrict a fundamental right *to the extent* that the limitation

tion must be reasonable; and (iii) that it must be justifiable in an open and democratic society. The first criterion represents a formal requirement that must be met before the inquiry can proceed to the proportionality test. The other two criteria are comparable to the elements of the principle of proportionality: The requirement that it must be "justifiable", is comparable to the inquiry whether a limitation is suitable or appropriate to achieve a specific objective, whereas "reasonableness" requires that a limitation may not be arbitrary, unfair or based upon irrational considerations. Further, section 36(1)(e) FC, which provides that less restrictive means should be invoked to achieve the objective, could be compared with proportionality in the narrower sense according to German theory.[1552]

This approach tunes in with Woolman's[1553] plea for the rearrangement of the factors in section 36(1)(a) to (e) FC. It is correctly indicated that, for a proper limitation analysis, the factors mentioned in section 36(1) FC should be rearranged in the correct order. First, the nature of the right infringed should be considered, as this will determine the level of scrutiny to which a specific limitation is subjected. Thereafter, the importance of the purpose of the limitation should be considered in order to determine whether it serves the values of openness, democracy, human dignity, freedom, equality and all the other values underlying the bill of rights and the Constitution as a whole. Then the relation between the limitation and its purpose should be considered, as it makes sense to inquire about the means employed to achieve the objective in their rational relation to the achievement of the objective. Once this has been determined, one can consider whether less restrictive means to achieve the purpose exist. The inquiry into the nature and extent of the limitation only becomes important after all the other factors have been considered. This calls for a genuine balancing of the values at stake; a consideration of the compromise of social interests reached by the government. This exercise might place the court under immense political pressure, because it in principle involves a policy decision. It should therefore be the very last resort in deciding whether a specific limitation of a fundamental right is justified.

---

is reasonable and justifiable in an open and democratic society based on human dignity, equality and freedom. This implies that a fundamental right must be left intact insofar as these requirements are not met. Moreover, the limitation must apply generally and not solely to an individual case. See 317 above.

[1552] See 289 ff. above.

[1553] *Woolman,* 1997 SAJHR, 110-111.

This approach furthermore ties in neatly with the function of the proportionality test in German constitutional property law. *Verhältnismäßigkeit* itself is tested only in the last stage of the inquiry as to the constitutional validity of an interference with property, but it is connected to the so-called *Abstufung* ("scaling") of the social function of property in the constitutional context.[1554] According to this approach, legislature is given greater freedom to delimit the content of property and to define the restrictions on property where it has a function of specific social relevance. Moreover, the legislature has more latitude to define restrictions on interests that are further removed from the property holder's personal liberty.[1555] For example, investment-based interests are protected to a lesser degree in the consitutitonal context than an individual's interest in having a roof over his or her head. In landlord-tenant relations, for instance, rent control and other forms of tenant protection are almost routinely affirmed, because the tenant's interest is personal and intimately connected with personal liberty, while the landlord's interest usually is strictly economic.[1556] In other words, the social importance and function of property interests contribute to deciding upon the degree of restriction of the constitutional right to property that would be justifiable in a specific case. This is relevant especially where different rights come into conflict with each other.

This "scaling" of the kind of protection afforded to different proprietary interests can be important in the determination of the proportionality of a specific interference with property, but can also be employed much earlier in the investigation as to the justifiability of a specific interference with property. It harks back to the principles of the constitutional state and social state underlying the constitutional orders of both Germany and South Africa,[1557] and therefore can be important not only in the process of restriction of the constitutional right to property, but also in its interpretation.

Applied to the South African context, this approach would enable a process of "interest-balancing" earlier in the investigation as to the con-

---

[1554] See 296 ff. above. See also *Alexander*, "Two Experiences, Two Dilemmas" in *Maclean* (ed), Property and the Constitution (1999), 106.

[1555] See 296 ff. above.

[1556] *Alexander*, "Two Experiences, Two Dilemmas" in *Maclean* (ed), Property and the Constitution (1999), 106. This example is based on BVerfGE 68, 361 and BVerfGE 89, 1.

[1557] See 115 ff. above.

stitutional validity of a specific interference with property, by a consideration and balancing of the principles underlying the constitution and thus also the property clause of section 25 FC. This kind of interest-balancing should, however, not be confused with an inquiry into the proportionality of a specific interference with property, which will still constitute the final stage of a rather formal process of determining justifiability. Instead, the importance of protecting specific interests at stake in a given case should simply, without resorting to weighing or ranking, be considered against the basic principles of the constitutional and social state.

3.4.4. Maintenance of Essential Content Required?

The *essential content* requirement that appeared in section 33(1) IC[1558] was omitted in the limitations clause of the Final Constitution. This was due to the difficulties experienced by the Constitutional Court in determining the exact meaning of the essential content requirement in section 33(1)(b) IC, and the consequent reluctance of the court[1559] to pronounce on the matter. The ommission of the essential content requirement could mean that the drafters of the Final Constitution consciously intended to depart from the model anticipated by the Interim Constitution and the German example, in which the essence of the right and the principle of proportionality were harmonised. Instead, it appears that room is left for the Constitutional Court to weigh and rank rights, allowing for one right to take precedence over another and ousting the other in the process. If such an approach is followed, it could mean that in specific cases guaranteeing a certain right could lead to the dissolution of another guarantee — even to the extent that the innermost core of one right is denied for the sake of upholding another.[1560] In the following paragraphs, the problems with the essential content requirement are explained with reference to the Interim Con-

---

[1558] Sec. 33(1) IC: "The rights entrenched in this Chapter may be limited by law of general application, provided that such limitation-(a) shall be permissible only to the extent that it is-(i) reasonable; and (ii) justifiable in an open and democratic society based on freedom and equality; and (b) *shall not negate the essential content* of the right in question, and provided further that ..." Emphasis added.

[1559] See *S v Makwanyane* (note 363 above), par. 132, 167, 281, 283-286, 298.

[1560] *Blaauw-Wolf*, 1999 SAPR/PL, 205.

stitution. In addition the extent to which courts are still obliged to respect the inviolable core of each fundamental right under the Final Constitution is investigated.

3.4.4.1. The Essential Content Provision of the Interim Constitution

Section 33(1)(b) IC provided that

> *"The rights entrenched in [the chapter on fundamental rights] may be limited by law of general application provided that such limitation — ... (b) shall not negate the essential content of the right in question ... "*

This meant that a limitation, even if reasonable and necessary, could not destroy the basic core of a right by rendering it impossible for the right to serve its intended social function or by permanently preventing an individual from exercising the right. The *essential content* requirement thus ensured that there would be a final boundary beyond which a limitation would result in a denial of the right.[1561] In practice this point was seldom reached, as limitations generally did not aim to destroy the essential content of a right. In most constitutional cases, courts would limit themselves to the balancing of governmental and individual interests in order to ensure that the limitation employed was proportionate to the objective pursued. The courts would only turn to the essential content requirements as a final resort. In the *Makwanyane* case, involving the constitutionality of the death penalty, six judges[1562] considered the essential content requirement, but preferred to base their decisions on other grounds after balancing competing interests in the context of reasonableness and the values of an open and democratic society. Provincial decisions have adopted a similar approach.[1563]

[1561] *Erasmus* in *Van Wyk/Dugard et al. (eds)*, Rights and Constitutionalism (1996), 650.

[1562] *S v Makwanyane* (note 363 above), Chaskalson (par. 132-134); Ackermann (par. 167); Didcott (par. 175); Kentridge (par. 193-195); Mahomed (par. 298) and O'Regan (par. 343).

[1563] See *Jeeva v Receiver of Revenue* 1995 2 SA 433 (SECLD), 445D-H; *Khala v Minister of Safety and Security* (note 432 above), 227-228; *S v Majuva* 1994 4 SA 26 (CK), 317. Only Marais J in *S v Bhulwana* 1995 1 SA 509 (C), 511 and *Nortje v AG, Cape* 1995 2 SA 460 (C), 481-484 has held that a limitation negated the essential content of a right. That he reached this conclusion too hurriedly without first attempting to balance the interests of the respective par-

The meaning of the *essential content* inquiry has been the subject of speculation, and has given rise to several, often contrasting, opinions. In the case of *Nortje v AG, Cape*[1564] Marais J stated[1565] that:

> "*The test of whether or not the essential content of a right has been negated may sometimes be quantitative, sometimes qualitative, and sometimes both. Everything turns, I think on the nature of the rights and its raison d'etre.*"

In the *Makwanyane* case, Chaskalson P raised the question[1566] whether the requirement of essential content should be determined subjectively (from the point of view of the individual affected by the invasion of the right) or objectively (from the point of view of the nature of the right and its place in the constitutional order) or in some other way. This issue was not decided. However, Mahomed J in the same case declared[1567] that

> "*it is possible to consider a third angle which focuses on the distinction between the 'essential content' of a right and some other content. This distinction might justify a relative approach to the determination of what is the essential content of a right by distinguishing the essential core of the right from its peripheral outgrowth and subjecting 'as law of general application' limiting an entrenched right, to the discipline of not invading the core, as distinct from the peripheral outgrowth. In this regard, there may conceivably be a difference between rights which are inherently capable of incremental invasion and those that are not.*"

The essential content requirement in the Interim Constitution, therefore, created rather difficult obstacles of interpretation in the South African context. In the *Explanatory Memoranda on the Draft Bill of*

---

ties in the context of proportionality and the values of an open and democratic society, is borne out by the fact that other judges dealing with the similar issues (sec. *v Zuma* (note 501 above) and *Jeeva v Receiver of Revenue*, 445D-H) did not find that the essential content of a right had been negated.

[1564] *Nortje v AG, Cape* (note 1563 above).

[1565] *Nortje v AG, Cape* (note 1563 above), 484E.

[1566] *S v Makwanyane* (note 363 above), par. 132.

[1567] *S v Makwanyane* (note 363 above), par. 298.

Rights,[1568] the difficulties with the "traditional" essential content test is explained:

> *"[I]t is a test that is not easily loosened from its German moorings and courts are likely to devote too much of their interpretative energies to ascertaining the meaning of this phrase in German law."*

Woolman[1569] further indicates that the court was more concerned with circumventing this clause than in applying it to specific cases:

> *"That is, the Court has had to find a way to make the limitation clause work without having recourse to the 'essential content' requirement. The Court has discovered that there is nothing that the essential content requirement can do that cannot be accomplished by simply tightening the rest of the tests undertaken during limitation analysis."*

Although it is necessary to recognize that there is a core content of most rights that may not be destroyed by limitation, it is questionable whether the *essential content* requirement was a useful component of the South African limitation clause. The requirement of essential content as it was found in the Interim Constitution was, therefore, omitted from the Final Constitution's limitation clause.

3.4.4.2. Consequence of Excluding the Essential Content Requirement from the Final Constitution

It is difficult at this stage to assess what implications the omission of the *essential content* provision would have in realising the constitutional objectives in general. Should courts interpret the constitution as a textual unity, there are apparently sufficient checks and balances built into the constitutional text to compensate for the lack of an essential content clause. Some authors, however, regarded the exclusion of the essential content clause as unfortunate.[1570] Blaauw-Wolf[1571] explains:

[1568] *Technical Committee of Theme Committee Four*, Explanatory Memoranda on the Draft Bill of Rights (09.10.1995).

[1569] *Woolman*, 1997 SAJHR, 106.

[1570] *Rautenbach*, General Provisions of the South African Bill of Rights (1995), 105.

[1571] *Blaauw-Wolf*, 1999 SAPR/PL, 205.

> *"the principle of proportionality which in a sense 'superseded' the es-*
> *sential-content guarantee in German constitutional theory, has not*
> *been interpreted in a similar manner in South Africa, where it re-*
> *mains embedded in the norm requiring the essential content of a*
> *right to be left intact."*

The *lacuna* created in this manner could too easily be filled by applying a "balancing of interests" in the sense of weighing and ranking of rights, allowing one right to unconditionally take precedence over another, and dismissing other rights in the process. This would be analogous to the doctrine of *Güterabwägung* in German law, which is not generally accepted. The omission of the essential content requirement could lead to a subjective weighing and ranking of rights and interests which is not in the interest of legal certainty and methodological clarity.[1572]

De Waal, Currie and Erasmus,[1573] for example, explains that the limitation test of the Final Constitution stipulates an investigation into the *reasonableness and justifiability in an open and democratic society based on human dignity, equality and freedom* of the limitation. This requires proof that the law in question serves a constitutionally acceptable purpose and that there is sufficient proportionality between the harm done by the law (the infringement of fundamental rights) and the benefits it is designed to achieve (the purposes of the law).[1574] Subsequently, in the course of discussing one of the factors (more specifically, the *nature of the right*) to be identified within the South African version of the proportionality test, the authors remark:

> *"Some rights weigh more heavily than others. It will therefore more*
> [sic] *difficult to justify the infringement of such rights than other, less*
> *weighty rights. ... A right that is of particular importance to the con-*
> *stitution's ambition to create an open and democratic society based*
> *on human dignity, freedom and equality will carry a great deal of*
> *weight in the exercise of balancing rights against justifications for*
> *their infringement."*

[1572] Such an extension could, however, probably be challenged on the basis that the court would exceed the scope of its constitutional powers.

[1573] *De Waal/Currie/Erasmus*, Bill of Rights Handbook (1999), 150-159.

[1574] *De Waal/Currie/Erasmus*, Bill of Rights Handbook (1999), 150.

This distinction can even be undertaken on a more fundamental level. Venter,[1575] for instance, argues that some of the constitutional *values* are more fundamental than others. In his opinion, the constitutional value of human dignity is the most fundamental constitutional value (that is to say the "nuclear value"),[1576] whereas equality and freedom, being described as "processes" in section 1(a) FC, cannot be considered as quite on the same level as human dignity. The latter are therefore "supporting nuclear values".[1577] If such an approach is supported, the bill of rights could be open to the interpretation that rights supporting human dignity rank above all other rights, even if support of these rights would further the aims of achieving equality and advancing freedom.

Proponents of this line of thought usually overlook the fact that these values are inextricably linked to each other and to the fundamental rights depending on them. Their case studies barely go beyond the infringement of the right to life as considered in the *Makwanyane* case.[1578] Thus the need for a "symbiotic unison" between, for example, human dignity and equality,[1579] and also the dialectic of freedom and equality — which Du Plessis[1580] described as a constructive interpretative aid to constrain one-sidedness in the interpretation of inherently dualistic provisions — can be quite easily ignored. It is, therefore, advisable that

---

[1575] *Venter*, A Hierarchy of Constitutional Values - Constitution and Law Seminar Report (1997), 17.

[1576] Upon a reading of sec. 1(a) FC and sec. 10 FC.

[1577] *Venter*, A Hierarchy of Constitutional Values - Constitution and Law Seminar Report (1997), 18.

[1578] *De Waal/Currie/Erasmus*, Bill of Rights Handbook (1999), 153, 154-155, 156, 157, 158.

[1579] This term has been used by *Du Plessis*, 1996 Stell LR, 7, where it is explained that the working draft text of the Final Constitution is, like the Interim Constitution, still strongly oriented towards equality. Nevertheless, it is explained, the text is wary of the interaction necessary between the concepts of human dignity and equality: "Equality transcends mathematical equations: it needs 'flesh and blood' to breathe a spirit conducive to the promotion of what is peculiarly human."

[1580] *Du Plessis*, 1996 Stell LR, 7. There it is explained that equality is also counterbalanced by freedom, "because it occurs in a dialectical relationship with freedom in key-provisions of the Bill of Rights" and because the achievement of equality is made a "fundamental goal on one footing with the advancement of (human) freedoms" in the working draft text of the Final Constitution.

the directives provided by Chaskalson P[1581] in the *Makwanyane* case itself,[1582] are followed:

> "*The fact that different rights have different implications for democracy, and in the case of our Constitution, for 'an open and democratic society based on freedom and equality,' means that there is no absolute standard which can be laid down for determining reasonableness and necessity.* Principles can be established, but the application of those principles to particular circumstances can only be done on a case by case basis. *This is inherent in the requirement of proportionality, which calls for the balancing of different interests.*"

The court, with the use of the term *balancing of interests* here probably intended a concept similar to that of *Verhältnismäßigkeit* and not really balancing-by-ranking, as is the case with *Güterabwägung*. This becomes clear when the court explains:[1583]

> "*In the balancing process, the relevant considerations will include the nature of the right that is limited, and its importance to an open and democratic society based on freedom and equality; the purpose for which the right is limited and the importance of that purpose to such a society; the extent of the limitation, its efficacy, and particularly where the limitation has to be necessary, whether the desired ends could reasonably be achieved through other means less damaging to the right in question. In the process regard must be had to the provisions of section 33(1), and the underlying values of the Constitution, bearing in mind that, as a Canadian Judge has said, 'the role of the Court is not to second-guess the wisdom of policy choices made by legislators'.*"

The situation that could arise in the context of land reform legislation and governmental reform policy (where constitutionality of the legislation or administrative action will have to be determined by weighing up the protection of existing property rights against the socio-economic rights created in support of security of land tenure, as well as the promotion of land restitution and redistribution), has not yet been considered against the issue of a ranking of rights. Nevertheless the compromise between liberty and equality in this context has kept the negotiators and drafters of the Constitution busy until practically the last mo-

---

[1581] *S v Makwanyane* (note 363 above), par. 104.

[1582] Emphasis added.

[1583] *S v Makwanyane* (note 363 above), par. 104.

ments of the drafting process.[1584] Surely here the "hierarchy conception" of constitutional values and fundamental rights will not be of much help in striking a balance between the rights and freedoms affected. Moreover, the ranking of fundamental rights could encourage a subjective assessment of constitutional norms, which would amount to legal uncertainty and thus to a denial of the constitutional state concept itself.[1585]

3.4.4.3. Implicit Adherence to the Essential Content Requirement?

The importance of the essential content requirement lies in the fact that it is a *Schranken-Schranke*, to use the German terminology: No matter how urgent the government's objectives may be, there is a point beyond which the government may not go in limiting the rights enshrined in the Constitution. The essential content requirement achieves this by focussing on the detrimental effect of a specific restriction of a fundamental right, rather than on the means and objectives of the restriction.[1586]

The requirement that a limitation should not negate the essential content of a right is undoubtedly controversial. However, in many of the fundamental rights provisions there is a core element that cannot be limited without destroying the intended social function of the right.[1587] The elimination of the essential content requirement means that the courts will have to devise another method for ensuring that the fundamental rights enshrined in the constitution are not undermined by an

---

[1584] See 60 and 64 above.

[1585] See 295 above. Also *Blaauw-Wolf*, 1999 SAPR/PL, 205.

[1586] *Woolman*, 1997 SAJHR, 106-107.

[1587] E.g., while many of the provisions of sec. 25 IC, dealing with the rights of detained, arrested and accused persons, could be limited where such limitation was according to law and was reasonable and necessary in an open and democratic society based on freedom and equality, the denial of the right of *habeas corpus* contained in sec. 25(1)(e) IC would destroy the foundation of sec. 25 IC and sec. 11(1) IC. The case is similar with sec. 11(2) IC which prohibits "torture of any kind, whether physical, mental or emotional." While certain methods of lawful police interrogation and imprisonment might cause mental stress amounting to mental and emotional torture, which might be justified as a lawful limitation, there must surely be a threshold of mental and physical torture beyond the protection of a limitation clause and which can never be justified.

unduly deferential limitation test.[1588] The crucial question is whether the courts are still under the Final Constitution compelled to concern themselves with the determination of what the inviolable core of any given fundamental rights is or should be.

The *nature of the right* was one of the limitation factors identified in the *Makwanyane* case, and later incorporated into the limitations clause of the Final Constitution.[1589] The *Explanatory Memoranda on the Draft Bill of Rights*[1590] suggested an "alternative" *essential content* test,[1591] requiring that the limitation should not be incompatible with the *nature of the right*. This emphasises that the interests of society in the restriction of a right are not the only consideration. The nature of the right itself should also be considered. Complete restriction of a right will never be compatible with the nature of the right.

Thus, the essential content requirement is, under the Final Constitution, built into the proportionality inquiry.[1592] This would mean that, even in the absence of a stipulation like section 33(1)(b) IC, the abolition of property as an institution would be in conflict with the proportionality principle contained in the limitation clauses of both the Interim and Final Constitution.[1593] However, this conclusion is based on the assumption that section 36(1) FC — and therewith also the provision as to the nature of the right — applies to the constitutional property clause. The following paragraphs will indicate that this assumption is also well founded, by analysing the South African courts' attempts to apply the validity requirements for interferences with property to a specific case.

[1588] *Woolman*, 1997 SAJHR, 107.

[1589] See 363 above.

[1590] *Technical Committee of Theme Committee Four*, Explanatory Memoranda on the Draft Bill of Rights (09.10.1995).

[1591] The so-called *compatibility test* based on art. 4 of the International Covenant on Economic, Social and Cultural Rights.

[1592] See 352 above.

[1593] *Kleyn*, 1996 SAPR/PL, 433.

3.5. The South African Judiciary's Attempts to Distinguish between Deprivation and Expropriation

From recent case law it seems as if the South African courts, like their counterparts in many jurisdictions, are willing to accept the notion of regulatory expropriation.[1594] If the "grey area" of regulatory expropriation or "inverse condemnations" between the constructions of *deprivation* and *expropriation* is not treated with circumspection, it might have a detrimental effect on the land reform initiative, because of the heavy burden on the state for compensation of impositions on property.[1595]

The effectiveness of the courts' approach will depend on the clarity with which they are able to construct and define the category of regulatory expropriations and the consequences of such actions for the parties involved. For this purpose, the interpretation clause[1596] and the limitations clause[1597] would be important. The factors that could play a role in delimiting a category of regulatory expropriations (like (i) the purpose of the regulation, (ii) the history and social function of the property involved, (iii) the effect of the regulation on society at large, and so on), could be identified with reference to the values and considerations underlying these provisions.[1598]

3.5.1. Harksen v Lane NO

An attempt at elucidating the distinction between regulation (deprivation) of property and expropriation has been made by the South African Constitutional Court in *Harksen v Lane NO*.[1599] The case involved the vesting of the property of the solvent spouse in the Master in terms

---

[1594] *Van der Walt*, Constitutional Property Clauses - A Comparative Analysis (1999), 336. See also the discussion of *Steinberg v South Peninsula Municipality* 2001 4 SA 1243 (SCA) at 379 ff. below.

[1595] *Chaskalson*, 1993 SAJHR, 407-408, 411; *Chaskalson*, 1994 SAJHR, 134-136.

[1596] Sec. 35 IC; sec. 39 FC.

[1597] Sec. 33 IC; sec. 36 FC.

[1598] *Van der Walt*, Constitutional Property Clauses - A Comparative Analysis (1999), 336.

[1599] *Harksen v Lane* (note 820 above).

of section 21(1)[1600] of the Insolvency Act. It was contended that section 21 of the Insolvency Act was in conflict with the equality guarantee[1601] and the property guarantee[1602] of the Interim Constitution. With regard to the property guarantee in particular, the applicant argued that section 21(1) of the Insolvency Act constituted an *expropriation* of the solvent spouse's property without any provision for compensation. The court thus had to decide, *inter alia*, whether section 21(1) of the Insolvency Act amounted to an expropriation in terms of the Interim Constitution, in which case it would not be justifiable, as the legislation did not provide for compensation.

In deciding that this provision did not amount to an expropriation of property, Goldstone J pointed out that the distinction between deprivation and expropriation of property, as it was described in sections 28(2) and 28(3) IC, has long been recognised in South African law.[1603] An analysis of this issue in other jurisdictions also indicates that this question is not peculiar to the South African context.[1604] On the basis of the authority quoted in this context, the court showed that the main difference between deprivation and expropriation was the fact that the former does not require that rights in property *must be acquired by a*

[1600] Sec. 21(1) of the Insolvency Act: "The additional effect of the sequestration of the separate estate of one of two spouses who are not living apart under a judicial order of separation shall be to vest in the Master, until a trustee has been appointed, and, upon the appointment of a trustee, to vest in him all the property (including property or the proceeds thereof which are in the hands of a sheriff or a messenger under a writ of attachment) of the spouse whose estate has not been sequestrated (hereinafter referred to as the solvent spouse) as if it were property of the sequestrated estate, and to empower the Master or trustee to deal with such property accordingly, but subject to the following provisions of this section." The remaining subsections of sec. 21 of the Insolvency Act provide for the interests of the solvent spouse to be safeguarded in certain ways. Property of the solvent spouse may be released by the trustee in certain circumstances.

[1601] Sec. 8 IC.

[1602] Sec. 28 IC.

[1603] As authority for this view, the case of *Beckenstrater v Sand River Irrigation Board* (note 1499 above), 515A-C is mentioned by the court.

[1604] *Harksen v Lane* (note 820 above), par. 33 (Zimbabwe): *Hewlett v Minister of Finance* (note 1499 above); *Davies v Minister of Lands, Agriculture and Water Development* (note 1499 above); *Harksen v Lane* (note 820 above), par. 34 (India): *HD Vora v State of Maharashtra* 1984 AIR 866 SC, 869.

public authority for a public purpose, which characterises the infringement in the latter case.[1605] A deprivation of rights in property, which did not include *transfer of ownership*, did in other words not amount to an expropriation.

By this reasoning, the *Harksen* decision has by no means cleared up the dogmatic confusion that exists with regard to the distinction between deprivation and expropriation of property. The court's approach has been criticised for being too restrictive and lacking in sophistication.[1606] Fundamental differences exist between the situation in the *Harksen* case and the decisions quoted as authority by the court.[1607] Moreover, the distinction between deprivation and expropriation is more complex. With reference to the Interim Constitution, against which section 21 of the Insolvency Act was tested in the *Harksen* case, the contrast between sections 28(3) and (2) IC made it apparent that expropriation had to be distinguished from deprivation of property in that expropriations were subject to additional requirements not applicable to deprivations. The Interim Constitution thus guaranteed that no deprivation of (rights in) property would be permitted otherwise than *in accordance with a law*. In the case of expropriation, further requirements had to be met: The expropriation had to be *for a public purpose* and against payment of *compensation*. Appropriation by the expropriator, being a public authority is not mentioned as a requirement in the Interim Constitution.

This does not necessarily mean that the court was wrong in finding that section 21 of the Insolvency Act did not constitute an expropriation. However, Van der Walt[1608] has summarised the main problem with the *Harksen* decision well when remarking that

> "The essential issue ... is that the purpose of the vesting of property in the master or trustee in terms of section 21 of the [Insolvency Act] resembles the logic of a forfeiture or a confiscation of property more closely than it resembles the logic of an expropriation, and conse-

---

[1605] *Harksen v Lane* (note 820 above), par. 32, 33, 34.

[1606] *Van der Walt*, Constitutional Property Clauses - A Comparative Analysis (1999), 338.

[1607] See *Van der Walt/Botha*, 1998 SAPR/PL, 21-22 for a discussion of the authority.

[1608] *Van der Walt*, Constitutional Property Clauses - A Comparative Analysis (1999), 338-339.

quently the procedural and evidential purpose and character of these provisions should have enjoyed more attention."

The reasoning of the court in the *Harksen* case already indicates that section 21 of the Insolvency Act has a regulatory, rather than an expropriatory character. Goldstone J explained that the purpose of section 21 of the Insolvency Act was to enable the master or trustee to ensure, for the sake of creditors of the insolvent estate, that property belonging to the insolvent estate should not be transferred unlawfully or fraudulently to the solvent spouse's separate estate. It therefore places the burden of proof of ownership upon the solvent spouse.[1609] Thus, this section protects the public interest by ensuring that property of an insolvent estate is available for fair distribution, and that property is not fraudulently disguised or withheld.

The eminent legal question in the *Harksen* case should have been whether the temporary and preventive vesting of the solvent spouse's property could be regarded as a valid *regulation (deprivation)* of the rights in that property;[1610] and not whether such a temporary vesting amounted to an *expropriation*. This question was never considered, due probably to the applicant's heads of argument, which did not raise this issue in the course of the proceedings.[1611] Instead, the applicant chose to build her attack only upon averments that the vesting amounted to an expropriation. The *Harksen* case could have been of considerable importance for restructuring the South African property law order if only the court had been able to investigate the more complex question whether the vesting of the solvent spouse's property in the master or trustee was a regulatory measure intended to protect innocent creditors of the insolvent estate and whether this regulation was reasonable and justifiable in terms of the general limitation provisions of the Interim Constitution.[1612]

[1609] *Harksen v Lane* (note 820 above), par. 35.

[1610] See *Van der Walt/Botha*, 1998 SAPR/PL,17-41.

[1611] *Van der Walt*, Constitutional Property Clauses - A Comparative Analysis (1999), 337.

[1612] *Van der Walt*, Constitutional Property Clauses - A Comparative Analysis (1999), 339.

3.5.2. Conjunctive Reading, Interest-balancing and Proportionality

The point of departure is of immense importance in any inquiry into the constitutional validity of an interference with property. In the following paragraphs, the *Harksen* case is used as an example of how the outcome of a decision is dependant on the initial assumptions in approaching a specific problem. To further illustrate this point, one could attempt to solve the problem posed to the court in the *Harksen* case by approaching it from another angle: Instead of focusing on the question considered by the court in that case (that is, whether section 21 of the Insolvency Act constituted expropriation of property which should be compensated), the following analysis will turn on the question whether section 21 of the Insolvency Act represents a justifiable deprivation of property.

As has been indicated,[1613] the disjunctive reading of section 25 FC and section 36 FC stands or falls with the acceptability of the solution this approach provides to the issue of the reversibility of a decision that a specific interference with property is constitutionally justifiable.[1614] A disjunctive reading of section 25 FC and section 36 FC either results in the conclusion that the proportionality principle contained in section 36 FC is not at all applicable to the constitutional property clause, or that section 36 FC provides the parties with another change, in the form of an additional "third stage" of the inquiry, to contest (or support) the justifiability of a specific interference with property. Van der Walt[1615] argues that these solutions are logically untenable:

> *"The problem is that the general limitation provisions in section 36 cannot and should not be regarded as a kind of default, add-on test that complements the specific limitation test in section 25 — the relationship between the two should be a much more integrated one."*

An analysis of the question which should have been raised in the *Harksen* case (that is to say, whether section 21 of the Insolvency Act constitutes a justifiable deprivation of property) from a disjunctive reading of section 25 FC and section 36 FC indicates that it would probably not effect a reversal of a decision regarding the (in)validity of an interference with property. A deprivation of property that is not in terms of a law of general application as required by section 25(1) FC

[1613] See the discussions at 93 ff., 108 ff., 270 ff. above.

[1614] *Van der Walt*, 1997 SAPR/PL, 326 ff. provides a good overview.

[1615] *Van der Walt*, 1997 SAPR/PL, 326-327.

would also not pass the test of section 36(1) FC, as the same requirement appears in the latter provision.[1616] For present purposes, it is more
interesting to determine how the requirement of non-arbitrariness in
section 25(1) FC can be distinguished from the proportionality test of
section 36(1) FC. Both an inquiry into the compliance with the requirement of non-arbitrariness and an analysis of the proportionality of
the interference with property brought about by section 21 of the Insolvency Act depends on a process of interest-balancing:

(i) First, the interference brought about by section 21 of the Insolvency
Act would comply with the requirement of non-arbitrariness as set in
section 25(1) FC in that (i) there is a reason justifiying the interference;
(ii) there is a rational connection between the interference and the purpose, and (iii) there are certain procedural safeguards in favour of the
person whose proprietary interests had been infringed. In the case of
Harksen, there would be a rational connection between the interference
(that is, the temporary attachment of the assets of the solvent spouse)
and the purpose of the interference (the need to establish an inventory
of assets belonging to the insolvent spouse). The reason for the interference establishes the rational connection between interference and purpose: the need to avoid the situation in which the claims of creditors in
liquidation proceedings are paralysed because of the indeterminability
of the assets of the insolvent person. Here, the broader public interest
(in the sense of the interests of the creditors and other stakeholders)
would seem to overshadow the interests of the individual (in this case
the solvent spouse whose assets are temporarily attached). Moreover,
through certain procedural safeguards (namely, the solvent spouse's opportunity to prove ownership of the temporarily attached assets in order to win them back) the interests of the individual enjoy the most optimal protection that can be afforded to him or her in view of the circumstances of the case and the importance of the interests of the public
at large. In answering the question as to compliance with the requirement of non-arbitrariness, the interests of the public at large and the individual seemingly form part of the inquiry. However, it is important to
note that an outright "balancing of interests" is not at the order of the
day. Much rather, the interest-balancing that does take place this early
in the inquiry, is a "subconscious" result of a consideration of the reason for the interference, the rational connection between the interference and its purpose, and the procedural safeguards that exist.

[1616] See 317 ff. above.

(ii) On another level, section 21 of the Insolvency Act would also have passed the scrutiny of the proportionality test (as codified in section 36(1)FC) upon more-or-less the same considerations as those which indicate compliance with the non-arbitrariness requirement of section 25(1) FC as discussed above. When the "true" proportionality of a specific interference is brought into play, and section 21 of the Insolvency Act must be found to be reasonable and justifiable in an open and democratic society, based on human dignity, freedom and equality, with adherence to the factors listed in section 36(1)(a) to (e) FC, the balancing process is apparently more outright, or less "subconscious". As such, it could also be more enticing to resort to a second-guessing of the wisdom of policy choices made by the legislature. Section 25 FC, with its specific requirements for the constitutional validity of an interference with property, therefore gives effect to the proportionality test of section 36 FC in the context of the constitutional property guarantee.

Several conclusions can be drawn from the analysis above. For one, it should indicate that a reversal of a finding as to the constitutional validity of an interference with property cannot be effected by a disjunctive reading of section 25 FC and section 36 FC. Instead, it is evident that the relationship between section 25 FC and section 36 FC can never be ignored. Conjunctive reading of the general limitations clause of section 36 FC and the specific limitation provisions within section 25 FC specifies and confirms the application of the proportionality test in the context of the constitutional property clause. It also indicates that the point of departure should not be that something "less than property" is protected from the outset.[1617] However, the relationship between section 25 FC and section 36 FC is not static. The mere presence of the interest-balancing procedure, regardless of whether it takes place consciously or subconsciously, introduces an element of flexibility in the process of determining the constitutional validity of an interference with property. This is what the "application of ... principles to particular circumstances ... on a case by case basis"[1618] is all about.

In short, therefore, an approach to the issue in the *Harksen* case which would have taken notice of the need for a balancing of interests on a case to case basis, and which would have combined this awareness with

---

[1617] See the discussion at 93 ff., 108 ff. above.

[1618] Chaskalson, P in *S v Makwanyane* (note 363 above), par. 104. See also 355 above.

a conjunctive reading of section 25 FC and section 36 FC, would have resulted in a finding correcting the argument regarding the arbitrariness of the provision[1619] and coupling the reasoning with the principle of proportionality. This process would also have illustrated that the balancing of interests can operate on different levels. This could, in particular, have influenced the manner in which the operation of the property clause on a horizontal level — in the resolution of the conflicting rights of private persons — could be perceived.

3.5.3. Constructive Expropriation

In view of the court's difficulty with distinguishing between actions of deprivation and actions amounting to expropriation of property, it is necessary to consider the existence of constructive (or indirect) expropriation within the South African legal framework.[1620] Constructive expropriation refers to actions of the state that do not qualify formally or explicitly as expropriation, but that imposes such strong regulation of private property that it is considered fair either to treat the deprivation as an expropriation and require payment of compensation, or to invalidate the deprivation. The Constitutional Court's rigid approach to the distinction between expropriation and deprivation in the *Harksen* case tends to suggest that a doctrine of constructive expropriation does not form part of South African law.[1621] The stance of the Supreme Court of Appeal in *Steinberg v South Peninsula Municipality*[1622] suggests the opposite.[1623]

[1619] See 323 ff. above.

[1620] *Van der Walt* has done much of the groundwork in this regard. See e.g. the forthcoming discussion "Moving Towards Recognition of Constructive Expropriation", 2002 THRHR, which entails an analysis of *Steinberg v South Peninsula Municipality* 2001 4 SA 1243 (SCA), and which forms the basis of the analysis above. I am grateful to André van der Walt for giving me access to the unpublished manuscript of this article.

[1621] See also *Southwood*, Compulsory Acquisition of Rights (2000), 14-15.

[1622] *Steinberg v South Peninsula Municipality* (note 1620 above).

[1623] *Van der Walt* (note 1620 above) explains that the Constitutional Court's absolute or categorical approach to the distinction between deprivation and expropriation of property in the *Harksen* case (note 820 above), appears from its treatment of the question whether the state actually acquired the property involved. This precludes the development of a doctrine of constructive expro-

The latter case involved a road scheme which was proclaimed and approved over the appellant's property between 1969 and 1974. The existence of the road scheme places no obligation on the part of the local authority to implement the scheme, or to build a road in terms of it. However, should the road scheme be implemented, it would necessitate expropriation of at least a part of the appellant's land. Although the appellant was aware of the existence of the road scheme when she purchased and took transfer of the land between 1994 and 1997, she later approached the court with the complaint that the existence of the road scheme diminished the value of her property to such an extent that she could not sell or develop the property. She therefore requested that the local authority be forced by court order to complete the expropriation of her property.[1624] In short, the appellant's arguments were that the road scheme proclaimed and approved by the local authority does not constitute a proper expropriation, but rather amounts to a constructive expropriation, and as such entitles her to a remedy in terms of section 25 FC.[1625] The court, however, dismissed her application, on the basis that the approval of the road amounted to nothing more than[1626]

> "advance notification of a possible intention to construct a road, which, if implemented, would result in a taking."

In the course of its decision, the court dwells upon the question whether the doctrine of constructive expropriation is part of South African law, in view of the clear distinction drawn in the South African constitution between deprivations and expropriations of property. Constructive expropriation is understood as a principle in terms of which deprivations of property would under certain circumstances give rise to an obligation to compensate the deprived owner, even though no rights vested in the institution effecting the deprivation.[1627] As such, it forms the "grey area" between deprivation and expropriation. The court then reasons that, despite the clear distinction between deprivation and expropriation in section 25 FC, there may be room for the development of a doctrine akin to constructive expropriation, in particu-

---

priation to a large degree (although not completely), since "the development of such a doctrine depends on the notion that the distinction represents two points on a continuum rather than two watertight categories".

[1624] *Steinberg v South Peninsula Municipality* (note 1620 above), par. 1.

[1625] As summarized by *Van der Walt* (note 1620 above).

[1626] *Steinberg v South Peninsula Municipality* (note 1620 above), par. 9, 12.

[1627] *Steinberg v South Peninsula Municipality* (note 1620 above), par. 6.

lar where a public body utilises a regulatory power in a manner which, when considered in isolation, can be categorised as a deprivation of property rights and not an expropriation, but which has the (indirect) effect of transferring rights to the public body involved.[1628]

The court is cautious of showing outright support for the adoption of a general doctrine of constructive expropriation. The reasons advanced are the possible confusion that might be introduced into the law, and the possible adverse effect such a doctrine might have on the constitutional imperative of land reform embodied in section 25(4), (6) and (8) FC. Nevertheless, it is apparent from the decision that section 25 FC could be open to an interpretation supporting the doctrine of constructive expropriation, expecially in situations where no formal expropriation of property is at stake, but the owner is still deprived of property in such a way that the public body undertaking the transfer benefits from it either directly or indirectly. In cases where the owner is deprived of the property without that transfer to the public body takes place, for instance when the state's action would simply destroy or extinguish the owner's rights, the application of a doctrine of constructive expropriation may be more undesirable.

The pragmatic and theoretical considerations advanced by the court[1629] in taking this stance, need to be examined briefly. As far as the court's reservations concerning the introduction of confusing principles in South African law is concerned, the demands placed on legal interpretation by the new constitutional order needs to be taken into account. It is indicated above[1630] that judicial precedent about the concept expropriation should be treated with caution, especially as far as attaching a meaning to the terms public interest and public purposes is concerned.[1631] Van der Walt[1632] further argues that the demands on legal interpretation under the new constitutional order renders a categorical distinction between expropriation and deprivation undesirable:

> "[T]he new constitutional order demands a more flexible, context-sensitive approach to interpretation and not the abstract, definitional approach in terms of which the effects of a state action are deduced

---

[1628] *Steinberg v South Peninsula Municipality* (note 1620 above), par. 8.

[1629] *Steinberg v South Peninsula Municipality* (note 1620 above), par. 8.

[1630] See 331 ff. above.

[1631] Contra *Southwood*, Compulsory Acquisition of Rights (2000), 15.

[1632] *Van der Walt*, (note 1620 above).

from the abstract characteristics of the category into which it is classified."

In any event, the distinction between deprivation and expropriation of property is artificial, and a categorical approach to the issue might do more harm than can be expected, as is evident from the myriad of possibilities for confusing the law opened up by the reasoning in the *Harksen* case. Therefore, the approach favoured by Van der Walt[1633] seems to be more acceptable. This entails that deprivation and expropriation of property are regarded as "to two points on a [continuous line], with a wide area of shading over from one into the other in between."[1634] Admittedly, the "continuum approach" does not propose a single or even clear-cut principle according to which constructive expropriation cases may be determined. It does, however, provide a starting point from which to determine (on a case by case basis and by means of conjunctive reading and the process of interest-balancing)[1635] how constructive expropriation should be construed in the South African process, and in which cases it should be applicable.

As regards the court's concerns about the possible detrimental effects of constructive expropriation on land reform, several considerations indicate that fears might be exaggerated, albeit not completely without substance. For one, it is likely that constructive expropriation will be more important for purposes of protecting commercial property.[1636] Nevertheless, the land reform programme is so clearly endorsed by section 25 FC, and so extensively relies on the format of expropriation that it is unlikely to be detrimentally affected by the application of a doctrine of constructive expropriation, even in situations involving land reform.[1637] The most obvious instance where land reform might be influenced by reliance on the doctrine of constructive expropriation is the case where a landowner's existing rights or entitlements are curtailed by legislative provisions or administrative actions for the sake of giving effect to land reform objectives like security of tenure, or more equitable access to

---

[1633] *Van der Walt,* (note 1620 above).

[1634] *Van der Walt,* (note 1620 above) bases this approach on the decision of the United States' Supreme Court in *Pennsylvania Coal Co v Mahon* 260 US 393 (1922), which is also used as authority in the *Steinberg* case.

[1635] See 375 ff. above.

[1636] *Van der Walt,* (note 1620 above). See also *Van der Walt* in *Jackson/Wilde, Property Law: Current Issues and Debates* (1999), 208-280.

[1637] *Van der Walt,* (note 1620 above).

land. However, even in such instances an application of the continuum approach would be sensible, when effected with the process of interest-balancing underlying the constitutional protection and regulation of property in mind.[1638]

4. Limitation through "Horizontal" Application: the Conflicting Rights of Private Persons

Bills of Rights are usually regarded as having the primary function of protecting the rights of individuals against the state, in other words, having vertical operation only. The constitutional property clauses in Germany and in South Africa are constructed so as to address the vertical operation of these guarantees. Legislative and administrative interference with and regulation of property would be controlled by these provisions. So, too, would expropriation.

Fundamental rights can, however, also operate horizontally when they affect legal relationships between individuals. In Germany, this is the so-called *Drittwirkung* of fundamental rights on private relations. A distinction is usually drawn between direct and indirect horizontal operation: Indirect horizontality refers to the influence of the values projected through a bill of rights on statutory interpretation and the development of the law. This includes the private law, where the relations between private parties are regulated. Direct horizontality refers to a situation where the bill of rights would be the immediate and direct source of one individual's right against another. Indirect horizontal operation of fundamental rights is referred to in German constitutional law as *"mittelbare Drittwirkung"* and direct horizontal operation as *"unmittelbare Drittwirkung."*

Both in Germany and in South Africa, the general issues arising from horizontality can rightly be described as "subtle and ... the subject of considerable debate."[1639] However, within the general discussion, the operation of the constitutional property guarantees in the relations between private parties *inter se* is generally afforded no more than a cursory reference in legal writing, not only in Germany, but also in

---

[1638] See 375 ff. above.

[1639] As per Kentridge J, *Du Plessis and Others v De Klerk and Another* (note 432 above), par. 41.

South Africa. In the following paragraphs, an attempt will be made at providing an overview of the issue of horizontal operation with regard to the constitutional property guarantee, without addressing the general issues, which gave rise to so many disputes already.

4.1. German "Drittwirkung" and the Property Clause

Article 1 III GG determines that the basic rights in the German constitution "shall bind the legislature, the executive and the judiciary as directly enforceable law." Since a similar provision is not found in respect of private persons, many authors concluded that, in general, the Basic Law does not explicitly support direct horizontal operation of the basic rights. The wording of certain provisions may point to a direct operation of the basic rights provisions on private law,[1640] but these are exceptional cases. The Federal Constitutional Court[1641] and most authors are of the opinion that the fundamental rights in the German Basic Law operate with *indirect* horizontality.[1642] This means that basic rights do not solve disputes in the field of private law in *specific* cases, but operate as an objective value system, thus "influencing" the relations in private law. The Federal Constitutional Court refers to the "radiating effect" (*Ausstrahlungswirkung*) of the basic rights on private law,[1643] and remarks:[1644]

[1640] E.g. art. 9 III 2 GG, where the right to form associations "in order to safeguard and improve working and economic conditions" is guaranteed and where it is provided that agreements restricting or intended to hamper the exercise of this right shall be null and void; and measures to achieve such an end shall be illegal. BVerfGE 73, 261, 269. See further art. 20 IV GG and art. 38 I GG read with art. 48 II GG. These provisions are not Basic Rights in the formal sense, but they are regarded as "quasi-fundamental rights" (*grundrechtsgleiche Rechte)* in terms of art. 93 I 4a GG.

[1641] BVerfGE 7, 198 *(Lüth);* BVerfGE 30, 173 *(Mephisto);* BVerfGE 42, 143.

[1642] See e.g. *Von Münch/Kunig,* Grundgesetz-Kommentar I (1992), Vorb. Art. 1-19, m.n. 31; *Jarass/Pieroth,* Grundgesetz für die Bundesrepublik Deutschland (1995), art. 1 m.n. 22, 24; *Hesse,* Grundzüge des Verfassungsrechts (1993), 19th ed m.n. 355; BVerfGE 7, 198, 203-207; BVerfGE 7, 230, 233 ff.; BVerfGE 42, 143, 148.

[1643] BVerfGE 7, 198 *(Lüth)* 207.

[1644] Transl by *Kommers,* Constitutional Jurisprudence of Germany (1997), 363-364.

*"The influence of the scale of values of the basic rights affects par-
ticularly those provisions of private law that contain mandatory rules
of law and thus form part of the* ordre public — *in the broad sense of
the term — that is, rules which for reasons of the general welfare also
are binding on private legal relationships and are removed from the
domination of private intent. Because of their purpose these provisions are closely related to the public law they supplement. Consequently, they are substantially exposed to the influence of constitutional law. In bringing this influence to bear, the courts may invoke
the general clauses which, like Article 826 of the Civil Code, refer to
standards outside private law. "Good morals" is one such standard.
In order to determine what is required by social norms such as these,
one has to consider first the ensemble of value concepts that a nation
has developed at a certain point in its intellectual history and laid
down in its constitution. That is why the general clauses have rightly
been called the points where basic rights have breached the [domain
of] private law ..."*

The "radiating effect" of the basic rights therefore means that, in interpreting concepts such as "justified," "wrongful," or "*contra bonos mores*" in the course of private litigation, the German courts have to take
the basic rights into account.[1645] The basic rights therefore have a "radiating effect" on the private law through provisions such as paragraph
138 BGB, which provides that legal acts which are "contrary to public
policy" are void.[1646] The basic rights can, similarly, be applied to other
rules of private law where the meaning is unclear.[1647] Through indirect
horizontal application, the whole body of existing law in German is
subject to cautious reform within its own framework.

[1645] *Pieroth/Schlink*, Grundrechte - Staatsrecht II (1994), 51 m.n. 193.

[1646] BVerfGE 73, 261, 269. See further e.g. par. 157 BGB, par. 242 BGB and
par. 826 BGB.

[1647] BVerfGE 7, 198, 206 ff.; BVerfGE 34, 269, 280; BVerfGE 54, 117, 124. See
further BVerfGE 89, 214 for an example of the application of the "general" provisions of par. 138 BGB as well as par. 242 BGB (which obliges the debtor to
perform in good faith) as a medium through which indirectly to apply art. 2 I
GG (guaranteeing a person's private autonomy) to a contract of suretyship. The
court struck down the suretyship, in which the surety had undertaken an exceptionally high risk without obtaining any benefit in the credit supplied, because the bank had failed to inform the surety about the nature and scope of her
obligations, thus violating the principle of contractual equality.

In the German context, the importance of the institutional guarantee[1648] of property explains the "radiating effect" of the constitutional guarantee of property best.[1649] When legislature determines the content and limits of property in the course of exercising its capacity in terms of article 14 I 2 GG, it is compelled to take the institution of property into account. The same is expected of the adminstration and judiciary in the exercise of their functions.

The principles pertaining to indirect horizontal operation of the property guarantee can be "translated" into the property context with reference to the protection of landlords and tenants under the Basic Law. The concept of property in the constitutional context is arguably wide enough to include personal rights like those created in a contract of lease. Consequently, this could mean that the constitutional guarantee of property has to be taken into account by legislature, administration or judiciary with regard to all parties involved in a specific legal relationship like that of landlord and tenant. For instance, if the rights of the landlord and tenant of a specific apartment come into conflict,[1650] the constitutional guarantee of property requires that the interests of both parties should be carefully balanced. A is the owner of a semi-detached, double storey house, of which she has leased the top storey to B. However, A is old and ill, and terminates the contract of lease with B on the basis that she wants her son, C, to live close by in order to take care of her as she becomes more dependent on help. C lives in the other half of the semi-detached house. B refuses to acknowledge the termination of the contract of lease, on the basis that it constitutes an unlawful infringement on his right in terms of article 14 GG.

The fact that the possessory right of the lessee falls within the protective ambit of article 14 GG,[1651] does not lead to the conclusion that article 14 GG is directly applicable to the relation between lessor and lessee.[1652] The function of article 14 GG in the relation between lessor and lessee is to compel the legislature, courts and administration to take the interests of both parties into account and balance them, objectively speak-

---

[1648] See 80 ff. above.

[1649] *Wieland* in *Dreier (ed)*, Kommentar I (1996), m.n. 149.

[1650] Example taken from the facts of BVerfGE 89, 1 8 ff.

[1651] See 231 above.

[1652] BVerfGE 89, 1, 5. *"Sie erhebt ... den Mieterschutz nicht zu einer subjektiven Grundrechtsverbürgung"*. See also BVerfGE 21, 73, 83; BVerfGE 80, 137, 150.

ing, in a suitable manner.[1653] The function of the property guarantee in securing the freedom of individuals in such a case should work both ways. It should acknowledge the interest of the lessee in the retention of the apartment as a method of securing his or her existence, but it should also acknowledge the interest of the landlord in using the apartment for purposes of advancing his or her self-esteem. These competing interests should be balanced in view of the indirect horizontal operation of art 14 GG. In this regard, the Federal Constitutional Court has made the constitutional justifiability of termination of the contract of lease dependent on whether the lessor/owner can furnish acceptable reasons for such a termination of the contract.[1654] The court thus accepted that the reasons for termination of the lease advanced by the lessor/owner in the above-mentioned example, namely use by a relative in exchange for rendering much-needed health care to the lessor/owner, would be sufficient justification for termination of the contract of lease.[1655]

Schwabe[1656] supports the theory that the courts (as state organs)[1657] are directly bound by the bill of rights in civil cases. He argues that article 14 III GG would also be applicable to the case where one individual is empowered, through statute or codified law, to interfere with the property right of another or to withdraw such a right. The provisions in the Civil Code dealing with infringement of property rights in self-defence or due to the creation of a way of necessity are mentioned as examples.[1658] More specifically, he relies on the *Feldmühle* case[1659] as an example of where article 14 III GG with an expanded interpretation should also have found application. This case involved the reorganisation of a company, by allowing shareholders owning more than three-

---

[1653] BVerfGE 89, 1, 5. See also BVerfGE 37, 132, 140 ff.

[1654] BVerfGE 89, 1, 10. *"Soweit nach einfachem Recht die Belange des Vermieters darauf zu prüfen sind, ob sie einen ernsthaften, vernünftigen und nachvollziehbaren Erlangungswunsch ergeben, kann der Mieter beanspruchen, daß das Gericht hiergegen gerichteten Einwänden in einer Weise nachgeht, die der Bedeutung und Tragweite seines Bestandsinteresses gerecht wird, also Beispielsweise nachprüft, ob der Selbstnutzungswunsch ernsthaft verfolgt wird ... "*

[1655] BVerfGE 89, 1.

[1656] *Schwabe,* Die sogenannte Drittwirkung der Grundrechte (1971), 118-139.

[1657] In terms of art. 1 III GG.

[1658] Par. 904 BGB; par. 917 BGB.

[1659] BVerfGE 14, 263.

fourths of the capital stock of a joint-stock company to convert the company, in spite of the objection of minority stockholders who were completely excluded from the decision. The minority stockholders contested the validity of the statute[1660] that authorised the conversion.

In deciding the issue, the court reasoned[1661] that it is logical that legislature is, in all cases of determination of the contents and limits of property, compelled to take the *"grundlegenden Wertentscheidungen des GG zugunsten des Privateigentums im herkömmlichen Sinne"*[1662] into account. Furthermore, legislation has to be in accordance with all the constitutional values (in particular the value of equality and the principles of the constitutional and social welfare state) and also has to consider the basic right to individual freedom and autonomy.[1663] In this case, it was decided that the legislature acted in the general interest by fostering the creation of larger business enterprises and that the three-fourths conversion rule was not manifestly out of proportion to the prejudice caused by the encroachment on the proprietary interests of minority shareholders.[1664]

The argument of Schwabe is, however, that this (justifiable) legislative interference with property, and the private law limitation of the owners' rights, create the possibility for further indirect infringement (or even "expropriation" in a material sense) by individuals (like the majority of the shareholders in the *Feldmühle* case). According to this argument, the courts should apply the requirements of expropriation in terms of article 14 III GG — in particular the requirement that the expropriation should be in the public interest — to test the justifiability of the limitation. This reasoning results in a circular argument. Almost every justifiable legislative interference with the content and limits of property which is "approved" by the court could have the effect of curtailing the rights of a holder, for the sake of either expanding the rights of other right holders (like neighbours, in terms of the Civil Code)[1665] or of em-

---

[1660] Par. 15, *Umwandlungsgesetz.*

[1661] BVerfGE 14, 263, 278.

[1662] Translation: "fundamental value decisions incorporated into the Basic Law, in favour of private ownership in its ordinary sense".

[1663] *"Grundrecht auf freie Entfaltung der Persönlichkeit."*

[1664] BVerfGE 14, 263, 277.

[1665] E.g. par. 912 BGB.

powering other individuals (like the public in general, in terms of a public right of way).

4.2. Horizontality and the Property Clause in the South African Context

In *Du Plessis and Others v De Klerk and Another*,[1666] the majority of the Constitutional Court held that the bill of rights in the Interim Constitution did not operate directly between relations on a horizontal level. The Interim Constitution was to be applied between relations on the vertical level and only indirectly on a horizontal level. However, the arguments of the majority in favour of indirect horizontal operation[1667] could not appease fears concerning the "privatisation" of apartheid and the socio-economic benefits unjustly gained thereunder.[1668] Therefore, some of the new provisions in the Final Constitution give the bill of rights in general a direct horizontal effect,[1669] within the limits set by these provisions themselves.

Section 8(1) FC determines that the bill of rights "applies to *all law* and binds the legislature, the executive, the *judiciary* and all other organs of state."[1670] *All law* encompasses also common-law disputes between private parties, which indicates direct operation of the bill of rights. Should it happen that a legal dispute is not covered by subjecting all law to the bill of rights, then subjecting all *judicial actions* to constitutional review should fill the gap.[1671]

[1666] *Du Plessis and Others v De Klerk and Another* (note 432 above).

[1667] It was pointed out in *Du Plessis v De Klerk* (note 432 above), par. 103-105, with particular reference to the German jurisprudence, that the "radiating effect" of the indirect horizontal operation of the Bill of Rights on the common law would adequately address any legitimate fears concerning the privatising of apartheid. See also the comments of the majority on the unsatisfactory jurisprudential features of direct horizontal operation, par. 37-41, 106-112.

[1668] See Kriegler J, *Du Plessis v De Klerk* (note 432 above), par. 120.

[1669] See *Protea Technology Ltd v Wainer* 1997 9 BCLR 1225 (W), 1238.

[1670] Emphasis added.

[1671] *Woolman* in *Chaskalson/Kentridge/Klaaren et. al. (eds)*, Constitutional Law of South Africa (1996), ch. 10, 57.

Section 8(3) FC[1672] should be read as a reminder that rules of common law are subject to direct constitutional review. This means that, where no express rule of common law exists to cover a private or public relationship, a rule must be formulated if necessary to give effect to the bill of rights; and that rules of common law can have their constitutionality tested in terms of the limitations clause.[1673] This interpretation is underscored by section 39(2) FC, which provides:

> *"When interpreting any legislation, and when developing the common law and customary law, every court, tribunal or forum must promote the spirit, purport and objects of the Bill of Rights."*

This section asserts that there is a core set of values underlying the South African legal system. Therefore, all law — also the common law — is, in terms of these provisions, subject to direct constitutional scrutiny. This further also applies to the conduct of juristic persons and natural persons, where appropriate. Where neither existing statutory law nor existing common law provides the causes of action or remedies needed in a particular instance to vindicate the new fundamental rights, the bill of rights directs the courts to create new causes of action and remedies necessary to protect and promote fundamental rights.[1674]

Section 8(2) FC[1675] could, however, pose an interpretative problem. This provision could be read as meaning that a right would apply to a natural person or a juristic person unless the right makes expressly clear that only certain kinds of relationships are destined for constitutional protection. This could mean that (certain aspects of) the property clause would preclude application to private relationships ungoverned by any express rule of law. The property clause contains provisions that limit

---

[1672] Sec. 8(3) FC: "When applying a provision of the Bill of Rights to a natural or juristic person in terms of subsection (2), a court-(a) in order to give effect to a right in the Bill, must apply, or where necessary develop, the common law to the extent that legislation does not give effect to that right; and (b) may develop rules of the common law to limit the right, provided that the limitation is in accordance with section 36(1)."

[1673] *Woolman* in *Chaskalson/Kentridge/Klaaren et. al. (eds)*, Constitutional Law of South Africa (1996), ch. 10, 60.

[1674] *Woolman* in *Chaskalson/Kentridge/Klaaren et. al. (eds)*, Constitutional Law of South Africa (1996), ch. 10, 56.

[1675] Section 8(2) FC: "A provision of the Bill of Rights binds a natural or a juristic person if, and to the extent that, it is applicable, taking into account the nature of the right and the nature of any duty imposed by the right."

the ambit of the guarantee to the relation between the individual and the state. However, it could also, upon an interpretation of section 8(2) FC read with section 25 FC, be decided that the latter is excluded from the outset from application to all private relationships, making it only vertically operational.[1676] It is submitted that the former possibility is the more acceptable interpretation of section 8(2) FC. Although it is true that some of the provisions in section 25 FC can be more easily applied to relations on the vertical level than on the horizontal level, it is submitted that the right to property also plays a significant role in the relations between private individuals.

Ackermann,[1677] in analysing the impact of the constitutional value of human dignity on the equality provisions in the Final Constitution, explains that

> *"[i]n developing the common law generally and in developing it to limit the right to horizontal equality, it would seem that the courts are in effect being enjoined to conduct a proportionality analysis and evaluation in the process of balancing what is in essence a clash of rights between different persons. A clash between, on the one hand, the right to equality and non-discrimination and, on the other, the rights to freedom (in its various forms), privacy, property (and possibly others), or combinations of such rights."*

In operating on a horizontal level, the right to property can, hypothetically, be invoked in the following circumstances:

(i) The rules of a sectional title scheme could contain exclusions on the basis of race, gender, sexual orientation, ethnic or social origin, age, religion, conscience or belief, an so on.[1678] Thus, it might be impossible for a cohabiting couple, or a couple with children, or someone under a specific age, or a black person, or a homosexual, to buy a unit in a specific scheme, because the present owners are prohibited in the rules from selling to certain categories of persons, or are restricted to sell

---

[1676] *Woolman* in *Chaskalson/Kentridge/Klaaren et. al. (eds),* Constitutional Law of South Africa (1996), ch. 10, 58-60.

[1677] *Ackermann,* 2000 ZaöRV, 537-556.

[1678] See *Van der Merwe/Mohr/Blumberg,* 2000 Stell LR, 167-180 for a more extensive discussion of restrictions in the rules of sectional title schemes and their compatability with the chapter on fundamental rights in the Final Constitution.

only to specific categories. [1679] In cases like these, the rights and duties attached to a specific kind of property (sectional title ownership) and freedom of contract would have to be balanced against the values of human dignity and the right not to be unfairly discriminated against. [1680] The relevant circumstances and impact, if evaluated in accordance with established jurisprudence of the Constitutional Court on vertical equality in relation to dignity, suggests that, depending on the nature thereof, restrictive conditions in the rules ought to be declared void and the transfer interdicted. [1681]

(ii) Q, a widow, rather capriciously, but in her sound and sober senses, makes a will leaving her entire estate to a friend she has not seen for years and who has no financial need. Her children, who had been the beneficiaries in all previous wills of Q, contest the will. [1682] In this example one is concerned with a clash between, on the one hand, the capacity to dispose freely of one's property and freedom of testation and, on the other, the right to equality. Ackermann remarks: [1683]

> "A court would have to consider how important the first mentioned rights are and how serious a limitation of these rights the enforcement of horizontal equality would cause; in particular how serious the impact on the testator's dignity would be. In considering the position of the complainants, the impact on their dignity of the testamentary provisions would have to be assessed and, in particular, the extent to which it can be said to be in [the] public [interest]."

Both the abovementioned examples depend on an application of the constitutional principle of equality (in its relation to human dignity) to private relations. Mostly, they would also require judicial interpretation of private law concepts, like freedom of testation, or freedom of contract, in which case private law is developed by constitutional law juris-

---

[1679] *Ackermann*, 2000 ZaöRV, 537-556. In *Shelley v Kraemer* 334 US 1 (1948), the United States Supreme Court unanimously reversed the judgments of state courts enforcing a racist restrictive covenant. While the result of the decision is universally applauded, the reasons for the decision of the Supreme Court have given rise to academic debate. See *Wechsler*, 1959 Harv L Rev, 1; *Henkin*, 1961 Univ Pa L Rev, 637; *Henkin*, 1962 Univ Pa L Rev, 473; *Greenawalt*, 1978 Colum L Rev, 982.

[1680] *Ackermann*, 2000 ZaöRV, 537-556.

[1681] *Van der Merwe/Mohr/Blumberg*, 2000 Stell LR, 167-180.

[1682] *Ackermann*, 2000 ZaöRV, 537-556.

[1683] *Ackermann*, 2000 ZaöRV, 537-556.

prudence. The private law concept of ownership would, in this regard, be a target of constitutional reform when evaluated against the constitutional values of human dignity, equality and individual freedom. Through horizontal operation of the bill of rights, the private law concept of ownership is bound to be influenced by the spirit, purport and objectives of the constitution, most noticeably that of "social justice" and "quality of life," but also that of individual "free potential".[1684] This could occur even though the constitutional protection of property itself is not invoked during the proceedings.

Woolman[1685] mentions a further example in the context of horizontal application of socio-economic rights:

(iii) A non-governmental organisation committed to providing adequate, affordable housing to poor people in South Africa, attempts to lease a large unused piece of land on the outskirts of a big city from the landowner. The landowner refuses, saying that he would prefer the land to lie fallow rather than to put it to any particular use, whether profitable or not. The NGO proceeds with judicial action against the landowner on the basis of the provision for access to housing in s 26 FC. It is reasoned that this provision, in view of the "spirit, purport and objects" of the bill of rights operates directly against the landowner and that it trumps the latter's right in terms of common law to dispose of his property as he wishes. The landowner could, of course, counter this argument by relying on the protection of the property guarantee, which would then require direct horizontal application. In such a case, the court would once again have to consider the importance of these rights weighed against the severity of the limitations thereon, caused by applying the bill of rights horizontally.

Accepting a hierarchy of rights in this regard would, in my submission, not be appropriate. The provisions in a bill of rights do not provide an unassailable basis for solving disputes between "equal" parties. Like in cases where the infringement of constitutionally protected rights by the state must be tested, it would be inappropriate to introduce weighing and ranking of rights in this context.[1686] Instead, one should endeavour to "harmonise" or "optimise" both (or all of) the conflicting rights,

---

[1684] See Preamble, FC.

[1685] *Woolman* in *Chaskalson/Kentridge/Klaaren et al. (eds)*, Constitutional Law of South Africa (1996), ch. 10, 59 refers to a discussion with Prof Frank Michelman, in the course of which this issue was raised.

[1686] See 292 above.

thereby achieving a relative equilibrium or "practical concordance" as is the case in German law.[1687] However, the same results could, in most cases, be achieved by applying concepts from private law and techniques that have up to now been used to resolve disputes between "equal" parties. The most appropriate role of the bill of rights in this context would be to correct possible imbalances in the relation between the parties in an attempt to level their respective positions, in order to place them on an equal footing in the true sense of the word.

5. Effect of Constitutional Limitations on the Existing Property Order

In keeping with the basic division between the functions of private and constitutional law, one must distinguish between legislative limitations on movable and immovable property, on the one hand, and constitutional limitations on property (whether movable or immovable)[1688] on the other hand. The latter category of limitations is relatively new in the South-African context, being a result of the inclusion of the property guarantees in the first two enforceable Bills of Rights in the Interim and Final Constitutions. However, since the Constitution in the new democratic order ranks higher than other "ordinary" legislation, these constitutional limitations on property are also of supreme importance for the whole system of property law in South Africa. On the one hand, the constitutional provisions determine which ordinary legislative limitations are justifiable in terms of the property guarantee. On the other hand, the constitutional provisions give rise to a whole new body of legislation influencing the existing landownership in particular.

Divergent methods are used in South Africa and Germany for determining justifiable constitutional limitations on property. Nevertheless, the effect of limitation in both systems is quite similar. Fundamental rights are limited individually within the respective provisions establishing the different basic rights in the German Basic Law. By contrast,

---

[1687] See 262 above. See also *Rautenbach,* General Provisions of the South African Bill of Rights (1995), 79, where both methods of "balancing" are discussed.

[1688] Section 25(4)(b) FC makes provision for the protection of (and limitations on) property of land *or otherwise* by expressly stating that for the purposes of section 25 FC , property is not limited to land.

both the Interim Constitution and the Final Constitution of South Africa contain general limitation clauses.[1689] These provisions apply to the same extent to the limitation of all rights included in the South African bill of rights. However, internal modifying components and specific limitation clauses included in many of the specific fundamental rights' guarantees of the South African Final Constitution result in a slight differentiation in the limitation of the various fundamental rights, according to the unique provisions in which they are framed.

Further; both in private and in constitutional law the scope of property rights are restricted, albeit on different levels. From a private law perspective, property rights are restricted on a "horizontal" level by the rights and interests of third parties. From a constitutional perspective, the scope of a person's property rights is determined by considering limitations in the public interest; that is, on a vertical level *vis-á-vis* the state authority. On both these levels restrictions can cause serious inroads in individual property rights, sometimes to the extent of withdrawing such rights completely. The following paragraphs provide an overview of the relevance of limitations in the public interest for private autonomy in property law.

5.1. Limitations, Private Autonomy and Public Interest

The first question to be considered is the extent to which individual interests should yield to public purpose (that is to say to what extent legislative actions taken for the sake of public benefit can override individual sovereignty with regard to property). Some of the areas where individual freedom with regard to property might, under specific circumstances, have to recede for the public benefit are: zoning and planning laws, pollution control, nature conservation and the protection of historic sites. The legislation[1690] arising from the commitment in section 25 FC to equitable access to land, legally protected land tenure, restitution of property and land reform[1691] should also be analysed against the provisions governing the interpretation of public interest (section 25(2)(a) FC read with section 25(4)(a) FC). Where land is to be expropriated from some individuals in order to provide land for housing or agricul-

---

[1689] Sec. 33 IC; sec. 36 FC.

[1690] Sec. 25(9) FC specifically provides for such legislation.

[1691] In particular sec. 25 (5), (6), (7) and (8) FC.

tural purposes to other individuals, the land reform programme could stand or fall by the interpretation of the public purposes / public interest requirement. *Public purpose* or *public interest* should not be understood to denote that private property could in no circumstance be expropriated to further housing for the disadvantaged. This would render effective land reform programmes impossible.

It is, furthermore, necessary to determine to what extent a *public interest / public purpose* qualification must be applied to the deprivation provision in section 25(1) FC.[1692] The deprivation provision of section 28(2) IC read with section 33 IC covered all legitimate state interference with private rights in property. Similar provisions are found in section 25(1) FC and section 36 FC. However, it is not provided that deprivations of property should be in the public interest or for public purposes. A deprivation of property simply has to comply with the due-process principle,[1693] and it must be authorised by a law that applies generally. It should also be reasonable and justifiable in an open and democratic society based on freedom and equality, and it should arguably not destroy the essence of the right to private property.[1694]

Van der Walt[1695] suggests that the *public purpose / public interest* requirement should be "read into" section 25(1) FC for purposes of regulation of property in the wide sense. This view is based on the fact that section 36(1) FC applies to the property clause, and is wide enough to be regarded as an "extended" *public purposes / public interest* requirement. If the courts follow this approach, even more reason exist for comparing the German and South African applications of the *public interest / public purposes* requirement.[1696]

The German Basic Law uses the term *"Wohle der Allgemeinheit"* to express a requirement similar to the *public interest / public purposes* requirement in the South African property clause. The role of these requirements within the property clauses of Germany and South Africa also correspond

---

[1692] See the discussion with reference to the application of the public interest / public purposes requirement in the context of expropriations at 330 ff. above.

[1693] It is stated, in both the Interim and Final Constitutions that deprivation of property rights can only take place if it is in accordance with a law of general application. This must be read in conjunction with the administrative justice clauses of both these Constitutions: sec. 24 IC, sec. 33 FC.

[1694] *Van der Walt/Pienaar*, Introduction (1996), 421.

[1695] *Van der Walt*, Constitutional Property Clause (1997), 137.

[1696] See 302 ff. above.

to some extent. It qualifies the limits for expropriation and determines an equitable amount of compensation. However, in the German context the requirement of *"Wohle der Allgemeinheit"* serves two different purposes. In the case of expropriation, it is supposed to limit the number of expropriations to the minimum, *in order to protect individual interests.*[1697] In the case of determining the amount of compensation[1698] it is meant *to protect the public interest as such.*[1699] This requires that the interpretation of the requirement varies, depending on the function it fulfils in a specific case.

If this reasoning is applied to the South African context, it would mean that in case of expropriation, the term *public interest / public purposes* must be interpreted restrictively, so as to give effect to the interests of individuals affected by the conduct of the state. An expropriation might be in the public interest, but might not constitute a public "necessity." Accordingly, expropriation would sometimes not be justifiable. In the case of compensation, a wider interpretation of the term *public interest / public purposes* can be used.[1700] If, however, expropriation for the benefit of private individuals were justifiable, the interpretation of the *public interest / public purposes* would also have to be adapted. In such a case, a wider interpretation of *public interest / public purposes* should also be followed in the context of expropriation, for the sake of giving effect to the land reform policies. This approach would tune in with the suggestion above[1701] that the importance of constitutionally protecting and restricting a specific proprietary interest can be measured through a balancing of the conflicting interests in a specific case against the background of the constitutional and social state principles. This would enable a consideration of the different interests at stake without resorting to weighing and ranking of interests, and without forcing a malapplication of the proportionality test too early in the investigation as to the constitutional validity of a specific interference with property.

[1697] See Böhmer J's minority decision in BVerfGE 56, 249.

[1698] And in the case of determining the justifiability of legislative regulation of property, if the approach of Van der Walt (n 1695 above) is endorsed for the South African context.

[1699] See Böhmer J's minority decision in BVerfGE 56, 249.

[1700] *Van der Walt,* Constitutional Property Clause (1997), 138.

[1701] See 359 ff. above.

5.2. Limitations and Horizontal Operation of the Bill of Rights

In both Germany and South Africa, two basic categories of limitations are justifiable on a vertical level: expropriation and regulation of property. On a horizontal level of limitation, however, considerable differences exist. In Germany the provisions of the various basic rights apply only indirectly to all relations between individuals. In South Africa, the bill of rights has been made directly horizontally applicable in the Final Constitution. Nevertheless, the primary function of horizontal application, whether applied directly or indirectly, is to create interaction between the protection of property in private and constitutional law. This enables the judiciary to correct imbalances that might exist in the relations between those who are perceived to be "equal" in terms of private law.

Especially in the context of the constitutional property guarantee, however, direct horizontal application can be problematic. It raises the issue of how far existing mechanisms in private law could and should be used to solve problems in the private law sphere. The proliferation of claims based on the right to property could be devastating in view of the expanded concept of property under the constitution. Moreover, direct application of the provisions of the bill of rights may result in a situation where well refined private law principles, developed over a long time and based upon fairness in the private law context, are deviated from in favour of the vague and general norms of the bill of rights. Considerations of legal certainty militate against such a result.[1702] Of course, in situations where the traditional private law remedies afford the parties to a dispute no relief, the direct horizontal application of the bill of rights could fill the gap. Moreover, if the values underlying the constitutional order cannot be given effect by interpreting or applying ordinary law with due regard to the spirit, purport and objects of the bill of rights, direct horizontal application becomes necessary.

5.3. Land Reform and Restitution as Limitation in the Public Interest

Du Plessis[1703] indicates that, in a society like that of South Africa, the limitation of the right to property under the constitution is imperative:

[1702] *De Waal*, 1995 SAHJR, 14.

[1703] *Du Plessis*, 1996 Stell LR, 21.

"To guarantee property in a Constitution which commits a nation to the achievement of equality as well as the promotion and protection of human dignity, is quite significant. If such guarantee has to serve the accomplishment of these laudable objectives, it should be seen to include empowerment to gain access to property as well as to redress inequities, especially the dispossession of large numbers of people under apartheid. Measures aimed at the restitution of property, therefore, do not constitute "exceptions to" the guarantee of property, but follow as its natural consequences."

The first steps towards transforming the South African concept of land-ownership have been taken through new land-use policies and programmes and innovative legislative reforms.[1704] In section 25(4) FC, land reform and equitable access to natural resources are explicitly mentioned as public purposes for the sake of expropriation in section 25(4) FC. This indicates that land reform and redistribution are sufficiently important to make regulation and expropriation of property for those purposes possible, even if existing property relations — and therewith also privileges built on apartheid — are protected through an individual property guarantee.[1705] The drafting history of the constitutional property clause and the tendency of the courts to prefer a purposive interpretation of the constitutional provisions suggest that the objectives of land reform, redistribution and restitution need not even be explicitly mentioned in the constitutional text in order to interpret them as elements of the *public interest / public purposes* requirement.

The constitutional dispensation pertaining to property and land rights provide the legal foundation for a new system of land tenure in South Africa.[1706] Simultaneously, the process of land reform, restitution and redistribution, both in Germany and in South Africa, is a perfect arena in which to examine the relationship between private and public law, in particular the interaction between individual and societal interests in the

---

[1704] E.g. Abolition of Racially Based Land Measures Act 108 of 1991; Upgrading of Land Tenure Rights Act 112 of 1991; Less Formal Township Establishment Act 113 of 1991; Restitution of Land Rights Act 22 of 1994; Land Reform Pilot Programme of 1995; Land Affairs General Amendment Act 11 of 1995; Upgrading of Land Tenure Rights Amendment Act 34 of 1996; Interim Protection of Informal Land Rights Act 31 of 1996; Extension of Security of Tenure Act 62 of 1997.

[1705] *Kleyn*, 1996 SAPR/PL, 417.

[1706] *Gutto*, Property and Land Reform (1995), 34.

private and public spheres of property law. Of course, the scope of constitutional property protection and regulation stretches much further than rights related to land and immovable property. Nevertheless, the interaction of the constitutional protection and regulation of property by legislation embodying the reform policies is highly significant at this point in South African legal history. Therefore, the remaining part of this thesis will be devoted to an analysis of the land reform and restitution programmes in South Africa, compared with those in Germany after the reunification.

Part Four

The Influence of Social Reform on Land Law in Germany and South Africa

Chapter 9: Meaning of the Constitutional Objective of Land Reform for the South African Property Law

1. Background: Incentives for and Institutions of Reform

With the advent of colonialisation in South Africa, a legislative process[1707] was started which eventually would restrict eighty percent of the South African population to ownership (or quasi-ownership) of thirteen percent of the country's land.[1708] These laws would form the cornerstone of the apartheid government's policy of absolute racial segregation,[1709] and was based mainly on the hierarchical "primacy" of ownership in terms of private law.[1710]

The South Africa Act,[1711] which paved the way for the formation of the Union of South Africa in 1910, effectively sanctioned all past acquisi-

---

[1707] See *Gutto*, Property and Land Reform (1995), 13-17 for a discussion of the revolutionary replacement of one system of dominant proprietary relations (i.e. the indigenous African non-capitalist property regime, which was familiar with concepts like none-property, common property, private property under slavery and feudalism) by another system of dominant proprietary relations (i.e. the colonial dominated capitalist property regime).

[1708] See e.g. *Bennett* in *Zimmermann/Visser (eds)*, Southern Cross (1996), ch. 2.

[1709] The most prominent of these laws were the Blacks Trust and Land Act 18 of 1936 and the two Group Areas Acts (41 of 1950 and 36 of 1996).

[1710] *Van der Walt*, 1999 Koers, 261-263 points out that the (im)possibility to acquire and exercise land-use rights was ultimately determined by the (im)possibility of owning land in a certain area.

[1711] 1909.

tions of land by colonialists.[1712] Further acquisition was enabled with the promulgation of the Black Land Act of 1913,[1713] the first in a long line of racially motivated land laws. This act provided the statutory basis for territorial segregation by dividing South Africa into the so-called "black spots" on the one hand and the "non-African" areas on the other hand.[1714] The latter comprised the rest (approximately 87% of the country's surface area) of the country and black South Africans could not purchase, hire or in any other way acquire rights to land in these areas.[1715] In further developments, the Group Areas Act[1716] effected racial fragmentation by assigning land to the so-called white, Indian and coloured race groups and securing the best agricultural and residential land for the whites. This resulted in large-scale forced removals, which affected approximately 3,5 million South Africans after 1913. The most extensive removals occurred in 1960 and 1983. Coupled with these policies of segregation, a double-standard system of land rights was introduced. White people enjoyed strong and efficient protection against infringement of their ownership of land, because they were backed up by the highly valued legal institution of property as it was understood in the civil-law oriented private-law system. Black people did not receive the same kind of protection of their land rights, and could mostly have only traditional tribal land rights, or statutory land "rights" based on "governmental grants" like residential permits or certificates of occupation. These "black" land rights were not strong enough or even secure enough to weigh up against "traditional" (white) civil-law land rights,[1717] not to mention the inability of these rights to serve as security for bonds or loans.

Although the supremacy of "white" land rights and the deficiencies of "black" land rights under the apartheid regime primarily resulted from political choices and the inequitable division of available land related to these policies, the hierarchical conception of property rights in the sys-

---

[1712] *Visser/Roux* in *Rwelamira/Werle (eds)*, Confronting Past Injustices (1996), 90.

[1713] 27 of 1913.

[1714] See maps and illustrations in *Van der Merwe/Pienaar* in *Jackson/Wilde (eds)*, Reform of Property Law (1997), 336-337.

[1715] *Murphy* in *Rwelamira/Werle (eds)*, Confronting Past Injustices (1996), 122.

[1716] 36 of 1966.

[1717] *Van der Walt*, 1999 Koers, 261-263.

tem of private law exacerbated the deficiencies of "black" land rights.[1718] Not surprisingly, the issue of land rights was espoused in both the Interim and Final Constitutions, as a fundamentally important factor in the process of redressing the wrongs of the past and ensuring full human and civil rights for all citizens.[1719] The inclusion of the objectives of land reform, and redistribution and restitution of land within the property clause of the Final Constitution in the chapter on fundamental rights, indicates the desperate need for such reform.

1.1. Problems Posed by the Existing Scheme of Landownership Law

The diversified and complex land control system with its racial basis necessitated land reform and the rationalisation of land control measures in South Africa.[1720] Most of the claims to land of black South Africans did not enjoy legal recognition under the apartheid-influenced property law.[1721] They could not be based on documents such as title deeds or lease agreements, as black South Africans were denied these rights in "white" areas. Instead, claims were based on certain principles and values, such as length of occupation, birthright, secure tenure preserved through due process and contractual obligations. These principles were often closely related to concepts recognised by the law, but were overreached and restricted by the apartheid land law.[1722] The land rights espoused by the law under the apartheid regime were thus based on the relative strength and security of "white" land rights coupled with the relative weakness and insecurity of "black" land rights. In this

---

[1718] *Van der Walt*, 1999 Koers, 262.

[1719] *Milton* in *Zimmermann/Visser (ed)*, Southern Cross (1996), 698.

[1720] In effect, fourteen different land control systems existed within South Africa before the introduction of a new constitutional dispensation. In each of the four provinces the rules on land control varied slightly. The four "independent" states of Transkei, Bophuthatswana, Venda and Ciskei all had unique sets of rules governing land control. Moreover, in the six self-governing states different systems of land control were also applied.

[1721] *Van der Walt*, 1999 Koers, 262-263.

[1722] *Swanson*, 1992 SAJHR, 332. Approximately one third of the persons forcibly removed between 1913 and 1989 were moved off white farms. Several had been there for generations, and believed that their rights to the land were based on birthright or on traditional patterns of occupation. *Murphy* in *Rwelamira/Werle (eds)*, Confronting Past Injustices (1996), 124.

way, the power relations[1723] implicit in the hierarchy of rights endorsed by the private law of property were exploited to ensure the political domination and legal security entrenching white privilege.[1724]

Furthermore, the need for a land reform programme was made all the more urgent on account of poverty (especially in the traditional rural areas), and the lack of suitable land for development and housing. Demographic factors, like population increase, urbanisation, city sprawling and increased informal settlements, together with pressure from foreign countries further contributed to the introduction of a full-scale land reform project. The challenge was to find a manner of addressing the existing inequalities in the system of land distribution, as well as the structural inequalities built into the hierarchical system of apartheid's land rights.[1725]

1.2. The First Attempts at Reform

In effect, property law reform in South Africa started off with the recognition of the fact that absoluteness has never been a characteristic of the ownership concept.[1726] In the eighties and during the early nineties, the first few insecure steps towards a new property order was taken. Most of the reforms were, however, directed at the upper land market, in attempts to accommodate the needs of the middle and higher income groups. Van der Walt explains:[1727]

> "[P]roperty lawyers have designed and implemented the quite complicated and imaginative system of property time-sharing in order to provide holiday accommodation for the rich, but were unable to devise a system of land rights that can provide security of tenure for those who live in rural areas or informal settlement. Likewise, property lawyers have already made possible the three-dimensional registration of air space units, but seem to be unable to

---

[1723] For an overview of the different perspectives on property theory, the power relations endorsed by them, and their application in South Africa at the turn of the 20th century, see *Van der Walt*, 1995 THRHR, 396-420.

[1724] *Van der Walt*, 1999 Koers, 263.

[1725] *Van der Walt*, 1999 Koers, 264.

[1726] See 191 ff. above.

[1727] *Van der Walt* in *Van der Walt (ed)*, Landownership in South Africa (1991), 27.

devise a registration system for unsurveyed land in the rural areas, which might have provided the occupants of such land with the security of tenure they need and deserve. ... The facade of property law has been developed magnificently, but the backyard is a dump."

During the latter part of the eighties and the early nineties, after the inevitability of a new political order was recognised, a few hasty legislative attempts were made at formally deracialising the existing property law and system of landownership.[1728] These steps were aimed at pragmatically addressing the unjust system of land distribution in South Africa, rather than at systematically eradicating the injustice ingrained in the system of property law as such.

1.2.1. Reform between 1991 and 1993

The "pre-transitional" reform process was embodied in the White Paper on Land Reform and corresponding legislation between 1991 and 1993. During these years, the groundwork for the unification of the South African land tenure system was completed, on the principles expressed in the White Paper of 1991 that (i) access to land was a basic human right and (ii) free enterprise and private ownership were the appropriate mechanisms to give effect to this right.[1729]

The land control system was deracialised by repealing most of the race-related land measures. The promulgation of the Abolition of Racially Based Land Measures Act,[1730] the Upgrading of Land Tenure Rights Act[1731] and the Less Formal Township Establishment Act[1732] accompanied the publication of the White Paper of 1991. This legislation aimed in general at creating speedier procedures for establishment of informal settlements, improving security of title and addressing the system of

---

[1728] E.g. the Abolition of Racially Based Land Measures Act 108 of 1991; Conversion of Certain Rights into Leasehold or Ownership Act 81 of 1988; the Upgrading of Land Tenure Rights Act 112 of 1991; the Less Formal Townships Establishment Act 113 of 1991. Most of these were also substantially amended by the General Law Second Amendment Act 108 of 1993.

[1729] *Van der Merwe/Pienaar* in *Jackson/Wilde (eds)*, Reform of Property Law (1997), 350.

[1730] 108 of 1991.

[1731] 112 of 1991.

[1732] 113 of 1991.

land use by way of a permit system. The purpose of the Abolition of Racially Based Land Measures Act was mainly to deracialise the land control system. This was done by repealing various pieces of primary legislation, wholly or partially, on which the policy of spatial separation of different races within South Africa were based.[1733] Regulations and proclamations issued under those acts, however, remained in force until explicitly repealed or abolished. An example of such subordinate legislation, which was not immediately repealed, is proclamation R293[1734] promulgated under the Black Administration Act.[1735] It made provision for the establishment of a special kind of township[1736] for African citizens in areas of land held by the "South African Native Trust,"[1737] *inter alia* by creating limited forms of tenure through "deeds of grant" and "certificates of occupation of a letting unit for residential purposes." These tenure rights were precarious and could be cancelled by the township "manager" if the holder of the right ceased, for instance, "to be in the opinion of the manager a fit and proper person to reside in the township."[1738] The insecure tenure rights established through this proclamation can clearly be regarded as one of the most visible prod-

---

[1733] I.e. Black Land Act 27 of 1913; Development and Trust Land Act 18 of 1936; Group Areas Act 36 of 1966.

[1734] Government Gazette 373, 16 November 1962. *Inter alia*, chapter 1 of the proclamation makes provision for the establishment of the townships. Chapter 2 provides for the demarcation of sites in the townships for various categories of occupation and regulates their occupation, sale or lease. It makes provision also for the issue of deeds of grant and certificates of occupation, as well as for their assignment or transfer. Chapter 3 relates to trading sites and the control of trading in the townships. Chapter 9 establishes special deeds registries in the office of every "Chief Bantu Affairs Commissioner" and for the registration therein of rights granted under the proclamation.

[1735] 38 of 1927.

[1736] By the (then) Minister of Bantu Administration and Development.

[1737] The South African Native Trust (later the South African Development Trust) was established by the Native Trust and Land Act, 18 of 1936. The short title of the statute and the title of the Minister and the Trust reflect the names used to refer to Africans at the time the statute was promulgated. Africans were initially referred to in statutes as "Natives." This term was later changed to "Bantu," and eventually to "Blacks." Even a cursory reading of the proclamation and the act can leave no doubt as to the distasteful character of the provisions thereof.

[1738] Regulation 23(1)(a)(iv) of the Proclamation.

ucts of the previous government's policy of apartheid and racial segregation.

The Upgrading of Land Tenure Rights Act provided for the conversion into ownership of the (lower ranking) more tenuous land rights granted to black South Africans during the apartheid era. For example, leasehold, quitrent and deeds of grant could be upgraded to ownership.[1739] The scope of the Upgrading of Land Tenure Rights Act was extended by the amendment of the Conversion of Certain Rights into Leasehold or Ownership Act[1740] so as to include other rights in formalised towns, not mentioned specifically in the Upgrading of Land Tenure Rights Act. The mechanisms introduced by these acts had a far-reaching influence on the South African system of land rights, since these rights in land were automatically converted into ownership[1741] and registered at a later stage.[1742] Although the larger aim of these acts was the eradication of inequalities in the system of land use in South Africa, the effect of the application of this legislation in specific circumstances were sometimes nevertheless still unjust. In the case of *Mnisi v Chauke*,[1743] the hidden irony of this system of reform is noticeable. The case involved an application for the eviction of some family members of Mrs Chauke from a house which belonged to Mr Mnisi and which was allegedly occupied unlawfully by them. From the history of the case it appeared that Mrs Chauke obtained a "right of occupation" with respect to the property[1744] by reason of her marriage in community of property with her late husband, who purchased such a right from the Atteridge Town Council. Upon her husband's death, a certificate of occupation was issued in her name, as she was his sole intestate heir. After the Conver-

---

[1739] Sec. 2(1)(a), Upgrading of Land Tenure Rights Act.

[1740] 81 of 1988, as amended by sec. 24 of the Second General Laws Amendment Act 108 of 1993, by adding "or ownership" into the title of the act.

[1741] 112 of 1991. The terms of this act were not of application in the TBVC states (the former "independent homelands" of Transkei, Bophuthatswana, Venda and Ciskei) until 28 September 1998, the date of promulgation of the Land Affairs General Amendment Act, 61 of 1998 (which inserted section 25A in the Upgrading of Land Tenure Rights Act and which made the provisions of this act applicable in the whole country).

[1742] Sec. 2(2)(a), Upgrading of Land Tenure Rights Act.

[1743] *Mnisi v Chauke and Others; Chauke v Provincial Secretary, Transvaal, and Others* 1994 4 SA 715 (T).

[1744] Situated in Atteridgeville near Pretoria.

sion of Certain Rights to Leasehold Act[1745] had come into operation, Mrs Chauke was granted leasehold in respect of the property in terms of this act. Subsequently, the Upgrading of Land Tenure Rights Act[1746] came into operation, whereupon a certificate of ownership with respect to the property was issued to Mrs Chauke in terms of this act. She then sold and transferred the property to Mr Mnisi. The rest of the Chauke family objected to the sale of the family residence, but their objections were overruled and they were evicted from the property, eviction being the remedy by which a landowner asserts the right of ownership. This outcome indicates that, in spite of the honourable objectives of the land reform process, the reform measures themselves could have disastrous results for people who were supposed to benefit from transformation. In anticipation of a system in which not only the existing inequalities in land distribution, but also the structural inequalities built into the hierarchical system of South Africa's land rights, are addressed,[1747] one would expect the courts to resort to a more sophisticated and layered system of interest-balancing in view of the constitutional prerogative of land reform.[1748]

New methods for the subdivision and transfer of certain land were also invented.[1749] The Less Formal Township Establishment Act provided for procedures to regulate the establishment of less formal settlements and townships. The main aim of this Act was to avoid the time-consuming and expensive procedures usually applied to township establishment (in terms of the provincial ordinances at the time). The aim was to provide a speedier and more effective type of informal settlement with the object of eventually upgrading it into a recognised township. The South African Development Trust[1750] was also abolished and the land under its control was transferred to various functionaries, like the provincial administrations, governments of the (then still) self-

---

[1745] 81 of 1988.

[1746] 112 of 1991.

[1747] *Van der Walt*, 1999 Koers, 264.

[1748] See also 411 below.

[1749] *Van der Merwe/Pienaar* in *Jackson/Wilde (eds)*, Reform of Property Law (1997), 354-357.

[1750] The organ established by the Development Trust and Land Act 18 of 1936, with the purpose of administering the land set aside for occupation by black South Africans under the policy of racial segregation.

governing territories, and the Department of Regional and Land Affairs.

In 1991 the Commission on Land Allocation was established with the specific purpose of identifying unallocated and undeveloped state land which was acquired in terms of the repealed racial legislation and which could be used for agricultural resettlement. The commission could also identify other rural land, which could be acquired by the state for the purpose of agricultural resettlement, with a view to the symbolic redress of approximately three and a half million victims of forced removals under apartheid.[1751] Urban claims were, however, excluded from the commission's brief. This lead to the perception that the commission lacked legitimacy. Consequently, its powers were expanded in 1993 so as to include jurisdiction over urban land and to grant the power to make awards in respect of land acquired by the state under apartheid laws. It also received the authority to make recommendations in relation to land that could be acquired by the state for allocation for agricultural purposes.[1752] The commission brought the need for a restitution process into sharper focus, although very few of the more than 2000 claims that were received were dealt with. In retrospect, it was more successful with implementing reforms in the rural areas than in urban areas. The inadequate infrastructure at the commission's disposal together with the passive and unrepresentative character of the commission itself explained why better results could not be achieved.[1753] The commission was eventually replaced with the permanent Commission on the Restitution of Land Rights.[1754]

In further developments, legislation was enacted to prepare the groundwork for the unification of the South African system of land control and to create new mechanisms for the division and transfer of certain land. The Joint Administration of Certain Matters Act[1755] enabled substitution of many individual departments within South Africa and the (then still) self-governing territories with a single governmental

---

[1751] *Murphy* in *Rwelamira/Werle (eds),* Confronting Past Injustices (1996), 114.

[1752] Act 110 of 1993. Sec. 88B of the amended legislation.

[1753] *Murphy* in *Rwelamira/Werle (eds),* Confronting Past Injustices (1996), 115.

[1754] See 422 below.

[1755] 99 of 1993.

department.[1756] This was further supported by the enactment of the Regulation of Joint Executive Action Act[1757] which provided for joint or co-ordinated executive action by the South African government and the governments of the territories relating to former South African Development Trust land. (These acts were eventually repealed during 1995 by the Land Affairs General Amendment Act.)[1758]

Division and transfer of certain land were regulated by the enactment of the Distribution and Transfer of Certain State Land Act[1759] and the Provision of Certain Land for Settlement Act.[1760] These acts regulated transfers of land belonging to state organs to specific persons or groups of persons where transfer coincided with land division;[1761] and provided for the designation and subdivision of state-owned land and privately owned land for resettlement, small-scale farming, residential, public, community and business purposes.[1762] The Land Titles Adjustment Act[1763] was another important statute enacted in the pre-transitional period of land reform. It regulated the allocation or devolution of certain land in respect of which one or more persons claimed ownership without having registered title deeds. The absence of the necessary documents could handicap development or utilisation of the property, to the disadvantage of the parties involved. Therefore, the Minister of Land Affairs was enabled to designate land in cases where absence of title deeds caused difficulties.

1.2.2. Evaluation

The idea of land restoration encountered severe opposition from the former minority government when apartheid was dismantled. The former government held the view that land restoration was not feasible because of practical complexity and the potential for conflict. Therefore, reforms in the period between 1991 and 1993 basically focussed only on

---

[1756] Sec. 3, Joint Administration Act.

[1757] 109 of 1993.

[1758] 11 of 1995.

[1759] 119 of 1993.

[1760] 126 of 1993.

[1761] Sec. 3, 5-12; Act 119 of 1993.

[1762] Sec. 5; Act 126 of 1993.

[1763] 111 of 1993.

removing the formal obstacles in the way of the acquisition of rights in land by black South Africans.[1764] Little attention was paid to addressing the problems of the landless, especially those in rural areas. Thus, these reforms did not succeed in breaking down the structural and dogmatic priviledge of landowners in terms of South African common law at all.[1765] This explains why the legislative attempts at solving the land issue in South Africa created probably as many problems as they purported to solve. The staying in force of subordinate legislation bred confusion; the distribution of land to different governmental functionaries after the abolishment of the Development Trust reinstated legal pluralism regarding land control; and land use, town planning and establishment measures were still complex. In fact, as long as no specific commitment to land restitution and redistribution was given, the overall objective of land reform would be doomed to fail.

1.2.2.1. The Continued Existence of Subordinate (Discriminating) Legislation

Carey-Miller[1766] pinpoints the difficulties arising from the pre-transitional land reform programme with his remark that

"*[t]he anomaly of a process of restitution adopted in advance of the controlling property clause being settled was an early indication of the ad hoc character of the land-reform process; ... symptomatic of an approach dictated by compelling circumstances and to that extent, consistent with retaining the established working infrastructure of property law.*"

Certain problems related to this *ad hoc* character of the reforms are illustrated in the decision of the Constitutional Court, *DVB Behuising (Pty) Ltd v North West Provincial Government and others*.[1767] Proclamation R293, linked with the Upgrading of Land Tenure Rights Act, was the subject of controversy. The tenure and registration provisions of Proclamation R293, read with the Upgrading of Land Rights Act,

---

[1764] *Murphy* in *Rwelamira/Werle (eds)*, Confronting Past Injustices (1996), 114.

[1765] *Van der Walt*, 1999 Koers, 289.

[1766] *Carey-Miller*, 1999 SALJ, 750.

[1767] *DVB Behuising (Pty) Ltd v North West Provincial Government and others* (note 612 above).

constituted a cheap and straightforward mechanism for providing access to land to people in townships. The rights initially acquired could, in due course, become ownership or at least secure tenure. The case arose from the enactment of the North West Local Government Laws Amendment Act[1768] by the legislature of the North West Province. Section 6 of this act purported to repeal Proclamation R293 in its entirety. This could have the effect that people whose claims to land were based on the "deed of grant" of the proclamation, coupled with the Upgrading of Land Rights Act, would lose any claim they could have had in relation to the relevant land, because the legal basis of their claim would fall away.

The applicant *(DVB Behuising)* challenged the constitutional validity of the section 6 of the North West Local Government Laws Amendment Act,[1769] contending that the purported repeal of chapters 1, 2, 3 and 9 of the proclamation was beyond the legislative competence of the North West province. In the court of first instance,[1770] it was held that the purported repeal of these chapters of the proclamation was unconstitutional. Pursuant to the provisions of section 172(2)(a) FC,[1771] the declaration of invalidity was referred to the Constitutional Court for confirmation.

The Constitutional Court was confronted with the question of whether the legislature of the North West Province had the competence to repeal the proclamation. It decided that the legislature of the North West

---

[1768] 7 of 1998.

[1769] It was averred that the repeal of those chapters made it impossible for persons to whom it had sold houses in a township established under the proclamation to have their deeds of grant registered by the Registrar of Deeds (the second respondent in the case). This was alleged to prejudice its business seriously, in particular, because the purchasers of such houses were not able to secure loans which would normally be offered to them by banks.

[1770] *DVB Behuising (Pty) Ltd v North West Provincial Government and Another*, Bophuthatswana High Court, Case No 308/99, 27 May 1999, (per Mogoeng J).

[1771] Sec. 172(2)(a) FC: "The Supreme Court of Appeal, a High Court or a court of similar status may make an order concerning the constitutional validity of an Act of Parliament, a provincial Act or any conduct of the President, but an order of constitutional invalidity has no force unless it is confirmed by the Constitutional Court."

Province did have the competence[1772] to repeal all provisions save for regulations 1 and 3 of chapter 1 and the provisions of chapter 9.[1773] These provisions dealt with the registration of deeds of grant, a matter that is required to be regulated by uniform norms and standards, and thus falls within the competence of the national legislature.[1774] In the majority judgment of the court, it was stated:[1775]

> "What the North West is in effect saying by the repeal of the Proclamation is that in that province apartheid forms of tenure will no longer be available in future. I should have thought that the provisions of section 25 of the Constitution and the Upgrading Act are a clear indication that apartheid forms of land tenure that are legally insecure are no longer to be tolerated in our new democratic dispensation. The repeal of the tenure provisions is consistent with this policy."

The minority judgement contains grave criticism of this approach. It is contended[1776] that the judgment of the majority of the court would have the effect that the speedy and accessible form of registration coupled with the deed of grant tenure is no longer available in the North West. The minority of the court regards this result as being in conflict with the constitutional scheme in terms of which land tenure reform and the manner in which it is achieved is a matter reserved for national government. It is then stated[1777] that

> "jurisprudence of the transitional era necessarily involves a measure of contradiction. Fundamental fairness at times requires that aspects of the old survive immediate obliteration and are kept alive pending their replacement by appropriate forms of the new. ... In the present matter, the meritorious desire manifested in the majority judgment for a clean sweep of the past in the name of modernisation and de-

---

[1772] In terms of sec. 235(8) IC. By implication, therefore, certain aspects of the legislative competence assigned to the national legislature can be exercised by the provincial legislatures, anomalous as it may be. See in general Schedules 4 and 5 FC.

[1773] As amended by Proclamation R9 of 1997.

[1774] In terms of sec. 126(3)(b) IC.

[1775] Per Ngcobo; *DVB Behuising* (note 612 above), par. 69 of the decision.

[1776] Per Goldstone, O'Regan and Sachs JJ; *DVB Behuising* (note 612 above), par. 109-110 of the decision.

[1777] *DVB Behuising* (note 612 above), par. 110.

racialisation has an unintended and ironic consequence. It deprives
underprivileged communities from gaining access to a cheap form of
land tenure which in terms of national legislation can be upgraded to
freehold. The Constitution requires government to foster access to
land. The repeal of the Proclamation by the North West province, in
one sense at least, does the reverse."

The irony inherent in the approach suggested by the minority is perhaps as striking as that ascribed by them to the majority decision. In
employing one of the most apparent pieces of racist and sexist subordinate legislation of the previous regime, exactly those people who were
previously discriminated against can benefit under the new system.
However, the alternative suggested by the majority, in response to this
criticism, is also fraught with difficulties.

Ngcobo J,[1778] for the majority of the court, reads into the provisions of
the Upgrading of Land Tenure Act providing for the upgrading of
"limited form[s] of ownership" into "full ownership" the policy that a
title which conferred a limited form of ownership was to be phased out.
The implication would be that the cheap, speedy method of obtaining
ownership would be available only to persons holding rights in terms of
the old apartheid legislation. The creation of rights in terms of this legislation would no longer be possible in the North West province. Further, Ngcobo J points to the Less Formal Township Establishment
Act[1779] and the Development Facilitation Act[1780] as mechanisms that
could be used to continue the cheap, speedy method of acquisition of
ownership of land.

Indeed, the Less Formal Township Establishment Act contains an accessible form of land tenure. It makes provision for the development of
less formal settlements and townships. It provides, among other things,
"for shortened procedures for the designation, provision and development of land, and the establishment of townships [and] for less formal
forms of residential settlement" and it also regulates the use of land by
rural communities for communal forms of residential settlement. In the
case of development of less formal settlements, section 3(5)(e) of the
Less Formal Township Establishment Act provides that laws regulating
township development and planning are not applicable. In addition,
provision is made in section 9(1) of the Less Formal Township Estab-

---

[1778] *DVB Behuising* (note 612 above), par. 8-9.

[1779] 113 of 1991.

[1780] 67 of 1995.

lishment Act for the acquisition and registration of ownership in respect of an erf allocated to a person. In the case of less formal townships, section 19(5)(a) of the Less Formal Township Establishment Act provides for the exclusion of such laws if their application "will have an unnecessary dilatory effect on the establishment of the contemplated township or will otherwise be inappropriate in respect of the establishment of the township." However, not all the land control measures provided for in terms of Proclamation R293 can be substituted by simply applying the Development Facilitation Act. Specifically in the case of the Meriteng township, the establishment of which gave rise to the present case, it is doubtful whether the Less Formal Township Establishment Act could have been used as a substitute for the procedure of allocating land rights in terms of proclamation R293 and then "upgrading" them. Similar situations could also in future arise where the Less Formal Township Establishment Act cannot simply be employed as a surrogate.

The suggestion is valuable in as far as it indicates a method of retaining the cheap, speedy way of upgrading lesser rights in land into ownership. Especially the Development Facilitation Act could be useful in this regard, as it is aimed at overhauling the tedious process of rationalising and improving (on the provincial level) the content of law inherited by the various provinces. The Development Facilitation Act addresses the need for legislation describing a common procedure that could be used nationally, parallel to existing, inherited land development laws and procedures.[1781] The Development Facilitation Act provides a national framework for the development of land in urban and rural areas for residential purposes, and for the grant of land tenure rights. It "lay[s] down general principles governing land development throughout the Republic." It makes provision for the grant of land tenure rights and their registration with the Registrar of Deeds.[1782] It also provides for the upgrading of informal settlements and for the conversion of "informal or unregistered tenure arrangements" into ownership.[1783] However, it still builds upon legislation created under apartheid, and therefore does not pass the standard that Ngcobo J sets.

[1781] *Latsky* in *Budlender/Latsky/Roux*, New Land Law (1998), ch. 2A, 9.

[1782] Chapter VII.

[1783] Sec. 63, Development Facilitation Act.

1.2.2.2. Social Restructuring

It was said that the White Paper of 1991, together with the legislation implemented pursuant to it, "changed the face of property relations" in South Africa.[1784] However, the implementation of the pre-transitional land reform programme achieved only limited results. It did not focus on the major socio-legal issues (already recognised by academics during the eighties),[1785] which property and land rights reform was supposed to address. These issues included redistribution to achieve class, racial and gender equality, restitution of property and land rights lost during forced removals and the policy of racial segregation, the improvement of the unacceptable status of labour tenants, urban homelessness and the extension of protected property and land rights to the dispossessed and marginalised. Moreover, local governments were until 1995 dominated by conservative white elite and private property owners, who were rather cautious of reform.

So, for instance, the administrator of the former province of Transvaal took steps in terms of the Less Formal Township Establishment Act to resettle the "Zevenfontein squatter community" in a less formal settlement in the Diepsloot area northwest of Johannesburg. The residents of a neighbouring upper class (white) residential area thereupon lodged an application for an interdict preventing settlement of the squatters in Diepsloot, on the basis that it constituted a public nuisance.[1786] One of the arguments raised by the applicant *(Diepsloot Residents' and Landowners' Association)*, was that the establishment of the less formal settlement would undermine the value of their property, because of increased air and water pollution, dust and noise, and a suspected increase in criminality. The case was heard before the Interim Constitution (and with it the first South African constitutional property guarantee) was enacted. The argument was raised, however, that it would be impossible for the administrator to fulfil his obligations in terms of the Less Formal Township Establishment Act without interfering with the private property rights of the applicants.

[1784] *Van der Merwe,* 1990 Stell LR, 321-335; *Roux,* 1993 SAJHR, 539.

[1785] *Van der Walt,* 1999 Koers, 259-294 explains the understructure of the South African system of property law and the problems it poses for land and property law reform. See also *Van der Walt,* 2001 SALJ, 258-311.

[1786] *Diepsloot Residents' and Landowners' Association v Administrator, Transvaal* 1993 1 SA 577 (T) per De Villiers J; 1993 3 SA 49 (T) per McCreath J; 1994 3 SA 336 (A) per Smalberger JA.

In the decision of the court of first instance, the temporary interdict was granted and the argument of the applicants concerning the interference with private law rights upheld.[1787] On the return day, the application for a final interdict was denied[1788] on various grounds. It was held that an interference with the private property rights of the applicants in this specific case was justified in terms of the Less Formal Township Establishment Act.[1789] Reference is made to the fact that the urgent need for resettlement of the Zevenfontein community was not in dispute.[1790] On appeal, this decision was upheld on the reasoning that the Less Formal Township Establishment Act by implication authorised interference with the common-law rights of neighbouring landowners.[1791] Smalberger J, acknowledges:[1792]

> *"I have sympathy for the genuine concerns of the Diepsloot residents and the financial loss they may suffer as a consequence of the necessary reconstruction of our society. What they conceive, rightly or wrongly, to be a burden may well have fallen elsewhere."*

However, it was found that the administrative authorities did not exercise their powers in a grossly unreasonable way. The Less Formal Township Establishment Act addressed the urgent need to provide for the speedy and orderly settlement of homeless persons near the place where they were or wanted to be, near their work or where employment opportunities existed. In these circumstances the settlement of persons next door to — or close to — established residential areas was unavoidable.[1793]

The decisions of the court of second instance (handed down in December 1992) and the appellate division (handed down in March 1994) certainly rectified the position. Nevertheless, the decision of De Villiers J in the court of first instance (handed down in July 1992) indicated the

---

[1787] *Diepsloot Residents' and Landowners' Association v Administrator, Transvaal* 1993 1 SA 577 (T) per De Villiers J, 584C; 585F-G.

[1788] *Diepsloot Residents' and Landowners' Association v Administrator, Transvaal* 1993 3 SA 49 (T) per McCreath J, 58A ff.

[1789] *Diepsloot* (note 1788 above), per McCreath J, 65F-G.

[1790] *Diepsloot* (note 1788 above), per McCreath J, 65B-C.

[1791] *Diepsloot Residents' and Landowners' Association v Administrator, Transvaal* 1994 3 SA 336 (A), per Smalberger JA, 348H-I.

[1792] *Diepsloot* (note 1791 above), per Smalberger JA, 353H-I.

[1793] *Diepsloot* (note 1791 above), per Smalberger JA, 349E-G.

kind of obstacles in the way of social restructuring early in the pre-transitional period. These included the long history of judicial conservatism with regard to statutory interpretation,[1794] which resulted, in the decision of the court of first instance. The court disregarded the broader context surrounding the enactment of a statutory provision (except as a last resort in cases where the so-called ordinary meaning of a provision would be unclear) and focused on an analysis of the content of the contested provisions of the act. Such an approach could all too easily be employed to undermine any legislative initiatives on social restructuring in the context of property.

In general, meaningful social restructuring in the areas of class, race and gender inequalities was not on the agenda during the pre-transitional land reform period.[1795] Reforms in this period basically focused on removing the formal obstacles in the way of the acquisition of land rights by black South Africans; opening up communal tenures to individual ownership and extending benefits of the dominant property rights regime to those who had the means to gain access to the market.[1796] Little attention was paid to addressing the problems of the landless, especially those in rural areas. Further, the dominant property relations were left unscathed by the changes.[1797] These reforms were therefore rather ineffective. The main problem was that they still took place within the existing legal order where ownership prevailed over other subordinated forms of land control, like leasehold and "communal" or "tribal" land rights. Even in the fast-changing political order of the beginning of the nineties, the diversification of land rights preferred by and predicted from academic quarters did not get the recognition it deserved from the legislative organs of the pre-transitional regime.

Two keywords signify the trend for property law reform and land reform during the period immediately preceding the political changes: *privatisation* and *communalisation*. This might seem like a contradiction in terms, but should be understood against the political goals of the previous out-going government: The chief aim was to protect existing landowners against a radical property law and land reform. To placate the traditional authorities developed under the Black Administration

---

[1794] *Roux*, 1993 SAJHR, 543.

[1795] *Gutto*, Property and Land Reform (1995), 58.

[1796] *Murphy* in *Rwelamira/Werle (eds)*, Confronting Past Injustices (1996), 114.

[1797] *Van der Walt*, 1999 Koers, 289.

Act[1798] and the Black Authorities Act,[1799] and to invest in their likely coalition in a conservative force against possible future radical property and land rights reform, the government in the last days of apartheid attempted to entrench the existing powers of these authorities. Thus conditions were created in which existing traditional leaders could amass wealth and consolidate their power.[1800] The success of these reforms was therefore questionable.

1.3. Constitutional Prerogative for the Overall Land Reform Programme

One of the clear purposes, and indeed one of the most devastating effects of apartheid policy, was to deny black South Africans access to land.[1801] Where access to land was recognised, tenure was generally precarious. It is not surprising that, with the advent of the new constitutional order, this deep injustice was acknowledged. The process of property reform gained renewed support in the Interim and Final Constitutions in that both contain express provisions pertaining to restitution and redistribution of land and access to land.[1802] An important part of the function of the new constitution is to free land and property distribution patterns from the shackles of apartheid, and to actively promote the establishment and maintenance of a more just distribution of property and of greater access to land and security of land tenure. The introduction of the property guarantee was an attempt to reverse the

---

[1798] 38 of 1927.

[1799] 126 of 1951.

[1800] *Gutto,* Property and Land Reform (1995), 59-60 mentions the example of the Lebowa Farmers' Title to Land Trust, which received illegal transfer of 400 large farms (around 30 percent of the total area of the former Lebowa) under the Chief Minister Nelson Ramodike, thereby causing complete ineffectiveness of the Upgrading of Land Tenure Rights Act to address the land needs of peasants.

[1801] *DVB Behuising (Pty) Ltd v North West Provincial Government and others* (note 612 above) per Goldstone, O'Regan and Sachs JJ, par. 103.

[1802] In the Interim Constitution, the commitment to land reform (or rather, land restitution) is not solely contained in the Bill of Rights, but in sec. 121-123 IC, that should, however, be read with the property guarantee in sec. 28 IC. In the Final Constitution, the land reform provisions are contained within the Bill of Rights itself: sec. 25(4)-(9) FC.

systematic process of erosion to which most "black" land rights were subjected during years of apartheid.[1803]

The Final Constitution, like the Interim Constitution did before it, plays an active role in land reform. Section 25(5) to (7) FC provides that:

> *(5) The state must take reasonable legislative and other measures, within its available resources, to foster conditions which enable citizens to gain access to land on an equitable basis.*

> *(6) A person or community whose tenure of land is legally insecure as a result of past racially discriminatory laws or practices is entitled, to the extent provided by an Act of Parliament, either to tenure which is legally secure or to comparable redress.*

> *(7) A person or community dispossessed of property after 19 June 1913 as a result of past racially discriminatory laws or practices is entitled, to the extent provided by an Act of Parliament, either to restitution of that property or to equitable redress.*

These provisions place an obligation on the national legislature to provide redress through legislative means for the discrimination that happened in the past. Further, legislature is obliged to transform insecure forms of tenure into legally protected tenure. By contrast, the interim property clause could, by itself, effectively have blockaded measures for general land redistribution. However, it had to be interpreted in conformity with the constitution as a whole. This meant, in particular, that provisions like the equality and affirmative action clauses had to be taken into account.[1804] Further, the detailed provisions of sections 121 to 123 IC[1805] left little doubt that the regulation of property rights and land

---

[1803] *Van der Walt*, Constitutional Property Clause (1997), 69.

[1804] Sec. 8(2) IC; 8(3)(a) and (b) IC.

[1805] Sec. 121 IC defined the type of legislation to be enacted to effect the requirements of sec. 8(3) IC. This section also permitted imposition of conditions, limitations and exclusions which only could have been challenged in court in terms of sec. 122 IC. Sec. 122 IC required the establishment of a commission of Restitution of Land Rights to carry out investigations on the merit of the claims, to mediate and settle disputes arising from such claims and to draw up reports on unsettled claims to be submitted to court for adjudication. The powers of a court to deal with unsettled claims were spelled out in sec. 123 IC. No provision in the Interim Constitution specifically required the establishment of a special court for land restitution claims. Nevertheless, the Land Claims Court

for purposes of restitution, redistribution and reform was regarded as being in the public interest and as constituting legitimate restriction of property rights. Thus, one can safely assume that section 25 FC elaborates in express terms upon what was implicit in the Interim Constitution.

The part in the Interim Constitution dealing with restitution of land rights had four objectives. (i) It obliged Parliament to enact legislation for realising the restitution of land rights.[1806] (ii) It conferred a constitutional right to restitution upon certain categories of dispossessed persons.[1807] (iii) It compelled Parliament to establish a Commission on the Restitution of Land Rights with competence to investigate the merits of claims, to mediate and settle disputes and to draw up reports and gather evidence for the adjudication of claims.[1808] (iv) It set the parameters of the power of the judiciary (the Land Claims Court, in particular) to make orders of restoration and compensation.[1809] Section 25 FC is a further manifestation of the constitutional goal of actively promoting and maintaining a more equitable distribution of property, easier access to land and security of land tenure. As such, section 25 FC also imposes certain legislative and other duties upon the government and legislature. Further, the text of the Final Constitution provides specifically that no legislative provision may impede land reform or equitable access to natural resources.[1810]

The constitutional objectives of land reform, expressed initially in sections 121 to 123 IC, and imbued with continued importance — albeit in different terms — within section 25 FC, were first given legislative effect through the enactment of the Restitution of Land Rights Act[1811] in 1994. This act created a Commission on the Restitution of Land Rights, as well as a Land Claims Court. Thus, a two-tier approach (similar to

---

was established in terms of ch. III of the Restitution of Land Rights Act, which was enacted on the basis of sec. 121-123 IC.

[1806] Sec. 121(1) IC. Parliament has heeded this duty with the enactment of Act.

[1807] Sec. 121(2) IC.

[1808] Sec. 122 IC.

[1809] Sec. 123 IC.

[1810] Sec. 25(8) FC.

[1811] 22 of 1994.

that in the German Federal Republic after reunification)[1812] of administrative proceedings followed by judicial intervention was established, so as to provide a framework within which land claims against the state could be resolved, where possible through negotiated settlements. Before discussing the land reform policy under the new constitutional order, the functions of the commission and the court will be addressed.

1.3.1. Commission on the Restitution of Land Rights

Section 4 of the Restitution of Land Rights Act, following section 122 IC, established a Commission on Restitution of Land Rights. The commission consists of a Chief and Deputy Land Claims Commissioner appointed by the Minister of Land Affairs, assisted by a number of regional land commissioners[1813] with special skills and knowledge in the area of law, land matters, planning, community development and the history of forced removals. The requirements for the appointment of the officials are set out in the act.[1814] Public servants, drawn from a representative cross section of the population, and experts appointed on an *ad hoc* basis complete the number.[1815] The main function of the commission was to orchestrate the procedure of land restitution initiated in the Interim Constitution. Claims had to be lodged on or before 31 December 1998. However, many claims are still not finalised. This necessitates the following inquiry into the functions and activities of the commission.

[1812] See 552 below. See also *Visser/Roux* in *Rwelamira/Werle (eds)*, Confronting Past Injustices (1996), 96 note 24.

[1813] See *Carey-Miller/Pope*, Land Title in South Africa (2000), 335 for a list of the names of the present commissioners.

[1814] Sec. 4(4), Restitution of Land Rights Act. These include that the officials have to be fit to hold the office, they have to be South African citizens, and they must have skills and knowledge relevant to the work of the Commission or such legal knowledge or qualifications that the Minister of Land Affairs deem necessary.

[1815] Sec. 4, 7, 8, 9, Restitution of Land Rights Act.

1.3.1.1. Functions and Activities

In *Farjas v Regional Land Claims Commissioner, KwaZulu Natal*[1816] the essential role of the Commission was seen to be investigative, facilitative and mediatory.[1817] The functions of the commission are set out in section 6(1) of the Restitution of Land Rights Act, which has been amended on several occasions.[1818] It provides for the commission to receive and acknowledge receipt of all claims for the restitution of rights in land lodged with or transferred to it in terms of the Act.[1819] The commission should also investigate the merits of these claims,[1820] and mediate and settle[1821] disputes arising from them.[1822] Further, the commission is supposed to take reasonable steps to ensure that claimants are assisted in the preparation and submission of claims.[1823] The commission should also upon reasonable request and at regular intervals advise claimants of the progress of their claims.[1824] If settlement is out of the question, the commission must define those issues that are in dispute between the claimants and other interested parties, in order to expedite the hearing of claims by the court.[1825] It also has to draw up reports on unsettled claims for submission as evidence to the court and present any other relevant evidence to the court.[1826] Furthermore, the commission has a duty to regularly publicise information about the ability to claim restitution, and the manner in which claims should be lodged.[1827]

[1816] *Farjas v Regional Land Claims Commissioner, KwaZulu Natal* 1998 2 SA 900 (LCC).

[1817] *Pienaar,* Land Reform (2003), forthcoming.

[1818] E.g. Act 63 of 1997; Act 78 of 1996.

[1819] Sec. 6(1)(a), Restitution of Land Rights Act.

[1820] Sec. 6(1)(cA), Restitution of Land Rights Act.

[1821] Sec. 6(1)(d), Restitution of Land Rights Act provides that the commission should, subject to the provisions of section 14, report to the Court on the terms of settlement in respect of successfully mediated claims.

[1822] Sec. 6(1)(cB), Restitution of Land Rights Act.

[1823] Sec. 6(1)(b), Restitution of Land Rights Act.

[1824] Sec. 6(1)(c), Restitution of Land Rights Act.

[1825] Sec. 6(1)(e), Restitution of Land Rights Act.

[1826] Sec. 6(1)(eA), Restitution of Land Rights Act.

[1827] Sec. 6(1)(f), Restitution of Land Rights Act.

Section 6(2) of the Restitution of Land Rights Act confers certain powers to the commission. It may, for instance, monitor and make recommendations concerning the implementation of orders made by the court.[1828] It may also advise the minister regarding the most appropriate form of alternative relief, if any, for those claimants who do not qualify for the restitution of rights in land in terms of the act.[1829] It is also capable of referring questions of law and interpretation to the court.[1830] The commission may ensure that priority is given to claims which affect a substantial number of persons, or persons who have suffered substantial losses as a result of dispossession or persons with particularly pressing needs.[1831] It may generally do anything necessarily connected with or reasonably incidental to the expeditious finalisation of claims.[1832]

Section 6(3) of the Restitution of Land Rights Act confers on the regional land claims commissioner the power to apply to the court for an interdict prohibiting the sale, exchange, donation, lease, subdivision, rezoning or development of land, which may be the subject of an order of the court, or in respect of which a person or community is entitled to claim restitution. The regional commissioner or an interested party must have reason to believe that the sale, exchange, donation, lease, subdivision, rezoning or development of the land will defeat the achievement of the objects of the Restitution of Land Rights Act. However, in order to obtain such an interdict, a claim must already have been lodged in respect of such land[1833] and the owner of the land must have been notified of such a claim.[1834] The court may, in respect to such an application, grant the interdict or make any other order it deems fit.[1835]

[1828] Sec. 6(2)(a), Restitution of Land Rights Act.

[1829] Sec. 6(2)(b), Restitution of Land Rights Act.

[1830] Sec. 6(2)(c), Restitution of Land Rights Act.

[1831] Sec. 6(2)(d), Restitution of Land Rights Act.

[1832] Sec. 6(2)(e), Restitution of Land Rights Act.

[1833] Sec. 6(3)(a), Restitution of Land Rights Act.

[1834] Sec. 6(3)(b), Restitution of Land Rights Act.

[1835] Sec. 6(3), Restitution of Land Rights Act.

The commission is, thus, empowered and obliged to assist claimants with preparing and submitting their claims[1836] and to endeavour to settle land claims by advising claimants to subject the claim to a process of mediation.[1837] To aid the commission in the exercise of these functions, it has the authority to appoint experts (like persons with expertise in dispute resolution) that could assist it in the phase of administrative adjudication.[1838] Moreover, the commission also has wide powers of investigation.[1839] It could, for instance, order the production of government files and help claimants to obtain information that they were unable to find on their own.[1840]

1.3.1.2. Interaction with the Land Claims Court

Section 14 of the Restitution of Land Rights Act governs the interaction between the commission and the Land Claims Court. The commission has the power to refer matters for adjudication to the Land Claims Court.[1841] Claims are referred to the court if:[1842] (i) the parties in dispute agree in writing that it is not possible to settle the claim by mediation and negotiation; or if (ii) the parties submit an agreement considered appropriate by the regional commissioner with the request that it is made an order of the court; or if (iii) the regional commissioner is of the opinion that the claim is ready to be heard by the court. Matters for adjudication have first to be certified by the Chief Land Claims Commissioner, after having consulted the parties and upon having reached an agreement that settlement of the claim by mediation and negotiation was not possible. The parties could, alternatively, agree upon a manner in which the matter could be finalised, or the Chief Land Claims

---

[1836] Sec. 6 read with sec. 14, Restitution of Land Rights Act. Further duties included (i) the provision of publicity of restitution claims, (ii) giving priority to group claims and claims involving hardship, (iii) defining issues for adjudication, and (iv) facilitating the implementation of court orders.

[1837] Sec. 13, Restitution of Land Rights Act.

[1838] Sec. 9, Restitution of Land Rights Act.

[1839] Sec. 12, Restitution of Land Rights Act.

[1840] The power of *subpoena duces tecum* as described in sec. 12, Restitution of Land Rights Act.

[1841] Sec. 6 read with sec. 14, Restitution of Land Rights Act.

[1842] Sec. 14, Restitution of Land Rights Act.

Commissioner has to be satisfied that the claim was ready for adjudication.[1843] A claim referred to the court must be accompanied by a report
setting out the details of interested parties and the results of any investigation into possible, but unsuccessful, mediation. The report must
also recommend the most appropriate way of resolving the dispute. If
the referral of the dispute to the court was delayed for more than nine
months, an additional report must be submitted, setting out the reasons
for the delay. The certification and reporting procedures are precondi-
tions for vesting jurisdiction in a specific matter in the court.[1844] In

---

[1843] Sec. 13 and 14, Restitution of Land Rights Act.

[1844] Sec. 14(6), Restitution of Land Rights Act. Cases that were referred to the
court had furthermore to observe the administrative procedure of feasibility.
This requirement was, however, abolished by the Land Restitution and Reform
Laws Amendment Act 63 of 1997. Feasibility addressed the question of
whether restoration, acquisition or designation of land is practically achievable,
not whether it is just and equitable. Only the court can pronounce on the justness or equitableness of restoring rights in land. The procedure entailed that the
commission had to request a certificate from the Minister of Land Affairs in
which it was stated-upon advice from the relevant commissioner-whether or
not the restitution would be feasible. In this document it was declared whether
it was feasible to restore the right, or to acquire it, or to designate alternative
state-owned land for the purposes of restitution. (sec. 15(1), (2) and (3)). When
deciding to designate alternative land for restitution, the minister also had to
take into account whether state land would be available in the area where dispossession took place and whether such land would be suitable to meet the
needs of the claimant. Sec. 15(7). Interested parties were given a reasonable opportunity to make submissions on the question of feasibility. In considering this
question, the minister had to take into account (i) whether the zoning of the
land was altered after dispossession in such a way as to make restoration of the
relevant right in the land impracticable, (ii) whether development plans have
been approved in respect of the land, as this would also impede restoration, (iii)
whether any other factor would make it unfeasible to restore or acquire the
land and (iv) whether and inherent defect in the land would make it dangerous
for human habitation. Sec. 15(5), Restitution of Land Rights Act. The minister's
decision could be reviewed by the Land Claims Court. The requirement concerning the issue of certificates of feasibility (as contained in section 15 of the
Restitution Act) was repealed by the Land Restitution and Reform Laws
Amendment Act 63 of 1997, as this was the cause of considerable delay in completion of claims. See Memorandum on the Objects of the Land Restitution and
Reform Laws Amendment Bill, 1997. The requirement of a certificate of feasibility placed the Minister of Land Affairs in a position of power in the determination of the scope and pace of the restitution process. The granting or refusal
of a certificate could have become the real focus of a decision of land claims,

short, therefore, the commission operates as the initial filter and first instance of adjudication. Its chief aim is to solve each land claim in a non-adversarial manner. Only if this process does not succeed, is the claim referred to the Land Claims Court for "conventional" adjudication.[1845]

In both the *Macleantown Residents Association* case[1846] and *In Re Elandskloof Vereniging*[1847] the relation between the functions of the commission and the court, as set out in section 14 of the Restitution of Land Rights Act, was at stake. Both cases concerned the referral of specific settlement agreements to the Land Claims Court. Both these cases were reported before the amendments to the Restitution of Land Rights Act that ultimately streamlined the referal procedure,[1848] which means that many of the comments on[1849] the shortcomings of the statutory procedure are now obsolete. However, the basic guidelines[1850] set out in both these decisions are presently still useful. In the *Elandskloof* case it was decided that a settlement was not invalid merely because the claim which was being settled was in fact open to doubt or the amount paid for the land was too high or too low.[1851] In the case of settlement agreements, the Land Claims Court does not investigate the validity of the claim or the reasonableness of compensation agreed on by the par-

---

thereby leaving the restitution process to the mercy of bureaucratic red tape. However, skilful use of the feasibility procedure could provide a useful device for managing the proliferating number of urban claims that threatened to overburden the restitution process. The certificate could, for instance, be withheld pending the design of an appropriate urban restructuring plan for the area concerned. It could also encourage cost-effective group awards or compromises. *Visser/Roux* in *Rwelamira/Werle (eds)*, Confronting Past Injustices (1996), 97.

[1845] *Visser/Roux* in *Rwelamira/Werle (eds)*, Confronting Past Injustices (1996), 96.

[1846] *In Re Macleantown Residents Association* 1996 4 SA 1272 (LCC).

[1847] *In Re Elandskloof Vereniging* 1999 1 SA 176 (LCC).

[1848] See 456 ff. below.

[1849] See *In Re Macleantown Residents Association* (note 1846 above), 1285G-1286B.

[1850] E.g. that if the transfer of state-owned property is involved, particulars of the property, particulars of the person to whom or community to which it will be transferred and particulars of the relevant state department have to be included into the agreement.

[1851] The case concerned a referral of a settlement agreement to the Court to be made an order of court under sec. 14(1)(c) of the Restitution of Land Rights Act, which has been repealed since.

ties. However, the court must ensure that the settlement does not prejudice the rights of persons who were not party to the agreement. The following requirements were listed in order for settlement agreements to be made orders of the court:[1852] (i) the settlement must be clear and enforceable; (ii) it must be properly executed; (iii) it must be signed by or on behalf of all interested parties or their representatives; (iv) it must not be against public policy; and (v) it must comply with the requirements of the Restitution of Land Rights Act. In the particular case, the formation of an association[1853] was also a condition of the agreement. This aspect can also be incorporated in the court order. In the course of its decision in the *Macleantown* case, the court pointed out[1854] the necessity of examining the legislation under which it is entitled to make an order upon referral of a settlement agreement, and of determining whether all requirements imposed by such legislation have been met. The court cited section 14(3) of the Restitution of Land Rights Act in order to indicate its awareness that it can only convert a settlement agreement into an order of the court if the competence of such an order is clear in terms of the Restitution of Land Rights Act.[1855] From these decisions, it seems clear that the court cannot waive compliance with the requirements of section 14 of the Restitution of Land Rights Act. However, the addition (by the Land Restitution and Reform Laws Amendment Act[1856]) of the provision that the court may, on good cause shown, condone noncompliance with the provisions of section 14 of the Restitution of Land Rights Act, seems to constitute a definite adjustment in the relation between the Land Claims Court and the commission.[1857]

Since 1997[1858] a claim for restitution of a right in land can under certain circumstances[1859] be made directly to the court. The claimant must ob-

---

[1852] *In Re Elandskloof Vereniging* (note 1847 above), decision of Gildenhuys J, 179G.

[1853] Under the Communal Property Associations Act 28 of 1996.

[1854] *In Re Macleantown Residents Association* (note 1846 above), 1276G.

[1855] *In Re Macleantown Residents Association* (note 1846 above), 1276H.

[1856] 18 of 1999.

[1857] *Carey-Miller/Pope*, Land Title in South Africa (2000), 358.

[1858] See the Land Restitution and Reform Laws Amendment Act 63 of 1997, which introduced ch. IIIA.

[1859] I.e. that a sec. 35 court order has already been made in respect of a right relating to specific land (sec. 38B(1)(a), Restitution of Land Rights Act), or that

tain leave from the court.[1860] Provision is also made for the necessary co-ordination between the commission and the court so that the investigation of a matter is suspended pending the outcome of an application for direct access. The insertion is intended to make the process of restitution more effective and efficient in terms of the delivery of results.[1861] It thus constitutes a further adjustment in the relation between the commission and the court for the sake of expediting restitution.

1.3.1.3. Influence on the Rights of Landowners

In the exercise of their powers, the commission and its functionaries could seriously restrict the rights of owners of land in dispute. The Restitution Act determines that once notice of the claim has been given, the land claims commissioner must be informed of any intention to alienate or develop the land.[1862] Such endorsement renders it a criminal offence to obstruct the passage of the claim in an improper manner, to evict claimants and to remove or destroy improvements upon the land without the written authority of the Chief Land Claims Commissioner.[1863] In order to police the process, the regional commissioner can also enter the land to prepare an inventory of assets, a list of persons employed or resident on the land and a report on the agricultural and mining activities on the land.[1864]

1.3.2. Creation and Functions of the Land Claims Court

The Land Claims Court has been established as a court of law, with the specific function of presiding over the realignment of property rights in South Africa, taking into account the history of racially based dispossession.[1865] Scollo-Lavizzari[1866] ascribes the establishment of a separate

---

a notice has been published in the Gazette in terms of either sec. 12(4) or 38D(1), Restitution of Land Rights Act, in respect of land and the period specified in the notice has expired (sec. 38B(1)(b), Restitution of Land Rights Act).

[1860] Sec. 38B(1), Restitution of Land Rights Act.

[1861] *Carey-Miller/Pope*, Land Title in South Africa (2000), 391.

[1862] In terms of sec. 11(7)(aA), Restitution of Land Rights Act.

[1863] Sec. 11(7), Restitution of Land Rights Act.

[1864] Sec. 11(8), Restitution of Land Rights Act.

[1865] *Chaskalson*, 1997 Consultus, 31.

court solely concerned with matters pertaining to land reform and restitution to fears that the unfortunate experience with land reform in India could be repeated in South Africa. The reluctance of the Indian judiciary to promote the parliamentary policy of land reform by rigidly upholding individual property rights in terms of the Indian Constitution resulted in the courts losing credibility among the members of the Indian society. A similar result in South Africa could be disastrous.

The Land Claims Court has the same status as the High Court.[1867] The Court consists of a President of the Court and five judges.[1868] The court, situated in Randburg, has national jurisdiction,[1869] similar to that of a provincial division of the Supreme Court in civil proceedings[1870] as well as all the ancillary powers necessary or reasonably incidental to the performance of its functions. The latter includes the power to grant interlocutory orders and interdicts. The procedural rules of the Land Claims Court also resemble those of the High Court, in so far as the President of the court has not exercised his or her capacity to make rules of procedure.[1871] The court frequently operates as a circuit court in

---

[1866] *Scollo-Lavizzari,* Restitution of Land Rights in an Administrative Law Environment (1996), 22.

[1867] Appeals against decisions of the Land Claims Court have to be directed either to the Constitutional Court or to the Appellate Division of the Supreme Court. Sec. 36, 37 and 38, Restitution of Land Rights Act.

[1868] Sec. 22(4)-(5), Restitution of Land Rights Act. Provision is also made for the appointment of acting judges in certain circumstances – sec. 22(8), Restitution of Land Rights Act. See sec. 23, Restitution of Land Rights Act for an exposition of the requirements for the appointment of land claims judges.

[1869] See sec. 28K, Restitution of Land Rights Act with regard to the scope and execution of process in Court.

[1870] Sec. 22(2), Restitution of Land Rights Act.

[1871] Special rules have been set out in Government Notice 300 of 21 February 1997 and published in Government Gazette 17804 of 21 February 1997. Arbitrations in terms of the Land Reform (Labour Tenants) Act 3 of 1996 are set out in Government Notice 299 of 21 February 1997. The following features can be mentioned: (i) judges are in some regards afforded the capacity to play a more active role in the development of cases; (ii) the introduction of a pre-trial conference to expedite cases and reduce litigation costs; (iii) video-conferencing facilities may be used in appropriate circumstances; (iv) the forms are written in plain language, making them more comprehensible to litigants; (v) a standard form in all eleven official languages accompanies documents served on persons, pointing to the importance of the documents, and advising persons affected to seek legal aid; (vi) the language used in the rules has also been modernised and

exercising its national jurisdiction. All hearings are conducted in open court, except if otherwise directed by the court in special cases.[1872]

The Land Claims Court is a product of the Interim Constitution and the Restitution of Land Rights Act. Section 121 to 123 IC contained the obligation for restitution or provision of equitable redress to individuals and communities dispossessed of rights in land under racially discriminatory laws in force in South Africa since 1913. Section 123 IC made provision for the type of court orders that could be issued with regard to the restitution of land rights, but without mandating that a special court had to be established for this purpose. In order to achieve this constitutional purpose of restitution, the Restitution of Land Rights Act established, among others, the Land Claims Court. Thus, section 121(6) IC, read with sections 11(5), 14(1), 22, 34(1) and 35 of the Restitution of Land Rights Act, conferred jurisdiction on the Land Claims Court.

1.3.2.1. Jurisdiction of the Court

The court deals with the justiciability of claims once the requirements in section 122 IC had been fulfilled. This meant that the court had jurisdiction over claims only after the Commission on Restitution of Land Rights, which had to be established in terms of section 122 IC, investigated the merits of a possible claim, and tried to mediate and settle disputes arising from such a claim.[1873] If settlement was not possible,[1874]

---

simplified; (vii) procedures have been devised to accommodate the system of investigation and referral by the Commission of the Restitution of Land Rights and the Director-General of Land Affairs; (viii) the court may override an agreement between parties which would delay the filing of documents, and may order parties to comply with a prescribed time period; (ix) provision is made for the admission of an *amicus curiae* in appropriate circumstances; and (x) there are flexible provisions regarding service and service addresses.

[1872] Sec. 28B, Restitution of Land Rights Act.

[1873] See 425 above.

[1874] Claims are referred to the court if, according to sec. 14, Restitution of Land Rights Act: (i) the parties in dispute agree in writing that it is not possible to settle the claim by mediation and negotiation; and (ii) the regional commissioner certifies that it is not feasible to resolve the dispute by mediation and negotiation; or if (iii) the parties reach an agreement considered appropriate by the regional commissioner which is submitted with the request to be made an order

the commission had to draw up a report for submission as evidence to the court. Any other relevant evidence also had to be presented to the court.

The jurisdiction of the court was originally limited to claims brought under sections 121 to 123 IC. Since 1996, however, the court's jurisdiction has been extended by the Land Reform (Labour Tenants) Act,[1875] so as to hear and adjudicate all disputes arising out of the provisions of this act. Jurisdiction of the court has been further extended through the Extension of Security of Tenure Act[1876] so as to decide on disputes arising out of the measures introduced by this act to extend the security of tenure in rural areas. The latter conferred the power to grant eviction orders on the magistrate's courts, and coupled it with an automatic review function of the Land Claims Court in terms of section 19(3) of the act until the end of 1999. Therefore, the Land Claims Court was also, albeit only temporarily, the instance for automatic review of decisions of the magistrate's courts related to the extension of security of tenure.

The court has the powers to grant restitution of any right in land and to award compensation.[1877] The court's powers are further supplemented by the act, in order to ensure that the restitution process is consistent with the broader reform programme, and that land is put to its best uses within the constraints of the prevailing formal and informal tenure arrangements.[1878] In terms of section 33 of the Restitution of Land Rights Act, the court has to consider certain factors when deciding whether or not to award restitution of rights in land, compensation or alternative relief:

33 (Factors to be taken into account by Court)

In considering its decision in any particular matter the Court shall have regard to the following factors: (a) The desirability of providing for restitution of rights in land to any person or community dispossessed as a result of past racially discriminatory laws or practices; (b) the desirability of remedying past violations of human rights; (c) the

---

of the court; or if (iv) the regional commissioner is of the opinion that the claim is ready to be heard by the court.

[1875] Sec. 29; sec. 32, Land Reform (Labour Tenants) Act 3 of 1996.

[1876] 62 of 1997, sec. 17 read with sec. 20.

[1877] These powers are circumscribed by section 123 IC, read with sections 33 to 36 of the Restitution of Land Rights Act.

[1878] See 429 above.

requirements of equity and justice; (cA) if restoration of a right in land is claimed, the feasibility of such restoration; (d) the desirability of avoiding major social disruption; (e) any provision which already exists, in respect of the land in question in any matter, for that land to be dealt with in a manner which is designed to protect and advance persons, or categories of persons, disadvantaged by unfair discrimination in order to promote the achievement of equality and redress the results of past racial discrimination; (eA) the amount of compensation or any other consideration received in respect of the dispossession, and the circumstances prevailing at the time of the dispossession; (eB) the history of the dispossession, the hardship caused, the current use of the land and the history of the acquisition and use of the land; (eC) in the case of an order for equitable redress in the form of financial compensation, changes over time in the value of money; (f) any other factor which the Court may consider relevant and consistent with the spirit and objects of the Constitution and in particular the provisions of section 9 of the Constitution.

The sole function of these rather vague factors is to direct the attention of the court to the fact that restitution is a legitimate and desirable goal. Thus, the restitution process more closely approximated a process of peace-making, reconciliation and affirmative action.[1879]

The duty of the court in section 33(c) of the Restitution of Land Rights Act to have regard to "the requirements of equity and justice" in deciding any particular matter, has induced Chaskalson[1880] to refer to this jurisdiction of the court as "equitable jurisdiction." There is no precedent in South African land law or property law that could provide the court with guidelines on how this equitable jurisdiction should be exercised. If the court chooses to draw on the experience of other countries, the treatment of restitution and reparation issues in the Federal Republic of Germany might be a helpful guideline.

[1879] *Scollo-Lavizzari*, Restitution of Land Rights in an Administrative Law Environment (1996), 25.

[1880] *Chaskalson*, 1997 Consultus, 32.

1.3.2.2. Relevance of the Land Claims Court for Property Reform in
South Africa

The Land Claims Court is an integral part of the mechanism established
by the Restitution of Land Rights Act to deal with the process of restitution. However, its powers stretch further than the restitution programme. In considering the court's role, it is important to keep the interaction of the court and commission in mind. The former is in many
regards complementary to the latter.[1881]

The Land Claims Court constantly considers claims for stability and
security by landowners, as well as claims for restitution and reparation
by the dispossessed. As such, it is constantly confronted with a difficult
challenge: it has to balance the protection of private property rights
against the need for social justice. The Land Claims Court is, therefore,
the place where the conflicting values as embodied in the constitutional
property clauses can gain material content. The treatment of these issues by the court will be discussed in the course of this chapter with
reference to the different elements constituting legislative attempts to
reform land law in South Africa. However, some general effects of the
Land Claims Court's powers should be mentioned at the outset.

(i) The court's power to order restoration includes the power to adjust
the nature of the right previously held by the applicant, and to determine the kind of title under which the right may be held in future.[1882]
The original right may therefore be either upgraded or downgraded,
and may even assume a different legal form. The court can also allocate
any right connected to the restored rights, like servitudes or other limited real rights. In view of the fact that the court is concerned with restoring certain rights to persons dispossessed as a result of the policy of
racial segregation, it seems unlikely that the rights of which restoration
is claimed will be further downgraded. The power of the court to upgrade title is therefore, apparently more important. In claims for the
restoration of rights in terms of quitrent or permission to occupy[1883]
which were lost as a result of forced removal or incorporation of land

---

[1881] *Carey-Miller/Pope*, Land Title in South Africa (2000), 367-368.

[1882] Sec. 35(4) of the Restitution of Land Rights Act.

[1883] Held in terms of the regulations in Proclamation R188 of 18 June 1969.
These tenures involved the imposition of limitations and conditions upon the
exercise of the entitlements of the real rights and gave the government excessive
powers in relation to the land. *Murphy* in *Rwelamira/Werle (eds)*, Confronting
Past Injustices (1996), 130.

into the bantustans, the court has jurisdiction not only to restore these rights, but also to upgrade them to freehold without the racially imposed restrictions.[1884] This is an important development, as the legal nature of these rights have not been sufficiently clarified in the Upgrading of Land Tenure Rights Act[1885] which formed part of the outgoing government's land reform programme between 1991 and 1993.

(ii) The court can furthermore use its power in terms of section 35(4) of the Restitution of Land Rights Act to introduce an equitable and functional division of ownership in respect of different aspects of the same piece of land. If labour tenancy and informal occupancy on farms are to be regarded as "rights in land", then the court, in the restoration process, could upgrade these "rights" into new forms of equitable tenure, providing the beneficiaries with better legal protection.[1886] In making such an order, however, the court must, with the utmost sensitivity, endeavour to balance commercially related land-use with the social security advantages deriving from tribal structures and group affiliations.

(iii) The court's power to restore rights in land owned by or falling within the area of jurisdiction of any national, provincial or local government body, is qualified by section 34 of the Restitution of Land Rights Act.[1887] The relevant public authority may apply to the court for an order that the rights in land shall not be restored to the claimant. The court will grant the order once it is satisfied that it is in the public interest and that the public or a substantial part thereof will suffer substantial prejudice if the land is restored to the claimant. This provision raises interesting possibilities. It could, for instance, be invoked by a local authority under pressure from the owners and residents on land neighbouring the land concerned on the grounds that restoration may result in a decline in standards or market values.[1888] On the other hand, this

---

[1884] In terms of sec. 35(4) of the Restitution of Land Rights Act.

[1885] 112 of 1991.

[1886] *Murphy* in *Rwelamira/Werle (eds)*, Confronting Past Injustices (1996), 130. The Land Reform (Labour Tenant) Act, however, also provides for the vesting of ownership in land by labour tenants (see 477 ff. below). Labour tenants can therefore, in terms of the provisions of this act become owners in own right.

[1887] See *Pienaar*, Land Reform (2003), forthcoming; *Singh v North Central and South Central Metropolitan Substructure Councils of the Durban Metropolitan Area* 1999 1 All SA 350 (LCC).

[1888] See the facts in the case of *Diepsloot Residents and Landowners Association v Administrator, Transvaal* (note 1787 above).

provision could also have been invoked more progressively by applying it, for example, to help the Cape Town local authority solve the District Six[1889] dilemma. The Land Claims Court recently found[1890] that, although it was true that the object of the Restitution of Land Rights Act was restitution, it is equally true that the act aims to achieve restitution in a way that is in harmony with the public interest. In *Ex Parte North Central and South Central Metropolitan Substructure Councils of the Durban Metropolitan Area*,[1891] the Land Claims Court developed the concept of *public interest* in this context.[1892] The case arose from the purported development of Cato Manor, an area from which a large group of persons have forcibly been removed during the times of apartheid. They applied for the section 34 order of exclusion from restitution, and were opposed by claimants for restoration. During the proceedings, the parties started negotiations and finally reached an agreement, which they then wanted to incorporate into the court order under section 34(5)(d) of the Restitution of Land Rights Act. The settlement entailed an agreement to proceed with the development as planned, but subject to the proviso that where restoration was feasible any respondent who wished to pursue a claim, would be entitled to do so. Respondents who wished to return to the area without insisting on restoration or for whom restoration was not a viable option were also able to benefit from the development. The court found that, in the instant case, both development and restoration were in the public interest.[1893] Any agreement that accommodated both, with the consent of all

---

[1889] This refers to the vacant land in the centre of Cape Town, previously owned by white landlords. The expropriation and clearance of District Six during the 1960's and 1970's is regarded by many Capetonians of all creeds and colours as the most brutal and insensitive act of the apartheid government towards their city, as it tore out a vibrant and colourful community from the heart of Cape Town. Many would like to see the still vacant land redeveloped and restored, not to the original landlords, but to the tenants who were shunted out to a variety of urban wastelands on the Cape Flats. *Preißler,* Rückgabe von Landrechten (1998), 95-105 provides an extensive analysis of this issue.

[1890] See the decision of *Singh v North Central & South Central Metropolitan Substructure Councils* (note 1887 above).

[1891] *Ex Parte North Central and South Central Metropolitan Substructure Councils of the Durban Metropolitan Area* (note 1464 above).

[1892] See the discussion of *Pienaar,* Land Reform (2003), forthcoming.

[1893] *Ex Parte North Central and South Central Metropolitan Substructure Councils of the Durban Metropolitan Area* (note 1464 above), 83B-C and E-F.

the parties concerned, would henceforth eminently be in the public interest. A section 34(5) order was consequently granted.[1894]

2. Legislation Shaping the Policy of Land Reform

The endorsement of the restitution and redistribution of land and access to land in the Interim and Final Constitutions has prompted the new government to initiate further legislative measures, amend existing legislation and introduce various programmes, strategies and policies. A two-pronged approach has been adopted: On the one hand, the government strives to create an environment in which these policies can be implemented, and on the other hand it provides direct financial and other support services.[1895] The general function of the land reform, redistribution and restitution legislation promulgated since 1994, is to give effect to the broad constitutional objectives of land reform,[1896] and thus to revive and restore the legal protection and commercial value of "black" land rights. Most of the legislation is apparently directed at balancing the competing interests of the landowners, on the one hand, and the landless, on the other, in the most suitable, rational, feasible and least intrusive manner possible.

In the course of 1997, the government published another White Paper,[1897] in which the policy pertaining to the land reform programme is

---

[1894] In *Singh and Others v North Central & South Central Local Councils* (note 1470 above) another application was brought before the court by participants and other claimants in respect of land in Cato Manor who were not party to the agreement that was incorporated into the sec. 34 court order. The applicants claimed that the respondents were in breach of numerous obligations under the said agreement and claimed, in most instances, orders of specific performance. The application was dismissed on the facts and did not undermine the principles relating to public interest as said out in the discussion above.

[1895] *Department of Land Affairs*, White Paper on South African Land Policy (1997). Online at http://www.polity.org.za/govdocs/white_papers/landwp.html [16.12.1998], par. 2.3.

[1896] *Van der Walt*, Constitutional Property Clause (1997), 69.

[1897] Cf note 1895 above.

set out. According to this document, the government's policy consists of three separate, but interconnected elements:[1898]

(i) The first element, *land restitution*, aims at redressing the wrongs caused by forced removals, which took place after 1913. The restitution process is, therefore, limited in scope[1899] as well as lifespan.[1900] In principle, the Restitution of Land Rights Act,[1901] which has been amended in some respects,[1902] determine how issues of restitution should be dealt with. The Land Claims Court and Commission on the Restitution of Land Rights give effect to the provisions of this act.[1903] However, the functions of these institutions are not limited to the restitution programme, but extend to the rest of the broad land reform programme as a whole.

(ii) The second element, *land redistribution*, aims at providing the disadvantaged and the poor with access to land for residential and productive purposes. It addresses the needs of the poorest urban and rural residents, labour tenants, farm workers as well as new entrants to agriculture. As such, it is a wider project aimed at rectifying some of the inequalities in the existing land distribution patterns in South Africa. It deals with a wide variety of different policies, strategies and projects. Legislative measures falling within the purview of land redistribution[1904] can be found in the Less Formal Township Establishment Act,[1905] the

---

[1898] White Paper (1997) par. 2.3. See *Van der Merwe/Pienaar* in *Jackson/Wilde (eds)*, Reform of Property Law (1997), 359.

[1899] See *Carey-Miller/Pope*, Land Title in South Africa (2000), 320-326.

[1900] See *Van der Walt*, 1999 Koers, 270-271 note 16.

[1901] 22 of 1994.

[1902] See e.g. Land Restitution and Reform Laws Amendment Act 63 of 1997. References to the amended texts are expressly indicated in the course of this chapter.

[1903] These bodies were established under the Restitution of Land Rights Act. See 422 ff. above.

[1904] Academics differ in opinion as to the classification of the legislation according to the three legs of the government's reform programme. This can be ascribed to the fact that the programmes and the different statutes sometimes overlap as far as objectives and the means to attain these objectives are concerned. See the classifications of *Van der Walt*, 1999 Koers, 275, 282-283; *Carey-Miller/Pope*, Land Title in South Africa (2000), 404-405, 459-461; *Pienaar*, Land Reform (2000), 11-12, 29.

[1905] 113 of 1991.

Provision of Certain Land and Assistance Act,[1906] the Development Facilitation Act,[1907] the Land Reform (Labour Tenants) Act,[1908] the Extension of Security of Tenure Act[1909] and the Housing Act.[1910] The redistribution programme overlaps to some extent with the third element of the overall reform programme (land tenure reform), as will be indicated in due course.

(iii) The third element, *land tenure reform*, reviews present land policy, administration and legislation with the aims of improving the security of tenure of all South Africans and of accommodating diverse forms of land tenure, including certain kinds of communal tenure. The problem[1911] with many of these "rights" is that they either do not provide sufficient security of title[1912] or that they are unsuitable for the purpose they are supposed to serve.[1913] Land tenure reform therefore represents that part of the reform process by which the land rights of people who do have land or access to land are strengthened and secured. Legislative measures falling within the purview of land tenure reform[1914] can be found in the Conversion of Certain Rights into Leasehold or Ownership Act,[1915] the Upgrading of Land Tenure Rights Act,[1916] the Development Facilitation Act,[1917] the Land Reform (Labour Tenants) Act,[1918]

[1906] 126 of 1993. Renamed from the "Provision of Certain Land for Settlement Act 126 of 1993" by the Provision of Certain Land for Settlement Amendment Act 26 of 1998.

[1907] 67 of 1995.

[1908] 3 of 1996.

[1909] 62 of 1997.

[1910] 107 of 1997.

[1911] *Van der Walt*, 1999 Koers, 281-282.

[1912] Because of the way in which they have been acquired or vested or because of the discriminatory laws that applied to them in the past.

[1913] E.g. because they do not provide access to financing, or because they feature within a problematic tribal or group structure that might disadvantage women or other land users.

[1914] See note 1904 above.

[1915] 81 of 1988.

[1916] 112 of 1991.

[1917] 67 of 1995.

[1918] 3 of 1996.

the Extension of Security of Tenure Act,[1919] the Communal Property Associations Act,[1920] the Interim Protection of Informal Land Rights Act[1921] and the Prevention of Illegal Eviction from and Unlawful Occupation of Land Act.[1922]

Each of these elements of reform has some consequences for the development of property law in the South African legal order. Selecting only specific legislative measures for discussion admittedly does injustice to the process of land and property reform in South Africa. For present purposes, however, a discussion of some of the legislation as examples of the broader reform process will have to suffice. For interest's sake, the process of redistribution and tenure reform will be discussed, albeit only briefly.[1923] However, in keeping with the objectives of the present exposition, the principles and procedures of land restitution are chosen as the main component of the discussion, because of the parallels with the German reform process introduced after the reunification in 1990.[1924] Nevertheless, it will be indicated in the course of this chapter, that the different processes of reform in South Africa are intertwined and their categorisation into programmes of restitution, (and especially) redistribution and tenure reform, can only be a superficial aid for understanding the reform process in its entirety. Accordingly, this exterior categorisation also serves to provide the structure of the following discussion.

2.1. Land Restitution (Restitution of Land Rights Act)

The Restitution of Land Rights Act was the practical embodiment of the constitutional directive[1925] that legislation enabling the restitution of

---

[1919] 62 of 1997.

[1920] 28 of 1996.

[1921] 31 of 1996.

[1922] 19 of 1998.

[1923] More detailed discussions can be found in *Van der Walt*, 1999 Koers, 275 ff.; *Carey-Miller/Pope*, Land Title in South Africa (2000), 398 ff., 456 ff.; *Pienaar*, Land Reform (2003), forthcoming; and *Erasmus*, Interaction between Property Rights and Land Reform (1998), 281 ff., in particular 415-421 and 421-436.

[1924] See 535 ff. below.

[1925] Sec. 121-123, read with sec. 28 IC.

land rights should be passed, and was the first act that was promulgated by the new government during December 1994.[1926] The Land Restitution and Reform Laws Amendment Act,[1927] which came into effect on 21 November 1997, brought the Restitution of Land Rights Act into line with section 25(7) FC. In the case of *Uitenhage Local Transitional Council v Zenza and Others*[1928] it was stated that the mere fact that provision is specifically made in the constitution[1929] for the restitution of land rights, does not mean that persons can take the law into their own hands and invade property thinking it is their constitutional right to do so. The Restitution of Land Rights Act is thus the only mechanism to realise these restitution rights and persons claiming restitution have to follow the correct procedure, as set out in the act.

The preamble to the Restitution of Land Rights Act confirms the constitutional right to restitution and the aim of the act to promote and to protect the advancement of persons, groups or categories of persons disadvantaged by unfair discrimination, in order to promote their full and equal enjoyment of rights in land. The act accordingly also prescribes the procedures to be followed in lodging claims at the Commission on Restitution of Land Rights[1930] and during the mediation and investigation process. It also established the Land Claims Court,[1931] which has to consider difficult claims that cannot be mediated and settled by the commission itself.[1932] Consequently, the operation of this act will be

---

[1926] *Pienaar,* Land Reform (2003), forthcoming. Proclamation R176 in GG 16166 of 02.12.1994.

[1927] 63 of 1997.

[1928] *Uitenhage Local Transitional Council v Zenza and Others* 1997 8 BCLR 115 (SE). This case concerned the invasion of land that was earmarked for the development of a housing project. The illegal occupants claimed that the invasion ought to be allowed because they formed part of the category of persons who would benefit from land reform in general and land restitution in particular.

[1929] Sec. 121 IC and sec. 25(7) FC.

[1930] Established in terms of sec. 122(1) IC (see *Farjas (Pty) Ltd v Regional Land Claims Commissioner, KwaZulu-Natal* (note 1816 above), 907C and the Restitution of Land Rights Act.

[1931] The Interim Constitution envisaged claims going to "a court of law," (sec. 122(1)(c) IC) but the Restitution of Land Rights Act created a specialised "Land Claims Court".

[1932] The Land Claims Court has since its implementation also obtained further functions. See 429 ff. above.

discussed and evaluated in the light of the constitutional protection and regulation of property in South Africa.

2.1.1. Operation of the Restitution of Land Rights Act

The definition of "restitution" should be determined by a cumulative reading of three separate definitions in section 1 of the Restitution of Land Rights Act.[1933] The event of restitution of a right in land is defined as the restoring of a right in land or the provision of equitable redress. *Restitution of a right in land* means "the return of a right in land or a portion of land dispossessed after 19 June 1913 as a result of past racially discriminatory laws or practices." A *right in land* is defined as "any right in land whether registered or unregistered." It can apparently include the interest of a labour tenant and sharecropper, a customary law interest, the interest of a beneficiary under a trust arrangement and a beneficial occupation for a continuous period of not less than 10 years prior to the dispossession in question. This understanding of the concept "restitution" is underscored by the provision in section 25(7) FC that[1934]

> "[a] person or community dispossessed of property after 19 June 1913 as a result of past racially discriminatory laws or practices is entitled, to the extent provided by an Act of Parliament, either to restitution of that property or to equitable redress."

This provision should be read with section 2 of the Restitution of Land Rights Act,[1935] which provides:

Section 2 (Entitlement to restitution):

(1) A person shall be entitled to restitution of a right in land if – (a) he or she is a person or community [sic] dispossessed of a right in land after 19 June 1913 as a result of past racially discriminatory laws or practices or a direct descendant of such a person; and (b) ... (c) the claim for such restitution is lodged not later than 31 December 1998.

(2) No person shall be entitled to restitution of a right in land if – (a) just and equitable compensation as contemplated in section 25(3) of the Constitution; or (b) any other consideration which is just and eq-

---

[1933] *Carey-Miller/Pope*, Land Title in South Africa (2000), 320.

[1934] Emphasis added.

[1935] Note that the numbering of this section was changed by Act 18 of 1999.

uitable, calculated at the time of any dispossession of such right, was received in respect of such dispossession.

In effect, this section sets seven requirements to qualify for restitution, thus also limiting the number of claims.

(i) The claimant must be a *person*[1936] (or direct descendant[1937] of such a person) or *community*.[1938] The term "person" probably extends to natural as well as legal persons, given the fact that "communities" are included as claimants in terms of the Restitution of Land Rights Act. The acknowledgement the right of a community to claim restitution is an endorsement of communal tenure systems in traditional and modern customary law. Community claims to restitution would then much rather be predicated upon the informal tenures underlying the formal land distribution system imposed by apartheid. This becomes apparent from the definition of "community" in the Restitution of Land Rights Act:[1939]

> " *'[C]ommunity' means any group of persons whose rights in land are derived from shared rules determining access to land held in common by such group, and includes part of any such group.* "

[1936] Read with Annexure A of the commission's rules, it seems as if the term *person* includes legal persons in the form of trusts. *Roux* in *Budlender/Latsky/ Roux*, New Land Law (1998), ch. 3A, 11 further submits that companies (like property-development companies which lost land rights in terms of the Group Areas Act) would also be entitled to claim, because any other interpretation would run contrary to the spirit of the act.

[1937] This term is defined as "including the spouse or partner in a customary union of such person whether or not such customary union has been registered." Registration of customary unions was only compulsory in Natal. In effect, therefore, most of these customary unions are not registered.

[1938] Sec. 121(2) IC; Sec. 25(7) FC read with sec. 2(1)(a), Restitution of Land Rights Act. The extent to which communities will exercise their rights to institute claims for restitution against the state, is not certain. It is not generally so that the victims of forced removals still form cohesive groups or communities. Mostly they have been dispersed over a wide geographical area, which renders it difficult to identify homogenous groups capable of demanding consolidated pieces of land. See *Murphy* in *Rwelamira/Werle (eds)*, Confronting Past Injustices (1996), 123. It is, however, not required that a community wanting to submit a claim need to still live together as a group. The community also need not have continued occupying land on a communal basis.

[1939] Sec. 1 *"community"*, Restitution of Land Rights Act.

The "shared rules" referred to in the definition could mean that in appropriate circumstances, mechanisms of land control could be based on status or on a specific understanding of legal personality. Thus, access to land need not involve the original rights of landowners to exclude others from the use and enjoyment of the land.[1940] As becomes apparent from an analysis of the nature of claims by communities, claims for restitution on the basis of informal tenure need not be permitted under all circumstances.[1941] The act provides for claims of rival groups within a single community.[1942]

(ii) The claimant must have been *dispossessed*. Neither the Restitution of Land Rights Act, nor the provisions of the Interim and Final Constitution contain a definition of "dispossession". From case law it appears that the claimant need not have been physically dispossessed of the land. The withdrawal of permission to control land is apparently sufficient. "Dispossession" apparently also includes "downgraded" in the sense that the person or community was forced, as a result of racially based legislation, to exchange a stronger right in land for a weaker one.[1943] In *Dulabh v Department of Land Affairs*[1944] it had to be decided whether the claimants would qualify as applicants under the Restitution of Land Rights Act, seeing that they never lost physical possession of the property concerned. The transfer of the property under a will to the heiress, being of the Indian group, was prohibited when the area was proclaimed a white area under the Group Areas Act[1945]. The Community Development Board obtained the property at a reduced price, but

---

[1940] *Murphy* in *Rwelamira/Werle (eds)*, Confronting Past Injustices (1996), 123.

[1941] *Murphy* in *Rwelamira/Werle (eds)*, Confronting Past Injustices (1996), 123.

[1942] See definition of "community"; sec. 13(1)(b), sec. 35(3), Restitution of Land Rights Act.

[1943] See *Nchabeleng v Phasha* 1998 3 SA 578 (LCC). This case involved the application for an interim interdict preventing the respondent from making any new allotments of the land concerned, the meaning of "dispossession" was also considered. Here both parties claimed that they had authority over the land at stake (595G-I). It was found that the requirement of "dispossession" would be complied with if the applicant could prove that his tribe had previously exercised exclusive control over the land in question, and that this control was reduced or removed by governmental action, he would be sucessful (595G-596F).

[1944] *Dulabh v Department of Land Affairs* 1997 4 SA 1108 (LCC), par. 25-31.

[1945] 36 of 1966.

the family remained on as tenants. The property was later sold to a white owner, but the family remained tenants. Subsequent to the abolition of the racially based land control system, the family bought back the property in 1994 and sent a letter to the commission setting out a fully motivated claim for compensation. With regard to the issue relating to dispossession, it was found that the fact that the claimants had leased the property for over 20 years indicated that they were never willing to part with it and were determined retain physical possession.[1946] It was found that the prohibition of the transfer of property to the heiress and the subsequent sale thereof to the Community Development Board constituted a dispossession of her right in land.[1947] Because all the other requirements were fulfilled,[1948] the court concluded that a dispossession had occurred.

(iii) The claimant had to have been deprived of a *right in land*. This term is defined to denote:

> "*any right in land whether registered or unregistered, [including] the interest of a labour tenant and sharecropper, a customary law interest, the interest of a beneficiary under a trust arrangement and beneficial occupation for a continuous period of not less than 10 years prior to the dispossession in question*".

This definition quite clearly includes "lesser" real rights and personal rights. No *numerus clausus* of rights in land is contemplated by the definition. The Land Claims Court has ruled that *rights in land* include the "right to inherit and take transfer of property"[1949] and "rights derived from occupation (in certain circumstances) or from customary law."[1950] It is thus clear that the definition of *rights in land* supports the argument for an extended category of rights, which does not readily comply with the categorisation of rights in private law as either real or personal.[1951] In fact, it stretches much further than "real rights"

[1946] *Dulabh v Department of Land Affairs* (note 1944 above), 1118F.

[1947] More specifically her right to inherit and take transfer of the property.

[1948] She was dispossessed of her right by sec. 23 of the Group Areas Act, a racially discriminatory law, and Proclamation 212 of 24 July 1968, which delineated the property to fall within a white group area (*Dulabh v Department of Land Affairs* (note 1944 above), 1120C-D).

[1949] *Re Dulabh: Re Erf 1687, King William's Town* LCC Case no 14/96, par. 25-31.

[1950] *Nchabeleng v Phasha* (note 1943 above), par. 27.

[1951] See *Carey-Miller/Pope*, Land Title in South Africa (2000), 323.

(whether properly registered in terms of the Deeds Registries Act[1952] or "embryonic" in the sense of susceptible of registration, but not duly registered as such[1953]). The express inclusion of "rights" (or claims) of labour tenancy[1954] and sharecropping[1955] supports the view that the category of *rights in land* is not determined on the basis of the traditional notion of *registrable real rights* alone. Similarly, the inclusion of customary law interests in the definition of rights in land indicates that the definition is quite wide, and that it does not support a categorisation of rights into either real or personal. In fact, the further incorporation of "beneficial occupation" as a right in land indicates the intention to bring even forms of possession not otherwise covered and possibly of dubious standing within the ambit of the restitution policy.[1956] This, together with the inclusion of the category of "beneficiaries under a trust agreement" indicates that the definition of rights in land is in principle aimed first and foremost at eliminating all possible forms of racial discrimination on the basis of land segregation by making the category of rights capable of restoration as wide as possible.

(iv) Dispossession must have taken place *after 19 June 1913*.[1957] This requirement reflects the view that land restitution in South Africa is not directed at restoring ancestral lands on the basis of pre-colonial entitlement.[1958] The moral basis for the South African restitution process is

---

[1952] 47 of 1937.

[1953] See the discussion of *Carey-Miller/Pope*, Land Title in South Africa (2000), 323.

[1954] See 477 ff. below.

[1955] The system of sharecropping involved black people living on and working parts of white-owned farmland. The significant feature was that the landowner provided the seed and the parties shared the crop on the basis of an agreement. This system was abolished by the Black Land Act 27 of 1913, which had the effect of stripping black African cash tenants and sharecroppers of their land. *Carey-Miller/Pope*, Land Title in South Africa (2000), 324.

[1956] *Carey-Miller/Pope*, Land Title in South Africa (2000), 324-325.

[1957] Sec. 121(3) IC, read with sec. 2(1)(a) of the Restitution of Land Rights Act.

[1958] *Carey-Miller/Pope*, Land Title in South Africa (2000), 316-317 points out that the White Paper of 1997 expresses the government's view that the judicial process system of the Restitution of Land Rights Act would be ineffective when applied to historic land claims. The reasons provided for the argument in the White Paper of 1997 that South Africa's ancestral land claims would create a number of problems and legal-political complexities that would be impossible

apparently found in the illegitimate and systematic monopolisation of the country's land surface, instrumentally consolidated by laws effecting racial segregation after 1913.[1959] The South African land restitution policy is, in principle, aimed at correcting these inequities administered by "internal" colonialism. The reversal of dispossession of land before 1913 is left to a later, more gradual process of land reform (in the redistribution and tenure reform programmes) and the economic empowerment of the landless.[1960]

(v) The dispossession must have had the *purpose of furthering the object of a racially discriminatory law or practice*.[1961] No definition exists of the term "racially based land measure." However, reference to sections 121 to 123 IC could be of some help.[1962] The historical and statutory context of a contested provision could, furthermore, provide the necessary in-

---

to unravel (par. 4.14.2.) are: (i) that most historic claims are justified on the basis of tribal affiliations and that entertaining such claims would awaken and/or prolong destructive ethnic and racial politics; (ii) that members of ethnically defined communities have increased in number more than eight times in the 20th century alone and do not form cohesive groups any more; and (iii) that large parts of South Africa could be subject to overlapping and competing claims where peices of land have been occupied in succession by, e.g. San, Khoi, Xhosa, Mfengu, Trekkers and British.

[1959] *Visser/Roux* in *Rwelamira/Werle (eds)*, Confronting Past Injustices (1996), 94. The cut-off date for dispossessions enabling restitution resembles that of the coming into force of the Black Land Act. A further consideration for not including restitution claims originating in the time before 1913 was found in the ANC's concern that such claims would be politically divisive. They feared that the Inkatha Freedom Party would use the land restitution process to stake an ethnic claim to the whole of KwaZulu-Natal.

[1960] *Visser/Roux* in *Rwelamira/Werle (eds)*, Confronting Past Injustices (1996), 95 note 18.

[1961] Sec. 25 FC read with sec. 2(1)(a), Restitution of Land Rights Act. Racially discriminatory laws under which forced removals were effected include: sec. 5(1)(b), Black Administration Act 38 of 1927; sec. 2, 3, 13(2), 26(5), 29(1), 33(5) and 37(3), Development Trust and Land Act 18 of 1936; sec. 2, 3(2), 9(1), 16(1)(a), 38(3)(1) and 38(3)(p), Blacks (Urban Areas) Consolidation Act 25 of 1945; "enabling provisions," National States Constitutions Act 21 of 1971; Borders of Particular States Extension Act 2 of 1980; sec. 27bis, Black Laws Amendment Act, 42 of 1964; sec. 41, Group Areas Act 36 of 1966; sec. 35, 38, Community Development Acts 3 of 1966 and 41 of 1984). See *Roux* in *Budlender/Latsky/Roux*, New Land Law (1998), ch. 3A, 19.

[1962] *Minister of Land Affairs v Slamdien* 1999 1 All SA 608 (LCC), par. 21.

terpretative background,[1963] especially if it is viewed in relation to the underlying purpose of the Restitution of Land Rights Act.[1964] The judgment of Bam, J in *Farjas (Pty) Ltd v Regional Land Claims Commissioner, KwaZulu Natal*[1965] indicates that deciding whether a particular expropriation had been effected under or for the purpose of furthering the object of a law which would have been inconsistent with the prohibition of racial discrimination contained in s 8(2) IC would require that commissioners delve deeply into complex issues.[1966] The reason for the complexity was explained with reference to the South African societal structure under apartheid:[1967]

> *"One of the reasons why this issue will frequently be a vexed and hotly contested one is precisely that South African society was saturated with laws which directly and indirectly discriminated against persons along the lines enumerated in s 8(2) [IC]. There was scarcely any aspect of life and activity that was not permeated with racial discrimination."*

> *"Consequently, there was many a law and many an expropriation which at first might appear innocuous, only to emerge to be serving or promoting racist interests upon closer scrutiny. The Expropriation Act was particularly vulnerable to abuse since there was no obligation on expropriators to state the specific purpose for which the expropriation was being made..."*

Although some statutory provisions effecting forced removals were quite obviously racially discriminatory; certain apparently "race-neutral" provisions could have similar effects.[1968] Unlawful dispossessions, although not strictly speaking effected "as a result of" racially discriminatory law, can also come under the purview of this require-

---

[1963] *Minister of Land Affairs v Slamdien* (note 1962 above), par. 27.

[1964] *Minister of Land Affairs v Slamdien* (note 1962 above), par. 28-29. The preamble of the Restitution of Land Rights Act might play an important role in such an inquiry.

[1965] *Farjas (Pty) Ltd v Regional Land Claims Commissioner* (note 1816 above).

[1966] *Farjas (Pty) Ltd v Regional Land Claims Commissioner* (note 1816 above), 937D.

[1967] *Farjas (Pty) Ltd v Regional Land Claims Commissioner* (note 1816 above), 937E-G.

[1968] Sec. 22, Slums Act 6 of 1959; sec. 15(5)(a), Community Development Act 3 of 1966; sec. 6F, Prevention of Illegal Squatting Act 52 of 1951.

ment.[1969] Furthermore, not only the actions of governmental organs can give rise to restitution. The inclusion of the term "discriminatory practice" implies that so-called "private-law evictions", that is, evictions carried out by private persons within a prevailing climate of racially based evictions, could also give rise to an entitlement to claim restitution.[1970] Accordingly, Bam J found that even though not each and every expropriation was invariably tinged with an element of racial discrimination, the appropriate approach in cases of dispossession by expropriation should be that [1971]

> *"only when it is patently clear that there is no racial discrimination that a Regional Land Claims Commissioner would be entitled to reject a claim."*

The Land Claims Court thus tends to interpret the requirement that dispossession had to occur in terms of a racially discriminatory law or practice generously,[1972] but seemingly attempts to relate the interpretation to practices with land in particular. The case of *Minister of Land Affairs v Slamdien*[1973] concerned land bought and registered in 1955, after which the area in which the land was situated was declared a "coloured group area" in terms of the Group Areas Act. The state purchased the land in 1970 and established a primary school on it. The applicant sought a declaratory order to the effect that the respondents were not dispossessed of a right in land as a result of past discriminatory laws or practice.[1974] It was decided, on applying a purposive ap-

---

[1969] *Roux* in *Budlender/Latsky/Roux,* New Land Law (1998), ch. 3A, 19.

[1970] See, for instance, the situation of the San-community in the Northern Cape. Approximately 12 800 hectares of land close to Kimberly (Platfontein) were handed over to them in 1999 (Daily Mail & Guardian, 20 May 1999). In 1998, a deal was made with the San community living in the area formerly known as the Kalahari Gemsbok National Park, enabling them to jointly own and manage a large part of this nature reserve (Daily Mail & Guardian, 23 December 1998).

[1971] *Farjas (Pty) Ltd v Regional Land Claims Commissioner* (note 1816 above), 938B.

[1972] See *Carey-Miller/Pope,* Land Title in South Africa (2000), 332, relying on the decision of *Farjas (Pty) Ltd v Regional Land Claims Commissioner* (note 1816 above).

[1973] *Minister of Land Affairs v Slamdien* (note 1962 above).

[1974] The issue was determined (*Minister of Land Affairs v Slamdien* (note 1962 above), par. 11) with regard to three questions: (a) was the Group Areas Act a *racially discriminatory law* as referred to in section 2(1)(a) and defined in

proach[1975] to interpretation of this requirement, that the Group Areas Act was plainly the type of law which was contemplated in section 2(1)(a) of the Restitution of Land Rights Act.[1976] It was, however, further decided that this finding as such did not constitute grounds for restitution. The dispossession itself also has to fall within the ambit of the Restitution Act. It was concluded[1977] that, in this case, the discriminatory component of the practice was not directed at the exercise of land rights, either directly or indirectly. The discrimination was directed at the school's prospective pupils who would have to be educated separately from other race groups. This type of racially discriminatory practice was, according to the decision, not contemplated in section 2(1)(a) of the Restitution of Land Rights Act. Moreover, it was found, dispossession in this case was not "a result" of the Group Areas Act.[1978] This indicatates that the existence of a causal link between dispossession and racial discrimination is an important factor to be taken into account when interpreting this requirement.

(vi) Dispossession must have taken place *without payment of just and equitable compensation.*[1979] This means that persons dispossessed of rights under the Expropriation Act[1980] and corresponding legislation would in principle be excluded from claiming restitution. However, if just and equitable compensation were not paid, a claim would be possible, provided that all other requirements are met. Just and equitable compensation in this context is determined by taking into account the factors listed in section 25(3)(a) to (e) FC, or circumstances that pre-

---

section 1 of the Restitution Act, (b) was the building of the coloured school a *racially discriminatory practice* and (c) was the dispossession of the property *as a result of* the law referred to in (a) or practice referred to in (b)?

[1975] Dodson J explained (*Minister of Land Affairs v Slamdien* (note 1962 above), par. 12-13) that the purposive approach should be applied, as the statutory measure originated directly from the bill of rights and was designed to give content to one of the rights included in the bill.

[1976] See also *Re Macleantown Residents Association* (note 1846 above), 1277, where the Group Areas Act is declared to "clearly [offend] the provisions of section 8(2) [IC]."

[1977] *Minister of Land Affairs v Slamdien* (note 1962 above), par. 33.

[1978] *Minister of Land Affairs v Slamdien* (note 1962 above), par. 41.

[1979] Sec. 2, Restitution of Land Rights Act.

[1980] Act 63 of 1975.

vailed at the time of the dispossession.[1981] Such circumstances might include the availability of alternative land, which could have been bought with the compensation received, and the suitability of any land, which might have been awarded in lieu of compensation.[1982] There are thus two bases upon which a bar against restitution might be established if the claimant had already received a fair *quid pro quo*.[1983] If just and equitable compensation was not paid at the time of dispossession, the amount that was actually paid for compensation may be set off by the court against an award of restitution in kind or restitution in money.

(vii) The claim for restitution had to be *lodged on or before 31 December 1998*. The Land Restitution and Reform Laws Amendment Act,[1984] extended the cut-off date for the lodgement of claims from 1 May 1995. Especially in the face of massive adult illiteracy in rural areas where no or only limited access to the public media by potential claimants exists, the three-years period for lodging claims can be regarded as fair.[1985] The deadline is subject to possible limitation on the basis of a special mechanism, which allows all the claims in respect of a particular area of land to be dealt with together as a matter of effective application of resource.[1986] In *Re Former Highlands Residents*[1987] the question whether a number of claimants who did not submit their claims timeously, could be allowed to piggy-back on claims timely lodged in respect of land in the same township.[1988] The late claimants *inter alia* submitted that, because of the constitutional right to restitution of persons dispossessed of their property as a result of racially discriminatory laws or practices,

---

[1981] Sec. 2(2), Restitution of Land Rights Act.

[1982] *Roux* in *Budlender/Latsky/Roux*, New Land Law (1998), ch. 3A, 22.

[1983] *Carey-Miller/Pope*, Land Title in South Africa (2000), 333.

[1984] 63 of 1997.

[1985] *Murphy* in *Rwelamira/Werle (eds)*, Confronting Past Injustices (1996), 120.

[1986] *Carey-Miller/Pope*, Land Title in South Africa (2000), 332, relying on sec. 12(4), Restitution of Land Rights Act.

[1987] *Re Former Highlands Residents* 2000 1 SA 489 (LCC).

[1988] The claimants or their forebears were the owners of properties in the Highlands township. They alleged that in the mid-1960s they or their forebears had been dispossessed of certain properties as a result of racially discriminatory laws or practices. With the exception of three intervening claimants, they had all lodged claims for restitution in terms of the Restitution of Land Rights Act before the cut-off date of 31 December 1998.

a generous rather than a legalistic perspective had to be favoured, which would allegedly have the effect of allowing their (admittedly late) claims. It was held[1989] that a purposive approach to the Restitution of Land Rights Act made it clear that the act was not focused simply on restoring the status quo ante, but that it instead limited the benefit of restitution to persons who had lodged their claims timeously. Accordingly, late claims did not gain validity just because other people lodged timely claims in respect of the same land. Accordingly, the intervening claimants were denied a right to restitution.

2.1.1.1. Administrative Proceedings

The restitution process is in essence administrative rather than adjudicatory. This means that claims reach the Land Claims Court only in circumstances where the Commission for the Restitution of Land Rights have done everything within its powers to resolve the claim, and was not successful. The powers of the commission and its relation to the Land Claims Court have been discussed above.[1990] This section concentrates only on the procedure for lodgement of claims.

A claim for restitution was lodged by completing and filing the prescribed forms at the office of the Commission on the Restitution of Land Rights.[1991] The claim had to include a description of the land in question,[1992] the nature of the right being claimed,[1993] and the claimant's needs and attitude towards receiving alternative land or compensation. The basis of the claim also determined the kind of documents and certificates that could accompany the claim.[1994] In case of a community

---

[1989] *Re Former Highlands Residents* (note 1987 above) par. 11.

[1990] See 422 ff. above.

[1991] Sec. 10, Restitution of Land Rights Act.

[1992] Sec. 10(1), Restitution of Land Rights Act. This will require details of the history of the title to the land, other interests in the land, the market value and the value of investments in the land and the present use to which the property is being put.

[1993] This requires details such as the relationship between the dispossessed person and the claimant, the history of dispossession, the hardship caused and the interests of the dispossessed, the amount of any compensation received, and the claimant's needs and attitude towards receiving alternative land as compensation.

[1994] See *Carey-Miller/Pope*, Land Title in South Africa (2000), 340-341.

claim, the basis of the applicant's representation and an appropriate resolution or document supporting the right to represent the community had to be provided.[1995] If the appropriate regional land commissioner was satisfied that the claim met the entry requirements and that it was not frivolous or vexatious,[1996] the claim was made public for the benefit of persons who may have had interests in the claim.[1997] Otherwise, the commissioner had to advise the claimant why the claim has not been approved.[1998]

The Restitution of Land Rights Act set certain "acceptance criteria" which should be met in order to enable the regional land claims commissioner with jurisdiction over a specific claim to publish notice of it in the Gazette.[1999] These include the seven "qualifying criteria"[2000] plus two[2001] additional requirements: (i) the claim had to be lodged in the prescribed manner;[2002] and (ii) the claim should not have been frivolous or vexatious.[2003] In the *Farjas* case,[2004] it was remarked that the acceptance criteria for the restitution process involved, on the one hand, matters in respect of which the commissioners could exercise no independent discretion, and on the other hand, discretionary criteria which

---

[1995] Sec. 10(3), Restitution of Land Rights Act.

[1996] *Farjas (Pty) Ltd v Regional Land Claims Commissioner, KwaZulu-Natal* (note 1816 above).

[1997] Sec. 11(1), Restitution of Land Rights Act.

[1998] Sec. 11(4), Restitution of Land Rights Act.

[1999] Sec. 11(1), Restitution of Land Rights Act. However, in the case of *Farjas (Pty) Ltd v Regional Land Claims Commissioner, KwaZulu-Natal* (note 1816 above), 923F it was indicated that the standard of proof is not as onerous as the Commission might have perceived it to be, and that the applicants are merely expected to show that they have an arguable case.

[2000] See 442 above.

[2001] A third requirement, that no order had been made by the court in terms of section 35 of the Restitution of Land Rights Act in respect of the land in question, was deleted by the Land Restitution and Reform Laws Amendment Act 18 of 1999.

[2002] Sec. 11(1)(a), Restitution of Land Rights Act. This entails compliance with the requirements of the prescribed claim form in Annexure A. *Carey-Miller/Pope*, Land Title in South Africa (2000), 342.

[2003] Sec. 11(1)(c) and (3), Restitution of Land Rights Act.

[2004] *Farjas (Pty) Ltd v Land Claims Commissioner, KwaZulu-Natal* (note 1816 above), 937A-B.

could involve complexities and needed to be approached with great caution. On the basis of this distinction, the acceptance criteria can be either classified as "substantive" or "formal".

The decision in the *Farjas* case was primarily concerned with the basis upon which a regional commissioner's discretion should be exercised. As such, the decision provides important guidelines as to the substantive acceptance criteria. The case concerned a review of the regional land claims commissioner's dismissal of a claim for restitution as being frivolous or vexatious. Upon review of the commissioner's decision, Dodson J emphasised that section 24 IC elevated the right to administrative justice to the status of a constitutional right and thereby widened the High Court's common law powers of review relating to an administrative action considerably.[2005] It was also indicated that the inquiry called for under section 11(3) of the Restitution of Land Rights Act involved two aspects:[2006] (i) reference to the legislation under which dispossession had been effected and (ii) the issue whether dispossession had been effected for the purpose of furthering the object of a law which today would be inconsistent with the equality clause. It was then found that the commissioner in this instance omitted the first aspect and failed to refer to the relevant legislation.[2007] It was further indicated that the commissioner erred in her finding as to the basis of the legislation upon which dispossession occurred.[2008] It was also found that the

---

[2005] *Farjas (Pty) Ltd v Land Claims Commissioner, KwaZulu-Nata l*(note 1816 above), 910F-G, 912H-913A.

[2006] It should be noted that the Restitution of Land Rights Act was amended and that no distinction between two different aspects of the inquiry is made since the amendment by Act 63 of 1997. Nevertheless, the new unitary requirement that the dispossession must be "a result of past racially discriminatory laws or practices" still admits the form of dispossession involved in the *Farjas* case. *Carey-Miller/Pope,* Land Title in South Africa (2000), 344.

[2007] *Farjas (Pty) Ltd v Land Claims Commissioner, KwaZulu-Natal* (note 1816 above), 920I-921E, 924F-925B.

[2008] She found that the land in question had been expropriated under the Expropriation Act 63 of 1975 and failed to consider the fact that the land was in fact expropriated under sec. 21(1)(a) of the Housing Development Act (House of Delegates) 4 of 1987, a provision that arguably would not survive scrutiny under sec. 8(2) IC. Thus, even had she conducted the first leg of the enquiry required by sec. 121(2)(b) IC, the commissioner had been completely mistaken as to the law under which it had been effected (*Farjas* (note 1816 above), 921F-G, 922G).

dismissal of the claim as being frivolous or vexatious was based on the commissioner's finding that just and equitable compensation had been paid when dispossession had occurred. This was not what was required of her: unless she had been convinced that the applicants had indisputably received just and equitable compensation as contemplated in section 121(4) IC and that their pursuit of the claim was an intentional abuse of the land claims process, she ought to have accepted the claims.[2009] Moreover, because the applicant was not invited even to show why the compensation was not just and equitable, there was also a general failure to comply with the *audi et alteram partem* rule.[2010] The applicant should also have been furnished with reasons for the dismissal and ought to have been given the opportunity to respond and amplify the claim. The commission was accordingly ordered to reconsider the applicant's claim under section 11(1) of the Restitution of Land Rights Act.

As far as the "frivolous or vexatious" nature of claims is concerned, the court found that a claim or legal proceeding would meet this description if it is pursued where there is plainly no prospect of success and the motive of the claimant or plaintiff is to harass the defendant.[2011] Thus, if it emerged from the documents submitted with the claim or otherwise available to the respondent that the applicants had indisputably received just and equitable compensation as contemplated in section 121(4) IC and that their pursuit of the claim was an intentional abuse of the land claims process, and this view was not altered by the hearing afforded to them, the commissioner would have been entitled to dismiss the claim for being frivolous or vexatious. This requirement was presumably introduced in order to provide the commission with the opportunity to dismiss summarily claims which are manifestly without substance or merit, and to avoid the waste of resources involved in the preliminary processing of a claim which is manifestly lacking in any merit or substance.[2012]

In the *Farjas* case, the court identified the lodging of the claim in the prescribed manner and the required date of 19 June 1913 as a limit to

---

[2009] *Farjas (Pty) Ltd v Land Claims Commissioner* (note 1816 above), 926I-927E.

[2010] *Farjas (Pty) Ltd v Land Claims Commissioner* (note 1816 above), 926G-I.

[2011] *Farjas (Pty) Ltd v Land Claims Commissioner* (note 1816 above), 927B-C.

[2012] *Carey-Miller/Pope*, Land Title in South Africa (2000), 346.

determine whether dispossessions qualify for restitution, as purely mechanical considerations involving no independent discretion.[2013] These would, therefore, constitute the formal acceptance criteria. The requirement that the claim has to be lodged in the prescribed manner indicates the significance of the fact that the restitution process is by nature rather administrative than litigious or adjudicatory.[2014] It is also directly connected to the effectiveness of the restitution process. The requirement that the dispossession must have occurred after 19 June 1913 is a matter of factual evidence.

In contrast to the deadline for lodging, no definite time limit is set for the settlement of claims. This might be detrimental to owners whose land is subject to restitution claims, as the mere threat of a restitution claim could sterilise property for years.[2015] Decades of wrongdoing, however, cannot be undone overnight.[2016]

2.1.1.2. Judicial Proceedings

Claims are justiciable by the Land Claims Court only once they have been dealt with by the commission. Matters may be referred to the Land Claims Court only if[2017] (i) the parties to a dispute arising from a claim have agreed, in writing, that settlement by mediation and negotiation is not possible,[2018] (ii) the regional land claims commissioner has certified that it is not feasible to resolve any dispute arising from the

---

[2013] *Farjas (Pty) Ltd v Land Claims Commissioner* (note 1816 above), 936-937.

[2014] *Carey-Miller/Pope,* Land Title in South Africa (2000), 347.

[2015] See also, in the German context, 552 below.

[2016] Sec. 14(7) of the Restitution of Land Rights Act, which has been repealed, made provision for expediting the process by requiring a special report, furnishing reasons for delays in cases that were not completed or referred to court within nine months after lodgement.

[2017] Certified confirmation by the Chief Land Claims Commissioner is necessary in all cases. Moreover, any claim referred to the court must be accompanied by a document incorporating the results of the commission's investigations into the merits of the claim, a report on the failure of any party to accede to mediation, a list of the parties with interest in the claim, and the commission's recommendations as to the most appropriate manner in which the claim can be resoved. Sec. 14(2), Restitution of Land Rights Act.

[2018] Sec. 14(1)(a), Restitution of Land Rights Act.

claim by mediation and negotiation,[2019] or (iii) the regional land claims commissioner is of the opinion that the claim is ready for hearing by the court.[2020] Parties may be represented by either an attorney or advocate, and where the Chief Land Claims Commissioner considers it necessary, legal representation may be arranged for parties unable to afford their own.[2021]

If the parties could come to an agreement, the regional land claims commissioner should provide a written validation, certifying that the agreement ought not to be referred to the court.[2022] However, referral of an agreement is still possible[2023] in terms of section 11 of the Restitution of Land Rights Act if (i) the regional land claims commissioner is of the opinion that a question of law arising out of the agreement needs to be resolved; (ii) there is doubt as to whether or not all parties who have an interest in the claim are parties to the agreement; (iii) there is doubt as to the validity of the agreement or any part of it; (iv) there is doubt as to the feasibility of the implementation of the agreement; (v) the agreement is not just and equitable in respect of any party; (vi) the agreement is contrary to the provisions of the Restitution of Land Rights Act; (vii) the authority of any signatory is in doubt; (viii) the agreement is vague and contradictory; (ix) the parties to the agreement agree that it is desirable that the agreement be made an order of court; or (x) the agreement ought to be referred to the court for any other good reason.[2024]

The court must, in terms of section 33 of the Restitution of Land Rights Act, consider certain factors when deciding whether or not to award restitution of rights in land, compensation or alternative relief. They

---

[2019] Sec. 14(1)(b), Restitution of Land Rights Act. Feasibility in this context is not connected to the now repealed general requirement of a feasibility certificate.

[2020] Sec. 14(1)(d), Restitution of Land Rights Act.

[2021] *Murphy* in *Rwelamira/Werle (eds)*, Confronting Past Injustices (1996), 127.

[2022] Sec. 14(3), Restitution of Land Rights Act.

[2023] In which case it should be accompanied by a copy of the relevant deed of settlement and a report providing the background information regarding the claim and the settlement, information necessary for the court to establish whether or not it has jurisdiction, the reasons for the referral of the matter, and any recommendations the regional land claims commissioners may make as to how the matter should be dealt with. Sec. 14(4), Restitution of Land Rights Act.

[2024] Sec. 14(3A)(i)-(xi), Restitution of Land Rights Act.

are: (i) the desirability of providing restitution to people dispossessed under discriminatory laws; (ii) the desirability of remedying past human rights violations; (iii) the requirements of equity and justice; (iv) the feasibility of a restoration order; (v) any affirmative action measure pertaining to the land in question; (v) the desirability of avoiding major social disruption; (vi) the amount of compensation received in respect of dispossession; (vii) the history of the dispossession, hardship caused, current use of the land and the history of the acquisition of the land, (viii) the changes over time in the value of money if an order for equitable redress is contemplated; and (ix) any other relevant factor consistent with the spirit and objects of the constitution and the principle of substantive equality.

After having considered the feasibility of a particular order and having determined whether any compensation has already been awarded to the claimant,[2025] the court may make one of several possible orders:[2026]

(i) The court may review an administrative act, an interdict or a mandamus or a declaration of rights upon application by an aggrieved party.[2027] In limited circumstances (for instance, where the facts are in dispute), the review may be sought through the action procedure.

(ii) The court may order that rights in respect of certain land specified in the application ought *not* to be restored. Such an order might bind the claimants and/or the state.[2028] The court should, accordingly, be satisfied that it is in the public interest that the rights in question should not be restored to a specific claimant and that the public or any substantial part thereof will suffer substantial prejudice unless a barring order is made.[2029] Consequently, the state may not confer such rights in respect of land by way of consent. Instead, the court could, for instance order that alternative land for restitution be allocated to the claimants, or that compensation be paid to them. In *Ex Parte North Central and South Central Metropolitan Substructure Councils, Durban*[2030] the ap-

---

[2025] See *Pienaar,* Nuwe Sakeregtelike Ontwikkelings op die Gebied van Grondhervorming (1997), 9.

[2026] In terms of sec. 123 IC.

[2027] See e.g. the *Farjas* case discussed 452 ff. above.

[2028] *Scollo-Lavizzari,* Restitution of Land Rights in an Administrative Law Environment (1996), 26.

[2029] Sec. 34(6), Restitution of Land Rights Act.

[2030] *Ex Parte North Central and South Central Metropolitan Substructure Councils, Durban* (note 1464 above).

plicant sough a so-called blocking order in terms of section 34(5)(b) of the Restitution of Land Rights Act. Potential claimants of restitution opposed it. Finally, a compromise order was made, based on a negotiated settlement. In the course of the judgement, however, the meaning of the twin prerequisites of the barring order of section 34(6) of the act was considered. Influenced by the procedure of balancing private and public interests in the context of Australian native title, the court concluded that it would be almost axiomatic that restoration of rights in that specific case would be in the public interest, given the history of dispossession and the resultant devastation and hardship suffered by the forcibly removed community.[2031]

(iii) As regards awards to claimants, four possibilities are foreseen: Where the land in question is owned by the state, the court may order the state to restore the rights in that land to the claimant.[2032] Where the land in question is under private ownership, the court may again order the state to purchase or expropriate the land and restore the relevant right to the claimant. Likewise, an order can also be made for expropriation or purchase of a part of such land or of rights in the land.[2033] Where restoration of the land in question is not feasible, the court may order the state, in lieu of restoration of the rights, to grant the claimant appropriate rights in alternative state-owned land designated by the state to the satisfaction of the court and certified by the state as feasible.[2034] The court may also order the state, in lieu of restoration of the right, to pay the claimant just and equitable compensation upon consideration of all relevant factors.[2035] The court may, however, also grant the claimant alternative relief.[2036] These awards can also be accompanied by ancillary orders to implement the main court order.

[2031] *Ex Parte North Central and South Central Metropolitan Substructure Councils, Durban* (note 1464 above), 86H.

[2032] Sec. 123(1)(a) IC.

[2033] Sec. 123(1)(b) IC. Expropriation is, however, a last resort according to the policy of the Department of Land Affairs. If it is ordered that privately owned land should be acquired for the purpose of restitution of land rights, attempts will first be made at purchasing the land in question.

[2034] Sec. 123(3)(a) IC.

[2035] Sec. 123(3)(b) IC.

[2036] Sec. 123(3)(c) IC.

(iv) If monetary compensation is decided upon, the court must determine the amount and manner of payment.[2037] If an amount is not negotiated between the Department of Land Affairs and the parties involved, this might prove difficult for the court. It is submitted that the standard applicable to the determination of compensation for expropriation should apply to the determination of monetary compensation as a substitute for restitution in kind. If the Land Claims Court orders an expropriation of private land, the requirement stated in section 25(3) FC,[2038] that "just and equitable" compensation should be paid, must be observed. This is determined by considering "all relevant circumstances," but especially including:[2039]

> (a) the current use of the property; (b) the history of the acquisition and use of the property; (c) the market value of the property; (d) the extent of direct state investment and subsidy in the acquisition and beneficial capital (e) improvement of the property; and the purpose of the expropriation.

Expropriation is, however, a last resort according to the policy of the Department of Land Affairs. If it is ordered that privately owned land should be acquired for the purpose of restitution of land rights, attempts will first be made at purchasing the land in question.

The court's powers are further supplemented by the Restitution of Land Rights Act, in order to ensure that the restitution process is consistent with the broader reform programme, and that land is put to its best uses within the constraints of the existing formal and informal tenure arrangements. Section 35(2) thus empowers the court to give directions for the implementation of its order. This can entail (i) ordering

---

[2037] Although the Land Claims Court has the exclusive jurisdiction to determine compensation in respect of an expropriation pursuant to an order made by the Court in terms of sec. 35(1)(a), read with sec. 35(5), of the Restitution of Land Rights Act after the expropriation has taken place, the court has no jurisdiction to determine the compensation in respect of such expropriation until the expropriation has actually taken place. *In Re Farmerfield Communal Property Trust* 1999 1 SA 936 (LCC), 942F-G, 942H-I.

[2038] Section 123(2) IC read with section 28(3) IC contained similar provisions.

[2039] Sec. 25(3)(a)-(e) FC. The corresponding provision in the Interim Constitution (sec. 123(2) IC) also provided for the taking into account of "all relevant factors," including the history of the dispossession, the hardship caused, the use to which the property is being put, the history of its acquisition by the owner, the interests of the owner, persons affected by the expropriation and the dispossessed. See 343 ff. above.

that any compensation received must be repaid; (ii) determining pre-conditions for restoration; (iii) providing for the manner in which rights are held under communal tenures; and also (iv) making recommendations to the minister concerning the priority to be given to some claimants for access to state resources for the sake of development.

2.1.2. Evaluation

Whereas restitution might not be explicitly focused on development of the property law order as such,[2040] the restitution policy and its implementation by the legislature and the courts have some important implications for the development of property law in South Africa. These implications are discussed in the following paragraphs.

2.1.2.1. The Extent to which Existing Rights have to Accommodate New Policies

The central concept, *rights in land,* was created in section 121(2) IC, but not defined. Instead, it was left to Parliament to decide what the scope of the land claims process, and therefore also the content of the term *rights in land* would be. If only dispossession of *real rights* "in land" would qualify for restitution, the number of possible claims would have been significantly less. Numerous persons forcibly removed under apartheid were not owners in the strict private law sense, and not even the holders of real rights in land, but possessors, labour tenants, share-croppers or lessees.[2041] In the case of sharecropping[2042] and cash tenancy[2043] limited real rights could, in appropriate circumstances, be established. Past dispossessions of rights under apartheid legislation,[2044] like quitrent, permission to occupy and commonage would probably

---

[2040] *Carey-Miller,* 1999 SALJ, 750.

[2041] *Murphy* in *Rwelamira/Werle (eds),* Confronting Past Injustices (1996), 123.

[2042] *Van der Merwe,* 1990 Stell LR, 333.

[2043] E.g. when the rule *huur gaat voor koop* comes into operation against the lessor's successor in title for the duration of a valid lease. See *Johannesburg Municipal Council v Rand Townships Registrar* 1910 TPD 1314.

[2044] E.g. GN R29, R 30, R402, R 404, R 405 of 9 March 1988 and GN R293 enacted in terms of Act 38 of 1927.

also amount to *real rights*. The dispossession of these "rights" might also have given rise to claims for restitution.[2045] However, rights in terms of a lease are contractual or personal rights, which would not qualify for restitution in terms of a strict interpretation of the term rights in land. The decision of *De Jager v Sisana*,[2046] although controversial,[2047] created the impression that labour tenancy rights were also personal in nature. Finally, possession is not considered to be a "right" but a factual circumstance, which would possibly also exclude restitution claims related to previous possession.

The decisions as to whether *only* the "black spot" removals should be reversed, whether the grievances of communities who never had more than informal rights to land should also be addressed, and whether urban claims should be included in the restitution programme, turned out to be a difficult political nut to crack.[2048] Eventually, the land claims process was given an extensive scope.[2049] Apart from previously held registered real rights also more "informal" rights in land, like share-cropping and labour tenancy are embraced in the definition of *rights in land*. Nevertheless it seems as if the executive interprets the scope of the land claims process more restrictively. In the White Paper of 1997,[2050] the Department of Land Affairs stipulated that certain categories of labour tenants and victims of "betterment" policies would not qualify for restitution, and should be accommodated within the other elements of the land reform programme. However, these categories of persons could, if all requirements were complied with, also have fallen within the ambit of the restitution process. For instance, victims of "betterment planning" — a policy furthering the objectives of apartheid land law — could have been entitled to enforce restitution if they could

---

[2045] *Murphy* in *Rwelamira/Werle (eds)*, Confronting Past Injustices (1996), 124.

[2046] *De Jager v Sisana* 1930 AD 71.

[2047] See 477 below.

[2048] *Roux* in *Budlender/Latsky/Roux*, New Land Law (1998), ch. 3A, 14.

[2049] See sec. 1 *"right in land"*, Restitution of Land Rights Act.

[2050] White Paper (1997), par. 4.14.3.

prove that they had a "customary law interest"[2051] in the land in question.[2052]

With the incorporation of the requirement that a claim should qualify as a "right in land" and with the exceptionally wide definition attached to this requirement, an effective break with the categorisation of rights as either "personal" or "real" has been achieved in the context of restitution. This is an important development as far as the distinction between private and constitutional property is concerned, as the restitution of land rights can operate in both the public and the private sphere. The programme is based on the constitutional directive for it, but can influence rights of individuals to a similar extent as it can influence the position of the state with regard to landownership. In other words, the restitution of "rights in land" is an important example of how the existing private law can be overridden by a constitutional correction of the imbalances (in this case in the distribution of land) that exist in the South African society.

The restitution process focuses on the provision of rights in and access to land, on the basis of the constitutional prerogative to address racial discrimination under the previous statutory order. The obvious question is to what extent existing property rights can be maintained in the face of severe policy changes. The *Diepsloot* decisions, which were handed down in the pre-transitional period, already indicated that inroads on existing property rights would be sanctioned in view of the urgent socio-economic need for housing and access to land, even if it would be to the economic disadvantage of the holders of existing rights.

The legislative measures implementing land restitution focus extensively on administrative proceedings in processing and effecting the restoration and restitution of rights. Recourse to the judiciary for the enforcement of rights is reserved as a last resort. From the review proceedings before the Land Claims Court,[2053] it seems as if existing right holders are to an increasing extent, in terms of the restitution legislation, left to the mercy of administrative authorities. These authorities can, in effect, decide when and to which extent existing rights should

---

[2051] *Nchabeleng v Phasha* (note 1943 above), par. 27 states that the definition of *right in land* contemplates "rights derived from occupation (in certain circumstances) or from customary law."

[2052] *Roux* in *Budlender/Latsky/Roux*, New Land Law (1998), ch. 3A, 14.

[2053] E.g. *Farjas (Pty) Ltd & another v Regional Land Claims Commissioner, KwaZulu-Natal* (note 1816 above).

yield to policies underlying the administrative decisions. Judging from the *ad hoc* character of the restitution process, the powers of the administration to determine the kinds of inroads on private property that should be tolerated is cause for concern. Such administrative decisions are not necessarily conducive to legal certainty. Moreover, such decisions could involve a violation of the element of trust inherent to the constitutional state principle, which would be difficult to monitor.

Nevertheless, the restitution policy is apparently guided by the principles of fairness and justice and driven by the just demands of claimants who have been dispossessed. Inherent in these principles of fairness and justice is a consideration of the broader development interests of the country and the responsible exploitation of limited state resources.[2054] The Restitution of Land Rights Act leaves room for restitution awards that reflect the difference between land and rights in land. It also provides for restitution awards that differ depending on whether the claimant is an individual or a community. It furthermore envisages land rights that suit the social and political position of individual members of a community, and accordingly provides for restitution awards that take the potential weaknesses and insecurities of dispossessed land rights into account and allow a suitable adjustment and strengthening of the rights that are restored.[2055] Yet, the hierarchy of property rights as it is known in private law is basically left intact, with dominium of land still being the highest aspiration.[2056]

2.1.2.2. Objectives and Character of Restitution Process

As has been indicated,[2057] the goal of the restitution policy is to restore land and to make other restitution remedies available to people dispossessed by racially discriminatory legislation.[2058] Since the promulgation

---

[2054] White Paper (1997), par. 4.10.

[2055] *Van der Walt,* 1999 Koers, 275.

[2056] Sec. 2, Communal Property Associations Act constitutes a possible exception in that restitutions involving communities may be structured in terms of the framework of communal property associations rather than in the form of individual common-law ownership. *Van der Walt,* 1999 Koers, 275.

[2057] See 437 above.

[2058] The original preamble to the Restitution of Land Rights Act reiterates this objective and links the act with the constitutional prerogative of land reform: "Whereas the Constitution ... provides for the restitution of a right in

of the Restitution of Land Rights Act, it has become clear that the restitution programme would take centre stage in the new government's approach to redressing past injustices. Roux[2059] summarises the policy considerations inherent in the Act as follows:

> "More than any other recent statute, the Restitution of Land Rights Act seems to epitomise the paradox at the heart of the struggle for social justice in South Africa. At its starkest, the question posed by the Act is whether a society can ever hope, by dint of a fresh round of law-making, to undo the effects of past unjust laws."

Restitution must be conducive to the process of reconciliation, reconstruction and development. The process of restitution is accordingly characterised by the extensive powers granted to the courts in making awards, coupled with a noticeable reticence as far as the nature or content of rights that could or should be included in an order for restitution is concerned.

The Land Restitution and Reform Laws Amendment Act[2060] broadened the process, so that it is no longer restricted to land or rights in land.[2061] Nevertheless, restitution is in principle aimed at the restoration of land and/or land rights. However, the Land Claims Court is granted wide powers to make alternative orders, like adjusting the nature of the right previously held by a possible claimant, or determining the form of title under which the right may be held in future.[2062] Thus, it is ensured that the restitution award addresses the possible insecurity connected to the specific land or right in land at stake, which could result in a situation where the restitution award conflicts with other rights, or is paralysed

---

land to a person or community dispossessed under or for the purpose of furthering the objects of any racially discriminatory law; and whereas legislation for this purpose is to be designed to promote the protection and advancement of persons, groups or categories of persons disadvantaged by unfair discrimination, in order to promote their full and equal enjoyment of rights in land ...".

[2059] Roux in Budlender/Latsky/Roux, New Land Law (1998), ch. 3A, 3.

[2060] 63 of 1997.

[2061] The preamble was amended by the Land Restitution and Reform Laws Amendment Act 63 of 1997 to make it clear that the restitution process is not restricted to actual restoration of land, but includes restitution of any property as well as equitable redress, and that a major purpose of the act is to achieve equality, in accordance with the Final Constitution. Van der Walt, 1999 Koers, 272.

[2062] Sec. 35(4), Restitution of Land Rights Act.

by subsequent eviction.[2063] Similarly, the Land Claims Court is also granted the power to take into account and make adequate provision for traditional or tribal land rights when making an order to a community, in order to ensure that all members of the community receive equal access to the land awarded and that the land is held in a manner appropriate under the circumstances.[2064]

The restitution process has been criticised by some as not being extensive enough. Indeed, restitution is, by nature, a process limited in scope and lifespan, although it can influence a wide variety of situations.[2065] This appears from the targets envisaged by the White Paper on Land Reform, which include: (i) a three year period for the lodgement of claims;[2066] (ii) a five year period for the Commission and Land Claims Court to finalise claims; and (iii) a ten year period for the implementation of all court orders. The Restitution of Land Rights Act and the programme of restitution coupled with it cannot by themselves alleviate all the injustice still inherent in the land control system in South Africa. There are several reasons for this, which are all connected to the limited scope and timespan of the restitution process:

(i) First, the restitution process does not provide for restoration of land rights lost because of "external colonialism," that is, the restoration of title on the basis of pre-colonial ancestral entitlement.[2067] Most certainly, the compromise reached concerning the cut-off date for claims does have harsh consequences for some interest groups not adequately represented at the negotiations, like the Nama inhabitants of the north-western Cape, who were dispossessed of their traditional land in 1848, when the boundaries of the Cape Colony were extended to the Orange

---

[2063] *Van der Walt,* 1999 Koers, 273.

[2064] Sec. 35, Restitution of Land Rights Act.

[2065] The process of restitution includes, but is not limited to land and "rights in land". The latter concept is understood as being fairly extensive. See 442 ff. above.

[2066] The three year period for lodgement of claims had to be calculated initially from 1 May 1995. The period for the lodgement of claims was, however, extended to the 31 December 1998 by the Land Restitution and Reform Laws Amendment Act 63 of 1997.

[2067] I.e. aboriginal title, as applied in Australia, New Zealand and North America.

River.[2068] Some argue that wholesale nationalisation of land, coupled with a more openly socialist system of wealth distribution would be the only fair and legitimate response to the dispossession of the indigenous inhabitants during the era of colonial conquest.[2069] However, arguments like these lose sight of the diversification of land rights over the past 400 years in South Africa, and the massive demographic shifts involved in a restitution of rights held during the earlier phases of colonialisation.[2070] A simplistic focus on an absolutist approach to ownership, which is inherent in these arguments, would not solve South Africa's land question. Moreover, the claim that settlers confiscated all South Africa's land from the indigenous people during the 17th century is not quite accurate. Whereas much land was indeed taken by illegitimate means, especially in the north and east of the country, the establishment of the early settlements and the circumstances in which land was transferred are more complex and even more controversial than this argument proposes. The nature and effect of original and derivative claims to title can mostly not be determined on the basis of legal and moral judgment. International law also recognises certain historical arguments that support the claim that some land was indeed *terra nullius/derelicta* at the time of settlement.[2071]

(ii) Second, in spite of the gender inequality persisting in the present system of land distribution in South Africa, women also do not gain considerable benefit from the restitution programme. In traditional tribal societies in particular, women were often not capable of holding any rights relating to land. Consequently, they cannot claim restitution, as no legal basis for the claim would exist.

(iii) Third, in order to limit restitution claims to a workable number, claims based exclusively on need were omitted from the land restitution process. These claims are to be addressed in the broader land reform

---

[2068] *Visser/Roux* in *Rwelamira/Werle (eds)*, Confronting Past Injustices (1996), 94. See also the decision in *Richtersveld Community and Others v Alexkor (Pty) Ltd and Another* 2001 3 SA 1293 (LCC).

[2069] See, e.g. policy of the Pan-Africanist Congress.

[2070] See *Murphy* in *Rwelamira/Werle (eds)*, Confronting Past Injustices (1996), 121; *Van der Merwe*, 1989 TSAR, 663, 672; *Bennett*, 1993 SAJHR, 463-465.

[2071] See *Murphy* in *Rwelamira/Werle (eds)*, Confronting Past Injustices (1996), 121; *Van der Merwe*, 1989 TSAR, 663, 672; *Bennett*, 1993 SAJHR, 463-465.

programme,[2072] that is, in the course of tenure reform and redistribution of land. It should also, where necessary, be linked to initiatives of establishing gender equality in the South African society. This point is important in determining the nature of the constitutional protection and regulation of land rights. Restitution seems to be based rather on historical circumstance than on social statistics.

The case of the *Richtersveld* community raised many of the issues mentioned above.[2073] It concerned the application of the requirements for restitution in terms of the Restitution Act. The Richtersveld forms part of a larger area known as Namaqualand, and is situated south of the Garib (Orange) River in the Northern Cape Province. Two groups of indigenous peoples originally inhabited the area, long before even the Dutch colonisation of the Cape from 1652 onwards. The (pastoralist) Khoi Khoi and the (hunter-gatherer) San peoples moved about in nomadic fashion, according to the seasons and the rainfall. By the 19th century, the two groups had merged with each other. Others who came to the area, in particular some white *"trekboere"* (itinerant farmers) and the so-called *basters* (who were people of mixed descent, mainly from white fathers and San or Khoi mothers), were also incorporated into the group. The people of this new formation are sometimes referred to as Khoisan/Nama. They were governed by a chief/leader, who held his position through descent, and who was assisted by an advisory council. The Richtersveld community is a small section of this people.

The Richtersveld was placed under British rule through annexation in 1847. Since then, the area was considered to be Crown land. Seventy years later (between 1925 and 1927), a rich deposit of diamonds was discovered in the area. By that time the British Colonial Government had been replaced by a South African government, although South Africa was still regarded as a British protectorate. The South African government considered the land upon which the diamonds were discovered to be unalienated Crown land, due to the annexation thereof. Hence, they proclaimed alluvial diggings and awarded mining rights to various stakeholders. Since this time, the Richtersveld people were progressively denied access to the land they previously occupied. The ousting of these people was, for instance, effected by the erection of a fence (in

---

[2072] *Murphy* in *Rwelamira/Werle (eds)*, Confronting Past Injustices (1996), 116.

[2073] *Richtersveld Community and Others v Alexkor (Pty) Ltd and Another* (note 2068 above).

1957), the creation of farms to act as buffers between the diamond-rich area and the rest of the territory occupied by the Richtersveld community, the creation of a reserve for these people, and the establishment of the Alexander Bay Development Corporation, which would hold most of the prospecting and mining rights. This corporation was state-owned. When it was eventually converted into a private stock company (Alexkor), the state remained the largest shareholder.

Before the court, the Richtersveld Community averred a number of dispossessions.[2074] These included the failure by previous governments to recognise their rights after annexation, coupled with the proclamation of the area in terms of the Precious Stones Act, and the granting of prospecting and mining leases. Moreover, the transfer of all rights to Alexkor, the mining company which succeeded the Alexander Bay Development Corporation, was also alleged to be a dispossession in terms of the Restitution Act. A restitution of the dispossessed land rights was claimed, because of the alleged compliance with all the qualifying criteria of the Restitution Act. Alexkor and the government of South Africa opposed the application.[2075] The court did not uphold the Richtersveld community's claim, because of non-compliance with some of the requirements of the Restitution Act.[2076] The combination of the criteria regarding the racially discriminatory nature of the laws or practices, which gave rise to the dispossessions, and the cut-off date of 1913 seemed to be the biggest hurdle in the way of the claimants.[2077] Another important element which was considered, was the nature of the land rights which the community allegedly held.[2078] The court's treatment of the qualifying criteria for restitution will be briefly analysed here, in order to indicate the general understanding of the purpose of the Restitution Act.

The previous government's failure to recognise and protect the claimants' legal rights to the land gave rise to an interesting argument by the court. The court indicated that there *were* no legal rights that *needed* protection.[2079] This might seem strange in view of the fact that the court

---

[2074] *Richtersveld v Alexkor (Pty) Ltd* (note 2068 above), par. 6; 96-113.

[2075] *Richtersveld v Alexkor (Pty) Ltd* (note 2068 above), par. 5.

[2076] *Richtersveld v Alexkor (Pty) Ltd* (note 2068 above), par. 115.

[2077] *Richtersveld v Alexkor (Pty) Ltd* (note 2068 above), par. 115.

[2078] *Richtersveld v Alexkor (Pty) Ltd* (note 2068 above), par. 37-65.

[2079] *Richtersveld v Alexkor (Pty) Ltd* (note 2068 above), par. 114.

first (in a very elaborate fashion) came to the conclusion that the claimants did have possession of the land, and that they were dispossessed.[2080] The court's statement regarding the lack of protected legal rights must be understood in the light of the argumentation regarding the kind of land right upon which the claimants built their case, together with the application of the cut-off date of 1913 as qualifying criterion. The claimants proposed three possible, alternative explanations as to the nature of the right in land for which restitution was sought:[2081] (i) *full ownership* of the land; (ii) rights based on *aboriginal title*; and (iii) rights founded in their *beneficial occupation* of the land. The court eventually based the claimant's right to land on the last of these, beneficial occupation.[2082] This refers to the possession of land by a person (or community) to which no legal title is held. The possession must be exercised openly, as if the possessor is owner of the land, and must last for at least ten years. This type of possession is expressly included as falling within the ambit of "rights in land" in terms of the Restitution Act. In this instance, however, the court's finding that the claimants had beneficial occupation of the land before each of the dispossessions, was not very helpful to the claimants. This was due to the poor combination of this requirement with the other criteria, namely that of the 1913-cut-off-date, and the requisite causal link with racial discrimination.[2083]

The other contentions (regarding the nature of the claimant's rights as either full ownership or aboriginal title) failed: On the one hand, the court did not consider itself to have jurisdiction to determine whether the doctrine of aboriginal title ever formed part of South African law[2084] The doctrine of aboriginal title refers to rights of land occupation and use that vested in a community at the time of colonialisation. Once established, aboriginal title enables the community to vindicate their land (in cases of dispossession), or to obtain adequate compensation (in cases of expropriation). Although this doctrine is applied in other Anglo-American legal systems, (eg the United States and Australia), it has never before been raised before a South African court. The Land Claims Court *in casu* considered itself incapable to pronounce on the

---

[2080] *Richtersveld v Alexkor (Pty) Ltd* (note 2068 above), par. 54-65, 75, 106-109.

[2081] *Richtersveld v Alexkor (Pty) Ltd* (note 2068 above), par. 37-65.

[2082] *Richtersveld v Alexkor (Pty) Ltd* (note 2068 above), par. 114.

[2083] *Richtersveld v Alexkor (Pty) Ltd* (note 2068 above), par. 83-115.

[2084] *Richtersveld v Alexkor (Pty) Ltd* (note 2068 above), par. 44-53, 117.

question whether aboriginal title forms part of South African law. It argued that, should the doctrine of aboriginal title exist at all in South African law, it would be a remedy alternative to that of the Restitution Act. The court argued that aboriginal title could by no means be included in the Restitution Act's reference to "rights in land." If at all, it would have to be introduced through the concept of a "customary law interest", which would mean that the concept of aboriginal title has to be developed. The Constitution permits South African courts to "develop the common law" in order to give effect to the spirit and purport of the constitution, of which land reform and restitution is part. However, the Land Claims Court interpreted this provision strictly in view of chapter 8 of the Constitution, which deals with the jurisdiction of the courts. It regarded this ability to develop the common law as an ancillary power, which could only be exercised when dealing with matters which did undoubtedly fall within its jurisdiction. Hence, the court refused to see aboriginal title as a customary-law interest, arguing that it would constitute exercise of an ancillary power in the absence of a matter falling truly within its jurisdiction. On the other hand, the court also rejected the argument that the claim was based on *ownership* of the land.[2085] Its argument here involved the application of International Law prevailing at the time of annexation. According to a specific provision of nineteenth century International law, land rights of indigenous people occupying annexed territories were only recognised if their usages and conceptions of rights and duties were reconcilable with the institutions and legal ideas of civil society. From the facts it appeared that, although the Richtersveld community frequently attempted to have their rights acknowledged by the British Colonial Government, the latter did not consider the Richtersveld people to have the sufficient degree of civilisation to warrant such recognition. Hence, the British Colonial Government during the 19th century simply assumed sovereignty of, and full ownership over, the entire southern Namaqualand (including the Richtersveld), which it viewed as being *terra nullius*. The court's rejection of the claimant's contentions as to their ownership of the land is important for understanding the manner in which the other requirements were interpreted.

Having established that rights in land did exist, in the form of beneficial occupation, the court proceeded to determine whether the claimants were dispossessed of these rights as a result of racially discriminatory

---

[2085] *Richtersveld v Alexkor (Pty) Ltd* (note 2068 above), par. 37-43.

laws or practices.[2086] The court had to consider a number of acts or omissions by government or its officials, which took place after the cut-off date of 1913, and which allegedly caused racially discriminatory dispossessions. These included (i) a number of proclamations relating to the exploitation of diamonds in the area; (ii) the creation of a reserve for the Richtersveld people, which excluded the area now claimed back by the community; (iii) the prospecting and mining leases issued to Alexkor; and (iv) the physical ousting of the Richtersveld people from the land. According to the court, these dispossessions related to the exploitation of diamonds in the area, and were aimed at heightening the security surrounding the diamond mining industry. They were, therefore, not racially discriminatory. Another argument which failed was based upon the categorisation of the area as "controlled land" in terms of the Group Areas Act. This apparently disqualified the Richtersveld people from holding land unless by permit; and no permit was ever issued to them, in spite of repeated requests. The court was, however, not satisfied with the manner in which the influence of the Group Areas Act on the claimants' rights was dealt with in the pleadings.

The only recognition of racial discrimination in the present case was an *obiter dictum* of the court concerning the disregard of the indigenous laws and private rights of the Richtersveld people by the British Colonial Government upon annexation.[2087] This incidence occurred long before the 1913 cut-off date. The court pointed out that - in view of the cut-off date requirement — it does not consider itself to have jurisdiction to decide whether the 1847 annexation was a dispossession as contemplated by the Restitution Act, and that this particular act of discrimination is therefore not covered by the Restitution Act.[2088] According to the court, the only relevance this occurrence had, is that it caused all subsequent governments in South Africa to view the land as unalienated Crown land, belonging to no private individual or community, and rightfully acquired by the British Colonial Government.[2089] The court did not explore the possibility that the dispossessions which occurred after 1913 could be causally linked with the original discriminatory dispossession of 1847. This is not done in spite of repeated acknowledgements that the South African Government might have been

---

[2086] *Richtersveld v Alexkor (Pty) Ltd* (note 2068 above), par. 97-113.

[2087] *Richtersveld v Alexkor (Pty) Ltd* (note 2068 above), par. 106.

[2088] *Richtersveld v Alexkor (Pty) Ltd* (note 2068 above), par. 109.

[2089] *Richtersveld v Alexkor (Pty) Ltd* (note 2068 above), par. 110.

wrong in assuming that the Richtersveld was unalienated Crown land at the time of proclamation and issuing of the mining licences.[2090] The court did not regard itself to have jurisdiction to make findings on the possible racially discriminatory nature of dispossessions that occurred before 1913.

Interestingly, moreover, the court in this context does not refer to the powers of ancillary jurisdiction conferred to it by section 22(2)(c) of the Restitution Act. This section provides that subject to chapter 8 of the Constitution, the Court shall have, among others, the power to decide an issue either *in terms of the act itself or in terms of any other law*, which is not ordinarily within its jurisdiction but which is *incidental to an issue* within its jurisdiction, if it is *in the interests of justice* to do so. This provision could arguably place the annexation of 1847, coupled with the later actions of the South African government with regard to the Richtersveld, within the jurisdiction of the court. Each of the post-1913 dispossessions, viewed independently and without considering the surrounding circumstances, admittedly cannot lead to a finding as to racial discrimination. However, the result might be different when all acts of dispossession are regarded as parts of a whole: The progressive expulsion of the Richtersveld community from the area upon the belief that they had no rights to the land, does at least create an assumption of racial discrimination. In view of the fact that all acts of dispossession were based on the (arguably mistaken) belief by the South African government that the Richtersveld people had no rights to the land, it could be argued that the court should have exercised its ancillary jurisdiction in terms of section 22(2)(c) of the Restitution Act.

The question then is whether such a wide interpretation of the court's powers, which would stretch the application of the seven qualifying criteria of the Restitution Act to the absolute limit, was intended by legislature in the enactment of the Restitution Act. The Restitution Act was, from the outset, not directed at so-called "external colonialism" or the restoration of ancestral lands on the basis of pre-colonial entitlement. The moral basis for the South African restitution process is found in the illegitimate and systematic monopolisation of the country's land surface, instrumentally consolidated by laws effecting racial segregation after 1913. The cut-off date for dispossessions enabling restitution resembles that of the coming into force of the Black Land Act. A further consideration for not including restitution claims originating in the time

---

[2090] *Richtersveld v Alexkor (Pty) Ltd* (note 2068 above), par. 110, 114, 98.

before 1913 was found in the ANC's concern that such claims would be politically divisive.[2091] Indeed, it is trite that the Restitution Act focuses only on this so-called "internal colonialism". In the *Richtersveld* decision, the Land Claims Court takes cognisance of this fact in its finding that the "mischief" against which the Restitution Act operates, is that of spatial apartheid (i.e. the formal segregation by law of the different South African races since the beginning of the twentieth century). The court refers to a dictum in *Minister of Land Affairs and Another v Slamdien and Others*,[2092] which confirms that a purposive interpretation of the Restitution Act indicates that its underlying purpose is to address the dispossession of land rights that resulted from the policy of the apartheid government to confine each racial and ethnic group to a particular racial zone.[2093] The court then remarks:

> "*The brushing aside of claims which persons of colour might have had in respect of land because they were considered insufficiently civilised, could well be a wrong for which the Restitution Act provides not remedy. A remedy for such a wrong, if it exists, will have to be sought elsewhere.*"

In the closing paragraph of its decision[2094] the court then recommends that the Minister of Land Affairs should consider granting alternative relief to the claimants.

As is apparent from the targets envisaged for restitution by the Department of Land Affairs in the 1997 White Paper, the restitution process cannot be described as a comprehensive attempt to undo all the injustices occasioned by apartheid land law. The White Paper acknowledged that a number of unfair dispossessions are not covered by the Restitution programme.[2095] Among these are dispossessions prior to

---

[2091] *Visser/Roux* in *Rwelamira/Werle* (eds), Confronting Past Injustices (1996), 94.

[2092] *Minister of Land Affairs and Another v Slamdien and Others* 1999 1 All SA 608 (LCC), par 26.

[2093] *Richtersveld v Alexkor (Pty) Ltd* (note 2068 above), par. 93-94.

[2094] *Richtersveld v Alexkor (Pty) Ltd* (note 2068 above), par. 120.

[2095] The White Paper, par. 4.14.3 indicates three distinct categories of unfair dispossessions which are not covered by the restitution programme: (i) victims of dispossession prior to 1913; (ii) labour tenants (the Land Reform (Labour Tenants) Act 3 of 1996 is designed to address the needs of this group); and (iii) inhabitants of the former Bantustans who were dispossessed under "betterment" policies (whose needs should be addressed through tenure security pro-

1913. However, the White Paper expresses[2096] the view that applying the Restitution Act to ancestral land claims would create a number of legal-political complexities impossible to unravel. For instance, most historic claims are justified on the basis of tribal affiliations and entertaining such claims would awaken and/or prolong destructive ethnic and racial politics; thus being detrimental to the ultimate goal of reconciliation. Moreover, members of ethnically defined communities have increased in number more than eight times in the twentieth century alone and do not form cohesive groups any more; and large parts of South Africa could be subject to overlapping and competing claims where pieces of land have been occupied in succession by, eg San, Khoi, Xhosa, Mfengu, Trekkers and British.[2097] The Restitution of Land Rights Act itself is therefore mainly concerned with keeping the possibilities of restitution of rights dispossessed within a limited scope and timespan as open as possible. This is proven by the broad distinction drawn between three categories of prejudice suffered through dispossession in the White Paper of 1997.[2098] Hence, the White Paper leaves the reversal of dispossession of land before 1913 to a later, more gradual process of land reform (in the redistribution and tenure reform programmes) and the economic empowerment of the landless. In view of the objectives of the White Paper, the case of the *Richtersveld* community exemplifies the fact that land restitution, limited as it may be, is part of the broader process of reconciliation of the different groupings within the South African society. It forms but a small part of the broader land reform process, and within the financial and logistic constraints placed upon the state, it can be no more than a politically symbolic gesture. Unfortunately, this gesture is not extended to certain groups of people who had been subject to unfair, racially discriminatory treatment for centuries.

In the end, restitution must be conducive to the process of reconciliation, reconstruction and development. The process of restitution is accordingly characterised by the extensive powers granted to the courts in

---

grammes, land administration reform and land redistribution support programmes).

[2096] White Paper (1997), par. 4.14.2.

[2097] See *Carey-Miller/Pope*, Land Title in South Africa (2000), 316-317.

[2098] In some circumstances, dispossession leads to landlessness. Prejudice has also been suffered through inadequate compensation for the value of the property. Dispossession has also lead to hardship that cannot be measured in financial or material terms. White Paper (1997), par. 4.14.1.

making awards, and noticeable self-restraint on the part of the judiciary as far as the nature or content of rights that could or should be included in an order for restitution is concerned. Restitution of proprietary interests like business goodwill and lost profits, as well as nonproprietary claims founded upon pain and suffering, will not be possible. Attempts at undoing the injustices of the past by providing restitution can, furthermore, only be successful as far as the state's fiscal limits allow. This contributes to the pressing need for a restitution framework designed to satisfy at least some of the demands social justice while, simultaneously minimising new grievances.[2099] Ironic as it may seem, the Land Claims Court's denial of the ancestral land rights of the Richtersveld community as qualifying for restitution serves the ultimate purpose of reconciliation, if one considers the goals envisaged by the White Paper on Land Reform. More importantly, though, the *Richtersveld* case shows that restitution alone cannot undo the effects of all past unjust laws. It seems as if the legislature has understood this when the broader land-reform project was developed. In terms of the other two legs of the South African land reform project, which involve large-scale land redistribution and upgrading of tenure rights, and which are incidentally much broader in scope and application than the restitution process, some of the injustice of the past can be addressed. This also seems to be in line with section 25 FC, which deals not only with the restitution of land rights, but also with the upgrading of insecure tenure and with more equitable access to land. The establishment of a more just land regime in South Africa, can therefore not be dependent only on the successful completion of the restitution programme. Carey-Miller[2100] points out that the history and circumstances of South Africa mean that comprehensive land reform is essential in any meaningful transition to a just society. At the same time, however, there appears to be a certain concern that a package of too radical reform proposals would not serve the general interest. The market economy is apparently potentially sensitive to nature and extent of this kind of reform.[2101] To eradicate racial domination in the context of land control, the restitution process must be viewed as part of a more comprehensive objective of land reform, not only by the legislature and judiciary, but also by the

---

[2099] *Visser/Roux* in *Rwelamira/Werle (eds)*, Confronting Past Injustices (1996), 96.

[2100] *Carey-Miller/Pope*, Land Title in South Africa (2000), 318.

[2101] The White Paper (1997), box 4.7. points out that restitution of land must be effected while maintaining public confidence in the land market.

Department of Land Affairs, which will have to accommodate those persons and communities that apparently does not fit into the system of the broader land reform programme, and for whom reconciliation can only begin once psychological redress of the injustice suffered by them at the hand of previous land regimes has taken place, and they are put on the road to economic independence.[2102] These issues are touched upon in the following sections of this chapter.

2.2. Land Redistribution

Whereas restitution involves restoring the control of some persons over land, which was withdrawn during the apartheid era, and tenure reform involves the strengthening of rights of those who have access to land, the redistribution effort is aimed mostly at those who did not have land before, and still do not have sufficient access to land.[2103] The purpose of land redistribution is therefore to provide land for the rural and urban landless and at the same time improve their standards of living, and the redistribution programme is intended to assist the urban and rural poor, like farm workers, labour tenants and emergent farmers.[2104] In this way, some of the inequalities in current land distribution patterns can be addressed.[2105] As such, this programme gives priority to the marginalised and to women in need through projects that can be implemented quickly and effectively. Land traditionally used for agriculture is, in particular, affected by this element of the activities of the Department of Land Affairs,[2106] although the redistribution programme also involves legislation dealing with residential land and housing.[2107]

[2102] See the Communal Property Associations Act 28 of 1996, which provides that a restitution award to a community shall be made in terms of the tenure reform programme. See also 497 below.

[2103] *Van der Walt*, 1999 Koers, 275.

[2104] *Pienaar*, Land Reform (2003), forthcoming.

[2105] *Van der Walt*, 1999 Koers, 275.

[2106] The most important initiatives are the Land Reform Pilot Project and the Land Reform (Labour Tenants) Act 3 of 1996. The Pilot Project was announced by the Minister of Land Affairs on 28.02.1995 as part of a Presidential Lead Programme envisaged by the White Paper on the Reconstruction and Development Programme. It was meant to "kick start" the land redistribution process in rural areas and involved the identification of areas in each province where existing land users could be assited in acquiring additional land, as well as

The scope of this programme is in principle much wider than the restitution programme, and it involves a wide variety of different policies, strategies and projects, which need to be viable and sustainable. In fact, this process is mainly embodied in state policies (on national, provincial and local level) regarding the allocation of funds for development of land and building of houses or for housing subsidies, and in laws that promote wider access to land and housing, in pursuance of the redistribution imperative embodied in section 25(5) FC. Therefore, redistribution is not a mere legal mechanism, but rather a more complex programme involving the promotion and provision of state aid and assistance — in the form of finance and infrastructure — for the acquisition of land by persons prejudiced by the unfair system of the old regime.[2108]

Although the redistributive land reform programme is supposed to be based on willing-buyer, willing-seller arrangements[2109] in the course of providing land to the landless, it also provides for the acquisition of land rights by tenants. In this regard, the Land Reform (Labour Tenants) Act[2110] is of particular importance. However, there are several other legislative measures that are equally significant to the effectivity of this programme.[2111] The Provision of Land and Assistance Act[2112] provides for the designation of certain land and regulates the subdivision of this land and the settlement of persons on such land. In principle, the act is aimed at bringing common-law ownership within the

---

financial and technical assitance, to help them achieve meaningful and sustainable land use. Six pilot land reform districts were identified, i.e. the Northern province (the so-called "White Finger," near Pietersburg); Eastern Cape (Queenstown); Free State (parts of Bloemfontein, Dewetsdorp, Thaba'Nchu, Botshabelo, Exelsior en parts of Brandfort); Gauteng (the Rust and De Winter areas); Northern Cape (the North-Eastern area); KwaZulu Natal (Weenen-Estcourt); and the Western Cape (Southern area). *Pienaar,* Land Reform (2003), forthcoming; *Van der Walt,* 1999 Koers, 279.

[2107] In this regard, see the Less Formal Township Establishment Act 112 of 1991, the Provision of Certain Land for Settlement Act 126 of 1993, the Development Facilitation Act 67 of 1995 and the Housing Act 107 of 1997.

[2108] *Carey-Miller/Pope,* Land Title in South Africa (2000), 398.

[2109] White Paper (1997), par. 4.3.

[2110] Act 3 of 1996.

[2111] See *Carey-Miller/Pope,* Land Title in South Africa (2000), 405-455 and *Van der Walt,* 1999 Koers, 275-281 for more detailed discussions.

[2112] 126 of 1993, renamed by the Provision of Certain Land for Settlement Amendment Act 26 of 1998.

reach of a wider part of the general public.[2113] The Development Facilitation Act[2114] has a multi-faceted agenda and is, inter alia, aimed at facilitating, simplifying and expediting the delivery of housing to the rural and urban poor.[2115] The Housing Act[2116] is meant to provide for the facilitation of a sustainable housing development process and applies to the provision of housing on national, provincial and local government levels.[2117] The Transformation of Certain Rural Areas Act[2118] introduces new procedures on the basis of which available land in certain areas can be transferred for the benefit of residents in substitution for the landholding system of the old Rural Areas Act.[2119]

On the whole, the redistribution programme will probably involve the most far-reaching innovations in South African property law, simply because of its scope and because of the wrongs it intends to address. In general, the redistribution policies and laws function within the common law conceptual and institutional structures already known in the times of apartheid. The constraints of racial discrimination have simply been removed and access to land and housing has been extended to people and communities who were previously excluded from it. Nevertheless, the policies of land redistribution involve a response to the demand that the maldistribution of land, brought about by centuries of colonialism and decades of apartheid government, must be restored. As such, it would contain excellent material from which examples of the influence of the constitutional concept property on existing land law could be drawn. However, it has been pointed out already[2120] that for purposes of the present legal-comparative inquiry, the redistribution

---

[2113] *Carey-Miller/Pope,* Land Title in South Africa (2000), 405-411 and *Van der Walt,* 1999 Koers, 276-277.

[2114] 67 of 1995.

[2115] See in particular ch. IV. *Carey-Miller/Pope,* Land Title in South Africa (2000), 411-449 and *Van der Walt,* 1999 Koers, 277-278; *Latsky* in *Budlender, Latsky & Roux,* New Land Law (1996), ch. 2A comments extensively on the provisions of this act. See also 511 ff. below.

[2116] 107 of 1997.

[2117] *Van der Walt,* 1999 Koers, 278-279.

[2118] 94 of 1998.

[2119] (House of Representatives) 9 of 1987. *Carey-Miller/Pope,* Land Title in South Africa (2000), 449-445.

[2120] 437 above.

and tenure reform aspects of the South African land reform programme will have to take the back seat.

2.2.1. The Land Reform (Labour Tenants) Act: an Example

In an attempt to select an example from the legislative arsenal of the redistribution programme that would indicate the extent to which reliance on existing law is intertwined with the legislature's need to be innovative, the most obvious choice should be the Land Reform (Labour Tenants) Act.[2121] Another option would be the Extension of Security of Tenure Act.[2122] The former relates to a more restricted category of disadvantaged people, namely labour tenants, whereas the latter concerns all persons occupying land of which they are not the registered owners. In both instances, the measures are aimed at providing protection against unfair eviction and the acquisition of rights in land, and are thus both aimed at redistribution as well as tenure reform.

In view of the fact that the system of labour tenancy resulted from racially discriminatory legislation and led to exploitation of individuals and denial of access to land, the promulgation of the Labour Tenants Act was seen as imperative to broaden access to land on the one hand and to provide adequate protection against recurrence of the wrongs induced by this system. The acquisition of land or rights in land by labour tenants result in the redistribution of existing land and thereby broadening the access to land.[2123] Since the present discussion is aimed at indicating the tension between existing rights and newly created rights within the context of the constitutional protection and regulation of property and its influence on structures of property in private law,

---

[2121] 3 of 1996. *Carey-Miller/Pope*, Land Title in South Africa (2000), 525 indicates that labour tenancy reforms are primarily about the enhancement of an existing form of tenure and hence should be categorised as tenure reform legislation. *Van der Walt*, 1999 Koers, 279 views the Labour Tenants Act as partially redistributory and partially tenure reform in its orientation. *Pienaar*, Land Reform (2003), forthcoming indicates that the promulgation of the act was seen as imperative to broaden access to land on the one hand and to provide adequate protection against this kind of discrimination being repeated in the future. The acquisition of land or rights in land by labour tenants hence result in the redistribution of existing land and thereby broadening the access to land.

[2122] 62 of 1997.

[2123] *Pienaar*, Land Reform (2003), forthcoming.

the redistributory objectives of the Land Reform (Labour Tenants) Act will enjoy precedence in the following paragraphs. In a subsequent discussion of the government's tenure reform initiative and other legislative measures,[2124] the protection of unfair eviction provided by the Extension of Security of Tenure Act will then be considered.

2.2.1.1. Labour Tenancy Under Apartheid

Labour tenancy is a contractual arrangement between an agricultural landlord and a tenant in terms of which the tenant is obliged to provide labour in exchange for the right to occupy and use a part of the farm for his or her own agricultural or residential purposes.[2125] This practice is found mainly in the north of KwaZulu-Natal and in the Mpumalanga, where there are between 30 000 and 40 000 labour tenants at present.[2126] Labour tenants in South Africa have occupied land for generations, usually with the expectation that the tenancy would endure irrespective of the changes in the ownership of the land. Traditionally the rights of the tenants would devolve automatically on death to their descendants.[2127]

The labour tenancy system is a direct result of the Black Land Act of 1913. Prior to that act many black South Africans, deprived of ownership by earlier conquests, occupied land as tenants, lessees, or sharecroppers. The Black Land Act of 1913 prohibited these arrangements. To continue farming, the only alternative for those affected was to become labour tenants. The nature of this right to labour tenancy was, at the outset, not clear. In *De Jager v Sisana*,[2128] it was held that labour tenancy could best be described as an innominate contract from which the tenant gains no real rights in land. Consequently, compliance with the rules of labour tenancy rested upon custom. Moreover, the system resulted in unfair discrimination and disadvantage in that labour tenants

---

[2124] See 494 ff. below.

[2125] *Murphy* in *Rwelamira/Werle (eds)*, Confronting Past Injustices (1996), 117 note 22.

[2126] *Haythorn/Hutchinson* in *Murray/O'Regan*, No Place to Rest (1990), 194.

[2127] *Murphy* in *Rwelamira/Werle (eds)*, Confronting Past Injustices (1996), 124.

[2128] *De Jager v Sisana* 1930 AD 71.

were denied access to land.[2129] Between 1966 and 1980, the labour tenancy system was progressively outlawed with the aim of reducing all black South Africans in so-called white rural areas to the status of temporary wage labourers. More than one million people were evicted under this scheme.[2130]

2.2.1.2. Objectives and Operation of the Land Reform (Labour Tenants) Act

Under the Labour Tenants Act, persons qualifying as "labour tenants" enjoy much better protection than during the era before its enactment. Considerations of equity emerging from the new constitutional order gave rise to the recognition of more secure tenure rights for labour tenants.[2131] The objectives of the Labour Tenants Act are twofold: On the one hand, the act provides for the protection of the existing rights of labour tenants. On the other hand, it makes provision for the acquisition of land for existing labour tenants by granting them the opportunity to obtain a settlement or land access grant of R15 000 per household,[2132] to enable them to become landowners in own right. The present discussion is primarily concerned with this second aspect, although mention will also be made of the first aim of the act.

2.2.1.2.1. Qualifying Criteria for Labour Tenant Protection

In order to enjoy the benefits of the Labour Tenants Act, a "labour tenant" has to comply with the requirements set out in the act. These are found in the definition of "labour tenant."[2133] In *Moshela v Sancor*[2134] it was confirmed that "labour tenant" is not a dictionary term, but a tech-

---

[2129] See preamble of Land Reform (Labour Tenants) Act.

[2130] *Haythorn/Hutchinson* in *Murray/O'Regan*, No Place to Rest (1990), 195-198; *Murphy* in *Rwelamira/Werle (eds)*, Confronting Past Injustices (1996), 117 note 22.

[2131] *Murphy* in *Rwelamira/Werle (eds)*, Confronting Past Injustices (1996), 124.

[2132] White Paper (1997), par. 4.10. See *Van der Merwe/Pienaar* in *Jackson/Wilde (eds)*, Reform of Property Law (1997), 359.

[2133] Sec. 1, Labour Tenants Act.

[2134] *Moshela v Sancor* 1999 1 SA 614 (T).

nical one. Accordingly, the facts have to be specified in order to support the allegation of labour tenancy. In general, a *labour tenant* can be described as a person (usually black), who lives on a (usually white-owned) farm, and who exchanges labour for the right to use cropping or grazing land on farm land of the owner.[2135] For purposes of the Labour Tenants Act, a labour tenant is someone[2136]

(a) who is residing or has the right to reside on a farm;

(b) who has or has had the right to use cropping or grazing land on the farm, referred to in paragraph (a), or another farm of the owner, and in consideration of such right provides or has provided labour to the owner or lessee; and

(c) whose parent or grandparent resided or resides on a farm or had the use of cropping or grazing land on such farm or another farm of the owner, and in consideration of such right provided or provides labour to the owner or lessee of such other farm,

including a person who has been appointed a successor to a labour tenant in accordance with the provisions of section 3(4) and (5), but excluding a farm worker.

In theory, this definition sets three requirements which should be complied with in order to qualify for the benefits of the redistribution programme: (i) the person must have had a right to reside on the farm, (ii) the person must have had cropping or grazing rights in consideration of which labour must have been provided, and (iii) the person's parent or grandparent (who also resided on a farm) had the previously mentioned rights and provided labour. In effect, however, the final part of the definition constitutes a fourth requirement: the person trying to establish labour tenancy must also be able to prove that he or she is not a farm worker. Therefore, *labour tenancy* is often contrasted with the contractual rights and duties of a *farmworker*.[2137] A *farmworker* is employed on the farm in terms of a contract of employment, which entails that in return for the labour, provided to the owner or lessee of the farm, payment shall be predominantly in cash or in *natura* (a share in the proceeds), and not predominantly in the right to occupy and use land. A farmworker is furthermore obliged to perform his or her ser-

---

[2135] See *Carey-Miller/Pope*, Land Title in South Africa (2000), 525-526.

[2136] According to sec. 1 read with sec. 3(4) and 3(5), Land Reform (Labour Tenants) Act.

[2137] See *Malangu v De Jager* 2000 3 SA 145 (LCC), par. 11-57.

vices personally.[2138] When compliance with the requirements in paragraphs (a), (b) and (c) of the definition, can be proved, a person shall be presumed not to be a farm worker, unless the contrary is proved.[2139] In this regard, the court must take into account the combined effect and substance of all agreements between the person who avers labour tenancy and the owner or lessee of the land concerned.[2140]

The reference in paragraph (b) to the provision of labour includes labour provided personally by a person who claims labour tenancy, or by way of a nominee. This would also include cases where applicants have never provided labour personally, but always through nominees.[2141] Although an agreement of some sort in which labour tenancy is embodied usually exists, a labour tenant contract is not essential to the issue of labour tenancy.[2142]

As far as paragraph (c) is concerned, the interpretation of the word "farm" initially was uncertain. The issue was apparently whether a person trying to establish labour tenancy and his or her parent or grandparent all had to have rights relating to the same farm. In *Zulu v Van Rensburg*[2143] Dodson J contended that if the farm referred to in paragraph (c) had to be the same farm as that referred to in paragraph (a), the legislature would have expressly mentioned it, as was the case in paragraph (b). It was also emphasised that if the approach were followed that the "same farm" was intended, a person whose predecessors had over generations consistently been labour tenants, but had been forced by eviction to move from farm to farm, would inevitably be excluded from protection. This could not have been the intention of the legislature, keeping in mind the redistributive objectives of the act. In

---

[2138] See sec. 1 (Definitions) of the act. The difference between farmworker and labour tenant has been discussed in the case of *Malangu v De Jager* 1996 3 SA 235 (LCC). See also *Ngcobo and others v Salimba CC* 1999 All SA 491 (A).

[2139] Sec. 2(5) was inserted by the Land Restitution and Reform Amendment Laws Amendment Act 63 of 1997 in order to relieve the heavy burden on persons claiming to be labour tenants.

[2140] Sec. 2(6) of the Labour Tenants Act.

[2141] *Mlifi v Klingenberg* 1999 2 SA 674 (LCC), 684I.

[2142] In *Mokwena v Marie Appel Beleggings* (LCC) 89/98 of 30.09.1998 the argument that the existence of labour agreement was imperative for proving labour tenancy was rejected.

[2143] *Zulu v Van Rensburg* 1996 4 SA 1236 (LCC), 1257H-1258A.

another case, *Mlifi v Klingenberg*,[2144] it was argued that paragraph (c) required the plaintiff to show that his parents or grandparents had resided and worked on a farm owned by the same owner or his successors or predecessors in title.[2145] Meer J found that the nexus is between the labour tenant and the land and not between the landowner and labour tenant (or generations of labour tenants) and confirmed the *Zulu* case on this matter.[2146]

The statutory definition of labour tenancy has also on a larger scale led to interpretative differences, and consequently different judgements. The vexing issue is apparently whether paragraphs (a) (b) and (c) of the definition should be interpreted disjunctively or conjunctively.[2147] Some decisions require compliance with paragraphs (a) and (b) or (a) and (c), but do not require compliance with all three paragraphs.[2148] Other decisions seem to place exceptional interpretative value on the connecter "and" between the paragraphs, and apply it in such a manner that compliance with all three paragraphs of the definition is required.[2149] The most probable explanation of the reason behind the different approaches is the obscure wording of paragraph (c), which is an open invitation to varied interpretations.[2150] If a disjunctive approach is followed, the burden of proof is eased, and more prospective claimants would be able to meet the requirements of the definition. If "cumula-

---

[2144] *Mlifi v Klingenberg* (note 2141 above).

[2145] Reference was also made to the unreported case of *Salimba v Ngcobo* (NPD) 340/96 of 4.11.1997 (see note 2138 above) in which a nexus between the same owner and his successors or predecessors in title and generations of labour tenants was suggested, but was rejected by the Court.

[2146] *Zulu v Van Rensburg* (note 2143 above), 690A. Meer J remarks that the legislature could not have intended such an "absurd and unfair result" (690F).

[2147] *Pienaar*, Land Reform (2003), forthcoming.

[2148] I.e. *Klopper v Mkhize* 1998 1 SA 406 (N) and *Tselentis Mining (Pty) Ltd v Mdlalose* 1998 1 SA 411 (N). For a detailed analysis, see *Pienaar*, 1998 Stell LR, 311-325.

[2149] I.e. *Malangu v De Jager* 1996 3 SA 235 (LCC) and *Zulu v Van Rensburg* (note 2143 above), *Moshela v Sancor* (note 2134 above) and *Mokwena v Marie Appel Beleggings* (LCC) 89/98 of 30.09.1998. See *Pienaar*, 1997 TSAR, 538-548 for a detailed analysis. Most recently, the ruling in *Ngcobo v Van Rensburg and Others* 1999 2 SA 525 (LCC) supported the (normal) conjunctive approach.

[2150] Galgut J in *Klopper v Mkhize* (note 2148 above), 408H; *Pienaar*, Land Reform (2003), forthcoming.

tive compliance"[2151] with the requirements is necessary, the application of the act would be more restricted. The *Zulu* case and the *Malangu* case required cumulative compliance with all three requirements.[2152] The *Klopper* case departed from this approach, but without giving reasons. Galgut J merely mentioned that the rigid approach followed in the latter case would substantively stultify the objectives of the Labour Tenants Act.[2153] The *Tselentis* case provides a valuable overview of case law concerning the matter of interpretation and attaches a broad interpretation to the definition of labour tenancy within the context and goal of the act.[2154] Meskin J concluded in this decision that persons have to comply either with paragraphs (a) and (b) or with (a) and (c). It is also said that paragraph (c) intends to provide for additional means of establishing labour tenancy.

Although paragraphs (a) and (b) are normally met by applicants, and paragraph (c) is problematic, the opposite happened in *Ngcobo v Van Rensburg*[2155] where applicants (the son and daughter of a deceased labour tenant) applied for an interdict preventing their ejectment from the premises they occupied. The daughter cared for her father and lived with him, but she never provided labour to the landowner. The son left the farm at a very early age and returned only after his father's death. Hence, neither of the respondents complied with paragraph (b) of the definition, but both complied with paragraph (c) in view of the terms of contract between their father and the respondent and his predecessors in title. It was argued that the daughter's presence on the farm was unlawful and consequently not in accordance with the requirements of the act. However, the court found that lawfulness of occupation was of no consequence under the circumstances.[2156] The more important question

---

[2151] This phrased was used by Gildenhuys J in *Malangu v De Jager* 1996 3 SA 235 (LCC), 241F.

[2152] Both decisions handed down by Dodson J.

[2153] *Klopper v Mkize* (note 2148 above), 408H.

[2154] In the *Tselentis* case (note 2148 above), other definitions such as "family member" and "associate" are also discussed. See also *Makhombothi v Klingenberg* 1999 1 SA 135 (T) with regard to the interpretation of "associate."

[2155] *Ngcobo v Van Rensburg* (note 2149 above).

[2156] This aspect was confirmed in *Mkwanazi v Bivane Bosbou, Msimango v De Villiers; Ngema v Van der Walt; Mdletshe v Nxumalo* 1999 1 All SA 59 (LCC), 771B. *Pienaar*, Land Reform (2003), forthcoming note 42 points out that the term "reside" is not limited to lawful residence. In cases where the

was whether the statutory requirements for qualification as "labour tenant" were met, seeing that she only complied with the requirements of paragraphs (a) and (c). This called for a decision in favour of either the disjunctive or the conjunctive approach. If the disjunctive approach would be followed, the daughter would succeed with the application. If the conjunctive approach would be followed, the non-compliance with paragraph (b) of the definition would disqualify her. In the judgment it was recognised that the word "and" can have both a conjunctive and a disjunctive meaning and that interpretation had to be based on the statute in its entirety, with constant consideration of the objectives of the act. Eventually, the decision was in favour of a conjunctive approach and against the applicant. The mere fact that the word "and" had been inserted before paragraph (c) apparently made it clear that the paragraph cannot be read on its own. Hence, the conjunctive approach as first set out in the cases of *Malangu* and *Zulu* enjoys stronger support.

2.2.1.2.2. Access to Land

The redistributory character of the Land Reform (Labour Tenants) Act is apparent from Chapter III of the act, which provides for the acquisition of ownership or rights in land by the labour tenant. Persons qualifying as "labour tenants" in terms of the statutory definition[2157] may apply for an award of land or land rights and for financial assistance.[2158] In applications concerning land allocation, tenants can apply for the specific parcel of land being occupied by the tenant or for land that was occupied by the tenant or predecessors for a period of five years prior to the commencement of the Act and of which they were illegally deprived.[2159] They can also apply for rights in land elsewhere on the farm or in the vicinity, which have been proposed by the landowner. Servitudes of water, way or any other servitude reasonably necessary or reasonably consistent with the rights previously enjoyed by the labour tenant may also be awarded.[2160]

---

contractual basis for residence had been terminated, such residence would still fall within the ambit of the Labour Tenants Act.

[2157] See 482 above.

[2158] Sec. 16, Labour Tenants Act. Advances and subsidies are made available under sec. 26 of the Labour Tenants Act.

[2159] Sec. 16(1)(a) and (b), Labour Tenants Act.

[2160] Sec. 16(1)(c) and (d), Labour Tenants Act.

The claim must be lodged with the Director-General of Land Affairs, after which notice is given to the landowner,[2161] who is entitled to dispute whether the applicant is indeed a labour tenant.[2162] If the status of the applicant is not disputed, he or she is presumed to be a labour tenant, unless proof to the contrary is produced.[2163] If the applicant's status is disputed, either party is entitled to institute judicial proceedings in order to determine the issue. Once the issue concerning the status of the applicant has been resolved, the owner may submit proposals to the director-general for alternative, equitable ways of dealing with the claim instead of allowing the acquisition of a right in the affected land.[2164] The applicant is also informed of these proposals, and can reject any proposal if he or she wants to persist with the original claim. If the matter cannot be resolved, the claimant may institute court proceedings for an order or apply to court for appropriate relief.[2165]

The application for the acquisition of ownership or other rights will thus be submitted to the court if the owner refrained from initiating settlement proposals; if such a proposal was offered, but rejected by the applicant; and in cases where parties have reached an agreement, but the agreement was not certified to be reasonable or equitable.[2166] If necessary, the issue will be referred to arbitration in which case the arbitrator has extensive powers in order to assist he parties in reaching an agreement.[2167] In the process of determining the nature of the order to be made by the court, various factors will be taken into account:[2168] (i) the desirability of assisting labour tenants to establish themselves on farms on a viable and sustainable basis; (ii) the achievement of the objectives of the Act; (iii) the requirements of equity and justice; (iv) the willingness of the owner of affected land and the applicant to make contributions towards the settlement of the application; and, where relevant, (v) the report of an arbitrator.

[2161] Sec. 17(1), Labour Tenants Act.

[2162] Sec. 17(4), Labour Tenants Act. The landowner has a month's time within which to dispute the applicant's status.

[2163] Sec. 17(5), Labour Tenants Act.

[2164] Sec. 18, Labour Tenants Act.

[2165] Sec. 17(4), Labour Tenants Act.

[2166] Sec. 17(7), Labour Tenants Act.

[2167] Sec. 20 and 22, Labour Tenants Act.

[2168] Sec. 22(5), Labour Tenants Act.

If the Land Claims Court decides that the labour tenant is eligible to obtain ownership, the owner and the labour tenant should try to reach agreement on the price to be paid. The act gives detailed prescriptions on the arbitration procedure to be applied in aiding the parties to come to an agreement.[2169] In terms of the land reform programme of the Department of Land Affairs, a "settlement/land acquisition grant" may be obtained to subsidise the purchase price of the land allocated to the labour tenant.[2170] If the labour tenant fails to make payment within three calendar months of reception of a notice claiming payment, the owner can lodge an application to have the court order granting ownership to the labour tenant nullified.[2171]

In exceptional circumstances expropriation will be resorted to. The owner of the land is entitled to just and equitable compensation, as set out in section 25(3) FC, which will be determined by the court or, if necessary, by an arbitrator.[2172] If the land in question is encumbered by a registered mortgage bond or is subject to a deed of sale, compensation will be paid only on terms agreed to by the owner and the mortgagee or buyer[2173] or, in the absence of such an agreement, only after a court order containing directions with regard to the payment of compensation has been issued.[2174] As is the case with land restitution issues, provision is also made for mediation.[2175]

2.2.1.2.3. Protection of Labour Tenants and Rights of Landowners

Presently, labour tenants for the first time enjoy a statutory right to occupation and use of the land, which can only be terminated in accordance with the provision of the Act.[2176] They are also protected against

---

[2169] Sec. 18 to 22, Labour Tenants Act.

[2170] White Paper (1997), par. 4.5.9 and 4.7.

[2171] Sec. 24, Labour Tenants Act.

[2172] Sec. 23, Labour Tenants Act.

[2173] Sec. 25(1), Labour Tenants Act.

[2174] Sec. 25(2), Labour Tenants Act.

[2175] See in general sec. 36, Labour Tenants Act.

[2176] The Labour Tenants Act mentions four possible circumstances under which the right of use and occupation is terminated: (i) in case of waiver, sec. 3(2)(a); (ii) death, sec. 3(2)(b); (iii) eviction in accordance with the act, sec. 3(2)(c); or (iv) acquiring of ownership or compensation, sec. 3(2)(d). Eviction may only take place according to the provisions of the act.

arbitrary eviction, in that eviction should take place in accordance with prescribed procedures and in the circumstances prescribed by the act.[2177] Extensive rights of reinstatement are granted to labour tenants who had to vacate the land or who were evicted between 2 June 1995 and the commencement of the act on 22 March 1996.[2178] Similarly, the act has strict provisions controlling the relocation of labour tenants in the case where the owner of the land requires it for agricultural purposes or development for the public benefit.[2179]

The rights of the landowner are, however, also protected: First, the successor proposed by the labour tenant should be acceptable to the owner. The owner is therefore entitled to refuse a proposed successor on reasonable grounds.[2180] Second, the owner can apply for eviction if he or she can prove that such an eviction is just and reasonable. One such instance is where the labour tenant (in spite of a one-month's written notice) acted contrary to their agreement by refusing to work for the owner. Alternatively it could be shown that a material breach of the relationship between the parties, which was practically impossible to remedy, has occurred.[2181]

The owner can under certain circumstances approach the court in urgent proceedings for the eviction of the labour tenant. If there were a real and imminent danger of substantial injury to the owner or damage to his or her property if the labour tenant is not removed from the farm, eviction would, for instance, be possible. Furthermore, no other effective remedy should be available to the owner or lessee and the likely harm to the owner or lessee in case of an order not being granted, should be disproportionately higher than the likely harm to the labour

---

[2177] Sec. 5-15, Labour Tenants Act. In some instances, eviction is not at all possible. See sec. 9(1), Labour Tenants Act.

[2178] Sec. 12, Labour Tenants Act.

[2179] Sec. 8(1), Labour Tenants Act. This section further stipulates the circumstances under which a court could grant an order for relocation (sec. 8(2), Labour Tenants Act); provides for the payment of compensation to the labour tenants to forestall unfair prejudice (sec. 8(3) and (4), Labour Tenants Act); determines the circumstances under which a labour tenant can claim reinstatement of his or her right to occupy and use the land (sec. 8(5), Labour Tenants Act) and in this regard grants the court a wide discretion in making any order deemed to be just and equitable (sec. 8(6), Labour Tenants Act).

[2180] Sec. 3(5), 4(1) and (2), Labour Tenants Act.

[2181] Sec. 6 and 7, Labour Tenants Act.

tenant against whom the order is sought.[2182] Under appropriate circumstances, the owner can also be entitled to just compensation where his or her rights are affected by the act, if it would amount to an expropriation.[2183]

2.2.2. Evaluation

In determining the influence of the government's redistribution policy on the development of land law as such, and in examining the influence of these developments on the existing concept of ownership in private law, a brief overview of the effects of redistribution in general is necessary. This will be provided in the following paragraphs. The effects of the Land Reform (Labour Tenants) Act as an example of the redistribution policy will be evaluated in more detail.

2.2.2.1. The Effects of the Land Reform (Labour Tenants) Act in Particular

In practice, the Land Reform (Labour Tenants) Act has brought long-needed relief to a large community of people disadvantaged by the existing land control system in South Africa. The Labour Tenants Act does not perpetuate the original form of labour tenancy with its numerous shortcomings.[2184] Instead, the institution of labour tenancy is revised, and a general phasing out of the institution and its replacement by common law ownership is envisaged.

For the person who has not applied for the acquisition of land or other rights in land, the basic elements of labour tenancy remain the same: the provision of labour and services in exchange for utilisation of land. Even in cases where no application was made for the acquisition of rights in land, the labour tenant has definite security of tenure in that eviction can only take place in accordance with the Labour Tenants Act.

The labour tenant, who has successfully applied for the acquisition of land or rights, does not fit the traditional mode of labour tenancy since

---

[2182] Sec. 15, Labour Tenants Act.

[2183] Sec. 23 read with sec. 2(1) and sec. 38(1)(b)(ii), Labour Tenants Act.

[2184] The practice of labour tenancy before the commencement of the Labour Tenants Act was equated with slavery. See the detailed discussion of *Pienaar*, 1998 Stell LR, 311-325.

one of the essential elements, namely exchange of labour for the use of the land, has lapsed.[2185] A successful applicant for the acquisition of land rights is technically no longer a labour tenant, but an independent land-owner. Of course, such a person is free to provide labour and services, but this will have nothing to do with the institution of labour tenancy. In fact, the implementation of the Labour Tenants Act introduced a to-tally new dispensation with regard to the provision of labour and serv-ices.[2186]

A point in favour of the act is its strongly negotiation-oriented nature, which means that conflict is regulated rather than generated.[2187] In terms of the act, the rights of labour tenants, on the one hand, and own-ers, on the other, must constantly be balanced. In *Van der Walt v Lange*[2188] the owners of the land in question applied for an order pro-hibiting the occupiers from keeping more than ten head of cattle each, while the labour tenants had applied for the acquisition of rights in land under section 16 of the Labour Tenants Act.[2189] The occupiers averred that they had permission to graze more cattle and that a curtailment of that right would amount to eviction in terms of the act. The applicants based their argument on the principle that rights are never absolute and above limitation, and indicated that they would suffer irreparable harm if an appropriate interim measure was not enforced. In its decision, the court included the restriction of grazing rights within the meaning of "eviction" for purposes of the act.[2190] The pending section-16-application prohibited an eviction of the labour tenants. The court nev-ertheless also established that it had the necessary jurisdiction to restrict the use of land by labour tenants by way of interim measures. Since "damage" was interpreted to include pecuniary loss[2191] over and above mere physical damage, it was found that the applicants would indeed suffer damage from an overgrazing by the cattle of the respondents. Moreover, the only remedy available to the court was an application to the court. The court thus granted interim relief, in spite of the pending

---

[2185] *Pienaar,* Land Reform (2003), forthcoming.

[2186] *Pienaar,* Land Reform (2003), forthcoming.

[2187] *Pienaar,* 1997 TSAR, 143.

[2188] *Van der Walt v Lange* 1999 1 SA 189 (LCC).

[2189] People cannot be evicted as long as section 16 applications are pending.

[2190] *Van der Walt v Lange,* 197G-H.

[2191] *Van der Walt v Lange,* 200C-E.

application for the acquisition of land rights. This constituted a restriction on the rights of the labour tenants.

In the final analysis, the Land Reform (Labour Tenants) Act is an example of legislation dealing with forms of possession circumscribed in a particular way.[2192] It enhances the security of tenure of persons qualifying as "labour tenants" and established a specifically controlled right to acquisition of property. As such, it reflects the process of transformation of the existing law pertaining to private ownership. Although the act is in the first place aimed at redressing past injustices with which labour tenants had to deal, and is therefore orientated to establishing social justice, existing owners are protected in several ways. On the one hand, strict procedures are prescribed to deal with the infringement of existing rights of owners, and provision is made for compensation in case of inevitable infringement. On the other hand, the Land Claims Court tends to follow a strict approach in interpreting the requirements of the act.[2193]

2.2.2.2. Redistribution in General

Because of the nature and purpose of the redistribution programme, most of the legislation comprised by it is aimed at increasing the speedy and cheap delivery of land and access to land, both in the residential and the agricultural sectors. Here the primary concern is the alteration of the unequal distribution of land and of means to gain access to land still prevalent in the South African society. This is done mainly by way of state intervention in the market process.[2194]

Within the context of the redistribution programme, the intention is to make provision for a variety of flexible land rights. In reality, most of the redistribution initiatives are aimed at enabling the beneficiaries in terms of the redistribution process to become owners in own right. The traditional hierarchy in which common law ownership forms the pinnacle of all rights in property is thus by and large upheld. Van der Walt[2195] indicates that even the initatives that mention a variety of rights explicitly, like the Housing Act, tend to create frameworks that either

---

[2192] *Carey-Miller*, 1999 SALJ, 752.

[2193] *Pienaar*, 1997 TSAR, 135; *Malangu v De Jager* 1996 3 SA 235 (LCC).

[2194] *Van der Walt*, 1999 Koers, 281.

[2195] *Van der Walt*, 1999 Koers, 281.

leave the question of a possible diversification of rights open, or openly priviledge "full" ownership as it is known in private law. Even the procedures of the Labour Tenants Act tend to fall back on an understanding of rights in the traditional classification, in which private law ownership remains supreme.

The redistribution programme should be understood within the context of the three-tiered land reform process as such. The success of this process depends to a large extent on the possible colaboration between the different aspects of land reform. Seeing that the overall aim of the land reform process is to establish a more equitable system of land control and to make land control more accessible to all members of society, the separate aspects of land reform must, to a large extent, be intertwined. That explains why certain legislative measures are on the one hand unique to a specific aspect of land reform, but on the other hand also leave room for supple boundaries between these different aspects.[2196] It also explains why some parliamentary acts serve two or more of the individual programmes simultaneously. For example, although the Restitution of Land Rights Act is unique to the restitution programme, but the Labour Tenants Act and the Extension of Security of Tenure Act are relevant to both the redistribution and the tenure reform programmes.

2.3. Land Tenure Reform

One of the most troublesome legacies of apartheid land law is its diversified land tenure system, in which forms of land control vary from race group to race group and from region to region, depending on the applicable legislation.[2197] In general, land rights for blacks, both in urban and in rural areas, were cast in legal forms that rendered them permanently insecure, weak, and open to the manipulation that characterised the forced removals and evictions of the apartheid era. Black holders and occupiers of land lived under the continuous threat that the precarious "priviledge" which characterised their relation with the land could be retracted at the whim and fancy of the controlling officials.[2198]

[2196] *Pienaar,* Land Reform (2003), forthcoming.

[2197] *Van der Merwe/Pienaar* in *Jackson/Wilde (eds),* Reform of Property Law (1997), 364.

[2198] *Van der Walt,* 1999 Koers, 281-282; *Pienaar,* Land Reform (2003), forthcoming.

Against this background, tenure reform was intended to restore at least some security and permanence to land rights, to formalise the land rights of those whose occupation or use of land justified it, and to establish land rights for those who needed it. Therefore, tenure reform is also defined as a process whereby insecure or unsuitable forms of existing land tenure are legally transformed to provide better or more suitable rights.[2199] This can concern the security of the landholding as such, or the possibility of procuring loans with the land right as security, or any aspect of the tenure under which the land right is held or exercised. In view of these policies and objectives of the tenure reform programme, it is understandable the the process of tenure reform is particularly complex, and its implementation is rendered all the more difficult by the intention to introduce new systems of land tenure, land rights and forms of ownership. In this regard, the Department of Land Affairs have set targets[2200] amongst which are (i) the movement away from a permits-based system to a rights-oriented system; (ii) development of a unitary, non-racial system of land rights for all South Africans; (iii) accommodation of individuals in tenure systems according to their circumstances and preferences; (iv) consistant adherence to the constitutional commitment to basic human rights and equality; (v) adoption of a rights-based approach to deliver security of tenure; and (vi) upgrading of the land registration system to facilitate new tenure systems.

Several legislative measures, like the Communal Properties Associations Act,[2201] Upgrading of Tenure Rights Act,[2202] the Interim Protection of Informal Land Rights Act,[2203] and in some regards also the Extension of Security of Tenure Act, contribute to the realisation of these objectives.

[2199] See White Paper (1997) vi, viii, 9 and 10. The constitutional provision controlling land tenure reform is sec. 25(5) FC. Legislation incorporating land tenure reform policies include: the Upgrading of Land Tenure Rights Act 112 of 1991, the Land Reform (Labour Tenants) Act 3 of 1996, read with the Land Restitution and Reform Laws Amendment Act 63 of 1997, the Communal Property Associations Act 28 of 1996, the Interim Protection of Informal Land Rights Act 31 of 1996, the Extension of Security of Tenure Act 62 of 1997, and the Prevention of Illegal Eviction from and Unlawful Occupation of Land Act 19 of 1998.

[2200] White Paper (1997), par. 4.16.

[2201] 28 of 1996.

[2202] 112 of 1991.

[2203] 31 of 1996.

The implications of this policy for the existing law pertaining to private ownership will be analysed in the following paragraphs. As the scope of this policy is exceptionally wide, the following analysis concentrates only on examples taken from the Interim Protection of Informal Land Rights Act, the Communal Property Associations Act and the Extension of Security of Tenure Act, and by no means purport to present an extensive analysis of the government's tenure reform programme. It merely indicates the degree to which the different legs of the South African land reform programme are intertwined.

2.3.1. Interim Protection of Informal Land Rights Act

The Interim Protection of Informal Land Rights Act is specifically aimed at protecting insecure tenure rights (for example unregistered communal tenure), held by a large number of South Africans (especially in areas previously part of the national states, the self-governing territories and land of the South African Development Trust) which exist *de facto*, but are still not legally recognised. In terms of the Interim Protection of Informal Land Rights Act a number of specifically defined "lesser" rights enjoys protection (on an interim basis, pending permanent reform measures) against the otherwise dominant rights of the title holder. In principle, the various "informal" rights protected pertain to the holding of state-owned land. However, where the protection of "beneficial occupation" is at stake, not only state-owned land is involved.

"Beneficial occupation" is defined in terms of this act as "the occupation of land by a person, as if he or she is the owner, without force, openly and without the permission of the registered owner."[2204] This kind of occupation then constitutes an "informal" land right if it has endured for a continued period of not less than 5 years prior to 31 December 1997. The definition of beneficial occupation in this act suggests a relation to prescription *nec vi, nec clam, nec precario*. It in effect provides for the protection of a non-precarious interest, which would otherwise be no more than an unprotected potential to mature into a right on the basis of acquisitive prescription after a period of thirty years.

The Interim Protection of Informal Land Rights Act thus reflects a departure from the previous position under the South African common

---

[2204] Sec. 1, Interim Protection of Land Rights Act.

law in terms of which the strong power of vindication of a title holder is regarded as a natural consequence of the supremacy of his or her ownership over other rights and against third parties. The absolute powers enforce the right to ownership are thereby watered down.

2.3.2. Communal Properties Associations Act

The Communal Property Associations Act aims at providing a framework for the registration of a new form of juristic person to acquire, hold or control property on behalf of and for the benefit of disadvantaged communities. Although innovatory, this act does not represent a radical move away from the existing property law. With its commitment to ensure non-discrimination, equity and democracy in the management of communal property,[2205] it is significant for future developments, though. It provides for the holding of movable and immovable property for the benefit of a community group, constituted as a new kind of juristic person, in a way similar to the establishment of the body corporate in terms of the Sectional Titles Act.[2206] However, the body corporate in terms of the Sectional Titles Act does not have ownership or rights of tenure, and is therefore not comparable to the juristic person created in terms of the Communal Property Associations Act.

2.3.3. Extension of Security of Tenure Act

The preamble to the Extension of Security of Tenure Act[2207] states that many South Africans presently do not have security of tenure of their homes and land and are consequently vulnerable to unfair eviction. It also acknowledges that these evictions have led and will continue to lead to great hardship, conflict and social instability. It thus shows the desirability of promoting the achievement of long-term security of tenure for occupiers of land and the extension of rights of occupiers through legislative measures. However, the rights, duties and legitimate interests of owners also need to be taken into consideration.[2208]

[2205] Preamble, Interim Protection of Land Rights Act.

[2206] Act 95 of 1986. See *Carey-Miller*, 1999 SALJ, 758.

[2207] 62 of 1997.

[2208] *Pienaar*, Land Reform (2003), forthcoming.

2.3.3.1. Objectives and Application

The objective of the Extension of Security of Tenure Act is to provide
security of tenure for farm labourers that do not benefit from the protection of the Land Reform (Labour Tenants) Act[2209] because they do
not qualify as labour tenants. As such, the act focuses on "occupiers" of
land, and applies to rural areas, nation wide.[2210] Like the Labour Tenants Act, the Extension of Security of Tenure Act is aimed at preventing
unfair evictions and creating alternative ways of acquiring independent
land rights. For purposes of illustrating the land tenure reform objectives of the overall land reform programme, focus will be placed on the
first aspect in the following discussion.

2.3.3.1.1. Definition of "Occupier"

The Extension of Security of Tenure Act defines "occupier" to denote
(i) a person residing on land which belongs to another person, and who
has or had on 4 February 1997 or thereafter consent or another right in

---

[2209] 3 of 1996.

[2210] Sec. 2, Extension of Security of Tenure Act. The provisions of the act do
not apply in a township established, approved, proclaimed or otherwise recognised in terms of any law. The act is, however, applicable to land within a township (of any kind) that has been designated for agricultural purposes and any
land within a township which has been established, approved, proclaimed or
otherwise recognised *after* 4 February 1997 (the date on which the bill was first
published) only if the person concerned was an occupier immediately prior to
the establishment, approval, proclamation or recognition (sec. 2(1), Extension
of Security of Tenure Act). This would give some protection to persons residing
on land in towns used for agricultural purposes and the land is then rezoned,
for whatever reason, resulting in the land not falling within the general ambit of
sec. 2, Extension of Security of Tenure Act, as a whole, except with regard to
the particular occupiers. This specific group would still have protection from
eviction. However, because the land has been rezoned, occupiers that take occupation after the rezoning would not fall under the scope of the act and cannot
benefit from the protective measures. The act therefore in essence applies to rural areas only and not to urban areas. In *Karabo v Kok* 1998 4 SA 1014 (LCC),
1019B it was found that the section does not relate to agricultural land only. In
this case the property was in fact used for industrial purposes in that a quarry
and brick work were operated from the farm. The conclusive considerations
were apparently the rural, farming nature of the land. See *Pienaar,* Land Reform
(2003), forthcoming; *Carey-Miller/Pope,* Land Title in South Africa (2000),
493-495.

law to do so; or (ii) a person who resides on land belonging to another who works for himself or herself and does not employ an outside person.[2211] Labour tenants, persons using or intending to use the land mainly for industrial, mining, commercial or commercial farming purposes, and persons whose income exceeds R5000 per month are explicitly excluded form the protection of the act.[2212] Persons claiming to be occupiers for purposes of the act, have to set out the facts upon which they rely. In *Ntuli v Smit*[2213] it was found to be insufficient for such persons merely to repeat the wording of the statutory requirements in their affidavits.

With regard to the consent requirement in the definition of "occupier" for purposes of the act, section 3(4) of the Extension of Security of Tenure Act provides that a person who has continuously and openly resided on land for a period of one year shall (for purposes of civil proceedings in term of the act) be presumed to have consent unless the contrary is proved. In this context, the treatment of the issue of tacit permission in *Rademeyer v Western Districts Council*[2214] is important. This case involved an application for an interdict prohibiting the council from allowing certain occupants of land belonging to the council to erect housing structures thereupon, and ordering the removal of the occupants. The occupants initially occupied the land without the permission of the council. The applicants accordingly argued that the provisions of the Extension of Security of Tenure Act did not apply,[2215] as the occupants did not fall within the ambit of "occupiers" in terms of this act. However, on the facts it was clear that the council had become aware of the occupants' presence before the commencement of the act and had done nothing to disturb their occupancy.[2216] It was consequently found that the act applied to the situation and that the strict requirements relating to eviction had not been adhered to.

[2211] Members of the family excluded.

[2212] Sec. 1 s v "occupier", Extension of Security of Tenure Act.

[2213] *Ntuli v Smit* 1999 2 SA 540 (LCC), 549C-D.

[2214] *Rademeyer v Western Districts Council* 1998 3 SA 1011 (SECLD).

[2215] Non-application of the act would expedite the eviction of the occupants who were causing a nuisance to the land owners in the vicinity.

[2216] *Rademeyer v Western Districts Council* (note 2214 above), 1016F-G, 1017C.

2.3.3.1.2. Long-term Security of Tenure

Chapter II of the Extension of Security of Tenure Act deals with the measures to facilitate long-term security of tenure for occupiers. In view of the importance of these measures for establishing security of tenure, this part of the act is too generally formulated and contains too little information concerning specific options open to claimants of long-term security of tenure.[2217] Nevertheless, two methods of achieving long-term security can be identified: by way of either on-site or off-site development.[2218] Off-site development takes place where occupants of land are provided with an independent tenure right on land owned by someone other than the owner of land on which they resided immediately prior to the development. The act envisages a balancing-of-interests process, in that applications accommodating the interests of both occupiers and landowners, and which are cost-effective, are given precedence.[2219] If the development is not on the farm itself and occupiers have indicated a preference towards on-site development, satisfactory reasons must be given why an on-farm development is not feasible.[2220]

If expropriation of land is necessary to enable developments in accordance with the Extension Act, the Minister of Land Affairs is called upon to exercise his or her powers in terms of section 26(1) of the Extension of Security of Tenure Act, which roughly resembles those powers conferred by the Expropriation Act.[2221] However, all expropriations for these purposes have to be preceded by a hearing[2222] and compensation has to be paid with due regard to the section 25(3) FC and sections 12(3) to (5) of the Expropriation Act.[2223]

2.3.3.1.3. Protection against Eviction

Chapter IV of the Extension of Security of Tenure Act deals with the termination of occupant's rights and evictions. The primary aim of the

---

[2217] *Pienaar,* Land Reform (2003), forthcoming.

[2218] Sec. 4(1), Extension of Security of Tenure Act.

[2219] Sec. 4(2), Extension of Security of Tenure Act.

[2220] Sec. 4(2)(c), Extension of Security of Tenure Act.

[2221] 63 of 1975.

[2222] Sec. 26(2), Extension of Security of Tenure Act.

[2223] Sec. 26(3), Extension of Security of Tenure Act.

act being the provision of security of tenure, rights vested under the act may only be terminated in accordance with the act.[2224] Circumstances are accordingly prescribed in terms of which occupants of land can be evicted legally.[2225] Applications for evictions or for the restoration of residence and use of land can either be made in the Magistrate's Court for the area concerned or in the Land Claims Court.[2226] If all parties agree, an application can also be made to the Provincial High Court.[2227]

[2224] In cases of legal eviction, proper alternative housing must be provided. Illegal removals will be punishable. Section 15, Extension of Security of Tenure Act provides for an alternative eviction procedure in cases of urgency. The order made in terms of this section resembles that order available in identical circumstances in terms of labour tenancy legislation. In *Conradie v Fortuin* 1999 3 SA 1027 (LCC), the order for eviction was set aside due to the fact that the applicant did not give the occupier notice of the intended eviction and also because the occupant was not present when the final proceedings were held under sec. 15 of the act. Even though it was an urgent application, it could not be granted in the absence of the person affected by it.

[2225] E.g. where a worker is dismissed in terms of the Labour Relations Act 66 of 1995 or when the lessees refuse to pay their rent.

[2226] Sec. 17(1), Extension of Security of Tenure Act. The Land Claims Court has national jurisdiction and has all the ancillary powers necessary or reasonably incidental to the performance of its functions, including the power to decide on any constitutional matter in relation to the act, to grant interlocutory orders, declaratory orders and interdicts and to review acts, omissions or decisions of functionaries under the act. See 429 ff. and 456 ff. above. The Land Claims Court has an automatic review function with regard to orders made by Magistrate's Courts until 31 December 1999. The number of reported cases immediately after the commencement of the act indicates that the provisions of the act with regard to eviction are generally not adhered to by the Magistrate's Courts. *Pienaar,* Land Reform (2003), forthcoming.

[2227] Sec. 19(2), Extension of Security of Tenure Act. The jurisdiction of the High Court with regard to granting an interdict relating to occupiers under the Extension Act was the issue in *Khumalo v Potgieter* 1999 (1) All SA 10 (N). The proceedings involved an application for an interdict to restrain the respondent/landowner from ejecting the applicant. A point *in limine* was whether the High Court had jurisdiction to entertain the application, since it ought to have been lodged in the Land Claims Court. Nicholson J investigated the relevance of the Extension of Security of Tenure Act to the facts and found that, the provisions of the act applied, in spite of certain conflicting factual statements in the papers. The landowner was accused of threatening and intimidation, and interference with the applicant's occupation and use of the land. This was *par exellence* the sort of conduct for which legislature reserved the relief of the Land Claims Court under section 19(1)(b)(i) of the act. Prior to the commencement

Since relationships between especially farm workers and landowners can be very volatile at times, the provision for mediation proceedings in section 21 of the Extension of Security of Tenure Act can be quite helpful.[2228] Provision has also been made for the establishment of a special tribunal[2229] authorised to grant eviction orders and to exclude persons from lodging applications in terms of the act if such a person had unlawfully obtained consent to reside on the land in question.[2230]

In the provisions made for evictions, a distinction is made between persons who were "occupiers" on 4 February 1997[2231] and persons who became "occupiers" after this date.[2232] Section 11(3) of the Security of Tenure Act lists specific factors that have to be considered in determining whether an eviction order would be just and equitable in cases where "occupation" in terms of the act commenced after 4 February 1997:[2233] (i) the period that the occupier had resided on the land; (ii) the fairness of the terms of any agreement between the parties; (iii) the availability of suitable alternative accommodation to the occupier;

---

of the Extension of Security of Tenure Act, such an interdict would have been granted by the High Court. Hence, the question was whether the jurisdiction of the High Court in these matters had been ousted by the Extension of Security of Tenure Act (16F). The decision attempts to indicate the specialised function of the Land Claims Court (16G-17E). The conclusion was reached that the Land Claims Court had the power to grant interdicts and that the legislature had sought to cater for situations which may arise for ancillary and incidental powers. It was therefore necessary to consider the aims and object of the Extension Act to determine whether an interdict to prevent the threats fell within the jurisdiction of the Land Claims Court (19H). The point *in limine* succeeded. *Pienaar*, Land Reform (2003), forthcoming.

[2228] Under sec. 21, Extension of Security of Tenure Act, any person may request the director-general to appoint someone to facilitate meetings and to attempt mediation. If the parties refer the dispute to arbitration in terms of the Arbitration Act 42 of 1965, a person may be appointed as arbitrator from the panel established under sec. 31(1) of the Labour Tenant Act.

[2229] Appointed in terms of the Special Investigating Units and Special Tribunals Act 74 of 1996.

[2230] Sec. 17(2A) inserted by sec. 27 of The Land Affairs General Amendment Act 61 of 1998.

[2231] Sec. 10, Extension of Security of Tenure Act.

[2232] Sec. 11, Extension of Security of Tenure Act.

[2233] According to decision of *Albertyn v Bhekaphezulu* 1999 2 SA 538 (LCC), these provisions are peremptory.

(iv) the reason for the proposed eviction; and (v) the interests of the landowner or person in charge, the occupier and the remaining occupiers.

Irrespective of the date of occupation, the right of residency may generally be terminated on any legal ground,[2234] including: (i) breach of section 6(3) of the Extension of Security of Tenure Act, which relates to the prohibitions on occupiers;[2235] (ii) breach of a material and fair term of any agreement reached by the occupier and the landowner, if the landowner has kept his or her part of the agreement;[2236] (iii) such a fundamental breach of the relationship between the occupant and the landowner that it is not practically possible to remedy it;[2237] (iv) voluntary resignation of an occupier who was simultaneously an employee of the landowner and whose right of residence arose solely from the employment,[2238] in circumstances not amounting to a constructive dismissal in terms of the Labour Relations Act.[2239] Since the commencement of the Extension of Security of Tenure Act, numerous cases have been reported relating to the requirements for eviction orders.[2240]

In *Lategan v Koopman*[2241] and in *Karabo v Kok*[2242] it was emphasised that the objectives of the act relating to security of title can only be achieved when there is compliance with all the requirements for eviction orders. Despite the legal requirements concerning the grounds for eviction, the applicant also has to satisfy the court that the eviction is fair. When an application for an eviction order is lodged, various factors

---

[2234] Sec. 8(1), Extension of Security of Tenure Act.

[2235] E.g. intentionally causing harm or damage.

[2236] Sec. 10(1)(b), Extension of Security of Tenure Act.

[2237] Sec. 10(1)(c), Extension of Security of Tenure Act.

[2238] Sec. 10(1)(d), Extension of Security of Tenure Act.

[2239] 66 of 1995.

[2240] Most of the reported cases resulted from the automatic review of orders granted by the Magistrate's Courts. *Pienaar,* Land Reform (2003), forthcoming. See *Lategan v Koopman* 1998 3 SA 457 (LCC), *Rademeyer v Western District Council* (note 2214 above), *Karabo v Kok* (note 2210 above), *Albertyn v Bhekaphezulu* (note 2233 above), *Conradie v Fortuin* (note 2224 above), *Springs v Occupants of the Farm Kwa-Thema* 1998 4 All SA 155 (LCC), *Uitkyk Farm Estates v Visser* (LCC) 60/98 (not reported), *Kanhym v Mashiloane* (LCC) 17R/98 and *Serole v Pienaar* 2000 1 SA 328 (LCC).

[2241] *Lategan v Koopman* (note 2240 above), 461C-D.

[2242] *Karabo v Kok* (note 2210 above), 1019B.

are taken into account, *inter alia* (i) the fairness of any agreement or provision in any law on which the owner or person in charge relies; (ii) the conduct of the parties giving rise to the termination; (iii) the interests of the parties and (iv) the fairness of the procedure followed by the owner or person in charge.[2243]

If the court orders eviction, a just and equitable date on which the vacation of the premises has to take place, as well as a date on which the eviction order will be carried out if not adhered to, have to be determined by the court.[2244] When determining these dates, the court has to consider all relevant factors, the main thrust of the process being to find a fair solution in the balancing of the interests of the parties.[2245] An eviction order can coincide with orders regarding the payment of compensation for structures and buildings erected by the occupier, as well as compensation for improvements or crops planted by the occupier.[2246] Eviction orders can also be made conditional on the payment of any outstanding wages.[2247] In cases where occupiers are evicted due to no fault or choice of the occupier, for example as a result of a retrenchment exercise by the owner, the provision of suitable accommodation by the land owner may be ordered.[2248]

Like in the case of labour tenants, the possibility of eviction has certain limits. The right of residence of occupiers who have resided on the land for ten years or longer and who have reached the age of 60 may normally not be terminated, unless a breach as contemplated in section 10(1)(a) to (c) of the Extension of Security of Tenure Act was committed. In short, there must be a legal ground for eviction, and an occupier may not be evicted merely on the ground of, for instance, old age.[2249]

[2243] Sec. 8(1), Extension of Security of Tenure Act.

[2244] Sec. 12(1), Extension of Security of Tenure Act.

[2245] Sec. 12(2), Extension of Security of Tenure Act.

[2246] Sec. 13(1)(a), Extension of Security of Tenure Act.

[2247] Sec. 13 (1)(b), Extension of Security of Tenure Act.

[2248] Alternative accommodation is accommodation that is safe and no less favourable than previous accommodation and suitable, having regard to the reasonable needs of occupiers, their joint earning abilities and the need to live close enough to employment opportunities or other economic activities.

[2249] This was common practice prior to the enactment of legislation. *Pienaar*, Land Reform (2003), forthcoming.

2.3.3.2. Protection, Rights and Duties of Occupiers and Owners

Chapter III of the Extension of Security of Tenure Act sets out the rights and duties of owners and occupiers respectively. Here the social nature[2250] of the Extension of Security of Tenure Act becomes clear.

The occupier first and foremost is entitled to security of tenure. Furthermore, he or she has the right to reside on the land and utilise it, in a manner, which takes the interests of the owner or person in charge into account. A list of special rights and privileges are also set out in section 6(2) of the Extension of Security of Tenure Act. These include the rights to receive postal and other communication, and to enjoy family life. An occupier is prohibited from intentionally and unlawfully causing harm to other persons or to cause material damage to property. The right to occupation is in some instances extended beyond the lifetime of the occupant concerned. Section 8(5) of the Extension of Security of Tenure Act provides that the right of residence of the occupier's spouse or dependant may only be terminated on written notice of twelve calendar months, unless such a spouse or dependant has committed a breach contemplated in section 10(1) of the act.[2251] In the latter instance, the court has a discretion to grant an eviction order on shorter notice if the landowner will be unfairly prejudiced. The rights of owners are likewise set out in section 7 of the Act and include for example the right to have an animal belonging to or under the care of an occupier impounded if there was no reaction to a notice to remove the animal. However, the landowner has to heed the provisions of the Extension of Security of Tenure Act in enforcing his or her rights. In this regard, it is of particular importance that the occupier may not be prejudiced in the

---

[2250] The social nature of the Land Reform (Labour Tenants) Act and the Extension of Security of Tenure Act is also illustrated by the treatment of costs orders espoused by this legislation. This entails that the Land Claims Court will refrain from making cost orders, provided that litigation is reasonably justified and properly conducted. See *Pienaar*, Land Reform (2003), forthcoming. See also *Ntuli v Smit* 1999 2 SA 540 (LCC), 550G-I. In that case the attorney could not take full instructions from the applicants and had accordingly been unable to present their case properly. It was found that litigation was not reasonably justified or properly conducted with the result that a costs order was allowed. In *Manana v Johannes* 1999 1 SA 181 (LCC), 183I-184C the attorneys were ordered to show cause why they should not pay the costs *de bonis propriis*. In that case the conduct of the legal representatives was below the expected quality.

[2251] All the rights of occupiers bind successors in title. Sec. 24, Extension of Security of Tenure Act.

past, present or anticipated exercise of a right conferred by section 7 of the act.[2252]

A person who has been evicted contrary to the provisions of the Extension of Security of Tenure Act may apply for reinstatement under section 14(3) of the act. A reinstatement order may be issued on such terms as the court deems fit. Such an order may include provisions regarding the repair, reconstruction or replacement of any building or structure and the payment of compensation. In *Karabo v Kok*[2253] reinstatement of occupiers was particularly problematic, because the case also involved a dispute about the validity of the termination of the employment of the labourers, an aspect which was being dealt within under the provisions of the Labour Relations Act. The court found that the termination of the employment had not taken effect for purposes of the Extension of Security of Tenure Act, because the dispute was still pending.[2254] It was clear that the Magistrate's Court should never have granted the eviction order. Nevertheless, reinstatement was problematic, because the hostel where the applicants previously resided was at that point already occupied by the new labourers hired by the landowner. The respondents accordingly alleged that the restoration of residence would lead to renewed violence.[2255] The court the ordered that the applicants should be placed in a position to reside elsewhere in an available hostel. Thus, reinstatement did not mean restoration of the exact *status quo ante*.

Section 5 of the Extension of Security of Tenure Act contains a catalogue of general rights for owners, persons in charge of the property and occupiers. These rights mirror those contained in the constitutional bill of rights, and include the right to human dignity, freedom and security of person, privacy, freedom of belief, and expression of opinion, freedom of association and freedom of movement. In view of the preference for contextual interpretation, this section holds interesting possibilities for further studies of the development of land law in view of the constitutional provisions regarding the protection and regulation of property. This is also illustrated by the existing case law.

[2252] *Du Plessis/Olivier/Pienaar*, 1997 SAPR/PL, 541.

[2253] *Karabo v Kok* (note 2210 above).

[2254] *Karabo v Kok* (note 2210 above), 1020E, 1022B.

[2255] *Karabo v Kok* (note 2210 above), 1023C-I.

Serole v Pienaar,[2256] for instance, entailed an inquiry into the question whether occupiers of land are allowed to bury their deceased relatives on that land. It was argued before the Land Claims Court that it was an important African custom for deceased family members to be buried close to the place where the surviving family members reside. The court nevertheless found that the rights set out in the Extension of Security of Tenure Act were all of a temporary nature and that the right to burial did not form part of it. Accordingly, it was found that graves would only be allowed if an agreement to that effect was reached between the occupier and the landowner.

The implementation of the Extension of Security of Tenure Act surely limits the exercise of a landowner's property rights considerably by creating basic human rights for occupiers of rural land and preventing unfair eviction. Hence it contributes to creating a (previously non-existent) culture of rights, especially in rural areas.[2257] Nevertheless, it should be approached cautiously, keeping in mind the interests of all parties involved.

2.3.4. Evaluation

On the whole, the redistribution policies and laws function within the common law conceptual and institutional structures. An attempt is made, however, to free access to land and housing from the shackles of apartheid and to extend it to people and communities previously excluded from it. Hence, the redistribution programme addresses the demand for restoring the balance in land law. The claims here are more general, relating to an imbalance in land holdings, and here the reconciliatory aspect of the land reform process is probably not as prevalent as the demands on the government to deliver on promises made to the

---

[2256] *Serole v Pienaar* (note 2240 above). The Magistrate's Court granted a temporary order refusing burial on the land. The Land Claims Court refused to hear the case on a procedural ground, but went ahead and dealt with the burial issue. See also the more recent decision of Nkosi v Bührmann 2002 1 SA 372 (SCA) where the right to burial was not regarded as incidental to the occupant's right to secure tenure, nor to the right to freedom of religion. The position has been altered since the handing down of this decision, by the insection of sec. 6 (dA) into the Extension of Security of Tenure Act.

[2257] *Pienaar*, 1998 SAPR/PL, 423-437 provides an extensive evaluation of the Extension of Security of Tenure Act.

landless and homeless. The purpose is not to restore land rights or to grant or improve access to land, but rather to transform the law in order to improve the security of tenure and the value of previously disregarded and unprotected land rights.[2258]

In the context of the Extension of Security of Tenure Act in particular, this means that a working relationship between landowners and the local government is paramount if the act is to be successfully applied. This holds true particularly with regard to off-site development. In view of the fact that the Act is generally not applicable to urban land, there is a risk involved that landowners would opt for new workers to settle in towns, thereby avoiding the impact of the Act. This could again lead to overcrowding and even longer waiting lists, exacerbating the huge backlog with regard to the provision of housing.[2259]

To some extent, the Communal Property Associations Act and the Interim Protection of Informal Land Rights Act manifest a tendency in South African legislation towards diversification of the ownership concept. In recognition of the fact that individual security is of the essence in the ownership concept, these statutes expand the categories of tenure holders that can claim ownership-like protection.[2260] Simultaneously, it adds new dimensions to the entitlements inherent in ownership, in that it circumvents the recourse to aspects of common law by providing for the community factor on the basis of rights to and control over the property-acquiring and property-holding entity of a communal property association.[2261]

2.4. Developments Pertaining to Land Administration and Regulation

Other pieces of legislation, not exactly falling within any single specific subcategory of the tripartite programme of land reform in South Africa, could also influence the development of property law. The issue of land tax[2262] and the initiatives of the Development Facilitation Act within the broader framework of the Reconstruction and Development policy of

---

[2258] *Van der Walt*, 1999 Koers, 288.

[2259] *Pienaar/Muller*, 1999 Stell LR, 370-396.

[2260] See also *Van der Walt*, 1999 Koers, 288.

[2261] *Carey-Miller*, 1999 SALJ, 758.

[2262] I am grateful to Mr Pieter Oosthuizen for discussing some of the intricacies of this subject with me.

the government are only mentioned here. The Prevention of Illegal Eviction from and Unlawful Occupation of Land Act[2263] will be discussed briefly.

2.4.1. Land Tax

Another innovation linked to land reform and relevant to the question of the limitation of the entitlements inherent in ownership, is the appointment of a subcommittee of the Tax Commission to investigate the possible introduction of a land tax. The functions of the commission include investigating the rationale for and the nature of land tax, its economic effects, the revenue raising potential thereof and the possibility of utilising funds for future land reform programmes and redistributional practices.

In South Africa land is a capital asset, and therefore the only taxation is in the form of transfer duties to be paid at sale and taxation raised on proof that land in a particular instance is not held as a capital asset, but as a source of income (like in the case of speculation with land).[2264] In the Third Interim Report of the Katz Commission,[2265] however, the sub-committee investigating the land-tax issue stated that there was no reason in principle why a rural land tax should not be seriously considered, primarily as a source of revenue for rural local authorities. The committee further recommended that such a tax should be levied at a local government level. It did not recommend the introduction of a national land tax on agricultural land.

Further proposals published during September 1996 aimed at including all land (that is to say privately owned land, state-owned land, tribal land and land used for any purpose within the jurisdiction of the local councils) be included in the tax base, with tax levied on the improved market value of the land. It was also suggested that the land tax should be levied on the owner and/or occupier to a maximum of 2% per annum for all jurisdictions. These principles have been translated into the

---

[2263] 19 of 1998.

[2264] Municipal rates and taxes are also levied on (in particular rural) immovable property.

[2265] *Commission of Enquiry into Certain Aspects of the Tax Structure of South Africa,* Third Interim Report, (November 1995).

South African Revenue Service's "Guide to Capital Gains Tax,"[2266] which is presently being put into legislation.

The *Draft Property Rates Bill*[2267] proposed that municipal authorities be granted the capacity to levy rates on property within a specific municipal area. Municipalities are given wide capacities in terms of the bill to decide upon the categories of property against which such rates could be levied, by taking into account the use and status of the property and the area in which it is situated.[2268] The property capable of being categorised as such by the municipal authorities range from residential property, commercial property through to a variety of farm land.[2269] It is suggested that the rates be levied on the improved value of the property as determined from time to time by the municipal authorities,[2270] for which specific provisions are prescribed.[2271] The Bill also provided for the recovery of rates so levied,[2272] and for the keeping of a register by the municipal authority portraying the different rates on property.[2273] Provision has further been made for appeal against a valuation of the property and the consequent assignment of a specific rate.

In the opinion of the Department of Land Affairs, the introduction of a land tax system might lead to a reduction in land speculation, which would in turn expedite the availability of land for land reform purposes.[2274] The question whether land tax would be constitutional in the South African context, has not yet been considered by the constitutional court. When confronted with this problem, the court would probably again have to weigh up the interests of individual owners against those of the South African society at large, but also the interests of the various "local" communities in particular. It is submitted that the bill in its present form does not portray a fair balance between the in-

---

[2266] *SARS*, Guide to Capital Gains Tax (23 February 2000).

[2267] See   http://www.polity.org.za/govdocs/bills/2000/property.pdf   [06.09. 2000].

[2268] Clause 3, Draft Property Rates Bill.

[2269] Clause 4, Draft Property Rates Bill.

[2270] Clauses 5 ff., Draft Property Rates Bill.

[2271] Clauses 21 ff., clauses 32 ff., Draft Property Rates Bill.

[2272] Clauses 15 ff., Draft Property Bill.

[2273] Clause 12, Draft Property Bill.

[2274] White Paper, par 3.4; *Van der Merwe/Pienaar* in *Jackson/Wilde (eds)*, Reform of Property Law (1997), 366-367.

terests of society (or, for that matter, the various local communities) and the interests of the individual. The municipal authorities are granted almost unlimited capacity to determine the amount of rates to be levied, as well as the capacity to discriminate against certain groups of owners on the basis of the status, situation and use of the property, by levying higher (or lower) rates.

2.4.2. Reconstruction and Development: Development Facilitation Act

In the broader context of the reconstruction and development policy of the government, the Development and Facilitation Act[2275] plays an important role in projects relating to land reform. Its primary thrust is to transform land law in its entirety on a uniform basis. It adopts an approach of extensive development, encompassing rural and urban areas, land tenure matters, general planning and conservation standards, financial measures and a new planning and developmental infrastructure.[2276]

The act covers the following matters:[2277] In the first place, it deals with the general principles relating to all land development[2278] and land development objectives.[2279] In the second place, it provides for the establishment of a new infrastructure consisting of the Development and Planning Commission[2280] and the Development Tribunals and Appeal Tribunals.[2281]. Finally, the act deals with the land development procedures, sometimes excluding[2282] and sometimes including, small-scale farming[2283] and land tenure matters.[2284] The provisions relating to general principles and objectives are important from the perspective of

---

[2275] 67 of 1995.

[2276] *Van der Merwe/Pienaar* in *Jackson/Wilde (eds)*, Reform of Property Law (1997), 368.

[2277] See 368.

[2278] Ch. I sec. 2-4.

[2279] Ch. IV sec. 27-29.

[2280] Ch. II sec. 5-14.

[2281] Ch. III sec. 15-26.

[2282] Ch. V sec. 30-47.

[2283] Ch. V sec. 30-47; ch. VI sec. 48-60.

[2284] Ch. VII sec. 61-66.

limitations on ownership. It contains conservation measures[2285] as well
as an additional commitment to the fundamental rights set out in the
Constitution.[2286]

At another level, the act also influences the existing ownership concept,
in that it provides for a new form of title, so-called "initial ownership,"[2287] thereby introducing land tenure developed in stages. By this
mechanism, full ownership is acquired in a number of steps.[2288] "Initial
ownership" can be registered in a deeds registry,[2289] enabling the holder
thereof to use and occupy the land *as if* he or she were the registered
owner in terms of the normal system of registration. The "initial"
owner therefore has almost[2290] all the entitlements usually afforded to
the owner.[2291] The "initial" owner can encumber the land by mortgage
or servitude, and significantly, can sell his right of "initial ownership" to
an outsider. At a later stage, when all the requirements for the registration of the land are met, "initial ownership" is converted into full ownership,[2292] without the payment of transfer or stamp duties. In other
words, automatic conversion to ownership occurs when certain prescribed conditions[2293] are met.

[2285] Sec. 3 (1)(c)(viii).

[2286] Sec. 3 (1)(g)(iv).

[2287] Sec. 62.

[2288] *Latsky* in *Budlender/Latsky/Roux,* New Land Law (1998), ch. 2A, 73.

[2289] Sec. 61(7) read with sec. 62, Development Facilitation Act.

[2290] The right of disposal over the object is restricted until conversion into
ownership has taken place, except in the contexts of the administration of a deceased estate, sale in execution, insolvency or liquidation, "or where some other
event occurs requiring the transfer of such initial ownership". See sec. 62(6),
Development Facilitation Act.

[2291] Sec. 62(4), Development Facilitation Act, provides that, upon the making
of the prescribed entries by the registrar of deeds, a transfer of initial ownership
vests in the holder the following rights: the right to occupy and use the erf as
owner; the right to acquire ownership of the erf under the Act; the right to encumber the initial ownership by means of a mortgage or a personal servitude
(but not the right otherwise to encumber or deal with the initial ownership);
and the right to sell the right of initial ownership.

[2292] Sec. 62(7), Development Facilitation Act.

[2293] Sec. 38, Development Facilitation Act.

The Deeds Registries Act[2294] defines immovable property as including "a registered right of initial ownership contemplated in section 62 of the Development Facilitation Act." *Prima facie*, initial ownership is therefore a real right, due to the fact that it is eligible for registration in the deeds register. Initial ownership is, however, a new kind of limited real right in that it amounts to a diminution of the parent right of ownership and is enforceable against the whole world.[2295] However, unlike other real rights,[2296] a registrar of deeds can cancel initial ownership.[2297] This indicates that initial ownership is not an ultimate reversionary right, because ownership can in principle only be terminated by the owner himself or herself (or a state authority in accordance with the provisions of the constitutional property guarantee).

Through this innovation, security of land tenure is guaranteed at a much earlier stage in the process of acquiring rights in land, thus diminishing the holding and selling costs thereof.[2298] This indicates that although the land reform policy of the government is, in the first instance, dedicated to establish social justice with regard to landownership through the principles of equality and fairness, it also places a premium on security of tenure inherent in the ownership of land. On a theoretical level, the introduction of initial ownership constitutes such a far-reaching deviation of the "traditional" private law definition of ownership, that the scope and content of private law ownership will have to be redefined.

The act also attaches another meaning to the concept of "beneficial occupation." It defines a "beneficial occupier" as "any person who has been in peaceful and undisturbed occupation of such land for a continuous period of not less than five years."[2299] Precarious occupation is not excluded. The main intention here is to legally recognise the factual circumstance of established peaceful occupation in the context of land

---

[2294] Sec. 102 of Act 47 of 1937.

[2295] *Carey-Miller*, 1999 SALJ, 754.

[2296] All other real rights except mortgage bonds need to be cancelled by a court order. See sec. 6, Deeds Registries Act 47 of 1937.

[2297] On concurrence of the owner of the parent entity of land, the holder of the right of initial ownership and parties with mortgage or personal servitude interests. See sec. 62(5)(b), Development Facilitation Act.

[2298] *Van der Merwe/Pienaar* in *Jackson/Wilde (eds)*, Reform of Property Law (1997), 369-370.

[2299] Sec. 1, Development Facilitation Act.

reform. A tribunal, in approving land development under the Development Facilitation Act is empowered to impose a condition of establishment regarding the manner in which the interests of any "beneficial occupier" will be provided for in the upgrading of an existing settlement.[2300]

2.4.3. Prevention of Illegal Eviction from and Unlawful Occupation of Land Act

Illegal land occupation is a national concern, but seems to be especially prevalent in the Western Cape.[2301] The slow pace, at which affordable housing is made available to those needing it and the insufficient provision of alternative land for settlement, most probably exacerbate the invasion of land.[2302] The Prevention of Illegal Squatting Act[2303] of 1951 criminalised, inter alia, invasion of land without a lawful reason and the occupation of it without permission.[2304]. The act furthermore made provision for the removal of informal settlers and the demolition of their buildings and structures.[2305] In the light of the provisions for housing and property in the Interim and Final Constitutions, the repeal of the Act was inevitable. In its stead, the Prevention of Illegal Eviction from and Unlawful Occupation of Land Act[2306] was promulgated in 1998. The long title of this act indicates that its purpose is, on the one hand, to provide for the prohibition of illegal eviction and, on the other hand, to provide procedures for the eviction of unlawful occupiers.[2307]

[2300] *Carey-Miller*, 1999 SALJ, 757.

[2301] In 1999, the estimated number of shacks in the metropolis alone was 72000. See *Brummer*, "Kaap Kreun onder Plakkery" Die Burger (04.08.1999), 1.

[2302] *Reitz*, "Huisagterstand meer as in 1994" Die Burger (10.09.1999), 10.

[2303] 52 of 1951.

[2304] Sec. 1(1)(a), Prevention of Illegal Squatting Act. Erecting a building without the necessary approval (sec. 3A(1)(a)(i), Prevention of Illegal Squatting Act), and permitting anyone to occupy such a building or structure and receiving or soliciting payment for facilitating squatting (also referred to as "squatter farming" sec. 4(1), Prevention of Illegal Squatting Act), was also prohibited.

[2305] Sec. 3, Prevention of Illegal Squatting Act.

[2306] 19 of 1998.

[2307] See the discussion of *Carey-Miller/Pope*, Land Title in South Africa (2000), 516 ff. on the relationship between the Prevention of Illegal Eviction Act and the Extension of Security of Tenure Act.

The Prevention of Illegal Eviction Act describes an unlawful occupant as a person who occupies land without the express or tacit consent of the person in charge,[2308] or without any other right in law to occupy.[2309] There is no provision in the Act that criminalises the illegal occupation of land as such. However, the eviction of occupiers from land other than on the authority of an order of a competent court constitutes an offence.[2310] Hence, this act has very little in common with the preceding legislation on squatting.[2311]

The Prevention of Illegal Eviction Act covers both evictions by private individuals[2312] as well as eviction at instance of a state organ.[2313] An urgent procedure for eviction is available to both private parties and state organs,[2314] should the circumstances require it. The act also provides for mediation, irrespective of whether the landowner is an organ of state or a private party.[2315] This constitutes a clear departure from the intolerant approach followed in earlier legislation.[2316]

As far as eviction at the instance of a private party is concerned, the proceedings may be instituted as soon as it comes to the attention of the owner or person in charge of the property that persons are occupying the land unlawfully. The court must serve[2317] a written and effective no-

---

[2308] Sec. 1(x), Prevention of Illegal Eviction Act, defines "Person in charge" as any person who has or at the relevant time had legal authority to give permission to a person to enter or reside upon the land in question.

[2309] Sec. 1(xi), Prevention of Illegal Eviction Act. Persons who qualify as occupiers for purposes of the Extension of Security of Tenure Act and persons whose rights to land would normally be protected by the Interim Protection of Informal Land Rights Act are excluded form the definition of "unlawful occupier".

[2310] Sec. 8, Prevention of Illegal Eviction Act. Persons are on conviction liable to a fine, or imprisonment not exceeding two years, or both.

[2311] *Pienaar*, Land Reform (2003), forthcoming.

[2312] Sec. 4, Prevention of Illegal Eviction Act.

[2313] Sec. 6, Prevention of Illegal Eviction Act.

[2314] Sec. 5, Prevention of Illegal Eviction Act.

[2315] Sec. 7.

[2316] *Pienaar*, Land Reform (2003), forthcoming.

[2317] Normally the manner and procedure for the serving and filing of notices would be as set out in the rules of the Magistrate's Court. Service of process takes place when the process is formally delivered to an opposing litigant, in accordance with the rules of the court. Rule 9 of the Magistrate's Court provides

tice of proceedings upon the unlawful occupier or occupiers and the municipality that has jurisdiction at least fourteen days before the contemplated hearing.[2318] If the court is satisfied that the prescribed manner is for specific reasons not acceptable,[2319] the court can determine the manner in which service should be effected. The notice must contain:[2320] (i) a statement that proceedings are being instituted in terms of section 4(1) of the Prevention of Illegal Eviction Act for an eviction order against the unlawful occupier; (ii) the date and time at which the court will consider the matter; (iii) the reasons for the proposed eviction and (iv) an indication of the unlawful occupier's entitlements to appear before the court, defend the case and where applicable, apply for legal aid. In *Cape Killarney Property Investments (Pty) Ltd v Mahamba and Others*[2321] the meaning of the requirement that the notice should be written and effective was considered. A rule *nisi* was obtained for the eviction of 542 families unlawfully occupying the property of the applicant. However, the eviction order was sought under section 4 of the Prevention of Illegal Eviction Act, which provides for written and effective notice of at least 14 days prior to the hearing. No such notice was given. Accordingly an application for setting aside the rule *nisi* followed. The Court confirmed, with reference to the right to housing,[2322] that eviction orders may only be granted after all relevant circumstances had been considered. It held that the purpose of the notice

---

for the following methods of service: (i) personal service, (ii) service upon an agent, (iii) service at the residence or place of business of the defendant, (iv) service at the defendant's place of employment, (v) service at the defendant's *domicilium citandi*, (vi) service upon a body corporate, (vii) service by registered post, (viii) service upon state organs and state officials, (ix) service by affixing a copy upon the defendant's door, (x) service upon a partnership, (xi) service upon curators, executors or guardians, (xii) service upon clubs and societies, and (xiii) service in terms of an order of court. *Paterson*, Eckard's Principles (1996), 96-103; *Erasmus/Barrow*, Hooggeregshof en Landdroshowe (1992), 88-91. *Pienaar*, Land Reform (2003), forthcoming.

[2318] Sec. 4(2), Prevention of Illegal Eviction Act.

[2319] The very nature of land invasion and the informal settlement of people on land can make the service of notices on unlawful occupiers in practice extremely problematic.

[2320] Sec. 4(5), Prevention of Illegal Eviction Act.

[2321] *Cape Killarney Property Investments (Pty) Ltd v Mahamba and Others* 2000 2 SA 67 (C).

[2322] More specifically sec. 26(3) FC.

was to protect occupants by warning them that their occupation was threatened, informing them of their rights and remedies in terms of the provisions of the Prevention of Illegal Eviction Act.[2323] It would therefore not be sufficient to merely have the notice in writing, because the effectiveness of the notice is as important as its form. In that particular case, the larger part of the community consisted of Xhosa-speaking, illiterate people. Effectiveness in that case would have meant that the written notice would have had to be accompanied by a Xhosa translation and that the contents thereof should have been broadcast, in Xhosa, by a megaphone throughout the community at times when many of the residents would be there.[2324]

The court can grant the eviction order after having taken into account all the relevant considerations. The order will set a just and equitable date on which the premises must be vacated and a date on which the eviction order is to be carried out failing vacation of the premises.[2325] The equitable date referred to is to be determined after all relevant factors have been taken into account, *inter alia* the period of occupation. An eviction order can coincide with an order regarding the demolition and removal. However, any such order is subject to conditions deemed reasonable by the court. The Prevention of Illegal Eviction Act compels the court to distinguish between unlawful occupiers who have occupied land for less than six months and those who have been in occupation of the land for more than six months in granting eviction orders. In both cases, the court will grant an eviction order if it is just and equitable to do so after considering all relevant circumstances,[2326] but with regard to occupiers who have been on the land for longer than six months, it should additionally be considered whether land has been made available

---

[2323] *Cape Killarney Property Investments (Pty) Ltd v Mahamba and Others* (note 2321 above), 74D-F.

[2324] *Cape Killarney Property Investments (Pty) Ltd v Mahamba and Others* (note 2321 above), 75F-G. Apart from the problems ensuing form the notice above, the rule *nisi* was discharged due to the following considerations: (a) the proceedings were initiated by obtaining a rule *nisi* in stead of issuing and serving a notice of motion, (b) the hearing took place without notice to the respondents, (c) the normal time periods were bypassed by the applicant and (d) only a copy of the court order, rather than a full copy of the founding papers, was served on each of the respondents (77D-E).

[2325] Sec. 4(8), Prevention of Illegal Eviction Act.

[2326] E.g. the rights and needs of the elderly, children, disabled persons and households headed by women.

or can reasonably be made available by a municipality or other organ of state or another landowner for the relocation of the unlawful occupiers.[2327] This aspect will be a consideration in all of these cases, except where the land is sold in a sale of execution pursuant to a mortgage. It must be stressed that the availability of alternative land is not a prerequisite for the issue of an eviction order, but that it is rather one of the factors that can be taken into account. Thus, it will not necessarily form part of all eviction proceedings. It is only relevant in cases where the land was occupied longer than six months.

The Prevention of Illegal Eviction Act provides for the initiation of eviction proceedings by a state organ directly or indirectly. If the eviction is to take place at the direct instance of an organ of state,[2328] such an order will be granted if just and equitable and after the court has considered all the relevant circumstances.[2329] This includes questions like whether the occupant is in occupation of land or has erected a structure without the necessary consent or whether it is in the public interest to grant such an order.[2330] The interests and safety of those occupying the land, as well as the interests of the general public need to be considered. Furthermore, the circumstances under which occupation took place and structures were erected, the period of occupation and the availability of suitable alternative accommodation or land can also influence the outcome of the court order. In contrast to the case where private parties apply for eviction, the court will normally consider the availability of alternative land or accommodation regardless of the period of occupation.[2331] Notice of the proceedings must be given not less than 14 days before they take place.[2332]

The Prevention of Illegal Eviction Act further provides that an organ of state can initiate eviction proceedings indirectly, by giving an owner or person in charge notice to institute eviction proceedings. This is usually relevant within the context of local authorities' responsibility to enforce

---

[2327] Sec. 4(7), Prevention of Illegal Eviction Act.

[2328] An organ of state may institute eviction proceedings with regard to land situated in its area of jurisdiction.

[2329] See *Carey-Miller/Pope*, Land Title in South Africa (2000), 522-523.

[2330] Sec. 6(1), Prevention of Illegal Eviction Act.

[2331] Where individuals apply for eviction orders, this aspect is only relevant if occupation had been longer than six months.

[2332] Sec. 4(2) and 5(2) as opposed to sec. 6(4).

town planning and spatial measures.[2333] In such cases, the court can order the private party to bear the costs of these proceedings, upon request by the state organ responsible for instigating the eviction order.[2334] If the relevant owners do not react within the stipulated period in the notice, the proceedings will nevertheless continue, on the authority of the organ of state.[2335]

Both individuals and state organs can make use of the urgent proceedings pending the outcome of proceedings for a final order. Such an order will be granted if the court is satisfied (i) that there is real and imminent danger of substantial injury or damage to any person or property if the unlawful occupier is not evicted; (ii) that the likely hardship to the owner if an order is not granted in relation to the likely suffering of the unlawful occupier against whom the order is sought if an order of eviction is granted; and (iii) that there is no other effective remedy available. As in the case of an ordinary order, the hearing has to be preceded by a notice. This must be in writing and must effectively indicate the owner's intention to obtain an eviction order, but no time period is set out in this section.[2336] The content of the notice is identical to that of a normal eviction notice.[2337]

Upon reading the provision of the Prevention of Illegal Eviction Act, it seems as if the intention is not to create any new land rights. It simply provides fair procedures for the eviction of unlawful occupants.[2338] However, illegal land invasion and informal settlement are still major concerns. The fact that a court order may entrench the position of unlawful occupiers of land is problematic. The question whether the unlawful occupation of the land becomes lawful upon an order of court against eviction, and the issue of the status of the occupiers of land pursuant to such an order, will in future have to be clarified. Obviously, the full impact of the Prevention of Illegal Eviction Act has not been completely realised in practice.

Also in the case of the Prevention of Illegal Eviction Act, the main purpose of the legislation seems to be the protection of both occupiers and

---

[2333] *Pienaar*, Land Reform (2003), forthcoming.

[2334] Sec. 6(5), Prevention of Illegal Eviction Act.

[2335] *Carey-Miller/Pope*, Land Title in South Africa (2000), 522.

[2336] Sec. 5(2), Prevention of Illegal Eviction Act.

[2337] *Pienaar*, Land Reform (2003), forthcoming.

[2338] *Van der Walt*, 1999 Koers, 288.

landowners. In *Port Elizabeth Municipality v Peoples Dialogue on Land and Shelter and Others*[2339] the underlying philosophy of this act and the unique circumstances and background which led to the drafting of it, were highlighted.[2340] Horn AJ emphasised that a legalistic approach to this kind of social welfare legislation was not appropriate. The legislation is inevitably linked to social and economic factors and fairness, morality and social values must influence it.[2341] In matters like these, the conflicting interests of the landowners and the homeless are always present. It is the duty of the court to balance these interests and to come to a decision that is "just and equitable" in the relevant circumstances.

3. Evaluation

The actual transformation of property law and landownership is presently curtailed by financial difficulties and the lack of a generally accepted theoretical framework. The legislative reforms must be accommodated within the current socio-political function and practise of landownership to establish an acceptable legal theoretical framework.

The land reform model currently advocated by the government promotes the individual self-esteem and interest as one of the primary incentives to efficient and optimal use.[2342] However, the three-fold divi-

---

[2339] *Port Elizabeth Municipality v Peoples Dialogue on Land and Shelter and Others* 2000 2 SA 1074 (SECLD). This case concerned land earmarked for housing development under carefully structured housing policies, but which was occupied illegally as a result of a well-organised, deliberate and premeditated act on the part of the occupants. The duty of the local authority to provide housing and shelter and the role that the Act had to play to regulate evictions in an orderly fashion, were underlined. The court pointed out the intolerability of allowing a small number of individuals to frustrate large-scale housing projects and henceforth granted the eviction order, pending the availability of suitable alternative land or accommodation.

[2340] *Port Elizabeth Municipality v Peoples Dialogue on Land and Shelter and Others* (note 2339 above), 1079A-1080I.

[2341] *Port Elizabeth Municipality v Peoples Dialogue on Land and Shelter and Others* (note 2339 above), 1081G.

[2342] *Murphy* in *Rwelamira/Werle (eds)*, Confronting Past Injustices (1996), 117.

sion of the South African land reform programme does not reflect a specific dogmatic structure.[2343] Instead, it represents the ad hoc nature of the process and its possible results. Consequently, substantive legal change would be a matter of chance.

The reform process has, up to now, been focused on according land rights by using existing procedures or by modifying existing procedures of acquisitions. As such, the land reform programme's most striking contribution to the transformation of property law is the expansion of a broad range of possessory "rights" at the expense of ownership.[2344] Fundamental transformation of the law of landownership is embodied in the introduction of the concepts of "initial ownership" and "beneficial occupation." However, these developments still take place within a framework resembling that of "traditional" common law, that is, a framework in which full ownership (of land, in these cases) is seen as the highest ideal. Within this framework, new mechanisms of access to land can be seen as exceptions to the old, established rules of private law.

Initial ownership, for instance, challenges the traditional South African common law concept of ownership in that it questions the element of absolute enforceability usually associated with private property. Initial ownership hovers somewhere between ownership and limited real rights in the traditional private law sense, as it encompasses the power to enforce the rights against anyone and everyone, but does not comprise the power of alienation. On the other hand, it might not constitute any inroad on the traditional common law understanding of ownership, if it is regarded as ownership "in name and anticipation"[2345] and already contains the essential elements of full ownership.

In the context of the constitutional property guarantee, the application of the principles of proportionality to a specific case will determine whether the legislation intentionally or accidentally resulting in an adaptation of the private law principles of property law will pass muster. The constitutionality of the legislation promoting the objectives of the broader land reform process and denying rights and entitlements existing under private law of property will most probably be supported by

---

[2343] *Carey-Miller*, 1999 SALJ, 749.

[2344] See e.g. Land Reform (Labour Tenants) Act; Interim Protection of Informal Land Rights Act; Extension of Security of Tenure Act; Prevention of Illegal Eviction from and Unlawful Occupation of Land Act.

[2345] *Carey-Miller*, 1999 SALJ, 755.

the affirmative action clauses, the broader context and the solemn language of the preamble which tip the scales in favour of the homeless and landless.[2346]

3.1. Land Reform and the Paradigm Shift Induced by the New Constitutional Order

The property law order under a system characterised by the predominance of private law in determining the principles and rules pertaining to property underwent a radical change when the new constitutional order induced a reconsideration of priorities in the context of land reform. The crux of the land reform programme concerns the introduction of measures to give effect to constitutionally declared policy commitments. Thus, land reform legislation embodies a critical statement of policies agreed upon in the course of drafting the Final Constitution. This of necessity entails an abandonment of existing laws and measures of control that represented a different policy orientation in the past.[2347]

In this regard the recent decision of the Witwatersrand High Court in *Joubert v Van Rensburg*[2348] serves as an example of the challenges awaiting the judiciary in the context of the shifting paradigm in South African Land Law.[2349] The case originated from an unlawful land invasion, but the main focus of the application was an unlawful land devel-

---

[2346] *Murphy* in *Rwelamira/Werle (eds)*, Confronting Past Injustices (1996), 119. As of yet, however, the judiciary has been cautious to opt for protection of rights in the land reform context, which challenges existing traditional private-law rights of landowners. Cf e.g. the decisions in *Bührmann v Nkosi* 2000 1 SA 1145 T and *Nkosi v Bührmann* 2002 1 SA 372 SCA; as well as the decision of Fleming J in *Joubert v Van Rensburg* 2001 1 SA 753 (W). The Supreme Court of Appeal has, however, warned explicitly against an approach in which judges use statutes of a socially contentious nature to vent their personal dissatisfaction with the political system, or to uphold the old regime (see par 26 of *Mkangeli v Joubert* case no 220/2001 SCA).

[2347] *Carey-Miller*, 1999 SALJ, 751.

[2348] *Joubert v Van Rensburg* 2001 1 SA 753 (W).

[2349] The scope of the present inquiry does not allow a detailed analysis of the decision in the *Joubert* case. *Van der Walt* addresses most of the issues related to land reform in a forthcoming case discussion ("Living with New Neighbours: Landownership, Land Reform and the Property Clause" forthcoming 2002 SALJ). I am grateful to André van der Walt for making the manuscript of this discussion available to me.

opment and not the land invasion as such. Briefly, the case involved the efforts of a couple of landowners to assist a homeless community in their vicinity to acquire agricultural land elsewhere, where the interests of the particular landowners would not be impaired. The new piece of land was purchased and managed by means of a trust created especially for that purpose. In essence, the trust was created and the land purchased in an attempt to address homelessness which had already resulted in land invasion, by establishing an unauthorised, informal residential township, which did not comply with the Town Planning and Township Ordinance,[2350] and without bringing the settlement under the auspices of statutory alternatives such as the Less Formal Township

---

[2350] 15 of 1986 (T). An overview of the features of township development in South Africa is provided in par 15.1-15.2 of the decision (*Joubert v Van Rensburg*, note 2348 above). Among others, it mentions the construction of roads to new townships and the provision of adequate water supplies for reasons of public health and fire hazards by the local authority; the installation of other services such as sewerage by developers or, when a service is not supplied itemwise, the cash contribution towards the creation of parks, ambulance services, markets, street lighting, cemeteries, etc by the community itself. An alternative method of township establishment was introduced to cater for urgent needs on a level which would be acceptable to people in need who would settle for lesser standards. The Communal Property Associations Act 28 of 1996 introduced a less rigorous system of requirements for alternative methods of township establishment. This act supports a philosophy of controlled permission to a group of people for 'township' development for themselves but excluding outsiders. However, the development still cannot be completely discretionary. The act controls the bona fides of the type of need that is served, including the background of the participants, but attention is given to certainty of and clarity about rights. The act and its schedule attends to a written exposition, inter alia, of the purposes for which each person may use the property and physical division; whether and to whom a member may sell rights; and how disputes are resolved. Operational effectiveness is promoted also by making the association a juristic person run by democratically elected persons with definite duties and controls but without power to simply sell the communal property. Finances are specifically attended to. The basic element of the association is protected by the creation of a statutory offence of, inter alia, wrongly granting another person access to the property. Sec. 14(1)(a) CPA. The court then criticises the lack of attention in the act to a list of clearly discernable and acceptable minimum standards for development of such townships, but remarks that the Minister, who has a discretion in terms of sec. 2(1) CPA whether or not to allow such development, would presumably not allow it if the end result would be nothing better that an unserviced site likely to be marked by squalor and dirt and unhealthy conditions.

Establishment Act,[2351] the Development Facilitation Act[2352] or the Communal Property Associations Act,[2353] on privately purchased agricultural land. The landless moved to the new settlement voluntarily and peacefully. The new settlement soon started causing problems because of overcrowding, lack of sanitation and refuse removal services, pollution and overburdening of inadequate road infrastructure.[2354] Other landowners in the vicinity of the new settlement thereupon approached the Court for an ejectment order against the trustees and beneficiaries of the trust and all other occupiers of the new settlement, as well as an abatement order to terminate the nuisance. The application was based on the alleged invalidity of the trust arrangement, lack of compliance with (and consequent contravention of) planning and development laws, and the nuisance caused by the settlement.

The occupants were ordered to abate the nuisance they were causing and to terminate their occupation of the land.[2355] The informal structures in which they were living were to be broken down and if they would fail to leave the land, they were to be ejected by the sheriff. In his judgment, Flemming DJP considered the constitutionality of the Extension of Security of Tenure Act in extremely negative terms, and concluded that its provisions are inconsistent with the Constitution. Nevertheless, the court then decided that the unconstitutionality of the Extension of Security of Tenure Act was not really in issue in this case, because the act is not directly involved in an application by someone who does not own the land upon which the occupiers to be evicted reside, and because the applicants in casu (the neighbouring owners) were not

---

[2351] 113 of 1991.

[2352] 67 of 1995.

[2353] 28 of 1996.

[2354] See the court's examination of the facts relating to the nuisance in *Joubert v Van Rensburg* (note 2348 above) at par. 17.2.1-17.3.7.2.

[2355] The court stated that it would be appropriate to grant an interdict against the nuisance created by the occupiers, but this would entail that the joint unlawful occupation had to be ceased, and the squatters evicted. (*Joubert v Van Rensburg* (note 2348 above), par 18.2, 20.2.3 and 20.3.) It also confirmed that an order could be obtained against the local authority, as argued by the respondents, but stated that this was not the only available remedy (par 21.4). The court refrained from postponing the application for an interdict against unlawful use of land, as that would have amounted to adopting a view that unlawful behaviour was temporarily in order, which could not be tolerated (par 22).

"burdened by" the act.[2356] The court did not consider the possible influence of section 26(3) FC on the position of the applicants. The result of the decision is that the anti-eviction provisions characterising the land reform effort in South Africa were ignored or bypassed in the search for a solution.[2357] Interestingly, in the subsequent, related decision of *Katazile Mkangeli v Joubert*,[2358] which dealt with an application for leave to appeal directly to the Constitutional Court against the decision in *Joubert*, the case was referred to the Supreme Court of Appeal in order for the substantive trust and nuisance questions to be resolved. Hence, Fleming DJP's remarks on ownership and land reform, the constitutional validity of the Extension of Security of Tenure Act, and anti-eviction procedures were apparently regarded as *obiter*. Nevertheless, these remarks (and the tone in which they are made) raise the important question of whether the judiciary is prepared for the imminent paradigm shift in South African Land Law under a new constitutional order.

Fleming DJP's decision that the Extension of Security of Tenure Act is arbitrary because it is forces fairness in favour of the land occupants, loses sight of the legitimate state purpose in the enactment of land reform legislation. Within the broader land reform programme, of which the Extension of Security of Tenure Act is a part, the state's intention to transform the unjust system of landholding and land control inherited from the apartheid regime. The judge's finding that the act is unconstitutional thus disregards the consideration of the legislature's objectives, and opts for a comparison of apples and oranges, by playing off land occupants against landowners. Ironically, in this case the occupants had consent from the landowners/trustees to occupy the land, and hence the proposed arbitrariness and lack of general application, which is ascribed to the Extension of Security of Tenure Act, makes even less sense in the specific circumstances. The decision acknowledges that section 25(5)-(8)

[2356] *Joubert v Van Rensburg* (note 2348 above), par. 44.2. See, however, the response of the Supreme Court of Appeal to this line of reasoning in their (still unreported) decision in the present matter (*Mkangeli and others v Joubert and others*, case 220/2001), par 8 et seq. where the provisions of the Extension of Security of Tenure Act are upheld in view of the purpose of the constitutional property clause.

[2357] The anti-eviction provisions of the Prevention of Illegal Eviction from and Unlawful Occupation of Land Act 19 of 1998 were also found to be not applicable. See *Joubert v Van Rensburg* (note 2348 above), par. 25.4.1.

[2358] *Mkangeli v Joubert* 2001 2 SA 1191 (CC).

FC was intended to keep the way clear for land reform, but the judge then remarks that[2359]

> *"allowing people to stay on another's property wherever they chose and simply because they so chose, at the expense of lawful rights, is clearly not land reform."*

The concern about uncontrolled land invasions is evident in this statement, but what happened in the *Joubert* case should much rather raise concern about the abuse of private rights to evade the state's policies on land control. In effect, a very basic principle of ownership should have informed the decision: owners of private land should be allowed to act as they please on their land, but not without a consideration of the limitations from public and private law, and not unreasonably. Similarly, the state should be allowed to interfere in private property relations, but only to an extent that may be reasonably tolerated by individual owners and holders of rights. The integrated application of the constitutional and social state principles can be employed to determine whether the private individual and the state's conduct in either situation would be reasonable.

The *Joubert* case indicates how mechanisms and structures of private property law could be invoked to side-step the effects of the broader land reform programme, and what could happen if the judiciary turns a blind eye to such manoevres. The original creators of the trust invoked ordinary private law mechanisms to deal with what they regarded as "the squatter problem" threatening their business interests: instead of resorting to the measures available in terms of administrative and legislative control, they decided rather to keep the state out of the situation and to acquire alternative land on which to resettle the squatters. This measure could have been laudable, and could even have exemplified the employment of individual liberty with regard to private property in a fashion indicating an awareness of social duty on the level of private parties *inter se*. But a closer look at the situation shows, as Fleming DJP also recognises,[2360] that " 'the problem' ...[is] merely move[d] to another address"; merely dumped, so to speak, on the doorstep of someone else. As such, it exemplifies anything but an individual awareness — and responsibility towards the resolution of — a socio-economic problem existing alongside any political view.

[2359] *Joubert v Van Rensburg* (note 2348 above), par. 43.6.

[2360] *Joubert v Van Rensburg* (note 2348 above), par. 3.2.

More importantly, however, the court never questions the sanctity of individual property rights in the present context. This is significant in view of the fact that this case gave the court the opportunity to determine its own role in enforcing liberty and social duty with regard to property within the realm of private law. The question that the court could have considered more carefully in the context of s 25 FC is whether the development of an informal settlement on the relevant land, pursuant to its purchase by the trust, and the conduct of the trustees in providing the beneficiaries with plots for occupation, can be regarded as a socially responsible exercise of individual freedom in the context of ownership. One would expect socially responsible conduct under circumstances as in the *Joubert* case to comprise more formal involvement in the eventual development of the settlement and the provision of services, with a view not only to the convenience of neighbouring owners, but also to the constitutional objective of improvement of living conditions. Moreover, the court should not allow itself or the parties calling upon its judgment to abuse the structures of private property law in order to evade the implications of land control measures anchored in public law.

In this regard, Van der Walt,[2361] upon an analysis of the issues of land reform, constitutionality and eviction in the *Joubert* decision, draws attention to the need

> "to develop a theory about factors that should, in view of the land reform programme and its roots in history and in the Constitution, weigh in favour of being lenient, flexible and accommodating rather than strict and formalistic about formal requirements and prescriptions that affect the establishment of housing for homeless communities."

Van der Walt[2362] then indicates that a development undertaken on private initiative and with private funds, should be regarded favourably, as should the fact that the development is set up in consultation with the community and structured to suit their needs and wishes. However, it would be preferable whenever possible to involve the whole local community within which the development takes place and local government structures — something that was not done in the case of *Joubert*. It is then suggested that, in view of the abnormal housing situation in South Africa and the fact that housing development apparently takes

---

[2361] *Van der Walt* (note 2349 above).

[2362] *Van der Walt* (note 2349 above).

place more quickly and naturally in the informal sector (where the development process is completely different from what is accepted as normal in the western tradition of urbanisation), attempts could be made to formalise the settlement, post hoc, in a manner satisfactory to the occupiers, the local farming community and the government. If such a compromise could be reached, the formalisation of the settlement is preferable to eviction of the occupants. The court's actual decision in favour of eviction of the occupants simply removed the homelessness problem to a different area and further postponed the possibility of a solution acceptable to all stakeholders.

Although the court paid lip-service to the idea of interest-balancing in the context of land reform,[2363] it displays a disturbing lack of understanding or openness to the necessity for and the justification of land reform in South Africa. Instead, the court makes it clear that the sanctity of private ownership is considered the highest public good, and that it perceives private ownership to be under threat from laws the court regards as permitting and supporting land invasions and general lawlessness. The court in the *Joubert* case saw its duty in protecting ownership against that threat. As Van der Walt explains,[2364]

> *"the decision is set up and stands as victory of the rule of law over lawlessness and of ownership over land invasions, but in fact it also stands as a victory of stability over change and of existing rights over land reform."*

As such, the *Joubert* case harshly highlights the choice the courts must make in decisions involving land reform, housing or shelter, and improvement of living standards. The dismissive view of land reform adopted by the court is ill-placed within the new constitutional order which supports the transformation of the oppressive land regime that characterised property law under apartheid through a process of reform.

3.2. Land Reform, Public Purposes and the Concept of Property

From the analysis of the Joubert case, it seems as if at least two general ideas should be kept in mind in any evaluation of the land reform programmes in South Africa: On the one hand, terms like public interest,

---

[2363] See *Joubert v Van Rensburg* (note 2348 above), par. 3.2.

[2364] *Van der Walt* (note 2349 above).

public good, and more specifically public purposes must be understood in the context of land reform itself. On the other hand, the influence of land reform and constitutional protection and regulation of property on the concept of ownership as it is understood in private law points to an inevitable shift away from a theory acclaiming private ownership as the pinnacle in a hierarchy of rights, to a theory of diversification.

3.2.1. Public Purposes

The term *public purposes* will play a prominent role in determining the constitutionality of aspects related to the land reform programme. An absolutist interpretation of this term would result in a prohibition of expropriation of one individual for the sake of restoring ownership to another. Such an interpretation would be contrary to the principles of restitution and reconstruction, which are central to the constitution.[2365] Already in terms of the Interim Constitution, the *use to which property is being put* as a factor relevant to the determination of compensation on expropriation suggested that expropriation of under-utilised property for the purposes of transferring it to new owners was anticipated.[2366] It appears that the distinction between situations where the specific aim of expropriation is to benefit a private party, and others where the private party is benefited as an ancillary result of the expropriation that was intended to fulfil a public policy, remains important. The ultimate purpose of the expropriation, as opposed to the mechanism of expropriation, is the determining factor.[2367]

Public purpose has obviously not been interpreted literally as *public use* in South Africa. It is understood in a broad sense. Instead of facilitating direct public use and access to the property, *public purpose* rather requires that the expropriation generate some particular advantage for the public in general. It includes expropriations whereby the entire population or a local community is affected and not only matters pertaining to the state or government.[2368] Therefore land redistribution programmes have been regarded as falling within the purview of the public purpose

---

[2365] See e.g. sec. 8, 121, 122, 123 and the Preamble and Postscript, IC.

[2366] *Chaskalson*, 1994 SAJHR, 137.

[2367] *Eisenberg*, 1995 SAJHR, 221.

[2368] *White Rocks Farm (Pty) Ltd v Minister of Community Development* (note 1419 above), 793I.

definition, even if private property is occasionally transferred from one private party to another.[2369]

3.2.2. Ownership and Other ("Lesser") Property Rights

The "traditional" property law division between ownership and other "possessory rights" or "rights in property" was dictated by the assumption that the all-pervading power of ownership, represented by seventeenth-century Roman-Dutch law, should not be open to challenge.[2370] The all-pervading power of ownership was perhaps best indicated by the prominence and scope of a landowner's powers of vindication. Exactly this power has been curtailed extensively as a result of the advancement of the so-called lesser rights through the process of reform. Although the idea that "full" ownership is supreme to other rights, still seems to be at the order of the day,[2371] the most recent legislative measure effecting land reform indicates a stronger tendency to break away from the existing structures.

Instances of the reinforcement of lesser rights are found in the Land Reform (Labour Tenants) Act and the Interim Protection of Informal Land Rights Act. In the Land Reform (Labour Tenants) Act, the formerly insecure tenure of labour tenants were granted better legal protection, and where a controlled right to acquisition of land was granted to persons who qualified for it in terms of the act. In terms of the Interim Protection of Informal Land Rights Act a specifically defined number of lesser rights enjoys protection (on an interim basis, pending permanent reform measures) against the otherwise dominant rights of the titleholder.

The concept *rights in land* could in future have a substantial influence on the concept of *property*, not only in the context of constitutional property protection, but also in the context of private-law enforcement of rights. The inclusion of *beneficial occupation* (for a period of 10 years prior to dispossession) as a *right in land* worthy of restitution in terms of the Restitution of Land Rights Act points, for instance, to some of the objective and subjective components which comprise informal land

---

[2369] *Eisenberg,* 1995 SAJHR, 221.

[2370] *Carey-Miller,* 1999 SALJ, 751.

[2371] *Van der Walt,* 1999 Koers, 289-290.

rights: occupation (usually of a specific period)[2372] plus the intention to benefit from the land to the exclusion of others. Beneficial occupation itself is not defined in the Restitution of Land Rights Act. Under the Development Facilitation Act,[2373] it is apparently understood to mean peaceful and undisturbed occupation of land for a continuous period of not less than five years. The Interim Protection of Informal Land Rights Act[2374] defines it as

"the occupation of land by a person, as if he or she is the owner, without force, openly and without the permission of the registered owner."

Carey-Miller[2375] shows that the concept of beneficial occupation has distinct roles in separate legislative contexts. In the context of restitution, it functions as a control mechanism to determine the beneficiaries of the restitution programme. In the context of protection of informal land rights, this concept serves to secure an otherwise very insecure form of possession. In the context of land reform, "beneficial occupation" is a condition of establishment in providing how the interests of parties will be upgraded in existing settlements. From these definitions it seems as if beneficial occupation is a concept similar to "statutory prescriptive title," which enjoys protection from infringement by third parties. The protection afforded to beneficial occupation within the context of land law in the transformation era is another indication of the growing importance of a theory of diversification of land rights.

3.3. Land Law Reform and the Constitution in Comparison

The chief purpose of the constitutional provisions on land reform in general is to redress the imbalance of existing patterns of ownership by promoting the development of a new property order, where rights in land are diversified and based upon considerations of fairness. This speaks against an elevation the courts elevating real rights above other interests, since such an approach would do nothing but confirm the ex-

---

[2372] Whereas the Restitution of Land Rights Act requires a period of 10 years for beneficial occupation, the Development Facilitation Act 67 of 1995 sets a minimum of 5 years as requirement.

[2373] Sec. 1 defines the term "beneficial occupier".

[2374] Sec. 1, Act 31 of 1996.

[2375] *Carey-Miller,* 1999 SALJ, 755 ff.

isting unjust patterns of title. Unfortunately, in a recent set of decisions[2376] involving a clash of interests of a landowner (one *Bührmann*) and a family of labourers' right to family burial on the land, the judiciary indicated a tendency to approach matters like these rather conservatively and restrictively.[2377]

Without dwelling upon the factual detail that underlies these decisions, the problem could be summarised as follows: Sections 5 and 6 of the Extension of Security of Tenure Act[2378] embodies a right to freedom of religion for families of farm labourers in situations resorting under the act. *In casu*, the labourer's family (*Nkosi*) claimed that they were entitled in terms of these provisions to bury a deceased relative on the farm, without it being necessary to obtain the permission of the farmer/landowner. The latter (*Bührmann*), however, relied on his right of ownership to refuse permission for the burial and to claim that an interdict had to be issued preventing the burial. Hence, the main issue was whether a landowner's right of ownership trumps a statutorily protected occupier's right to freedom of religion, which is protected by land reform legislation (in particular the Extension of Security of Tenure Act) as part of the occupier's right to security of tenure.[2379] The

---

[2376] *Nkosi v Bührmann* 2002 1 SA 372 (SCA), discussed in conjunction with *Bührmann v Nkosi* 2000 1 SA 1145.

[2377] A detailed analysis of these cases is provided by *Van der Walt* "Property Rights v Religious Rights: Bührmann v Nkosi", forthcoming in 2002 Stell LR. I am grateful to André van der Walt for allowing me access to the manuscript thereof. My discussion here builds upon his own.

[2378] Sec. 5 ESTA mirrors constitutional provisions for fundamental rights by providing that an occupier, an owner and a person in charge of land affected by ESTA shall, subject to limitations which are reasonable and justifiable in an open and democratic society based on human dignity, equality and freedom, and with due regard to the objects of the Constitution and of the Act, have the right to human dignity, freedom and security of the person, privacy, freedom of religion, belief and opinion and of expression, freedom of association and freedom of movement. Sec. 6(2) ESTA provides that an occupier in terms of ESTA shall have the right to security of tenure, to receive bona fide visitors at reasonable times and for reasonable periods (subject to certain safeguards), to receive postal and other communications, to family life in accordance with the culture of that family, not to be denied or deprived of access to water, and not to be denied or deprived of access to educational or health services.

[2379] Note that the Nkosi family does not rely on constitutional protection of religious freedom under sec. 15 FC, but on the indirect protection of freedom

Nkosi family did not rely on the direct constitutional protection of religious freedom espoused by section 15 FC, but filtered their claim for protection of religious freedom through the land reform legislation mentioned. Their arguments for the establishment of a right to burial of relatives on the land formed a complex system of reliance partly on established practice, agreements and implicit servitudes, to indicate that the right of burial has vested in or has been acquired by the family; and partly on the proposition that the right to burial constitutes one aspect of the right to freedom of religion, thereby emphasising the conflict between freedom of religion, land reform legislation and ownership.

The final decision was handed down by the Supreme Court of Appeal.[2380] It establishes that land occupiers' right to freedom of religion and free exercise of religious practice, as embodied in section 5 of the Extension of Security of Title Act, is limited and does not include the right to take land for burial sites unilaterally, without the landowner's consent.[2381] The landowner's rights are, therefore, taken as the point of departure. The likelihood of allowing religious freedom of the occupants to trump the owner's rights is limited unless there is a clear indication to the contrary. The decision further suggests that a strong, permanent occupation right resembling a limited real right is required before the court will be willing to consider the possibility that a burial right has been created and amounts to a dimuntion of ownership.[2382]

It is impossible to deal with all aspects of the decision within the confines of the present inquiry.[2383] However, it needs to be remarked that the case illustrates the strong influence of traditional private-law thinking on the manner in which the court deals with issues related to fundamental rights and freedoms. Van der Walt quite correctly indicates that a more constitution-sensitive, flexible and sophisticated analysis of land rights and burial rights is needed if the land reform angle to matters like these gets the attention it should.[2384]

---

of religion in ESTA, which seeks to provide security of tenure to weak and marginalised occupiers of agricultural land.

[2380] *Nkosi v Bührmann* (note 2376 above).

[2381] *Nkosi v Bührmann* (note 2376 above).

[2382] Van der Walt (note 2377 above).

[2383] See, however, the detailed analysis of Van der Walt (note 2377 above).

[2384] Van der Walt (note 2377 above).

The following chapter aims at providing a comparative balance to that part of the South African land reform programme involved in restitution, and to indicate how issues of land law reform were resolved elsewhere. It indicates the extent to which the balancing of interests inherent to a system of constitutional protection of Germany (and arguably also South Africa) pervades the law-making process in cases where land law reform is necessary. Simultaneously, it provides examples of how certain issues with regard to compensation and restitution have been resolved.

Chapter 10: German Reunification and the Property Order

1. Background to the Property Questions Raised by Reunification

After World War II, it was assumed that the division of Germany, which was effected by the Allied forces, was only of a temporary nature.[2385] Instead, the relationship between the three Western powers[2386] on the one hand, and the Soviet Union, on the other, deteriorated with the commencement of the Cold War, and German unification seemed to be out of the question. In the East German occupation zone a socialistic constitution was enacted in 1949, replaced in 1968, and extensively revised again in 1974 to remove all references to a possible reunification of Germany. In the West, the Basic Law, which was intended to be a temporary constitution, came into force in 1949 and remained so until reunification in 1990.[2387] In fact, it still forms the basis of the German state.

German reunification eventually took place in 1990, with the "accession" of the German Democratic Republic to the Federal German Republic. Due to the different political and social models that developed during the forty years of separation, many obstructions impeded reunification, among them also the issue of how the property order in Germany would be influenced by attaching two such different socio-political and legal systems to each other. In particular, the treatment of the property order of the former German Democratic Republic would place new, unexpected demands on the courts, legislature and administration of the new reunified Federal German Republic. This contributed to the development of the concept of constitutional protection and regulation of property in German law. This chapter provides an overview of the legislative innovations to the property order brought about by reunification, as well as the treatment thereof by the judiciary.

[2385] *Robbers*, Introduction to German Law (1998), 41.

[2386] Britain, France and the USA.

[2387] See 45 ff. above.

1.1. Property Order in the German Democratic Republic Before Reunification

After the war, but before the establishment of the German Democratic Republic, the eastern part of Germany was under Soviet occupation. During this period (between 1945 and 1949), a series of expropriations were effected under the so-called *Bodenreform* programme, in order to lay the foundation for a socialist society. The ostensible legal basis for this large-scaled property reform programme was the Treaty of Potsdam, concluded by the four Allied Powers in July 1945, although the true purpose of this treaty was rather the elimination of militarism and national-socialism in Germany.[2388] Almost all large businesses were expropriated. The land seized formed about one-third of the entire Soviet zone.[2389]

Large industrial enterprises and all estates larger than 100 hectares (for instance, the estates of the aristocratic land barons called the *Junkers*) were confiscated,[2390] the latter on the basis that owners of such vast landholdings were automatically regarded as "enemies of the People".[2391] Many thousands of holdings under 100 hectares were confiscated too with the objective of large-scale social restructuring. All in all, this comprised around 3,3 million hectares.[2392] Some 60% of the confiscated land was distributed to poor farmers who did not pose any political threat to the government.[2393] The rest was reorganised for purposes of societal use or municipal administration, or developed into state research and educational institutions.[2394]

Orders that all land registers relating to land confiscated in the time of Soviet occupation had to be destroyed, were apparently not obeyed.[2395]

[2388] *Pries,* Neubauerneigentum (1993), 13.

[2389] *Southern,* 1993 ICLQ, 691.

[2390] No compensation was paid. *Pries,* Neubauerneigentum (1993), 16.

[2391] *Quint,* The Imperfect Union (1997), 125; *Pries,* Neubauerneigentum (1993), 7-12.

[2392] *Southern,* 1993 ICLQ, 691.

[2393] This property was referred to as *Neubauerneigentum, Bodenreform-eigentum* or *Siedlungseigentum.* See *Pries,* Neubauerneigentum (1993), 1-2; *Kommers,* Constitutional Jurisprudence of Germany (1997), 256.

[2394] *Pries,* Neubauerneigentum (1993), 19-24.

[2395] Most of the old land registers were collected and stored in Castle Barby, and forgotten for decades. With the reunification, they were rediscovered by

Crossings-out, erasures, obliteration or gummed paper were, nevertheless, used to remove evidence of former ownership.[2396] Thus, the land registers as such were left intact, but the process of tracing the original owners after reunification and during the restitution process was complicated. The new holders received "title" to the land attributed to them by the Soviet occupation regime in so far as that they were allowed to use it and that the land could be bequeathed to a descendant, but the holders did not have the capacity to alienate, divide or mortgage it. Further, the holders were obliged to deliver a specific share of their harvests to the government.[2397]

Extensive expropriations of property by the state for public purposes[2398] took place after the establishment of the German Democratic Republic in 1949 and during its forty year existence. Virtually all industrial and agricultural property, such as land, buildings, installations, machinery, raw materials, industrial products, copyright and patents, were converted into *Volkseigentum* (People's Property).[2399] In most cases extremely low compensation was awarded. The agrarian land distributed to individual farmers during the period between 1945 and 1949 was reorganised into agricultural co-operatives.[2400] Many of the small and middle-sized businesses remained — at least partly — in the hands of private owners until 1972 when practically all private businesses were placed under government ownership. The thousands of state-owned enterprises were also regarded as People's Property.[2401]

---

anxious former landowners wanting restitution of their property. The arson attack on the archive at Castle Barby in 1993 caused considerable damage, and seriously dislocated the restitution process. *Southern*, 1993 ICLQ, 692.

[2396] *Pries*, Neubauerneigentum (1993), 18.

[2397] *Pries*, Neubauerneigentum (1993), 26-34; 36-40.

[2398] This included expropriation of land for the building of cities and development of belowstructure; for industrial settlements, energy management and for military purposes. *Visser/Roux* in *Rwelamira/Werle (eds)*, Confronting Past Injustices (1996), 100.

[2399] *Quint*, The Imperfect Union (1997), 124.

[2400] The so-called *Landwirtschaftlichen Produktionsgenossenschaften (LPG-en)*. See *Pries*, Neubauerneigentum (1993), 41-45.

[2401] *Quint*, The Imperfect Union (1997), 146.

Part Four: Influence of Social Reform on Land Law

Land and property had a consciously diversified, subordinated and artificially reduced status in the socialist socio-economic system.[2402] In Socialist law, a premium was placed on "control" rather than "ownership."[2403] The following types of "control" could be identified:

(i) *Socialist Property* consisted of *Peoples Property*,[2404] *Co-Operative Socialist Property*,[2405] and *Property of Civic Associations*.[2406] It is difficult to determine exactly where ownership of *People's Property* lay. It was owned by everybody and nobody. The ownership entitlements were exercised by the socially owned firms of the state, which means that it was indeed not the People, but rather the State, that could be regarded as the legal subject of People's Property.[2407] *Co-Operative Socialist Property* belonged to the industrial and agricultural co-operatives. They could use and control the property in the interests of their enterprise. *Property of Civic Associations* constituted the belongings of mass organisations and parties.

[2402] *Fieberg* in *Rwelamira/Werle (eds)*, Confronting Past Injustices (1996), 83; *Pries*, Neubauerneigentum (1993), 119; *Kimminich*, Die Eigentumsgarantie im Prozeß der Wiedervereinigung (1990), 53.

[2403] *Pries*, Neubauerneigentum (1993), 45-65 indicates, for instance, that the members of the agricultural co-operatives had specific rights and duties with regard to the land, but that the co-operative itself had extensive rights of use over this land against the members. A member had, upon entry into the co-operative, to submit an inventory of the land and related property under his or her control, and had to hand it over to the co-operative. In return, the member was entitled to a just proportion of the land under control of the co-operative, for control by the member himself or herself. This also included the right to determine a successor upon death of the member. The member further had the right to terminate his membership, but only once the Members' Assembly agreed to it. He or she would also lose the means of production. The co-operative had the right to claim handing over of all fruits from the land, to use the land for agricultural purposes, and to erect buildings upon it. It could exploit the mineral resources of the land, and could exercise the rights of an owner, without that it was necessary for the controller to be joined to any action pertaining to the property.

[2404] *Volkseigentum.*

[2405] *Genossenschaftlich-sozialistisches Eigentum.*

[2406] *Eigentum gesellschaftlicher Organisationen der Bürger.*

[2407] *Pries*, Neubauerneigentum (1993), 120-121.

(ii) *Personal Property*[2408] included objects for personal use, like furniture, books and so on, aimed at satisfying the material and cultural needs of citizens. It was not intended to be used as source of income. Land and buildings could also qualify as personal property. This property could be alienated, used and exploited at will of the owner.[2409]

(iii) *Property of Labourers*[2410] comprised property connected to certain kinds of professions, like that of craftsmen, labourers and small-scale farmers.[2411]

Where immovable property was concerned, the existing land registers were closed and a new land register opened,[2412] designating the land as People's Property, and indicating the authority or enterprise holding the property. Agriculture and industry were organised into different "enterprises" *(Kombinate)* and each enterprise controlled a number of "socially owned firms" *(Volkseigener Betrieb / VEB)*. Moreover, state and party organisations acquired extensive land holdings.[2413]

The application of the rules of economic criminal law led to the gradual *de facto* expropriation of the middle class. It provided for total expropriation of industrial and other property on even minor offences against provisions on, for example, the delivery of goods.[2414] In addition, property could be seized by the state from the owners if permissible rental under the law of the German Democratic Republic proved insufficient to maintain the property.[2415]

The small sphere of private property left was held under a comprehensive system of government administration. The institution of long leasehold *(Überlassungsvertrag)* was introduced and the number of titles thus created proliferated between 1952 and 1976. The occupiers had the same entitlements as owners, but were not registered as such in the land register.[2416] In some instances, property — especially houses or

---

[2408] *Persönliches Eigentum.*

[2409] *Pries,* Neubauerneigentum (1993), 122-123.

[2410] *Eigentum der Handwerker und Gewerbetreibenden.*

[2411] *Pries,* Neubauerneigentum (1993), 123.

[2412] *Pries,* Neubauerneigentum (1993), 22.

[2413] *Southern,* 1993 ICLQ, 692.

[2414] *Fieberg* in *Rwelamira/Werle (eds),* Confronting Past Injustices (1996), 82.

[2415] *Quint,* The Imperfect Union (1997), 129.

[2416] *Southern,* 1993 ICLQ, 692.

other residences — remained in private ownership and could still be alienated. Both the 1949 and 1968/1974 constitutions of the German Democratic Republic protected private property to some extent and even seemed to contemplate at least a low rate of compensation for expropriation.[2417]

The socialist property order in the German Democratic Republic at the time of reunification, together with the haphazard system of land registration, created serious obstacles for the development of a just property law regime in the reunified Germany. The property issues were amongst the most controversial to be solved.

1.2. Problems Posed for the Property Order due to Reunification

At the start of negotiations for reunification, there were many unsettled property questions. This resulted from the different ideologies which formed the basis of property law in the eastern and western parts of Germany, and the discriminatory way in which the German Democratic Republic treated the property of people who fled its territory, who left with its permission and who were domiciled outside its later territory (including the Soviet sector of Berlin) before the end of World War II in Europe.[2418] The following paragraphs provide a brief overview of these problems.

1.2.1. The "Bodenreform" and its Implications

The Soviet occupation regime's *Bodenreform* — the land or agrarian reform programme of 1945 to 1949 — caused dogmatic difficulties after

---

[2417] In the 1949 Constitution (art 22, 23, 27) property was protected subject to "the social duties in favour of the community." Expropriation was allowed "only for the good of the community on the basis of a statute," and required compensation, "as long as the law does not determine otherwise." In the 1968/1974 Constitution (art 11, 16), "personal property" was guaranteed, but in a much narrower sense than what is usually understood to be personal property in the "western" sense of the word: it referred in principle only to "property in consumer goods purchased from income from work." It was also stipulated that "the use of property may not contradict the interests of the community." Expropriation could be undertaken "in return for appropriate compensation."

[2418] 8 May 1945.

the reunification.[2419] It was primarily aimed at the punishment of fascism by dividing agricultural areas more "justly" and thus indirectly improving the use of land.[2420] It therefore did not qualify as confiscated foreign assets, and the purpose of the confiscation was neither reparation, nor debilitation of the German national economy. Consequently it did not fall into any of the categories of confiscation qualifying for compensation set earlier[2421] by the Federal Constitutional Court.[2422] It was also speculated whether the *Bodenreform* could have been an unconstitutional infringement in terms of article 3 III GG, which provides protection against discrimination on the basis of class or social origin.[2423]

1.2.2. "Wiedergutmachung" in the Federal Republic and its Implications

A further problem was to what extent the reparation arrangements of the Federal Republic of Germany and the Allied powers influenced the measures undertaken in the former East zone and also in the German Democratic Republic. Refugees who left Germany between 1933 and 1945 were forced to sell their immovable property and could only take a restricted amount of currency out of the country. The persecuted that did not flee, only rarely survived the large-scale massacre of so-called state enemies. In any event, their land often ended up in the hands of party organisations or members, without any systematic alterations to the land register.[2424]

The *Wiedergutmachung* programme in the German Federal Republic was aimed at providing some kind of reparation for the victims of national socialism. The Federal Court of Justice declared on one occasion that the reparation arrangements in the Federal Republic of Germany

---

[2419] BVerfGE 1991 *NJW* 1597.

[2420] *Kimminich*, Die Eigentumsgarantie im Prozeß der Wiedervereinigung (1990), 81; *Pries*, Neubauerneigentum (1993), 13.

[2421] In 1976 in BVerfGE 41, 126.

[2422] *Leisner*, 1991 NJW, 1569 ff. provides a discussion of the reasons forwarded by the Federal Constitutional Court for not granting compensation.

[2423] *Kimminich*, Die Eigentumsgarantie im Prozeß der Wiedervereinigung (1990), 72.

[2424] *Southern*, 1993 ICLQ, 691.

were compatible with article 14 GG.[2425] No comprehensive rehabilitation was ever envisaged in the German Democratic Republic for the victims of national socialism,[2426] and in particular no restitution of property which had been lost as a consequence of persecution in the period between 1933 and 1945.[2427] After reunification it was, however, not clear how the forcible dispossession or confiscation of property, situated in what would later become the German Democratic Republic, could be brought into line with the Basic Law.[2428] The victims[2429] or their relatives demanded the necessary relief from the two German governments.[2430]

1.2.3. Expropriation Policy in German Democratic Republic

In 1949, the Soviet occupied zone became the German Democratic Republic. Expropriation legislation was enacted and on this basis countless expropriations and other infringements of property rights, in particular with regard to land, apartment ownership and means of production, took place. The main purpose of these expropriations was to give effect to a socialist concept of ownership,[2431] and to transform individual ownership to so-called *Volkseigentum*.[2432] A difficult problem, which resulted from this, was whether the expropriation legislation of the former German Democratic Republic would continue to apply after reunification had taken place.

[2425] BGHZ 52, 371 381.

[2426] *Tappert,* Die Wiedergutmachung von Staatsunrecht der SBZ / DDR (1995), 19-71 gives a detailed analysis of the attempts at *Wiedergutmachung* that were undertaken.

[2427] *Visser/Roux* in *Rwelamira/Werle (eds),* Confronting Past Injustices (1996), 99.

[2428] *Kimminich,* Die Eigentumsgarantie im Prozeß der Wiedervereinigung (1990), 80.

[2429] These were mostly Jews who survived the holocaust, or their descendants, but also included relatives of the conspirators of 20 July (the day on which a failed assassination attempt on Hitler took place).

[2430] *Fieberg* in *Rwelamira/Werle (eds),* Confronting Past Injustices (1996), 82.

[2431] *Fieberg* in *Rwelamira/Werle (eds),* Confronting Past Injustices (1996), 82.

[2432] *Visser/Roux* in *Rwelamira/Werle (eds),* Confronting Past Injustices (1996), 99.

This crucial question in this regard was whether the requirement of article 14 III 2 GG was applicable to expropriatory legislation of the former German Democratic Republic. This provision states that expropriation could only take place if compensation was provided for and if the type and extent of such compensation was expressly stipulated by legislation. The confiscation and expropriations in the German Democratic Republic were undertaken in terms of regulations applying to all inhabitants of the German Democratic Republic, citizens of the German Federal Republic as well as foreigners. They were thus not necessarily arbitrary, and not necessarily aimed at putting a particular group or person at a disadvantage, even if the compensation amounts offered (if any) were very low. Instead, they could be regarded as part of the socialist system of the German Democratic Republic. The only exception to the rule in article 14 III 2 GG pertains to expropriatory legislation enacted before the coming into force of article 14 GG. It therefore had to be determined whether the German Democratic Republic's expropriation legislation would be subject to article 14 III 2 GG, or whether this article was not applicable because of the rule against retrospectivity.[2433]

The confiscation of property in East Germany that qualified for compensation[2434] confronted the legislative authorities with the question about the manner in which the amount of compensation should be determined. In discussions on this topic, the social function of property as it is described in article 14 GG played an important role.[2435] Under the Defence Act[2436] of the German Democratic Republic, property was for instance expropriated (with payment of normal GDR compensation) for building the Berlin Wall and clearing the surrounding territory. Most of the "Wall Property" ran through the centre of Berlin, and became extremely valuable after reunification. The administration in Bonn was particularly adamant on retaining this property, at essentially no cost, for governmental purposes or lucrative resale. This created an uproar among many interested parties, some even calling it a retroactive

---

[2433] *Kimminich*, Die Eigentumsgarantie im Prozeß der Wiedervereinigung (1990), 79.

[2434] Mostly those taking place after 1949.

[2435] *Kimminich*, Die Eigentumsgarantie im Prozeß der Wiedervereinigung (1990), 83.

[2436] 1961.

endorsement of the Berlin Wall by the legal system of the former western part of the Federal Republic of Germany.[2437]

1.2.4. Administration of Emigrants' and Refugees' Property and its Implications

Between 1945 and 1990, but especially before 1961, about 3,5 million people fled the German Democratic Republic.[2438] At first, no special legal regulation governed the immovable property abandoned by these refugees. In 1952, however, the property of all people who fled the German Democratic Republic since the end of the war, was confiscated.[2439] Regulations pertaining to obligatory state regulation were also imposed against the property of all property holders who lived outside the German Democratic Republic after the end of the war. This legislation was repealed in 1953, but without undoing the retrospective confiscation of property abandoned before 1952.

Movement from East to West was severely constrained after the Berlin Wall was erected in 1961. Citizens of the German Democratic Republic could, however, still apply for official permission to leave. In spite of the legal protection offered to emigrants, permission to leave was in effect only granted once these "emigrants" had been forced to alienate their land to the state or third parties, often at very low prices.[2440]

From this time onwards, until the opening of the inner-German borders in 1989, property abandoned by refugees was not confiscated, but placed under the obligatory administration of the state, which was in fact nothing less than *de facto* expropriation.[2441] The obligatory administration of the state effectively removed all the rights and commercial

---

[2437] *Quint*, The Imperfect Union (1997), 134.

[2438] *Fieberg* in *Rwelamira/Werle (eds)*, Confronting Past Injustices (1996), 80.

[2439] *Verordnung zur Sicherung von Vermögenswerten* 17 July 1952 (GDR Law Gazette 615).

[2440] A decree from the Ministry of the Interior permitting emigrants to have the property administered was never put into effect or made public. Emigrants regarded themselves as having no choice but to alienate their property to the state.

[2441] Regulation no 2 *(Anordnung über die Behandlung des Vermögens von Personen, die die Deutsche Demokratische Republik nach dem 10. Juni 1953 verlassen)* GDR Law Gazette I, 664.

opportunities usually associated with ownership. Although still registered as owners in the title deeds of land, they were no longer responsible for the administration of their own property, they had no control over it and received no information about its use and condition. Proceeds did not befall the owners, but were regarded as People's Property or as state resources. The state used this property for a variety of purposes, for instance for the construction of industries or for state housing schemes. Land belonging to the state was let to tenants from as early as 1954. State administered property was also often used for this purpose. Tenants received the right to use state property, free of charge and without any time limit. Property under obligatory state administration could be sold to its users subject to specific conditions. Even after this regulation had been repealed,[2442] the obligatory administration of property continued. This system gave rise to several problems after reunification:

(i) In practice these regulations created two separate groups of refugees with different legal rights, although their positions were practically identical. The one group was *de iure* and *de facto* completely dispossessed, whereas the other group still retained title, but was economically dispossessed and "expropriated" for all practical purposes.[2443] This situation made the decision as to the form of rehabilitation controversial: confiscated or similar assets, could be returned to the original owners, state control could be removed,[2444] or the expropriated owners could be financially recompensed.[2445] The former option eventually turned out to be more equitable in view of the anomalous categorisation of refugees' property. Restitution was the only possible way in which both categories of "refugee property" could receive equal and equitable treatment. Compensation would have had the unacceptable result that victims of the obligatory state administration system would not have been regarded as having lost their property in the first place. The compensation option would then either have had to be restricted to cases of loss of ownership through expropriation or alienation, or

---

[2442] 11 November 1989.

[2443] *Fieberg* in *Rwelamira/Werle (eds)*, Confronting Past Injustices (1996), 81.

[2444] This option was preferred by the Federal Republic of Germany, as the expropriation of refugees' property had never been recognised by its government.

[2445] This option was preferred by the German Democratic Republic and its inhabitants.

would have had to provide in the Unification Treaty for formal expropriation of hitherto state-administered property. The consequence of the latter would be a sanctioning of the discriminatory confiscation that was effected economically by the German Democratic Republic, by the Unification Treaty.[2446] This could have had a disruptive effect on the restoration of German unity. Thereby a step would have been taken in the unification process that not even the German Democratic Republic's authorities wanted to take.

(ii) This system also caused serious disagreement between the so-called East- and West-Germans. On the one hand, former owners who previously fled to the West regarded the reunification negotiations as their chance of having their property returned. They regarded any interests of third parties that vested in the property after confiscation or the commencement of obligatory administration by the government of the former German Democratic Republic as unworthy of protection. They argued that these parties almost always knew that the property belonged to refugees, and thus were accomplices of the corrupt state. On the other hand, fear and insecurity prevailed within the German Democratic Republic itself, among landowners, but also among the larger contingent of land tenants: In fact, not many citizens of the German Democratic Republic were landowners. Most were *tenants*, often of property (which was abandoned by refugees) under the obligatory state administration system.[2447] This property was mostly not maintained properly by the state and the tenants themselves often financed fundamental repairs and maintenance, to keep the land and dwellings in habitable conditions. Tenants in the German Democratic Republic were subsidised by the state and enjoyed the strong protection of the socialist rent legislation. However, their situation became precarious with reunification and property reform pending. They faced possible eviction from their long-term homes by the original owners who had no real interest in these dwelling places any more. Besides, practically no provision was made for remuneration, regardless of the extent of their expenditure for maintenance of the property over years of residence.[2448] The problems of *landowners* in the German Democratic Republic were also manifold. The assets acquired by them — mostly with great per-

---

[2446] *Fieberg* in *Rwelamira/Werle (eds),* Confronting Past Injustices (1996), 84-85.

[2447] *Quint,* The Imperfect Union (1997), 132.

[2448] *Quint,* The Imperfect Union (1997), 133.

sonal effort and under harsh economic, social and legal conditions —
were all of a sudden to be placed at the disposal of the previous owners.
The security of title that landowners in the eastern part of Germany
enjoyed under the legal system of the German Democratic Republic
vanished. Economic and social re-evaluation of land and property in a
new market-oriented economy loomed. A satisfactory solution for all
parties concerned could only include compromises. This involved substantial inroads in the respective interests of the parties concerned.[2449]

1.2.5. Business Property

The large-scale expropriation of businesses under Soviet occupation
rule and in the later German Democratic Republic led to more problems at reunification. It was uncertain how these enterprises should be
treated. In the last days of the German Democratic Republic, a trust
agency *(Treuhand)* was created by the transitional government for the
administration of these businesses. Provision was made to convert
state-owned businesses into stock companies or private companies.[2450]

2. Legislative Arrangements

The framework within which certain property, expropriated or confiscated in the German Democratic Republic was to be returned to its
original owners was first set out in the *Joint Declaration in regard to the
Regulation of Unresolved Property Questions*.[2451] The Joint Declaration
formed the political and legal basis for the regulation of property in a
new, reunified Germany. Its aim was to return expropriated property in
the German Democratic Republic to its original owners or their
heirs,[2452] although several pragmatic considerations restricted this general intention of restitution. Although the Joint Declaration was a po-

---

[2449] *Fieberg* in *Rwelamira/Werle (eds)*, Confronting Past Injustices (1996), 83.

[2450] *Quint*, The Imperfect Union (1997), 146.

[2451] *Gemeinsame Erklärung zur Regelung offener Vermögensfragen*, 15 June
1990, BGBl 1990 II, 1273.

[2452] *Kommers*, Constitutional Jurisprudence of Germany (1997), 256.

litical document, it was incorporated[2453] into the Unification Treaty,[2454] and thus was binding upon the contracting parties.[2455] It therefore forms part of the foundations of modern German property law.[2456]

2.1. Giving Legislative Effect to the Revision of the Property Order

For the purpose of clarifying the general provisions of the Joint Declaration, the Unification Treaty also provided for more detailed measures regulating property issues: (i) The *Law on the Regulation of Unsolved Property Questions* (the "Property Act")[2457] regulated the circumstances under which the principle of natural restitution would apply. (ii) The *Act on Special Investments in the German Democratic Republic* (the "Investment Act")[2458] and its successors (the "Investment Acceleration Act"[2459] and the "Investment Priority Act")[2460] provided additional conditions to regulate the principle of natural restitution.

2.1.1. Restitution Before Compensation

The policy of natural restitution *(Rückgabe vor Entschädigung)* is laid down and simultaneously limited in articles 41(1) and (2) of the Unification Treaty.[2461] The chief mechanism for giving this principle practical

---

[2453] Incorporated into the Unification Treaty as Exhibit III, the agreement covered seized businesses and real estate – nearly all the industrial and landed property in the German Democratic Republic.

[2454] Art. 41(1) of *Vertrag zwischen der Bundesrepublik Deutschland und der Deutschen Demokratischen Republik über die Herstellung der Einheit Deutschlands – Einigungsvertrag –* 31 August 1990, BGBl 1990 II, 889.

[2455] *Fieberg* in *Rwelamira/Werle (eds)*, Confronting Past Injustices (1996), 83.

[2456] *Diekmann*, Das System der Rückerstattungstatbestände (1992), 43-55.

[2457] *Gesetz zur Regelung von offenen Vermögensfragen*, BGBl 1990 II, 1159.

[2458] *Gesetz über besondere Investitionen in der Deutschen Demokratischen Republik*, BGBl 1990 II, 1157.

[2459] *Gesetz zur Beseitigung von Hemmnissen bei der Privatisierung von Unternehmen und zur Förderung von Investitionen*, BGBl 1991 I, 766.

[2460] *Gesetz über den Vorrang für Investitionen bei Rückübertragungsansprüchen nach dem Vermögensgesetz – Investitionsvorranggesetz –* BGBl 1992 I, 1268.

[2461] *Diekmann*, Das System der Rückerstattungstatbestände (1992), 66-74.

implication, was the "Property Act." Section 1 is the key provision. Subsections (1) to (7) enumerate the various categories of property which could be the subject of restitution claims, while subsection (8) excludes restitution in a further number of categories. An amendment to the Property Act in 1992[2462] makes express provision for interpretation difficulties arising from the Property Act in connection with descendants of former owners or right holders that might qualify for restitution.[2463]

Restitution before compensation did not mean that rehabilitation in the economic sphere would necessarily be guided by present market values. It merely established the precedence of rehabilitation in kind over rehabilitation in money.[2464] However, this principle does reflect an almost absolutist conception of property with the right of recovery extending to 1949 and even earlier; thus, over a period of more than fifty years. Even though descendants had no personal relation to the property, they were still able to pursue the claims for restitution.[2465]

A profound ideological gulf lay between the supporters and opponents of restitution.[2466] Supporters of this policy regarded restitution as a moral and pragmatic necessity, because respect for and protection of property is a prerequisite for creation of wealth. Opponents of this policy saw in this process the making of an economic and administrative disaster, which produced greater injustice than that it intended to relieve.[2467] By the end of 1994, however, about half of all the restitution claims had been processed and most of the claims for return or privatisation of businesses had been completed. The claims to restitution of land and buildings were more time-consuming.

[2462] See 2. *Vermögensrechtsänderungsgesetz* (BGBl 1992 I, 1257) incorporated in art. 233 EGBGB.

[2463] See in general *Försterling*, Recht der offenen Vermögensfragen (1993), m.n. 225 ff.

[2464] *Fieberg* in *Rwelamira/Werle (eds)*, Confronting Past Injustices (1996), 84-85.

[2465] *Quint*, The Imperfect Union (1997), 128-129.

[2466] *Du Sold*, Restitution vor Entschädigung (1993), discusses in detail the arguments against and in favour of this policy.

[2467] *Southern*, 1993 ICLQ, 696-697.

2.1.1.1. Restitution of Land

The principal object of the Property Act was the restitution of land seized by the German Democratic Republic state without adequate compensation. The main categories for which restitution could be claimed were: (i) property that was converted into People's Property after the establishment of the German Democratic Republic on 7 October 1949,[2468] (ii) property acquired *mala fide* by third parties after this date; and (iii) property lost between 30 January 1933 and 8 May 1945 as a result of religious, political or racial persecution.[2469] The Joint Declaration also stated that property under obligatory state administration, namely property placed under state administration in consequence of forced emigration, renunciation, and flight to West Germany and non-consensual sale or property appropriated by the state,[2470] would be restored to the original owners.[2471]

The Property Act initially provided that expenses for fundamental repairs and maintenance to keep the land and dwellings in habitable conditions could be reclaimed by the tenants. This provision was, however, subsequently repealed.[2472]

2.1.1.2. Restitution of Business Property

The property settlement in the Unification Treaty also addressed the fate of thousands of business enterprises in the German Democratic Republic. After it had been accepted that the former German Democratic Republic would adopt the legal and economic principles conforming with those of the Federal Republic, including the principle of

---

[2468] See art. 41(1), Unification Treaty.

[2469] Sec. 1(6), Property Act; Claims of restitution involving victims of National-Socialism would take precedence over claims of later holder of the same property who may have been subject to expropriation. Sec. 3(2), Property Act.

[2470] *Pries*, Neubauerneigentum (1993), 161-164; *Kommers*, Constitutional Jurisprudence of Germany (1997), 256.

[2471] Attachment III par. 2, Unification Treaty; sec. 1(4), 11-15 Property Act. The original owner could, however, choose compensation in stead of restitution.

[2472] See sec. 19, 1990 version of Property Act.

private property in land and means of production, the *Treuhand* Act[2473] was promulgated to assist in the privatisation of People's Property.

It was decided that the general policy of restitution would also apply to business property expropriated by the German Democratic Government. Yet, some legal, technical and economic problems related to business property necessitated a specialised treatment of restitution. In contrast with land, business property is a rather fluid entity. It would make little sense to return a firm that might have the same name but otherwise bore no resemblance to the expropriated enterprise.[2474] Thus, under the Property Act, a business enterprise could only be returned to its prior owner if the enterprise remained *comparable* with the business at the time of expropriation, taking into account intervening changes in technology and general economic development.[2475] The original owner could, however, in many cases also choose compensation instead of return of the enterprise.[2476]

If the business was *comparable*, and therefore capable of being returned to the original owner, adjustments had to be made for substantial changes in the value of the business in the intervening period. The Property Act contains complicated rules for measuring substantial increases or decreases in value and regulating the problems of joint owners and stockholders caused by intervening mergers and splitting of businesses. Those business concerns that were not comparable, and could consequently not be returned to the original owners, as well as the business enterprises that were founded by the state and therefore had no prior owners, posed a serious administrative problem.[2477] The task of determining the destiny of these concerns fell to the *Treuhand*. It was decided that the concerns would mostly be sold to private owners. However, due to lack of governmental participation and the currency union established after unification, many of the *Treuhand*-concerns were unable to pay their debts, and the *Treuhand* administration itself was incapable of handling this problem effectively. Consequently, the economic conditions and the escalation of unemployment

---

[2473] *Gesetz zur Privatisierung und Reorganisation des volkseigenen Vermögens (Treuhandgesetz)*, 17 June 1990, GBl DDR I no 33, 300; art. 25, Unification Treaty.

[2474] *Quint*, The Imperfect Union (1997), 146.

[2475] Sec. 6(1)-(4), Property Act; see attachment III, sec. 7, Unification Treaty.

[2476] Sec. 6(7), Property Act.

[2477] *Quint*, The Imperfect Union (1997), 147.

rates in the east of Germany were attributed by German society to the *Treuhand*.[2478] The *Treuhand* ceased its activities in 1994, and a number of smaller agencies continued the necessary administrative duties.

2.1.1.3. Procedure for Claiming Restitution

Restitution claims usually had to be registered at one of the 221 local *Open Property Offices* in Germany. These local Property Offices are subject to one of six superior (provincial) Property Offices.[2479] Restitution claims had to be registered in the local Property Office of the district where the claimant (or the deceased in the case of a claim by the descendants) last lived, but could also be directed to the office in the district where the property in question was situated. The victims of persecution under national-socialism and foreign residents had to register their claims at the Federal Ministry of Justice in Bonn. Applications by corporate bodies and businesses had to be made to one of the six provincial property offices. Once a restitution claim had been lodged, the person with the power of disposition over the property — usually the *Treuhand* or another state or local authority — could not sell, lease or rent the land,[2480] unless an investment priority decision or investment certificate had been granted. In such cases, the right to restitution was overridden.[2481]

The deadline for lodging restitution claims *(Rückübertragungsansprüche)* was set at 31 December 1992. Property not claimed by that date would belong to the person with *de facto* power of disposal over it.[2482] Over 1,2 million applications were lodged, the majority concerning landownership and affecting over one-third of the land area of the former German Democratic Republic.

[2478] *Quint*, The Imperfect Union (1997), 148-151 gives a detailed explanation of the factors contributing to the fall of the *Treuhand* institution.

[2479] *Scollo-Lavizzari*, Restitution of Land Rights in an Administrative Law Environment (1996), 45.

[2480] Sec. 3(3)1 and 15(2), Property Act.

[2481] *Scollo-Lavizzari*, Restitution of Land Rights in an Administrative Law Environment (1996), 45-50; *Southern*, 1993 ICLQ, 695.

[2482] *Gesetz zur Änderung des Vermögensgesetzes und anderer Vorschriften (2. Vermögensrechtsänderungsgesetz)* 14 July 1992; 1992 BGBl, 1257.

After a restitution claim had been registered, the relevant property office had to establish what exactly was being claimed in each case. Claims were often unsubstantiated, vague, contradictory or conflicting. In favoured areas, like the suburbs of Berlin and central areas of cities, two or more claims, seeking recovery of the same piece of land to different "prior" owners, were sometimes encountered.[2483] It was up to the federal, provincial and local property offices to trace the original owners of such property with proper title to it. Once a claim had been sufficiently clarified, the office would make a provisional decision (*Vorbescheid*), either to reject or uphold the claim, or find that the applicant is only entitled to compensation, and not restitution.[2484] Appeals against such a decision have to be directed to the superior Property Office in a specific territory, where they will be decided by a committee established especially for this purpose.[2485]

If the claim for restitution was endorsed, an application could be brought to the local Land Registry for the entry of the correct particulars of the proprietor. Such an application would be successful, if no investment certificate was sought or granted in respect of the property. In case of a successful entry, the property was charged with a levy for the purpose of subsidising the compensation fund. The rights and duties of parties who had contracted in good faith were returned with the property to the original owner. The original owner would then step into the position of the party with whom bona fide third parties had concluded agreements pertaining to the property. In many instances the original owners had to take over the roles of contracting parties, with all the rights and duties arising form the contractual relationships.[2486]

Upon rejection of a claim by the property office in the provisional decision, an appeal could be lodged first at the provincial and subsequently at the federal property office. After exhausting internal appeals, the applicant could appeal to the Administrative Court.[2487] Only a limited number of the numerous restitution claims resulted in court proceedings. Most reached only the administrative pre-trial phase of the proc-

---

[2483] *Southern*, 1993 ICLQ, 696.

[2484] *Scollo-Lavizzari*, Restitution of Land Rights in an Administrative Law Environment (1996), 50 ff.

[2485] *Scollo-Lavizzari*, Restitution of Land Rights in an Administrative Law Environment (1996), 46 ff.

[2486] *Fieberg* in *Rwelamira/Werle (eds)*, Confronting Past Injustices (1996), 85.

[2487] *Southern*, 1993 ICLQ, 695.

ess. Eventually about 9000 cases were heard by the administrative courts. Several must still be decided.[2488]

2.1.2. Exclusion of Restitution

The revision of property law was not intended to remedy the disastrous consequences of a 40-year-old socialist economic and property policy. Rather, it was regarded as a form of rehabilitation, covering only cases of political disadvantage or discrimination.[2489] Complete revision of property measures applicable in the fourty years of German Democratic Republic rule was therefore never on the cards. For instance, the Joint Declaration regarded the expropriations "for the public interest"[2490] effected during socialist rule in the German Democratic Republic as valid. They were consequently not subject to review and could not be reopened for restitution claims.[2491]

Under the principle of *restitution before compensation*, it had to be decided how the interests of third parties to affected property were to be treated. Extensive inroads on the principle of restitution were required to maintain the social viability of the compromised reached on the property question in the course of reunification.[2492] The Joint Declaration consequently contained some exceptions to the policy of restitution which were incorporated into the Property Act. Restitution was excluded in the following instances: (i) where property was confiscated in the period from 8 May 1945 to 6 October 1949, prior to the establishment of the German Democratic Republic; and (ii) where property was acquired by an individual, church or charitable organisation between 7 October 1949 and 18 October 1989 in a *bona fide* transaction. In some instances, restitution was also excluded on the ground that the use of the property had changed after expropriation, for example

---

[2488] *Fieberg* in *Rwelamira/Werle (eds)*, Confronting Past Injustices (1996), 88.

[2489] *Pries*, Neubauerneigentum (1993), 160; *Fieberg* in *Rwelamira/Werle (eds)*, Confronting Past Injustices (1996), 84.

[2490] *Visser/Roux* in *Rwelamira/Werle (eds)*, Confronting Past Injustices (1996), 100.

[2491] For a discussion, see *Du Sold*, Restitution vor Entschädigung (1993); *Försterling*, Recht der offenen Vermögensfragen (1993); *Diekmann*, Das System der Rückerstattungstatbestände (1992).

[2492] *Fieberg* in *Rwelamira/Werle (eds)*, Confronting Past Injustices (1996), 85.

through the erection or alteration of buildings, or through communal-ising industrial or social use.

2.1.2.1. "Bodenreform" Property

The Soviet Union and the German Democratic Republic refused to undo the expropriations undertaken in terms of the Soviet Occupation Regime's *Bodenreform* of the period between 1945 and 1949. Business concerns expropriated before 1949 by the Soviet occupation regime would also not be returned to their former owners. The *Bodenreform* property distributed amongst individual farmers therefore became the property of those farmers after reunification, upon a reading of the *Bodenreform* Act (enacted in the last days of the German Democratic Republic) together with article 233 II 1 of the Act on Introductory Provisions to the Civil Code.[2493] Furthermore, the agricultural co-operatives were to be dissolved in order to create more competitive agricultural and industrial structures.[2494]

Because of the vast amount of property involved, restitution of the property expropriated in the Soviet occupation period would have caused a major social obstacle for reunification. It would have involved about one third of the agricultural property in the former German Democratic Republic, and would have left thousands of farming families landless and homeless.[2495] The Soviet Union would not have signed the final peace treaty without this concession on the part of the Allies and the Federal Republic of Germany.[2496] Former owners of land in eastern Germany challenged the Treaty's exemption clause on the ground that it violated their right to property secured by article 14 III GG, their right to equality under article 3 I GG, and the rule of law.[2497]

A compromise was eventually included in the Compensation and Equalisation Payments Act.[2498] Instead of settlement payments, original

---

[2493] EGBGB (*Einführungsgesetz zum Bürgerlichen Gesetzbuch*).

[2494] See *Gesetz über die strukturelle Anpassung der Landwirtschaft an die soziale und ökologische Marktwirtschaft in der Deutschen Demokratischen Republik (Landwirtschaftsanpassungsgesetz / LAnpG)* 19 June 1990 GBl I, 642.

[2495] See *Quint*, The Imperfect Union (1997), 128.

[2496] *Pries*, Neubauerneigentum (1993), 151.

[2497] *Kommers*, Constitutional Jurisprudence of Germany (1997), 256.

[2498] 1994.

owners could choose to purchase a portion of the land at a favourable price. However, the act determined that the proportion of land subject to a favourable purchase price depended on the extent of the land previously owned. The larger the original property was, the smaller the piece that could be favourably repurchased would be. Besides, any individual leasing the property at that moment would have a prior right of repurchase. In enacting this legislation, the interests of modern society in accessibility of landownership for a larger part of the population ostensibly enjoyed precedence over considerations of the individual autonomy of previous owners in the likes of the land barons of the pre-war era. This legislation met with oppositions from both sides, the original owners complaining about an alleged disregard of the *Junker* system of landownership, and the present possessors pointing out that the agricultural co-operatives in the eastern parts of Germany would be greatly disadvantaged if the land were put up for sale to the former owners.

The legislation was eventually adapted. Former land barons, farmers from the east and west of Germany, as well as the agricultural co-operatives in the east could repurchase the property at favourable prices. However, purchasers who did not intend to use the land for agricultural purposes, could only repurchase half of what they would otherwise have been entitled to purchase.[2499]

2.1.2.2. Bona Fide Transactions

Bona fide acquisitions of private property were in principle excluded from the ambit of claims for restitution.[2500] In such cases, a socially acceptable exchange had to be effected.[2501] The original owners were therefore entitled to compensation at a rate less than market value,[2502] or they could receive land of comparable value. The recognition of rights obtained in good faith was considered the foundation necessary for a solution that was to be both just and socially practicable. The interpretation of the term *bona fide* acquisition *(gutgläubiger Erwerb)* would

---

[2499] *Quint,* The Imperfect Union (1997), 142-143.

[2500] Sec. 4(2), Property Act.

[2501] *Quint,* The Imperfect Union (1997), 131.

[2502] *Visser/Roux* in *Rwelamira/Werle (eds),* Confronting Past Injustices (1996), 100.

determine exactly how much land would remain in the hands of former citizens of the German Democratic Republic.[2503]

Good faith acquisitions entailed the acquisition of property consistent with the prevailing law or administrative practice of the German Democratic Republic. The acquirer should not have been aware of any inconsistency, the transaction should not have been influenced by corruption or exploitation of a personal position of power, and should not have been the result of coercion or deception. Moreover, the reasonableness of the purchase price would serve as evidence of whether the property was acquired through corruption, coercion or deception.[2504] However, it was not easy to determine *bona fides* in all cases. For instance, it was questionable whether purchase of land abandoned — or forcibly sold — by refugees could be regarded as having been obtained in good faith. Mere knowledge of the fact that the object purchased was part of the property of a refugee, however, eventually did not hinder an acquisition in good faith.[2505]

The situation was more problematic where the property had become the object of real rights of use as they existed in the legal system of the German Democratic Republic.[2506] The original owner's interest in restitution had to be balanced against the interests of such right holders in retaining their rights of use. From a social viability viewpoint, this balancing of interests could only fall in favour of the current right holders. They had obtained the rights in good faith, under the relevant legal position of the German Democratic Republic at the time.

In cases where land was obtained during the collapse of the German Democratic Republic — within sight of the new economic and social order and the obvious changes that would accompany it — the problem was even more critical. At first, an acquisition in good faith under these circumstances was excluded and the former owners could always recover their property. Legislature[2507] regarded the interests of the original owners as taking precedence over those of current owners, if the property was acquired at a time when the changes in the German Demo-

---

[2503] *Quint,* The Imperfect Union (1997), 132.

[2504] *Quint,* The Imperfect Union (1997), 131.

[2505] *Fieberg* in *Rwelamira/Werle (eds),* Confronting Past Injustices (1996), 85.

[2506] This right of use was unlimited in time, free of charge, and could be inherited.

[2507] *Gesetz zur Regelung offener Vermögensfragen* 23 September, 1990 BGBl II 889, 1159; BGBl 1994 I 3610.

cratic Republic could be anticipated.[2508] The exception applies to acquisitions of property from autumn 1989 until the time of reunification. However, because of the fierce political debate resulting from this point, the rule had been adjusted considerably in favour of later right holders.

2.1.2.3. Restitution Impossible

If restitution of property was impossible, impractical or inequitable "in the nature of the matter,"[2509] the principle of *restitution before compensation* did not apply. Anticipated here were cases defined in the Joint Declaration (i) in favour of society in general and the administration; (ii) to secure the position attained by the German Democratic Republic in the field of public housing construction and settlement; and (iii) to ensure the survival of business undertakings.[2510] In some instances property had merged with other property so completely[2511] that separation of the different parts was not possible any more. In case of restitution being impossible, the original owners were entitled to receive compensation to the extent that compensation had not already been paid under German Democratic Republic law to one of its own citizens.[2512]

2.1.3. Special Arrangement for "Wall Property"

Although property surrounding the infamous Berlin Wall (the "wall property" or *"Mauergrundstücke"*) was expropriated around 1961

[2508] *Quint*, The Imperfect Union (1997), 131-132 reports that in the last days before the opening of the Berlin Wall, high party functionaries of the SED purchased villas in East Berlin and elsewhere for what was said to be, by all calculations, bargain prices. The exclusion of "good faith" acquisitions after 18 October 1989 (Honecker's capitulation) was apparently intended to invalidate these purchases. However, this regulation endangered the purchases of ordinary citizens for whom it was easier under the legislation of the transitional period under Modrow to purchase the dwellings they had occupied and maintained for years.

[2509] See Joint Declaration; Property Act sec. 4(1).

[2510] *Fieberg* in *Rwelamira/Werle (eds)*, Confronting Past Injustices (1996), 86.

[2511] E.g. in the development of sites for large apartment buildings or as part of a business enterprise.

[2512] *Quint*, The Imperfect Union (1997), 130.

against the payment of compensation by the German Democratic Republic, thereby strictly disqualifying it from further compensation or restitution, the public pressure for restitution was so strong that particular provision was made for restitution of the "wall property" to its original owners. In 1996 it was enacted that the "wall property" would be returned to its former owners, upon payment of one-fourth of its current market value. The owners of property retained by the government, or sold by it "in the public interest" could receive compensation equal to 75 percent of its present market value. The original owners of "wall property" were nevertheless not satisfied, and threatened with a Federal Constitutional Court action.[2513]

2.1.4. Investment Before Restitution

The restitution principle was further limited by the priority given to investment.[2514] This limitation sought to strike the necessary balance between maintaining the sovereignty of individual ownership of the former owners and the need to attract investment, create employment opportunities and reduce subsidies in the eastern part of Germany.[2515]

The provisions of the Investment Priority Act[2516] when read with the Property Act[2517] provided for alienation of the land to certain kinds of prospective investors, despite any restitution claims already lodged. The "special investment purposes" provided for in the act included: (i) the safeguarding or creation of jobs, in particular through the establishment or preservation of industrial or service-providing enterprises; (ii) the creation of new housing space or the repair of housing space which was not habitable or in danger of being lost; or the building or repair of one- or two-family houses; and (iii) the creation of infrastructure necessary for (or imperative because of) investment. The former owner's

---

[2513] *Quint*, The Imperfect Union (1997), 134.

[2514] See art. 41(2), Unification Treaty.

[2515] *Southern*, 1993 ICLQ, 604.

[2516] *Gesetz über besondere Investitionen in der Deutschen Demokratischen Republik* 23 September 1990, BGBl II, 889, 1157. Now *Gesetz über den Vorrang von Investitionen bei Rückübertragungsansprüchen nach dem Vermögensgesetz* 14 July 1992 (BGBl I, 1257, 1268); *Berichtigung des zweiten Vermögensrechtsänderungsgesetzes* (BGBl 1993 I, 1811).

[2517] Art. 1, Property Act.

right of restitution was overridden and converted into a right to compensation, if an investor obtained the approval for a proposal which satisfies a "special investment purpose."[2518]

The Property Act introduced a priority procedure for obtaining business property for investment purposes.[2519] A similar provision was contained in the Investment Act for other immovable property, like land and buildings.[2520] The original procedure for investment claims, the Investment Act and the provisions of the Property Act related to the priority of investment have, however, been revised several times,[2521] due to the conflicting interests, the time pressure under which the initial provisions had to be formulated and the lack of experience with regard to the unification of property law, as well as the large variety of property regulations in the German Democratic Republic.[2522] During 1991, statutory amendments were also made to the existing legislation in order to accelerate privatisation. This applied to both land and business property. The 1991 amendments pertaining to investments, for instance, also extended the special rules on investment to expropriated enterprises.[2523] Accordingly, a former owner expropriated of a business concern could be excluded from restitution by a purchaser with an investment plan. The former owner would then receive the purchase price or

---

[2518] *Southern*, 1993 ICLQ, 694.

[2519] Sec. 3(6)-(8), Property Act.

[2520] Sec. 1, Investment Act.

[2521] See sec. 3a, *Gesetz zur Beseitigung von Hemmnissen bei der Privatisierung von Unternehmen und zur Förderung von Investitionen*, (Investment Acceleration Act), 22 March 1991, BGBl I, 766. The various procedures were combined in sec. 2 of the Investment Priority Act of 14 July 1992. This Act also introduced the new procedure of the "investment priority certificate," to be granted by the municipality in which the land in question was situated, were the person with power of disposition over the land a private individual. In other cases, the certificate was to be issued by the body with power of disposal over the land. The certificate annulled the right to reconveyance, transforming it into a right to compensation. All reconveyance claims finally had to be registered by 31 December 1992. As soon as the Property Office was informed of the investment priority application, the restitution process is suspended for a maximum of three months. *Southern*, 1993 ICLQ, 694.

[2522] *Fieberg* in *Rwelamira/Werle (eds)*, Confronting Past Injustices (1996), 87.

[2523] Sec. 3a(1)(2), Property Act (1991 version); sec. 1, Investment Preference Act.

other compensation.[2524] All this reduced the status of the original owner in the administrative process and his or her legal protection against investors.[2525] However, the economic disadvantages were minor, as the original owner is entitled to claim payment of the selling price or at the least the current market value of the property.[2526]

2.1.5. Compensation as Alternative to Restitution

As an alternative to restitution,[2527] the original owners could in many cases choose compensation instead of return of the land or business enterprise.[2528] If the claim for restitution was endorsed by the property office or one of the bodies of appeal, the applicant had to decide whether he or she preferred restitution or compensation. If the applicant preferred compensation, or could only claim compensation, an application for payment of it had to be made to the local valuation office.[2529]

Compensation would constitute only 30 to 50 percent of the current market value of the property under discussion. Payments of over DM 100 000 were to be reduced on a sliding scale:[2530] compensation was based on 1.3 times the 1935 rateable value of the property, up to a maximum figure of DM 250 000. Payment of compensation was to begin on 1 January 1996, depending on the available funds. A minimal compensation would also be paid to those who lost property between 8 May 1945 and 6 October 1949, even though these cases were excluded from restitution.

In overview, the compensation alternatives to restitution can be summarised as follows:

(i) Generally, compensation for land seized during the time of Soviet occupation was not envisaged, as the rehabilitation programme did not cover such confiscation. However, for some of the *Junker* expropria-

---

[2524] Sec. 18, Investment Preference Act.

[2525] *Quint,* The Imperfect Union (1997), 129.

[2526] *Fieberg* in *Rwelamira/Werle (eds),* Confronting Past Injustices (1996), 86.

[2527] *Kommers,* Constitutional Jurisprudence of Germany (1997), 256.

[2528] Sec. 6(7), Property Act.

[2529] *Southern,* 1993 ICLQ, 695.

[2530] *Southern,* 1993 ICLQ, 694.

tions, certain "equalisation measures" in the form of compensation for less-than-market-value were envisaged.[2531] Legislation providing for a more extensive right of compensation was enacted during 1994.[2532] This followed the public row that arose because of the initial decision neither to return the *Bodenreform* property to its original owners, nor to pay compensation. Accordingly, fixed property was compensated up to a maximum of ten percent of its present market value. This provision has since been criticised for not living up to the standards of the German equality guarantee, as it ostensibly pointed to a discrepancy of ninety percent between monetary reimbursement and restitution in kind.[2533]

(ii) In case of expropriations "for the public interest"[2534] effected during the forty years of socialist rule in the German Democratic Republic, less-than-market-value compensation could be claimed, provided that no compensation had been paid previously in terms of other compensatory measures, regardless of how unfair such amounts were.[2535] Thus, claims for increasing the compensation already paid by the German Democratic Republic were not allowed.[2536]

(iii) *Bona fide* acquisitions of private property were in principle excluded from the ambit of claims for restitution.[2537] At first, neither the Unification Treaty, nor the Property Act provided for compensation of former owners who could not obtain restitution of their property due to it having been acquired by a *bona fide* third person. In later legislation it was provided that compensation would be payable in such cases, but at a rate lower than market value.[2538]

[2531] Joint Declaration par. 1; Property Act sec. 1(8)(a).

[2532] *Gesetz über die Entschädigung nach dem Gesetz zur Regelung offener Vermögensfragen und über staatliche Ausgleichsleistungen für Enteignungen auf besatzungsrechtlicher oder besatzungshoheitlicher Grundlage* 27 September 1994 (1994 BGBl I, 2624).

[2533] *Fieberg* in *Rwelamira/Werle (eds)*, Confronting Past Injustices (1996), 87.

[2534] *Visser/Roux* in *Rwelamira/Werle (eds)*, Confronting Past Injustices (1996), 100.

[2535] *Fieberg* in *Rwelamira/Werle (eds)*, Confronting Past Injustices (1996), 84.

[2536] Joint Declaration par. 3a.

[2537] Sec. 4(2), Property Act.

[2538] *Visser/Roux* in *Rwelamira/Werle (eds)*, Confronting Past Injustices (1996), 100.

(iv) Where restitution was impossible, the original owners were entitled to receive compensation to the extent that compensation had not already been paid under German Democratic Republic law to one of its own citizens.[2539] In other words, a second compensation could not be claimed as equalisation for the low compensation rates existing in the German Democratic Republic.

(v) An exception to the compensation and restitution regulations was made for former owners of property that was expropriated for purposes of building the Berlin Wall. These owners had received compensation before, and were strictly speaking disqualified from receiving further compensation or restitution. Nevertheless, the public pressure was so strong that former owners of property retained by the government, or sold by it "in the public interest" could receive compensation equal to 75 percent of its present market value.[2540]

(vi) In case of an investor obtaining the approval for a proposal which satisfies a *special investment purpose*,[2541] the former owner's right of restitution was overridden and converted into a right to compensation. In such a case, the former owner could claim payment of the current market value of the property.[2542]

(vii) In 1992, amendments were made to legislation governing the return of business property. This entailed the identification of specific territories where the principle of restitution was not applicable. In those areas, restitution of business property was excluded altogether, and claimants were only able to claim compensation.[2543]

2.2. Restitution and the Basic Law

In order to avoid constitutional challenges to the decision not to include expropriations in the period of Soviet occupation in the restitution programme, the Basic Law was also amended by the Unification Treaty.[2544] A provision was added to the Basic Law to the effect that the

---

[2539] *Quint*, The Imperfect Union (1997), 130.

[2540] *Quint*, The Imperfect Union (1997), 134. See also 558 *above*.

[2541] *Southern*, 1993 ICLQ, 694.

[2542] *Fieberg* in *Rwelamira/Werle (eds)*, Confronting Past Injustices (1996), 86.

[2543] Sec. 18, Investment Preference Act.

[2544] *Quint*, The Imperfect Union (1997), 136.

Treaty and related regulations would remain permanent to the extent that they provide that incursions on property in eastern Germany are not to be undone.[2545] This would make the non-return of land expropriated between 1945 and 1949 permanent, provided that it was in accordance with the basic principles of the German constitutional order.[2546]

3. The Treatment of the Restitution / Compensation Questions by the Courts

The ambiguities and insufficiently negotiated compromises incorporated in the Joint Declaration and its related statues, will probably ensure decades of litigation on the property questions that arose from the German reunification. According to estimates, the restitution issue in Germany will take another 30 years to resolve.[2547] More than one million claims have been filed for the return of property in the east of Germany, and in many areas the understaffed claims offices have been hopelessly clogged.[2548] This claims process will probably be rendered even more difficult by the likely problems of proof that will arise in individual cases. The following paragraphs briefly survey the way in which restitution of property situated in the former German Democratic Republic is treated by the German courts.

3.1. Federal Administrative Court

The development in case law, particularly the judgements of the superior courts had a significant effect on the work of the state offices in the sphere of property law. The Federal Administrative Court has handed down some important decisions on the Property Act, thus resolving some of the interpretation problems experienced.

Several attempts were made to obtain property outside the confines of the revised and reunified property law. One specific problem is that the decision to exclude specific expropriations from the restitution programme were in certain cases perceived to be unjust. Particularly where

---

[2545] Art. 4(5), Unification Treaty; art. 143 III GG.

[2546] See 122 ff. above.

[2547] *Southern*, 1993 ICLQ, 697.

[2548] *Quint*, The Imperfect Union (1997), 151.

the initial aim behind the expropriation had not been realised and could no longer be realised due to the changes that have taken place, or where the earlier goal disappeared completely during German reunification, the exclusions from restitution were challenged. This would include property expropriated in Berlin in order for the Wall to be built. These attempts mostly failed before the Federal Administrative Court.[2549]

3.2. Federal Constitutional Court

Many of the property related cases to reach the Federal Constitutional Court in the 1990s involved procedural irregularities.[2550] For example, the court granted the former owner of property expropriated by the German Democratic Republic an injunction, restraining the present owner from building upon that property, because the court of first instance failed to grant the former owner a hearing on the validity of the claim, thus violating article 103 GG.[2551]

On policy issues the court continually sustained the political considerations embodied in various laws and treaties. For instance, the political decision not to allow restitution of property expropriated during the time of Soviet occupation from 1945 to 1949, met with considerable resistance and eventually was challenged before the Federal Constitutional Court. Several arguments were put forward to support the allegations that the practice of excluding the expropriations during the time of Soviet occupation from restitution were unconstitutional:

(i) It was argued that the expropriations were *ab initio* void on several grounds. They violated the Weimar Constitution's property guarantees, which were, arguably, effective until 1949. Alternatively, they violated the rules of international law, such as the Hague Convention,[2552] in terms of which the occupying powers were bound to respect the laws in force in the occupied country, and which prohibited expropriation. A further possible ground for the invalidity of the expropriations was that they allegedly violated the principles of natural law binding on all nations.[2553]

[2549] *Fieberg* in *Rwelamira/Werle (eds)*, Confronting Past Injustices (1996), 84.

[2550] *Kommers*, Constitutional Jurisprudence of Germany (1997), 256.

[2551] BVerfGE 84, 286.

[2552] 1907.

[2553] *Quint*, The Imperfect Union (1997), 135.

(ii) A second series of arguments maintained that, even if the expropriations were not illegal at that time, the social welfare state principle imposed a positive duty on the present government to undo those past actions. When applying the social welfare state principle in an extraordinarily conservative manner so as to recreate a previously existing *status quo*, rather than to affirm present economic and social equality, it could be sustained that the state had to alleviate the misfortune that part of the community affected by the expropriations.[2554] In earlier cases, similar obligations were placed on the government of the Federal Republic of Germany to alleviate certain forms of prejudice incurred during the war and period of occupation.[2555]

(iii) Further, the validity of the added article 143 GG was challenged on the basis that it eroded the "core" values of articles 1 to 20.[2556]

(iv) It was also argued that exclusion of the expropriations between 1945 and 1949 from the restitution programme would violate the guarantee of equality contained in article 3 I GG. It would make the restitution process applicable only to certain groups of deprived owners, namely those who lost their property in terms of the Nazi-expropriations and the expropriations of the German Democratic Republic. The government would ostensibly create substantial inequality by granting redress to some groups and denying it to others.[2557]

The Federal Constitutional Court, however, in 1990 unanimously upheld the provision of the Unification Treaty stating that the 1945 to 1949 expropriations could not be undone,[2558] thus affirming the validity of the exemption clauses. Faced with the Soviet Union's non-negotiable stance against any rollback of properties expropriated during the occupation, the court accepted the government's argument that the exemption was a compromise necessary to achieve the higher constitutional goal of reunification.[2559] The court thus concluded that the legislature

---

[2554] *Quint*, The Imperfect Union (1997), 136.

[2555] BVerfGE 27, 253, 283; BVerfGE 41, 153, 154.

[2556] BVerfGE 84, 90, 121.

[2557] *Quint*, The Imperfect Union (1997), 136.

[2558] BVerfGE 84, 90.

[2559] BVerfGE 84, 90, 127-128.

had not exceeded its authority in giving constitutional endorsement to the decision not to return the expropriated property.[2560]

The view that the expropriations were illegal at the time when they were undertaken was rejected. Under Soviet occupation law, the expropriations were according to the court clearly legal. At the time neither the Basic Law nor the law of the German Democratic Republic applied to the territory where the expropriations were undertaken. This reasoning also by implication rejects the arguments of illegality on the basis of the Weimar Constitution or natural law.[2561] With regard to the international law, the court noted that Germany was not responsible for the expropriation between 1945 and 1949, since the affected property was subject to a legal system other than that of the Federal Republic of Germany. In any event, the Basic Law did not become enforceable until after the property had been taken.[2562]

The court took a positivistic stance and argued that the question of whether someone has a specific legal interest could only be answered in light of a specific legal order. In this case, the Soviet occupation regime's expropriations deprived the original owners of any legal interest in the property.[2563] Nevertheless, the court reasoned that the Basic Law requires affirmative governmental action in favour of the original owners. The social welfare state principle might even, according to the court, require that the legislature effect an equalisation of burdens to some extent: not necessarily return of the property, but some degree of compensation to the former owners.

The core of the court's ruling, on the basis of the equality guarantee, also supported this point. The final effect of the decision was that excluding the Soviet occupation regime's expropriations from the restitution programme did not violate the principle of equality. However, the equality principle also necessitated some kind of compensation to the original owners, albeit not at market value. Lesser compensation was regarded as reasonable in light of the government's other obligations in-

---

[2560] The court sustained the validity of article 143 over the objection that it amounted to an unconstitutional amendment to the Basic Law. BVerfGE 84, 90 117-121.

[2561] *Quint*, The Imperfect Union (1997), 137.

[2562] BVerfGE 84, 90, 122-125.

[2563] BVerfGE 84, 90, 122-125.

curred upon unification, such as the cost of economic renewal in the former German Democratic Republic.[2564]

It is debatable whether the mediating technique employed by the court in this case, in choosing no clear winners or losers but rather seeking to create a political compromise, resulted in an acceptable balancing of the interests on both sides of the former inner-German border.[2565] It has also been contended that the court's ruling is based on the false assumption that the Soviet Union would not have agreed to reunification of Germany if the *Bodenreform* would have been treated differently.[2566] In addition, disputes about the equitable amount of compensation to be paid to the original owners were complicated by the budget deficit of the state. After a few unsuccessful initial attempts,[2567] legislation providing for compensation of owners whose property was expropriated during the Soviet occupation of East Germany was eventually enacted during 1994.[2568] However, this still did not satisfy some of the parties involved, as the legislation could not solve the practical ninety percent discrepancy between monetary reimbursement and restitution in

---

[2564] BVerfGE 84, 90, 130-131.

[2565] See *Quint*, The Imperfect Union (1997), 139 for a summary of the polemical discussion that resulted from this decision.

[2566] *Pries*, Neubauerneigentum (1993), 154.

[2567] The first proposed statute of 1992 envisaged settlement payments that would not burden the federal treasury. According to this, original owners would be entitled to 1,3 times the worth of the property in 1935. A special tax was also to be imposed on original owners who received a return of expropriated property under the Unification Treaty. The tax, equalling one third of the actual value of the returned property, would be used to help finance compensation under the statute. This proposal was withdrawn in the face of severe attacks on it by some interest groups. A second proposal (in 1993) significantly increased the amounts offered as compensation, and omitted the planned taxation of property restitution. But compensation would not be paid in the form of immediate cash. That would have burdened the treasury too much. Instead, promissory notes payable after the year 2004 would have been issued, and a bonus would be paid if the property were to be used for investment in the east of Germany. This proposal also met with fierce opposition because it did not foresee compensation of the original owners in the form of real property of the state. *Quint*, The Imperfect Union (1997), 142.

[2568] *Gesetz über die Entschädigung nach dem Gesetz zur Regelung offener Vermögensfragen und über staatliche Ausgleichsleistungen für Enteignungen auf besatzungsrechtlicher oder besatzungshoheitlicher Grundlage 27 September 1994* (1994 BGBl I, 2624).

kind.[2569] It is questionable whether this provision lives up to the standards of the German equality guarantee as set out in the decision.

In 1993, the court reaffirmed its view that former owners of land expropriated between 1945 and 1949 as part of an agrarian reform program would not have a right to return of their property.[2570] In addition, the court summarily dismissed a claim by a German citizen that the German-Polish Frontier Treaty of 1990 violated his right to property, noting that Germans could no longer claim expropriated or abandoned property they once owned within the present boundaries of Poland.[2571] Finally, in rejecting motions for injunctions that would have undermined the general willingness to invest in the former German Democratic Republic, the court demonstrated considerable sensitivity to the plight of eastern Germany's economy, by refusing to stop the sale of a former owner's property to a third party for development[2572] and refusing to bar the *Treuhand*[2573] from implementing a contract by which it had sold property for investment purposes.[2574] In the latter case, the applicant's main claim in respect of the property had to be decided before it could be determined whether the original owner would be entitled to restoration of title.

4. Influence on the Reunification's Property Issues on the Property Order in Germany

Section 3(3)1 and 15(2) of the Property Act provide that the owner of the land is not entitled to sell, transfer or rent it if restitution claims had been registered against it. As such, these provisions paralyse commercial traffic with the property, and constitute a serious curtailment of the interests of the present landowners. Because the restitution process ef-

---

[2569] *Fieberg* in *Rwelamira/Werle (eds)*, Confronting Past Injustices (1996), 87.

[2570] Property Confiscation II case, Chamber decision of 15 April 1993 (1 BvR 1885/92) NJW (1993) 366.

[2571] German-Polish Frontier Treaty case, Chamber decision of 5 June 1992, EuGZ 19 (1992).

[2572] BVerfGE 85, 130.

[2573] The agency charged with privatising state-owned property in the old German Democratic Republic and clarifying questions of ownership.

[2574] Chamber decision of 21 April 1993 (1 BvR 1422/92).

fectively prohibited circulation of affected property, an orderly property market could not develop straight away. The prices of freely disposable pieces of land were, moreover, driven to unrealistic heights. Besides, investment in the east of Germany was hindered by the fact that investors could not be certain that the property they wanted to develop belonged to them. Banks refused finance, because of the inability to register mortgages over property subject to a restitution dispute.[2575] This uncertainty affected small investors and entrepreneurs in particular. Larger businesses had, after all, the capacity to fend for themselves, without state protection. This could also lead to unbalanced economic development.

The social dislocation caused by the property provisions in the Unification Treaty and legislation enacted subsequently, could well have created a permanent division between east and west. Quint[2576] explains the position in the following terms:

> *"In certain towns in the outskirts of Berlin, for example, more than half of the dwellings are being claimed by former owners or the heirs of former owners, leading to the prospect of homelessness (virtually unknown in the old GDR) and even, apparently, suicides of householders fearing eviction. Often, the claimants are people from the west who do not want to live on the property, but intend to sell it, as real-estate prices in Berlin and its suburbs have increased enormously since unification. Here, as in most other aspects of the property rules, the structure of the Unification Treaty has the effect of pitting east against west in a very clearly perceptible manner."*

The market strategies reflected in the action of the *Treuhand* represent a massive extension of western structures and western personnel to the business enterprises of the east. The surviving concerns were mainly purchased by business people from the west of Germany, as citizens of the former German Democratic Republic rarely had the resources to purchase old concerns or establish new enterprises. Moreover, from the time of the currency union onwards, many eastern enterprises have gone out of business or have been closed by the *Treuhand*. With them, many social structures, like day care centres for children and vacation resorts disappeared. Even where the enterprises — with help from the

---

[2575] *Southern*, 1993 ICLQ, 696.

[2576] *Quint*, The Imperfect Union (1997), 133.

west — survived, practically no attempts were made to preserve the social structures.[2577]

The restitution policy also resulted in the extension of western control over the eastern part of Germany. Apart from the few exceptions to this rule, with regard to bona fide acquisition and investment, this policy has resulted in displacements of large communities, especially in areas which became politically or financially important after reunification, like the suburbs around Berlin. Instead of maintaining the existing residential structures, the western landowners preferred to lease or sell their property to those who could pay market prices, mostly also people from the west.[2578] This also deepened the division between rich owners of assets in the western part of Germany and asset-poor wage earners and unemployed in the eastern part.[2579]

Agricultural property in the east of Germany also raised complex problems. After the ruling of the Federal Constitutional Court with regard to the non-restitution of the lands expropriated by the Soviet occupation regime, the agricultural structures of the east — large farming co-operatives — will probably continue to exist as an alternative to the smaller family farms which are more usual in the western parts of Germany.[2580]

In general, the strong property principles of conservative ideology prevalent in the west of Germany before reunification, together with the large-scale extension of capitalist values to the eastern part of Germany, have significantly contributed to the creation of these problems. These principles prevailed in the decision to prefer restitution to compensation.[2581] In years to come, the reorganisation of the German property order after reunification will significantly influence the issue of whether a strongly individual property concept is compatible with the social market economy under the Basic Law.

[2577] *Quint,* The Imperfect Union (1997), 152.

[2578] *Du Sold,* Restitution vor Entschädigung (1993), 159 ff.

[2579] *Southern,* 1993 ICLQ, 696.

[2580] *Quint,* The Imperfect Union (1997), 152.

[2581] *Du Sold,* Restitution vor Entschädigung (1993), 159 ff.

5. The Significance of the German Experience with Land Reform for South Africa

From the treatment of the post-reunification land reform, and more specifically the issue of restitution in Germany, it becomes apparent that the success of such a process of reform depends on the importance attached to the social welfare and individual functions of property. In South Africa it could be problematic to find a balance between these different functions of property within the legal order, due to the extensive scope that the land reform programme would have to take in order to effect a socially just system of land control and distribution.

After the re-unification in Germany, approximately one fifth of the entire population was involved in claims pertaining to land situated in the former German Democratic Republic. In South Africa, the claims of four-fifths of the entire population to land have to be satisfied. With the financial means available, this is practically impossible.[2582] This also, at least partially, explains why only one percent of the estimated thirty percent of land that had to be distributed between 1994 and 2000 has, in fact, been so distributed. Other factors further complicate the process of reform. The system of land redistribution, restitution and tenure reform has turned out to be more complex than was expected at the outset. The proliferating number of reform statutes, which are not always interpreted uniformly, slow processes[2583] and lack of co-ordination within the Department of Land Affairs[2584] all ostensibly contribute to

---

[2582] An estimated 25 million hectares (almost 30%) of South Africa's agricultural land are supposed to be redistributed. This will cost billions of Rands. In 2000, the budget for redistribution was set at R424 million. The budget for restitution of land, which is set at R150 million for 2000 and can be doubled within the next two years, seems more realistic in view of the objectives of this leg of the reform programme. See Van Zyl, Finansies en Tegniek, 5-05-2000, 10-12.

[2583] By December 1998, only 40 of the more than 63 000 claims had been finalised. See Van Zyl, Finansies en Tegniek, 5-05-2000, 10-12.

[2584] Van Zyl, Finansies en Tegniek, 5-05-2000, 10-12 provides a brief account of the quick succession of key players within the structure of the Department of Land Affairs within the first four years of the reform project. The previous Minister of Agriculture and Land Affairs, Mr Derek Hanekom discharged the Chief Commissioner of Land Affairs (Mr Joe Seremane) in 1998, before leaving the department himself later that year. In the mean time Geoff Budlender, the former Director General of Land Affairs, also left office. Dr Peter Mayende has recently been appointed in this position. The new Minister of Agriculture and

the frustration of the constitutional objectives pertaining to land reform.

Land Affairs, Ms Thoko Didiza, has introduced new policy guidelines for land distribution.

Part Five

Conclusion

Chapter 11: Property in Private Law and its Constitutional Protection and Regulation: Some Considerations

1. General Remarks

Under the surface of the property order espoused by section 28 IC and section 25 FC, the unfortunate history of ownership and property rights in South Africa and the present disparities of wealth in society meet to create the need for reform. Private property is one of the socio-legal institutions inherited from — and thoroughly influenced by the inherent injustice of — the old South African order. South Africa's constitution is the embodiment of a new social, political and legal order. The main virtue of the constitution is its potential to correct the injustices integrated in the law and society inherited from the old order. In the case of private property, the challenge to the new constitutional order is to eliminate the injustice of the apartheid era (so deeply ingrained in the South African system of property law) without crippling the institution of private property as such. This is no easy task, especially because property, and especially land, is a limited resource (in South Africa, like in the rest of the world) and the need for it is greater than the supply of it can be. The acute need for legislative programmes of reconstruction and reparation will inevitably disturb existing property relations in South Africa.[2585] Emotions are running high, especially where the principles of private property meet policies of land tenure reform, restitution and redistribution. Because these issues are highly emo-

---

[2585] *Chaskalson/Lewis* in *Chaskalson/Kentridge/Klaaren et al. (eds)*, Constitutional Law of South Africa (1996), ch. 31, 21.

tional, they are also prone to political abuse, as the example of our neighbouring country Zimbabwe shows.[2586]

The present investigation set out to determine to what extent constitutional development of the private law of property could result in a property law order serving the socio-economic and political goals of economic growth and empowerment of the individual and development of individual self-esteem. As such, this dissertation is an attempt at reconciling the existing (and until recently predominant) private law concept of ownership and the property rights sustained by the new constitutional order. Attempts at restitution and redistribution in South Africa and Germany were used as specific examples of the manner in which the existing law of property in both these legal systems could be developed through legislative and judicial initiative.

This final chapter summarises the conclusions that can be drawn from the preceding inquiry. It attempts to distinguish the function of property in private and constitutional law. Then it provides a discussion of the significance of a new property order for the economic growth of South Africa and for the empowerment and development of the self-esteem of all South Africans. Furthermore, it also attempts to provide some guidelines for the development of a new property order in South Africa.

2. The Distinction between Property in Private and Constitutional Law

Part of the confusion surrounding the study of property and land law is its proper place in the overall structure of the law. The classification of property and land law as belonging either to public law or private law is, for instance, one issue that causes general confusion. Property takes a

---

[2586] The Zimbabwean crisis has pushed the South African land reform programmes into the public eye. The South African situation parallels that of Zimbabwe only to a limited extent. In Zimbabwe, corrupt politicians had abused the land reform question in attempts to retain political power. Most politicians in South Africa still refrain from using this line of argument to gain political support. However, the slow pace at which land reform, redistribution and restitution is taking place could be used to ignite emotions similar to those experienced by the landless in Zimbabwe. See *Van Zyl*, Finansies en Tegniek, 5-05-2000, 10-12 for different viewpoints on this issue.

central place in the study of constitutional and human rights law, public and private international law, delict, criminal law, contract, commercial law, tax law, planning and environmental law, mining and minerals law and family law. The scope and limits of property law and aspects of property in the law can, therefore, be confusing. One of the questions that could be posed in this regard is to what extent the distinction between private law and constitutional law will remain intact.

2.1. Property and Ownership

In the wake of the new South African land reform policies and practises, the demise of "traditional" property law[2587] (or rather private law property) inevitably raises profound theoretical questions. It has been indicated that the definition of property and ownership is not the exclusive domain of private law. In fact, *property* means something different from *ownership*, and the constitutional *property* concept is much wider than the private law concept of *ownership*. Even though not explicitly defined in either the German or South African constitutions, the term *property* in the constitutional context usually designates a concept broader than the concept *thing (res)* of private law. It includes not only *ownership* as it is known in private law, but also several other patrimonial and incorporeal rights, regarded as "lesser" rights in private law, and which mostly do not even qualify as limited real rights.

The varying definitions of property in private law and constitutional law underscores the dichotomy between individual security and freedom reflected by the institution of property, on the one hand, and the obligatory social welfare function of property on the other. This raises the question of how the predominantly liberalist principles of property in private law can be adapted to the values of social democracy underlying the new constitutional order.[2588] The introduction of a wider property concept in the constitutional context would obviously bring about some changes to the property law order. However, the private law concept of ownership and the meaning of property in the constitutional context remain poles apart.

[2587] I.e. the law of property cast in the mould prepared by the most important Roman-Dutch authors, and supplemented by the perspectives of the Pandectist interpreters. The foundations for this approach were laid in *Van der Merwe, Sakereg* (1979) and (1989).

[2588] *Van der Merwe*, 1998 TSAR, 10.

2.2. Function of Constitutional Law and Private Law with regard to Property

The polarisation of property in private and constitutional law is connected to the different functions of private law and constitutional law in general: private law regulates (*inter alia*) the acquisition, protection and transfer of private property and constitutional law regulates the liberty and equality of citizens. From a private law perspective, property rights are restricted on a "horizontal" level by the rights and interests of third parties. From a constitutional perspective, the scope of a person's property rights is determined by considering limitations in the public interest; that is, on a vertical level *vis-à-vis* the state authority. The private law concept of ownership influences the constitutional concept of property insofar as it provides a point of departure for an investigation about the scope of protection under the constitution, but the constitutional property concept will necessarily be a protective shield to a broader variety of interests.

The reason for limiting the protection of property in private law to corporeals only lies in the fact that other kinds of proprietary relations are protected and regulated elsewhere in private law or in public law. Contractual rights fall under the law of contract, statutory rights are regulated and protected by the statutes creating them, rights arising from the social security benefits granted by different state organs fall within the ambit of administrative law, labour law and the like. However, all these rights — as far as they relate to the patrimony of individuals — are *constitutionally* protected by the property clause: against arbitrary state authority in the first instance, but also against an "unjust" balance of power between individuals *inter se*, which should be eradicated on the initiative of the state. In case of an imminent danger to the common good, or in times of social change, the constitutional provisions will, therefore, be used to correct the effect of private law principles on the patrimonial interests of individuals.

From an analysis of the range and intensity of the constitutional property guarantee, the significance of a constitutional right to property becomes clear. The right to property has a distinct individual or personal function, because it is the means through which the individual can secure his or her material existence, and assert his or her independence and freedom. Further, the right to property has a distinct social function. For society, private property is a prerequisite for promoting private initiative under the conditions of a decentralised economy. It is, however, also in the interest of society at large that the state exercises its power of control against dangers and disadvantages arising from private, autonomous use of property and allocation of things.[2589]

These different functions of the constitutional property guarantee are in a sense antagonistic. When the function of property as a safeguard for individual freedom is emphasised, the constitutional guarantee of individual ownership tends to be expanded. When the social welfare function is emphasised, the legislature is allowed to restrict the individual owner's powers of disposal over the property.[2590] The German example illustrates that the constitutional protection and regulation of property serves as a guarantee of personal freedom within a social dimension. The fact that the legislature may limit property rights only to that extent, in which the public weal could be served best, restricts the power of the state and compels it to respect private property.[2591] Whereas certain kinds of property interests are protected or guaranteed by the property clause, not every single property entitlement will be protected or guaranteed in a specific situation. Property is therefore not protected in the sense that existing property interests are guaranteed absolutely against any interference or invasion not authorised or consented to by the owner.[2592]

The constitutional protection of property is, therefore, different from the private-law protection of property. The main purpose is not to guarantee and insulate the *status quo* and the existing position of the individual property holder against any interference. The purpose of the constitutional property guarantee is to establish and maintain a balance between the individual's existing position and the public interest, which often means that the individual's interest has to be subjected to controls, regulations, restrictions, levies and other measures that advance or protect the public interest, often without compensation.[2593] In the constitu-

---

[2589] *Badura* in *Benda/Maihofer/Vogel (eds)*, Handbuch des Verfassungsrechts (1994), 329: *"Aber auch den staatlichen Auftrag der Sozialbindung und Machtkontrolle gegenüber den Gefahren und Nachteilen einer privatautonomen Eigentumsnutzung und Güterallokation."* Kimminich in Starck (ed), Rights, Institutions and Impact of International Law (1987), 79.

[2590] *Schuppert* in *Karpen (ed)*, Constitution of Germany (1988), 108.

[2591] *Kleyn*, 1996 SAPR/PL, 414.

[2592] *Van der Walt*, Constitutional Property Clause (1997), 68.

[2593] *Van der Walt*, Constitutional Property Clause (1997), 68.

tional framework, an owner might be free to act with his or her own property, but only within the limits set by the interests of the public.[2594]

Because property is not a legal institution exclusively dealt with in private law,[2595] the imbalances that might occur through an emphasis of private autonomy and individual freedom in the private law of property as it stands at present, will have to be corrected through the horizontal application of constitutional values. The application of the constitutional values of equality and human dignity on a horizontal level (that is, to private relations) might, for instance, influence an owner's capacity to restrict resale thereof.[2596] Similarly, it might also influence an owner's capacity to dispose of property *inter vivos* or upon his or her death. An even more severe restriction of powers can be effected by the enforcement of socio-economic rights on a horizontal level. Changes in the area of customary property law can also be expected,[2597] in particular where upholding existing proprietary relations will result in discrimination on the basis of sex, marital status, and the like.

Private property ownership does not have the same prominent position in constitutional law as it has in private law. Instead, the nature of the constitutional guarantee of property and the land reform prerogative attach importance to individual security in the sphere of land tenure, regardless of what the nature of rights emanating from it might be in private law. Moreover, a wide range of proprietary interests is protected.

Long before the introduction of the constitutional property clause in South Africa, Van der Merwe[2598] has explained that the place of prop-

---

[2594] *Pienaar,* Nuwe Sakeregtelike Ontwikkelings op die Gebied van Grondhervorming (1997), 6-7.

[2595] Contra *Gutto,* Property and Land Reform (1995), xiv.

[2596] See 388 ff. above.

[2597] *Kleyn,* 1996 SAPR/PL, 423.

[2598] *Van der Merwe,* Sakereg (1989), 6-7 explains his statement that the *law of things* forms part of private law and not of public law by pointing immediately to the difference between these two spheres of the law: *"[Die sakereg] reël die verhouding tussen individuele regsubjekte ..., en nie soos die publiekreg die verhouding tussen die owerheid en 'n onderdaan nie."* The role that public law plays in the formation legal structures within the law of things is expressly acknowledged: *"Dit beteken egter nie dat die sakereg heeltemal onafhanklik van publiekregtelike beperkings wat die uitoefening en inhoud van saaklike regte*

erty law in the South African legal system stretches far beyond that of private law. The law of things probably most closely resembles the place of property in the Roman-Dutch oriented private law structure of the South African legal system. However, even in this sphere of law, far-reaching public law (restrictive and/or developing) adjustments continuously influenced the understanding of the property concept in terms of private law. The most obvious example of such adjustments remains legislation aimed at establishing the apartheid government's ideal of a "racially segregated" society by allocating specific land for specific races on a discriminatory basis. The legitimacy the existing private law of property was, consequently, also rightly challenged, because of its succeptibility to influences from the apartheid government's legislature, whose enactments were clearly not always for the weal of the general South African public.

In spite of the questionable legitimacy of the existing property order in private law, one should not exclude the possibility that the private law of property could still play an important role in developing the property law under the new constitution in South Africa. However, the continued significance of private property law under the new constitution is closely connected to the question of how successful the new constitutional order will be in fulfilling its self-assigned objectives of healing the divisions of the past, establishing a society based on democratic values, social justice and fundamental human rights, improving the quality of life of all citizens and freeing the potential of every individual.[2599]

3. Property, Economic Growth and Empowerment

The state has to foster the ideals of governance through legality, the promotion and protection of fundamental rights and the constitutional and social state principles. This is important for the formulation and implementation of policies on social and economic development. It can be done either through legislative regulation, or through providing the necessary infrastructure, or both. In this regard, the German and South African systems are comparable, although by no means similar. Owner-

---

beperk, bestudeer kan word nie. Aangesien sodanige beperkings in die moderne tyd al hoe meer toeneem, moet die sakereg wel deeglik daarvan kennis neem."

[2599] See Preamble, FC.

ship of land can, for instance, be a stabilising element in society. However, this stabilising role can also be undertaken by the state; for instance, through the provision of social security, licences and permits. The extent to which the state assumes responsibility for providing in the socio-economic needs of individuals, influences the importance attached to private ownership in a given society.

Social and economic development implies the increase and the effective and equitable distribution of wealth within a society so as to enhance material, cultural, intellectual and spiritual well being. For proprietary relations in South Africa, this means that the constitutional property clause should be aimed at enhancing the individual's ability to participate in important societal changes, while simultaneously upholding the individual's ability to determine his or her own economic destiny. However, the success of a venture like this will be determined by the ability of the courts and legislature to resolve the inherent conflict between individual autonomy and equality (or freedom and social duty) in the property clause.

South Africa has one of the worst records in the world in terms of income equality and social indicators like health, education, safe water and fertility.[2600] The inclusion of socio-economic rights in the bill of rights represents a strong commitment to overcome this legacy and to put the principle of the social state into motion.[2601] However, at present the indications of the state's ability to deliver on the promises of providing social security, ensuring social justice and raising living standards, are rather disappointing. One could, therefore, assume that individuals will have to fend for themselves at least until the economic tide has taken a turn for the better in South Africa. This would be reason enough to support an interpretation of the constitutional property clause that would also provide individuals with the autonomy to determine their own economic destiny to a large extent, along with the responsibility to partake in social change.

[2600] See *Pienaar/Muller*, 1999 Stell LR, 373.

[2601] In this sense, the South African constitution goes even further than the German Basic Law, by extensive coverage of socio-economic rights in the chapter on fundamental rights. In Germany the *Sozialstaatsprinzip* is the constitutional anchor for the socio-economic rights, which by no means enjoy the same constitutional coverage as in South Africa and are mostly not explicitly mentioned in the Basic Law as such. In Germany the socio-economic rights are effected on the level of ordinary legislation.

3.1. A Framework for Legal Reform: Liberalism and Social Democracy

In the previous chapters, an attempt was made to indicate that the constitutional protection and regulation of private property in South Africa is a tool for protecting individual freedom and security as well as initiating social change. The judicial task of balancing the protection of ownership of individuals against the need for regulation and expropriation of property rights for the common good is enormous. An overzealous protection of property rights will do injustice to the broader objectives of national unity and reconciliation espoused in recent legislation; a fanatical focus on the redistributive character of the property clauses might lose sight of the importance of maintaining individual security in the context of property law.

The practical consequences of a failure to find the balance would be devastating. South Africans need look no further than the neighbouring country of Zimbabwe to get an idea of what could happen if the urgent need for socio-economic upliftment is left smouldering for too long and then abused for political ends. Even though the constitutional order and land reform process in Zimbabwe differs from that of South Africa, it still illustrates the dismal consequences of a complete disregard of individual freedom and autonomy of landowners and disrespect for the courts' attempts to keep the rule of law intact.

No property guarantee can survive the maintenance and absolute insulation of an unjust and inequitable system of distribution of property for too long. It is therefore always in the public interest that at least some reform and some redistributive initiatives be undertaken to preserve the property system itself.[2602] An effective balance between collective and individual interests would further require a continuation of the compromise reached between the ideologies of libertarianism and liberationism/egalitarianism in the drafting of the South African constitutions. This is proved by the German example, where a constant balancing of the values of liberalism and social democracy takes place. Classical liberalism, on which also the human rights ideology of libertarianism is based, affords owners and other right holders a high degree of individual freedom and autonomy. In terms of social democratic theory, on which liberationism/egalitarianism is based, stronger regulatory measures — also upon private property — are in general accepted as permissible. But, if the application of a property order with hybrid ideological foundations is to be successful, it is important that the state

---

[2602] *Van der Walt*, Constitutional Property Clause (1997), 68-69.

seriously endeavours to give effect to social justice and to improve the quality of life of its citizens. It is equally important that property rights of citizens are respected by the state administration, legislature and private persons alike. The role of the courts is to supervise the process of reform. It is, therefore, also indispensable that the judiciary is independent and perceived as legitimate and that its decisions are enforceable.

Political and economic equality in the sphere of landownership cannot be effected merely by importing a short-term policy of redistribution of wealth coupled with a disregard for individual autonomy. On the long run, it would be in the political and economic interests of the larger South African society that the institution of property is protected by attaching fundamental importance to the value of individual freedom. However, protection and regulation of property based on individual freedom alone will not be able to address all social welfare issues prevalent in modern day South African society successfully.

Here, the German constitutional order is an important example of a system where a working balance was achieved between an individual interest in property and social responsibility inherent in the concept of private property. The German example indicates that existing proprietary relations can sometimes cause inequality in certain individuals' chances of participation in social life. In some instances, the inequality can be so severe that "justice" would require state intervention. A purely legalistic interpretation of property and ownership is not possible in a legal system in which the constitutional and social state principles interact. In such a system, the demands of equity influence the approach to property. This means that material needs, historical changes and the social function of property rights qualify the definition and application of a constitutional property guarantee. In the process, a system of "scaled" protection of property in the constitutional context developed, according to the interest of the society at large in the protection and regulation of specific interests.[2603] For instance, in landlord-tenant relations, the tenant's interest (as expounded through rent control legislation or other forms of tenant protection) is intimately connected with personal liberty, while the landlord's interest is usually of a more economic nature. The former therefore usually enjoys a higher level of protection than the latter.

[2603] See the discussion of *Alexander* in *McLean (ed)*, Property and the Constitution (1999), 106 ff.

The German example teaches us that, although personal freedom and private property are two separate ethical values, they influence each other reciprocally, particularly in modern, industrialised societies. To be integrated in society, the individual needs a strictly protected sphere of property, to enable him or her to develop as a person among equals. The right to private property is a crucial component of the values of freedom and human dignity, which enables the individual to develop his or her own personality and self-esteem in a responsible way and to be more than the mere object of an overwhelming state power. In the German context, this individual freedom and responsibility underlying the constitutional protection of property has influenced the courts' treatment of rent control legislation, the determination of a fair amount of compensation in cases of expropriation, and the definition of the scope of entitlements pertaining to property (like excavations, gardening leases, and exclusion of third parties), to mention but a few.

The approach developed by the Federal Constitutional Court could be well applied in South Africa, not only to the abovementioned issues, but also to a broader range of issues, like labour rights, land reform and property taxation. By interpreting the property guarantee so as to secure personal liberty for the individual, and tempering this liberty with the duty to participate in the development and functioning of the community, it might be possible to achieve a working balance between liberalism and social justice in the context of section 25 FC. The willingness of the courts to continue the spirit of compromise and reconciliation established during the period of negotiations preceding the coming into effect of the new constitutional order will determine whether the attempts at striking such a balance will be successful.

3.2. Property, Individuals and the General Public

As far as the constitutional property guarantee is concerned, the basic premise of the South African Constitution is clear: property can be limited in terms of legal norms which are generally applicable, and a person can be deprived of ownership if the legal norm is not arbitrary. If property is completely withdrawn, compensation should be paid. On various levels public interest shapes the property law in general and the concept of ownership in particular, both in Germany and in South Africa. In the constitutional context, property regulation and property protection has to be viewed against the unique function and purpose of the bill of rights. The inclusion of certain interests in and the exclusion of other interests from the constitutional protection of property, is usually undertaken by determining whether it would serve or frustrate the constitutional purpose of establishing and maintaining an equitable balance between private property interests and the public interest in controlling and regulating the use of property and the distribution of property.[2604]

The development of the law of landownership within the framework of the new constitutional order in South Africa is regulated by the general constitutional objectives mentioned in the preamble of the Final Constitution. For South Africa, the significance of the German experience with property, liberty and social duty lies in the balancing of individual autonomy and the public good pertaining to private property. It indicates that in a democracy supported by constitutional values like the constitutional and social state, proprietary relations must always be characterised by an interaction between liberty and social duty.[2605] The Basic Law also establishes that, in the recurring tension between the property interest of the individual and the needs of the public, the public interest may in case of conflict take precedence over the legally guaranteed position of the individual. The Basic Law does not leave the resolution of this conflict to the legislature but settles the issue in the provisions of article 14 GG.

This framework is important in the South African context where, with the dawning of a new constitutional order, the legal system will be confronted with the question as to what interests should enjoy precedence in situations where the interests of individual property owners and the public in general come into conflict with each other. The policy of the Department of Land Affairs is quite clear with regard to the future of South African law of landownership. The primary focus should be on the protection of both the interests of individual owners and the society at large. Nevertheless, the inherent dichotomy between individual autonomy and social responsibility inevitably requires balancing of interests. In such a process, the eradication of past injustice and continued inequality seems to be a decisive consideration. It is also likely to have the same importance if a court is required to balance the interests of the individual against those of the general public.

The inevitable implication of the constitutional purpose to establish and maintain a just and equitable balance between individual property in-

---

[2604] *Van der Walt*, Constitutional Property Clause (1997), 68.

[2605] *Kimminich*, Die Eigentumsgarantie im Prozeß der Wiedervereinigung (1990), 24.

terests and the public interest is that the constitutional property clause itself must support a just and equitable distribution of property, even in the absence of explicit land reform provisions like those in section 25 FC. A constitutional property clause cannot guarantee existing property holdings indefinitely, absolutely or without qualification, without destroying the dynamic nature of property relations. This probably also indicates the approach that could be followed in examining interference on property in the light of proportionality.

4. Property, Interference, Proportionality and Balancing of Interests

In the course of this exposition,[2606] an attempt was made at indicating the importance of the approach chosen in the investigation of interferences with property. The different approaches, and the arguments supporting and countering them, will not be repeated here. It is necessary, however, to briefly recapitulate the approach favoured in this exposition.

It is submitted that the constitutional property clause in South Africa needs to be approached from the premise that property itself, and not something "less than property" is protected.[2607] This eliminates the problems which could be experienced at a later stage in the inquiry as to the constitutional protection and regulation of property and its interaction with the general limitations clause in the South African bill of rights.[2608] It is further submitted that the property clause and the general limitations clause apply cumulatively in an investigation as to the justifiability of a specific infringement on property.[2609]

The problems with selecting the appropriate point of departure in an investigation into the constitutional regulation and protection of property are, submittedly, linked to the structure and stages of the inquiry to be followed.[2610] In the South African system, the contraction of the "threshold" question and the question as to the existence of an infringement into a single stage might lead to a disregard of the latter

---

[2606] See e.g. 80, 93, 108, 165, 352, 375, 394 above.

[2607] 108, 200 above.

[2608] 264 above.

[2609] 271 above.

[2610] 99 above.

question. Skipping the process of identifying the infringement (that is, identifying the nature of the action complained of, without attempting to determine its justifiability), could result in a confusion as to the kind of validity requirements that would be applicable to determine justifiability at a later stage in the inquiry.[2611] If more focus is placed on the nature of the action earlier in the process of determining the constitutionality of that action, it would in many cases not even be necessary to resort to the proportionality inquiry. For such an approach, the German theory on protection and regulation of property can provide valuable examples.[2612]

Proportionality (in the sense of the suitability, necessity and moderation) of an infringement,[2613] it is submitted, should be tested only as a very last step in the investigation, so as to exclude the probability of the court making decisions on the basis of a ranking of rights. This does not mean, however, that interest-balancing will practically never take place. The values underlying the constitution in its entirety, like those of the constitutional state and the social state,[2614] require that throughout the whole process the interests of the parties to a dispute as well as the general public interest be taken into account. This, however, can be done on a case by case basis, and need not be based on a preconceived hierarchy of rights.

5. Land Law Reform and the Balancing of Interests as Example

Within the system of social reform legislation pertaining to land, the system of a continuous balancing of the individual interest and the interests of society at large seems to be established already. In the discussion of certain pieces of this land reform legislation above,[2615] an attempt was made at indicating how the legislature considered the inter-

---

[2611] The decision in *Harksen* (see 327, 350, 371 above) is an example of how the issue of whether compensation was payable could have been avoided if more focus was place on the kind of infringement, before an attempt was made at determining whether the validity requirements for expropriation of property were complied with.

[2612] 281, also 99 above.

[2613] 352 above.

[2614] Ch. 6 (115 ff.) above.

[2615] 437 ff. above.

ests on both sides of the scale in drafting the relevant legislation. First and foremost, the interests of the poor and landless are addressed by reform legislation. However, provision is nearly always made for a certain degree of protection of existing rights. As such, the body of land reform legislation provides an example of how individual autonomy can be coupled with the duties of the same individuals towards the development of society.

Simultaneously, the land reform legislation represents an example of how the interaction between private law and constitutional law could operate. The private law remedies of owners are upheld as far as possible, and land and ownership of land are made more readily accessible for all members of the South African society. This could result in a diversification of land rights,[2616] although indications to this effect are still few and far apart. More recent land reform legislation seems to follow this tendency to a larger extent than the earlier legislative efforts pertaining to land reform.

What can be deducted from viewing the land reform effort as a whole, however, is the intention of legislature to correct the imbalances existing in land control relations within the structure of private law, by adherence to the constitutional mandate of reform. In effect, the constitutional provisions, either directly or indirectly, can be employed to regulate the effects that private law protection and regulation of property could have on particular cases. However, the fact that the application of the constitutional provisions to specific cases vary according to the particular facts and circumstances, does not justify an ad hoc approach to the interaction of private and constitutional law in the sphere of property. A reading of the constitutional property clause in conformity with the rest of the Final Constitution and the adherence to the values underlying the constitutional system would dictate against such an approach.

The extent to which the private law of property will eventually be influenced by the constitutional provisions on property remains to be seen. At this point, it can only be estimated that the degree of interaction will vary according to the nature and content of the specific property interests at stake. For the time being, these issues need not be pursued into the finest detail. Submittedly, it is more important to identify a structure within which such an interaction between the principles of property in private and constitutional law could take place.

[2616] See the argument of *Van der Walt*, 1999 Koers, 289 ff.

6. The Way Forward?

This exposition indicates that individual security and freedom, which are characteristics of private law property, remain important amidst the changes effected by the constitution or the reform legislation to the property law order in general. However, the private law rights and entitlements of owners need to be viewed against the interests of these people in a society based on equality, freedom and human dignity. A new constitutional order cannot insulate property from the influence of these basic values. Because of the different functions of property protection in private law and constitutional law, an owner's private law rights alone will in any event not provide much assistance if his or her position is challenged by the general interests of the public.

If property law can be developed according to a set of principles, abstracted from the constitution itself, in which land reform takes place against a consideration of the constitutional spirit of reconciliation, unity and compromise, but without discarding the importance of the institution of private property, many of the problems relating to the constitutional protection of property could be satisfactorily solved. However, the courts' task of abstracting a set of values from the constitutional property guarantee to regulate the function of property law and to monitor compliance with these values is by no means easy. The omnipresent dichotomy between social justice and individual freedom in the realm of property law should not be underestimated. The treatment of this issue will influence the definition of the constitutional property concept, for which no extensive guidelines are provided in section 25 FC itself.

Indeed, the South African constitutional property clause itself is not of much assistance in the determination of the protective scope of section 25 FC, nor in the weight that the public interest requirement should have in the process of balancing competing interests. The policy of the state administrative authorities in reforming the law of landownership is to protect the interests of both individual owners and the society at large. The relevant statutory provisions and policy documents are, however, subject to varying interpretation. It is vital that the judiciary more clearly defines a process through which more legal certainty can be achieved in the application of the principle of balancing the competing interests of the individual and society, as espoused by the constitutional property clause. This approach should, moreover, not apply only to issues emanating from the reform of the system of landownership, but should also be assimilated on a broader basis so as to apply to all issues related to property.

In particular, major socio-economic issues have to be tackled in South Africa through the chosen method of constitutionalism. In this regard, substantive legal change should not be a matter of chance. In German law, the treatment of the values of individual freedom and social justice through application of the constitutional principles have resulted in a clear-cut framework within which the interests of the individual property owner can be weighed against those of the community at large. This framework is important in the South African context, where, under a new constitutional order, the legal system will be confronted with the question as to which of these considerations should enjoy precedence in situations where both are at stake and compete with each other.

Considerable differences exist between the German and South African property law orders and societies. Nevertheless, the issues arising for constitutional adjudication in terms of the property clauses of both these legal systems show significant similarities. These issues relate to the balancing of individual autonomy and the public good pertaining to private property. They are to a large extent still unsolved in South Africa, and were in most instances effectively treated by the German judiciary. This is where the German experience with property, liberty and social duty becomes important. Translating the relevant principles, which have crystallised in German law through a process of trial and error, into the South African context is a challenge well worth embracing. In embarking upon such a venture, the present exposition, as a whole, can be no more than an introduction.

Summary

This dissertation is an attempt at reconciling the existing (and until recently predominant) private law concept of ownership and the property rights espoused by the new constitutional order. The endeavours at land reform in South Africa and Germany are used as specific examples of the manner in which the whole property law order in both these legal systems is developed through legislative and judicial initiative, on the basis of the constitutional provisions concerning property protection and regulation. The purpose of the investigation is to determine to what extent constitutional development of the private law of property will result in a property law order serving the socio-economic and political goals of economic growth and self-fulfilment and empowerment of the individual. Focus is placed on the influence of the constitutional protection and regulation of property as a mechanism for developing the private law of ownership in Germany and South Africa.

In the first part of the exposition, the choice of legal comparison as course of inquiry is substantiated, and the terminological difficulties connected with an investigation into the development of the private law of property by the constitutional protection and regulation of property are discussed. Attention is given to the use of the terms "ownership" and "property" in the private law and in the constitutional context. The term "tenure" is also discussed in the context of land reform in South Africa. Further, the use of terms such as "public interest", "common weal" and "public purposes" is discussed. The use of these terms are particularly complicated by the fact that each of them are often used in more than one sense, and that the use of these different terms overlap to varying extents.

The second part of the exposition contains information on the background of the constitutional property orders as they are found in Germany and South Africa. The drafting histories of the South African and German constitutional property clauses indicate that in both these legal systems, the constitutional property clauses have hybrid ideological foundations. Both contain a compromise between, on the one hand, classical liberalism (which affords the holders of rights a high degree of individual freedom and autonomy) and, on the other hand, social democracy (which allow stronger regulatory measures, also upon private property). Further, some of the structural aspects connected to constitutional protection and regulation of property in Germany and South Africa are discussed. The positively phrased property guarantee in art 14 GG is compared with the negatively phrased "guarantee" of section 25 FC, whereby the transitional property guarantee in section 28 IC is also considered. Further, the basic structure and stages of an inquiry into the constitutional property clause are discussed, with reference to differences between the German and South African methods. These differences do not exclude further comparison. However, it is necessary to keep the differences in the judicial system in mind when conducting a comparison of the present nature. Therefore, a brief overview of the judicial systems of Germany and South Africa is provided, with specific reference to the manner in which the courts resolved certain property questions. The principles underlying the constitutional orders of Germany and South Africa are also discussed with specific reference to their significance for the treatment of property issues. In particular, the meaning of the constitutional state *(Rechtsstaat)* and the social welfare state *(Sozialstaat)* for the solution of problems connected to property is discussed. It is indicated that the legitimacy of the legal order in general and property law in particular, depends on the degree of success in the implementation of these values. Further, it is indicated that the implementation of these values also determines the importance of private property and/or regulation thereof in a specific legal system.

In the third part of the exposition, the relevance of the constitutional protection and regulation for the private law of ownership is discussed. The expansion of the concept of property by the application of a "purely" constitutional definition thereof raises the question as to the continued relevance of the private law concept of ownership. This issue is discussed with reference to the protection of property in terms of the constitution in comparison with the scope of property in private law. It is indicated that the "exclusively constitutional" concept of property is by no means based only on Constitutional law. The role of the private law concept of ownership in a constitutional order is then elucidated. The discussion then turns to an analysis of the limitations on property endorsed by the constitutional order. Two main kinds of limitation are possible: (i) limitation of property through vertical operation of the constitution (ie a broad category of legislative and administrative deprivation (regulation), and a more specialised category, namely expropriations), and (ii) limitation through horizontal operation of the constitution (ie through the inroads allowed on property rights by the protection of other rights in the Bill of Rights). It is indicated that the application of the public interest / public purposes requirements are sometimes intended to protect individual interests rather than those of society in general. In other cases, the public interest / public purposes requirements are aimed at securing the interests of the society at large. Further, it is indicated that the purpose of constitutional "interference" in the area of private property law is to correct imbalances in the relations among private persons which are regarded by the law as "equals," even if they are not equal for all practical purposes.

The fourth part of the exposition concentrates on the land reform programmes in Germany (after the reunification of 1990) and South Africa (since 1991) in order to analyse the endeavours by the legislature and judiciary to give effect to the improved property order as anticipated by constitutional development of property. In both Germany and South Africa political changes made land reform programmes essential: In South Africa the land reform programme was introduced to reverse the injustices created by colonialism and apartheid. A tripartite programme is employed for this purpose. The new kinds of land rights created through this system of land reform are indicated. The manner in which this body of law is treated by the courts is also analysed with reference to its relevance for the development of Property Law in general. In Germany a property and land reform programme became necessary with the reunification. On the one hand, the socialist property order in the former GDR had to be replaced by the property order already existing in the FGR, and on the other hand the individual claims for restitution of the land and enterprises taken by the GDR state or its Soviet predecessor had to be balanced against the claims that present occupiers of such land have to it. The influence of legislation and litigation connected to these issues on the development of Property Law is discussed.

The final part of the exposition is a summary of the conclusions drawn during the course of the analysis.

Afrikaanse Opsomming

In 'n poging om in hierdie uiteensetting die bestaande (en tot onlangs nog oorheersende) privaatregtelike begrip "eiendom" te versoen met die breër eiendomsbegrip wat deur die nuwe grondwetlike bestel gepropageer word, word die grondhervormingsprogramme in Suid Afrika en Duitsland gebruik as voorbeelde van die wyse waarop die bestaande eiendomsreg konsep in beide regsisteme deur die wetgewer en die howe ontwikkel word. Die doel van die ondersoek is om vas te stel tot watter mate die grondwetlike ontwikkeling van privaatregtelike eiendomsreg sal bydra tot die totstandkoming van 'n eiendomsregtelike regsorde waarin die sosio-ekonomiese en politieke doelwitte van ekonomiese groei en die vrye ontwikkeling en bemagtiging van die individu gedien word. Die klem word geplaas op die grondwetlike beskerming en regulering van eiendom as 'n meganisme waardeur die privaatregtelike eiendomsreg in Duitsland en Suid-Afrika ontwikkel kan word.

Die eerste deel van die uiteensetting begrond die keuse van regsvergelyking as metode van analise en bespreek die terminologiese probleme wat in 'n ondersoek na die grondwetlike ontwikkeling van die privaatregtelike eiendomsreg kan opduik. Aandag word gegee aan die gebruik van begrippe wat verband hou met eiendom en publieke belang in sowel die privaatreg as in die grondwetlike konteks. Die gebruik van verskillende terme, veral in Engels, kan problematies wees, en daarom word dit breedvoeriger bespreek.

In die tweede deel van die uiteensetting word die agtergrond waarteen die grondwetlike bestelle van Duitsland en Suid-Afrika funksioneer, bespreek: Eers word die formulering van die eiendomsklousules in Suid-Afrika en Duitsland vanuit 'n historiese perspektief ondersoek. In beide regsisteme is die grondwetlike eiendomsklousules op 'n kompromis tussen verskillende ideologieë gebaseer. Enersyds op klassieke liberalisme, in terme waarvan eienaars en ander reghebbendes 'n hoë mate van individuele vryheid en outonomie toegeken word; andersyds op sosiaal-demokratiese denke, in terme waarvan strenger regulerende maatreëls (ook op privaat eiendom) geduld moet word. Dan word sommige van die strukturele aspekte verbonde aan die grondwetlike beskerming en regulering van eiendom in Duitsland en Suid-Afrika bespreek. Die positief geformuleerde eiendomswaarborg in art 14 GG word vergelyk met die negatiewe formulering in art 25 FG en die positiewe waarborg in art 28 IG. Verder word die basiese struktuur en fases van 'n grondwetlike ondersoek in die beskerming en regulering van eiendom bespreek, met spesifieke verwysing na die verskille in die Duitse en Suid-Afrikaanse benaderings. Hierdie verskille is nie van so 'n aard dat dit regsvergelyking kortwiek nie. Nogtans is dit noodsaaklik dat die benaderingsverskille in ag geneem word vir 'n meer diepgaande vergelyking. Daarom word 'n vlugtige oorsig oor die rol van die howe in die hantering van eiendomsvraagstukke in grondwetlike konteks verskaf. Verder word die beginsels onderliggend aan die grondwetlike bestelle in Duitsland en Suid-Afrika bespreek met spesifieke verwysing na die betekenis daarvan vir die beskerming en regulering van eiendom. Daar word veral klem gelê op die regstaat- en sosiaalstaatbeginsels. Die legitimiteit van die regsorde in die algemeen, en meer spesifiek die bepaalde eiendomsregime, hang af van die mate van sukses waarmee hierdie beginsels in die gemeenskap geïmplementeer word. Daar word verder aangedui dat die toepassing van hierdie beginsels die mate van individuele vryheid in die uitoefening van eiendomsreg en/of die graad van regulering van eiendomsreg in 'n bepaalde regstelsel bepaal.

Die derde deel van die uiteensetting konsentreer op die betekenis van die grondwetlike beskerming en regulering van eiendom vir die privaatregtelike eiendomsreg. Die uitgebreide eiendomsbegrip wat in die grondwetlike konteks aangewend word, gee aanleiding tot die vraag na die sin van 'n voortgesette enger eiendomsbegrip in die privaatreg. Hierdie kwessie word bespreek met verwysing na die beskerming van eiendom in terme van die grondwet, en word vergelyk met die omvang van die eiendomsbegrip in die privaatreg. Daar word aangedui dat die sogenaamde uitsluitlik grondwetlike eiendomsbegrip geensins eksklusief aan die Grondwetlike Reg is nie. Die rol van die privaatregtelike eiendomsbegrip in 'n grondwetlike bestel word vervolgens uiteengesit. Verder word die beperkings op eiendom in die grondwetlike konteks geanaliseer. In beginsel is twee soorte beperkings regverdigbaar: (i) Beperking van eiendomsreg deur die vertikale aanwending van die grondwet, dit wil sê deur die breër kategorie wetgewende en administratiewe ontnemings (regulerings) van eiendomsreg en deur 'n enger en meer spesifieke kategorie, naamlik onteiening; en (ii) beperking van eiendomsreg deur horisontale aanwending van die grondwet, dit wil sê deur die inbreuk op eiendomsregte wat toegelaat word as gevolg van die uitwerking van die beskerming van ander regte in die Handves vir Menseregte. Daar word aangedui dat die vereiste van publieke belang in twee teenoorstaande opsigte gebruik word: Enersyds om die individuele belang bo dié van die gemeenskap te stel, en andersyds om die gemeenskap se belange as sulks te beskerm. Daar word ook aangedui dat grondwetlike "inmenging" met privaatregtelike eiendomsreg daarop gemik is om ongebalanseerdhede in die regsverhoudings tussen persone wat deur die reg as "gelykes" bejeën word en in effek nie gelyk is nie, uit te skakel.

In die vierde deel van die uiteensetting word die grondhervormings-programme in Duitsland (sedert hervereniging in 1990) en Suid-Afrika (sedert 1991) bespreek. Die klem val op die pogings van die wetgewer en howe om die verbeterde eiendomsbestel, soos wat dit in die grondwet in die vooruitsig gestel word, te konkretiseer. In beide regstelsels het politieke veranderinge 'n grondhervormingsprogram onontbeerlik gemaak: Die grondhervormingsprogram in Suid-Afrika het ten doel om die ongeregtighede in die grondbesitstelsel wat ontstaan het as gevolg van kolonialisme en apartheid uit te skakel. Vir dié doel berus die grondhervormingsprogram op drie verwante, maar uiteenlopende, beginsels. Die nuwe vorme van grondregte wat uit hierdie sisteem ontstaan, word aangedui, en die wyse waarop hierdie deel van die reg deur die howe hanteer word, word bespreek met verwysing na die betekenis daarvan vir die ontwikkeling van die grondregime. In Duitsland is die noodwendigheid van 'n grondhervormingsprogram aan die hervereniging van die DDR en die BRD gekoppel. Die sosialisties-georienteerde eiendomsbestel wat in die "oostelike" deel van Duitsland aanwending gevind het, moes vervang word deur die bestel wat reeds in die "westelike" deel van die "nuwe" staat in werking was. Verder moet die grondeise van persone wat grond of besigheidseiendom verloor het gedurende die sosialistiese regeringstyd en die voorafgaande Sowjetiese besetting, opgeweeg word teen die aansprake wat huidige besitters op sulke grond het. Die invloed van wetgewing en regspraak hieroor op die Eiendomsreg word geanaliseer.

Die laaste deel van die uiteensetting bevat 'n samevatting van die gevolgtrekkings wat deur die loop van die analise gemaak is.

Bibliography

Commentaries, Books, Articles, Papers and Dissertations

A

ACKERMANN, L., "Equality and the South African Constitution: The Role of Dignity", *Bram Fischer Lecture delivered at Rhodes House, Oxford (26 May 2000)*, 2000 *Zeitschrift für ausländisches öffentliches Recht und Völkerrecht*, 537 – 556

ALEXANDER, G., "Constitutionalising Property: Two Experiences, Two Dilemmas" in MCLEAN, J. (ed), *Property and the Constitution*, Oxford, Hart, (1999)

ALLEN, T., "Commonwealth Constitutions and the Right not to be Deprived of Property", 1993 *International and Comparative Law Quarterly (Int & Comp LQ / ICLQ)*, 523 – 552

ATKINSON, D., "Insuring the future? The Bill of Rights" in FRIEDMAN, S. & ATKINSON, D. (eds), *South African Review 7 – The Small Miracle: South Africa's Negotiated Settlement*, Johannesburg, Ravan Press, (1994), chapter 5

AVENARIUS, H., *Die Rechtsordnung der Bundesrepublik Deutschland* 2nd ed, Bonn, Bundeszentrale für Politische Bildung, (1997)

B

BADURA, P., "Eigentum" in BENDA, E., MAIHOFER, W. & VOGEL, H.-J. (eds), *Handbuch des Verfassungsrechts der Bundesrepublik Deutschland* 2nd ed, Berlin, De Gruyter, (1994), chapter 10

BARRY, M. (ed), *Proceedings of International Conference on Land Tenure in the Developing World* (held at the University of Cape Town in January 1998); online at http://www.gtz.de/orboden/capetown/capetown.htm [13.05.2000]

BAUMAN, R.W., "Property Rights in the Canadian Constitutional Context", 1992 *South African Journal on Human Rights (SAJHR)*, 344 – 361

BAUR, F. & STÜRNER, R., *Sachenrecht* 17th ed, München, Beck, (1999)

BEEKHUIS, J.H., LAWSON, F.H., KNAPP, V., ET AL, "Structural Variations in Property Law" in LAWSON, F.H. (chief ed), *Property and Trust*, International Encyclopaedia of Comparative Law VI, (1975), chapter 2

BENDA, E., MAIHOFER, W. & VOGEL, H.-J. (eds), *Handbuch des Verfassungsrechts der Bundesrepublik Deutschland* 2nd ed, Berlin, De Gruyter, (1994)

BENNETT, T.W., "Redistribution of Land and the Doctrine of Aboriginal Title in South Africa" 1989, 1993 *South African Journal of Human Rights (SAJHR)*, 443 – 476

BENNETT, T.W., "African land: a History of Dispossession" in ZIMMERMANN, R. & VISSER, D.P. (eds), *Southern Cross*, Cape Town, Juta, (1996), chapter 2

BENNETT, T.W., *Human Rights & African Customary Law*, Cape Town, Juta, (1995)

BENNUN, M. & NEWITT, M. (eds), *Negotiating Justice – A New Constitution For South Africa*, Exeter, University of Exeter Press, (1995)

BIRKS, P., "The Roman Law Concept of Dominium and the Idea of Absolute Ownership", 1985 *Acta Juridica*, 1 – 37

BIXIO, A., "Property Ownership and Social Concern" in FERRARI, V. (ed), *Laws and Rights* – Proceedings of the International Congress of Sociology of Law for the Ninth Centenary of the University of Bologna May 30 – June 3, 1988 (1991), 967 – 981

BLAAU, L. [sic], "The Rechtsstaat Idea Compared with the Rule of Law as a Paradigm for Protecting Rights", 1990 *South African Law Journal (SALJ)*, 76 – 96

BLAAUW, L., *The Constitutional Tenability of Group Rights*, Unpublished Doctoral Dissertation, University of South Africa, (1988)

BLAAUW-WOLF, L., "The 'Balancing of Interests' with Reference to the Principle of Proportionality and the Doctrine of Güterabwägung – A Comparative Analysis", 1999 *SA Publiekreg / Public Law (SAPR/PL)*, 178 – 214

BLAAUW-WOLF, L. & WOLF, J., "A Comparison between German and South African Limitation Provisions", 1996 *South African Law Journal (SALJ)*, 267 – 296

BOOYSEN, H., "South Africa: In Need of a Federal Constitution for its Minority Peoples", 1997 *Loyola of Los Angeles International and Comparative Law Journal (Loy LA Int'l & Comp LJ)*, 789 – 809

BRYDE, B., "Artikel 14" in VON MÜNCH, I. & KUNIG, P., *Grundgesetz Kommentar* I 4th ed (1992), 821 – 904

BUB, W.-R. (ed), *Festschrift für Johannes Bärmann und Hermann Weitnauer*, München, Beck, (1990)

BUCHWALD, D., *Prinzipien des Rechtsstaats – Zur Kritik der gegenwärtigen Dogmatik des Staatsrechts anhand des allgemeinen Rechtsstaatsprinzips nach dem Grundgesetz der Bundesrepublik Deutschland*, Aachen, Shaker, (1996)

BUDLENDER, G., "The Constitutional Protection of Property Rights" in BUDLENDER, G., LATSKY, J. & ROUX, T., *Juta's New Land Law*, Cape Town, Juta, (1998), chapter 1

BUDLENDER, G., "The Right to Equitable Access to Land", 1992 *South African Journal on Human Rights (SAJHR)*, 295 – 304

BUDLENDER, G. & LATSKY, J., "Unravelling Rights to Land and Agricultural Activity in Rural Race Zones", 1990 *South African Journal of Human Rights (SAJHR)*, 155 – 177

BUDLENDER, G., LATSKY, J. & ROUX, T., *Juta's New Land Law*, Cape Town, Juta, (1998)

C

CACHALIA, A., CHEADLE, H., DAVIS, D. ET AL., *Fundamental Rights in the New Constitution* Cape Town, Juta, (1994)

CAIGER, A., "The Protection of Property in South Africa" in BENNUN & NEWITT (eds), *Negotiating Justice – A New Constitution for South Africa*, Exeter, University of Exeter Press, (1995), chapter 5

CAREY-MILLER, D.L., "A new property?", 1999 *South African Law Journal (SALJ)*, 749 – 759

CAREY-MILLER, D.L., "Revision of Priorities in South African Land Law" in BARRY, M. (ed), *Proceedings of International Conference on Land Tenure in the Developing World* (held at the University of Cape Town in January 1998), 49 – 60

CAREY-MILLER, D.L. & POPE, A., *Land Title in South Africa*, Cape Town, Juta, (2000)

CHASKALSON, M., "The Land Claims Court" (May 1997) *Consultus* 31 – 33

CHASKALSON, M., "Stumbling towards Section 28: Negotiations over the Protection of Property Rights in the Interim Constitution", 1995 *South African Journal on Human Rights (SAJHR)*, 222 – 240

CHASKALSON, M., "The Problem with Property: Thoughts on the Constitutional Protection of Property in the United States and the Commonwealth", 1993 *South African Journal on Human Rights (SAJHR)*, 388 – 411

CHASKALSON, M., "The Property Clause: Section 28 of the Constitution", 1994 *South African Journal on Human Rights (SAJHR)*, 131 – 139

CHASKALSON, M. & LEWIS, C., "Property" in CHASKALSON, M., KENTRIDGE, J. ET AL. (eds), *Constitutional Law of South Africa*, Cape Town, Juta, (1996), chapter 31

CHASKALSON, M., KENTRIDGE, J., KLAAREN, K., ET AL., "Introduction" in CHASKALSON, M., KENTRIDGE, J. ET AL. (eds), *Constitutional Law of South Africa*, Cape Town, Juta, (1996), chapter 1

CHASKALSON, M., KENTRIDGE, J., KLAAREN, K., ET AL. (eds), *Constitutional Law of South Africa*, Cape Town, Juta, (1996)

CLAASSENS, A., "Compensation for Expropriation: The Political and Economic Parameters of Market Value", 1993 *South African Journal of Human Rights (SAJHR)*, 422 – 427

COHEN, D. & SIMON, D. (eds), *Collected Studies in Roman Law II*, Frankfurt am Main, Klosterman, (1991)

CORDER, H. & DAVIS, D., "Law and Social Practice: An Introduction" in CORDER (ed), *Essays on Law & Social Practice in South Africa*, Cape Town, Juta, (1988), chapter 1

CORDER, H., KAHANOVITZ, S., MURPHY, S., ET AL., *A Charter for Social Justice – A Contribution to the South African Bill of Rights Debate*, Cape Town, Juta, (1992)

COWEN, D.V., *New Patterns of Landownership – The Transformation of the Concept of Ownership as Plena in Re Potestas*, Unpublished paper, read at the University of the Witwatersrand (Johannesburg) on 26 April 1984

CRONJÉ, D.S.P., Barnard Cronjé & Olivier's *The South African Law of Persons and Family Law* 2nd ed, Durban, Butterworths, (1990)

CURRIE, D.P., *The Constitution of the Federal Republic of Germany*, Chicago, University of Chicago Press, (1994)

D

DAUBE, D., "Fashions and Idiosyncracies in the Exposition of the Roman Law of Property" in COHEN, D. & SIMON, D. (eds), *Collected*

Studies in Roman Law II (1991), Frankfurt am Main, Klosterman, 1325 – 1339

DAVEL, C.J. & JORDAAN, R.A., *Personereg Studentehandboek*, Cape Town, Juta (1995)

DAVIS, D., CHASKALSON, M. & DE WAAL, J., "Democracy and constitutionalism: the role of constitutional interpretation" in VAN WYK, DUGARD ET AL. (eds), *Rights and Constitutionalism – The New South African Legal Order*, Oxford, Clarendon, (1996), 1 – 130

DAVIS, D., CHEADLE, H., & HAYSOM, N., *Fundamental Rights in the Constitution – Commentary and Cases*, Cape Town, Juta, (1997)

DAVIS, D.M., "The Case against the Inclusion of Socio-Economic Demands in a Bill of Rights Excerpt as Directive Principles", 1992 *South African Journal on Human Rights (SAJHR)*, 475 – 490

DE GROOT, H., *Inleidinge tot de Hollandsche Rechtsgeleerdheyd*, 's-Gravenhage, (1631)

DE VILLIERS, B., "Directive Principles of State Policy and Fundamental Rights: The Experience of India", 1992 *South African Journal on Human Rights (SAJHR)*, 29 – 49

DE VILLIERS, B., "The Socio-Economic Consequences of Directive Principles of State Policy: Limitations on Fundamental Rights", 1992 *South African Journal on Human Rights (SAJHR)*, 188 – 199

DE VILLIERS, B. (ed), *Birth of a Constitution*, Cape Town, Juta, (1994)

DE VOS, P., "A Bill of Rights as an Instrument for Social and Economic Transformation in a New South African Constitution: Lessons from India" in BENNUN, M. & NEWITT, M. (eds), *Negotiating Justice – A New Constitution For South Africa*, Exeter, University of Exeter Press, (1995), chapter 4

DE WAAL, J., "A Comparative Analysis of the Provisions of German Origin in the Interim Bill of Rights", 1995 *South African Journal on Human Rights (SAJHR)*, 1 – 29

DE WAAL, J., CURRIE, I. & ERASMUS, G., *The Bill of Rights Handbook*, Cape Town, Juta, 2nd ed (1999); 3rd ed (2000)

DE WET, E., "Can the Social State Principle in Germany Guide State Action in South Africa in the Field of Social and Economic Rights?", 1995 *South African Journal on Human Rights (SAJHR)*, 30 – 49

DE WET, E., *The Constitutional Enforceability of Economic and Social Rights – The Meaning of the German Constitutional Model for South Africa*, Durban, Butterworths, (1996)

DEGENHART, C., *Staatsrecht I – Staatszielbestimmungen, Staatsorgane, Staatsfunktionen* 4th ed, Karlsruhe/Heidelberg, Müller, (1998)

DEVENISH, G.E., A *Commentary on the South African Constitution*, Durban, Butterworths, (1998)

DIEKMANN, B., *Das System der Rückerstattungstatbestände nach dem Gesetz zur Regelung offener Vermögensfragen*, Frankfurt am Main, Lang, (1992)

DIOSDI, G., *Ownership in Ancient and Pre-Classical Roman Law*, Budapest, Akadémiai Kiadó, (1970)

DLAMINI, C.R., "Landownership and Customary Law Reform" in VAN DER WALT (ed), *Land Reform and the Future of Landownership in South Africa*, Cape Town, Juta, (1991), 37 – 44

DOLZER, R., *Property and Environment: The Social Obligation inherent in Ownership – A Study of the German Constitutional Setting*, Morges, International Union for Conservation of Nature an Natural Resources, (1976)

DOMANSKI, A., "Landownership and Natural Law", 1989 *Tydskrif vir Hedendaagse Romeins-Hollandse Reg (THRHR)*, 433 – 443

DU PLESSIS, L.M., "A Background to Drafting the Chapter on Fundamental Rights" in DE VILLIERS (ed), *Birth of a Constitution*, Cape Town, Juta, (1994), 89 – 100

DU PLESSIS, L.M., "Constitutional Construction and the Contradictions of Social Transfromation in South Africa", 2000 *Scriptura*, 31 – 52

DU PLESSIS, L.M., "The Bill of Rights in the Working Draft of the New Constitution: an Evaluation of Aspects of a Constitutional Text Sui Generis", 1996 *Stellenbosch Law Review (Stell LR)*, 3 – 24

DU PLESSIS, L.M., "The Evolution of Constitutionalism and the Emergence of a Constitutional Jurisprudence in South Africa: An Evaluation of the South African Constitutional Court's Approach to Constitutional Interpretation", 1999 *Saskatchewan Law Review*, 300 – 328

DU PLESSIS, L.M., "The Genesis of the Chapter on Fundamental Rights in South Africa's Transitional Constitution", 1994 *SA Publiekreg / Public Law (SAPR/PL)*, 1 – 21

DU PLESSIS, L.M. & CORDER, H., *Understanding South Africa's Transitional Bill of Rights*, Cape Town, Juta, (1994)

DU PLESSIS, W., " 'n Regsteoretiese Ondersoek na die Begrip 'Openbare Belang' ", 1987 *Tydskrif vir Hedendaagse Romeins-Hollandse Reg (THRHR)*, 290 – 298

DU PLESSIS, W. & OLIVIER, N., "The Old and the New Property Clause", 1997 (1) 5 *Human Rights and Constitutional Law Journal of South Africa (HRCLJSA)*, 11 – 15

DU PLESSIS, W., OLIVIER, N. & PIENAAR, J.M., "Land Reform continues during 1997", 1997 *SA Publiekreg / Public Law (SAPR/PL)*, 531 – 550

DU SOLD, A., *Restitution vor Entschädigung: Wiedervereinigung zu welchem Preis? Analyse und Wertung nach rechtlichen, wirtschaftlichen und politischen Gesichtspunkten*, Baden-Baden, Löw & Vorderwülbecke, (1993)

E

EBKE, W.F. & FINKIN, M.W. (eds), *Introduction to German Law*, The Hague, Kluwer, (1996)

ECKERT, J., *Sachenrecht*, Baden-Baden, Nomos (1999)

EISENBERG, A., " 'Public Purpose' and Expropriation: some Comparative Insights and the South African Bill of Rights", 1995 *South African Journal on Human Rights (SAJHR)*, 207 – 221

ERASMUS, G., "Limitation and Suspension" in VAN WYK, J., DUGARD, J., ET AL. (eds), *Rights and Constitutionalism – The New South African Legal Order*, Oxford, Clarendon, (1996), 629 – 663

ERASMUS, H.J. & BARROW, O.J., *Die Wet op die Hooggeregshof 59 van 1959 en die Wet op Landdroshowe 32 van 1944* 8th ed, Cape Town, Juta, (1994)

ERASMUS, J., *The Interaction between Property Rights and Land Reform in the New Constitutional Order in South Africa*, Unpublished Doctoral Dissertation, University of South Africa, (1998)

ESCHENBACH, J., *Der verfassungsrechtliche Schutz des Eigentums*, Berlin, Duncker und Humblot, (1996)

F

FIEBERG, G., "Legislation and Judicial Practice in Germany: Landmarks and Central Issues in the Property Question" in RWELA-MIRA, M.R. & WERLE, G. (eds), *Confronting Past Injustices – Approaches to Amnesty, Punishment, Reparation and Restitution in South Africa and Germany*, Durban, Butterworths, (1996), 79 – 88

FINER, S.E., BOGDANOR, V. & RUDDEN, B., *Comparing Constitutions*, Oxford, Clarendon Press, (1995)

FÖRSTERLING, W., *Recht der offenen Vermögensfragen*, München, Beck, (1993)

FOSTER, N.G., *German Legal System and Laws* 2nd ed, London, Blackstone Press, (1996)

FRAENKEL, E., *Der Doppelstaat*, Frankfurt, Europ. Verlagsanst., (1974)

FRECKMANN, A. & WEGERICH, T., *The German Legal System*, London, Sweet & Maxwell, (1999)

FRIEDMAN, S. & HUMPHRIES, R. (eds), *Federalism and its Foes* – Proceedings of the Institute for Multi-Party Democracy and the Centre for Policy Studies Workshop, "The Politics and Economics of Federalism: a South African Debate" held at Breadwater Lodge, Cape Town 21 – 23 August 1992 (1993)

FRIEDMAN, S. & ATKINSON, D. (eds), *South African Review 7 – The Small Miracle: South Africa's Negotiated Settlement*, Johannesburg, Ravan Press, (1994)

FROWEIN, J.A. & PEUKERT, W., *Europäische Menschenrechtskonvention-Kommentar* 2nd ed, Kehl, Engel, (1996)

FROWEIN, J.A., *Report on German Law concerning the Protection of Property in Relation to Taxation* Unpublished report (25 July 1996)

G

GREENAWALT, K., "The Enduring Significance of Neutral Principles", 1978 *Columbia Law Review (Colum L Rev)*, 982

GROTE, R., *Die Lehre von den Rechtskreisen und ihre Bedeutung für die Rechtsvergleichung auf dem Gebiete des öffentlichen Rechts – Zugleich ein Beitrag zu Aufgaben und Methode der öffentlich-rechtlichen Rechtsvergleichung*, Paper read at Max Planck Institut für ausl. öff. Recht und Völkerrecht, Heidelberg on 19 February 1999

GRUPP, T.M., *Südafrikas neue Verfassung – Mit vergleichender Betrachtung aus deutscher und europäischer Sicht,* Baden-Baden, Nomos, (1999)

GUEST, A.G. (ed), *Oxford Essays in Jurisprudence* (1961)

GUTTO, S.B., *Property and Land Reform – Constitutional and Jurisprudential Perspectives,* Durban, Butterworths, (1995)

H

HARRIS, J.W., Property Problems from Genes to Pension Funds, (1997)

HAYSOM, N., "Constitutionalism, Majoritatian Democracy and Socio-Economic Rights", 1992 *South African Journal on Human Rights (SAJHR),* 451 – 463

HAYTHORN, M. & HUTCHINSON, D., "Labour Tenants and the Law" in MURRAY, C. & O'REGAN, K., *No Place to Rest,* Cape Town, Oxford University Press, (1990), chapter 11

HEGEL, G.W., *Grundlinien der Philosophie des Rechts* (1896) translated by DYDE, S.W., *Philosophy of Right,* Repr. of the ed. London, Bell, 1896, Amherst, NY, Prometheus Books, (1996)

HENKIN, L., "Shelley v Kraemer : Notes for a Revised Opinion", 1962 *University of Pennsylvania Law Review (Univ Pa L Rev),* 473

HENKIN, L., "Some Reflections on Current Constitutional Controversy", 1961 *University of Pennsylvania Law Review (Univ Pa L Rev),* 637

HESSE, K., *Grundzüge des Verfassungsrechts* 19th ed, Heidelberg, Müller Jur. Verl., (1993)

HÖFT, E., *Öffentlichrechtliche Eigentumsbeschränkungen im römischen Bauwesen,* Unpublished Doctoral Dissertation, (1952)

HONORÉ, A.M., "Ownership" in GUEST, A. (ed), *Oxford Essays in Jurisprudence,* Oxford, Oxford University Press, (1961), chapter 5

HUMPHRIES, R., RAPOO, T. & FRIEDMAN, S., "The Shape of the Country – Negotiating Regional Government" in FRIEDMAN, S. & ATKINSON, D. (eds), *South African Review 7 – The Small Miracle: South Africa's Negotiated Settlement,* Johannesburg, Ravan Press, (1994), chapter 6

I

IPSEN, H.P., "Enteignung und Sozialisierung" in VON HIPPEL, IPSEN, VOIGT ET AL., *Verhandlungen der Tagung der Deutschen Staatsrechtslehrer zu Göttingen am 18. und 19. Oktober 1951*, Berlin, De Gruyter, (1952), 74 – 177

ISENSEE, J. & KIRCHHOF, P., *Handbuch des Staatsrechts der Bundesrepublik Deutschland* V, Heidelberg, Müller Jur. Verl., (1992)

ISENSEE, J. & KIRCHHOF, P., *Handbuch des Staatsrechts der Bundesrepublik Deutschland* VI, Heidelberg, Müller Jur. Verl., (1989)

J

JARASS, H.D. / PIEROTH, B., *Grundgesetz für die Bundesrepublik Deutschland,* 3rd ed München, Beck, (1995)

JEFFRESS, D.A., "Resolving Rival Claims on East German Property Upon German Unification", 1991 *Yale Law Journal (Yale LJ)*, 527 – 549

JUNG, Y., *Das deutsche und das koreanische Enteignungsinstitut – Insbesondere die Enteignung zugunsten privater Unternehmen nach dem Grundgesetz der Bundesrepublik Deutschland sowie nach der Verfassung der Republik Korea*, Rechtswissenschaftliche Forschung und Entwicklung Band 274, München, VVF, (1991)

K

KA MDUMBE, F., "Socio-Economic Rights: Van Biljon versus Soobramoney", 1998 *SA Publiekreg / Public Law (SAPR/PL)*, 460 – 470

KASER, M., *Eigentum und Besitz im älteren römischen Recht*, Weimar, (1943)

KENTRIDGE, J. & SPITZ, D., "Interpretation" in CHASKALSON, M., KENTRIDGE, J. ET AL. (eds), *Constitutional Law of South Africa*, Cape Town, Juta, (1996), chapter 11

KIMMINICH, O., "Artikel 14" in VON MANGOLDT, H. / KLEIN, F., *Bonner Kommentar*, Hamburg, Heitmann, (1992)

KIMMINICH, O., "Eigentum und Freiheit" in ABELEIN, M. & KIMMINICH, O. (eds), *Studien zum Staats- und Völkerrecht – Festschrift für Hermann Raschhofer zum 70. Geburtstag am 26. Juli 1975*, Kallmünz, Lassleben, (1977), 105 – 121

KIMMINICH, O., "Property Rights" in STARCK C (ed) *Rights, Institutions and Impact of International Law according to the Basic Law*, Baden-Baden, Nomos, (1987), 75 – 91

KIMMINICH, O., *Die Eigentumsgarantie im Prozeß der Wiedervereinigung – Zur Bestandskraft der agrarischen Bodenrechtsordnung der DDR*, Frankfurt am Main, Landwirtschaftl. Rentenbank, (1990)

KIMMINICH, O., *Eigentum Enteignung Entschädigung – Eine Kommentierung des Art. 14 GG*, Hamburg, Heitmann, (1976)

KLEYN, D., "The Constitutional Protection of Property: a Comparison between the German and the South African Approach", 1996 *SA Publiekreg / Public Law (SAPR/PL)*, 402 – 445

KLEYN, D., BORAINE, A. & DU PLESSIS, W., *Silberberg & Schoeman's Law of Property* 3rd ed (1992)

KÖTZ, H., "The Role of the Judge in the Court-room: The Common Law and Civil Law Compared", 1987 *Tydskrif vir die Suid-Afrikaanse Reg (TSAR)*, 35 – 43

KOMMERS, D.P., *The Constitutional Jurisprudence of the Federal Republic of Germany* 2nd ed, Durham, Duke University Press, (1997)

KROEZE, I., *Between Conceptualism and Constitutionalism: Private-law and Constitutional Perspectives on Property* Unpublished Doctoral Dissertation, University of South Africa, (1997)

KROEZE, I., *Between Conceptualism and Constitutionalism: The South African Property Concept*, Unpublished paper, (1997)

KROEZE, I.J., "The Impact of the Bill of Rights on Property Law", 1994 *SA Publiekreg / Public Law (SAPR/PL)*, 322 – 331

KUNIG, P., "German Constitutional Law and the Environment", 1983 *Adelaide Law Review (Adel LR)*, 318 – 332

KUNIG, P., "Staatsorganisationsrechtliche Grundentscheidungen des Grundgesetzes", 1990 *Jura (Special edition for first semester in East and West)*, 49 – 60

KUNIG, P., "The Principle of Social Justice" in KARPEN (ed), *The Constitution of the Federal Republic of Germany – Essays on the Basic Rights and Principles of the Basic Law with a Translation of the Basic Law*, Baden-Baden, Nomos, (1988), 187 – 204

L

LANDSBERG, E., *Das Recht des bürgerlichen Gesetzbuches vom 18. VIII. 1896*, vol I, Berlin, (1906)

LATSKY, J., "The Development Facilitation Act 67 of 1995" in BUDLENDER, G., LATSKY, J. & ROUX, T., *Juta's New Land Law* (1998)

LAWSON, F.H. (chief ed), *Property and Trust* International Encyclopaedia of Comparative Law VI (1975)

LEE, R.W., *Introduction to Roman Dutch Law* 5th ed, London Clarendon Press (1953)

LEISNER, W., "Das Bodenreform-Urteil des Bundesverfassungsgerichts: Kriegsfolge- und Eigentumsentscheidung", 1991 *Neue Juristische Wochenschrift (NJW)*, 1569 – 1575

LEISNER, W., "Eigentum" in ISENSEE, J. & KIRCHHOF, P., *Handbuch des Staatsrechts der Bundesrepublik Deutschland* VI, Heidelberg, Müller Jur. Verl., (1989), 1023 – 1097

LEISNER, W., "Eigentumswende? Liegt der Grundwasser-Entscheidung des Bundesverfassungsgerichts ein neues Eigentumsverständnis zugrunde?", 1983 *Deutsches Verwaltungsblatt (DVBl)*, 61 – 67

LEISNER, W., *Eigentum – Schriften zu Eigentumsgrundrecht und Wirtschaftsverfassung 1970 – 1996*, Berlin, Duncker & Humblot, (1996)

LERCHE, P., "Grundrechtlicher Schutzbereich, Grundrechtsprägung und Grundrechtseingriff" in ISENSEE, J. & KIRCHHOF, P. (eds), *Handbuch des Staatsrechts der Bundesrepublik Deutschland* V, Heidelberg, Müller Jur. Verl., (1992), 739 – 773

LETSOALO, E.M., *Land Reform in South Africa – A Black Perspective*, Braamfontein, Skotaville Publ., (1987)

LEWIS, C., "The Modern Concept of Ownership of Land", 1985 *Acta Juridica*, 241 – 266

LEWIS, C., "The Right to Private Property in a New Political Dispensation in South Africa", 1992 *South African Journal on Human Rights (SAJHR)*, 389 – 430

LIMPENS, H., *Funktion & Grenzen der Inhaltsbestimmung des Eigentums im Sinne von Art. 14 Absatz 1 Satz 2 des Grundgesetzes*, Doctoral Dissertation, University of Köln, (1973)

M

MAASDORP, A.F.S., *Institutes of South African Law* 10th ed, (Hall) Cape Town Juta (1976)

MALHERBE, E.F.J., "Die Sertifisering van die 1996 Grondwet", 1997 *Tydskrif vir die Suid-Afrikaanse Reg (TSAR)*, 356 – 370

MARCUS, T., "Land Reform – Considering National, Class and Gender Issues", 1990 *South African Journal on Human Rights (SAJHR)*, 178 – 194

MAURER, H., *Allgemeines Verwaltungsrecht (Grundrisse des Rechts)* 11ᵗʰ ed, München, Beck, (1997)

MCLEAN, J. (ed), *Property and the Constitution* Oxford, Hart, (1999)

MEIER-HAYOZ, A., "Vom Wesen des Eigentums" in KELLER, M. (ed), *Revolution der Technik Evolutionen des Rechts – Festgabe zum 60. Geburtstag von Karl Oftinger*, Zürich, Schulthess, (1969)

MEYER-ABICH, J., *Der Schutzzweck der Eigentumsgarantie*, Berlin, Duncker & Humblot, (1980)

MICHELMAN, F., " Property as a Constitutional Right ", 1981 *Washington & Lee Law Review*, 1097

MILTON, J.R., "Ownership" in ZIMMERMANN, R. & VISSER, D.P. (eds), *Southern Cross – Civil Law and Common Law in South Africa*, Cape Town, Oxford University Press, (1996), chapter 20

MOELLENDORF, D., "Reasoning about Resources: Soobramoney and the Future of Socio-Economic Rights Claims", 1998 *South African Journal on Human Rights (SAJHR)*, 327 – 333

MOHNHAUPT, H., "Zur Geschichte des Rechtsstaats in Deutschland: Begriff und Funktion eines schwierigen Verfassungsprinzips", 1993/94 *Acta Facultatis Politico-Iuridicae Universitatis Scientiarum Budapestinensis de Rolando Eötvös Nominatae*, 39 – 60

MÜLLER, K., *Sachenrecht* 4th ed Köln, Heymann (1997)

MUNZER, S.R., *A Theory of Property*, Cambridge, Cambridge University Press, (1990)

MUREINIK, E., "Beyond a Charter of Luxuries: Economic Rights in the Constitution", 1992 *South African Journal on Human Rights (SAJHR)*, 464 – 474

MURPHY, J., "Insulating Land Reform from Constitutional Impugnment: An Indian case study", 1992 *South African Journal on Human Rights (SAJHR)*, 362 – 388

MURPHY, J., "Interpreting the Property Clause in the Constitution Act of 1993", 1995 *SA Publiekreg / Public Law (SAPR/PL)*, 107 – 130

MURPHY, J., "Property Rights and Judicial Restraint: a Reply to Chaskalson", 1994 *South African Journal on Human Rights (SAJHR)*, 385 – 398

MURPHY, J., "The Ambiguous Nature of Property Rights", 1993 *Journal for Juridical Science (JJS)*, 35 – 66

MURPHY, J., "The Restitution of Land after Apartheid: Constitutional and Legislative Framework" in RWELAMIRA, R.W. & WERLE, G. (eds), *Confronting Past Injustices – Approaches to Amnesty, Punishment, Reparation and Restitution in South Africa and Germany*, Durban, Butterworths, (1996), 113 – 132

MURRAY, C. & O'REGAN, K., *No Place to Rest*, Cape Town, Oxford University Press, (1990), chapter 11

MUßGNUG, R., "Verfassungsrechtlicher und gesetzlicher Schutz vor konfiskatorischen Steuern", 1991 *Juristen Zeitung (JZ)*, 993 – 999

O

OLZEN, D., "Die geschichtliche Entwicklung des zivilrechtlichen Eigentumsbegriffs", 1984 *Juristische Schulung (JuS)*, 328 – 336

OSSENBÜHL, F., "Economic and Occupational Rights" in KIRCHHOF, P. & KOMMERS, D. (eds), *Germany and its Basic Law*, Baden-Baden, Nomos, (1993), 251 – 282

P

PAPIER, H.J., "Artikel 14" in MAUNZ, T. & DÜRIG, G., *Grundgesetz Kommentar*, München, Beck, (1994), chapter 14

PAPIER, H.J., *Recht der öffentlichen Sachen* 3rd ed, Berlin, De Gruyter, (1998)

PATERSON, T., *Eckard's Principles of Civil Procedure in the Magistrates' Courts* Cape Town, Juta (1996)

PIENAAR, G., "Ontwikkelings in die Suid-Afrikaanse Eiendomsbegrip in Perspektief", 1986 *Tydskrif vir die Suid-Afrikaanse Reg (TSAR)*, 295 – 308

PIENAAR, G., "Huurarbeiders – Baas of Klaas?", 1997 *Tydskrif vir die Suid-Afrikaanse Reg (TSAR)*, 131 – 144

PIENAAR, J.M., "Farm Workers: Extending Security of Tenure in Terms of Recent Legislation", 1998 *SA Publiekreg / Public Law (SAPR/PL)*, 423 – 437

PIENAAR, J.M., "Labour Tenancy: Recent Developments in Case Law", 1998 *Stellenbosch Law Review (Stell LR)*, 311 – 325

PIENAAR, J.M., "Land Reform" (2003) in forthcoming, updated edition of Silberberg & Schoeman's Law of Property (2002/2003)

PIENAAR, J.M., "Land Reform, Labour Tenants and the applications of the Land Reform (Labour Tenants) Act", 1997 *Tydskrif vir die Suid-Afrikaanse Reg (TSAR)*, 538 – 548

PIENAAR, J.M., *Nuwe Sakeregtelike Ontwikkelings op die Gebied van Grondhervorming*, Inaugural Address University of Stellenbosch, (1997)

PIENAAR, J.M. & MULLER, A., "The Impact of the Prevention of Illegal Eviction from and Unlawful Occupation of Land Act 19 of 1998 on Homelessness and Unlawful Occupation within the Present Statutory Framework", 1999 *Stellenbosch Law Review (Stell LR)*, 370 – 396

PIEROTH, B. & SCHLINK, B., *Grundrechte – Staatsrecht II* 10th ed, Heidelberg, Müller Jur. Verl., (1994)

PIEROTH, B. & SCHLINK, B., *Grundrechte – Staatsrecht II* 14th ed, Heidelberg, Müller Jur. Verl., (1998)

PIEROTH, B. & SCHLINK, B., *Grundrechte – Staatsrecht II* 7th ed Heidelberg, Müller Jur. Verl., (1991)

PREIßLER, S., *Die Rückgabe von Landrechten in Südafrika*, Sinzheim, Pro-Universitate-Verl., (1998)

PRETORIUS, J.L., *Die Begrip Openbare Belang en die Burgervryheidsbeperking* Unpublished Doctoral Dissertation, University of the Orange Free State (1986)

PRIES, S., *Das Neubauerneigentum in der ehemaligen DDR*, Frankfurt am Main, Lang, (1993)

Q

QUINT, P.E., *The Imperfect Union – Constitutional Structures of German Unification*, Princeton, Princeton Univ. Press, (1997)

R

RAUTENBACH, I.M., *General Provisions of the South African Bill of Rights*, Durban, Butterworths, (1995)

REICH, C.A., "The New Property", 1964 *Yale Law Journal (Yale LJ)*, 733 – 787

RICHTER, I. & SCHUPPERT, G.F., *Casebook Verfassungsrecht* 3rd ed, München, Beck, (1996)

RITTSTIEG, H., *Eigentum als Verfassungsproblem – zu Geschichte und Gegenwart des Bürgerlichen Verfassungsstaates*, Darmstadt, Wiss. Buchges., (1976)

ROBBERS, G., *An Introduction to German Law*, Baden-Baden, Nomos, (1998)

ROBERTSON, M., "Land and Human Rights in South Africa: (A reply to Marcus and Skweyiya)", 1992 *South African Journal on Human Rights (SAJHR)*, 215 – 227

ROUX, T., "Balancing competing Property Interests", 1993 *South African Journal on Human Rights (SAJHR)*, 539 – 548

ROUX, T., "The Restitution of Land Rights Act" in BUDLENDER, G., LATSKY, J. & ROUX, T., *Juta's New Land Law*, Cape Town, Juta, (1998) original service; (1998) service 1

RWELAMIRA, M.R. & WERLE, G. (eds), *Confronting Past Injustices – Approaches to Amnesty, Punishment, Reparation and Restitution in South Africa and Germany*, Durban, Butterworths, (1996)

RYCROFT, A.J., "The Protection of Socio-Economic Rights" in CORDER (ed), *Essays on Law & Social Practice in South Africa*, Cape Town, Juta, (1988), chapter 10

S

SACHS, A., "Constitutional Developments in South Africa", 1996 *New York Journal of International Law and Politics (NYU J Int'l L & P)*, 695 – 709

SACHS, A., *Advancing Human Rights in South Africa*, Cape Town, Oxford University Press, (1992)

SALTER, M.G., "Hegel and the Social Dynamics of Property Law" in HARRIS (ed), *Property Problems from Genes to Pension Funds*, London, Kluwer, (1997), chapter 19

SCHNAUDER, F., "Die Relativität der Sondernutzungsrechte" in BUB, W.-R. (ed), *Festschrift für Johannes Bärmann und Hermann Weitnauer* (1990), 567

SCHOCH, F., "Die Haftung aus enteignungsgleichem und enteignendem Eingriff", 1990 *Juristische Ausbildung (Jura)*, 140 – 150

SCHULTZ, F., *Classical Roman Law*, Oxford, Clarendon Press, (1951; reprinted in 1992), 334 – 380

SCHUPPERT, G.F., "The Right to Property" in KARPEN, U. (ed), *The Constitution of the Federal Republic of Germany*, Baden-Baden, Nomos, (1988), 107 – 119

SCHWABE, J., *Die sogenannte Drittwirkung der Grundrechte*, München, Goldmann, (1971)

SCOLLO-LAVIZZARI, C.E., *Restitution of Land Rights in an Administrative Law Environment – The German and South African Procedures Compared* LL M Research Dissertation, University of Cape Town, (1996)

SEILER, H.H., "§ 903" and "§ 904" in STAUDINGER, J., *Kommentar zum Bürgerlichen Gesetzbuch mit Einführungsgesetz und Nebengesetzen (Drittes Buch Sachenrecht §§ 903 – 924)* BEITZKE, G. (ed), 13th revised edition, Berlin, Sellier-de Gruyter (1996)

SEILER, H.H., "Vorbemerkungen zu §§ 903 ff" in STAUDINGER, J., *Kommentar zum Bürgerlichen Gesetzbuch mit Einführungsgesetz und Nebengesetzen (Drittes Buch Sachenrecht §§ 903 – 924)* BEITZKE, G. (ed), 13th revised edition, Berlin, Sellier-de Gruyter (1996)

SHAPIRO, F.R., "The Most-Cited Law Review Articles", 1985 *California Law Review*, 1540 – 1554

SKWEYIYA, Z., "Towards a Solution to the Land Question in Post-Apartheid South Africa: Problems and Models", 1990 *South African Journal on Human Rights (SAJHR)*, 195 – 214

SOBOTA, K., *Das Prinzip Rechtsstaat – Verfassungs- und verwaltungsrechtliche Aspekte*, Tübingen, Mohr, (1997)

SONTIS, J.M., "Strukturelle Betrachtungen zum Eigentumsbegriff" in PAULUS, G., *Festschrift für Karl Larenz zum 70. Geburtstag*, München, Beck, (1973), 981–1002

SOUTHERN, M., "Restitution or Compensation: The Land Question in East Germany", 1993 *ICLQ (International and Comparative Law Quarterly)*, 690 – 697

SOUTHWOOD, M.D., *Compulsory Acquisition of Rights*, Cape Town, Juta (2000)

STAUDINGER, J., *Kommentar zum Bürgerlichen Gesetzbuch mit Einführungsgesetz und Nebengesetzen (Drittes Buch Sachenrecht §§ 903 – 924)* BEITZKE, G. (ed), 13th revised edition, Sellier-de Gruyter, (1996)

STERN, K., "A Society based on the Rule of Law and Social Justice: Constitutional Model of the Federal Republic of Germany", 1981 *Tydskrif vir die Suid-Afrikaanse Reg (TSAR)*, 241 – 250

SWANSON, E., "A Land Claims Court for South Africa: Report on work in Progress", 1992 *South African Journal on Human Rights (SAJHR)*, 332 – 343

T

TAPPERT, W., *Die Wiedergutmachung von Staatsunrecht der SBZ/DDR durch die Bundesrepublik Deutschland nach der Wiedervereinigung*, Berlin, Berlin-Verl. Spitz (1995)

THORMANN, M., *Abstufungen in der Sozialbindung des Eigentums – Zur Bestimmung von Inhalt und Schranken des Eigentums nach Art. 14 Absatz 1 Satz 2 GG im Spannungsfeld von Eigentumsfreiheit und Gemeinwohl*, Stuttgart, Boorberg, (1996)

U

UNDERKUFFLER, L.S., "On Property: an Essay", 1990 *Yale Law Journal (Yale LJ)*, 127 – 148

V

VAN DER KEESSEL, D.G., *Praelectiones Iuris Hodierni ad Hugonis Grotii Introductionem ad Iurisprudentiam Hollandicam* (Van Warmelo/Coertze/Gonin/Pont, Cape Town, Balkema (1961–1967))

VAN DER LINDEN, J., *Regtsgeleerd, Practicaal en Koopmans Handboek* Amsteldam, Allart (1806)

VAN DER MERWE, C.G., *LAWSA Things* XXVII, Durban, Butterworths, 3 – 195

VAN DER MERWE, C.G., "Die Wet op Deeltitels in die Lig van ons Gemeenregtelike Saak- en Eiendomsbegrip", 1974 *Tydskrif vir Hedendaagse Romeins-Hollandse Reg (THRHR)*, 113 – 132

VAN DER MERWE, C.G. & PIENAAR, J., "Land Reform in South Africa" in JACKSON, P. AND WILDE, D.C. (eds), *The Reform of Property Law*, Vermont, Dartmouth, (1997), chapter 18

VAN DER MERWE, C.G., *Sakereg* 2nd ed, Durban, Butterworths, (1989)

VAN DER MERWE, C.G., MOHR, P. & BLUMBERG, M., "The Bill of Rights and the Rules of Sectional Title Schemes: a Comparative Perspective", 2000 *Stellenbosch Law Review / Regstydskrif (Stell LR)*, 155 – 181

VAN DER MERWE, D., "Land Tenure in South Africa: a Brief History and some Reform Proposals", 1989 *Tydskrif vir die Suid-Afrikaanse Reg (TSAR)*, 663

VAN DER MERWE, D., "Land Tenure in South Africa: Changing the face of Property Law", 1990 *Stellenbosch Law Review (Stell LR)*, 321 – 335

VAN DER MERWE, D., "The Roman-Dutch Law: From Virtual Reality to Constitutional Resource", 1998 *Tydskrif vir die Suid-Afrikaanse Reg (TSAR)*, 1 – 19

VAN DER VYVER, J.D., "Expropriation, Rights, Entitlements and Surface Support of Land", 1988 *South African Law Journal (SALJ)*, 1 – 16

VAN DER VYVER, J.D., "The Doctrine of Private-Law Rights" in STRAUSS, S.A. (ed), *Huldigingsbundel vir WA Joubert*, Durban, Butterworths, (1988), 201 – 246

VAN DER WALT, A.J., " 'Double' Property Guarantees: a Structural and Comparative Analysis", 1998 *South African Journal on Human Rights (SAJHR)*, 560 – 586

VAN DER WALT, A.J., "Bartolus se Omskrywing van Dominium en die Interpretasies daarvan sedert die Vyftiende Eeu", 1986 *Tydskrif vir Hedendaagse Romeins-Hollandse Reg (THRHR)*, 305 – 321

VAN DER WALT, A.J., "Comparative Notes on the Constitutional Protection of Property Rights", 1993 *Recht & Kritiek*, 263 – 297

VAN DER WALT, A.J., "Gedagtes oor die Herkoms en Ontwikkeling van die Suid-Afrikaanse Eiendomsbegrip", 1988 *De Jure* 16 – 35; 306 – 325

VAN DER WALT, A.J., "Introduction" in VAN DER WALT, A.J. (ed), *Land Reform and the Future of Landownership in South Africa*, Cape Town, Juta, (1991), 1 – 8

VAN DER WALT, A.J., "Living with New Neighbours: Landownership, Land Reform and the Property Clause", forthcoming 2002 *South African Law Journal (SALJ)*

VAN DER WALT, A.J., "Marginal Notes on Powerful(l) Legends: Critical Perspectives on Property Theory", 1995 *Tydskrif vir die Hedendaagse Romeins-Hollandse Reg (THRHR)*, 396 – 420

VAN DER WALT, A.J., "Moving Towards Recognition of Constructive Expropriation", forthcoming 2002 *Tydskrif vir die Hedendaagse Romeins-Hollandse Reg (THRHR)*

VAN DER WALT, A.J., "Notes on the Interpretation of the Property Clause in the New Constitution", 1994 *Tydskrif vir Hedendaagse Romeins-Hollandse Reg (THRHR)*, 181 – 203

VAN DER WALT, A.J., "Ownership and Personal Freedom: Subjectivism in Bernhard Windscheid's Theory of Ownership", 1993 *Tydskrif vir Hedendaagse Romeins-Hollandse Reg (THRHR)*, 569 – 589

VAN DER WALT, A.J., "Property Rights and Hierarchies of Power: a Critical Evaluation of Land-Reform Policy in South Africa", 1999 *Koers*, 259 – 294

VAN DER WALT, A.J., "Property Rights, Land Rights, and Environmental Rights" in VAN WYK, D., DUGARD, J., ET AL. (eds), *Rights and Constitutionalism – The New South African Legal Order* (1996)

VAN DER WALT, A.J., "Property Rights v Religious Rights: Bührmann v Nkosi", forthcoming 2002 *Stellenbosch Law Review (Stell LR)*

VAN DER WALT, A.J., "Rights and Reforms in Property Theory – A Review of Property Theories and Debates in Recent Literature: Part III", 1995 *Tydskrif vir die Suid-Afrikaanse Reg (TSAR)*, 493 – 526

VAN DER WALT, A.J., "Roman Law, Fundamental Rights, and Land Reform in Southern Africa", 1998 *Tydskrif vir Hedendaagse Romeins-Hollandse Reg (THRHR)*, 400 – 422

VAN DER WALT, A.J., "Subject and Society in Property Theory – a Review of Property Theories and Debates in Recent Literature: Part II", 1995 *Tydskrif vir die Suid-Afrikaanse Reg (TSAR)*, 322 – 345

VAN DER WALT, A.J., "The Constitutional Property Clause and Police Power Regulation of Intangible Commercial Property – A Comparative Analysis of Case Law" in JACKSON, P. & WILDE, D.C., *Property Law: Current Issues and Debates*, Vermont, Dartmouth (1999), 208–280

VAN DER WALT, A.J., "The Fragmentation of Land Rights", 1992 *South African Journal on Human Rights (SAJHR)*, 431 – 450

VAN DER WALT, A.J., "The Future of Common Law Landownership" in VAN DER WALT, A.J. (ed), *Land Reform and the Future of Land-ownership in South Africa*, Cape Town, Juta, (1991), 21 – 36

VAN DER WALT, A.J., "The Impact of the Bill of Rights on Property Law", 1993 *SA Publiekreg / Public Law (SAPR/PL)*, 296 – 319

VAN DER WALT, A.J., "The Limits of Constitutional Property", 1997 *SA Publiekreg / Public Law (SAPR/PL)*, 275 – 330

VAN DER WALT, A.J., "Towards a Theory of Rights in Property: Exploratory Observations on the Paradigm of Post-Apartheid Property Law", 1995 *SA Publiekreg / Public Law (SAPR/PL)*, 298 – 345

VAN DER WALT, A.J., "Towards the Development of Post-Apartheid Land Law: An Exploratory Survey", 1990 *De Iure*, 1 – 45.

VAN DER WALT, A.J., "Tradition on Trial: a Critical Analysis of the Civil-Law Tradition in South African Property Law", 1995 *South African Journal on Human Rights (SAJHR)*, 169 – 206

VAN DER WALT, A.J., "Unity and Pluralism in Property Theory – a Review of Property Theories and Debates in Recent Literature: Part I", 1995 *Tydskrif vir die Suid-Afrikaanse Reg (TSAR)*, 15 – 42

VAN DER WALT, A.J. & BOTHA, H., "Coming to Grips with the New Constitutional Order: Critical Comments on Harksen v Lane NO", 1998 *SA Publiekreg / Public Law (SAPR/PL)*, 17 – 41

VAN DER WALT, A.J. & PIENAAR, G.J., *Introduction to the Law of Property*, Cape Town, Juta, (1996)

VAN DER WALT, A.J. & PIENAAR, G.J., *Introduction to the Law of Property* 2nd ed, Cape Town, Juta, (1997)

VAN DER WALT, A.J., *Constitutional Property Clauses – A Comparative Analysis*, Cape Town, Juta, (1999)

VAN DER WALT, A.J., *Die Ontwikkeling van Houerskap*, Doctoral Dissertation Potchefstroom University for Christian Higher Education, (1985)

VAN DER WALT, A.J., *The Constitutional Property Clause – A Comparative Analysis of Section 25 of the South African Constitution of 1996*, Cape Town, Juta, (1997)

VAN MAANEN, G., "Ownership as a Constitutional Right in South Africa – Articles 14 & 15 of the Grundgesetz: the German Experience", 1993 *Recht & Kritiek*, 74 – 95

VAN WYK, D., " 'n Paar opmerkings en vrae oor die nuwe Grondwet", 1997 *Tydskrif vir Hedendaagse Romeins-Hollandse Reg (THRHR)*, 377 – 394

VENTER, F., "A Hierarchy of Constitutional Values" in *Constitution and Law* (Seminar Report of the papers delivered at the Colloquium of the Faculty of Law of the Potchefstroomse Universiteit vir Christelike Hoër Onderwys on 31 October 1997), 17 – 19

VENTER, F., "Aspects of the South African Constitution of 1996: An African Democratic and Social Federal Rechtsstaat?", 1997 *Zeitschrift für ausländisches öffentliches Recht und Völkerrecht (ZaöRV)*, 51 – 82

VENTER, F., VAN DER WALT, C.F., VAN DER WALT, ET AL., *Regsnavorsing Metode en Publikasie*, Cape Town, Juta, (1990)

VISSER, D. & ROUX, T., "Giving back the Country: South Africa's Restitution of Land Rights Act, 1994 in Context" in RWELAMIRA, R.W. & WERLE, G. (eds), *Confronting Past Injustices – Approaches to Amnesty, Punishment, Reparation and Restitution in South Africa and Germany*, Durban, Butterworths, (1996), 89 – 111

VISSER, D.P., "The 'Absoluteness' of Ownership: the South African Common Law in Perspective", 1985 *Acta Juridica*, 39 – 52

VOET, J., *Elementa Juris*, Leiden (1737)

VON BRÜNNECK, A., "Die Eigentumsordnung im Nationalsozialismus", 1979 *Kritische Justiz*, 151 – 172

VON BRÜNNECK, A., *Die Eigentumsgarantie des Grundgesetzes*, Baden-Baden, Nomos, (1984)

VON DOEMMING, K., FÜSSLEIN, R. & MATZ, W., "Entstehungsgeschichte der Artikel des Grundgesetzes", 1951 (1) *Jahrbuch des öffentlichen Rechts der Gegenwart (Neue Fassung)*, 144 – 154

VON HEINEGG, W.H. & HALTERN, U.R., "Keine Angst vor Art. 14 GG!", 1993 *Juristische Schulung – Zeitschrift für Studium und Ausbildung (JuS)*, 121 – 126; 213 – 217

VON MANGOLDT, H. / KLEIN, F., *Bonner Kommentar*, München, Vahlen, (1992)

VON MÜNCH, I. / KUNIG, P., *Grundgesetz-Kommentar I*, 4th ed, München, Beck, (1992), Artikel 1 – 19

W

WATTS, R.L., "Is the New Constitution Federal or Unitary?" in DE VILLIERS, B. (ed), *Birth of a Constitution*, Cape Town, Juta, (1994), 75 – 88

WEBER, W., "Das Eigentum und seine Garantie in der Krise" in PAW-LOWSKI, H.-M. & WIEACKER, F. (eds), *Festschrift für Karl Michaelis zum 70. Geburtstag am 21. Dezember 1970*, Göttingen, Vandenhoeck & Ruprecht, (1972), 316 – 336

WECHSLER, H., "Towards Neutral Principles of Constitutional Law", 1959 *Harvard Law Review (Harv L Rev)*, 1

WENDT, R., "Art. 14 [Eigentum, Erbrecht und Enteignung]" in SACHS, M. (ed), *Grundgesetz Kommentar*, München, Beck (1996), 482 – 528

WENDT, R., *Eigentum und Gesetzgebung*, Hamburg, Heitmann, (1985)

WESTERMANN, H.P., *BGB-Sachenrecht*, 9th ed, Heidelberg, Müller, Jur. Verl., (1994)

WIECHERS, M., "Grondslae van die Moderne Rechtsstaat / Foundations of the Modern Rechtsstaat", 1998 *Tydskrif vir Hedendaagse Romeins-Hollandse Reg (THRHR)*, 624 – 634

WIELAND, J., "Artikel 14 [Eigentum Erbrecht, Enteignung]" in DREI-ER, H. (ed), *Grundgesetz Kommentar I*, Tübingen, Mohr-Siebeck, (1996)

WIELING, H.J., *Sachenrecht*, Berlin, Springer, 2nd ed (1994); 3rd ed (1997)

WOOLMAN, S., "Application" in CHASKALSON, M., KENTRIDGE, J. ET AL. (eds), *Constitutional Law of South Africa*, Service Issue 2 Cape Town, Juta, (1996), chapter 11

WOOLMAN, S., "Limitation" in CHASKALSON, M., KENTRIDGE, J. ET AL. (eds), *Constitutional Law of South Africa*, Cape Town, Juta, (1996), chapter 12

WOOLMAN, S., "Out of Order? Out of Balance? The Limitation Clause of the Final Constitution", 1997 *South African Journal of Human Rights (SAJHR)*, 102 – 134

Z

ZACHER, H.F., "Was können wir über das Sozialstaatsprinzip wissen?" in STÖDTER, R. & THIEME, W. (eds), *Hamburg, Deutschland, Europa – Beiträge zum deutschen und europäischen Verfassungs-, Verwaltungs- und Wirtschaftsrecht – Festschrift für Hans Peter Ipsen zum siebzigsten Geburtstag*, Tübingen, Mohr, (1977), 207 – 267

Zimmermann, R. & Visser, D., "Introduction: South African Law as a Mixed Legal System" in Zimmermann, R. & Visser, D. (eds), *Southern Cross – Civil Law and Common Law in South Africa*, Cape Town, Oxford University Press (1996), 1 – 30

Newspaper articles

Daily Mail & Guardian (1998-12-23): "Bushmen get a stake in game park" online at http://www.mg.co.za [21.05.1999]

Daily Mail & Guardian (1999-05-20): "New farm, but not home for former guerrilla trackers" online at http://www.mg.co.za [21.05. 1999]

Die Burger (04-08-1999) 1: Brummer "Kaap kreun onder plakkery"

Die Burger (10-09-1999) 10: Reitz "Huisagterstand meer as in 1994"

Finansies en Tegniek (2000-05-05) 10 - 12: Van Zyl "Grond – So lyk SA hervorming" / "Wat Zimbabwe vir die rand inhou" / "Maak plan of ly honger" / "SA is nie Zimbabwe nie" / "So lyk die wette nou"

Sunday Independent (1997-10-19) 11: "The law created apartheid, but apartheid didn't quite destroy the law" Edited version of the submission of Mohamed, Chaskalson, Corbett, Van Heerden, and Langa to the Truth and Reconciliation Commission

Digest of cases

South Africa*

Administrator Natal and Another v Sibiya 1992 4 SA 532 (A)

---

* Where cases have been reported in more than one publication, references to the different reports are provided and separated by a semi-colon. References in the footnotes are, however, limited to one per decision. In general, the decisions handed down by the Land Claims Court and the Constitutional Court are also available online at http://www.law.wits.ac.za [09.10.2000]. Those decisions that have not yet been reported in either the South African Law Reports or the Butterworths Constitutional Law Reports at the time of completion of this dissertation, are quoted by means of their case numbers, and where possible an online reference.

Administrator Transvaal and Another v J van Streepen (Kempton Park) (Pty) Ltd 1990 4 SA 644 (A)

African Farms and Townships Ltd v Cape Town Municipality 1961 3 SA 392 (C)

Albertyn v Bhekaphezulu 1999 2 SA 538 (LCC); 1999 (2) SA 538 (LCC)

Beckenstrater v Sand River Irrigation Board 1964 4 SA 510 (T)

Bührmann v Nkosi 2000 1 SA 1145 (T)

Cape Killarney Property Investments (Pty) Ltd v Mahamba and Others 2000 2 SA 67 (C).

Certification of the Constitution of the Republic of South Africa 1996 (First Certification case) 1996 BCLR 1253 (CC); 1994 4 SA 744 (CC)

Chetty v Naidoo 1974 3 SA 13 (A)

Conradie v Fortuin (LCC) 1999 (3) SA 1027 (LCC)

Dawood and Another v Minister of Home Affairs and others; Shalabi and Another v Minister of Home Affairs and Others; Thomas and Another v Minister of Home Affairs and Others 2000 (3) SA 936 (CC)

De Jager v Sisana 1930 AD 71

De Lange v Smuts NO and Others 1998 3 SA 785 (CC); 1998 7 BCLR 779 (CC)

Diepsloot Residents' and Landowners' Association and Others v Administrator Transvaal and Others 1993 1 SA 577 (T); 1993 3 SA 49 (T); 1994 3 SA 336 (A)

Du Plessis and Others v De Klerk and Another 1996 3 SA 850 (CC); 1996 5 BCLR 658 (CC)

Dulabh and Another v Department of Land Affairs 1997 4 SA 1108 (LCC) also reported as Re Dulabh: Re Erf 1687, King William's Town 1997 All SA 635 (LCC)

Durban City Council v SA Board Mills Ltd 1961 3 SA 397 (A)

DVB Behuising (Pty) Ltd v North West Provincial Government and Another Bophuthatswana High Court Case No 308/99 (27 May 1999) as yet unreported

Elektrisiteitsvoorsieningskommissie v Fourie en Andere 1988 2 SA 627 (T)

Ex parte Geldenhuys 1926 OPD 155

Ex Parte North Central and South Central Metropolitan Substructure Councils of the Durban Metropolitan Area and Another 1998 1 SA 78 (LCC)

Farjas (Pty) Ltd and Another v Regional Land Claims Commissioner, KwaZulu-Natal 1998 2 SA 900 (LCC)

Ferreira v Levin and Others; Vryenhoek and Others v Powel NO and Others 1996 1 BCLR 1 (CC); 1996 1 SA 984 (CC)

Fose v Minister of Safety and Security 1997 3 SA 786 (CC); 1997 7 BCLR 851 (CC)

Fourie v Minister van Lande en 'n Ander 1970 4 SA 165 (O)

Gien v Gien 1979 2 SA 1113 (T)

Harksen v Lane NO and Others 1997 11 BCLR 1489 (CC); 1998 (1) SA 300 (CC)

Holomisa v Argus Newspapers Ltd 1996 2 SA 588 (W); 1996 6 BCLR 836 (W)

Jeeva and Others v Receiver of Revenue Port Elizabeth and Others 1995 2 SA 433 (SE)

Johannesburg Municipal Council v Rand Townships Registrar 1910 TPD 1314

Joubert and Others v Van Rensburg and Others 2001 1 SA 753 (W)

Kanhym v Mashiloane 1999 (2) SA 55 (LCC)

Karabo v Kok 1998 4 SA 1014 (LCC).

Kerksay Investments (Pty) Ltd v Randburg Town Council 1997 1 SA 511 (T)

Katazile Mkangeli v Joubert 2001 2 SA 1191 (CC)

Katazile Mkangeli v Joubert and Others (SCA) as yet unreported. Available online at http://wwwserver.law.wits.ac.za/scrtappeal/2002/2001.doc

Khala v Minister of Safety and Security 1994 4 SA 218 (W); 1995 2 BCLR 89 (W)

Khumalo and others v Potgieter and others 1999 1 All SA 10 (N)

Klopper and Others v Mkhize and Others 1998 1 SA 406 (N)

Lategan v Koopman en Andere 1998 3 SA 457 (LCC)

Makhombothi v Klingenberg 1999 (1) SA 135 (T)

Malangu v De Jager 1996 3 SA 235 (LCC)

Malangu v De Jager 2000 3 SA 145 (LCC)

Manana and Others v Johannes 1999 1 SA 181 (LCC)

Minister of Land Affairs v Slamdien 1999 (1) All SA 608 (LCC)

Minister of the Interior v Lockhat and Others 1961 2 SA 587 (A)

Mkwanazi v Bivane Bosbou, Msimango v De Villiers; Ngema v Van der Walt; Mdletshe v Nxumalo 1999 1 All SA 59 (LCC)

Mlifi v Klingenberg 1999 2 SA 647 (LCC) (1998) 3 B All SA 636 (LCC)

Mnisi v Chauke and Others; Chauke v Provincial Secretary, Transvaal, and Others 1994 4 SA 715 (T)

Mokwena v Marie Appel Beleggings (LCC) 89/98

Mosehla v Sancor 1999 1 SA 614 (T)

Chief Nchabeleng v Chief Phasha 1998 3 SA 578 (LCC)

New National Party of South Africa v Government of the Republic of South Africa and Others 1999 (3) SA 191 (CC); 1999 5 BCLR 489 (CC)

Ngcobo and others v Salimba CC 1999 2 SA 1057 (SCA)

Ngobo and Another v Van Rensburg and Others 1999 2 SA 525 (LCC)

Nkosi v Bührmann 2002 (1) SA 372 (SCA)

Nortje and Another v AG Cape 1995 (2) SA 460 (C); 1995 2 BCLR 236

Ntuli and Others v Smit and Another 1999 2 SA 540 (LCC).

Park-Ross v Director: Office for Serious Economic Offences 1995 2 SA 148 (C); 1995 2 BCLR 198 (C)

Port Elizabeth Municipality v Peoples Dialogue on Land and Shelter and Others 2000 2 SA 1074 (SECLD).

Pretoria City Council v Walker 1998 (2) SA 363 (CC); 1998 3 BCLR 257

Protea Technology Ltd v Wainer 1997 9 BCLR 1225 (W) 1238

Qozeleni v Minister of Law and Order 1994 3 SA 625 (E); 1995 1 BCLR 75 (E)

Rademeyer and Others v Western Districts Council and Others 1998 3 SA 1011 (SECLD).

Re Dulabh: Re Erf 1687 King William's Town LCC 14/96; later reported as Dulabh and Another v Department of Land Affairs 1997 4 SA1108 (LCC)

Re Elandskloof Vereniging 1999 1 SA 176 (LCC)

Re Farmerfield Communal Property Trust 1999 (1) SA 936 (LCC)

Re Former Highlands Residents 2000 1 SA 489 (LCC)

Re Macleantown Residents Association: Re Certain Erven and Commonage in Macleantown 1996 4 SA 1272 (LCC)

Rondebosch Municipal Council v Trustees of the Western Province Agricultural Society 1911 AD 271

S v Bhulwana 1995 1 SA 509 (C); 1996 1 SA 388 (CC)

S v Lawrence; S v Negal; S v Solberg 1997 4 SA 1176 (CC); 1997 10 BCLR 1345 (CC)

S v Makwanyane and Another 1995 3 SA 391 (CC); 1995 6 BCLR 665 (CC)

S v Mhlungu and Others 1995 3 SA 867 (CC); 1995 7 BCLR 793 (CC)

S v Zuma and Others 1995 2 SA 642 (CC); 1995 4 BCLR 401 (CC)

Sanderson v Attorney-General, Eastern Cape 1998 2 SA 38 (CC); 1997 12 BCLR 1675 (CC)

Sandton Town Council v Erf 89 Sandown Extension 2 (Pty) Ltd 1988 3 SA 122 (A)

Serole v Pienaar 2000 (1) SA 328 (LCC)

Singh v North Central and South Central Metropolitan Substructure Councils of the Durban Metropolitan Area 1999 1 All SA 350 (LCC)

Slabbert v Minister van Lande 1963 3 SA 620 (T)

Soobramoney v Minister of Health KwaZulu-Natal 1998 1 SA 765 (CC), 1997 BCLR 1696 (CC)

Springs v Occupants of the Farm Kwa-Thema (1998) 4 All SA 155 (LCC)

Steinberg v South Peninsula Municipality 2001 4 SA 1243 (SCA)

Tselentis Mining (Pty) Ltd and Another v Mdlalose and Others 1998 1 SA 411 (N)

Uitenhage Local Transitional Council v Zenza and Others 1997 8 BCLR 115 (ES)

Uitkyk Farm Estates v Visser (LCC) 60/98

Van Biljon and Others v Minister of Correctional Services and Others 1997 4 SA 441 (C); 1997 6 BCLR 789 (C)

Van der Walt and Others v Lange and Others 1999 1 SA 189 (LCC)

Western Cape Provincial Government and Others: In re DVB Behuising (Pty) Ltd v North West Provincial Government and Another 2001 (1) SA 500 (CC)

White Rocks Farm (Pty) Ltd and Others & Another v Minister of Community Development 1984 3 SA 785 (N)

Woolworths (Pty) Ltd v Whitehead (Women's Legal Centre Trust Intervening) 2000 3 SA 529 (LAC)

Zulu and Others v Van Rensburg and Others 1996 4 SA 1236 (LCC)

Germany
Federal Constitutional Court
BVerfGE 1 14

BVerfGE 1 264 (Schornsteinfeger)

BVerfGE 1 97

BVerfGE 3 377

BVerfGE 3 58

BVerfGE 4 7 (Investitionshilfe)

BVerfGE 5 85

BVerfGE 6 32

BVerfGE 6 389

BVerfGE 7 129

BVerfGE 7 198 (Lüth)

BVerfGE 8 71

BVerfGE 8 210

BVerfGE 8 277

BVerfGE 9 137

BVerfGE 11 64

BVerfGE 28, 119

BVerfGE 11 105

BVerfGE 12 205

BVerfGE 13 225

BVerfGE 13 248

BVerfGE 14 263 (Feldmühle)

BVerfGE 14 288

BVerfGE 16 147

BVerfGE 16 194

BVerfGE 16 286

BVerfGE 16 94

BVerfGE 17 108

BVerfGE 17 306

BVerfGE 18 121

BVerfGE 18, 132

BVerfGE 18 315

BVerfGE 18 392

BVerfGE 19 206

BVerfGE 19 342

BVerfGE 20 351 (Tollwut)

BVerfGE 20 45

BVerfGE 21 150

BVerfGE 21 73

BVerfGE 22 180

BVerfGE 23 127

BVerfGE 23 288

BVerfGE 24 367 (Deichordnung)

BVerfGE 25 112 (Niedersächsisches Deichgesetz)

BVerfGE 25 371

BVerfGE 27 253

BVerfGE 27 344

BVerfGE 28 119

BVerfGE 30 292

BVerfGE 30 173 *(Mephisto)*

BVerfGE 31 229

BVerfGE 31 239

BVerfGE 31 275

BVerfGE 32 111

BVerfGE 34 165

BVerfGE 34 210

BVerfGE 35 263

BVerfGE 35 85

BVerfGE 36 281

BVerfGE 37 132 (Wohnraumkündigung)

BVerfGE 38 175

BVerfGE 38 348

BVerfGE 40 121

BVerfGE 40 65

BVerfGE 41 126

BVerfGE 41 153

BVerfGE 41 29

BVerfGE 41 65

BVerfGE 42 143

BVerfGE 42 263 (Contergan)

BVerfGE 45 142

BVerfGE 45 297 (Hamburger U-Bahn-Bau)

BVerfGE 45 376

BVerfGE 47 268

BVerfGE 49 382

BVerfGE 50 290 (Mitbestimmung)

BVerfGE 50 57

BVerfGE 51 115

BVerfGE 51 150

BVerfGE 51 193 (Schloßberg)

BVerfGE 52 1 (Kleingärten)

BVerfGE 53 257

BVerfGE 53 366

BVerfGE 56 249 (Dürkheimer Gondelbahn)

BVerfGE 58 137 (Pflichtexemplar)

BVerfGE 58 300 (Naßauskiesung)

BVerfGE 58 81

BVerfGE 59 275

BVerfGE 61 82

BVerfGE 62 169

BVerfGE 62 320

BVerfGE 66 234

BVerfGE 66 248 (Hochspannungsleitung)

BVerfGE 68 193

BVerfGE 68 361

BVerfGE 69 272

BVerfGE 70 191

BVerfGE 70 278

BVerfGE 72 175

BVerfGE 72 278

BVerfGE 72 66

BVerfGE 72 9

BVerfGE 73 261

BVerfGE 74 12

BVerfGE 74 129

BVerfGE 74 203

BVerfGE 74 264 (Boxberg)

BVerfGE 76 220

BVerfGE 77 84

BVerfGE 78 205

BVerfGE 78 58

BVerfGE 79 1

BVerfGE 79 174

BVerfGE 79 29

BVerfGE 80 137

BVerfGE 81 12

BVerfGE 82 159 190

BVerfGE 83 201 (Vorkaufsrecht)

BVerfGE 84 286

BVerfGE 84 90

BVerfGE 85 130

BVerfGE 87 114

BVerfGE 89 1 (Besitzrecht des Mieters)

BVerfGE 91 294 (Fortgeltung der Mietpreisbindung)

BVerfGE 1991 *NJW* 1597

BVerfG 1976 *NJW* 101 (Vermögenssteuer)

BVerfG 1988 *KTS* 564 - 565 (3K)

Decision of 21 April 1993 (1 BvR 1422/92)

Decision of 3 April 1990 (1 BvR 269/90, 1 BvR 270/90)

Decision of 7 July 1985, 1985 *DVBl* 1015

Decision of 5 June 1992, 1992 *Europäische Grundrechte Zeitung* 19

Decision of 16 July 1985 - (1 BvL 5/80), 1985 *BB* 1537 - 1540

Decision of 18 October 1993 I BvR 1335/91 1994 *NJ* 25

Decision of 15 April 1993 (1 BvR 1885/92) 1993 *NJW* 366

Federal Court of Justice

BGHZ 6 270 (1952 *NJW* 972)

BGHZ 6 276

BGHZ 23 157

BGHZ 23 235

BGHZ 23 30

BGHZ 30 241

BGHZ 30 338

BGHZ 30 338

BGHZ 37 44

BGHZ 39 198

BGHZ 44, 288.

BGHZ 45 83 (Knäckebrot)

BGHZ 48 65

BGHZ 52 371

BGHZ 55 261

BGHZ 62 96

BGHZ 72 211

BGHZ 73 146

BGHZ 77 179

BGHZ 80 111

BGHZ 90 17

BGHZ 90 4

BGHZ 91 20
BGHZ 92 34
BGHZ 97 369
BGH 1975 *NJW* 1017
BGH 1976 *NJW* 1313
BGH 1980 *NJW* 387
BGH 1986 *NVwZ* 76
BGH 1990 *NJW* 898
BGH 1994 *NJW* 188

Federal Administrative Court
BVerwGE 3 335
BVerwGE 32 135
BVerwGE 38 209
BVerwGE 4 57
BVerwGE 5 143
BVerwGE 62 224
BVerwG 1990 *DVBl* 585

Other
BayVfGH 13 141 (b)
BSG 1987 *NJW* 463
RGZ 109 319
RGZ 111 320
RGZ 129 146

Other Jurisdictions
City of Ownensboro v McCormack 581 SW 2d 3 (Ky 1979)
Davies v Minister of Lands Agriculture and Water Development 1997 1
    SA 228 (ZSC)
Flemming v Nestor 363 US 603 (1960)
Goldberg v Kelly 397 US 254 (1970)
Handyside decision 1977 *EuGRZ* 38

HD Vora v State of Maharashtra 1984 AIR 866 SC 869

Hewlett v Minister of Finance 1982 1 SA 490 (ZSC)

Holland v Scott 1882 EDC 307

Karesh v City Council 247 SE 2d 342

Marckx decision 1979 *EuGRZ* 454

Pennsylvania Coal Co v Mahon 260 US 393 (1922)

Pointe Gourde Quarrying and Transport Co Ltd v Sub-intendent of Crown Lands [1947] AC 565

Poletown Neighbourhood City Council v City of Detroit 304 NW 2d 455

R v Oakes 1986 19 CRR 308; 1986 1 SCR 103; 1986 26 DLR 4th 200 SCC; 1987 LRC (Const) 477

Shelley v Kraemer 334 US 1 (1948)

Silver v United Kingdom (1983) 5 EHRR 347

State of Bihar v Kameshwar Singh AIR (1952) SC 252

Sunday Times v United Kingdom (1980) 2 EHRR 245

Digest of statutes and policy documents

South Africa
Constitutions
(Interim) Constitution of the Republic of South Africa, 200 of 1993
(Final) Constitution of the Republic of South Africa, 1996

Legislation
Abolition of Racially Based Land Measures Act 108 of 1991; 110 of 1993
Abuse of Dependence-producing Substances and Rehabilitation Centres Act 41 of 1971
Advertising on Roads and Ribbon Development Act 21 of 1940
Agricultural Pests Act 36 of 1983
Aliens Control Act 96 of 1991
Animals Protection Act 71 of 1962
Arbitration Act 42 of 1965

Arms and Ammunition Act 75 of 1969

Atmospheric Pollution Prevention Act 45 of 1965

Black Administration Act 38 of 1927

Black Authorities Act 126 of 1951

Black Land Act 27 of 1913

Black Laws Amendment Act 42 of 1964

Black Trust and Land Act 18 of 1936

Blacks (Urban Areas) Consolidation Act 25 of 1945

Borders of Particular States Extension Act 2 of 1980

Communal Properties Associations Act 28 of 1996

Community Development Act 3 of 1966

Companies Act 61 of 1973

Conservation of Agricultural Resources Act 43 of 1983

Constitution of the Republic of South Africa Amendment Act 2 of 1994

Conversion of Certain Rights into Leasehold or Ownership Act 81 of 1988

Deeds Registries Act 47 of 1937

Development Facilitation Act 67 of 1995

Development Trust and Land Act 18 of 1936

Distribution and Transfer of Certain State Land Act 119 of 1993

Electricity Act 40 of 1958

Environment Conservation Act 73 of 1989

Expropriation Act 63 of 1975

Expropriation Amendment Act 31 of 1958

Expropriation of Lands and Arbitration Clauses Proclamation 5 of 1902 (Transvaal)

Extension of Security of Tenure Act 62 of 1997

Films and Publications Act 65 of 1996

General Law Second Amendment Act 108 of 1993

Group Areas Act 36 of 1966; 41 of 1950; 77 of 1957

Health Act 63 of 1977

Housing Act 107 of 1997

Housing Development Act (House of Delegates) 4 of 1987

Interim Protection of Informal Land Rights Act 31 of 1996

Joint Administration of Certain Matters Act 99 of 1993

Labour Relations Act 66 of 1995

Land Affairs General Amendment Act 11 of 1995

Land Reform (Labour Tenants) Act 3 of 1996

Land Restitution and Reform Laws Amendment Act 18 of 1999; 63 of 1997; 78 of 1996

Land Titles Adjustment Act 111 of 1993

Land Use Planning Ordinance 15 of 1985 (Cape)

Less Formal Township Establishment Act 112 of 1991; 113 of 1991

Local Government Ordinance 17 of 1939 (T)

Minerals Act 50 of 1991

Municipal Act 45 of 1882

National Building Regulations and Building Standards Act 103 of 1977

National Road Traffic Act 1993 of 1996

National States Constitutions Act 21 of 1971

Physical Planning Act 125 of 1991

Prevention of Illegal Eviction from and Unlawful Occupation of Land Act 19 of 1998

Prevention of Illegal Squatting Act 52 of 1951

Property Time-Sharing Control Act 75 of 1983

Provision of Certain Land and Assistance Act 126 of 1993 (now: Provision of Certain Land for Settlement Act 126 of 1993)

Provision of Certain Land for Settlement Amendment Act 26 of 1998

Public Service Act 1994 (Transkei)

Publications Act 42 of 1974

Regulation of Joint Executive Action Act 109 of 1993

Restitution of Land Rights Act 22 of 1994

Rural Areas Act (House of Representatives) 9 of 1987

Second General Laws Amendment Act 108 of 1993

Share Block Control Act 59 of 1980

Slums Act 6 of 1959; 76 of 1979

South Africa Act 1909

Special Investigating Units and Special Tribunals Act 74 of 1996

Transformation of Certain Rural Areas Act 94 of 1998

Upgrading of Land Tenure Rights Act 112 of 1991

Upgrading of Land Tenure Rights Amendment Act 34 of 1996

Government Notices R29, R 30, R402, R 404, R 405 of 9 March 1988
 and R293

Proclamation R176 of 02 December 1994

Proclamation R188 of 18 June 1969

Proclamation R293 of 16 November 1962

Proclamation R9 of 1997

Telecommunications Act 103 of 1996

Town Planning and Township Ordinance 15 of 1986 (Transvaal)

Town Planning Ordinance 27 of 1949 (Natal)

Townships Ordinance 9 of 1969 (OFS)

Transvaal Roads Ordinance 22 of 1957

Political and Governmental Policy Documents and Papers

ANC: *"A Bill of Rights for a New South Africa."* Appendix A vol 21
 1989 Columbia Human Rights Law Review 235 - 239

ANC: *"African Claims in Africa"* 1943 online at http://www.anc.org.
 za/ancdocs/history/keydocs.html [12.03.2000]

ANC: *"Freedom Charter"* 1955 online at http://www.anc.org.za/
 ancdocs/history/keydocs.html [12.03.2000]

ANC: *"Ready to Govern: ANC Policy Guidelines for a Democratic
 South Africa"* online at http://www.anc.org.za/ancdocs/history/
 readyto.html [13.02.2000]

Department of Land Affairs *White Paper on South African Land Policy*
 (1997) online at http://www.polity.org.za/govdocs/white_papers/
 landwp.html [16.12.1998]

Draft Property Rates Bill, online at http://www.polity.org.za/govdocs/
 bills/2000/property.pdf [06.09.2000]

Memorandum on the Objects of the Land Restitution and Reform
 Laws Amendment Bill 1997

NP "Proposals on a Charter of Fundamental Rights" (2 February 1993)

Panel of Constitutional Experts' *Memorandum (Re: panel memo on
 "special limitations"/"qualifiers" and general limitation) of 20-02-*

1996, online at http://www.constitution.org.za/exmemo/cp320026.
html [19.01.2000]

South African Law Commission Working Paper 25 Project 58 Group
and Human Rights (1989)

South African Revenue Service (SARS): *Guide to Capital Gains Tax* 23
February 2000

Technical Committee/Theme Committee Four *Explanatory Memoranda on the Draft Bill of Rights (09.10.1995) "Overview of Method
of Work"* online at http://www.constitution.org.za/cgi-bin/
vdkw_cgi/xb45ff20b-10/Search/x2ccdbc/3#HL0 [04.02.2000]

Germany**

Basic Law

Grundgesetz für die Bundesrepublik Deutschland 23 May 1949, BGBl 1

Statutes and Treaties

*Anordnung über die Behandlung des Vermögens von Personen, die die
Deutsche Demokratische Republik nach dem 10. Juni 1953 verlassen*
10 June 1953, GBl DDR I 664

Atomgesetz 31 October 1975 as amended on 15 July 1984, BGBl I 1565

Baugesetzbuch 8 December 1986, BGBl I 2253

Berichtigung des zweiten Vermögensrechtsänderungsgesetzes 1993,
BGBl I 1811

Bundesfernstraßengesetz 19 April 1994, BGBl I 85

Bundesimmissionsschutzgesetz 14 May 1990, BGBl I 880

Bundesnaturschutzgesetz 29 December 1976, BGBl I 889

Bundeswaldgesetz 2 May 1975, BGBl I 1037

Bundeswasserstraßengesetz 23 August 1990, BGBl 818

Bürgerliches Gesetzbuch 18 August 1896, RGBl 195 / BGBl III 400

Energiewirtschaftsgesetz 24 April 1998, BGBl I 730

Flurbereinigungsgesetz 16 March 1976, BGBl I 546

** The German legislation quoted is based on the law as it stands on 1 June
2001, unless the contrary appears from the context in which it is used in the
text.

Gemeinsame Erklärung zur Regelung offener Vermögensfragen 15 June 1990, BGBl II 1273

Gerichtsverfassungsgesetz 27 January 1877, RGBl I 41 / 9 May 1975, BGBl III 300

Gesetz über besondere Investitionen in der Deutschen Demokratischen Republik 23 September 1990, BGBl II 889, 1157

Gesetz über das Wohnungseigentum und das Dauerwohnrecht 15 March 1951, BGBl I 175 / 11 January 1993, BGBl I 50

Gesetz über den Vorrang für Investitionen bei Rückübertragungsansprüchen nach dem Vermögensgesetz (Investitionsvorranggesetz) 14 July 1992, BGBl I 1257, 1268

Gesetz über den Widerruf von Einbürgerungen und die Aberkennung der deutschen Staatsangehörigkeit 14 July 1933, RGBl I 480

Gesetz über die Entschädigung nach dem Gesetz zur Regelung offener Vermögensfragen und über staatliche Ausgleichsleistungen für Enteignungen auf besatzungsrechtlicher oder besatzungshoheitlicher Grundlage 27 September 1994, BGBl I 2624

Gesetz über die strukturelle Anpassung der Landwirtschaft an die soziale und ökologische Marktwirtschaft in der Deutschen Demokratischen Republik (Landwirtschaftsanpassungsgesetz) 19 June 1990, GBl I 642

Gesetz über Maßnahmen zur Verbesserung der Agrarstruktur und zur Sicherung land- und forstwirtschaflicher Betriebe 28 July 1961, BGBl I 1091 / 8 December 1986, BGBl I 2191

Gesetz zur Änderung des Vermögensgesetzes und anderer Vorschriften (2. Vermögensrechtsänderungsgesetz) 14 July 1992, BGBl 1257

Gesetz zur Anpassung der Rechtspflege im Beitrittsgebiet 30 June 1992, BGBl I S 1147

Gesetz zur Beseitigung von Hemmnissen bei der Privatisierung von Unternehmen und zur Förderung von Investitionen (Investment Acceleration Act) 22 March 1991, BGBl I 766

Gesetz zur Ordnung deichrechtlicher Verhältnisse der Freien und Hansestadt Hamburg, 29 April 1964, GVBl I 79

Gesetz zur Privatisierung und Reorganisation des volkseigenen Vermögens (Treuhandgesetz) 17 June 1990, GBl DDR I 33 300

Gesetz zur Regelung offener Vermögensfragen (Open Property Questions Act / Property Act) 23 September 1990, BGBl II 1159 / 2 December 1994, BGBl I 3610

Grundbuchordnung 26 May 1994, BGBl I 1114

Grundstücksverkehrsgesetz 28 July 1961, BGBl I 1091, 1652, 2000

Hamburger Denkmalschutzgesetz 3 December 1973, GVBl 466

Landesenteignungsgesetz von Baden-Württemberg 6 April 1982, GBl Ba-Wü 97

Landesenteignungsgesetz von Rheinland-Pfalz 1966 GVBl 103 / 27 June 1974, GVBl 290

Luftverkehrgesetz 14 January 1981, BGBl I 61

Pachtkreditgesetz 5 August 1951, BGBl I 494 / 8 November 1985, BGBl I 2065

Telegraphenwegegesetz 24 April 1991, BGBl I 1053

Umwandlungsgesetz 28 October 1994, BGBl I 3210 / 1995 BGBl 428

Verordnung des Reichspräsidenten zum Schutz von Volk und Staat 28 February 1933, RGBl I 83

Verordnung zur Sicherung von Vermögenswerten 17 July 1952, GBl DDR 615)

Vertrag zwischen der Bundesrepublik Deutschland und der Deutschen Demokratischen Republik über die Herstellung der Einheit Deutschlands (Einigungsvertrag / Unification Treaty) 31 August 1990, BGBl 1990 II 889

Wasserhaushaltsgesetz 1 March 1960 (amended version of 16 October 1976), 23 September 1986, BGBl I 1529

Zwangsversteigerungsgesetz 24 March 1897, RGBl 97 / 20 May 1898, RGBl 713 / BGBl. III/FNA 310 -314

Other

Canadian Bill of Rights, 1960

Canadian Charter of Rights and Freedoms, 1982

Constitution of India, 1950

European Convention on Human Rights, 1950

First Protocol to the European Convention on Human Rights, 1950

Index

Max-Planck-Institut für ausländisches öffentliches Recht und Völkerrecht

Beiträge zum ausländischen öffentlichen Recht und Völkerrecht

Hrsg.: J. A. Frowein, R. Wolfrum

Bde. 27–59 erschienen im Carl Heymanns Verlag KG Köln, Berlin (Bestellung an:
Max-Planck-Institut für Völkerrecht, Im Neuenheimer Feld 535, 69120 Heidelberg);
ab Band 60 im Springer-Verlag Berlin, Heidelberg, New York, London,
Paris, Tokyo, Hong Kong, Barcelona

---

138 Britta *Specht:* **Die zwischenstaatliche Geltung des Grundsatzes** *ne bis in idem.* 1999. XXII, 237 Seiten. Geb. 119,– DM

137 Hans-Konrad *Ress:* **Das Handelsembargo.** 2000. XXVI, 532 Seiten. Geb. 186,– DM

136 Georg *Nolte:* **Eingreifen auf Einladung.** 1999. XXXIV, 699 Seiten. Geb. 218,– DM

135 Volkmar *Götz,* Peter *Selmer,* Rüdiger *Wolfrum* (Hrsg.): **Liber amicorum Günther Jaenicke – Zum 85. Geburtstag.** 1998. XXV, 1038 Seiten. Geb. 298,– DM

134 Peter *Rädler:* **Verfahrensmodelle zum Schutz vor Rassendiskriminierung.** 1999. XVII, 454 Seiten. Geb. 148,– DM

133 Volker *Röben:* **Die Einwirkung der Rechtsprechung des Europäischen Gerichtshofs auf das Mitgliedstaatliche Verfahren in öffentlich-rechtlichen Streitigkeiten.** 1998. XXX, 478 Seiten. Geb. 168,– DM

132 Frank *Hoffmeister:* **Menschenrechts- und Demokratieklauseln in den vertraglichen Außenbeziehungen der Europäischen Gemeinschaft.** 1998. XXII, 654 Seiten. Geb. 186,– DM

131 Stefan *Schuppert:* **Neue Steuerungsinstrumente im Umweltvölkerrecht am Beispiel des Montrealer Protokolls und des Klimaschutzrahmenübereinkommens.** 1998. XXII, 297 Seiten, Geb. 128,– DM

130 Jochen Abr. *Frowein,* Thilo *Marauhn* (Hrsg.): **Grundfragen der Verfassungsgerichtsbarkeit in Mittel- und Osteuropa.** 1998. IX, 583 Seiten. Geb. 178,– DM

129 David *Weissbrodt,* Rüdiger *Wolfrum* (Eds.): **The Right to a Fair Trial.** 1997. X, 779 Seiten. Geb. 198,– DM

128 Stefan *Lehr:* **Einstweiliger Rechtsschutz und Europäische Union.** 1997. XXXVI, 693 Seiten (12 Seiten English Summary). Geb. 198,– DM

127 Grace *Nacimiento:* **Die Amerikanische Deklaration der Rechte und Pflichten des Menschen.** 1997. XII, 208 Seiten (14 Seiten English Summary). Geb. 98,– DM

126 Ralf *Alleweldt:* **Schutz vor Abschiebung bei drohender Folter oder unmenschlicher oder erniedrigender Behandlung oder Strafe.** 1996. XXI, 228 Seiten (7 Seiten English Summary). Geb. 98,– DM

125 Rüdiger *Wolfrum* (Ed.): **Enforcing Environmental Standards: Economic Mechanisms as Viable Means?** 1996. VIII, 640 Seiten. Geb. 198,– DM

124 Christian *Walter:* **Vereinte Nationen und Regionalorganisationen.** 1996. XX, 407 Seiten (5 Seiten English Summary). Geb. 128,– DM

123 Gunnar *Schuster:* **Die Internationale Anwendung des Börsenrechts.** 1996. XXV, 729 Seiten (3 Seiten English Summary). Geb. 220,– DM

122 Michael J. *Hahn:* **Die einseitige Aussetzung von GATT-Verpflichtungen als Repressalie.** 1996. XVIII, 439 Seiten (4 Seiten English Summary). Geb. 148,– DM

121 Jochen Abr. *Frowein*/Rüdiger *Wolfrum*/Gunnar *Schuster* (Hrsg.): **Völkerrechtliche Fragen der Strafbarkeit von Spionen aus der ehemaligen DDR.** 1995. XVI, 193 Seiten. Geb. 98,– DM

120 **Recht zwischen Umbruch und Bewahrung. Festschrift für Rudolf Bernhardt.** 1995. XVI, 1397 Seiten. Geb. 398,– DM

119 Werner *Meng:* **Extraterritoriale Jurisdiktion im öffentlichen Wirtschaftsrecht.** 1994. XXIV, 810 Seiten (16 Seiten English Summary). Geb. 198,– DM

118 Rainer *Hofmann:* **Grundrechte und grenzüberschreitende Sachverhalte.** 1994. XVIII, 374 Seiten (5 Seiten English Summary). Geb. 148,– DM

117 Rudolf *Bernhardt* (Ed.): **Interim Measures Indicated by International Courts.** 1994. XII, 156 Seiten. Geb. 98,– DM

116 Thilo *Marauhn:* **Der deutsche Chemiewaffen-Verzicht.** 1994. XXII, 400 Seiten (7 Seiten English Summary). Geb. 128,– DM